Situationist International Anthology

Revised and Expanded Edition

The *Situationist International Anthology*, edited and translated by Ken Knabb, was originally published by the Bureau of Public Secrets in 1981. A revised and expanded version was published in 2006. The present edition, published in 2024 by PM Press, is a revised and updated version of the 2006 edition.

ISBN: 979-8-887440-57-6
ISBN (ebook): 979-8-887440-66-8
Library of Congress Control Number: 2024930604

Cover image: from a 1957 psychogeographical map of Paris by Guy Debord
Cover and book design: Jeanne Smith

PM Press
PO Box 23912
Oakland, CA 94623
www.pmpress.org

Printed in the USA.

Contents

*Excerpts

PREFACE

In 1957 a few European avant-garde groups came together to form the Situationist International. Over the next decade the SI developed an increasingly incisive and coherent critique of modern society and of its bureaucratic pseudo-opposition, and its new methods of agitation were influential in leading up to the May 1968 revolt in France. Since then—although the SI itself was dissolved in 1972—situationist theses and tactics have been taken up by radical currents in dozens of countries all over the world.

In this anthology I have tried to present a useful selection of situationist writings while at the same time illustrating the SI's origins and development. Thus some early texts are included even though they express positions that were later repudiated by the situationists. But even the later texts reveal mistakes, contradictions, projects that never materialized, problems that remain to be solved. In other publications I have presented my own views on a few of these issues, but here I have as far as possible let the SI speak for itself.

The major portion of the anthology is drawn from the French journal *Internationale Situationniste* (it includes about a third of the *IS* articles). The rest consists of various shorter publications and documents. I have not included any excerpts from the situationist books, Debord's *The Society of the Spectacle,* Vaneigem's *Treatise on Living for the Young Generations,* Viénet's *Enragés and Situationists in the Occupations Movement,* and Debord and Sanguinetti's *The Real Split in the International.* Anyone who is serious will want to read these books in their entirety. The English translations of them that have appeared are all unsatisfactory, but sooner or later someone will publish accurate versions.

The only previous English-language SI anthology, Christopher Gray's *Leaving the Twentieth Century,* is particularly bad. In *Bureau of Public Secrets* #1 I have already criticized the superficiality of Gray's commentaries on the SI. His translations are on the same level. Not only do his chummy paraphrases obscure the precise sense of the original, but there is scarcely a page in which he has not left out sentences or paragraphs without any indication of the omission, or even made completely gratuitous additions of his own.

About half the texts in the present anthology have been translated into English for the first time. All the others have been freshly translated, but I have gone through all the previous translations and incorporated many of their best renderings. I received an immense help from Nadine Bloch and Joël Cornuault, who answered hundreds of questions regarding the French texts, then checked the entire manuscript, correcting many errors and suggesting many further improvements. Dan Hammer also made a number of good suggestions.

Asterisks refer to my notes at the end of the book. The only notes original to the SI are the numbered footnotes in *On the Poverty of Student Life*. Within the text, all annotations in square brackets are mine and my omissions are indicated by [. . .]. I have not generally annotated references to historical events, etc., that enterprising readers can easily find out about for themselves. Nor have I tried to explain supposed difficulties in the SI's language. After the usual diet of ideological pabulum it may be a momentary shock to be forced to think; but those who are really confronting their lives and therefore this society will soon understand how to use these texts. Those who aren't, won't, regardless of explanations. Situationist language is difficult only to the extent that our situation is. "The path to simplicity is the most complex of all."

KEN KNABB
December 1981

Note for the 2006 revised and expanded edition:

In 1998–1999 I posted the entire *SI Anthology* at my new Bureau of Public Secrets website (www.bopsecrets.org). In the process of preparing the online versions, I rechecked all my translations against the French originals, taking the opportunity to make numerous minor stylistic improvements, and since that time I have continued to fine-tune them. The translations in the original edition remain completely reliable, but I believe that the present versions are somewhat more clear and idiomatic.

Some of the articles that were abridged in the original edition have now been translated complete. I have also translated several additional texts, added a large number of new notes, updated the bibliography, and created a more detailed index.

Special thanks to Jeanne Smith for the superb book and cover design and for extensive technical assistance.

Note for the 2024 PM Press edition:

This new edition includes the same selection of texts and the same pagination as the 2006 edition, but I have made numerous minor stylistic revisions to the translations and updated the bibliography to include comments on the many newer books by or about the situationists.

Thanks to the folks at PM Press for their enthusiastic collaboration, and once again special thanks to Jeanne Smith for her superb design work and for her immensely helpful technical assistance.

Pre-SI Texts

(1953–1957)

Formulary for a New Urbanism

SIRE, I AM FROM THE OTHER COUNTRY

We are bored in the city, there's no longer any Temple of the Sun. Between the legs of the women walking by, the dadaists imagined a monkey wrench and the surrealists a crystal cup. That's lost. We know how to read every promise in faces—the latest stage of morphology. The poetry of the billboards lasted twenty years. We are bored in the city, we really have to strain to still discover mysteries on the sidewalk billboards, the latest state of humor and poetry:

> *Showerbath of the Patriarchs*
> *Meat-Cutting Machines*
> *Notre-Dame Zoo*
> *Sports Pharmacy*
> *Martyrs Provisions*
> *Translucent Concrete*
> *Golden-Touch Sawmill*
> *Center for Functional Recuperation*
> *Saint-Anne Ambulance*
> *Café Fifth Avenue*
> *Prolonged Volunteers Street*
> *Family Boarding House in the Garden*
> *Hotel of Strangers*
> *Wild Street*

And the swimming pool on the Street of Little Girls. And the police station on Rendezvous Street. The medical-surgical clinic and the free placement center on the Quai des Orfèvres. The artificial flowers on Sun Street. The Castle-Cellars Hotel, the Ocean Bar, and the Coming-and-Going Café. The Hotel of the Epoch.*

And the strange statue of Dr. Philippe Pinel, benefactor of the insane, fading in the last evenings of summer. Exploring Paris.

And you, forgotten, your memories ravaged by all the consternations of both hemispheres, stranded in the Red Cellars of Pali-Kao, without music and without geography, no longer setting out for the hacienda *where the roots think of the child and where the wine is finished off with fables from an old almanac.* Now that's all gone. You'll never see the hacienda. It doesn't exist.

The hacienda must be built.

1

All cities are geological. You can't take three steps without encountering ghosts bearing all the glamour of their legends. We move within a *closed* landscape whose landmarks constantly draw us toward the past. Certain *shifting* angles, certain *receding* perspectives, allow us to glimpse original conceptions of space, but this vision remains fragmentary. It must be sought in the magical locales of fairy tales and surrealist writings—castles, endless walls, little forgotten bars, mammoth caverns, casino mirrors.

These dated images retain a slight catalyzing power, but it is almost impossible to use them in a *symbolic urbanism* without rejuvenating them by giving them a new meaning. There was a certain charm in horses born from the sea or magical dwarves dressed in gold, but they are in no way adapted to the demands of modern life. For we are in the twentieth century, even if few people are aware of it. Our imaginations, haunted by the old archetypes, have remained far behind the sophistication of the machines. The various attempts to integrate modern science into new myths remain inadequate. Meanwhile abstraction has invaded all the arts, contemporary architecture in particular. Pure plasticity, inanimate and storyless, soothes the eye and cools the mind. Elsewhere other fragmentary beauties can be found—while the promised land of new syntheses continually recedes into the distance. Everyone wavers between the emotionally still-alive past and the already-dead future.

We don't intend to prolong the mechanistic civilizations and frigid architecture that ultimately lead to boring leisure.

We propose to invent new, changeable decors.

* * *

We will leave Monsieur Le Corbusier's style to him, a style suitable for factories and hospitals, and no doubt eventually for prisons. (Doesn't he already build churches?) Some sort of psychological repression dominates this individual—whose face is as ugly as his conceptions of the world—such that he wants to squash people under ignoble masses of reinforced concrete, a noble material that should rather be used to enable an aerial articulation of space that could surpass the flamboyant Gothic style. His cretinizing influence is immense. A Le Corbusier model is the only image that arouses in me the idea of immediate suicide. He is destroying the last remnants of joy. And of love, passion, freedom.

* * *

Darkness and obscurity are banished by artificial lighting, and the seasons by air conditioning. Night and summer are losing their charm and dawn is disappearing. The urban population think they have escaped from cosmic reality, but there is no corresponding expansion of their dream life. The reason is clear: dreams spring from reality and are realized in it.

The latest technological developments would make possible the individual's unbroken contact with cosmic reality while eliminating its disagreeable aspects. Stars and rain can be viewed through glass ceilings. The mobile house turns with the sun. Its sliding walls enable vegetation to invade life. Mounted on tracks, it can go down to the sea in the morning and return to the forest in the evening.

Architecture is the simplest means of *articulating* time and space, of *modulating* reality and engendering dreams. It is a matter not only of plastic articulation and modulation expressing an ephemeral beauty, but of a modulation producing influences in accordance with the perpetual evolution of human desires and the progress in fulfilling them.

The architecture of tomorrow will thus be a means of modifying present conceptions of time and space. It will be both a means of *knowledge* and a *means of action*.

Architectural complexes will be modifiable. Their appearance will change totally or partially in accordance with the will of their inhabitants.

* * *

A new architecture can express nothing less than a new civilization. (It is clear that there has been neither civilization nor architecture for centuries, but only experiments, most of which were failures. We can speak of Gothic architecture, but there is no Marxist or capitalist architecture, though these two systems are revealing similar tendencies and goals.)

Anyone thus has the right to ask us on what vision of civilization we are going to found an architecture. I briefly sketch the points of departure for a civilization:

—A new conception of space (a religious or nonreligious cosmogony).

—A new conception of time (counting from zero, various *modes* of temporal development).

—A new conception of behaviors (moral, sociological, political, legal; economy is only a part of the laws of behavior accepted by a civilization).

Past collectivities offered the masses an absolute truth and incontrovertible mythical exemplars. The appearance of the notion of *rela-*

tivity in the modern mind allows one to surmise the EXPERIMENTAL aspect of the next civilization (though I'm not satisfied with that word; I mean that it will be more flexible, more "playful"). (For a long time it was believed that the Marxist countries were on this path. We now know that this endeavor followed the old normal evolution, arriving in record time at a rigidification of its doctrines and at forms that have become ossified in their decadence. A renewal is perhaps possible, but I will not examine this question here.)

On the bases of this mobile civilization, architecture will, at least initially, be a means of experimenting with a thousand ways of modifying life, with a view to an ultimate mythic synthesis.

* * *

A mental disease has swept the planet: banalization. Everyone is hypnotized by production and conveniences—sewage systems, elevators, bathrooms, washing machines.

This state of affairs, arising out of a struggle against poverty, has overshot its ultimate goal—the liberation of humanity from material cares—and become an omnipresent obsessive image. Presented with the alternative of love or a garbage disposal unit, young people of all countries have chosen the garbage disposal unit. It has become essential to provoke a complete spiritual transformation by bringing to light forgotten desires and by creating entirely new ones. And by carrying out an *intensive propaganda* in favor of these desires.

* * *

Guy Debord has already pointed out the construction of situations as being one of the fundamental desires on which the next civilization will be founded. This need for *total* creation has always been intimately associated with the need to *play* with architecture, time, and space. One example will suffice to demonstrate this—a leaflet distributed in the street by the Palais de Paris (manifestations of the collective unconscious always correspond to the affirmations of creators):

BYGONE NEIGHBORHOODS
Grand Events
PERIOD MUSIC
LUMINOUS EFFECTS
PARIS BY NIGHT
COMPLETELY ANIMATED

The Court of Miracles: an impressive 300-square-meter reconstruction of a Medieval neighborhood, with rundown houses inhabited by robbers, beggars, bawdy wenches, all subjects of the frightful KING OF THIEVES, who renders justice from his lair.

The Tower of Nesle: The sinister Tower profiles its imposing mass against the somber, dark-clouded sky. The Seine laps softly. A boat approaches. Two assassins await their victim. . . .*

Other examples of this desire to construct situations can be found in the past. Edgar Allan Poe and his story of the man who devoted his wealth to the construction of landscapes ["The Domain of Arnheim"]. Or the paintings of Claude Lorrain. Many of the latter's admirers are not quite sure to what to attribute the charm of his canvases. They talk about his portrayal of light. It does indeed have a rather mysterious quality, but that does not suffice to explain these paintings' ambience of *perpetual* invitation to voyage. This ambience is provoked by an *unaccustomed architectural space.* The palaces are situated right on the edge of the sea, and they have "pointless" hanging gardens whose vegetation appears in the most unexpected places. The incitement to drifting is provoked by the palace doors' proximity to the ships.

De Chirico remains one of the most remarkable architectural precursors. He was grappling with the problems of absences and presences in time and space.

We know that an object that is not consciously noticed at the time of a first *visit* can, by its absence during subsequent visits, provoke an indefinable impression: as a result of this sighting backward in time, *the absence of the object becomes a presence one can feel.* More precisely: although the quality of the impression generally remains indefinite, it nevertheless varies with the nature of the removed object and the importance accorded it by the visitor, ranging from serene joy to terror. (It is of no particular significance that in this specific case memory is the vehicle of these feelings; I only selected this example for its convenience.)

In De Chirico's paintings (during his Arcade period) an *empty space* creates a *richly filled time.* It is easy to imagine the fantastic future possibilities of such architecture and its influence on the masses. We can have nothing but contempt for a century that relegates such *blueprints* to its so-called museums. De Chirico could have been given free reign over Place de la Concorde and its Obelisk, or at least commissioned to design the gardens that "adorn" several entrances to the capital.

This new vision of time and space, which will be the theoretical basis of future constructions, is still imprecise and will remain so until experimentation with patterns of behavior has taken place in cities specifically established for this purpose, cities bringing together—in addition to the facilities necessary for basic comfort and security—

buildings charged with evocative power, symbolic edifices representing desires, forces, and events, past, present, and to come. A rational extension of the old religious systems, of old tales, and above all of psychoanalysis into architectural expression becomes more and more urgent as all the reasons for becoming impassioned disappear.

Everyone will, so to speak, live in their own personal "cathedrals." There will be rooms more conducive to dreams than any drug, and houses where one cannot help but love. Others will be irresistibly alluring to travelers.

This project could be compared with the Chinese and Japanese *trompe-l'oeil* gardens—with the difference that those gardens are not designed to be lived in all the time—or with the ridiculous labyrinth in the Jardin des Plantes, at the entry to which (height of absurdity, Ariadne* unemployed) is the sign: *No playing in the labyrinth.*

This city could be envisaged in the form of an arbitrary assemblage of castles, grottos, lakes, etc. It would be the baroque stage of urbanism considered as a means of knowledge. But this theoretical phase is already outdated. We know that a modern building could be constructed which would have no resemblance to a medieval castle but which could nevertheless preserve and enhance a "Castle" type of poetic power (by the conservation of a strict minimum of lines, the transposition of certain others, the positioning of openings, the topographical location, etc.).

The districts of this city could correspond to the whole spectrum of diverse feelings that one encounters by *chance* in everyday life.

Bizarre Quarter—Happy Quarter (specially reserved for habitation)—Noble and Tragic Quarter (for good children)—Historical Quarter (museums, schools)—Useful Quarter (hospital, tool shops)—Sinister Quarter, etc. And an *Astrolarium* which would group plant species in accordance with the relations they manifest with the stellar rhythm, a Planetary Garden along the lines the astronomer Thomas wants to establish at Laaer Berg in Vienna. Indispensable for giving the inhabitants a consciousness of the cosmic. Perhaps also a Death Quarter, not for dying in but so as to have somewhere to *live in peace*—I'm thinking here of Mexico and of a principle of cruelty in innocence that appeals more to me every day.

The Sinister Quarter, for example, would be a good replacement for those ill-reputed neighborhoods full of sordid dives and unsavory characters that many peoples once possessed in their capitals: they symbolized all the evil forces of life. The Sinister Quarter would have no need to harbor real dangers, such as traps, dungeons, or mines; but it would be difficult to get into, with a hideous decor (piercing whistles, alarm bells, sirens wailing intermittently, grotesque sculptures, power-driven mobiles, called *Auto-Mobiles*), and as poorly lit at night as it was blindingly lit during the day by an intensive use of reflection. At the center, the "Square of the Appalling Mobile." Saturation of the market with a product causes the product's market value to fall: thus, as they explored the Sinister Quarter, children would learn not to fear the anguishing occasions of life, but to be amused by them.

The main activity of the inhabitants will be CONTINUOUS DRIFTING.* The changing of landscapes from one hour to the next will result in total disorientation.

Couples will no longer pass their nights in the home where they live and receive guests, which is nothing but a banal *social* custom. The chamber of love will be more distant from the center of the city: it will naturally recreate for the partners a sense of *exoticism* in a locale less open to light, more hidden, so as to recover the atmosphere of secrecy. The opposite tendency, seeking a center for intellectual discourse, will proceed through the same technique.

Later, as the activities inevitably grow stale, this drifting will partially leave the realm of direct experience for that of representation.

Note: A certain Saint-Germain-des-Prés,* about which no one has yet written, has been the first group functioning on a historical scale within this ethic of drifting. This magical group spirit, which has remained underground up till now, is the only explanation for the enormous influence that a mere *three city blocks* have had on the world, an influence that others have inadequately attempted to explain on the basis of styles of clothing and song, or even more stupidly by the neighborhood's supposedly freer access to prostitution. (And Pigalle?)*

In forthcoming books we will elucidate the coincidence and *incidences* of the Saint-Germain days (Henry de Béarn's *The New Nomadism*, Guy Debord's *Beautiful Youth*, etc.).* This should serve to clarify not only an "aesthetic of behaviors" but practical means for forming new groups, and above all a complete *phenomenology* of couples, encounters, and duration which mathematicians and poets will study with profit.

Finally, to those who object that a people cannot live by drifting, it is useful to recall that in every group certain characters (priests or heroes) are charged with representing various tendencies as specialists, in accordance with the dual mechanism of projection and identification. Experience demonstrates that a dérive is a good replacement for a Mass: it is more effective in making people enter into communication with the ensemble of energies, seducing them for the benefit of the collectivity.

The economic obstacles are only apparent. We know that the more a place is *set apart for free play*, the more it influences people's behavior and the greater is its force of attraction. This is demonstrated by the immense prestige of Monaco and Las Vegas—and of Reno, that caricature of free love—though they are mere gambling places. Our first experimental city would live largely off of tolerated and controlled tourism. Future avant-garde activities and productions would naturally tend to gravitate there. In a few years it would become the intellectual capital of the world and would be universally recognized as such.

IVAN CHTCHEGLOV*
1953

Introduction to a
Critique of Urban Geography

Of all the affairs we participate in, with or without interest, the groping quest for a new way of life is the only thing that remains really exciting. Aesthetic and other disciplines have proved glaringly inadequate in this regard and merit the greatest indifference. We should therefore delineate some provisional terrains of observation, including the observation of certain processes of chance and predictability in the streets.

The word *psychogeography*, suggested by an illiterate Kabyle as a general term for the phenomena a few of us were investigating around the summer of 1953, is not too inappropriate. It is not inconsistent with the materialist perspective that sees life and thought as conditioned by objective nature. Geography, for example, deals with the determinant action of general natural forces, such as soil composition or climatic conditions, on the economic structures of a society, and thus on the corresponding conception that such a society can have of the world. Psychogeography sets for itself the study of the precise laws and specific effects of the geographical environment, whether consciously organized or not, on the emotions and behavior of individuals. The charmingly vague adjective *psychogeographical* can be applied to the findings arrived at by this type of investigation, to their influence on human feelings, and more generally to any situation or conduct that seems to reflect the same spirit of discovery.

It has long been said that the desert is monotheistic. Is it illogical or devoid of interest to observe that the district in Paris between Place de la Contrescarpe and Rue de l'Arbalète conduces rather to atheism, to oblivion, and to the disorientation of habitual reflexes?

Historical conditions determine what is considered "useful." Baron Haussmann's urban renewal of Paris under the Second Empire, for example, was motivated by the desire to open up broad thoroughfares enabling the rapid circulation of troops and the use of artillery against insurrections. But from any standpoint other than that of facilitating police control, Haussmann's Paris is a city built by an idiot, full of sound and fury, signifying nothing. Present-day urbanism's main problem is ensuring the smooth circulation of a rapidly increasing number of motor vehicles. A future urbanism may well apply itself to no less utilitarian projects, but in the rather different context of psychogeographical possibilities.

The present abundance of private automobiles is one of the most astonishing successes of the constant propaganda by which capitalist production persuades the masses that car ownership is one of the privileges our society reserves for its most privileged members. But anarchical progress often ends up contradicting itself, as when we savor the spectacle of a police chief issuing a filmed appeal urging Parisian car owners to use public transportation.

We know with what blind fury so many unprivileged people are ready to defend their mediocre advantages. Such pathetic illusions of privilege are linked to a general idea of happiness prevalent among the bourgeoisie and maintained by a system of publicity that includes Malraux's aesthetics as well as Coca-Cola ads—an idea of happiness whose crisis must be provoked on every occasion by every means.

The first of these means is undoubtedly the systematic provocative dissemination of a host of proposals tending to turn the whole of life into an exciting game, combined with the constant depreciation of all current diversions (to the extent, of course, that these latter cannot be détourned to serve in constructions of more interesting ambiances). The greatest difficulty in such an undertaking is to convey through these apparently extravagant proposals a sufficient degree of *serious seduction*. To accomplish this we can envisage an adroit use of currently popular means of communication. But a disruptive sort of abstention, or demonstrations designed to radically frustrate the fans of these means of communication, can also easily promote an atmosphere of uneasiness extremely favorable for the introduction of a few new conceptions of pleasure.

The idea that the creation of a chosen emotional situation depends only on the thorough understanding and calculated application of a certain number of concrete techniques inspired this somewhat tongue-in-cheek "Psychogeographical Game of the Week," published in *Potlatch* #1:

> In accordance with what you are seeking, choose a country, a large or small city, a busy or quiet street. Build a house. Furnish it. Use decorations and surroundings to the best advantage. Choose the season and the time of day. Bring together the most suitable people, with appropriate records and drinks. The lighting and the conversation should obviously be suited to the occasion, as should be the weather or your memories. If there has been no error in your calculations, the result should prove satisfying.

We need to flood the market—even if for the moment merely the intellectual market—with a mass of desires whose fulfillment is not beyond the capacity of humanity's present means of action on the material world, but only beyond the capacity of the old social organization. It is thus not without political interest to publicly counterpose such desires to the elementary desires that are endlessly rehashed by the film industry and in psychological novels like those of that old hack Mauriac. (As Marx explained to poor Proudhon, "In a society based on *poverty*, the *poorest* products are inevitably consumed by the greatest number.")*

The revolutionary transformation of the world, of all aspects of the world, will confirm all the dreams of abundance.

The sudden change of ambiance in a street within the space of a few meters; the evident division of a city into zones of distinct psychic atmospheres; the path of least resistance that is automatically followed in aimless strolls (and which has no relation to the physical contour of the terrain); the appealing or repelling character of certain places—these phenomena all seem to be neglected. In any case they are never envisaged as depending on causes that can be uncovered by careful analysis and turned to account. People are quite aware that some neighborhoods are gloomy and others pleasant. But they generally simply assume that elegant streets cause a feeling of satisfaction and that poor streets are depressing, and let it go at that. In fact, the variety of possible combinations of ambiences, analogous to the blending of pure chemicals in an infinite variety of mixtures, gives rise to feelings as differentiated and complex as any other form of spectacle can evoke. The slightest demystified investigation reveals that the qualitatively or quantitatively different influences of diverse urban decors cannot be determined solely on the basis of the historical period or architectural style, much less on the basis of housing conditions.

The research that we are thus led to undertake on the arrangement of the elements of the urban setting, in close relation with the sensations they provoke, entails bold hypotheses that must be constantly corrected in the light of experience, by critique and self-critique.

Certain of De Chirico's paintings, which were clearly inspired by architecturally originated sensations, exert in turn an effect on their objective base to the point of transforming it: they tend themselves to become blueprints or models. Disquieting neighborhoods of arcades could one day carry on and fulfill the allure of these works.

I scarcely know of anything but those two harbors at dusk painted by Claude Lorrain*—which are in the Louvre and which juxtapose extremely dissimilar urban ambiances—that can rival in beauty the Paris Metro maps. I am not, of course, talking about mere physical beauty—the new beauty can only be a beauty of situation—but simply about the particularly moving presentation, in both cases, of a *sum of possibilities*.

Along with various more difficult means of intervention, a renovated cartography seems appropriate for immediate utilization.

The production of psychogeographical maps, or even the introduction of alterations such as more or less arbitrarily transposing maps of two different regions, can contribute to clarifying certain wanderings that express not subordination to randomness but total *insubordination* to habitual influences (influences generally categorized as tourism, that popular drug as repugnant as sports or buying on credit).

A friend recently told me that he had just wandered through the Harz region of Germany while blindly following the directions of a map of London. This sort of game is obviously only a feeble beginning in comparison to the complete creation of architecture and urbanism that will someday be within the power of everyone. Meanwhile we can distinguish several stages of partial, less difficult projects, beginning with the mere displacement of elements of decoration from the locations where we are used to seeing them.

For example, in the preceding issue of this journal Marcel Mariën proposed that when global resources have ceased to be squandered on the irrational enterprises that are imposed on us today, all the equestrian statues of all the cities of the world be assembled in a single desert. This would offer to the passersby—the future belongs to them—the spectacle of an artificial cavalry charge which could even be dedicated to the memory of the greatest massacrers of history, from Tamerlane to Ridgway. It would also respond to one of the main demands of the present generation: educative value.

In fact, nothing really new can be expected until the masses in action awaken to the conditions that are imposed on them in all domains of life, and to the practical means of changing them.

"The imaginary is that which tends to become real," wrote an author* whose name, on account of his notorious intellectual degradation, I have since forgotten. The involuntary restrictiveness of such a statement could serve as a touchstone exposing various farcical literary revolutions: That which tends to remain unreal is empty babble.

Life, for which we are responsible, presents powerful motives for discouragement and innumerable more or less paltry diversions and compensations. A year doesn't go by when people we loved haven't succumbed, for lack of having clearly grasped the present possibilities, to some glaring capitulation. But the enemy camp objectively condemns people to imbecility and already numbers millions of imbeciles; the addition of a few more makes no difference.

The primary moral deficiency remains indulgence, in all its forms.

GUY DEBORD
1955

Proposals for Rationally Improving the City of Paris

The Lettrists present at the September 26 meeting jointly proposed the following solutions to the various urbanistic problems that came up in discussion. They stress that no constructive action was considered, since they all agreed that the most urgent task is to clear the ground.

The subways should be opened at night after the trains have stopped running. The corridors and platforms should be poorly lit, with dim lights flickering on and off intermittently.

The rooftops of Paris should be opened to pedestrian traffic by modifying fire-escape ladders and by constructing bridges where necessary. Public gardens should remain open at night, unlit. (In a few cases, a steady dim illumination might be justified on psychogeographical grounds.)

Street lamps should all be equipped with switches so that people can adjust the lighting as they wish.

With regard to churches, four different solutions were proposed, all of which were considered defensible until appropriate *experimentation* can be undertaken, which should quickly demonstrate which is best.

G.-E. Debord argued for the total destruction of religious buildings of all denominations, leaving no trace and using the sites for other purposes.

Gil J Wolman proposed that churches be left standing but stripped of all religious content. They should be treated as ordinary buildings, and children should be allowed to play in them.

Michèle Bernstein suggested that churches be partially demolished, so that the remaining ruins give no hint of their original function (the Tour Jacques on Boulevard de Sébastopol being an unintentional example). The ideal solution would be to raze churches to the ground and then build ruins in their place. The first method was proposed purely for reasons of economy.

Lastly, Jacques Fillon favored the idea of transforming churches into *houses of horror* (maintaining their current ambience while accentuating their terrifying effects).

Everyone agreed that aesthetic objections should be rejected, that admirers of the portals of Chartres should be silenced. Beauty, *when it is not a promise of happiness*, must be destroyed. And what could be more repugnant representations of unhappiness than such monuments to everything in the world that remains to be overcome, to the numerous aspects of life that remain inhuman?

Train stations should be left as they are. Their rather poignant ugliness contributes to the feeling of transience that makes these buildings mildly attractive. Gil J Wolman proposed removing or scrambling all information regarding departures (destinations, timetables, etc.) in order to facilitate *dérives*. After a lively debate, those opposing this motion retracted their objections and it was wholeheartedly approved. It was also agreed that background noise in the stations should be intensified by broadcasting recordings from many other stations, as well as from certain harbors.

Cemeteries should be eliminated. All corpses and related memorials should be totally destroyed, leaving no ashes and no remains. (It should be noted that these hideous remnants of an alienated past constitute a subliminal reactionary propaganda. Is it possible to see a cemetery and not be reminded of Mauriac, Gide, or Edgar Faure?)

Museums should be abolished and their masterpieces distributed to bars (Philippe de Champaigne's works in the Arab cafés of Rue Xavier-Privas; David's *Sacre* in the Tonneau on Rue Montagne-Geneviève).

Everyone should have free access to the prisons. They should be available as tourist destinations, with no distinction between visitors and inmates. (To spice things up, monthly lotteries might be held to see which visitor would win a real prison sentence. This would cater to those imbeciles who feel an imperative need to undergo uninteresting risks: spelunkers, for example, and everyone else whose *craving for play* is satisfied by such paltry pseudogames.)

Buildings whose ugliness cannot be put to any good use (such as the Petit or Grand Palais) should make way for other constructions. Statues that no longer have any meaning, and whose possible aesthetic refurbishing would inevitably be condemned by history, should be removed. Their usefulness could be extended during their final years by changing the inscriptions on their pedestals, either in a political sense (*The Tiger Named Clemenceau* on the Champs Élysées) or for purposes of disorientation (*Dialectical Homage to Fever and Quinine* at the intersection of Boulevard Michel and Rue Comte, or *The Great Depths* in the cathedral plaza on the Île de la Cité).

In order to put an end to the cretinizing influence of current street names, names of city councilors, heroes of the Resistance, all the Émiles and Édouards (55 Paris streets), all the Bugeauds and Gallifets,* and in general all obscene names (such as Rue de l'Évangile) should be obliterated.

In this regard, the appeal launched in *Potlatch* #9 for ignoring the word "saint" in place names is more pertinent than ever.

LETTRIST INTERNATIONAL
October 1955*

A User's Guide to Détournement*

Every reasonably aware person of our time is aware of the obvious fact that art can no longer be justified as a superior activity, or even as a compensatory activity to which one might honorably devote oneself. The reason for this deterioration is clearly the emergence of productive forces that necessitate other production relations and a new practice of life. In the civil-war phase we are engaged in, and in close connection with the orientation we are discovering for certain superior activities to come, we believe that all known means of expression are going to converge in a general movement of propaganda that must encompass all the perpetually interacting aspects of social reality.

There are several conflicting opinions about the forms and even the very nature of educative propaganda, opinions that generally reflect one or another currently fashionable variety of reformist politics. Suffice it to say that in our view the premises for revolution, on the cultural as well as the strictly political level, are not only ripe, they have begun to rot. It is not just returning to the past which is reactionary; even "modern" cultural objectives are ultimately reactionary since they depend on ideological formulations of a past society that has prolonged its death agony to the present. The only historically justified tactic is extremist innovation.

The literary and artistic heritage of humanity should be used for partisan propaganda purposes. It is, of course, necessary to go beyond any idea of mere scandal. Since opposition to the bourgeois notion of art and artistic genius has become pretty much old hat, [Marcel Duchamp's] drawing a mustache on the *Mona Lisa* is no more interesting than the original version of that painting. We must now push this process to the point of negating the negation. Bertolt Brecht, revealing in a recent interview in *France-Observateur* that he makes cuts in the classics of the theater in order to make the performances more educative, is much closer than Duchamp to the revolutionary orientation we are calling for. We must note, however, that in Brecht's case these salutary alterations are narrowly limited by his unfortunate respect for culture as defined by the ruling class—that same respect, taught in the newspapers of the worker parties as well as in the primary schools of the bourgeoisie, which leads even the reddest worker districts of Paris always to prefer *The Cid* over [Brecht's] *Mother Courage*.

It is in fact necessary to eliminate all remnants of the notion of personal property in this area. The appearance of new necessities outmodes previous "inspired" works. They become obstacles, dangerous habits. The point is not whether we like them or not. We have to go beyond them.

Any elements, no matter where they are taken from, can be used to make new combinations. The discoveries of modern poetry regarding the analogical structure of images demonstrate that when two objects are brought together, no matter how far apart their original contexts may be, a relationship is always formed. Restricting oneself to a personal arrangement of words is mere convention. The mutual interference of two worlds of feeling, or the juxtaposition of two independent expressions, supersedes the original elements and produces a synthetic organization of greater efficacy. Anything can be used.

It goes without saying that one is not limited to correcting a work or to integrating diverse fragments of out-of-date works into a new one; one can also alter the meaning of those fragments in any appropriate way, leaving the imbeciles to their slavish reference to "citations."

Such parodistic methods have often been used to obtain comical effects. But such humor is the result of contradictions within a condition whose existence is taken for granted. Since the world of literature seems to us almost as distant as the Stone Age, such contradictions don't make us laugh. It is thus necessary to envisage a parodic-serious stage where the accumulation of detourned elements, far from aiming to arouse indignation or laughter by alluding to some original work, will express our indifference toward a meaningless and forgotten original, and concern itself with rendering a certain sublimity.

Lautréamont advanced so far in this direction that he is still partially misunderstood even by his most ostentatious admirers. In spite of his obvious application of this method to theoretical language in *Poésies*—where Lautréamont (drawing particularly on the maxims of Pascal and Vauvenargues) strives to reduce the argument, through successive concentrations, to maxims alone—a certain Viroux caused considerable astonishment three or four years ago by conclusively demonstrating that *Maldoror* is one vast détournement of Buffon and other works of natural history, among other things. The fact that the prosaists of *Figaro*, like Viroux himself, were able to see this as a justification for disparaging Lautréamont, and that others believed they had to defend him by praising his insolence, only testifies to the senility of these two camps of dotards in courtly combat with each other. A slogan like "Plagiarism is necessary, progress depends on it" is still as poorly understood, and for the same reasons, as the famous phrase about the poetry that "must be made by all."*

Apart from Lautréamont's work—whose appearance so far ahead of its time has to a great extent preserved it from a detailed examination—the tendencies toward détournement that can be observed in contemporary expression are for the most part unconscious or accidental. It is in the advertising industry, more than in the domain of decaying aesthetic production, that one can find the best examples.

We can first of all define two main categories of detourned elements, without considering whether or not their being brought together is accompanied by corrections introduced in the originals. These are *minor détournements* and *deceptive détournements*.

Minor détournement is the détournement of an element which has no importance in itself and which thus draws all its meaning from the new context in which it has been placed. For example, a press clipping, a neutral phrase, a commonplace photograph.

Deceptive détournement, also termed premonitory-proposition détournement, is in contrast the détournement of an intrinsically significant element, which derives a different scope from the new context. A slogan of Saint-Just, for example, or a film sequence from Eisenstein.

Extensive detourned works will thus usually be composed of one or more series of deceptive and minor détournements.

Several laws on the use of détournement can now be formulated:

It is the most distant detourned element which contributes most sharply to the overall impression, and not the elements that directly determine the nature of this impression. For example, in a metagraph relating to the Spanish Civil War the phrase with the most distinctly revolutionary sense is a fragment from a lipstick ad: "Pretty lips are red." In another metagraph (*The Death of J.H.*) 125 classified ads of bars for sale express a suicide more strikingly than the newspaper articles that recount it.*

The distortions introduced in the detourned elements must be as simplified as possible, since the main impact of a détournement is directly related to the conscious or semiconscious recollection of the original contexts of the elements. This is well known. Let us simply note that if this dependence on memory implies that one must determine one's public before devising a détournement, this is only a particular case of a general law that governs not only détournement but also any other form of action on the world. The idea of pure, absolute expression is dead; it only temporarily survives in parodic form as long as our other enemies survive.

Détournement is less effective the more it approaches a rational reply. This is the case with a rather large number of Lautréamont's altered maxims. The more the rational character of the reply is apparent, the more indistinguishable it becomes from the ordinary spirit of repartee, which similarly uses the opponent's words against him. This is naturally not limited to spoken language. It was in this connection that we objected to the project of some of our comrades who proposed to detourn an anti-Soviet poster of the fascist organization "Peace and Liberty"—which proclaimed, amid images of overlapping flags of the Western powers, "Union makes strength"—by adding onto it a smaller sheet with the phrase "and coalitions make war."

Détournement by simple reversal is always the most direct and the least effective. Thus, the Black Mass reacts against the construction of an ambience based on a given metaphysics by constructing an ambience within the same framework that merely reverses—and thus simultaneously conserves—the values of that metaphysics. Such reversals may nevertheless have a certain progressive aspect. For example, Clemenceau [nicknamed "The Tiger"] could be referred to as "The Tiger Named Clemenceau."

Of the four laws that have just been set forth, the first is essential and applies universally. The other three are practically applicable only to deceptive detourned elements.

The first visible consequences of a widespread use of détournement, apart from its intrinsic propaganda powers, will be the revival of a multitude of bad books, and thus the extensive (unintended) participation of their unknown authors; an increasingly extensive transformation of phrases or plastic works that happen to be in fashion; and above all an ease of production far surpassing in quantity, variety, and quality the automatic writing that has bored us for so long.

Détournement not only leads to the discovery of new forms of talent; in addition, clashing head-on with all social and legal conventions, it cannot fail to be a powerful cultural weapon in the service of a real class struggle. The cheapness of its products is the heavy artillery that breaks through all the Chinese walls of understanding.* It is a real means of proletarian artistic education, the first step toward a *literary communism*.

Ideas and creations in the realm of détournement can be multiplied at will. For the moment we will limit ourselves to showing a few concrete possibilities in various current sectors of communication—it being understood that these separate sectors are significant only in relation to present-day technologies, and are all tending to merge into superior syntheses with the advance of these technologies.

Apart from the various direct uses of detourned phrases in posters, records, and radio broadcasts, the two main applications of detourned prose are metagraphic writings and, to a lesser degree, the adroit perversion of the classical novel form.

There is not much future in the détournement of complete novels, but during the transitional phase there might be a certain number of undertakings of this sort. Such a détournement gains by being accompanied by illustrations whose relationships to the text are not immediately obvious. In spite of undeniable difficulties, we believe it would be possible to produce an instructive psychogeographical détournement of George Sand's *Consuelo*, which thus decked out could be relaunched on the literary market disguised under some innocuous title like "Life in the Suburbs," or even under a title itself detourned, such as "The Lost Patrol." (It would be a good idea to reuse in this way many titles of deteriorated old films of which nothing else remains, or of the films that continue to deaden the minds of young people in the cinema clubs.)

Metagraphic writing, no matter how outdated its plastic framework may be, presents far richer opportunities for detourning prose, as well as other appropriate objects or images. One can get some idea of this from the project, conceived in 1951 but eventually abandoned for lack of sufficient financial means, which envisaged a pinball machine arranged in such a way that the play of the lights and the more or less predictable trajectories of the balls would form a metagraphic-spatial composition entitled *Thermal Sensations and Desires of People Passing by*

the Gates of the Cluny Museum Around an Hour after Sunset in November.
We have since come to realize that a situationist-analytic enterprise
cannot scientifically advance by way of such works. The means nevertheless remain suitable for less ambitious goals.

It is obviously in the realm of the cinema that détournement can
attain its greatest effectiveness and, for those concerned with this
aspect, its greatest beauty.

The powers of film are so extensive, and the absence of coordination of those powers is so glaring, that virtually any film that is above
the miserable average can provide matter for endless polemics among
spectators or professional critics. Only the conformism of those people
prevents them from discovering equally appealing charms and equally glaring faults even in the worst films. To cut through this absurd
confusion of values, we can observe that Griffith's *Birth of a Nation* is
one of the most important films in the history of the cinema because
of its wealth of innovations. On the other hand, it is a racist film and
therefore absolutely does not merit being shown in its present form.
But its total prohibition could be seen as regrettable from the point of
view of the secondary, but potentially worthier, domain of the cinema.
It would be better to detourn it as a whole, without necessarily even
altering the montage, by adding a soundtrack that made a powerful
denunciation of the horrors of imperialist war and of the activities of
the Ku Klux Klan, which are continuing in the United States even now.

Such a détournement—a very moderate one—is in the final analysis nothing more than the moral equivalent of the restoration of old
paintings in museums. But most films only merit being cut up to com-
pose other works. This reconversion of preexisting sequences will obviously be accompanied by other elements, musical or pictorial as well as
historical. While the cinematic rewriting of history has until now been
largely along the lines of Sacha Guitry's burlesque re-creations, one
could have Robespierre say, before his execution: "In spite of so many
trials, my experience and the grandeur of my task convinces me that all
is well." If in this case an appropriate reuse of a Greek tragedy enables
us to exalt Robespierre, we can conversely imagine a neorealist-type
sequence, at the counter of a truck stop bar, for example, with one of
the truck drivers saying seriously to another: "Ethics was formerly confined to the books of the philosophers; we have introduced it into the
governing of nations." One can see that this juxtaposition illuminates
Maximilien's idea, the idea of a dictatorship of the proletariat.*

The light of détournement is propagated in a straight line. To the
extent that new architecture seems to have to begin with an experimental baroque stage, the *architectural complex*—which we conceive

as the construction of a dynamic environment related to styles of behavior—will probably detourn existing architectural forms, and in any case will make plastic and emotional use of all sorts of detourned objects: careful arrangements of such things as cranes or metal scaffolding replacing a defunct sculptural tradition. This is shocking only to the most fanatical admirers of French-style gardens. It is said that in his old age D'Annunzio, that pro-fascist swine, had the prow of a torpedo boat in his park. Leaving aside his patriotic motives, the idea of such a monument is not without a certain charm.

If détournement were extended to urbanistic realizations, not many people would remain unaffected by an exact reconstruction in one city of an entire neighborhood of another. Life can never be too disorienting: détournement on this level would really spice it up.

Titles themselves, as we have already seen, are a basic element of détournement. This follows from two general observations: that all titles are interchangeable and that they have a decisive importance in several genres. The detective stories in the "Série Noir" are all extremely similar, yet merely continually changing the titles suffices to hold a considerable audience. In music a title always exerts a great influence, yet the choice of one is quite arbitrary. Thus it wouldn't be a bad idea to make a final correction to the title of the Eroica Symphony by changing it, for example, to "Lenin Symphony."*

The title contributes strongly to the détournement of a work, but there is an inevitable counteraction of the work on the title. Thus one can make extensive use of specific titles taken from scientific publications ("Coastal Biology of Temperate Seas") or military ones ("Night Combat of Small Infantry Units"), or even of many phrases found in illustrated children's books ("Marvelous Landscapes Greet the Voyagers").

In closing, we should briefly mention some aspects of what we call ultra-détournement, that is, the tendencies for détournement to operate in everyday social life. Gestures and words can be given other meanings, and have been throughout history for various practical reasons. The secret societies of ancient China made use of quite subtle recognition signals encompassing the greater part of social behavior (the manner of arranging cups; of drinking; quotations of poems interrupted at agreed-on points). The need for a secret language, for passwords, is inseparable from a tendency toward play. Ultimately, any sign or word is susceptible to being converted into something else, even into its opposite. The royalist insurgents of the Vendée,* because they bore the disgusting image of the Sacred Heart of Jesus, were called the Red Army. In the limited domain of political war vocabulary this expression was completely detourned within a century.

Outside of language, it is possible to use the same methods to detourn clothing, with all its strong emotional connotations. Here again we find the notion of disguise closely linked to play. Finally, when we have got to the stage of constructing situations—the ultimate goal of all our activity—everyone will be free to detourn entire situations by deliberately changing this or that determinant condition of them.

The methods that we have briefly examined here are presented not as our own invention, but as a generally widespread practice which we propose to systematize.

In itself, the theory of détournement scarcely interests us. But we find it linked to almost all the constructive aspects of the presituationist period of transition. Thus its enrichment, through practice, seems necessary.

We will postpone the development of these theses until later.

GUY DEBORD, GIL J WOLMAN
1956

The Alba Platform

September 2-8 a Congress was held in Alba, Italy, convoked by Asger Jorn and Giuseppe Gallizio in the name of the International Movement for an Imaginist Bauhaus, a grouping whose views are in agreement with the Lettrist International's program regarding urbanism and its possible uses (see *Potlatch* #26). Representatives of avant-garde groups from eight countries (Algeria, Belgium, Czechoslovakia, Denmark, France, Great Britain, Italy, Netherlands) met there to establish the foundations for a united organization. The tasks toward this end were dealt with in all their implications.

Christian Dotremont,* who had been announced as a member of the Belgian delegation despite the fact that he has for some time been a collaborator in the *Nouvelle Nouvelle Revue Française,* refrained from appearing at the Congress, where his presence would have been unacceptable for the majority of the participants.

Enrico Baj, representative of the "Nuclear Art Movement," was excluded the very first day. The Congress affirmed its break with the Nuclearists by issuing the following statement: "Confronted with his conduct in certain previous affairs, Baj withdrew from the Congress. He did not make off with the cash-box."

Meanwhile our Czechoslovakian comrades Pravoslav Rada and Kotik were prevented from entering Italy. In spite of our protests, the Italian government did not grant them visas to pass through its national iron curtain until the end of the Alba Congress.

The statement presented by Wolman, the Lettrist International delegate, particularly stressed the necessity for a common platform specifying the totality of current experimentation:

> Comrades, the parallel crises presently affecting all modes of artistic creation result from general, interrelated tendencies and cannot be resolved outside a comprehensive general perspective. The process of negation and destruction that has manifested itself at an accelerated pace against all the former conditions of artistic activity is irreversible: it is the consequence of the appearance of superior possibilities of action on the world. . . . Whatever prestige the bourgeoisie may today be willing to grant to fragmentary or deliberately retrograde artistic endeavors, creation can now be nothing less than a synthesis aiming at the construction of entire atmospheres and styles of life. . . . A unitary urbanism—the synthesis we call for, incorporating arts and technologies—must be created in accordance with new values of life, values which we now need to distinguish and disseminate. . . .

The Congress concluded by expressing a substantial agreement in the form of a six-point resolution, declaring the "necessity of an integral construction of the environment by a unitary urbanism that must utilize all the arts and modern techniques"; the "inevitable outmodedness of any renovation of an art within its traditional limits"; the "recognition of an essential interdependence between unitary urbanism and a future style of life" which must be situated "in the perspective of a greater genuine freedom and a greater domination of nature"; and finally, "unity of action among the signers on the basis of this program" (the sixth point going on to enumerate the various specifics of mutual support).

In addition to this final resolution—signed by J. Calonne, Constant, G. Gallizio, A. Jorn, Kotik, Rada, Piero Simondo, E. Sottsass Jr., Elena Verrone, Wolman—the Congress unanimously declared itself against any relations with participants in the Festival de la Cité Radieuse, thus following through with the boycott initiated the preceding month.

At the conclusion of the Congress Gil J Wolman was added to the editorial board of *Eristica*, the information bulletin of the International Movement for an Imaginist Bauhaus, and Asger Jorn was placed on the board of directors of the Lettrist International.

The Alba Congress will probably one day be seen as a key moment, one of the difficult stages in the struggle for a new sensibility and a new culture, a struggle which is itself part of the general revolutionary resurgence characterizing the year 1956, visible in the upsurge of the masses in the USSR, Poland, and Hungary (although in the latter case we see the dangerously confusing revival of rotten old watchwords of clerical nationalism resulting from the fatal error of the prohibition of any Marxist opposition), in the successes of the Algerian revolt, and in the major strikes in Spain. These developments allow us the greatest hopes for the near future.

LETTRIST INTERNATIONAL
November 1956

Notes on the Formation of an Imaginist Bauhaus

What was the Bauhaus?

The Bauhaus was an answer to the question: What kind of "education" do artists need in order to take their place in the machine age?

How was the Bauhaus idea implemented?

It was implemented with a "school" in Germany, first at Weimar, then at Dessau. Founded in 1919 by the architect Walter Gropius, it was destroyed by the Nazis in 1933.

What is the International Movement for an Imaginist Bauhaus?

It is the answer to the question *where and how* to find a justified place for artists in the machine age. This answer demonstrates that the education carried out by the old Bauhaus was mistaken.

How has the idea of an International Movement for an Imaginist Bauhaus been implemented?

The Movement was founded in Switzerland in 1953 as a tendency aimed at forming a united organization capable of promoting an integral revolutionary cultural approach. In 1954 the experience of the Albissola gathering demonstrated that experimental artists must get hold of industrial means and subject them to their own nonutilitarian ends. In 1955 an imaginist laboratory was founded at Alba. Conclusion of the Albissola experience: complete inflationary devaluation of modern values of decoration (cf. ceramics produced by children).

In 1956 the Alba Congress dialectically defined unitary urbanism. In 1957 the Movement is promulgating the watchword of psychogeographical action.

What we want

We want the same economic and practical means and possibilities that are already at the disposal of scientific research, of whose momentous results everyone is aware.

Artistic research is identical to "human science," which for us means "concerned" science, not purely historical science. This research should be carried out by artists with the assistance of scientists.

The first institute ever formed for this purpose is the experimental laboratory for free artistic research founded 29 September 1955 at Alba. This type of laboratory is not an instructional institution; it simply offers new possibilities for artistic experimentation.

The leaders of the old Bauhaus were great masters with exceptional talents, but they were poor teachers. The students' works were only pious imitations of their masters. The real influence of the latter was indirect, by force of example: Ruskin on Van de Velde, Van de Velde on Gropius.

This is not at all a criticism, it is simply a recognition of reality, from which the following conclusions may be drawn: The direct transfer of artistic gifts is impossible; artistic adaptation takes place through a series of contradictory phases: Shock—Wonder—Imitation—Rejection —Experimentation—Possession.

None of these phases can be avoided, though they need not all be gone through by any one individual.

Our practical conclusion is the following: We are abandoning all efforts at pedagogical action and moving toward experimental activity.

ASGER JORN
1957

Report on the Construction of Situations and on the International Situationist Tendency's Conditions of Organization and Action

Revolution and Counterrevolution in Modern Culture

First of all, we think the world must be changed. We want the most liberating change of the society and life in which we find ourselves confined. We know that such a change is possible through appropriate actions.

Our specific concern is the use of certain means of action and the discovery of new ones, means which are more easily recognizable in the domain of culture and customs, but which must be applied in interrelation with all revolutionary changes.

A society's "culture" both reflects and prefigures its possible ways of organizing life. Our era is characterized by the lagging of revolutionary political action behind the development of modern possibilities of production which call for a more advanced organization of the world.

We are going through a crucial historical crisis which each year poses more acutely the global problem of rationally mastering the new productive forces and creating a new civilization. Yet the international working-class movement, on which depends the prerequisite overthrow of the economic infrastructure of exploitation, has registered only a few partial local successes. Capitalism has invented new forms of struggle (state intervention in the economy, expansion of the consumer sector, fascist governments) while camouflaging class oppositions through various reformist tactics and exploiting the degenerations of working-class leaderships. In this way it has succeeded in maintaining the old social relations in the great majority of the highly industrialized countries, thereby depriving a socialist society of its indispensable material base. In contrast, the underdeveloped or colonized countries, which over the last decade have engaged in the most direct and massive battles against imperialism, have begun to win some very significant victories. These victories are aggravating the contradictions of the capitalist economy and (particularly in the case of the Chinese revolution) could be a contributing factor toward a renewal of the whole revolutionary movement. Such a renewal cannot limit itself to reforms within the capitalist or anticapitalist countries, but must develop conflicts posing the question of power everywhere.

The shattering of modern culture is the result, on the plane of ideological struggle, of the chaotic crisis of these antagonisms. The new desires that are taking shape are presented in distorted form: present-day resources could enable them to be fulfilled, but the anachronistic economic structure is incapable of developing these resources to such ends. Ruling-class ideology has meanwhile lost all coherence because of the depreciation of its successive conceptions of the world (a depreciation which leads the ruling class to historical indecision and uncertainty); because of the coexistence of a range of mutually contradictory reactionary ideologies (such as Christianity and social-democracy); and because of the mixing into contemporary Western culture of a number of only recently appreciated features of several foreign civilizations. The main goal of ruling-class ideology is therefore to maintain this confusion.

Within culture (it should be understood that throughout this text we are ignoring the scientific or educational aspects of culture, even if the confusion we have noted is also visibly reflected at the level of general scientific theories and notions of education; we are using the term to refer to a complex of aesthetics, sentiments, and customs: the reaction of an era on everyday life) there are two parallel counterrevolutionary confusionist tactics: the partial co-option of new values, and a deliberately anticultural, industrially facilitated production (novels, films), the latter being a natural continuation of the imbecilization of young people begun in their schools and families. The ruling ideology sees to it that subversive discoveries are trivialized and sterilized, after which they can be safely spectacularized. It even manages to make use of subversive individuals—by falsifying their works after their death, or, while they are still alive, by taking advantage of the general ideological confusion and drugging them with one or another of the many mystiques at their disposal.

One of the contradictions of the bourgeoisie in its period of decline is that while it respects the abstract principle of intellectual and artistic creation, it resists actual creations when they first appear, then eventually exploits them. This is because it needs to maintain a certain degree of criticality and experimental research among a minority, but must take care to channel this activity into narrowly compartmentalized utilitarian disciplines and avert any holistic critique and experimentation. In the domain of culture the bourgeoisie strives to divert the taste for innovation, which is dangerous for it in our era, toward certain confused, degraded, and innocuous forms of novelty. Through the commercial mechanisms that control cultural activity, avant-garde tendencies are cut off from the segments of society that could support them, segments already limited because of the general social conditions. The people within these tendencies who become well known are generally accepted as exceptional individuals, on the condition that they accept various renunciations: the essential point is always the renunciation of a comprehensive opposition and the acceptance of fragmentary works susceptible to diverse interpretations. This is what gives the very term "avant-garde," which in the final analysis is always defined and manipulated by the bourgeoisie, a dubious and ridiculous aspect.

The very notion of a collective avant-garde, with the militant aspect it implies, is a recent product of the historical conditions that are simultaneously giving rise to the necessity for a coherent revolutionary program in culture and to the necessity to struggle against the forces that impede the development of such a program. Such groups are led to transpose into their sphere of activity certain organizational methods originally created by revolutionary politics, and their action is henceforth inconceivable without some connection with a political critique. In this regard there is a notable progression from Futurism through Dadaism and Surrealism to the movements formed after 1945. At each of these stages, however, one discovers the same desire for total change; and the same rapid disintegration when the inability to change the real world profoundly enough leads to a defensive withdrawal to the very doctrinal positions whose inadequacy had just been revealed.

Futurism, whose influence spread from Italy in the period preceding World War I, adopted an attitude of revolutionizing literature and the arts which introduced a great number of formal innovations, but which was only based on an extremely simplistic application of the notion of mechanical progress. Futurism's puerile technological optimism vanished with the period of bourgeois euphoria that had sustained it. Italian Futurism collapsed, going from nationalism to fascism without ever attaining a more complete theoretical vision of its time.

Dadaism, initiated in Zurich and New York by refugees and deserters from World War I, expressed the rejection of all the values of a bourgeois society whose bankruptcy had just become so grossly evident. Its violent manifestations in postwar Germany and France aimed mainly at the destruction of art and literature and to a lesser degree at certain forms of behavior (deliberately imbecilic spectacles, speeches, and excursions). Its historic role is to have delivered a mortal blow to the traditional conception of culture. The almost immediate dissolution of dadaism was an inevitable result of its purely negative definition. The dadaist spirit has nevertheless influenced all subsequent movements; and any future constructive position must include a dadaist-type negative aspect as long as the social conditions that impose the repetition of rotten superstructures—conditions that have intellectually already been definitively condemned—have not been wiped out by force.

The creators of surrealism, who had participated in the dadaist movement in France, endeavored to define the terrain of a constructive action on the basis of the spirit of revolt and the extreme depreciation of traditional means of communication expressed by dadaism. Setting out from a poetic application of Freudian psychology, surrealism extended the methods it had discovered to painting, to film, and to some aspects of everyday life; and its influence, in more diffuse forms, spread much further. Now, what is important in an enterprise of this nature is not whether it is completely or relatively right, but whether it succeeds in catalyzing for a certain time the desires of an era. Surrealism's period of progress, marked by the liquidation of idealism and a moment of rallying to dialectical materialism, came to a halt soon after 1930, but its decay only became evident after World War II. Surrealism had by then spread to numerous countries. It had also initiated a discipline whose rigor must not be overestimated and which was often tempered by commercial considerations, but which was nevertheless an effective means of struggle against the confusionist mechanisms of the bourgeoisie.

The surrealist program, asserting the sovereignty of desire and surprise and proposing a new way of life, is much richer in constructive possibilities than is generally realized. The limited scope of surrealism was in large part due to the lack of material means for fulfilling its aims. But the devolution of its original proponents into spiritualism, and above all the mediocrity of its later members, obliges us to search for the failed development of surrealist theory in the very origin of that theory.

The error that is at the root of surrealism is the idea of the infinite richness of the unconscious imagination. The cause of surrealism's ideological failure was its belief that the unconscious was the finally discovered ultimate force of life, and the fact that the surrealists revised the history of ideas in accordance with that simplistic perspective and never went any further. We now know that the unconscious imagination is poor, that automatic writing is monotonous, and that the whole ostentatious genre of would-be "strange" and "shocking" surrealistic creations has ceased to be very surprising. The formal fidelity to this style of imagination ultimately leads back to the polar opposite of the modern conditions of imagination: back to traditional occultism. The extent to which surrealism has remained dependent on its hypothesis regarding the unconscious can be seen in the theoretical investigations attempted by the second-generation surrealists: Calas and Mabille relate everything to the two successive aspects of the surrealist practice of the unconscious—the former to psychoanalysis, the latter to cosmic influences. The discovery of the role of the unconscious was indeed a surprise and an innovation; but it was not a law of future surprises and innovations. Freud had also ended up discovering this when he wrote: "Whatever is conscious wears out. What is unconscious remains unalterable. But once it is freed, it too falls to ruin."

Opposing an apparently irrational society in which the clash between reality and the old but still vigorously proclaimed values was pushed to the point of absurdity, surrealism made use of the irrational to destroy that society's superficially logical values. The very success of surrealism has a lot to do with the fact that the most modern side of this society's ideology has renounced a strict hierarchy of factitious values and openly uses the irrational, including vestiges of surrealism. The bourgeoisie must above all prevent a new beginning of revolutionary thought. It was aware of the danger of surrealism. Now that it has been able to co-opt it into ordinary aesthetic commerce, it would like people to believe that surrealism was the most radical and disturbing movement possible. It thus cultivates a sort of nostalgia for surrealism at the same time that it discredits any new venture by automatically pigeonholing it as a rehash of surrealism, a rerun of a defeat which according to it is definitive and can no longer be brought back into question by anyone. Reacting against the alienation of Christian society has led some people to admire the completely irrational alienation of primitive societies. But we need to go forward, not backward. We need to make the world *more* rational—the necessary first step in making it more exciting.

Decomposition: The Ultimate Stage of Bourgeois Thought

The two main centers of "modern" culture are Paris and Moscow. The styles originating in Paris (the majority of whose elaborators are not French) influence Europe, America, and the other developed countries of the capitalist zone such as Japan. The styles imposed administratively by Moscow influence all the workers' states and also have a slight effect on Paris and its European zone of influence. The Moscow influence is directly political. The persistence of the traditional influence of Paris stems partly from its long-entrenched position as a professional cultural center.

Because bourgeois thought is lost in systematic confusion and Marxist thought has been profoundly distorted in the workers' states, conservatism reigns both East and West, especially in the domain of culture and customs. This conservatism is overt in Moscow, which has revived the typically petty-bourgeois attitudes of the nineteenth century. In Paris it is hidden, disguised as anarchism, cynicism, or humor. Although both of these ruling cultures are fundamentally incapable of dealing with the real problems of our time, relevant experimentation has been carried further in the West. In the context of this sort of cultural production, the Moscow zone functions as a region of underdevelopment.

In the bourgeois zone, where an appearance of intellectual freedom has generally been tolerated, the knowledge of the movement of ideas and the confused vision of the multiple transformations of the social environment tend to make people aware of an ongoing upheaval whose motivating forces are out of control. The reigning sensibility tries to adapt itself to this situation while resisting new changes that present new dangers. The solutions offered by the retrograde currents ultimately come down to three main attitudes: prolonging the fashions produced by the dada–surrealism crisis (which crisis is simply the sophisticated cultural expression of a state of mind that spontaneously manifests itself wherever previously accepted meanings of life crumble along with previous lifestyles); settling into mental ruins; or returning to the distant past.

In the first case, a diluted form of surrealism can be found everywhere. It has all the tastes of the surrealist era and none of its ideas. Its aesthetic is based on repetition. The remnants of orthodox surrealism have arrived at the stage of occultist senility, and are as incapable of articulating an ideological position as they are of inventing anything whatsoever. They lend credence to increasingly crude charlatanisms and engender others.

Setting up shop in nullity is the cultural solution that has been most visible in the years following World War II. This solution includes two possibilities, each of which has been abundantly illustrated: dissimulating nothingness by means of an appropriate vocabulary, or openly flaunting it.

The first of these options has become particularly famous since the advent of existentialist literature, which has reproduced, under the cover of a borrowed philosophy, the most mediocre aspects of the cultural evolution of the preceding three decades and augmented its mass-media-based notoriety by doses of fake Marxism and psychoanalysis and by successive announcements of more or less arbitrary political engagements and resignations. These tactics have generated a very large number of followers, avowed or unacknowledged. The continuing proliferation of abstract painting and its associated theories is another example of the same nature and scope.

The complacent affirmation of total mental nullity is exemplified by the recent neoliterary phenomenon of "cynical young right-wing novelists," but is by no means limited to right-wingers, novelists, or semiyouth.

Among the tendencies calling for a return to the past, the doctrine of Socialist Realism has proven to be the most durable, because its indefensible position in the domain of cultural creation seems to be supported by its appeal to the conclusions of a revolutionary movement. At the 1948 conference of Soviet musicians, Andrei Zhdanov* revealed the stake of theoretical repression: "Haven't we done well to preserve the treasures of classic painting and to suppress the liquidators of painting? Wouldn't the survival of such 'schools' have amounted to the liquidation of painting?" Faced with this liquidation of painting and with many other liquidations, and recognizing the crumbling of all its systems of values, the advanced Western bourgeoisie is banking on total ideological decomposition, whether out of desperate reaction or out of political opportunism. In contrast, Zhdanov—with the taste characteristic of the parvenu—recognizes himself in the petty-bourgeoisie that opposes the decomposition of nineteenth-century cultural values, and can see nothing else to do than to undertake an authoritarian restoration of those values. He is unrealistic enough to believe that short-lived local political circumstances will give him the power to evade the general problems of this era, if only he can force people to return to the study of superseded problems after having repressed all the conclusions that history has previously drawn from those problems.

The form (and even some aspects of the content) of this Socialist Realism is not very different from the traditional propaganda of religious organizations, particularly of Catholicism. By means of an invariable propaganda, Catholicism defends a unitary ideological structure that it alone, among all the forces of the past, still possesses. But at the same time, in a parallel operation designed to recapture the increasingly numerous sectors that are escaping its influence, the Catholic Church is attempting to take over modern cultural forms, particularly those representing complicated theoretical nullity ("spontaneous" painting, for example). The Catholic reactionaries have the advantage over other bourgeois tendencies of being able to rely on a permanent hierarchy of values; this inalterable foundation enables them all the more freely to push decomposition to the extreme in whatever discipline they engage in.

The crisis of modern culture has led to total ideological decomposition. Nothing new can be built on these ruins. Critical thought itself becomes impossible as each judgment clashes with others and each individual invokes fragments of outmoded systems or follows merely personal inclinations.

This decomposition can be seen everywhere. It is no longer a matter of noting the increasingly massive use of commercial publicity to influence judgments about cultural creation. We have arrived at a stage of ideological absence in which advertising has become the only active factor, overriding any preexisting critical judgment or transforming such judgment into a mere conditioned reflex. The complex operation of sales techniques has reached the point of surprising even the ad professionals by automatically generating pseudosubjects of cultural debate. This is the sociological significance of the Françoise Sagan phenomenon* in France over the last three years, an experience whose repercussions have even penetrated beyond the cultural zone centered on Paris by provoking some interest in the workers' states. The professional judges of culture, seeing such a phenomenon as an unpredictable effect of mechanisms with which they are unfamiliar, tend to attribute it to mere crude mass-media publicity. But their profession nevertheless obliges them to come up with bogus critiques of these bogus works. (Moreover, a work whose interest is inexplicable constitutes the richest subject for bourgeois confusionist criticism.) They naturally remain unaware of the fact that the intellectual mechanisms of criticism had already escaped them long before the external mechanisms arrived to exploit this void. They avoid facing the fact that Sagan is simply the ridiculous flip side of the change of means of expression into means of action on everyday life. This process of supersession has caused the life of the author to become increasingly more important than her work. As the period of important expressions arrives at its ultimate reduction, nothing of any possible importance remains except the personality of the author, who in turn is no longer capable of possessing any notable quality beyond her age, or some fashionable vice, or some picturesque old craft.

The opposition that must now be united against this ideological decomposition must not get caught up in criticizing the buffooneries appearing in outmoded forms such as poems or novels. We have to criticize activities that are important for the future, activities that we need to make use of. One of the most serious signs of the present ideological decomposition is the fact that the functionalist theory of architecture is now based on the most reactionary conceptions of society and morality. That is, the temporarily and partially valid contributions of the original Bauhaus or of the school of Le Corbusier have been distorted so as to reinforce an excessively backward notion of life and of the framework of life.

Everything indicates, however, that since 1956 we have been entering a new phase of the struggle, and that an upheaval of revolutionary forces, attacking the most appalling obstacles on all fronts, is beginning to change the conditions of the preceding period. Socialist Realism is beginning to decline in the countries of the anticapitalist camp, along with the reactionary Stalinism that produced it, while in the West the Sagan culture is marking a depth of bourgeois decadence beyond which it is probably impossible to go, and there seems to be an increasing awareness of the exhaustion of the cultural expedients that have served since the end of World War II. In this context, the avant-garde minority may be able to rediscover a positive value.

The Role of Minority Tendencies in the Ebbing Period

The ebbing of the international revolutionary movement, which became apparent within a few years after 1920 and increasingly obvious over the next three decades, was followed, with a time-lag of five or six years, by an ebbing of the movements that had tried to promote liberatory innovations in culture and everyday life. The ideological and material importance of such movements has continually diminished, to the point that they have become totally isolated. Their action, which under more favorable conditions was able to lead to a sudden renewal of the climate of feeling, has weakened to the point that conservative tendencies have been able to exclude them from any direct penetration into the rigged arena of official culture. Once these movements have been deprived of their role in the production of new values, they end up serving as a reserve pool of intellectual labor from which the bourgeoisie can draw individuals capable of adding innovative nuances to its propaganda.

At this point of dissolution, the social importance of the experimental avant-garde is apparently less than that of the pseudomodernist tendencies which don't even bother to pretend to seek change, but which represent the modern, media-reinforced face of accepted culture. But those who have a role in the actual production of modern culture, and who are discovering their interests as producers of this culture (all the more acutely as they are reduced to a purely negative position), are developing a consciousness that is inevitably lacking among the modernist representatives of the declining society. The poverty of the accepted culture and its monopoly on the means of cultural production lead to a corresponding impoverishment of the theory and manifestations of the avant-garde. But it is only within this avant-garde that a new revolutionary conception of culture is imperceptibly taking shape. Now that the dominant culture and the beginnings of oppositional culture are arriving at the extreme point of their separation and impotence, this new conception should assert itself.

The history of modern culture during the period of revolutionary ebbing is thus also the history of the theoretical and practical defeat of the movement of renewal, to the point that the minority tendencies became completely isolated and decomposition reigned everywhere.

Between 1930 and World War II surrealism continually declined as a revolutionary force at the same time that its influence was being extended beyond its control. The postwar period led to the rapid destruction of surrealism by the two factors that had already blocked its development around 1930: the lack of possibilities for theoretical renewal and the ebbing of revolution, developments which were reflected in the political and cultural reaction within the workers' movement. The latter factor is directly determinant, for example, in the disappearance of the surrealist group of Romania. On the other hand, it is above all the first of these factors that condemned the Revolutionary Surrealism movement in France and Belgium to a rapid collapse. Except in Belgium, where a fraction issuing from surrealism has maintained a valid experimental position [the *Lèvres Nues* group], all the surrealist tendencies scattered around the world have joined the camp of mystical idealism.

Some of the Revolutionary Surrealists were among those who formed the "Experimental Artists' International" (1949–1951), which included participants from Denmark, Belgium, Holland, and eventually also Germany, and which published the journal *Cobra* (Copenhagen–Brussels–Amsterdam).* The merit of these groups was to have understood that such an organization is necessitated by the complexity and extent of present-day problems. But their lack of ideological rigor, the limitation of their pursuits to mainly plastic experimentation, and above all the absence of a comprehensive theory of the conditions and perspectives of their experience led to their breakup.

Lettrism, in France, had started off by totally opposing the entire known aesthetic movement, whose continual decaying it correctly analyzed. Striving for the uninterrupted creation of new forms in all domains, the Lettrist group carried on a salutary agitation between 1946 and 1952. But the group generally took it for granted that aesthetic disciplines should take a new departure within a general framework similar to the former one, and this idealist error limited its productions to a few paltry experiments. In 1952 the Lettrist left wing organized itself into a "Lettrist International" and expelled the backward fraction.* In the Lettrist International the quest for new methods of intervention in everyday life was pursued amidst sharp struggles among different tendencies.

In Italy—with the exception of the antifunctionalist experimental group that in 1955 formed the most solid section of the International Movement for an Imaginist Bauhaus—the efforts toward avant-garde formations have remained attached to the old artistic perspectives and have not even succeeded in expressing themselves theoretically.

During the same period the most innocuous and massified aspects of Western culture have been massively imitated all over the world, from the United States to Japan. (The US avant-garde, which tends to congregate in the American colony in Paris, lives there in the most tame, insipidly conformist manner, isolated ideologically, socially, and even ecologically from everything else going on.) As for the productions of peoples who are still subject to cultural colonialism (often caused by political oppression), even though they may be progressive in their own countries, they play a reactionary role in the advanced cultural centers. Critics who have based their entire career on outdated systems of creation pretend to discover engaging new developments in Greek films or Guatemalan novels—an exoticism of the antiexotic, the revival of old forms long since exploited and exhausted in other countries; an exoticism which does, however, serve the primary purpose of exoticism: escape from the real conditions of life and creation.

In the workers' states only the experimentation carried out by Brecht in Berlin, insofar as it puts into question the classic spectacle notion, is close to the constructions that matter for us today. Only Brecht has succeeded in resisting the stupidity of Socialist Realism in power.

Now that Socialist Realism is falling apart, we can expect much from a revolutionary confrontation of the intellectuals in the workers' states with the real problems of modern culture. If Zhdanovism has been the purest expression not only of the cultural degeneration of the workers' movement but also of the conservative cultural position in the bourgeois world, those in the Eastern Bloc who are presently revolting against Zhdanovism cannot do so—whatever their subjective intentions—merely in the name of a greater creative freedom à la Cocteau, for example. A negation of Zhdanovism objectively means the negation of the Zhdanovist negation of "liquidation." Zhdanovism can be superseded only through the real exercise of freedom, which is consciousness of present necessity.

Here, too, the recent years have at most been a period of confused resistance to the confused reign of reactionary imbecility. There weren't many of us really working against it. But we should not linger over the tastes or trivial findings of this period. The problems of cultural creation can be resolved only in relation with a new advance of world revolution.

Platform for a Provisional Opposition

A revolutionary action within culture must aim to enlarge life, not merely to express or explain it. It must attack misery on every front. Revolution is not limited to determining the level of industrial production, or even to determining who is to be the master of such production. It must abolish not only the exploitation of humanity, but also the passions, compensations, and habits which that exploitation has engendered. We have to define new desires in relation to present possibilities. In the thick of the battle between the present society and the forces that are going to destroy it, we have to find the first elements of a more advanced construction of the environment and new conditions of behavior—both as experiences in themselves and as material for propaganda. Everything else belongs to the past, and serves it.

We now have to undertake an organized collective work aimed at a unitary use of all the means of revolutionizing everyday life. That is, we must first of all recognize the interdependence of these means in the perspective of increased freedom and an increased control of nature. We need to construct new ambiences that will be both the products and the instruments of new forms of behavior. To do this, we must from the beginning make practical use of the everyday processes and cultural forms that now exist, while refusing to acknowledge any inherent value they may claim to have. The very criterion of formal invention or innovation has lost its sense within the traditional framework of the arts—insufficient, fragmentary forms whose partial renovations are inevitably outdated and therefore impossible.

We should not simply refuse modern culture; we must seize it in order to negate it. No one can claim to be a revolutionary intellectual who does not recognize the cultural revolution we are now facing. An intellectual creator cannot be revolutionary by merely supporting some party line, not even if he does so with original methods, but only

by working alongside the parties toward the necessary transformation of all the cultural superstructures. What ultimately determines
whether or not someone is a bourgeois intellectual is neither his social
origin nor his knowledge of a culture (such knowledge may be the basis
for a critique of that culture or for some creative work within it), but
his role in the production of the historically bourgeois forms of culture. Authors of revolutionary political opinions who find themselves
praised by bourgeois literary critics should ask themselves what they've
done wrong.

The union of several experimental tendencies for a revolutionary
front in culture, begun at the congress held at Alba, Italy, at the end of
1956, presupposes that we not neglect three important factors.

First of all, we must insist on a complete accord among the persons
and groups that participate in this united action; and this accord must
not be facilitated by allowing certain of its consequences to be dissimulated. Jokers or careerists who are stupid enough to think they can
advance their careers in this way must be rebuffed.

Next, we must recall that while any genuinely experimental attitude is usable, that word has very often been misused in the attempt
to justify artistic actions within an already-existing structure. The
only valid experimental proceeding is based on the accurate critique
of existing conditions and the deliberate supersession of them. It must
be understood once and for all that something that is only a personal
expression within a framework created by others cannot be termed a
creation. Creation is not the arrangement of objects and forms, it is the
invention of new laws on such arrangement.

Finally, we have to eliminate the sectarianism among us that opposes unity of action with possible allies for specific goals and prevents our
infiltration of parallel organizations.* From 1952 to 1955 the Lettrist
International, after some necessary purges, continually moved toward
a sort of absolutist rigor leading to an equally absolute isolation and
ineffectuality, and ultimately to a certain immobility, a degeneration
of the spirit of critique and discovery. We must definitively supersede
this sectarian conduct in favor of real actions. This should be the sole
criterion on which we join with or separate from comrades. Naturally
this does not mean that we should renounce breaks, as everyone urges
us to do. On the contrary, we think that it is necessary to go still further in breaking with habits and persons.

We should collectively define our program and realize it in a disciplined manner, using any means, even artistic ones.

Toward a Situationist International

Our central idea is the construction of situations, that is to say, the concrete construction of momentary ambiences of life and their transformation into a superior passional quality. We must develop a systematic intervention based on the complex factors of two components in perpetual interaction: the material environment of life and the behaviors which that environment gives rise to and which radically transform it.

Our perspectives of action on the environment ultimately lead us to the notion of unitary urbanism. Unitary urbanism is defined first of all as the use of all arts and techniques as means contributing to the composition of a unified milieu. Such an interrelated ensemble must be envisaged as incomparably more far-reaching than the old domination of architecture over the traditional arts, or than the present sporadic application to anarchic urbanism of specialized technologies or of scientific investigations such as ecology. Unitary urbanism must also, for example, determine the acoustic environment and the distribution of different varieties of food and drink. It must include both the creation of new forms and the détournement of previous forms of architecture, urbanism, poetry, and cinema. Integral art, which has been talked about so much, can be realized only at the level of urbanism. But it can no longer correspond to any of the traditional aesthetic categories. In each of its experimental cities unitary urbanism will act by way of a certain number of force fields, which we can temporarily designate by the classic term "district." Each district will tend toward a specific harmony distinct from neighboring harmonies; or else will play on a maximum breaking up of internal harmony.

Secondly, unitary urbanism is dynamic, in that it is directly related to styles of behavior. The most elementary unit of unitary urbanism is not the house, but the architectural complex, which combines all the factors conditioning an ambience, or a series of clashing ambiences, on the scale of the constructed situation. Spatial development must take into account the emotional effects that the experimental city is intended to produce. One of our comrades has advanced a theory of "states-of-mind" districts, according to which each district of a city would be designed to provoke a specific basic sentiment to which people would knowingly expose themselves. It seems that such a project draws appropriate conclusions from the current tendency to depreciate randomly encountered primary sentiments, and that its realization could contribute to accelerating that depreciation. The comrades who call for a new, free architecture must understand that this new architecture will primarily be based not on free, poetic lines and forms—in the sense that today's "lyrical abstract" painting uses those terms—but rather on the atmospheric effects of rooms, hallways, streets—atmospheres linked to the activities they contain. Architecture must advance by taking emotionally moving situations, rather than emotionally moving forms, as the material it works with. And the experiments conducted with this material will lead to new, as yet unknown forms.

Psychogeographical research, "the study of the exact laws and specific effects of geographical environments, whether consciously organized or not, on the emotions and behavior of individuals," thus takes on a double meaning: active observation of present-day urban agglomerations and development of hypotheses on the structure of a situationist city. The progress of psychogeography depends to a great extent on the statistical extension of its methods of observation, but above all on experimentation by means of concrete interventions in urbanism. Before this stage is attained we cannot be certain of the objective truth of our initial psychogeographical findings. But even if those findings should turn out to be false, they would still be false solutions to what is nevertheless a real problem.

Our action on behavior, linked with other desirable aspects of a revolution in customs and behaviors, can be briefly defined as the invention of games of an essentially new type. The most general goal must be to expand the nonmediocre part of life, to reduce the empty moments of life as much as possible. One could thus speak of our enterprise as a project of quantitatively increasing human life, an enterprise more serious than the biological methods currently being investigated, and one that automatically implies a qualitative increase whose developments are unpredictable. The situationist game is distinguished from the classic notion of games by its radical negation of the element of competition and of separation from everyday life. On the other hand, it is not distinct from a moral choice, since it implies taking a stand in favor of what will bring about the future reign of freedom and play.

This perspective is obviously linked to the continual and rapid increase of leisure time resulting from the level of productive forces our era has attained. It is also linked to the recognition of the fact that a battle of leisure is taking place before our eyes, a battle whose importance in the class struggle has not been sufficiently analyzed. So far, the ruling class has succeeded in using the leisure the revolutionary proletariat wrested from it by developing a vast industrial sector of leisure activities that is an incomparable instrument for stupefying the proletariat with by-products of mystifying ideology and bourgeois tastes. The abundance of televised imbecilities is probably one of the reasons for the American working class's inability to develop any political consciousness. By obtaining through collective pressure a slight rise in the price of its labor above the minimum necessary for the production of that labor, the proletariat not only extends the power of its struggle, it also extends the terrain of that struggle. New forms of this struggle then arise alongside directly economic and political conflicts. It can be said that up till now revolutionary propaganda has been constantly overcome within these new forms of struggle in all the countries where advanced industrial development has introduced them. That the necessary changing of the infrastructure can be delayed by errors and weaknesses at the level of superstructures has unfortunately been demonstrated by several experiences of the twentieth century. New forces must be brought into the battle of leisure, and that is where we'll take our stand.

A rough experimentation toward a new mode of behavior has already been made with what we have termed the *dérive:* the practice of a passional journey out of the ordinary through a rapid changing of ambiences, as well as a means of psychogeographical study and of situationist psychology. But the application of this striving for playful creativity must be extended to all known forms of human relationships, so as to influence, for example, the historical evolution of sentiments such as friendship and love. Everything leads us to believe that the essential elements of our research lie in our hypothesis of the construction of situations.

A person's life is a succession of fortuitous situations, and even if none of them is exactly the same as another the immense majority of them are so undifferentiated and so dull that they give a definite impression of sameness. As a result, the rare intensely engaging situations found in life only serve to strictly confine and limit that life. We must try to construct situations, that is to say, collective ambiences, ensembles of impressions determining the quality of a moment. If we take the simple example of a gathering of a group of individuals for a given time, it would be desirable, while taking into account the knowledge and material means we have at our disposal, to study what organization of the place, what selection of participants, and what provocation of events are suitable for producing the desired ambience. The powers of a situation will certainly expand considerably in both time and space with the realizations of unitary urbanism or the education of a situationist generation.

The construction of situations begins beyond the ruins of the modern spectacle. It is easy to see how much the very principle of the spectacle—nonintervention—is linked to the alienation of the old world. Conversely, the most pertinent revolutionary experiments

in culture have sought to break the spectators' psychological identification with heroes, so as to draw them into activity by provoking
their capacities to revolutionize their own lives. The situation is thus
designed to be lived by its constructors. The role played by a passive or
merely bit-part playing "public" must constantly diminish, while that
played by those who cannot be called actors, but rather, in a new sense
of the term, "livers," must steadily increase.

We have to multiply poetic subjects and objects—which are now
unfortunately so rare that the slightest ones take on an exaggerated emotional importance—and we have to organize games for these
poetic subjects to play with these poetic objects. This is our entire program, which is essentially transitory. Our situations will be ephemeral,
without a future. Passageways. Our only concern is real life; we care
nothing about the permanence of art or of anything else. Eternity is
the grossest idea people can conceive of in connection with their acts.

Situationist techniques have yet to be invented. But we know that
a task presents itself only when the material conditions necessary to
its realization already exist, or at least are in the process of formation.
We have to begin with a phase of small-scale experimentation. It will
probably be necessary to prepare plans or scenarios for the creation
of situations, despite their inevitable inadequacy at the beginning. To
this end we must develop a system of notations, which will become
more precise as we learn more from the experiences of construction.
We will also need to discover or verify certain laws, such as that according to which situationist emotions depend on extreme concentration
or extreme dispersal of actions (classical tragedy giving a rough idea of
the former, dérives of the latter). In addition to the direct means that
will be used for specific ends, the positive phase of the construction
of situations will require a new application of reproductive technologies. One can envisage, for example, televised images of certain aspects
of one situation being communicated live to people taking part in
another situation somewhere else, thereby producing various modifications and interferences between the two. More simply, a new style of
documentary film could be devoted to "current events" that really are
current and eventful by preserving (in situationist archives) the most
significant moments of a situation before the evolution of its elements
has led to a different situation. Since the systematic construction of
situations will give rise to previously unknown sentiments, film will
find its greatest educational role in the dissemination of these new
passions.

Situationist theory resolutely supports a noncontinuous conception of life. The notion of unity must cease to be seen as applying to

the whole of one's life (where it serves as a reactionary mystification based on the belief in an immortal soul and, in the final analysis, on the division of labor). Instead, it should apply to the construction of each particular moment of life through the unitary use of situationist methods. In a classless society there will no longer be "painters," but only situationists who, among other things, sometimes paint.

The main emotional drama of life, aside from the perpetual conflict between desire and reality hostile to desire, seems to be the sensation of the passage of time. In contrast to the aesthetic modes that strive to fix and eternalize some emotion, the situationist attitude consists in going with the flow of time. In so doing, in pushing ever further the game of creating new, emotionally provocative situations, the situationists are gambling that change will usually be for the better. In the short term the odds are obviously against that bet. But even if we have to lose it a thousand times, we see no other choice for a progressive attitude.

The situationist minority first emerged as a tendency in the Lettrist left wing, then in the Lettrist International which it ended up controlling. The same objective movement has led several recent avant-garde groups to similar conclusions. Together we must eliminate all the relics of the recent past. We now believe that an accord for a united action of the revolutionary avant-garde in culture must be carried out on the basis of such a program. We have neither guaranteed recipes nor definitive results. We only propose an experimental research to be collectively led in a few directions that we are presently defining and toward others that have yet to be defined. The very difficulty of succeeding in the first situationist projects is a proof of the newness of the domain we are penetrating. Something that changes our way of seeing the streets is more important than something that changes our way of seeing paintings. Our working hypotheses will be reexamined at each future upheaval, wherever it comes from.

Various people (particularly among the revolutionary artists and intellectuals who have resigned themselves to a certain impotence) will respond that this "situationism" seems rather disagreeable; that we have not created any beautiful works; that we would do better to talk about André Gide; and that no one will see any clear reasons to be interested in us. They will evade facing the issues we have raised by reproaching us for using scandalous tactics in order to call attention to ourselves, and will express their indignation at the procedures we have sometimes felt obliged to adopt in order to dissociate ourselves from certain people. We answer: It's not a matter of knowing whether this interests you, but whether you yourselves are capable of doing anything interesting in the context of the new conditions of cultural creation. Your role, revolutionary artists and intellectuals, is not to complain that freedom is insulted when we refuse to march alongside the enemies of freedom. Your role is not to imitate the bourgeois aesthetes who try to restrict people to what has already been done because what has already been done doesn't bother them. You know that creation is never pure. Your role is to find out what the international avant-garde is doing, to take part in the critical development of its program, and to call for its support.

Our Immediate Tasks

We must call attention, among the worker parties or the extremist tendencies within those parties, to the need to undertake an effective ideological action in order to combat the emotional influence of advanced capitalist methods of propaganda. On every occasion, by every hyper-political means, we must publicize desirable alternatives to the spectacle of the capitalist way of life, so as to destroy the bourgeois idea of happiness. At the same time, taking into account the existence, within the various ruling classes, of elements that have always tended (out of boredom and thirst for novelty) toward things that lead to the disappearance of their societies, we should incite the persons who control some of the vast resources that we lack to provide us with the means to carry out our experiments, out of the same motives of potential profit as they do with scientific research.

We must everywhere present a revolutionary alternative to the ruling culture; coordinate all the researches which are currently taking place but which lack a comprehensive perspective; and incite, through critiques and propaganda, the most advanced artists and intellectuals of all countries to contact us in view of a collective action.

We should declare ourselves ready to renew discussion, on the basis of this program, with those who, having taken part in an earlier phase of our action, are still capable of rejoining us.

We must put forward the slogans of unitary urbanism, experimental behavior, hyper-political propaganda, and the construction of ambiences. The passions have been sufficiently interpreted; the point now is to discover new ones.

GUY DEBORD
June 1957*

French Journals

(1958–1969)

The Sound and the Fury

There is a lot of talk these days about angry, raging youth. The reason people are so fond of talking about them is that, from the aimless riots of Swedish adolescents to the proclamations of England's would-be literary movement, the "Angry Young Men," there is the same utter innocuousness, the same reassuring flimsiness. Products of a period in which the dominant ideas and lifestyles are decomposing, a period that has seen tremendous breakthroughs in the domination of nature without any corresponding increase in the real possibilities of everyday life; reacting, often crudely, against the world they find themselves stuck in, these youth outbursts are somewhat reminiscent of the surrealist state of mind. But they lack surrealism's points of leverage in culture and its revolutionary hope. Hence the tone underlying the spontaneous negativity of American, Scandinavian, and Japanese youth is one of resignation. During the first years after World War II, Saint-Germain-des-Prés had already served as a laboratory for this kind of behavior (misleadingly termed "existentialist" by the press), which is why the present intellectual representatives of that generation in France (Françoise Sagan, Robbe-Grillet, Vadim, the atrocious Buffet) are all such extreme caricatural images of resignation.

Although this intellectual generation exhibits more aggressiveness outside France, its consciousness still ranges from simple imbecility to premature self-satisfaction with a very inadequate revolt. The rotten-egg smell exuded by the idea of God envelops the mystical cretins of America's "Beat Generation" and is not even entirely absent from the declarations of the Angry Young Men (e.g. Colin Wilson). These latter have just discovered, thirty years behind the times, a certain moral subversiveness that *England* had managed to completely hide from them all this time; and they think they're being daringly scandalous by declaring themselves antimonarchists. "Plays continue to be produced," writes Kenneth Tynan, "that are based on the ridiculous idea that people still fear and respect the Crown, the Empire, the Church, the University and Polite Society." This statement is indicative of how tepidly *literary* the Angry Young Men's perspective is. They have simply come to change their opinions about a few social conventions without noticing the fundamental *change of terrain* of all cultural activity so evident in every avant-garde tendency of this century. The Angry Young Men are in fact particularly reactionary in attributing a privileged, redemptive value to the practice of literature, thereby defending a mystification that was denounced in Europe around 1920 and whose survival today is of greater counterrevolutionary significance than that of the British Crown.

In all this pseudorevolutionary sound and fury there is a common lack of understanding of the meaning and scope of surrealism (itself naturally distorted by its bourgeois artistic success). A continuation of surrealism would in fact be the most consistent attitude to take if nothing new arose to replace it. But because the young people who now rally to surrealism are aware of surrealism's profound demands while being incapable of overcoming the contradiction between those demands and the stagnation accompanying its apparent success, they take refuge in the reactionary aspects present within surrealism from its inception (magic, belief in a golden age elsewhere than in history to come). Some of them even take pride in still standing under surrealism's *arc de triomphe*, so long after the period of real struggle. There they will remain, says Gérard Legrand proudly (*Le Surréalisme même* #2), faithful to their tradition, "a small band of youthful souls resolved to keep alive the true flame of surrealism."

A movement more liberating than the surrealism *of 1924*—a movement Breton promised to rally to if it were to appear—cannot easily be formed because its liberativeness now depends on its seizing the more advanced material means of the modern world. But the surrealists of 1958 have not only become incapable of rallying to such a movement, they are even determined to combat it. But this does not eliminate the necessity for a revolutionary movement in culture to appropriate, with greater effectiveness, the freedom of spirit and the concrete freedom of mores demanded by surrealism.

For us, surrealism has been only a beginning of a revolutionary experiment in culture, an experiment that almost immediately ground to a practical and theoretical halt. We have to go further. Why is becoming a surrealist no longer a meaningful option? Not because of the ruling class's constant encouragement of "avant-garde" movements to dissociate themselves from the scandalous aspects of surrealism. (This encouragement is not made in the name of promoting originality at all costs—how could it be, when the ruling order has nothing really new to propose to us, nothing going beyond surrealism? On the contrary, the bourgeoisie stands ready to applaud any regressions we might lapse into.) If we are not surrealists, it is because *surrealism has become a total bore.*

Decrepit surrealism, raging and ill-informed youth, well-off adolescent rebels without perspectives (though certainly not without a cause)—boredom is what they all have in common. The situationists will execute the judgment that contemporary leisure is pronouncing against itself.

Preliminary Problems in Constructing a Situation

"The construction of situations begins beyond the ruins of the modern spectacle. It is easy to see how much the very principle of the spectacle—nonintervention—is linked to the alienation of the old world. Conversely, the most pertinent revolutionary experiments in culture have sought to break the spectators' psychological identification with heroes so as to draw them into activity. . . . The situation is thus designed to be lived by its constructors. The role played by a passive or merely bit-part playing 'public' must constantly diminish, while that played by those who cannot be called actors, but rather, in a new sense of the term, 'livers,' must steadily increase."

—*Report on the Construction of Situations*

Our conception of a "constructed situation" is not limited to an integrated use of artistic means to create an ambience, however great the force or spatiotemporal extent of that ambience might be. A situation is also an integrated ensemble of behaviors in time. It is composed of actions contained in a transitory decor. These actions are the product of the decor and of themselves, and they in their turn produce other decors and other actions. How can these forces be oriented? We are not going to limit ourselves to merely empirical experimentation with environments in quest of mechanistically provoked surprises. The really experimental direction of situationist activity consists in setting up, on the basis of more or less clearly recognized desires, a temporary field of activity favorable to these desires. This alone can lead to the further clarification of these simple basic desires, and to the confused emergence of new desires whose material roots will be precisely the *new reality* engendered by situationist constructions.

We must thus envisage a sort of situationist-oriented psychoanalysis in which, in contrast to the goals pursued by the various currents stemming from Freudianism, each of the participants in this adventure would discover desires for specific ambiences *in order to fulfill them*. Each person must seek what he loves, what attracts him. (And here again, in contrast to certain endeavors of modern writing—Leiris, for example—what is important to us is neither our individual psychological structures nor the explanation of their formation, but their possible application in the construction of situations.) Through this method one can tabulate elements out of which situations can be constructed, along with *projects to dynamize these elements*.

This kind of research is meaningful only for individuals working practically toward a construction of situations. Such people are *presituationists* (either spontaneously or in a conscious and organized manner) inasmuch as they have sensed the objective need for this sort of construction through having recognized the present cultural emptiness and having participated in recent expressions of experimental awareness. They are close to each other because they share the same specialization and have taken part in the same historical avant-garde of that specialization. It is thus likely that they will share a number of situationist themes and desires, which will increasingly diversify once they are brought into a phase of real activity.

A constructed situation must be collectively prepared and developed. It would seem, however, that, at least during the initial period of rough experiments, a situation requires one individual to play a sort of "director" role. If we imagine a particular situation project in which, for example, a research team has arranged an *emotionally moving gathering* of a few people for an evening, we would no doubt have to distinguish: a *director* or producer responsible for coordinating the basic elements necessary for the construction of the decor and for working out certain *interventions* in the events (alternatively, several people could work out their own interventions while being more or less unaware of each other's plans); the *direct agents* living the situation, who have taken part in creating the collective project and worked on the practical composition of the ambience; and finally, a few passive *spectators* who have not participated in the constructive work, who should be *forced into action*.

This relation between the director and the "livers" of the situation must naturally never become a permanent specialization. It's only a matter of a temporary subordination of a team of situationists to the person responsible for a particular project. These perspectives, or the provisional terminology describing them, should not be taken to mean that we are talking about some continuation of theater. Pirandello and Brecht have already revealed the destruction of the theatrical spectacle and pointed out a few of the requirements for going beyond it. It could be said that the construction of situations will replace theater in the same sense that the real construction of life has increasingly tended to replace religion. The principal domain we are going to replace and *fulfill* is obviously poetry, which burned itself out by taking its position at the vanguard of our time and has now completely disappeared.

Real individual fulfillment, which is also involved in the artistic experience that the situationists are discovering, entails the collective takeover of the world. Until this happens there will be no real individuals, but only specters haunting the things anarchically presented to them by others. In chance situations we meet separated beings moving at random. Their divergent emotions neutralize each other and maintain their solid environment of boredom. We are going to undermine these conditions by raising at a few points an incendiary beacon heralding a *greater game*.

In our time functionalism (an inevitable expression of technological advance) is attempting to entirely eliminate play. The partisans of "industrial design" complain that their projects are spoiled by people's playful tendencies. At the same time, industrial commerce crudely exploits those tendencies by diverting them to a demand for constant superficial renovation of utilitarian products. We obviously have no interest in encouraging the continuous artistic renovation of refrigerator designs. But a moralizing functionalism is incapable of getting to the heart of the problem. The only progressive way out is to liberate the tendency toward play elsewhere, and on a larger scale. Short of this, all the naïve indignation of the theorists of industrial design will not change the basic fact that the private automobile, for example, is primarily an idiotic toy and only secondarily a means of transportation. As opposed to all the regressive forms of play—which are regressions to its infantile stage and are invariably linked to reactionary politics—it is necessary to promote the experimental forms of a game of revolution.

Definitions

constructed situation
A moment of life concretely and deliberately constructed by the collective organization of a unitary ambience and a game of events.

situationist
Relating to the theory or practical activity of constructing situations. One who engages in the construction of situations. A member of the Situationist International.

situationism
A meaningless term improperly derived from the above. There is no such thing as situationism, which would mean a doctrine for interpreting existing conditions. The notion of situationism is obviously devised by antisituationists.

psychogeography
The study of the specific effects of the geographical environment (whether consciously organized or not) on the emotions and behavior of individuals.

psychogeographical
Relating to psychogeography. That which manifests the geographical environment's direct emotional effects.

psychogeographer
One who explores and reports on psychogeographical phenomena.

dérive
A mode of experimental behavior linked to the conditions of urban society: a technique of rapid passage through varied ambiences. The term also designates a specific uninterrupted period of dériving.

unitary urbanism
The theory of the combined use of arts and techniques as means contributing to the construction of a unified milieu in dynamic relation with experiments in behavior.

détournement
Short for "détournement of preexisting aesthetic elements." The integration of present or past artistic productions into a superior construction of a milieu. In this sense there can be no situationist painting or music, but only a situationist use of those means. In a more elementary sense, détournement within the old cultural spheres is a method of propaganda, a method which reveals the wearing out and loss of importance of those spheres.

culture
The reflection and prefiguration of the possibilities of organization of everyday life in a given historical moment; a complex of aesthetics, feelings, and mores through which a collectivity reacts on the life that is objectively determined by its economy. (We are defining this term only in the perspective of creating values, not in that of teaching them.)

decomposition
The process in which traditional cultural forms have destroyed themselves as a result of the emergence of superior means of controlling nature which make possible and necessary superior cultural constructions. We can distinguish between the active phase of the decomposition and effective demolition of the old superstructures—which came to an end around 1930—and a phase of repetition that has prevailed since that time. The delay in the transition from decomposition to new constructions is linked to the delay in the revolutionary liquidation of capitalism.

Theses on Cultural Revolution

1

The traditional goal of aesthetics is to produce, by means of art, impressions of certain past elements of life in circumstances where those elements are lacking or absent, in such a way that those elements escape the disorder of appearances subject to the ravages of time. The degree of aesthetic success is thus measured by a beauty that is inseparable from duration, and that even goes so far as pretensions of eternity. The goal of the situationists is immediate participation in a passionate abundance of life by means of deliberately arranged variations of ephemeral moments. The success of these moments can reside in nothing other than their fleeting effect. The situationists consider cultural activity in its totality as an experimental method for constructing everyday life, a method that can and should be continually developed with the extension of leisure and the withering away of the division of labor (beginning with the division of artistic labor).

2

Art can cease being a report about sensations and become a direct organization of more advanced sensations. The point is to produce ourselves rather than things that enslave us.

3

Mascolo is right in saying (in *Le Communisme*) that the reduction of the work day by the dictatorship of the proletariat is "the most certain sign of the latter's revolutionary authenticity." Indeed, "if man is a commodity, if he is treated as a thing, if human relations are relations of thing to thing, this is because it is possible to buy his time." But Mascolo is too quick to conclude that "the time of a man freely employed" is always well spent, and that "the purchase of time is the sole evil." There can be no freely spent time until we possess the modern tools for the construction of everyday life. The use of such tools will mark the leap from a utopian revolutionary art to an experimental revolutionary art.

4

An international association of situationists can be seen as a coalition of workers in an advanced sector of culture, or more precisely as a coalition of all those who demand the right to work on a project that is obstructed by present social conditions; hence as an attempt at organizing professional revolutionaries in culture.

5

We are excluded from real control over the vast material powers of our time. The communist revolution has not yet occurred and we are still living within the confines of decomposing old cultural superstructures. Henri Lefebvre rightly sees that this contradiction is at the heart of a specifically modern discordance between the progressive individual and the world, and he terms the cultural tendency based on this discordance "revolutionary romanticism." The inadequacy of Lefebvre's conception lies in the fact that he makes the mere expression of this discordance a sufficient criterion for revolutionary action within culture. Lefebvre abandons in advance any experimentation involving profound cultural change, contenting himself with mere awareness of possibilities that are as yet impossible (because they are still too remote), an awareness that can be expressed in any sort of form within the framework of cultural decomposition.

6

Those who want to supersede the old established order in all its aspects cannot cling to the disorder of the present, even in the sphere of culture. In culture as in other areas, it is necessary to struggle without waiting any longer for some concrete appearance of the moving order of the future. The possibility of this ever-changing new order, which is already present among us, devalues all expressions within existing cultural forms. If we are ever to arrive at authentic direct communication (in our working hypothesis of higher cultural means: the construction of situations), we must bring about the destruction of all the forms of pseudocommunication. The victory will go to those who are capable of creating disorder without loving it.

7

In the world of cultural decomposition we can test our strength but never use it. The practical task of overcoming our discordance with this world, that is, of surmounting its decomposition by some more advanced constructions, is not romantic. We will be "revolutionary romantics," in Lefebvre's sense, precisely to the degree that we fail.

GUY DEBORD

The Situationists and Automation

It is rather astonishing that almost no one until now has dared to examine the ultimate implications of automation. Instead of debating its various possible consequences, one has rather the impression that engineers, scientists, and sociologists are trying to smuggle automation into the society.

Yet automation is now at the heart of the problem of the socialist control of production and of the preponderance of leisure time over labor time. The issue of automation is bursting with positive and negative possibilities.

The goal of socialism is abundance—the greatest number of goods for the greatest number of people, which statistically implies reducing the unexpected to the level of the improbable. Increasing the number of goods reduces the value of each. This devaluation of all human goods to a level of "total neutrality" will be the inevitable consequence of a purely scientific development of socialism. It is unfortunate that many intellectuals fail to get beyond this idea of mechanical reproduction, and are instead contributing toward the adaptation of humanity to this bland and symmetrized future. Artists, whose specialty is seeking uniqueness, are consequently turning in increasing numbers against socialism. Conversely, socialist politicians are suspicious of every expression of artistic power or originality.

Attached to their conformist positions, both of these sides display a certain antagonism to automation because it threatens to undermine their economic and cultural conceptions. The various "avant-garde" currents all show a defeatist attitude in the face of automation. At best, they underestimate the positive aspects of the future that is being so suddenly revealed by the early stages of automation. Meanwhile the reactionary forces flaunt their moronic optimism.

A revealing anecdote: Last year, in the journal *Quatrième Internationale*, the militant Marxist Livio Maitan reported that an Italian priest had already suggested that increasing free time might necessitate adding a second weekly Mass. Maitan responded: "The error consists in supposing that man in the new society will be the same as in the present one, whereas he will in fact have completely different needs that are difficult for us to even imagine." But Maitan's error is to leave to a vague future the new needs he finds "difficult to even imagine." The dialectical role of spirit is to steer the possible toward desirable forms. Maitan forgets that "the elements of a new society are formed *within the old"* (*Communist Manifesto*). The elements of a new life should already be in formation among us—in the realm of culture—and it's up to us to draw on them to liven up the debate.

Socialism, which strives for the fullest liberation of the energies and potentials in each individual, will be obliged to see automation as an inherently antiprogressive tendency, a tendency that can be rendered progressive only by relating it to new provocations capable of bringing forth the latent energies of man. If, as the scientists and technicians claim, automation is a new means of liberating man, it should imply the supersession of previous human activities. This means that man's active imagination has to go beyond the realization of automation itself. Where can we find such perspectives, perspectives that will make man the master and not the slave of automation?

In his study *L'Automation*, Louis Salleron explains that automation, "as almost always happens in matters of progress, *adds* more than it *replaces or eliminates.*" What does automation, as such, add to man's possibilities of action? We have learned that it completely eliminates man within its own domain.

The crisis of industrialization is a crisis of consumption and production. The crisis of production is more important than the crisis of consumption, the latter being conditioned by the former. Transposed to the individual level, this amounts to the thesis that it is better to give than to receive, better to be capable of *adding* than of *suppressing.* Automation thus contains two opposing perspectives: it deprives the individual of any possibility of adding anything personal to automated production, thus representing a *fixation* of progress, yet at the same time it saves human energies by massively liberating them from reproductive and uncreative activities. The value of automation thus depends on projects that supersede it and open the way for the expression of new human energies on a higher plane.

Today, experimental activity in culture has this incomparable field of play. A defeatist attitude here, a failure to confront the possibilities of our time, is symptomatic of the old avant-gardes that remain content, as Edgar Morin puts it, "to gnaw on the bones of the past." A surrealist named Benayoun says in the latest expression of the movement (*Le Surréalisme même* #2): "The problem of leisure is already tormenting the sociologists. . . . Technicians will no longer be in demand, but rather clowns, sexy singers, ballerinas, freaks. One day of work for six of rest: the balance between the serious and the frivolous, between the lazy and the laborious, is at great risk of being upset. . . . The idle 'worker' will be cretinized by convulsive and invasive television that is short of both ideas and talent." This surrealist fails to see that a week of six days of rest will not lead to "upsetting the balance" between the frivolous and the serious, but to *changing the nature* of both the serious and the frivolous. Looking at the world through his faded surrealist glasses, he sees it as a sort of vaudeville show and can imagine nothing but reruns of its ludicrous routines and misadventures. Why should this future be nothing but an overdevelopment of present-day vulgarities? And why should it be "short of ideas"? Does that mean that it will be short of 1924 surrealist ideas as updated in 1956?* Very likely. Or does it mean that the imitation surrealists are short of ideas? We are already well aware of that.

The new leisure time appears as an empty space that present-day society can imagine filling only by multiplying the pseudoplay of pathetic hobbies. But this leisure time is also the basis on which could be built the most magnificent cultural construction that has ever been imagined. This goal is obviously outside the concerns of the partisans of automation. It is in fact antagonistic to the direct tendency of automation. If we want to talk with the engineers, we will have to enter their field of interest. Maldonado, who currently directs the Hochschule für Gestaltung in Ulm, explains that the development of automation is in jeopardy because young people show little enthusiasm for going into advanced engineering, except for those specializing in automation itself, who lack any general cultural perspective. But Maldonado himself fails to present, or even to be aware of, any such perspective: *Automation can develop rapidly only once it has established as a goal a perspective contrary to its own establishment, and only if it is known how to realize such a general perspective in the process of the development of automation.*

Maldonado proposes the opposite sequence: first establish automation, then figure out what to use it for. This schema might be worth discussing if its goal were not precisely automation. The problem is that automation is not an action in a domain, which would provoke a counteraction. It is the neutralization of a domain, which will also end up neutralizing other domains if conflicting actions are not undertaken at the same time.

Pierre Drouin (*Le Monde*, 5 January 1957) sees the growth of hobbies as fulfilling the potentialities that workers can no longer express in their professional activity, and concludes that "a creator lies dormant" in each person. This old platitude is now of vital importance if we relate it to the real material possibilities of our time. The sleeping creator must awaken, and that waking state could be termed "situationist."

The idea of standardization is an attempt to reduce and simplify the greatest number of human needs to the greatest degree of equality.

It's up to us whether standardization opens up more interesting realms of experience than it closes. Depending on the outcome, we may arrive at a total degradation of human life or at the possibility of perpetually discovering new desires. But these new desires will not appear by themselves within the oppressive context of our world. There must be a collective action to detect, express, and fulfill them.

ASGER JORN

No Useless Leniency

(excerpts)

"Intellectual" or "artistic" collaboration in a group devoted to the type of experimentation we are engaged in involves our everyday life. It is always accompanied with an element of friendship.

Consequently, when we think of those who have participated in this joint activity and then been excluded from it, we are obliged to admit that they were once our friends. Sometimes the memory is pleasant. In other cases it's ridiculous and embarrassing.

On the whole, later developments have confirmed the correctness of our reproaches and the irredeemability of the people who have not proved capable of remaining with us. A few of them have even ended up joining the Church or the colonial troops. Most of the others have retired to one or another little niche in the intelligentsia. [. . .]

The recent formation of the Situationist International has given a new relevance to the questions of accord and breaks. A period of discussions and negotiations on a footing of equality between several groups, beginning with the Alba Congress, has been concluded with the formation at Cosio d'Arroscia of a disciplined organization. The result of these new objective conditions has been to force certain opportunist elements into open opposition, leading to their immediate elimination (the purging of the Italian section). Certain wait-and-see attitudes have also ceased to be tolerable, and those of our allies who have not seen fit to join us immediately have thereby unmasked themselves as adversaries. It is on the basis of the program since developed by the majority of the SI that all the new elements have joined us, and we would risk cutting ourselves off from these elements, and especially from those we will meet in the future, if we consented to pursue the slightest dialogue with those who, since Alba, have demonstrated that their creative days are over.

We have become stronger and therefore more seductive. We don't want innocuous relationships and we don't want relationships that might serve our enemies. [. . .]

It should be clearly understood that all the situationists will maintain the enmities inherited from the former groupings that have constituted the SI, and that there is no possible return for those whom we have ever been forced to despise. But we don't have an idealist, abstract, absolutist conception of breaks. It is necessary to recognize when an encounter in a concrete collective task becomes impossible, but also to see if such an encounter, in changed circumstances, does not once again become possible and desirable between persons who have been able to retain a certain respect for each other.

There are a few people—two or three perhaps*—whom we have known and worked with, and who left or were asked to leave for reasons that are now superseded. And who have since avoided sinking into resignation, at least as far as we know. From having known them and having recognized their potentialities, we think that those potentialities are equal or superior now and that their place might once again be with us. As I said at the beginning, a collective project such as the one we have undertaken and are pursuing cannot avoid being accompanied by friendship. But it is also true that it cannot be identified with friendship and that it should not be subject to the same weaknesses. Nor to the same modes of continuity or looseness.

MICHÈLE BERNSTEIN

Action in Belgium
Against the International
Assembly of Art Critics

On April 12, two days before the gathering in Brussels of an international assembly of art critics, the situationists widely distributed an address to that assembly signed—in the name of the Algerian, Belgian, French, German, Italian, and Scandinavian sections of the SI—by Khatib, Korun, Debord, Platschek, Pinot-Gallizio, and Jorn:

> To you, this gathering is just one more boring event. The Situationist International, however, considers that while this assemblage of so many art critics as an attraction at the Brussels Fair is laughable, it is also significant.

Inasmuch as modern cultural thought has proved itself completely stagnant for over twenty-five years, and inasmuch as a whole era
that has understood nothing and changed nothing is now becoming
aware of its failure, its spokesmen are striving to transform their
activities into institutions. They thus solicit official recognition
from the completely outmoded but still materially dominant society, for which most of them have been loyal watchdogs.

The main inadequacy of modern art criticism is that it has never
looked at the culture as a whole nor at the conditions of an experimental movement that is constantly superseding it. At this point in time
the increased domination of nature permits and necessitates the use
of superior powers in the construction of life. These are today's problems; and those intellectuals who hold back, through fear of a general
subversion of a certain form of existence and of the ideas which that
form has produced, can no longer do anything but struggle irrationally against each other as defenders of one or another detail of the old
world—of a world whose day is done and whose meaning they have not
even understood. And so we see these art critics assembling to exchange
the crumbs of their ignorance and doubts. We know of a few people here
who are presently making some effort to understand and support new
ventures; but by coming here they have accepted being mixed up with an
immense majority of mediocrities, and we warn them that they cannot
hope to retain the slightest interest on our part unless they break with
this milieu.

Vanish, art critics, partial, incoherent, and divided imbeciles! In
vain do you stage the spectacle of a fake encounter. You have nothing in common but the role you cling to; you are only in this market
to parade one of the aspects of Western commerce: your confused
and empty babble about a decomposed culture. History has depre-
ciated you. Even your audacities belong to a past now forever closed.

Disperse, fragments of art critics, critics of fragments of art!
The Situationist International is now organizing the integral artistic activity of the future. You have nothing more to say.

The Situationist International will leave no place for you. We
will starve you out.

Our Belgian section carried out the necessary direct attack. Beginning April 13, on the eve of the opening of the proceedings, when the
art critics from two hemispheres, led by the American Sweeney, were
being welcomed to Brussels, the text of the situationist proclamation
was brought to their attention in several ways. Copies were mailed to
a large number of critics or given to them personally. Others were tele-
phoned and read all or part of the text. A group forced its way into the
Press Club where the critics were being received and threw the leaflets among the audience. Others were tossed onto the sidewalks from

upstairs windows or from a car. (After the Press Club incident, art critics were seen coming out in the street to pick up the leaflets so as to remove them from the curiosity of passersby.) In short, all steps were taken to leave the critics no chance of being unaware of the text. These art critics did not shrink from calling the police, and used their World Exposition influence in order to block the reprinting in the press of a text harmful to the prestige of their convention and their specialization. Our comrade Korun is now being threatened with prosecution for his role in the intervention.

Theory of the Dérive

One of the basic situationist practices is the *dérive*,* a technique of rapid passage through varied ambiences. Dérives involve playful-constructive behavior and awareness of psychogeographical effects, and are thus quite different from the classic notions of journey or stroll.

In a dérive one or more persons during a certain period drop their relations, their work and leisure activities, and all their other usual motives for movement and action, and let themselves be drawn by the attractions of the terrain and the encounters they find there. Chance is a less important factor in this activity than one might think: from a dérive point of view cities have psychogeographical contours, with constant currents, fixed points, and vortexes that strongly discourage entry into or exit from certain zones.

But the dérive includes both this letting-go and its necessary contradiction: the domination of psychogeographical variations by the knowledge and calculation of their possibilities. In this latter regard, ecological science, despite the narrow social space to which it limits itself, provides psychogeography with abundant data.

Ecological analysis of the absolute or relative character of fissures in the urban network, of the role of microclimates, of distinct neighborhoods with no relation to administrative boundaries, and above all of the dominating action of centers of attraction, must be utilized and completed by psychogeographical methods. The objective passional terrain of the dérive must be defined in accordance both with its own logic and with its relations with social morphology.

In his study *Paris et l'agglomération parisienne* (Bibliothèque de Sociologie Contemporaine, P.U.F., 1952) Chombart de Lauwe notes that "an urban neighborhood is determined not only by geographical and economic factors, but also by the image that its inhabitants and those of other neighborhoods have of it." In the same work, in order to illustrate "the narrowness of the real Paris in which each individual lives . . . within a geographical area whose radius is extremely small," he diagrams all the movements made in the space of one year by a student living in the 16th Arrondissement. Her itinerary forms a small triangle with no significant deviations, the three apexes of which are the School of Political Sciences, her residence, and that of her piano teacher.

Such data—examples of a modern poetry capable of provoking

sharp emotional reactions (in this particular case, outrage at the fact that anyone's life can be so pathetically limited)—or even Burgess's theory of Chicago's social activities as being distributed in distinct concentric zones, will undoubtedly prove useful in developing dérives.

If chance plays an important role in dérives, this is because the methodology of psychogeographical observation is still in its infancy. But the action of chance is naturally conservative and in a new setting tends to reduce everything to habit or to an alternation between a limited number of variants. Progress means breaking through fields where chance holds sway by creating new conditions more favorable to our purposes. We can say, then, that the randomness of a dérive is fundamentally different from that of the stroll, but also that the first psychogeographical attractions discovered by dérivers may tend to fixate them around new habitual axes, to which they will constantly be drawn back.

An insufficient awareness of the limitations of chance, and of its inevitably reactionary effects, condemned to a dismal failure the famous aimless wandering attempted in 1923 by four surrealists, beginning from a town chosen by lot: Wandering in open country is naturally depressing, and the interventions of chance are poorer there than anywhere else. But this mindlessness is pushed much further by a certain Pierre Vendryes (in *Médium*, May 1954), who thinks he can relate this anecdote to various probability experiments, on the ground that they all supposedly involve the same sort of antideterminist liberation. He gives as an example the random distribution of tadpoles in a circular aquarium, adding, significantly, "It is necessary, of course, that such a population be subject to no external guiding influence." From that perspective, the tadpoles could be considered more spontaneously liberated than the surrealists, since they have the advantage of being "as stripped as possible of intelligence, sociability, and sexuality," and are thus "truly independent from one another."

At the opposite pole from such imbecilities, the primarily urban character of the dérive, in its element in the great industrially transformed cities that are such rich centers of possibilities and meanings, could be expressed in Marx's phrase: "People can see nothing around them that is not their own image; everything speaks to them of themselves. Their very landscape is alive."

One can dérive alone, but all indications are that the most fruitful numerical arrangement consists of several small groups of two or three people who have reached the same level of awareness, since cross-checking these different groups' impressions makes it possible to arrive at more objective conclusions. It is preferable for the composition of these groups to change from one dérive to another. With more than four or five participants, the specifically dérive character rapidly diminishes, and in any case it is impossible for there to be more than ten or twelve people without the dérive fragmenting into several simultaneous dérives. The practice of such subdivision is in fact of great interest, but the difficulties it entails have so far prevented it from being organized on a sufficient scale.

The average duration of a dérive is one day, considered as the time between two periods of sleep. The starting and ending times have no necessary relation to the solar day, but it should be noted that the last hours of the night are generally unsuitable for dérives.

But this duration is merely a statistical average. For one thing, a dérive rarely occurs in its pure form: it is difficult for the participants to avoid setting aside an hour or two at the beginning or end of the day for taking care of banal tasks; and toward the end of the day fatigue tends to encourage such an abandonment. But more importantly, a dérive often takes place within a deliberately limited period of a few hours, or even fortuitously during fairly brief moments; or it may last for several days without interruption. In spite of the cessations imposed by the need for sleep, certain dérives of a sufficient intensity have been sustained for three or four days, or even longer. It is true that in the case of a series of dérives over a rather long period of time it is almost impossible to determine precisely when the state of mind peculiar to one dérive gives way to that of another. One sequence of dérives was pursued without notable interruption for around two months. Such an experience gives rise to new objective conditions of behavior that bring about the disappearance of a good number of the old ones.*

The influence of weather on dérives, although real, is a significant factor only in the case of prolonged rains, which make them virtually impossible. But storms or other types of precipitation are rather favorable for dérives.

The spatial field of a dérive may be precisely delimited or vague, depending on whether the goal is to study a terrain or to emotionally disorient oneself. It should not be forgotten that these two aspects of dérives overlap in so many ways that it is impossible to isolate one of them in a pure state. But the use of taxis, for example, can provide a clear enough dividing line: If in the course of a dérive one takes a taxi, either to get to a specific destination or simply to move, say, twenty minutes to the west, one is concerned primarily with personal disorientation. If, on the other hand, one sticks to the direct exploration of a particular terrain, one is concentrating primarily on research for a psychogeographical urbanism.

In every case the spatial field depends first of all on the point of departure—the residence of the solo dériver or the meeting place selected by a group. The maximum area of this spatial field does not extend beyond the entirety of a large city and its suburbs. At its minimum it can be limited to a small self-contained ambience: a single neighborhood or even a single block of houses if it's interesting enough (the extreme case being a static-dérive of an entire day within the Saint-Lazare train station).

The exploration of a fixed spatial field entails establishing bases and calculating directions of penetration. It is here that the study of maps comes in—ordinary ones as well as ecological and psychogeographical ones—along with their correction and improvement. It should go without saying that we are not at all interested in any mere exoticism that may arise from the fact that one is exploring a neighborhood for the first time. Besides its unimportance, this aspect of the problem is completely subjective and soon fades away.

In the "possible rendezvous," on the other hand, the element of exploration is minimal in comparison with that of behavioral disorientation. The subject is invited to come alone to a certain place at a specified time. He is freed from the bothersome obligations of the ordinary rendezvous since there is no one to wait for. But since this "possible rendezvous" has brought him without warning to a place he may or may not know, he observes the surroundings. It may be that the same spot has been specified for a "possible rendezvous" for someone else whose identity he has no way of knowing. Since he may never even have seen the other person before, he will be encouraged to start up conversations with various passersby. He may meet no one, or he may even by chance meet the person who has arranged the "possible rendezvous." In any case, particularly if the time and place have been well chosen, his use of time will take an unexpected turn. He may even telephone someone else who doesn't know where the first "possible rendezvous" has taken him, in order to ask for another one to be specified. One can see the virtually unlimited resources of this pastime.

Our rather anarchic lifestyle and even certain amusements considered dubious that have always been enjoyed among our entourage—slipping by night into houses undergoing demolition, hitchhiking nonstop and without destination through Paris during a transportation strike in the name of adding to the confusion, wandering in subterranean catacombs forbidden to the public, etc.—are expressions of a more general sensibility which is no different from that of the dérive. Written descriptions can be no more than passwords to this great game.

The lessons drawn from dérives enable us to draft the first surveys of the psychogeographical articulations of a modern city. Beyond the discovery of unities of ambience, of their main components and their spatial localization, one comes to perceive their principal axes of passage, their exits, and their defenses. One arrives at the central hypothesis of the existence of psychogeographical hubs. One measures the distances that actually separate two regions of a city, distances that may have little relation with the physical distance between them. With the aid of old maps, aerial photographs, and experimental dérives, one can draw up hitherto lacking maps of influences, maps whose inevitable imprecision at this early stage is no worse than that of the earliest navigational charts. The only difference is that it is no longer a matter of precisely delineating stable continents, but of changing architecture and urbanism.

Today the different unities of atmosphere and of dwellings are not precisely marked off, but are surrounded by more or less extended bordering regions. The most general change that dérive experiences lead to proposing is the constant diminution of these border regions, up to the point of their complete suppression.

Within architecture itself, the taste for dériving tends to promote all sorts of new forms of labyrinths made possible by modern techniques of construction. Thus in March 1955 the press reported the construction in New York of a building in which one can see the first signs of an opportunity to dérive inside an apartment:

> The apartments of the helicoidal building will be shaped like slices of cake. One will be able to enlarge or reduce them by shifting movable partitions. The half-floor gradations avoid limiting the number of rooms, since the tenant can request the use of the adjacent section on either upper or lower levels. With this setup three four-room apartments can be transformed into one twelve-room apartment in less than six hours.

(To be continued.)

GUY DEBORD

Détournement as
Negation and Prelude

Détournement, the reuse of preexisting artistic elements in a new ensemble, has been a constantly present tendency of the contemporary avant-garde, both before and since the formation of the SI. The two fundamental laws of détournement are the loss of importance of each detourned autonomous element—which may go so far as to completely lose its original sense—and at the same time the organization of another meaningful ensemble that confers on each element its new scope and effect.

Détournement has a peculiar power which obviously stems from the double meaning, from the enrichment of most of the terms by the coexistence within them of their old and new senses. And it is very practical because it's so easy to use and because of its inexhaustible potential for reuse. Concerning the negligible effort required for détournement, we have already noted that "the cheapness of its products is the heavy artillery that breaks through all the Chinese walls of understanding" ("A User's Guide to Détournement," May 1956). But these points would not by themselves justify recourse to this method, which the same text describes as "clashing head-on against all social and legal conventions." Détournement has a historical significance. What is it?

"Détournement is a game made possible by the capacity of *devaluation*," writes Jorn in his study *Detourned Painting* (May 1959), and he goes on to say that all the elements of the cultural past must be "reinvested" or disappear. Détournement is thus first of all a negation of the value of the previous organization of expression. It arises and grows increasingly stronger in the historical period of the decomposition of artistic expression. But at the same time, the attempts to reuse the "detournable bloc" as material for other ensembles express the search for a vaster construction, a new genre of creation at a higher level.

The SI is a very special kind of movement, different in nature from preceding artistic avant-gardes. Within culture, the SI can be likened to a research laboratory, for example, or to a party in which we are situationists but nothing that we do can yet be situationist. This is not a disavowal for anyone. We are partisans of a certain future of culture and of life. Situationist activity is a particular craft that we are not yet practicing.

Thus the signature of the situationist movement, the sign of its presence and contestation within contemporary cultural reality (since we cannot represent any common style whatsoever), is first of all the use of détournement. Examples of our use of detourned expression include Jorn's altered paintings; Debord and Jorn's book *Mémoires*, "composed entirely of prefabricated elements," in which the writing on each page runs in all directions and the reciprocal relations of the phrases are invariably uncompleted; Constant's projects for detourned sculptures; and Debord's detourned documentary film, *On the Passage of a Few Persons Through a Rather Brief Unity of Time*. At the stage of what the "User's Guide" calls "ultra-détournement, that is, the tendencies for détournement to operate in everyday social life" (e.g. passwords or the wearing of disguises, belonging to the sphere of play), we might mention, at different levels, Gallizio's industrial painting; Wyckaert's "orchestral" project for assembly-line painting with a division of labor based on color; and numerous détournements of buildings that were at the origin of unitary urbanism. But we should also mention in this context the SI's very forms of "organization" and propaganda.

At this point in the world's development, all forms of expression are losing their grip on reality and being reduced to self-parody. As the readers of this journal can frequently verify, present-day writing invariably has an element of parody. As the "User's Guide" notes: "It is necessary to envisage a parodic-serious stage where the accumulation of detourned elements, far from aiming to arouse indignation or laughter by alluding to some original work, will express our indifference toward a meaningless and forgotten original, and concern itself with rendering a certain sublimity."

This combination of parody and seriousness reflects the contradictions of an era in which we find ourselves confronted with both the urgent necessity and the near impossibility of initiating and carrying out a totally innovative collective action—an era in which the most serious ventures are masked in the ambiguous interplay between art and its necessary negation, and in which the essential voyages of discovery have been undertaken by such astonishingly incapable people.

Situationist Theses on Traffic

1

A mistake made by all the city planners is to consider the private automobile (and its by-products, such as the motorcycle) as essentially a means of transportation. In reality, it is the most notable material symbol of the notion of happiness that developed capitalism tends to spread throughout the society. The automobile is at the heart of this general propaganda, both as supreme good of an alienated life and as essential product of the capitalist market: It is generally being said this year that American economic prosperity is soon going to depend on the success of the slogan "Two cars per family."

2

Commuting time, as Le Corbusier rightly noted, is a surplus labor which correspondingly reduces the amount of "free" time.

3

We must replace travel as an adjunct to work with travel as a pleasure.

4

To want to redesign architecture to accord with the needs of the present massive and parasitical existence of private automobiles reflects the most unrealistic misapprehension of where the real problems lie. Instead, architecture must be transformed to accord with the whole development of the society, criticizing all the transitory values linked to obsolete forms of social relationships (in the first rank of which is the family).

5

Even if, during a transitional period, we temporarily accept a rigid division between work zones and residence zones, we must at least envisage a third sphere: that of life itself (the sphere of freedom and leisure—the essence of life). Unitary urbanism acknowledges no boundaries; it aims to form an integrated human milieu in which separations such as work/leisure or public/private will finally be dissolved. But before this is possible, the minimum action of unitary urbanism is to extend the terrain of play to all desirable constructions. This terrain will be at the level of complexity of an old city.

6

It is not a matter of opposing the automobile as an evil in itself. It is its extreme concentration in the cities that has led to the negation of its function. Urbanism should certainly not ignore the automobile, but even less should it accept it as a central theme. It should reckon on gradually phasing it out. In any case, we can envision the banning of auto traffic from the central areas of certain new complexes, as well as from a few old cities.

7

Those who believe that the automobile is eternal are not thinking, even from a strictly technological standpoint, of other future forms of transportation. For example, certain models of one-man helicopters currently being tested by the US Army will probably have spread to the general public within twenty years.

8

The breaking up of the dialectic of the human milieu in favor of auto-mobiles (the projected freeways in Paris will entail the demolition of thousands of houses and apartments although the housing crisis is continually worsening) masks its irrationality under pseudopractical justifications. But it is practically necessary only in the context of a specific social set-up. Those who believe that the particulars of the problem are permanent want in fact to believe in the permanence of the present society.

9

Revolutionary urbanists will not limit their concern to the circulation of things, or to the circulation of human beings trapped in a world of things. They will try to break these topological chains, paving the way with their experiments for a human journey through authentic life.

GUY DEBORD

Another City for Another Life

The crisis in urbanism is worsening. The layout of neighborhoods, old and new, conflicts with established patterns of behavior and even more with the new ways of life that we are seeking. The result is a dismal and sterile ambience in our surroundings.

In the older neighborhoods, the streets have degenerated into free-ways and leisure activities are being commercialized and corrupted by tourism. Social relations become impossible. The newly built neighborhoods have only two all-pervasive themes: automobile traffic and household comfort—an impoverished expression of bourgeois content-ment, lacking any sense of play.

To meet the need to rapidly construct entire cities, cemeteries of reinforced concrete are being built in which masses of the population are condemned to die of boredom. What's the point of all the extraor-dinary technical inventions the world now has at its disposal if the conditions are lacking to derive any benefit from them, if they contrib-ute nothing to leisure, if imagination is absent?

We demand adventure. Not finding it on earth, some want to seek it on the moon. We, however, are committed to changing life here on earth. We intend to create situations, new situations, breaking the laws that prevent the development of meaningful ventures in life and cul-ture. We are at the dawn of a new era, and we are already attempting to sketch out the image of a happier life, of a unitary urbanism—an urbanism designed for pleasure.

Our domain is thus the urban network, the natural expression of a collective creativity, capable of incorporating the creative energies liberated by the decline of a culture based on individualism. In our opinion the traditional arts will have no role in the creation of the new environment in which we want to live.

We are in the process of inventing new techniques; we are examining the possibilities offered by existing cities; and we are making models and plans for future cities. We know that we need to avail ourselves of all the new technological inventions, and we know that the future con-structions we envisage will have to be flexible enough to respond to a dynamic conception of life, which means creating our own surround-ings in direct relation to continually changing modes of behavior.

We thus have a social conception of urbanism. We are opposed to the notion of a garden city in which the spacing apart of isolated skyscrapers inevitably reduces people's direct relations and collective activities. To create a close connection between surroundings and behavior, urban concentration is indispensable. Those who think that telecommunications and rapid transportation are going to break up the shared life of the conurbations have little understanding of humanity's true needs. In contrast to the garden city idea favored by most modern architects, we envisage covered cities in which the layout of roads and separate buildings will be replaced by a continuous spatial construction elevated above the ground, including clusters of dwellings as well as public spaces (permitting changes in use according to the needs of the moment). Since all traffic, in the functional sense of the term, will pass on the ground level below or on overhead terraces, streets can be eliminated. The multitude of different traversable spaces of which the city is composed will form a complex and vast social space. Far from a return to nature—from the notion of living in a park, as solitary aristocrats once did—we see in such immense constructions the possibility of overcoming nature and of regulating the climate, light, and sounds in these different spaces in accordance with our desires.

Do we intend this to be a new functionalism, which would promote an even greater idealization of utilitarian life? It should not be forgotten that once functions are established, they are followed by play. For a long time now, architecture has become a game of space and ambiences. Garden cities lack ambiences. We, on the contrary, want to make more conscious use of ambiences so that they correspond to all our needs.

The future cities we envisage will offer a wholly new variability of sensations in this realm, and unforeseen games will become possible through the inventive use of material conditions, such as modifications of air, sound, and light. City planners are already studying the possibility of harmonizing the cacophony that reigns in present-day cities. This problem will soon give rise to a new field of creation, as will many other such problems that will present themselves. Space travel, which seems likely in the near future, might also influence this development, since establishing bases on other planets will immediately raise the problem of sheltered cities, which may provide models for our study of future urbanism.

Above all, however, the reduction in the work necessary for production (resulting from extensive automation) will create a need for leisure, a diversity of behavior, and a change in the very nature of human behavior that will inevitably lead to a new conception of a collective habitat with a maximum of social space, in contrast to the garden city where social space is reduced to a minimum. The city of the future must be conceived as a continuous construction on pillars, or as an extended system of different structures from which are suspended premises for housing, recreation, production, distribution, etc., leaving the ground level free for traffic circulation and public meetings. The use of ultralightweight and insulating materials that are currently being tested will permit light construction with supports spaced well apart. In this way it will be possible to create a multilayered city: underground, ground level, upper stories, and terraces, with areas ranging from that of a present-day neighborhood to that of a metropolis. It should be noted that in such a city the built-up surface will be 100% and the free surface 200% (ground level plus terraces), whereas in traditional cities the figures are approximately 80% and 20%, and even a garden city can at most reverse this latter proportion. The terraces, forming an outdoor terrain that extends over the whole surface of the city, can be used as sports fields, as landing pads for airplanes and helicopters, and for vegetation. They will be accessible everywhere by stairways and elevators. The different floors will be divided into adjoining, communicating, and climate-controlled spaces, making it possible to create an infinite variety of ambiences and facilitating the wanderings of the inhabitants and their frequent chance encounters. The ambiences will be regularly and consciously changed, using all technical means, by teams of specialized creators, who will thus be professional situationists.

An in-depth study of the means of creating ambiences, and of the latter's psychological influence, is one of the tasks we are currently undertaking. Studies concerning the technical implementation of the load-bearing structures as well as their aesthetic aspects are the specific task of visual artists and engineers. The contribution of the latter, in particular, is urgently needed for the preparatory work we are undertaking.

If the project we have roughly outlined here risks being taken for a fantastic dream, we insist on the fact that it is feasible from the technical standpoint, desirable from the human standpoint, and indispensable from the social standpoint. The increasing dissatisfaction of the whole of humanity will reach a point where we will all be compelled to execute projects for which we possess the means, projects that will contribute to the realization of a richer and more fulfilled life.

CONSTANT

The Use of Free Time

The most superficial and constantly reiterated platitude of leftish sociologists during recent years is that leisure has become a major factor in advanced capitalist society. This platitude is the basis of countless debates for or against the importance of a reformist rise in the standard of living, or of workers' participation in the prevailing values of the society into which they are becoming increasingly integrated. What is counterrevolutionary about all this verbiage is that it equates free time with passive consumption, as if the only use of free time was the opportunity to become an increasingly full-time spectator of the prevailing absurdities. The illusions manifested in a particularly ponderous symposium of these sociologists (*Arguments* #12–13) were soundly refuted in two articles in *Socialisme ou Barbarie #27*. In the first, Canjuers wrote: "While modern capitalism constantly develops new needs in order to increase consumption, people's dissatisfaction remains the same as ever. Their lives no longer have any meaning beyond a rush to consume, and this consumption is used to justify the increasingly radical frustration of any creative activity or genuine human initiative—to the point that people no longer even see this lack of meaning as important." In the second article, Jean Delvaux noted that the issue of consumption has not superseded the qualitative distinction between the poor and the wealthy (four out of five wage workers are still constantly living at a level of extreme poverty). More significantly, he pointed out that there is no reason to worry about whether or not the proletariat participates in the prevailing social or cultural values, because *"there no longer are any such values."* And he added the essential point that the present culture, "increasingly separated from society and from people's lives (painters painting for other painters, novelists writing novels read only by other novelists about the impossibility of writing a novel)—this culture, insofar as it has any originality, is no longer anything but a constant self-denunciation: a denunciation of the society and a rage against culture itself."

The emptiness of leisure stems from the emptiness of life in present-day society, and it cannot be filled within the framework of that society. This emptiness is simultaneously expressed and concealed by the entire cultural spectacle, in three basic forms.

The "classic" form of culture continues to exist, whether reproduced in its pure form or in latter-day imitations (tragic theater, for example, or bourgeois politeness). Secondly, there are the countless degraded spectacular representations through which the prevailing society presents itself to the exploited in order to mystify them (televised sports, virtually all films and novels, advertising, the automobile as status symbol). Finally, there is an avant-garde negation of the spectacle, a negation which is often unconscious of its basis but which is the only "original" aspect of present-day culture. The "rage against culture" expressed within this latter form ends up arriving at the same *indifference* that proletarians as a class have toward all the forms of spectacular culture. Until the spectacle has been totally negated, the audience watching the negation of the spectacle can no longer be distinguished from that suspect and unhappy audience consisting of *isolated* artists and intellectuals. When the revolutionary proletariat manifests itself as such, it will not be as a new audience for some new spectacle, but as people actively participating in every aspect of their lives.

There is no revolutionary problem of leisure—of an emptiness to be filled—but a problem of free time. As we have already said: "There can be no freely spent time until we possess the modern tools for the construction of everyday life. The use of such tools will mark the leap from a utopian revolutionary art to an experimental revolutionary art" (Debord, "Theses on Cultural Revolution," *Internationale Situationniste* #1). The supersession of leisure through the development of an activity of free creation-consummation can only be understood in relation with the dissolution of the traditional arts—with their transformation into superior modes of action which do not reject or abolish art, but *fulfill* it. That is how art will be superseded, conserved, and surmounted within a more complex activity. Its traditional elements may still be partially present, but transformed, integrated, and modified by the totality.

Previous avant-garde movements presented themselves by declaring the excellence of their methods and principles, which were to be immediately judged on the basis of their *works*. The SI is the first artistic organization to base itself on the radical inadequacy of all permissible works; and whose significance, and whose success or failure, will be able to be judged only with the revolutionary praxis of its time.

Gangland and Philosophy

"The *Beijing-Bao* is the oldest daily newspaper in the world. It has appeared for over fifteen centuries, its first number having been printed in Beijing in the 4th century. The editors have often incurred the anger of the Chinese rulers for attacking the infallibility of religion and the state. The paper has nevertheless continued to appear every day, even though the editors have often paid for it with their lives. During those fifteen centuries, 1500 editors of the *Beijing-Bao* have been hung."

(Ujvidéki Magyar Szo, 1957)

The situationist tendency is not aimed at preventing the construction of situations. This first restriction in our attitude has numerous consequences. We are striving to provoke the development of these consequences.

" 'Protection' is the key word in the Garment Center racket. The process is as follows: One day you receive a visit from a gentleman who kindly offers to 'protect' you. If you are really naïve, you ask, 'Protection against what?' " (Groueff and Lapierre, *The Gangsters of New York.*)

If, for example, the head honcho of existentialism assures us that it is hard for him to adopt any sort of vulgar materialism because culture is an integral part of our lives, we can agree substantially with the latter point but without being sure that we should be so proud of this fact. That's one consequence.

How can we comprehend the formation of our culture and of our philosophical and scientific information? Modern psychology has eliminated many of the doctrines that used to obscure this question. It looks for the motives: why do we accept or refuse an "idea" or an imperative? "One of the most important results of the process of socialization is the development of a system of normative equilibrium, which superimposes itself on the system of biological equilibrium. The latter system regulates the body's responses to various needs and necessities (nourishment, defense against cold or against physical attack, etc.), whereas the former one determines which actions can be considered 'practicable' or even 'thinkable' " (P.R. Hofstätter). For example, someone becomes aware of situationist activity. He "understands" it and "rationally" follows its arguments. Then, in spite of his momentary intellectual agreement, he relapses: the next day he no longer understands us. We propose a slight modification of the psychological description quoted above, in order to understand the play of forces that have prevented him from considering various things as "practicable" or even "thinkable" when we know they are possible. Let us examine this striking experimental reaction: "The trial of Dio and his accomplices begins. Then something extraordinarily scandalous takes place. The first witness, Gondolfo Miranti, refuses to talk. He denies all the statements he has made to the FBI. The judge loses all patience. Furious, he resorts to the ultimate argument: 'I order you to answer. If you do not, you will be sentenced to five years' imprisonment!' Without hesitation, Miranti accepts the five long years of prison. In the defendant's box Johnny Dio, well dressed and smooth shaven, smiles ironically." (Groueff and Lapierre, *op. cit.*) It is difficult not to recognize an analogous pattern of behavior in someone who doesn't dare speak of problems as he knows they are. We have to ask: Is he a victim of intimidation? He is indeed. What is the mechanism common to these two kinds of fear?

Miranti had lived in *gangland* since his youth. This explains many things. "Gangland," in Chicago gangster slang, means the domain of crime, of rackets. I propose to study the basic functioning of "the Organization," in spite of the risks of getting involved: "As for the man who would try to set them free and lead them up to the light, do you not think that they would seize him and kill him if they could?" (Plato.)* Philosophy must not forget that it has always spoken its part in the most burlesque and melodramatic settings.

We should develop a little *glossary of detourned words*. I propose that "neighborhood" should often be read *gangland*. Similarly, social organization = *protection*. Society = *racket*. Culture = *conditioning*. Leisure activity = *protected crime*. Education = *premeditation*.

The systematic falsification of basic information (by the idealist conception of space, for example, of which the most glaring expression is conventional cartography) is one of the basic reinforcements of the big lie that the racketeering interests impose on the whole gangland of social space.

According to Hofstätter, "we are as yet incapable of examining the process of socialization in a truly 'scientific' manner." We, on the contrary, believe that we are capable of constructing a model for examining the production and reception of information. If we were allowed to *monitor*, by means of an exhaustive survey, the entire social life of some specific urban sector during a short period of time, we could obtain a precise cross-sectional representation of the daily *bombardment of news and information* that is dropped on present-day urban populations. The SI is naturally aware of all the modifications that its very monitoring would immediately produce in the occupied sector, profoundly perturbing the usual informational monopoly of gangland.

"Integral art, which has been talked about so much, can be realized only at the level of urbanism" (Debord). That is indeed where the limit is. At that level we can already *remove* certain decisive elements of conditioning. But if, beyond such salutary eliminations, we expect the largeness of scale in itself to generate favorable results, we will have committed the most serious error.

Neocapitalism has also discovered some advantages in large scale. Day and night it talks of nothing but city planning and national development. But its real concern is obviously the conditioning of commodity production, which it senses escaping it unless it resorts to this new scale. Academic urbanism has accordingly defined "slums" from the standpoint of postwar neocapitalism. Its techniques of urban renewal are based on sterile, antisituationist criteria.

We must make this critique of Mumford: If neighborhoods are not considered as pathological elements (ganglands), we will not be able to develop new techniques (therapies).

The constructors of situations must learn how to *read* the constructive and reconstitutable elements of situations. In so doing, they begin to understand the language spoken by situations. They learn how to speak and how to *express themselves* in this language; and eventually, by means of constructed and quasi-natural situations, how to say what has never yet been said.

ATTILA KOTÁNYI

The Adventure

The conditions of the SI's activity explain both its discipline and the forms of hostility it encounters. The SI is not interested in finding a niche within the present artistic establishment, but in undermining it. The situationists are in the catacombs of visible culture.

Anyone who is at all familiar with the social milieu of those with special status in cultural affairs is well aware of how they all despise each other and are bored by each other. This fact is not hidden, they are all quite aware of it; it's even the first thing they talk about whenever they get together. What is the cause of their resignation? Clearly the fact that they are incapable of being bearers of a collective project. Each recognizes in the others his own insignificance and his own conditioning—the resignation he has had to accept in order to participate in this separate milieu and its established aims.

Within such a community people have neither the need nor the objective possibility for any sort of collective discipline. They all politely agree about the same things and nothing ever changes. Personal or ideological disagreements remain secondary in comparison with what they have in common. But for the SI and the struggle it sets for itself, exclusion is a possible and necessary weapon.

It is the only weapon of any group based on complete freedom of individuals. None of us likes to control or judge; if we do so it is for a practical purpose, not as a moral punishment. The "terrorism" of the SI's exclusions can in no way be compared to the same practices in political movements by power-wielding bureaucracies. It is, on the contrary, the extreme ambiguity of the situation of artists, who are constantly tempted to integrate themselves into the modest sphere of social power reserved for them, that makes some discipline necessary in order to clearly define an incorruptible platform. Otherwise there would be a rapid and irremediable osmosis between this platform and the dominant cultural milieu because of the number of people going back and forth. It seems to us that the question of a present-day cultural avant-garde can only be posed at a holistic level—a level not only of collective works but of collectively interacting problems.

This is why certain people have been excluded from the SI. Some of them have rejoined the world they previously fought; others merely console themselves in a pathetic community with each other, although they have nothing in common but the fact that we broke with them—often for opposite reasons. Others retain a certain dignity in isolation, and we have been in a good position to recognize their talents. Do we think that in leaving the SI they have ceased being avant-garde? Yes, we do. There is, for the moment, no other organization constituted for a task of this scope.

The sentimental objections to these breaks seem to us to reflect the greatest mystification. The entire socioeconomic structure tends to make the past dominate the present, to rigidify living persons, to reify them as commodities. A sentimental world in which the same sorts of tastes and relations are constantly *repeated* is the direct product of the economic and social world in which gestures *must be repeated* every day in the slavery of capitalist production. The taste for false novelty reflects its unhappy nostalgia.

The violent reactions against the SI, especially those coming from people who were previously excluded from its collective activity, are first of all a reflection of the personal passion that this enterprise has been able to bring into play. Reversed into a boundless hostility, this passion has spread it about that we are loafers, Stalinists, imposters, and a hundred other clever characterizations. One person claimed that the SI was a cunningly organized economic association for dealing in modern art. Others have suggested that it was rather for the purpose of dealing in drugs. Still others have declared that we have never sold any drugs since we have too great a propensity for taking them ourselves. Others go into detail about our sexual vices. Others have gotten so carried away as to denounce us as social climbers.

These attacks have long been whispered around us by the same people who publicly pretend to be unaware of our existence. But this silence is now beginning to be broken more and more frequently by sharp public critiques. The recent special issue of *Poésie Nouvelle*, for example, mixes several accusations of the above sort with two or three possibly sincere misunderstandings. These people characterize us as "vitalists," despite the fact that we have made the most radical critique of the poverty of all presently permitted life; and they are so completely caught up in the world of the spectacle that when they try to relate our notion of a "situation" to something they are familiar with, they can only imagine that it must refer to some form of theatrical presentation. Last June these same neo-lettrists put on an exhibition of "supertemporal" art calling for audience participation, and wanted to include in it the SI's antiart, particularly some of Asger Jorn's detourned paintings. This would have amounted to putting our antiart in the context of their metaphysical system of permanent, signed spectacles, thereby attributing the ridiculous ambitions of the official art of the last century to a total attack on art itself.

In a sense, certain expressions of critical art now being used by the situationist current could be considered as part of the general cultural disintegration. Not only detourned paintings, but a film like *Critique of Separation*, for example, or the "scenic unity" evoked elsewhere in the present issue of this journal. The difference is that our actions within culture are all linked to the project of overthrowing this culture itself, and to the formation and development of a new organized situationist instrumentation.

Strange emissaries journey across Europe and beyond, meeting each other, bearing incredible instructions.

To the question, Why have we promoted such an impassioned regrouping in this cultural sphere whose present reality we reject? the answer is: Because culture is the center of meaning of a society without meaning. This empty culture is at the heart of an empty existence, and the reinvention of a project of transforming the world as a whole must also and first of all be posed on this terrain. To give up demanding power in culture would be to leave that power to those who now possess it.

We are quite aware that the culture to be overthrown will really fall only with the totality of the socioeconomic structure that supports it. But without waiting any longer, the Situationist International intends to confront it in its entirety, on every front, to the point of imposing an autonomous situationist control and instrumentation against those held by the present cultural authorities; that is, to the point of a *state of dual power in culture*.

The Fourth SI Conference in London
(excerpts)

The 4th Conference of the Situationist International was held in London, at a secret address in the East End, September 24–28, 1960, seventeen months after the Munich Conference (April 1959). The situationists assembled in London were: Debord, Jacqueline de Jong, Jorn, Kotányi, Katja Lindell, Jörgen Nash, Prem, Sturm, Maurice Wyckaert, and H.P. Zimmer. [. . .]

The discussion of these perspectives leads to posing the question: "To what extent is the SI a political movement?" Various responses state that the SI is political, but not in the ordinary sense. The discussion becomes somewhat confused. Debord proposes, in order to clearly bring out the opinion of the Conference, that each person respond in writing to a questionnaire asking if he considers that there are "forces in the society that the SI can count on? What forces? Under what conditions?" This questionnaire is agreed upon and filled out. The first responses express the view that the purpose of the SI is to establish a program of general liberation and to act in accord with other forces on a social scale. (Kotányi: "To rely on what we call free." Jorn: "We are against specialization and rationalization, but not against them as means. . . . Movements of social groups are determined by the character of their desires. We can accept other social movements only to the extent that they are moving in our direction. We are the new revolution . . . we should act with other organizations that seek the same path.") The session is then adjourned.

At the beginning of the second session, on September 26, Heimrad Prem reads a declaration of the German section in response to the questionnaire. This very long declaration attacks the tendency in the responses read the day before to count on the existence of a revolutionary proletariat, for the signers strongly doubt the revolutionary capacities of the workers against the bureaucratic institutions that have dominated their movement. The German section considers that the SI should prepare to realize its program on its own by mobilizing avant-garde artists, who are placed by the present society in intolerable conditions and can count only on themselves to take over the weapons of conditioning. Debord responds with a sharp critique of these positions.

An evening session resumes discussion of the German declaration. Nash speaks against it, asserting the capacity of the SI to act directly on the terrain of social and political organizations, and advocating systematic infiltration by clandestine situationist elements wherever they might prove useful. Nash's statement is approved in principle by everyone, with minor reservations. But the debate on the German positions continues, brought back to its central core: the hypothesis of contented workers. Kotányi reminds the German delegates that even if since 1945 they have seen apparently passive and satisfied workers in Germany and legal strikes organized with music to divert union members, in other advanced capitalist countries "wildcat" strikes have multiplied. He adds that in his opinion they vastly underestimate the German workers themselves. Jorn responds to Prem, who had made a distinction between spiritual and material questions, that it is necessary to put an end to this distinction, that "material values must reacquire a 'spiritual' significance and that spiritual capacities must be valued only insofar as they are materially realized; or to put it in other terms, that the world must become artistic *in the sense defined by the SI.*" Jacqueline de Jong asks that in order to simplify the discussion, which has become obscure in addition to being complicated by certain translations (the dominant language of the Conference being German), each member declare whether or not he or she approves of Jorn's statement. Everyone agrees with it. Debord then proposes that the majority openly declare that it rejects the German theses. It is agreed that the two tendencies will separately decide on their positions. The German minority withdraws to an adjoining room to deliberate. When they return Zimmer announces, in the name of his group, that they retract the preceding declaration, not because they think it unimportant, but in order not to obstruct current situationist activity. He concludes: "We declare that we are in complete agreement with all the acts already done by the SI, with or without us, and with those that will be done in the foreseeable future. We are also in agreement with all the ideas published by the SI. We consider the question debated today as secondary in relation to the SI's overall development, and propose to reserve further discussion of it for the future." Everyone agrees to this. Kotányi and Debord, however, ask that it be noted in the minutes that they do not consider the question discussed today to be secondary. The German situationists agree to delete their reference to it as such. The session is adjourned, very late at night. [. . .]

Instructions for an Insurrection*

If it seems somewhat absurd to talk of revolution, this is obviously because the organized revolutionary movement has long since disappeared from the modern countries where the possibilities of a decisive social transformation are concentrated. But *all the alternatives* are even more absurd, since they imply accepting the existing order in one way or another. If the word "revolutionary" has been neutralized to the point of being used in advertising to describe the slightest changes in an ever-changing commodity production, this is because the possibilities of a fundamental *desirable* change are no longer expressed anywhere. Today the revolutionary project stands accused before the tribunal of history—accused of having failed, of having simply engendered a new form of alienation. This amounts to recognizing that the ruling society has proved capable of defending itself, on all levels of reality, much better than revolutionaries expected. Not that it has become more tolerable. The point is simply that revolution has to be reinvented.

This poses a number of problems that will have to be theoretically and practically overcome in the next few years. We can briefly mention a few points that it is urgent to understand and resolve.

Of the tendencies toward regroupment that have appeared over the last few years among various minorities of the working-class movement in Europe, only the most radical current is worth preserving: that centered on the program of workers' councils. Nor should we overlook the fact that a number of confusionist elements are seeking to insinuate themselves into this debate (see the recent accord among "leftist" philosophico-sociological journals of different countries).

The greatest difficulty confronting groups that seek to create a new type of revolutionary organization is that of establishing new types of human relationships within the organization itself. The forces of the society exert an omnipresent pressure against such an effort. But unless this is accomplished, by methods yet to be experimented with, we will never be able to escape from specialized politics. The demand for participation on the part of everyone often degenerates into a mere abstract ideal, when in fact it is an absolute practical necessity for a really new organization and for the organization of a really new society. Even if militants are no longer mere underlings carrying out the decisions made by masters of the organization, they still risk being reduced to the role of spectators of those among them who are the most qualified in politics conceived as a specialization; and in this way the passivity relation of the old world is reproduced.

People's creativity and participation can only be awakened by a collective project explicitly concerned with all aspects of lived experience. The only way to "arouse the masses" is to expose the appalling contrast between the potential constructions of life and the present poverty of life. Without a critique of everyday life, a revolutionary organization is a separated milieu, as conventional and ultimately as passive as those holiday camps that are the specialized terrain of modern leisure. Sociologists, such as Henri Raymond in his study of Palinuro, have shown how in such places the spectacular mechanism recreates, on the level of play, the dominant relations of the society as a whole. But then they go on naïvely to praise the "multiplicity of human contacts," for example, without seeing that the mere quantitative increase of these contacts leaves them just as insipid and inauthentic as they are everywhere else. Even in the most libertarian and antihierarchical revolutionary group, communication between people is in no way guaranteed by a shared political program. The sociologists naturally support efforts to reform everyday life, or to organize compensation for it in vacation time. But the revolutionary project cannot accept the traditional notion of play, the notion of a game limited in space, in time, and in qualitative depth. The revolutionary game—the creation of life—is opposed to all memories of past games. To provide a three-week break from the kind of life led during forty-nine weeks of work, the holiday villages of Club Med draw on a shoddy Polynesian ideology—a bit like the French Revolution presenting itself in the guise of republican Rome, or like the revolutionaries of today who define themselves primarily in accordance with how well they fit the Bolshevik or some other style of *militant role*. The revolution of everyday life cannot draw its poetry from the past, but only from the future.

The experience of the empty leisure produced by modern capitalism has provided a critical correction to the Marxian notion of the *extension of leisure time:* It is now clear that full freedom of time requires first of all a transformation of work and the appropriation of this work in view of goals, and under conditions, that are utterly different from those of the forced labor that has prevailed up till now (see the activity of the groups that publish *Socialisme ou Barbarie* in France, *Solidarity* in England,* and *Alternative* in Belgium). But those who put all the stress on the necessity of changing work itself, of rationalizing it and of interesting people in it, and who pay no attention to the free content of life (i.e. the development of a materially equipped creative power that goes beyond the traditional categories of work time and rest-and-recreation time) run the risk of providing an ideological cover for a harmonization of the present production system in the direction of *greater efficiency and profitability* without at all having called in question the experience of this production or the necessity of this kind of life. The free construction of the entire space-time of individual life is a demand that will have to be defended against all sorts of dreams of harmony in the minds of aspiring managers of social reorganization.

The different moments of situationist activity up till now can only be understood in the perspective of a reappearance of revolution, a revolution that will be social as well as cultural and whose field of action will right from the start have to be broader than during any of its previous endeavors. The SI does not want to recruit disciples or partisans, but to bring together people capable of applying themselves to this task in the years to come, by every means and without worrying about labels. This means that we must reject not only the vestiges of specialized artistic activity, but also those of specialized politics; and particularly the post-Christian masochism characteristic of so many intellectuals in this area. We don't claim to be developing a new revolutionary program all by ourselves. We say that this program in the process of formation will one day practically oppose the ruling reality, and that we will participate in that opposition. Whatever may become of us individually, the new revolutionary movement will not be formed without taking into account what we have sought together; which could be summed up as the passage from the old theory of limited permanent revolution to a theory of generalized permanent revolution.

Basic Program of the Bureau of Unitary Urbanism

1. NOTHINGNESS OF URBANISM AND NOTHINGNESS OF THE SPECTACLE

Urbanism* doesn't exist; it is only an "ideology" in Marx's sense of the word. Architecture does really exist, like Coca-Cola: though coated with ideology, it is a real production, falsely satisfying a falsified need. Urbanism is comparable to the advertising about Coca-Cola—pure spectacular ideology. Modern capitalism, which organizes the reduction of all social life to a spectacle, is incapable of presenting any spectacle other than that of our own alienation. Its urbanistic dream is its masterpiece.

2. CITY PLANNING AS CONDITIONING AND FALSE PARTICIPATION

The development of the urban milieu is the capitalist domestication of space. It represents the choice of one particular materialization, to the exclusion of other possibilities. Like aesthetics, whose course of decomposition it is going to follow, it can be considered as a rather neglected branch of criminology. What characterizes it at the "city planning" level—as opposed to its merely architectural level—is its insistence on popular consent, on individual integration into its bureaucratic production of conditioning.

All this is imposed by means of a blackmail of utility, which hides the fact that this architecture and this conditioning are really useful only in reinforcing reification. Modern capitalism dissuades people from making any criticism of architecture with the simple argument that they need a roof over their heads, just as television is accepted on the grounds that they need information and entertainment. They are made to overlook the obvious fact that this information, this entertainment, and this kind of dwelling place are not made for them, but without them and against them.

City planning must be understood as a society's field of publicity-propaganda, i.e. as the organization of participation in something in which it is impossible to participate.

3. TRAFFIC CIRCULATION, SUPREME STAGE OF CITY PLANNING

Traffic circulation is the organization of universal isolation. As such, it constitutes the major problem of modern cities. It is the opposite of encounter: it absorbs the energies that could otherwise be devoted to encounters or to any sort of participation. Spectacles compensate for the participation that is no longer possible. Within this spectacular society one's status is determined by one's residence and mobility (personal vehicles). You don't live somewhere in the city, you live somewhere in the hierarchy. At the summit of this hierarchy the ranks can be ascertained by the degree of mobility. Power is objectively expressed in the necessity of being present each day at more and more places (business dinners, etc.) further and further removed from each other. A VIP could be defined as someone who has appeared in three different capitals in the course of a single day.

4. DISTANCIATION FROM THE URBAN SPECTACLE

The spectacle system that is in the process of integrating the population manifests itself both as organization of cities and as permanent information network. It is a solid framework designed to reinforce the existing conditions of life. Our first task is to enable people to stop identifying with their surroundings and with model patterns of behavior. This is inseparable from making possible free mutual recognition in a few initial zones set apart for human activity. People will still be obliged for a long time to accept the era of reified cities. But the attitude with which they accept it can be changed immediately. We must encourage their skepticism toward those spacious and brightly colored kindergartens, the new dormitory cities of both East and West. Only a mass awakening will pose the question of a conscious construction of the urban environment.

5. AN INDIVISIBLE FREEDOM

The main achievement of contemporary city planning is to have made people blind to the possibility of what we call unitary urbanism, namely a living critique of this manipulation of cities and their inhabitants, a critique fueled by all the tensions of everyday life. A living critique means setting up bases for an experimental life where people can come together to create their own lives on terrains equipped to their ends. Such bases cannot be reservations for "leisure" activities separated from the society. No spatio-temporal zone is completely separable. The whole society exerts continual pressure even on its present vacation "reservations." Situationist bases will exert pressure in the opposite direction, acting as bridgeheads for an invasion of everyday life as a whole. Unitary urbanism is the contrary of a specialized activity; to accept a separate urbanistic domain is already to accept the whole urbanistic lie and the falsehood permeating the whole of life.

Urbanism promises happiness. It shall be judged accordingly. The coordination of artistic and scientific means of denunciation must lead to a complete denunciation of existing conditioning.

6. THE LANDING

All space is already occupied by the enemy, which has even reshaped its basic laws, its geometry, to its own purposes. Authentic urbanism will appear when the absence of this occupation is created in certain zones. What we call construction starts there. It can be clarified by the *positive void* concept developed by modern physics. Materializing freedom means beginning by appropriating a few patches of the surface of a domesticated planet.

7. THE ILLUMINATION OF DÉTOURNEMENT

The basic practice of the theory of unitary urbanism will be the transcription of the whole theoretical lie of urbanism, detourned for the purpose of de-alienation. We have to constantly defend ourselves from the poetry of the bards of conditioning—to jam their messages, to turn their rhythms inside out.

8. CONDITIONS OF DIALOGUE

Functional means practical. The only thing that is really practical is the resolution of our fundamental problem: our self-realization (our escape from the system of isolation). This and nothing else is useful and utilitarian. Everything else is nothing but by-products of the practical, mystifications of the practical.

9. RAW MATERIAL AND TRANSFORMATION

The situationist destruction of present conditioning is already at the same time the construction of situations. It is the liberation of the inexhaustible energies trapped within a petrified daily life. With the advent of unitary urbanism, present city planning (that geology of lies) will be replaced by a technique for defending the permanently threatened conditions of freedom, and individuals—who do not yet exist as such—will begin freely constructing their own history.

10. END OF THE PREHISTORY OF CONDITIONING

We are not contending that people must return to some stage previous to the era of conditioning, but rather that they must go beyond it. We have invented the architecture and the urbanism that cannot be realized without the revolution of everyday life—without the appropriation of conditioning by everyone, its endless enrichment and fulfillment.

ATTILA KOTÁNYI, RAOUL VANEIGEM

Perspectives for Conscious
Changes in Everyday Life

To study everyday life would be a completely absurd undertaking, unable even to grasp anything of its object, if this study was not expressly for the purpose of transforming everyday life.

The practice of lecturing (the exposition of certain intellectual considerations to an audience) is an extremely commonplace form of human relations in a rather large sector of society, and is thus itself part of the everyday life that must be criticized.

Sociologists, for example, are only too inclined to exclude from everyday life things that happen to them every day, and to transfer them to separate and supposedly superior spheres. In this way habit in all its forms—beginning with the habit of handling a few professional concepts (concepts produced by the division of labor)—masks reality behind privileged conventions.

It is thus desirable to demonstrate, by a slight alteration of the usual procedures, that everyday life is right here. These words are being communicated by way of a tape recorder,* not, of course, in order to illustrate the integration of technology into this everyday life on the margin of the technological world, but in order to take the simplest opportunity to break with the appearance of pseudocollaboration, of artificial dialogue, between the "in person" lecturer and his spectators. This slight discomforting break with accustomed routine may serve to bring directly into the field of questioning of everyday life (a questioning otherwise completely abstract) the very practice of lecturing, as well as any number of other forms of using time or objects, forms that are considered "normal" and not even noticed, and which ultimately condition us. With such a detail, as with everyday life as a whole, alteration is always the necessary and sufficient condition for experimentally bringing into clear view the object of our study, which would otherwise remain uncertain—an object which is itself less to be studied than to be changed.

I have just said that the reality of an observable entity designated by the term "everyday life" stands a good chance of remaining hypothetical for many people. Indeed, the most striking feature of the present "Group for Research on Everyday Life" is obviously not the fact that it has not yet discovered anything, but the fact that the very existence of everyday life has been disputed from its very inception, and increasingly so with each new session of this conference. Most of the talks we have heard so far have been by people who are not at all convinced that everyday life exists, since they haven't encountered it anywhere. A group for research on everyday life with this attitude is comparable in every way to an expedition in search of the Yeti, which might similarly come to the conclusion that its quarry was merely a popular hoax.

To be sure, everyone agrees that certain gestures repeated every day, such as opening doors or filling glasses, are quite real; but these gestures are at such a trivial level of reality that it is rightly objected that they are not of sufficient interest to justify a new specialized branch of sociological research. A number of sociologists seem disinclined to recognize any aspects of everyday life beyond these trivialities. They thus accept the definition of it proposed by Henri Lefebvre—"whatever remains after one has eliminated all specialized activities"—but draw a different conclusion: that everyday life is nothing. The majority of sociologists—and we know how much they are in their element in specialized activities, in which they generally have the blindest faith!—recognize specialized activities everywhere and everyday life nowhere. Everyday life is always elsewhere. Among others, somewhere in the nonsociologist classes of the population. Someone said here that it would be interesting to study the workers as guinea pigs who have probably been infected with this virus of everyday life because they, having no access to specialized activities, have no life except everyday life. This condescending manner of investigating the common people in search of an exotic primitivism of everyday life—and above all this ingenuously avowed self-satisfaction, this naïve pride in participating in a culture whose glaring bankruptcy no one can dream of denying, and the radical inability to understand the world that produces this culture—all this never ceases to astonish.

This attitude clearly reveals a desire to hide behind a development of thought based on the separation of artificial fragmentary domains, so as to reject the useless, vulgar, and disturbing concept of "everyday life." Such a concept covers an uncatalogued and unclassified residue of reality, a residue some people don't want to face because it at the same time represents the standpoint of the totality and thus implies the necessity of a holistic political judgment. Certain intellectuals seem to flatter themselves with an illusory personal participation in the dominant sector of society through their possession of one or more cultural specializations, though those specializations have put them in the best position to see that this whole dominant culture is moth-eaten. But whatever one's opinion of the coherence of this culture or of the interest of one or another of its fragments, the particular alienation it has imposed on these intellectuals is to make them imagine, from their lofty sociological position, that they are quite outside the everyday life of the common people, or to give them an exaggerated idea of their sociopolitical rank, as if their lives were not as *fundamentally impoverished* as everyone else's.

Specialized activities certainly exist; they are even put to certain general uses which should be recognized in a demystified manner. Everyday life is not everything—although its overlapping with specialized activities is such that in a sense we are never outside of everyday life. But to use a somewhat simplistic spatial image, we still have to place everyday life at the center of everything. Every project begins from it and every accomplishment returns to it to acquire its real significance. Everyday life is the measure of all things: of the (non)fulfilment of human relations; of the use of lived time; of artistic experimentation; and of revolutionary politics.

It is not enough to recall that the old stereotypical image of the detached scientific observer is fallacious in any case. It must be stressed that disinterested observation is even less possible here than anywhere else. What makes for the difficulty of even recognizing a terrain of everyday life is not only the fact that it has already become the ostensible meeting ground of an empirical sociology and a conceptual elaboration, but also the fact that it presently happens to be the stake in any revolutionary renewal of culture and politics.

To fail to criticize everyday life means accepting the prolongation of the present thoroughly rotten forms of culture and politics, forms whose extreme crisis is expressed in increasingly widespread political apathy and neoilliteracy, especially in the most modern countries. On the other hand, a radical critique in acts of the prevailing everyday life could lead to a supersession of culture and politics in the traditional sense, that is, to a higher level of intervention in life.

"But," you may ask, "how does it happen that the importance of this everyday life, which according to you is the only real life, is so completely and directly underrated by people who, after all, have no direct interest in doing so—many of whom are even far from being opposed to some kind of renewal of the revolutionary movement?"

I think this happens because everyday life is organized within the limits of a scandalous poverty, and above all because there is nothing accidental about this poverty of everyday life: it is a poverty that is constantly imposed by the coercion and violence of a society divided into classes, a poverty historically organized in line with the evolving requirements of exploitation.

The use of everyday life, in the sense of a consumption of lived time, is governed by the reign of scarcity: scarcity of free time and scarcity of possible uses of this free time.

Just as the accelerated history of our time is a history of accumulation and industrialization, so the backwardness and conservative tendencies of everyday life are products of the laws and interests that have presided over this industrialization. Everyday life has until now resisted the historical. This represents first of all a *verdict against the historical* insofar as it has been the heritage and project of an exploitive society.

The extreme poverty of conscious organization and creativity in everyday life reflects the fundamental need for unconsciousness and mystification in a society of exploitation and alienation.

Henri Lefebvre has extended the idea of uneven development so as to characterize everyday life as a lagging sector, out of joint with the historical but not completely cut off from it. I think that one could go so far as to term this level of everyday life a colonized sector. We know that underdevelopment and colonization are interrelated at the level of global economy. Everything suggests that the same thing applies at the level of socioeconomic structure, at the level of praxis.

Everyday life, policed and mystified by every means, is a sort of reservation for the good natives who keep modern society running without understanding it—this society with its rapid growth of technological powers and the forced expansion of its market. History (the transformation of reality) cannot presently be used in everyday life because the people who live that everyday life are the product of a history over which they have no control. It is of course they themselves who make this history, but they do not make it freely or consciously.

Modern society is viewed through specialized fragments that are virtually incommunicable; and so everyday life, where all questions are liable to be posed in a unitary manner, is naturally the domain of ignorance.

Through its industrial production this society has emptied the gestures of work of all meaning. And no model of human behavior has retained any real relevance in everyday life.

This society tends to atomize people into isolated consumers and to prohibit communication. Everyday life is thus private life, the realm of separation and spectacle.

It is thus also the sphere of the specialists' resignation and failure. It is the reason, for example, that one of the rare individuals capable of understanding the latest scientific conception of the universe will make a fool of himself by earnestly pondering Alain Robbe-Grillet's aesthetic theories or by sending petitions to the President in the hope of convincing him to change his policies. It is the sphere of personal disarmament, of an avowed incapability of living.

Thus the underdevelopment of everyday life cannot be characterized solely by its relative inability to put various technologies to good use. This inability is only one consequence (though an important one) of everyday alienation as a whole, which could be defined as the inability to invent a technique for the liberation of everyday experience.

Many technologies do, in fact, more or less markedly alter certain aspects of everyday life—not only housework, as has already been mentioned here, but also telephones, television, music on long-playing records, mass air travel, etc. These developments arise anarchically, by chance, without anyone having foreseen their interrelations or consequences. But there is no denying that, on the whole, this introduction of technology into everyday life ultimately takes place within the framework of modern bureaucratized capitalism and tends to reduce people's independence and creativity. The new prefabricated cities clearly exemplify the totalitarian tendency of modern capitalism's organization of life: the isolated inhabitants (generally isolated within the framework of the family cell) see their lives reduced to the pure triviality of repetition combined with the obligatory consumption of an equally repetitive spectacle.

One can thus conclude that if people censor the question of their own everyday life, it is both because they are aware of its unbearable impoverishment and because sooner or later they sense—whether they admit it or not—that all the real possibilities, all the desires that have been frustrated by the functioning of social life, are focused there, and not at all in the various specialized activities and distractions. Awareness of the profound richness and energy abandoned in everyday life is inseparable from awareness of the poverty of the dominant organization of this life. The awareness of this untapped richness leads to the contrasting definition of everyday life as poverty and as prison; which in turn leads to the repression of the whole problem.

In these conditions, repressing the political question posed by the poverty of everyday life means repressing the most profound demands bearing on the possible richness of this life—demands that can lead to nothing less than a reinvention of revolution. Of course an evasion of politics at this level is in no way incompatible with being active in the Parti Socialiste Unifié, for example, or with reading *L'Humanité* [the French Communist Party newspaper] with confidence.

Everything really depends on the level at which this problem is posed: How do we live? In what ways are we satisfied or unsatisfied with our life? Without for a moment letting ourselves be intimidated by the various advertisements designed to persuade us that we can be happy because of the existence of God or Colgate toothpaste or the National Center for Scientific Research.

It seems to me that the phrase "critique of everyday life" could and should also be understood in this reverse sense: as everyday life's sovereign critique of everything that is external or irrelevant to itself.

The question of the use of technological means, in everyday life and elsewhere, is a political question. Out of all the potential technological means, those that actually get implemented are selected in accordance with the goal of maintaining the rule of a particular class. When one imagines a future such as that presented in science fiction, in which interstellar adventures coexist with a terrestrial everyday life kept in the same old material poverty and archaic morality, this implies precisely that there is still a class of specialized rulers maintaining the proletarian masses of the factories and offices in their service; and that the interstellar adventures are nothing but the particular enterprise chosen by those rulers, the way they have found to develop their irrational economy, the pinnacle of specialized activity.

Someone posed the question, "What is private life [vie privée] deprived [privée] of?" Quite simply of life itself, which is cruelly absent. People are as deprived as possible of communication and of self-fulfillment; deprived of the opportunity to personally make their own history. Positive responses to this question about the nature of this privation can thus only take the form of projects of enrichment; the project of developing a style of life different from the present one (if the present way of life can even be said to have a "style"). Or to put it another way, if we regard everyday life as the frontier between the dominated and the undominated sectors of life, and thus as the terrain of chance and uncertainty, it would be necessary to replace the present ghetto with a constantly moving frontier; to work ceaselessly toward the organization of new chances, new opportunities.

The question of intensity of experience is posed today—with drug use, for example—in the only terms in which the society of alienation is capable of posing any question: namely, in terms of false recognition of falsified projects, in terms of fixation and attachment. It should also be noted how much the image of love elaborated and propagated in this society has in common with drugs. A passion is first of all presented as a denial of all other passions; then it is frustrated, and finally it reappears only in the compensations of the reigning spectacle. La Rochefoucauld wrote: "What often prevents us from abandoning ourselves to a single vice is that we have several."* This can be taken as a very positive observation if we ignore its moralistic presuppositions and put it back on its feet as the basis of a program for the realization of human capacities.

All these questions are now relevant because our time is clearly dominated by the emergence of the project borne by the working class—the abolition of every class society and the inauguration of human history—and is thus also dominated by the fierce resistance to this project and by the distortions and failures it has encountered up till now.

The present crisis of everyday life takes its place among the new forms of the crisis of capitalism, forms that remain unnoticed by those who cling to classical calculations of the dates of the next cyclical crises of the economy.

The disappearance in developed capitalism of all the old values and of all the frames of reference of past communication; and the impossibility of replacing them with any others before having rationally dominated, within everyday life and everywhere else, the new industrial forces that escape us more and more—these facts give rise not only to the virtually official dissatisfaction of our time, a dissatisfaction particularly acute among young people, but also to the self-negating tendency of art. Artistic activity had always been alone in expressing the clandestine problems of everyday life, albeit in a veiled, deformed, and partially illusory manner. Modern art now provides us with undeniable evidence of the destruction of all artistic expression.

If we consider the whole extent of the crisis of contemporary society, I don't think it is possible to still regard leisure activities as a negation of the everyday. It has been recognized here that it is necessary to study "wasted time." But let us look at the recent evolution of this notion of wasted time. For classical capitalism, wasted time was time that was not devoted to production, accumulation, saving. The secular morality taught in bourgeois schools instilled this rule of life. But it so happens that by an unexpected turn of events modern capitalism needs to increase consumption and "raise the standard of living" (bearing in mind that that expression is completely meaningless). Since at the same time production conditions, compartmentalized and clocked to the extreme, have become indefensible, the new morality already being conveyed in advertising, propaganda, and all the forms of the dominant spectacle now frankly admits that wasted time is the time spent at work, the only purpose of which is to earn enough to enable one to buy rest, consumption, and entertainments—a daily passivity manufactured and controlled by capitalism.

If we now consider the artificiality of the consumer needs prefabricated and ceaselessly stimulated by modern industry—if we recognize the emptiness of leisure activities and the impossibility of rest—we can pose the question more realistically: What would *not* be wasted time? Or to put it another way, the development of a society of abundance should lead to an abundance of what?

This can obviously serve as a touchstone in many regards. When, for example, in one of those papers where the flabby thinking of "leftist intellectuals" is displayed (*France-Observateur*) one reads a title like "The Little Car Out to Conquer Socialism" heading an article that explains that nowadays the Russians are beginning to pursue an American-style private consumption of goods, beginning naturally with cars, one cannot help thinking that one need not have mastered all of Hegel and Marx to realize that a socialism that gives way in the face of an invasion of the market by small cars is in no way the socialism for which the labor movement fought. The bureaucratic rulers of Russia must be opposed not because of their particular tactics or dogmas, but more fundamentally: because the meaning of people's lives has not really changed. And this is not some obscure, inevitable fate of an everyday life supposedly doomed to remain reactionary. It is a fate imposed on everyday life from the outside by the reactionary sphere of specialized rulers, regardless of the label under which they plan and regulate poverty in all its aspects.

The present depoliticization of many former leftist militants, their withdrawal from one type of alienation to plunge into another, that of private life, represents not so much a return to privacy, a flight from "historical responsibility," but rather a withdrawal from the specialized political sector that is always manipulated by others—a sector where the only responsibility they ever took was that of leaving all responsibility to uncontrolled leaders; a sector where the communist project was sidetracked and betrayed. Just as one cannot simplistically oppose private life to public life without asking: what private life? what public life? (for private life contains the factors of its negation and supersession, just as collective revolutionary action harbored the factors of its degeneration), so it would be a mistake to assess the alienation of individuals within revolutionary politics when it is really a matter of the alienation of revolutionary politics itself. The problem of alienation should be tackled dialectically, so as to draw attention to the constantly recurring possibilities of alienation arising within the very struggle against alienation; but we should stress that this applies to the highest level of research (to the philosophy of alienation as a whole, for example) and not to the level of Stalinism, the explanation of which is unfortunately more gross.

Capitalist civilization has not yet been superseded anywhere, but it continues to produce its own enemies everywhere. The next rise of the revolutionary movement, radicalized by the lessons of past defeats and with a program enriched in proportion to the practical potentials of modern society (potentials that already constitute the material basis that was lacked by the "utopian" currents of socialism)—this next attempt at a total contestation of capitalism will know how to invent and propose a different use of everyday life, and will immediately base itself on new everyday practices and on new types of human relationships (being no longer unaware that any conserving, within the revolutionary movement, of the relations prevailing in the existing society imperceptibly leads to a reconstitution of one or another variant of that society).

Just as the bourgeoisie, in its ascendant phase, had to ruthlessly liquidate everything that transcended earthly life (heaven, eternity), so the revolutionary proletariat—which can never, without ceasing to be revolutionary, recognize itself in any past or any models—will have to renounce everything that transcends everyday life. Or rather, everything that claims to transcend it: the spectacle, "historical" acts or pronouncements, the "greatness" of leaders, the mystery of specializations, the "immortality" of art and its supposed importance outside of life. In other words, it must renounce all the by-products of eternity that have survived as weapons of the world of the rulers.

The revolution in everyday life, breaking its present resistance to the historical (and to every kind of change), will create conditions in which *the present dominates the past* and the creative aspects of life always predominate over the repetitive ones. We must therefore expect that the side of everyday life expressed by the concepts of ambiguity (misunderstandings, compromises, misuses) will decline considerably in importance in favor of their opposites: conscious choices and gambles.

The present artistic calling in question of language—appearing at the same time as that metalanguage of machines which is nothing other than the bureaucratized language of the bureaucracy in power—will then be superseded by higher forms of communication. The present notion of a decipherable social text will lead to new methods of writing this social text, in the direction my situationist comrades are presently seeking with unitary urbanism and some preliminary ventures in experimental behavior. The central aim of an entirely reconverted and redirected industrial production will be the organization of new configurations of everyday life, the free creation of events.

The critique and perpetual re-creation of the totality of everyday life, before being carried out naturally by everyone, must be undertaken within the present conditions of oppression, in order to destroy those conditions.

An avant-garde cultural movement, even one with revolutionary sympathies, cannot accomplish this. Neither can a revolutionary party on the traditional model, even if it accords a large place to criticism of culture (understanding by that term the entirety of artistic and conceptual means through which a society explains itself to itself and shows itself goals of life). This culture and this politics are both worn out and it is not without reason that most people take no interest in them. The revolutionary transformation of everyday life—which is not reserved for some vague future but is placed immediately before us by the development of capitalism and its unbearable demands (the only alternative being the reinforcement of the modern slavery)—this transformation will mark the end of all unilateral artistic expression stocked in the form of commodities, at the same time as the end of all specialized politics.

This is going to be the task of a new type of revolutionary organization, from its inception.

GUY DEBORD
May 1961

Geopolitics of Hibernation

The "balance of terror" between two rival groups of states—the most visible basic aspect of global politics at the present moment—is also a balance of resignation: the resignation of each antagonist to the permanence of the other; and within their frontiers, the resignation of people to a fate that is so far out of their control that the very existence of the planet is far from certain, hinging on the prudence and skill of inscrutable strategists. This in turn reinforces a more general resignation to the existing order, to the coexisting powers of the specialists who organize this fate. These powers find an additional advantage in this balance since it facilitates the rapid liquidation of any original liberatory experience arising on the margin of their systems, particularly within the current movement of the underdeveloped countries. The same method of neutralizing one menace with another—regardless of who the victorious protector may be in any particular case—can be seen in the crushing of the revolutionary impetus of the Congo by sending in the United Nations Expeditionary Corps (two days after their arrival in early July 1960 the Ghanian troops, the first on the scene, were used to break a transportation strike in Leopoldville) and in the crushing of the revolutionary impetus of Cuba by the formation of a one-party system (in March 1962 General Lister, whose role in the repression of the Spanish revolution is well known, was named Assistant Chief of Staff to the Cuban Army).

In reality the two camps are not actually preparing for war, but for the indefinite preservation of this balance, which mirrors the internal stabilization of their power. It goes without saying that this will entail an enormous mobilization of resources, since it is imperative to continually escalate the spectacle of possible war. Thus Barry Commoner, head of the scientific committee assigned by the United States government to estimate the destruction that would result from a thermonuclear war, announces that after one hour of such a war 80 million Americans would be killed and that the survivors would have no hope of living normally afterwards. The Chiefs of Staff, who in their projections now count only in "megabodies" (one megabody = one million corpses), have admitted the impossibility of calculating beyond the first half day since experimental evidence is lacking to make any meaningful estimates at such a level of destruction. According to Nicolas Vichney (*Le Monde*, 5 January 1962), one extremist faction of American defense doctrine has gone so far as to argue that "the

best deterrent would consist of the possession of an enormous thermonuclear bomb buried underground. If the enemy attacked, the bomb
would be detonated and the Earth would be blown apart."

The theorists of this "Doomsday System" have certainly found the
ultimate weapon for enforcing submission; they have for the first time
translated the refusal of history into precise technological powers. But
the rigid logic of these doctrinaires only responds to one aspect of the
contradictory needs of the society of alienation, whose indissoluble
project is to prevent people from living while it organizes their survival
(see the opposition of the concepts of life and survival described by
Vaneigem in "Basic Banalities"). Thus the Doomsday System, through
its contempt for survival—which is still the indispensable condition for
the present and future exploitation of human labor—can only play the
role of last resort for the ruling bureaucracies: the insane proof of their
seriousness. But in order to be fully effective in reinforcing people's
submission, the spectacle of a war to come must henceforth extend its
sway over the organization of our present peacetime existence, while
simultaneously accommodating itself to the basic requirements of
that organization.

In this regard the extraordinary development of fallout shelters
during 1961 is certainly a decisive turning point in the Cold War, a
qualitative leap that will one day be seen as of immense importance
in the formation of a cybernetized totalitarian society on a global
scale. It began in the United States, where Kennedy in his State of the
Union Address last January was already able to assure the Congress:
"The nation's first serious civil defense shelter program is under way,
identifying, marking and stocking fifty million spaces; and I urge
your approval of federal incentives for the construction of public
fallout shelters in schools and hospitals and similar centers." This
state-controlled organization of survival has rapidly spread, more or
less secretly, to other major countries of the two camps. West Germany,
for example, was first of all concerned with the survival of Chancellor
Adenauer and his team (its disclosure of the plans to this end led to
the seizure of the Munich magazine *Quick*). Sweden and Switzerland
are in the process of installing collective shelters under their moun-
tains, where workers buried with their factories will be able to continue to produce without interruption until the grand finale of the
Doomsday System. But the home base of the civil defense policy is
the United States, where a number of flourishing companies, such as
the Peace o' Mind Shelter Company (Texas), the American Survival
Products Corporation (Maryland), Fox Hole Shelter, Inc. (California), and the Bee Safe Manufacturing Company (Ohio), are advertising

and installing countless individual shelters built as private property to ensure the survival of each family. This fad is giving rise to a new interpretation of religious morality, certain clergymen expressing the opinion that one's duty will clearly consist of refusing entry to friends or strangers, even by means of arms, in order to guarantee the salvation of one's own family. Morality has had to be adapted to this process of intensifying the terrorism of conformity that underlies all the publicity of modern capitalism. It was already hard, faced with one's family and neighbors, not to have the given model of automobile which a given salary level enables one to buy on credit (a salary level always recognizable in the American-type urban housing developments because the location of the dwelling is precisely determined by the level of salary). It will be even more difficult not to guarantee one's family's *survival status* once that commodity is on the market.

It is generally estimated that in the United States since 1955 the relative saturation of the demand for "durable goods" has led to an insufficiency of the consumer stimulus necessary for economic expansion. Hence the enormous vogue for trendy gadgets of all sorts, which represent an easily manipulable development in the semidurable goods sector. It is easy to see the shelters' important role in this necessary boost of expansion. With the installation of shelters and their foreseeable offshoots and by-products, all the appurtenances of life on the surface will need to be duplicated for the new duplicate life underground. These investments in subterranean strata as yet unexploited by the affluent society are boosting the sale both of semidurable goods already in use on the surface (as with the boom in canned foods, of which each shelter needs a huge supply) and of particular new gadgets, such as plastic bags for the bodies of people who will die in the shelter and, naturally, continue to lay there with the survivors.

It is easy to see that these (already widespread) individual shelters could not possibly work, if only because of such gross technical oversights as the absence of an independent oxygen supply; and that even the most sophisticated collective shelters would offer only the slightest possibility for survival if a thermonuclear war was actually accidentally unleashed. But here, as in every racket, "protection" is only a pretext. The real purpose of the shelters is to test—and thereby reinforce—people's submissiveness, and to manipulate this submissiveness to the advantage of the ruling society. The shelters, as a creation of a new consumable commodity in the society of abundance, prove more than any previous commodity that people can be made to work to satisfy highly artificial needs, needs that most certainly "remain needs without ever having been desires" ("Preliminaries Toward Defining a Unitary Revolutionary Program") and that do not have the slightest chance of becoming desires. The power of this society, its formidable automatic genius, can be measured by this extreme example. If this system were to go to the point of bluntly proclaiming that it imposes such an empty and hopeless existence that the best solution for everyone would be to go hang themselves, it would still succeed in managing a healthy and profitable business by producing standardized ropes. But regardless of all its capitalist wealth, the concept of survival means *suicide on the installment plan*, a renunciation of life *every day*. The network of shelters—which are not intended to be used for a war, but right now—presents a bizarre caricatural picture of existence under a perfected bureaucratic capitalism. A neo-Christianity has revived its ideal of renunciation with a new humility compatible with a new boost of industry. The world of shelters acknowledges itself as an *air-conditioned vale of tears*. The coalition of all the managers and their various types of priests will be able to agree on one unitary program: mass hypnosis plus superconsumption.

Survival as the opposite of life, if rarely voted for so clearly as by the buyers of shelters in 1961, can be found at all levels of the struggle against alienation. It is found in the old conception of art, which stressed survival through one's works, an admission of a renunciation of life—art as excuse and consolation (especially since the bourgeois era of aesthetics, that secular substitute for the religious otherworld). And it is found just as much at the level of the most basic needs, those of food and shelter, with the "blackmail of utility" denounced in the "Basic Program of Unitary Urbanism" (*Internationale Situationniste* #6), the blackmail that eliminates any human critique of the environment "with the simple argument that people need a roof over their heads."

The new habitat that is now taking shape with the large housing developments is not really distinct from the architecture of the shelters; it merely represents a less advanced level of that architecture. (The two are closely related and the direct passage from one to the other is already envisaged: the first example in France is a development presently being built in Nice, the basement of which is designed to serve as an atomic shelter for its inhabitants.) The concentration-camp organization of the surface of the earth is the normal state of the present society in formation; its condensed subterranean version merely represents that society's pathological excess. This subterranean sickness reveals the real nature of the "health" at the surface. The urbanism of despair is rapidly becoming dominant on the surface, not only in the population centers of the United States but also in those of much more backward countries of Europe and even, for example, in the Algeria of the neocolonialist period proclaimed since the "Constantine Plan." At the end of 1961 the first version of the national plan for French territorial development (whose formulation was later toned down) complained in its chapter on Paris of "an inactive population's stubborn insistence on living in the capital" despite the fact that the authors of the report, licensed specialists of happiness and practicality, pointed out that "they could live more agreeably outside Paris." They therefore urged the elimination of this distressing irrationality by the enactment of legal measures to "systematically discourage this inactive population from living in Paris."

Since the main worthwhile activity in this society obviously consists in systematically discouraging the plans made by its managers (until such point as the latter are concretely eliminated), and since those managers are much more constantly aware of this danger than are the drugged masses of underlings, the planners are erecting their defenses in all the modern projects of territorial organization. The planning of shelters for the population, whether in the normal form of dwellings or in the "affluent" form of family tombs for preventive habitation, in reality serves to shelter the planners' own power. The rulers who control the architectural incarceration and isolation of their subjects also know how to entrench themselves for strategic purposes. The Haussmanns of the twentieth century no longer stop at facilitating the deployment of their repressive forces by partitioning the old urban clusters into manageable city blocks divided by wide avenues. At the same time that they disperse the population over a vast area in the new prefabricated cities which represent this partitioning in its *purest state* (where the inferiority of the masses, disarmed and deprived of means of communication, is sharply increased compared with the continually more technically equipped police), they erect *inaccessible capital cities* where the ruling bureaucracy, for greater security, can constitute the whole of the population.

Different stages of development of these government-cities can be noted. The "Military Zone" of Tirana is a section cut off from the city and defended by the army, wherein are concentrated the homes of the rulers of Albania, the Central Committee building, and the schools, hospitals, stores, and diversions for this autarkic elite. The administrative city of Rocher Noir, which was built in a single year to serve as the capital of Algeria when it became evident that the French authorities were no longer capable of maintaining themselves normally in a large city, has exactly the same function as the "Military Zone" of Tirana, though it was erected in open country. Finally, there is the supreme example, Brasilia, the bureaucratic capital that is also the classic expression of functionalist architecture. Parachuted into the center of a vast desert, its inauguration came just at the moment when President Quadros was dismissed by his military and there were premonitions of civil war in Brazil.

Things having gone this far, many specialists are beginning to denounce a number of disturbing absurdities. This is due to their having failed to comprehend the central rationality (the rationality of a coherent delirium) that governs these partial, apparently accidental absurdities, to which their own activities inevitably contribute. Their denunciations of the absurd are thus themselves inevitably absurd, both in their forms and in their means. What is one to think of the naïveté of the nine hundred professors of all the universities and research institutes of the New York–Boston region who in the *New York Herald Tribune* (30 December 1961) solemnly addressed themselves to President Kennedy and Governor Rockefeller—a few days before Kennedy proudly issued an initial order for fifty million shelter spaces—in order to convince them of the perniciousness of "civil defense" development? Or of the horde of sociologists, judges, architects, policemen, psychologists, teachers, hygienists, psychiatrists, and journalists who never cease gathering in congresses, conferences, and committee meetings of all sorts, all urgently seeking some way to *humanize* the housing developments? Humanizing housing developments is as ridiculous a notion as humanizing atomic war, and for the same reasons. The shelters reduce not war but the threat of war to "human proportions"—"human" in modern capitalist terms: marketable human consumption. This sort of investigation of possible humanization strives quite explicitly for a joint working out of the most effective lies for the repression of people's resistance. While boredom and total lack of social life characterize the suburban housing developments in a way as immediate and tangible as a Siberian cold wave, some women's magazines now go to those new suburbs to photograph their fashion models and interview satisfied people. Since the stupefying power of such environments is discernable in the intellectual underdevelopment of the children, their maladjustment is blamed on their previous slum upbringing. The latest reformist theory places its hopes in a sort of culture center—though without using that particular term so as not to scare anyone away. In the plans of the Seine Architects Union (*Le Monde*, 22 December 1961) the prefabricated "bistro-club" that will everywhere humanize their work is presented as a cubic "plastic cell" (28 x 18 x 4 meters) comprising "a stable element: the *bistro*, which will sell tobacco and magazines, but not alcohol; the remainder will be reserved for various craft activities. . . . It should become a seductive showcase. Hence the aesthetic conception and the quality of the materials will be carefully designed to give their full effect night and day. The play of lights should in fact *communicate* the life of the bistro-club."

Thus is presented to us, in profoundly revealing terms, a discovery that "could facilitate social integration on a level that would forge the spirit of a small city." The absence of alcohol will be little noticed: in France youth gangs no longer need alcohol to inspire them to go on rampages. The French delinquents seem to have broken with the French tradition of mass alcoholism, which is still so important in the "hooliganism" of the Eastern bloc, while not having yet come around, like American youth, to the use of marijuana or stronger drugs. Though stuck in such an empty transitional period between the stimulants of two distinct historical stages, they are nevertheless expressing a sharp violence in response to this world we are describing and to the horrible prospect of occupying their dismal niche in it. In any case, if we leave aside the factor of revolt, the unionized architects' project has a certain coherence: their glass bistros are intended as a means of supplementary control on the way to that *total surveillance* of production and consumption that actually constitutes the famous integration they aim at. The candidly avowed recourse to the aesthetics of the show-window is perfectly illuminated by the theory of the spectacle: in these nonalcoholic bars the consumers themselves become as spectacular as the objects of consumption, for lack of any other attraction. Totally reified man has his place in the show-window as a desirable image of reification.

The internal defect of the system is that it cannot totally reify people; it also needs to make them act and participate, without which the production and consumption of reification would come to a stop. The reigning system is thus in conflict with history—including its own history, which is at once the history of its reinforcement and the history of the opposition to it.

Today (after a century of struggles and after the traditional or newly formed rulers' liquidation, between the two world wars, of the entire classical working-class movement which represented the force of general contestation), in spite of certain appearances, the dominant world *more than ever presents itself as permanent* on the basis of an enrichment and an infinite extension of an irreplaceable model. We can comprehend this world only by contesting it. And this contestation is neither true nor realistic except insofar as it is a contestation of the totality.

This explains the astonishing lack of ideas evident in all the acts of culture, of politics, of the organization of life, and in everything else—

the lameness of the modernist builders of functionalist cities is only a particularly glaring example. The intelligent specialists are intelligent only in playing the game of specialists; hence the timid conformity and fundamental lack of imagination that make them grant that this or that product is useful, or good, or necessary. The root of the prevailing *lack of imagination* cannot be grasped unless one is able to *imagine what is lacking*—that is, what is missing, hidden, forbidden, and yet possible, in modern life.

This is not a theory without links to the way people see their own lives; it is, on the contrary, a reality in the minds of people as yet without links with theory. Those who really "cohabit with the negative" (in the Hegelian sense) and explicitly recognize this lack as their platform and their power will bring to light the only *positive project* that can overthrow the wall of sleep; and the measures of survival; and the doomsday bombs; and the megatons of architecture.

The Bad Days Will End*

As the world of the spectacle extends its reign it approaches the climax of its offensive, provoking new resistances everywhere. These resistances are very little known precisely because the reigning spectacle is designed to present an omnipresent hypnotic image of unanimous submission. But they do exist and are spreading.

Everyone talks about the youth rebellion in the advanced industrial countries, though without understanding much about it (see "Unconditional Defense" in issue #6 of this journal). Militant publications such as *Socialisme ou Barbarie* (Paris) and *Correspondence* (Detroit) have published well-documented articles on workers' continual on-the-job resistance to the whole organization of work and on their depoliticization and their disillusionment with the unions, which have become a mechanism for integrating workers into the society and a supplementary weapon in the economic arsenal of bureaucratized capitalism. As the old forms of opposition reveal their ineffectiveness, or more often their complete inversion into complicity with the existing order, an irreducible dissatisfaction spreads subterraneanly, undermining the edifice of the affluent society. The "old mole" that Marx evoked in his "Toast to the Proletarians of Europe"* is still digging away; the specter is reappearing in all the nooks and crannies of our televised Elsinore Castle, whose political mists are dissipated as soon as workers' councils come into existence and for as long as they continue to reign.

Just as the first organization of the classical proletariat was preceded, during the end of the eighteenth century and the beginning of the nineteenth, by a period of isolated "criminal" acts aimed at destroying the machines of production that were depriving people of their work, we are presently witnessing the first appearance of a wave of vandalism against the *machines of consumption* that are just as certainly depriving us of our life. In both cases the significance obviously does not lie in the destruction itself, but in the rebelliousness which could potentially develop into a positive project going to the point of reconverting the machines in a way that increases people's real power over their lives. Leaving aside the havoc perpetrated by groups of adolescents, we can point out a few examples of actions by workers that are in large part incomprehensible from the classical "protests and demands" perspective.

On 9 February 1961 in Naples, factory workers coming off the day shift found that the streetcars that ordinarily took them home were not running, the drivers having launched a lightning strike because several of them had just been laid off. The workers demonstrated their solidarity with the strikers by throwing various projectiles at the company offices, and then bottles of gasoline which set fire to part of the streetcar station. They then burned several buses while successfully holding off police and firemen. Several thousand of them spread through the city, smashing store windows and electric signs. During the night troops had to be called in to restore law and order, and armored cars prowled the streets of Naples. This aimless and totally spontaneous demonstration was obviously a direct revolt against *commuting time*, which is such a burdensome addition to wage-slavery time in modern cities. Sparked by a chance minor incident, this revolt immediately began to extend to the whole consumer-society decor (recently plastered over the traditional poverty of southern Italy): the store windows and neon signs, being at once its most symbolic and most fragile points, naturally drew the first attacks, just as happens during the rampages of rebellious youth.

On August 4 in France, striking miners at Merlebach attacked twenty-one cars parked in front of the management buildings. All the commentators pointed out dumbfoundedly that nearly all these automobiles belonged to the workers' *fellow employees* at the mine. Who can fail to see in this action—over and beyond the innumerable reasons that always justify aggression on the part of the exploited—a gesture of self-defense against the central object of consumer alienation?

The strikers of Liège [Belgium] who attempted to destroy the machinery of the newspaper *La Meuse* on 6 January 1961 attained one of the peaks of consciousness of their movement in thus attacking the *means of information* held by their enemies. (Since the means of transmitting information are jointly monopolized by the government and the leaders of the socialist and union bureaucracies, this is precisely the crucial point of the struggle, the barrier that continues to bar workers' "wildcat" struggles from any perspective of power and thus condemns them to disappear.) Another symptom, though less interesting because more contingent on the de Gaulle regime's clumsy propagandistic excesses, is nevertheless worth noting in the following communiqué of the unions of French journalists and radio and television technicians last February 9: "Our fellow reporters and technicians who were covering the demonstration Thursday evening *were attacked by the crowd merely because they were bearing the 'Radio-Télévision Française' insignia.* This fact is significant. This is why the SJRT and SUT unions consider themselves justified in stressing in all seriousness that *the lives of our fellow reporters and technicians depend on the respect in which their reports are held.*" Of course, along with the first concrete reactions against the forces of conditioning we cannot close our eyes to the extent to which this conditioning continues to prove successful, even within very combative workers' actions. Thus, when at the beginning of the year the Decazeville miners delegated twenty of their number to go on a hunger strike, they were fighting on the spectacular terrain of the enemy by relying on the tear-jerking potential of twenty stars. They thus inevitably lost, since their only chance of success would have been to do whatever was necessary to extend their collective intervention beyond their limited sector (the only industry they were blocking having already been losing money anyway). Capitalist social organization and its oppositional by-products have so effectively propagated *parliamentary* and *spectacular* ideas that revolutionary workers often tend to forget that *representation* must always be kept to the essential minimum and used as little as possible. But it isn't only industrial workers who are fighting against spectacular stupefaction. The Berlin actor Wolfgang Neuss perpetrated a most suggestive act of sabotage last January by placing a notice in the paper *Der Abend* giving away the identity of the killer in a television detective serial that had been keeping the masses in suspense for weeks.

The assault of the first workers movement against the whole organization of the old world came to an end long ago, and nothing can bring it back to life. It failed. Certainly it achieved immense results, but not the ones it had originally intended. No doubt such deviation toward partially unexpected results is the general rule in human actions; but the one exception to this rule is precisely the moment of revolutionary action, the moment of the all-or-nothing qualitative leap. The classical workers movement must be reexamined without any illusions, particularly without any illusions regarding its various political and pseudotheoretical heirs, because all they have inherited is its failure. The apparent successes of this movement are actually its fundamental failures (reformism or the establishment of a state bureaucracy), while its failures (the Paris Commune or the 1934 Asturian revolt) are its most promising successes so far, for us and for the future. This movement must be precisely delineated in time. The classical workers movement can be considered to have begun a couple decades before the official formation of the International,* with the first linkup of communist groups of several countries that Marx and his friends organized from Brussels in 1845. And it was completely finished after the defeat of the Spanish revolution, that is, after the Barcelona May days of 1937.

We need to rediscover the whole truth of this period and to reexamine all the oppositions between revolutionaries and all the neglected possibilities, without any longer being impressed by the fact that some won out over others and dominated the movement; for we now know that the movement within which they were successful was an overall failure. Marx's thought is obviously the first which must be rediscovered—a task that should not present much difficulty in view of the extensive existing documentation and the crudeness of the lies about it. But it is also necessary to reassess the anarchist positions in the First International, Blanquism, Luxemburgism, the council movement in Germany and Spain, Kronstadt, the Makhnovists, etc.* Without overlooking the practical influence of the utopian socialists. All this, of course, not with the aim of scholarship or academic eclecticism, but solely in order to contribute toward the formation of a new, profoundly different revolutionary movement, a movement of which we have seen so many premonitory signs over the last few years, one of which is our own existence. We must understand these signs through the study of the classical revolutionary project, and vice versa. It is necessary to rediscover the history of the very movement of history, which has been so thoroughly hidden and distorted. It is, moreover, only in this enterprise (and in a few experimental artistic groups generally linked to it) that seductive modes of behavior have appeared—modes that enable people to take an objective interest in modern society and the possibilities it contains.

There is no other way to be faithful to, or even simply to understand, the actions of our comrades of the past than to profoundly reconceive the problem of revolution, which has been increasingly deprived of thought as it has become posed more intensely in concrete reality. But why does this reconception seem so difficult? Starting from an experience of free everyday life (that is, from a quest for freedom in everyday life) it is not so difficult. It seems to us that this question is quite concretely felt today among young people. And to feel it with enough urgency enables people to rediscover *lost history*, to salvage it, and to rejudge it. It is not difficult for thought that concerns itself with questioning everything that exists. It is only necessary not to have *abandoned* philosophy (as have virtually all the philosophers), not to have abandoned art (as have virtually all the artists), and not to have abandoned contestation of *present reality* (as have virtually all the militants). When they are not abandoned, these questions all converge toward the same supersession. The specialists, whose power is geared to a society of specialization, have abandoned the *critical truth* of their disciplines in order to preserve the personal advantages of their *function*. But all real researches are converging toward a totality, just as real people are going to come together in order to try once again to escape from their prehistory.

Many people are skeptical about the possibility of a new revolutionary movement, continually repeating that the proletariat has been integrated or that the workers are now satisfied, etc. This means one of two things: either they are declaring themselves satisfied (in which case we will fight them without any equivocation); or they are identifying themselves with some category separate from the workers, such as artists (in which case we will fight this illusion by showing them that the new proletariat is tending to encompass virtually everyone).

There are related misconceptions about the Third World. Apocalyptic fears or hopes regarding the movements of revolt in the colonized or semicolonized countries overlook this central fact: the revolutionary project must be realized in the industrially advanced countries. Until it is, the movements in the underdeveloped zone seem doomed to follow the model of the Chinese revolution, which began just as the classical workers movement was being destroyed and whose entire subsequent evolution has been dominated by the mutation it suffered due to that destruction. It remains true that the existence of these anticolonialist movements, even if they are polarized around the bureaucratic Chinese model, creates a disequilibrium in the external confrontation of the two great counterbalanced blocs, destabilizing any division of the world by their rulers and owners. But the security of the stakes in the planetary poker game is threatened just as much by the internal disequilibrium that still prevails in the factories of Manchester and East Berlin.

The radical minorities that in obscurity managed to survive the crushing of the classical workers movement (whose force the ruse of history transformed into state police) have handed down the truth of that movement, but only as an abstract truth of the past. Their honorable resistance to force has succeeded in preserving a maligned tradition, but not in redeveloping it into a new force. The formation of new organizations depends on a deeper critique, translated into acts. There must be a complete break with *ideology*, in which revolutionary groups think they possess official titles guaranteeing their function (that is, we must resume the Marxian critique of the role of ideologies). It is thus necessary to leave the terrain of specialized revolutionary activity—the terrain of the self-mystification of "serious politics"—because it has long been seen that such specialization encourages even the best people to demonstrate stupidity regarding all other questions, with the result that they end up failing even in their merely political struggles, since the latter are inseparable from all other aspects of the overall problem of our society. Specialization and pseudoseriousness are among the primary defensive outposts that the organization of the old world occupies in everyone's mind. A revolutionary association of a new type will also break with the old world by permitting and demanding of its members an authentic and creative participation, instead of expecting a participation of militants measurable in *atten dance time*, which amounts to recreating the sole control possible in the dominant society: the quantitative criterion of hours of labor. A genuine enthusiastic participation on the part of everyone is necessitated by the fact that the classical political militant, who "devotes himself" to his radical duties, is everywhere disappearing along with classical politics itself; and even more by the fact that devotion and sacrifice always engender *authority* (even if only purely moral authority). *Boredom is counterrevolutionary.* In every way.

The groups that recognize the fundamental (not merely circumstantial) failure of the old politics must also recognize that they can claim to be an *ongoing avant-garde* only if they themselves exemplify a new style of life, a new passion. There is nothing utopian about this lifestyle criterion: it was constantly evident during the emergence and rise of the classical workers movement. We believe that in the coming period this will not only hold true to the extent it did in the nineteenth century, but will go much further. Otherwise the militants of these groups would only constitute dull propaganda societies, proclaiming quite correct and basic ideas but with virtually no one listening. The spectacular unilateral transmission of a revolutionary teaching—whether within an organization or in its action directed toward the outside—has lost all chance of proving effective in the society of the spectacle, which simultaneously organizes a completely different spectacle and infects every spectacle with an element of nausea. Such specialized propaganda thus has little chance of leading to timely and fruitful intervention during situations when the masses find themselves obliged to wage real struggles.

It is necessary to recall and revive the nineteenth-century social war of the *poor*. The word can be found everywhere, in songs and in all the declarations of the people who worked for the objectives of the classical workers movement. One of the most urgent tasks confronting the SI and other comrades now advancing along convergent paths is to define the *new poverty*. Certain American sociologists over the last few years have played a role in the exposure of this new poverty* analogous to that played by the first utopian philanthropists vis-à-vis workers' action in the previous century: the problem is revealed, but in an idealistic and artificial way; because since understanding resides in praxis alone, one can really comprehend the nature of the enemy only in the process of fighting it (this is the terrain on which are situated, for example, G. Keller's* and R. Vaneigem's projects of *introducing the aggressiveness of the delinquents onto the plane of ideas*).

Defining the new poverty also entails defining the new wealth. To the image propagated by the dominant society—according to which it has evolved (both on its own and in response to acceptable reformist pressure) from an economy of profit to an economy of needs—must be counterposed *an economy of desires,* which could be defined as: technological society plus the imagination of what could be done with it. The economy of needs is falsified in terms of habit. Habit is the natural process by which fulfilled desire is degraded into need and is confirmed, objectified, and universally recognized as need. The present economy is directly geared to the fabrication of habits, and manipulates people by forcing them to repress their desires.

Complicity with the world's false opposition goes hand in hand with complicity with its false wealth (and thus with a retreat from defining the new poverty). Sartre's disciple Gorz is a good case in point. In *Les Temps Modernes* #188 he confesses how embarrassed he is that, thanks to his career as a journalist (which indeed is nothing to write home about), he can afford the good things of this society; among which he respectfully mentions taxis and trips abroad—at a time when taxis inch forward behind the mass of cars that everyone has been forced to buy; and when foreign travel presents us with the same boring spectacle of the same alienation endlessly duplicated around the world. He also waxes enthusiastic—like Sartre did once upon a time about the "total freedom of criticism in the USSR"—about "the youth" of the only "revolutionary generations," those of Yugoslavia, Algeria, Cuba, China, and Israel. The other countries are old, says Gorz, in order to justify his own senility. He thus relieves himself of the necessity of making any more precise analyses of, or distinctions among, "the youth" of those or other countries, where not everyone is so old or so visible, and where not every revolt is so Gorz.

Fougeyrollas, the latest thinker to have "gone beyond" Marxism, is somewhat disconcerted over the fact that while all previous major stages of historical development were characterized by a change in the mode of production, the communist society heralded by Marx, if it were to come about, would seem to be no more than a continuation of the society of industrial production. Go to the back of the class, Fougeyrollas. The next form of society will not be based on industrial production. It will be a society of *realized art*. The "absolutely new type of production supposedly in gestation in our society," whose absence Fougeyrollas laments in *Marxisme en question*, is the construction of situations, the free construction of the events of life.

The Fifth SI Conference in Göteborg
(excerpts)

The 5th Conference of the Situationist International was held in Göteborg, Sweden, 28–30 August 1961, eleven months after the London Conference. The situationists of nine countries were represented by Ansgar-Elde, Debord, J. de Jong, Kotányi, D. Kunzelmann, S. Larsson, J.V. Martin, Nash, Prem, G. Stadler, Hardy Strid, H. Sturm, R. Vaneigem, Zimmer. [. . .]

Next the Conference hears an orientation report by Vaneigem, who says notably:

> The Situationist International finds itself, due both to the present historical conjuncture and to its internal evolution, at a stage of development such that the activity it considers itself capable of carrying out, within the world of bureaucratization and reification, depends henceforth on its ability to maintain critical rigor, a rigor that will serve as a cohesive force. Its weakness in the face of the tasks to come and of the foreseeable repression can be turned into a strength only if each of its members is clearly aware of what threatens him personally and what threatens the nature and aims of the SI itself. This is the price of sectional autonomy.
>
> The existing world, in both its capitalist and its supposedly anti-

capitalist variants, organizes life in the form of spectacles. . . . The point is not to elaborate a spectacle of refusal, but to refuse the spectacle. In order for their elaboration to be *artistic* in the new and authentic sense defined by the SI, the elements of the destruction of the spectacle must precisely cease to be works of art. There is no such thing as *situationism*, or a situationist work of art, or a spectacular situationist. Once and for all.

Such a perspective means nothing if it is not directly linked to revolutionary praxis, to the desire to *change life* (which is not at all the same as merely changing the *bosses* of existing occupations). [. . .]

Our position is that of combatants between two worlds—one that we don't acknowledge, the other that does not yet exist. We have to bring the two together, to hasten the end of a world, the *disaster where the situationists will recognize their own.*

[. . .] The second session begins with reports from the various sections, primarily concerning the publication and translation of SI texts. The Scandinavian section also raises the issue of the production of experimental films in Sweden, in which several of its members have been collectively involved. The Swedes present in Göteborg have been discussing among themselves which of these films attain a level worthy of being termed "situationist," and ask the Conference to help settle this question. Debord replies that since he himself has never made a situationist film, he is in no position to judge.*

Kunzelmann expresses a strong skepticism as to the powers the SI can bring together in order to act on the level envisaged by Vaneigem. Kotányi responds to Nash and Kunzelmann: "Since the beginning of the movement there has been a problem as to what to call artistic works by members of the SI. It was understood that none of them was a situationist production, but what to call them? I propose a very simple rule: *to call them 'antisituationist.'* We are against the dominant conditions of artistic inauthenticity. I don't mean that anyone should stop painting, writing, etc. I don't mean that that has no value. I don't mean that we could continue to exist without doing that. But at the same time we know that such works will be co-opted* by the society and used against us. Our impact lies in the elaboration of certain truths which have an explosive power as soon as people are ready to struggle for them. The movement is only in its infancy regarding the elaboration of these essential points. It has yet to attain the degree of purity found in modern explosives. Until we attain this purity, i.e. this necessary degree of clarity, we cannot count on the explosive effects of our approaches to everyday life and to the critique of everyday life. I urge you not to forget that our present productions are antisituationist. The clarity that comes from recognizing this fact is indispensable for attaining any greater clarification. If we sacrifice this principle, Kunzelmann would be right in a negative sense: the SI would be unable to attain the most meager power."

The responses to Kotányi's proposal are all favorable. It is noted that would-be avant-garde artists are beginning to appear in various countries who have no connection with the SI but who refer to themselves as adherents of "situationism" or describe their works as being more or less situationist. This trend is obviously going to increase and it would be hopeless for the SI to try and prevent it. While various confused artists nostalgic for a positive art call themselves situationist, *antisituationist* art will be the mark of the best artists, those of the SI, since genuinely situationist conditions have as yet not at all been created. Admitting this is the mark of a situationist.

With one exception, the Conference unanimously decides to adopt this rule of antisituationist art, binding on all members of the SI. Only Nash objects, his spite and indignation having become increasingly sharp throughout the whole debate, to the point of uncontrolled rage. [...]

Prem resumes in more detail the objections of his friends to Kotányi's perspectives. He agrees with calling our art antisituationist; and also with the project of organizing a situationist base. But he does not think the SI's tactics are good. There is talk of people's dissatisfaction and revolt, but in his view, as his tendency already expressed it at London, "most people are still primarily interested in comfort and conveniences." He feels that the SI systematically neglects its real chances in culture. It rejects favorable occasions to intervene in existing cultural politics, whereas, in his view, the SI has no power but its power in culture—a power which could be very great and which is visibly within our reach. The SI majority sabotages the chances for effective action on the terrain where it is possible. It castigates artists who might be capable of accomplishing something, and it throws them out the moment they get in a position to accomplish anything. [...]

Other German situationists strongly oppose Prem, some of them accusing him of having expressed positions in their name that they do not share (but it seems, rather, that Prem simply had the frankness to clearly express the line that dominates in the German section). Finally the Germans come around to agreeing that none of them conceives of theory as separate from its practical results. With this the third session is adjourned in the middle of the night, not without violent agitation and uproar (from one side there are shouts of "Your theory is going to fly right back in your faces!" and from the other, "Cultural pimps!"). [...]

The German situationists stress the urgency, already made evident by the Conference, for them to unify their positions and projects with the rest of the SI. Kunzelmann feels that a useful focus for this discussion could be Vaneigem's report, which they will carefully study when they are back in Germany. The Germans also commit to rapidly augmenting their propagation and elaboration of situationist theory, as they have already begun to do in issues #5 and #6 of their journal *Spur*. On their request, the Conference adds Attila Kotányi and J. de Jong to the editorial committee of *Spur* in order to verify this process of unification. (But in January this decision is flouted by their putting out, without Kotányi and de Jong's knowledge, an issue #7 marking a distinct regression from the preceding ones—which leads to the exclusion of those responsible.) [. . .]

It is voted to hold the 6th Conference at Anvers, after the rejection of the Scandinavian proposal to hold it secretly in Warsaw. The Conference does decide, however, to send a delegation of three situationists to Poland to develop our contacts there. [. . .]

Basic Banalities

(Part 1)

1

Bureaucratic capitalism has found its legitimation in Marx. I am not referring here to orthodox Marxism's dubious merit of having reinforced the neocapitalist structures whose present reorganization is an implicit homage to Soviet totalitarianism; I am stressing the extent to which crude versions of Marx's most profound analyses of alienation have become generally recognized in the most commonplace realities— realities which, stripped of their magical veil and materialized in each gesture, have become the sole substance of the daily lives of an increasing number of people. In a word, bureaucratic capitalism contains the tangible reality of alienation; it has brought it home to everybody far more successfully than Marx could ever have hoped to do, it has banalized it as the reduction of material poverty has been accompanied by a spreading mediocrity of existence. As poverty has been reduced in terms of survival, it has become more profound in terms of our way of life—this is at least one widespread feeling that exonerates Marx from all the interpretations a degenerate Bolshevism has made of him. The "theory" of peaceful coexistence has accelerated this awareness and revealed, to those who were still confused, that exploiters can get along quite well with each other despite their spectacular divergences.

2

"Any act," writes Mircea Eliade, "can become a religious act. Human existence is realized simultaneously on two parallel planes, that of temporality, becoming, illusion, and that of eternity, substance, reality." In the nineteenth century the brutal divorce of these two planes demonstrated that power would have done better to have maintained reality in a mist of divine transcendence. But we must give reformism credit for succeeding where Bonaparte had failed, in dissolving becoming in eternity and reality in illusion. This union may not be as solid as the sacraments of religious marriage, but it *lasts*, which is all that the managers of coexistence and social peace can ask of it. This is also what leads us to define ourselves—in the illusory but inescapable perspective of duration—as the end of abstract temporality, as the end of the reified time of our acts; to define ourselves—does it have to be spelled out?—at the positive pole of alienation as the end of social alienation, as the end of humanity's term of social alienation.

3

The socialization of primitive human groups reveals a will to struggle more effectively against the mysterious and terrifying forces of nature. But struggling in the natural environment, at once with it and against it, submitting to its most inhuman laws in order to wrest from it an increased chance of survival—doing this could only engender a more evolved form of aggressive defense, a more complex and less primitive attitude, manifesting on a higher level the contradictions that the uncontrolled and yet influenceable forces of nature never ceased to impose. In becoming socialized, the struggle against the blind domination by nature triumphed inasmuch as it gradually assimilated primitive, natural alienation, but in another form. The struggle against natural alienation gave rise to social alienation. Is it by chance that a technological civilization has developed to such a point that this social alienation has been revealed by its conflict with the last areas of natural resistance that technological power hadn't managed (and for good reasons) to subjugate? Today the technocrats propose to put an end to primitive alienation: with a stirring humanitarianism they exhort us to perfect the technical means that "in themselves" would enable us to conquer death, suffering, discomfort, and boredom. But to eliminate death would be less of a miracle than to eliminate suicide and the desire to die. There are ways of abolishing the death penalty than can make one miss it. Up till now the particular uses that have been made of technology—or more generally the socioeconomic context in which human activity is confined—while quantitatively reducing the number of occasions of pain and death, have allowed death itself to eat like a cancer into the heart of each person's life.

4

The prehistoric food-gathering age was succeeded by the hunting age during which clans formed and strove to increase their chances of survival. Hunting grounds and preserves were staked out from which outsiders were absolutely excluded—the welfare of the whole clan depended on it. As a result, the freedom gained by settling down more safely and comfortably within the natural environment engendered its own negation outside the boundaries laid down by the clan and forced the group to modify its customary rules in organizing its relations with excluded and threatening groups. From the moment it appeared, socially engendered economic survival implied the existence of boundaries, restrictions, conflicting rights. It should never be forgotten that until now both history and our own nature have developed in accordance with the development of private appropriation: the seizing of control by a class, group, caste, or individual of a general power over a socioeconomic survival whose form remains complex, ranging from ownership of land, territory, factories, or capital to the "pure" exercise of power over people (hierarchy). Beyond the struggle against regimes whose vision of paradise is a cybernetic welfare state lies the necessity of a still vaster struggle against a fundamental and initially natural state of things, in the development of which capitalism plays only an incidental, transitory role; a state of things that will only disappear with the disappearance of the last traces of hierarchical power—along with the "swine of humanity," of course.

5

To be an owner is to claim a good one prevents others from using— while at the same time acknowledging everyone's abstract, potential right to ownership. By excluding people from a real right of ownership, the owner extends his dominion over those he has excluded (absolutely over nonowners, relatively over other owners), without whom he is nothing. The nonowners have no choice in the matter. The owner appropriates and alienates them as producers of his own power, while the necessity of ensuring their own physical existence forces them despite themselves to collaborate in producing their own exclusion and to survive without ever being able to live. Excluded, they participate in ownership through the mediation of the owner, a mystical participation characterizing from the outset all the clan and social relationships that gradually replaced the principle of obligatory cohesion in which each member was an integral part of the group ("organic interdependence"). Their guarantee of survival depends on their activity within the framework of private appropriation; they reinforce a property right from which they are excluded. Due to this ambiguity each of them sees himself as participating in ownership, as a living fragment of the right to possess, and this belief in turn reinforces their condition as excluded and possessed. (Extreme cases of this alienation: the faithful slave, the cop, the bodyguard, the centurion—creatures who, through a sort of union with their own death, confer on death a power equal to the forces of life and identify in a destructive energy the negative and positive poles of alienation, the absolutely submissive slave and the absolute master.) It is of vital importance to the exploiter that this appearance is maintained and made more sophisticated; not because he is especially Machiavellian, but simply because he wants to stay alive. The organization of appearances depends on the survival of the owner and his privileges, which in turn depend on the physical survival of the nonowner, who can thus remain alive while being exploited and excluded from being a real person. Private appropriation and domination are thus originally imposed and felt as a positive right, but in the form of a negative universality. Valid for everyone, justified in everyone's eyes by divine or natural law, the right of private appropriation is objectified in a general illusion, in a universal transcendence, in an essential law under which everyone individually manages to tolerate the more or less narrow limits assigned to his right to live and to the conditions of life in general.

6

In this social context the function of alienation must be understood as a *condition of survival*. The labor of the nonowners is subject to the same contradictions as the right of private appropriation. It transforms them into possessed beings, into producers of their own expropriation and exclusion, but it represents the only chance of survival for slaves, for serfs, for workers—so much so that the activity that allows their existence to continue by emptying it of all content ends up, through a natural and sinister reversal of perspective, by taking on a positive appearance. Not only has value been attributed to work (as a form of self-sacrifice during the old regime, and in its most mentally degrading forms in bourgeois ideology and in the so-called People's Democracies), but very early on to work for a master, to alienate oneself willingly, became the honorable and scarcely questioned price of survival. The satisfaction of basic needs remains the best safeguard of alienation; it is best dissimulated by being justified on the grounds of undeniable necessities. Alienation multiplies needs because it can satisfy none of them; nowadays lack of satisfaction is measured in the number of cars, refrigerators, TVs: the alienating objects have lost the ruse and mystery of transcendence, they are there in their concrete poverty. To be rich today is to possess the greatest *quantity* of poor objects.

Up till now surviving has prevented us from living. This is why much is to be expected of the increasingly obvious impossibility of survival, an impossibility that will become all the more obvious as the glut of conveniences and elements of survival reduces life to a single choice: suicide or revolution.

7

The sacred presides even over the struggle against alienation. As soon as the relations of exploitation and the violence that underlies them are no longer concealed by the mystical veil, there is a breakthrough, a moment of clarity—the struggle against alienation is suddenly revealed as a ruthless hand-to-hand fight with naked power, power exposed in its brute force and its weakness, a vulnerable giant whose slightest wound confers on the attacker the infamous notoriety of an Erostratus.*Since power survives, the event remains ambiguous. Praxis of destruction, sublime moment when the complexity of the world becomes tangible, transparent, within everyone's grasp; inexpiable revolts—those of the slaves, the Jacques, the iconoclasts, the Enragés, the Fédérés,* Kronstadt, the Asturias, and—promises of things to come—the hooligans of Stockholm and the wildcat strikes. Only the destruction of all hierarchical power will allow us to forget these. We intend to make sure that it does.

The deterioration of mythical structures and their slowness in regenerating themselves, which make possible the awakening of consciousness and the critical penetration of insurrection, are also responsible for the fact that once the "excesses" of revolution are past, the struggle against alienation is grasped on a theoretical plane, subjected to an "analysis" that is a carryover from the demystification preparatory to revolt. It is at this point that the truest and most authentic aspects of a revolt are reexamined and repudiated by the "we didn't really mean to do that" of the theoreticians charged with explaining the meaning of an insurrection to those who made it—to those who aim to demystify by acts, not just by words.

All acts contesting power call for analysis and tactical development. Much can be expected of:

(a) the new proletariat, which is discovering its destitution amid consumer abundance (see the development of the workers' struggles presently beginning in England, and the attitudes of rebellious youth in all the modern countries);

(b) countries that have had enough of their partial, sham revolutions and are consigning their past and present theorists to the museums (see the role of the intelligentsia in the Eastern bloc);

(c) the Third World, whose mistrust of technological myths has been kept alive by the colonial cops and mercenaries, the last, over-zealous militants of a transcendence against which they are the best possible vaccination;

(d) the force of the SI ("our ideas are in everyone's mind"), capable of forestalling remote-controlled revolts, "crystal nights"* and sheepish resistance.

8

Private appropriation is linked to the dialectic of particular and general. In the mystical realm where the contradictions of the slave and feudal systems are resolved, the nonowner, excluded as a particular individual from the right of ownership, strives to ensure his survival through his labor: the more he identifies with the interests of the master, the more successful he is. He knows the other nonowners only through their joint plight: the compulsory surrender of their labor power (Christianity recommended voluntary surrender: once the slave "willingly" offered his labor power, he ceased to be a slave), the search for the optimum conditions of survival, and mystical identification. Struggle, though born of a universal will to survive, takes place on the level of appearances where it brings into play identification with the desires of the master and thus introduces a certain individual rivalry that mirrors the rivalry between the masters. Competition develops on this plane as long as the exploitive relations remain dissimulated behind a mystical veil and as long as the conditions producing this veil persist; or to put it another way, as long as the degree of slavery determines the slave's consciousness of the degree of lived reality. (We are still at the stage of calling "objective consciousness" what is in reality the consciousness of being an object.) The owner, for his part, depends on the general acknowledgment of a right from which he alone is not excluded, but which is seen on the plane of appearances as a right accessible to each of the excluded taken individually. His privileged position depends on such a belief, and this belief is also the basis for the strength that is essential if he is to hold his own among the other owners; it is his strength. If he seems to renounce exclusive appropriation of everything and everybody, if he poses less as a master than as a servant of the public good and defender of collective security, then his power is crowned with glory and to his other privileges he adds that of denying, on the level of appearances (which is the only level of reference in the world of one-way communication), the very notion of personal appropriation. Denying that anyone has this right, he repudiates the other owners. In the feudal perspective the owner is not integrated into appearances in the same way as the nonowners, slaves, soldiers, functionaries, and servants of all kinds. The lives of the latter are so squalid that the majority can live only as a caricature of the Master (the feudal lord, the prince, the major-domo, the taskmaster, the high priest, God, Satan). But the master himself is also forced to play one of these caricatural roles. He can do so without much effort since his pretension to total life is already so caricatural, isolated as he is among those who can only survive. He is already one of our own kind (with the added grandeur of a past epoch, which adds a poignant savor to his sadness); he, like each of us, was anxiously seeking the adventure where he could find himself on the road to his total perdition. Could the master, at the very moment he alienates the others, see that he has reduced them to dispossessed and excluded beings, and thus realize that he is only an exploiter, a purely negative being? Such an awareness is unlikely, and would be dangerous. By extending his dominion over the greatest possible number of subjects, isn't he enabling them to survive, giving them their only chance of salvation? ("What would become of the workers if the capitalists weren't kind enough to employ them?" the high-minded souls of the nineteenth century liked to ask.) In fact, the owner officially excludes himself from all claim to private appropriation. To the sacrifice of the nonowner, who through his labor exchanges his real life for an apparent one (thus avoiding immediate death by allowing the master to determine his variety of living death), the owner replies by appearing to sacrifice his nature as owner and exploiter; he excludes himself mythically, he puts himself at the service of everyone and of myth (at the service of God and his people, for example). With an additional gesture, with an act whose gratuitousness bathes him in an otherworldly radiance, he gives renunciation its pure form of mythical reality: renouncing the common life, he is the poor man amidst illusory wealth, he who sacrifices himself for everyone while all the other people only sacrifice themselves for their own sake, for the sake of their survival. He turns his predicament into prestige. The more powerful he is, the greater his sacrifice. He becomes the living reference point of the whole illusory life, the highest attainable point in the scale of mythical values. "Voluntarily" withdrawn from common mortals, he is drawn toward the world of the gods, and his more or less recognized participation in divinity, on the level of appearances (the only generally acknowledged frame of reference), consecrates his rank in the hierarchy of the other owners. In the organization of transcendence the feudal lord—and through association with him the other owners of power or means of production, in varying degrees—is led to play the principal role, the role that he really does play in the economic organization of the group's survival. As a result, the existence of the group is bound on every level to the existence of the owners as such, to those who, owning everything because they own everybody, force everyone to renounce their lives on the pretext of the owners' unique, absolute, and divine renunciation. (From the god Prometheus, punished by the gods, to the god Christ, punished by men, the sacrifice of the Owner becomes vulgarized, it loses its sacred aura, becomes humanized.) Myth thus unites owner and nonowner, enveloping them in a common form in which the necessity of survival, whether mere physical survival or survival as a privileged being, forces them to live on the level of appearances and of the inversion of real life, the inversion of the life of everyday praxis. We are still there, waiting to live a life less than or beyond a mystique against which our every gesture protests while submitting to it.

9

Myth—the unitary absolute in which the contradictions of the world find an illusory resolution, the harmonious and constantly harmonized vision that reflects and reinforces the reigning order—is the sphere of the sacred, the extrahuman zone where an abundance of revelations are manifested but where the revelation of the process of private appropriation is carefully suppressed. Nietzsche saw this when he wrote: "All becoming is a criminal revolt from eternal being, and its price is death." When the bourgeoisie claimed to replace the pure Being of feudalism with Becoming, all it really did was to desacralize Being and resacralize Becoming to its own profit. It elevated its own Becoming to the status of Being, no longer that of absolute ownership but rather that of relative appropriation: a petty democratic and mechanical Becoming, with its notions of progress, merit, and causal succession. The owner's life hides him from himself; bound to myth by a life-and-death pact, he cannot see himself in the positive and exclusive enjoyment of any good except through the lived experience of his own exclusion. (And isn't it through this mythical exclusion that the nonowners will come to grasp the reality of their own exclusion?) He bears the responsibility for a group, he takes on the burden of a god. Submitting himself to its benediction and its retribution, he swathes himself in austerity and wastes away. Model of gods and heroes, the master, the owner, is the true reality of Prometheus, of Christ, of all those whose spectacular sacrifice has made it possible for "the vast majority of people" to continue to sacrifice themselves to the extreme minority, to the masters. (Analysis of the owner's sacrifice should be examined more carefully: isn't the case of Christ really the sacrifice of the owner's son? If the owner can never sacrifice himself except on the level of appearances, then Christ stands for the real immolation of the owner's son when circumstances leave no other alternative. As a son he is only an owner at an early stage of development, an embryo, little more than a dream of future ownership. In this mythic dimension belongs Maurice Barrès's famous remark in 1914, when war had arrived and made his dreams come true at last: "Our youth, as is proper, has gone to shed torrents of *our blood*.") This rather distasteful little game, before it became transformed into a symbolic rite, knew a heroic period when kings and tribal chiefs were ritually put to death according to their "will." Historians assure us that these august martyrs were soon replaced by prisoners, slaves, or criminals. The penalty was delegated, but the rulers kept the halo.

10

The concept of a common fate is based on the sacrifice of the owner and the nonowner. Put another way, the notion of a "human condition" is based on an ideal and tormented image whose purpose is to try to resolve the irresolvable opposition between the mythical sacrifice of the minority and the really sacrificed life of everyone else. The function of myth is to unify and eternalize, in a succession of static moments, the dialectic of "will-to-live" and its opposite. This universally dominant factitious unity attains its most tangible and concrete representation in communication, particularly in language. Ambiguity is most manifest at this level; it leads to a lack of real communication, it puts the analyst at the mercy of ridiculous phantoms, at the mercy of words— eternal and changing instants—whose content varies according to who pronounces them, as does the notion of sacrifice. When language is put to the test, it can no longer dissimulate the misrepresentation and thus it provokes the crisis of participation. In the language of an era one can follow the traces of total revolution, unfulfilled but always imminent. They are the exalting and terrifying signs of the upheavals they foreshadow, but who takes them seriously? The discredit striking language is as deeply rooted and instinctive as the suspicion with which myths are viewed by people who at the same time remain firmly attached to them. How can key words be defined by other words? How can phrases be used to point out the signs that refute the phraseological organization of appearances? The best texts still await their justification. When a poem by Mallarmé becomes the sole explanation for an act of revolt, then poetry and revolution will have overcome their ambiguity. To await and prepare for that moment is to manipulate information not as the last shock wave whose significance escapes everyone, but as the first repercussion of an act still to come.

11

Born of man's will to survive the uncontrollable forces of nature, myth is a public welfare policy that has outlived its necessity. It has consolidated its tyrannical force by reducing life to the sole dimension of survival, by negating it as movement and totality.

When contested, myth homogenizes the diverse attacks on it; sooner or later it engulfs and assimilates them. Nothing can withstand it, no image or concept that attempts to destroy the dominant spiritual structures. It reigns over the expression of facts and of lived experience, on which it imposes its own interpretive structure (dramatization). Private consciousness is the consciousness of lived experience that finds its expression on the level of organized appearances.

Myth is sustained by rewarded sacrifice. Since every individual life is based on its own renunciation, lived experience must be defined as sacrifice and recompense. As a reward for his asceticism, the initiate (the promoted worker, the specialist, the manager—new martyrs canonized democratically) is granted a niche in the organization of appearances; he is made to feel at home in alienation. But collective shelters disappeared with unitary societies, all that's left is their later concrete embodiments for the use of the general public: temples, churches, palaces . . . memorials of a universal protection. Shelters are private nowadays, and even if their protection is far from certain there can be no mistaking their price.

12

"Private" life is defined primarily in a formal context. It is, to be sure, engendered by the social relations created by private appropriation, but its essential form is determined by the expression of those relations. Universal, incontestable but constantly contested, this form makes appropriation a right belonging to everyone and from which everyone is excluded, *a right one can obtain only by renouncing it*. As long as it fails to break free of the context imprisoning it (a break that is called revolution), the most authentic experience can be grasped, expressed, and communicated only by way of an inversion through which its fundamental contradiction is dissimulated. In other words, if a positive project fails to sustain a praxis of radically overthrowing the conditions of life—which are nothing other than the conditions of private appropriation—it does not have the slightest chance of escaping being taken over by the negativity that reigns over the expression of social relationships: it is co-opted like an inverted mirror image. In the totalizing perspective in which it conditions the whole of everyone's life, and in which its real and its mythic power can no longer be distinguished (both powers being both real and mythical), the process of private appropriation has made it impossible to express life any way except negatively. Life in its entirety is immersed in a negativity that corrodes it and formally defines it. To talk of life today is like talking of rope in the house of a hanged man. Since the key of will-to-live has been lost we have been wandering in the corridors of an endless mausoleum. The dialogue of chance and the throw of the dice* no longer suffices to justify our lassitude; those who still accept living in well-furnished weariness picture themselves as leading an indolent existence while failing to notice in each of their daily gestures a living denial of their despair, a denial that should rather make them despair only of the poverty of their imagination. Forgetting life, one can identify with a range of images, from the brutish conqueror and brutish slave at one pole to the saint and the pure hero at the other. The air in this shit-house has been unbreathable for a long time. The world and man as representation stink like carrion and there's no longer any god around to turn the charnel houses into beds of lilies. After all the ages people have died while accepting without notable change the explanations of gods, of nature, and of biological laws, it wouldn't seem unreasonable to ask if we don't die because so much death enters—and for very specific reasons—into every moment of our lives.

13

Private appropriation can be defined notably as the appropriation of things by means of the appropriation of people. It is the spring and the troubled water where all reflections mingle and blur. Its field of action and influence, spanning the whole of history, seems to have been characterized until now by a fundamental double behavioral determination: an ontology based on sacrifice and negation of self (its subjective and objective aspects respectively) and a fundamental duality, a division between particular and general, individual and collective, private and public, theoretical and practical, spiritual and material, intellectual and manual, etc. The contradiction between universal appropriation and universal expropriation implies that the master has been seen for what he is and isolated. This mythical image of terror, destitution, and renunciation presents itself to slaves, to servants, to all those who can't stand living as they do; it is the illusory reflection of their participation in property, a natural illusion since they really do participate in it through the daily sacrifice of their energy (what the ancients called pain or torture and we call labor or work) since they themselves produce this property in a way that excludes them. The master can only cling to the notion of work-as-sacrifice, like Christ to his cross and his nails; it is up to him to authenticate sacrifice, to apparently renounce his right to exclusive enjoyment, and to cease to expropriate with purely *human* violence (that is, violence without mediation). The sublimity of the gesture obscures the initial violence, the nobility of the sacrifice absolves the commando, the brutality of the conqueror is bathed in the light of a transcendence whose reign is internalized, the gods are the intransigent guardians of rights, the short-tempered shepherds of a peaceful, law-abiding flock of owners and owner wannabes. The gamble on transcendence and the sacrifice it implies are the masters' greatest conquest, their most accomplished submission to the necessity of conquest. Anyone who intrigues for power while refusing the purification of renunciation (the brigand or the tyrant) will sooner or later be tracked down and killed like a mad dog, or worse: as someone who only pursues his own ends and whose blunt disdain for "work" lacks any tact toward others' feelings: serial killers like Troppmann, Landru, Petiot were doomed to defeat because they murdered people without justifying it in the name of defending the Free World, the Christian West, the State, or Human Dignity. By refusing to play the rules of the game, pirates, gangsters, and outlaws disturb those with good consciences (whose consciences are a reflection of myth); but the masters, by killing the encroacher or enrolling him as a cop, reestablish the omnipotence of the "eternal truth": namely, that those who don't

sell themselves lose their right to survive and those who do sell themselves lose their right to live. The sacrifice of the master is the essence of
humanism, which is what makes humanism—and let this be understood
once and for all—the miserable negation of everything human. Humanism is the master taken seriously at his own game, acclaimed by those
who see in his apparent sacrifice (that caricatural reflection of their real
sacrifice) a reason to hope for salvation. Justice, Dignity, Nobility, Freedom—these words that yap and howl, are they anything but household
pets who have continued to reliably return home to their masters since the
time when heroic lackeys won the right to walk them on the streets? To use
them is to forget that they are the ballast that enables power to rise out
of reach. And if we imagine a regime deciding that the mythical sacrifice
of the masters should not be promoted in such universal forms, and setting about tracking down these word-concepts and wiping them out, we
could well expect the Left to be incapable of combating it with anything
more than a plaintive battle of words whose every phrase, invoking the
"sacrifice" of a previous master, calls for an equally mythical sacrifice of
a new one (a leftist master, a regime mowing down workers in the name
of the proletariat). Bound to the notion of sacrifice, humanism is born of
the mutual fear of masters and slaves: it is nothing but the solidarity of a
shit-scared humanity. But those who reject all hierarchical power can use
any word as a weapon to punctuate their action. Lautréamont and the
illegalist anarchists were already aware of this; so were the dadaists.

The appropriator thus becomes an owner from the moment he puts
the ownership of people and things in the hands of God or of some
universal transcendence, whose omnipotence is reflected back on him
as a grace sanctifying his slightest gesture. To oppose an owner thus
consecrated is to oppose God, nature, the fatherland, the people. In
short, to exclude oneself from the whole physical and spiritual world.
"We must neither govern nor be governed," writes Marcel Havrenne
so neatly. For those who add an appropriate violence to his humor,
there is no longer any salvation or damnation, no place in the universal
order, neither with Satan, the great co-opter of the faithful, nor in any
form of myth, since they are the living proof of the uselessness of all
that. They were born for a life yet to be invented; insofar as they lived,
it was on this hope that they finally came to grief.

Two corollaries of singularization in transcendence:

(a) If ontology implies transcendence, it is clear that any ontology automatically justifies the being of the master and the
hierarchical power wherein the master is reflected in degraded,
more or less faithful images.

(b) Over the distinction between manual and intellectual work, between practice and theory, is superimposed the distinction between work-as-real-sacrifice and the organization of work in the form of apparent sacrifice.

It would be tempting to explain fascism—among other reasons for it—as an act of faith, the auto-da-fé of a bourgeoisie haunted by the murder of God and the destruction of the great sacred spectacle, dedicating itself to the devil, to an inverted mysticism, a black mysticism with its rituals and its holocausts. Mysticism and high finance.

It should not be forgotten that hierarchical power is inconceivable without transcendence, without ideologies, without myths. Demystification itself can always be turned into a myth: it suffices to "omit," most philosophically, demystification *by acts*. Any demystification so neutralized, with the sting taken out of it, becomes painless, euthanasic, in a word, humanitarian. Except that the movement of demystification will ultimately demystify the demystifiers.

RAOUL VANEIGEM

(Concluded in the next issue)

- What will become of the totality inherent in unitary society when it comes up against the bourgeois demolition of that society?

- Will an artificial reconstitution of unity succeed in hoodwinking the worker alienated in consumption?

- But what can be the future of totality in a fragmented society?

- What unexpected supersession of this society and of its whole organization of appearances will finally bring us to a happy ending?

IF YOU DON'T ALREADY KNOW, FIND OUT IN PART TWO!

Ideologies, Classes, and the Domination of Nature

The human appropriation of nature is the *real adventure we have embarked on*. It is the central, indisputable project, the issue that encompasses all other issues. What is always fundamentally in question in modern thought and action is the possible use of the dominated sector of nature. A society's basic perspective on this question determines the choices among the alternative directions presented at each moment of the process, as well as the rhythm and duration of productive expansion in each sector. The lack of such a comprehensive, long-term perspective—or rather the monopoly of a single untheorized perspective automatically produced by the present power structure's blind economic growth—is at the root of the emptiness of contemporary thought during the last forty years.

The advances in production and in constantly improving technological potentials are proceeding even faster than nineteenth-century communism predicted. But we have remained at a stage of over-equipped prehistory. A century of revolutionary attempts has failed: human life has not been rationalized and impassioned; the project of a classless society has yet to be achieved. We find ourselves caught up in an endless expansion of material means that continues to serve fundamentally static interests and notoriously obsolete values. The spirit of the dead weighs very heavily on the technology of the living. The economic planning that reigns everywhere is insane, not so much because of its academic obsession with organizing the enrichment of the years to come as because of the rotten blood of the past that circulates through its veins, continually pumped forth with each artificial pulsation of this "heart of a heartless world."

Material liberation is only a precondition for the liberation of human history, and can only be judged as such. A country's decision regarding which kind of minimum level of development is to be given priority depends on the particular project of liberation chosen, and therefore on who makes this choice—the autonomous masses or the specialists in power. Those who accept the ideas of one or another type of specialist organizers regarding what is *indispensable* may be liberated from any deprivation of the objects those organizers choose to produce, but they will never be liberated from the organizers themselves. The most modern and unexpected forms of hierarchy will always turn out to be nothing but costly remakes of the old world of passivity, impotence, and slavery—the antithesis of humanity's mastery of its history and its surroundings—regardless of the material forces abstractly possessed by the society.

Because of the fact that in present-day society the domination of nature presents itself both as an increasingly aggravated alienation and as the single great ideological justification for this social alienation, it is criticized in a one-sided, undialectical, and insufficiently historical manner by some of the radical groups who are halfway between the old degraded and mystified conception of the workers movement, which they have superseded, and the new form of total contestation which is yet to come. (See, for example, the very significant theories of Cardan and others in the journal *Socialisme ou Barbarie*.) These groups, rightly opposing the increasingly thorough reification of human labor and its modern corollary, the passive consumption of a leisure activity manipulated by the ruling class, often end up unconsciously harboring a sort of nostalgia for earlier forms of work, for the truly "human" relationships that were able to flourish in the societies of the past or even during the less developed phases of industrial society. As it happens, this attitude fits in quite well with the system's efforts to obtain a higher yield from existing production by doing away with both the waste and the inhumanity that characterize modern industry (in this regard see "Instructions for an Insurrection" in *Internationale Situationniste* #6). But in any case, these conceptions abandon the very core of the revolutionary project, which is nothing less than the suppression of work in the usual present-day sense (and of the proletariat) and of all the justifications of previous forms of work. It is impossible to understand the sentence in the *Communist Manifesto* that says "the bourgeoisie has played an eminently revolutionary role in history" if one ignores the possibility, opened up to us by the domination of nature, of replacing work with a *new type of free activity*; or if one ignores the role of the bourgeoisie in the "dissolution of old ideas," that is, if one follows the unfortunate tendency of the classical workers movement to define itself positively in terms of "revolutionary ideology."

In "Basic Banalities" Vaneigem has elucidated the process of the dissolution of religious thought and has shown how its function as anesthetic, hypnotic, and tranquilizer has been taken over, at a lower level, by ideology. Like penicillin, ideology has become less effective as its use has become more widespread. As a result, the dosage has to be continually increased and the packaging made more sensational (one need only recall the diverse excesses of Nazism or of today's consumer propaganda). Since the disappearance of feudal society the ruling classes have been increasingly ill-served by their own ideologies: these ideologies (as petrified critical thought), after having been used by them as general weapons for seizing power, end up presenting contradictions to their particular reign. What was originally an unconscious falsification (resulting from an ideology's having stopped at partial conclusions) becomes a systematic lie once certain of the interests it cloaked are in power and protected by a police force. The most modern example is also the most glaring: it was by taking advantage of the element of ideology present in the workers movement that a bureaucracy was able to establish its power in Russia. Any attempt to modernize an ideology—whether an aberrant one like fascism or a consistent one like the ideology of spectacular consumption in developed capitalism—tends to preserve the present, which is itself dominated by the past. An ideological reformism hostile to the established society can never be effective because it can never get hold of the means of force-feeding thanks to which this society can still make effective use of ideologies. Revolutionary theory must mercilessly criticize all ideologies—including, of course, that particular ideology called "the death of ideologies" (whose title is already a confession since ideologies have always been dead thought), which is merely an empiricist ideology rejoicing over the downfall of envied rivals.

The domination of nature implies the question "For what purpose?" but this very questioning of human praxis must itself dominate this domination, though it could not take place except on the basis of it. Only the crudest answer is automatically rejected: "To carry on as before, producing and consuming more and more," prolonging the reifying domination that has been inherent in capitalism from its beginnings (though not without "producing its own gravediggers"). We have to expose the contradiction between the positive aspects of the transformation of nature—the great project of the bourgeoisie— and its co-option and trivialization by hierarchical power, which in all its contemporary variants remains faithful to the same model of bourgeois "civilization." In its massified form, this bourgeois model has been "socialized" for the benefit of a composite petty bourgeoisie that is taking on all the capacities for mindless manipulability characteristic of the former poor classes and all the signs of wealth (themselves massified) that signify membership in the ruling class. The bureaucrats of the Eastern bloc are objectively led to follow the same pattern; and the more they produce, the less need they have for police in maintaining their particular schema for the elimination of class struggle. Modern capitalism loudly proclaims a similar goal. But they're all riding the same tiger: a world in rapid transformation in which they desire the dose of immobility necessary for the perpetuation of one or another variant of hierarchical power.

The criticisms of the present social order are all interrelated, just as are the apologetics for that order. The interrelation of the apologetics is less apparent in that they have to praise or lie about numerous mutually contradictory details and antagonistic variants within the system. But if you truly renounce all the variants of apologetics, you get straight to the critique that does not suffer from any guilty conscience because it is not compromised with any present ruling force. If some people think that a hierarchical bureaucracy can be a revolutionary power, and also agree that mass tourism as it is globally organized by the society of the spectacle is a good thing and a pleasure, then, like Sartre, they can pay a visit to China or somewhere else. His mistakes, lies, and stupidity should surprise no one. Everybody finds their own level (other travelers, such as those who go to serve Tshombe* in Katanga, are even more detestable and are paid in more real coin). The intellectual witnesses of the left, eagerly toddling to wherever they are invited, bear witness to nothing so much as their own abdication of thinking—to the fact that their "thought" has for decades been abdicating its freedom as it oscillates between competing bosses. The thinkers who admire the present achievements of the East or the West and who are taken in by all the spectacular gimmicks have obviously never thought about anything at all, as anyone can tell who has read them. The society they reflect naturally encourages us to admire its admirers. In many places they are even allowed to play their little game of "social commitment," in which they ostentatiously proclaim their support (with or without regretful reservations) for the form of established society whose label and packaging inspires them.

Every day alienated people are shown or informed about new successes they have obtained, successes for which they have no use. This does not mean that these advances in material development are bad or uninteresting. They could be turned to good use in real life— but *only along with everything else.* The victories of our day belong to star-specialists. Gagarin's exploit shows that man can *survive* farther out in space, under increasingly unfavorable conditions. But just as is the case when medicine and biochemistry enable a prolonged survival in time, this quantitative extension of survival is in no way linked to a qualitative improvement of life. You can survive farther away and longer, but never live more. Our task is not to celebrate such victories, but to make celebration victorious—celebration whose infinite possibilities in everyday life are potentially unleashed by these technical advances.

Nature has to be rediscovered as a "worthy opponent." The game with nature has to be exciting: each point scored must concern us directly. The conscious construction of a moment of life is an example of our (shifting and transitory) control of our time and our environment. Humanity's expansion into the cosmos is—at the opposite pole from the postartistic construction of individual life (though these two poles of the possible are intimately linked)—an example of an enterprise in which the pettiness of specialized military competition clashes with the objective grandeur of the project. The cosmic adventure will be extended, and thus opened up to a participation totally different from that of specialist guinea pigs, farther and *faster* when the collapse of the miserly reign of specialists on this planet has opened the floodgates of *everyone's* creativity—a creativity which is presently blocked and repressed, but which is potentially capable of leading to an exponential progress in dealing with all human problems, supplanting the present cumulative growth restricted to an arbitrary sector of industrial production. The old schema of the contradiction between productive forces and production relations should obviously no longer be understood as a short-term death warrant for the capitalist production system, as if the latter were inevitably doomed to stagnate and become incapable of continuing its development. This contradiction should be seen rather as a judgment (which remains to be executed with the appropriate weapons) against the miserable development generated by this self-regulating production—a development that must be condemned for its paltriness as well as for its dangerousness—in view of the fantastic *potential development* that could be based on the present economic infrastructure.

The only questions that are openly posed in the present society are loaded questions, questions that already imply certain obligatory responses. When people point out the obvious fact that the modern tradition is a tradition of innovation, they shut their eyes to the equally obvious fact that this innovation does not extend everywhere. During an era when ideology could still believe in its role, Saint-Just declared: "In a time of innovation everything that is not new is pernicious." God's numerous successors who organize the present society of the spectacle know very well what asking too many questions can lead to. The decline of philosophy and the arts also stems from this suppression of questioning. The revolutionary elements of modern thought and art have with varying degrees of precision demanded a praxis that would be the minimum terrain necessary for their development—a praxis that is still absent. The nonrevolutionary elements add new embellishments to the official questions, or to the futile questioning of pure speculation (the specialty of *Arguments*).

There are many ideological rooms in the House of the Father, i.e. in the old society, whose fixed frames of reference have been lost but whose law remains intact (God doesn't exist, but nothing is permitted).* Every facility is granted to the modernisms that serve to combat the truly modern. The gang of hucksters of the unbelievable magazine *Planète*, which so impresses the school teachers, epitomizes a bizarre demagogy that profits from the gaping absence of contestation and revolutionary imagination, at least in their intellectual manifestations, over the last nearly half a century (and from the numerous obstacles still placed in the way of their resurgence today). Playing on the truism that science and technology are advancing faster and faster without anyone knowing where they are going, *Planète* harangues ordinary people with the message that henceforth everything must be changed—while at the same time taking for granted 99% of the life really lived in our era. The daze induced by the barrage of novelties can be taken advantage of to calmly reintroduce outmoded nonsense that has virtually died out even in the most backward regions. The drugs of ideology will end their history in an apotheosis of vulgarity that even Pauwels [editor of *Planète*], for all his efforts, cannot yet imagine.

Ideology, in its various fluid forms that have replaced the solid mythical system of the past, has an increasingly large role to play as the specialist rulers need to increasingly regulate all aspects of an expanding production and consumption. Use value—indispensable still, but which had already tended to become merely implicit since the predominance of a market economy—is now explicitly manipulated (or artificially created) by the planners of the modern market. It is the merit of Jacques Ellul, in his book *Propaganda* (1962), which describes the unity of the various forms of conditioning, to have shown that this advertising-propaganda is not merely an unhealthy excrescence that could be prohibited, but is at the same time a remedy in a generally sick society, a remedy that makes the sickness tolerable while aggravating it. People are to a great extent accomplices of propaganda, of the reigning spectacle, because they cannot reject it without contesting the society as a whole. The single important task of contemporary thought must center upon this question of reorganizing the theoretical and material forces of contestation.

The alternative is not only between real life and a survival that has nothing to lose but its modernized chains. It is also posed within survival itself, with the constantly aggravated problems that the masters of survival are not able to solve. The risks of atomic weapons, of global overpopulation, and of the increasing material impoverishment of the great majority of humanity are subjects of official alarm, even in the popular press. One very banal example: in an article on China (*Le Monde*, September 1962) Robert Guillain writes, without irony, on the population problem: "The Chinese leaders seem to be giving it fresh consideration and apparently want to deal with it. They are coming back to the idea of birth control, which was tried out in 1956 and then abandoned in 1958. A national campaign has been launched against early marriages and in favor of family planning in young households." The oscillations of these specialists, immediately followed by official orders, reveal the sort of interest they really have in the liberation of the people just as completely as the opportunistic religious conversions of princes in the sixteenth century (*cuius regio, eius religio*)* revealed the real nature of their interest in the mythical arsenal of Christianity. The same journalist notes that "the USSR is not helping China because its available resources are now being devoted to the conquest of space, which is fantastically expensive." The Russian workers have no more say in determining the quantity of surplus "available resources" produced by their labor, or in deciding whether that surplus is to be devoted to the moon rather than to China, than the Chinese peasants have in deciding whether or not they will have children. The epic of modern rulers at grips with real life, which they are driven to take complete charge of, has found its best literary expression in the Ubu cycle.* The only raw material that has yet to be tried out in this experimental era of ours is *freedom* of thought and behavior.

In the vast drugstores of ideology, of the spectacle, of social planning and the justification of that planning, the specialized intellectuals have their jobs, their particular departments to take care of. (We are referring here to those who have a significant role in the actual production of culture—a stratum that should not be confused with the growing mass of "intellectual workers" whose conditions of work and life are becoming increasingly indistinguishable from those of ordinary blue-collar and white-collar workers as all of them evolve in accordance with the requirements of modern industry.) There's something for every taste. A certain Roberto Guiducci, for example, demonstrates his understanding of "The Difficult Quest for a New Politics" (*Arguments* #25-26) by writing that the present social backwardness "leaves us caught between the stupidity of living among the ruins of dead institutions and the mere ability to express proposals that are as yet scarcely realizable." In order to avoid this painful dilemma, he confines his own proposal within the most modest and "realizable" limits: After having succeeded in lumping Hegel and Engels in the same sentence with Stalin and Zhdanov, he proposes that we grant that "the romantic impatience of the young Marx and the tormented exegeses of Gramsci are equally moth-eaten and outdated." Although the blasé tone gives the impression that he has been through all that and succeeded in recovering from such illusions, it is in fact quite obvious from reading him that he was never capable of reading Hegel or Gramsci in the first place. Instead, he probably passed many years venerating Zhdanov and Togliatti. Then one fine day, like the other puppets of *Arguments* (whatever the particular Communist Party of their origin), he decided to call everything into question. Some of these people may have had dirtier hands than others, but they've all had clogged-up minds. Like the others, Mr. Guiducci undoubtedly spent some weeks "reconsidering" the young Marx. But if he had ever really been capable of understanding Marx, or even simply of understanding the time in which we live, how could he have failed to see through Zhdanov from the very beginning? It's been so many years since he and others reconsidered revolutionary thought, it all naturally appears to him as very "outdated." But did he reconsider anything whatsoever ten years ago? It's very unlikely. We can say, then, that Mr. Guiducci is a man who reconsiders more quickly than does history, because he is never in step with history. His stereotypical nullity will never need to be reconsidered by anyone.

At the same time, a part of the intelligentsia is working out the new contestation, beginning to develop the real critique of our era and to envisage correspondingly appropriate actions. Within the spectacle, which is its factory, this intelligentsia struggles against the speedups in the rhythm of production and against the very aims of that production. Engendering its own critics and saboteurs, it is joining with the new lumpen, the lumpen of consumer capitalism that is expressing its rejection of the goods that present-day work enables one to acquire. It is also beginning to reject the conditions of individual competition, and thus the servility, to which the creative intelligentsia is subjected: the movement of modern art can be considered as a continual *de-skilling* of intellectual labor power by the creators (whereas the workers as a whole, insofar as they accept the hierarchical strategy of the ruling class, compete by categories).

The revolutionary intelligentsia has now to accomplish an immense task, beginning with an uncompromising departure from the long period during which "the sleep of dialectical reason engendered monsters"—a period which is now drawing to a close. The new world that must be understood comprises both the continual increase of material powers that have yet to be put to good use and the spontaneous acts of personal opposition engaged in by people without any conscious perspective. In contrast to the old utopianism, which put forward more or less arbitrary theories that went beyond any possible practice (though not without having some significant influence), there is now, within the various problematics of modernity, *a mass of new practices that are seeking their theory.*

The "intellectual party" that some dream of is impossible, because the collective intelligence of such a union of intellectuals would only be on the miserable level of people like Guiducci or Morin or Nadeau. The officially recognized intelligentsia is fundamentally satisfied with things as they are (if it is dissatisfied with anything, it is nevertheless quite satisfied with its own mediocre literary expression of that dissatisfaction). Even if it votes for the Left, so what? It is in fact the social sector that is most instinctively antisituationist. Like a preview audience, it tastes and tests the consumer products that will gradually be made available to all the workers of the developed countries. We intend to disillusion this stratum of intellectuals, to expose the fraudulence of all their trendy values and tastes ("modern" furniture, the writings of Queneau). Their shame will be a revolutionary sentiment.

It is necessary to distinguish, within the intelligentsia, between the tendencies toward submission and the tendencies toward refusal of the employment offered; and then, by every means, to strike a sword between these two fractions so that their total mutual opposition will illuminate the first advances of the coming social war. The careerist tendency, which basically expresses the condition of all intellectual service within class society, leads this stratum, as Harold Rosenberg notes in *The Tradition of the New,* to expatiate on its own alienation without engaging in any oppositional actions because this alienation has been made comfortable. But as the whole of modern society moves toward this comfort—a comfort which is at the same time becoming increasingly poisoned by boredom and anxiety—the practice of sabotage can be extended to the intellectual terrain. Thus, just as in the first half of the nineteenth century revolutionary theory arose out of philosophy (out of critical reflections on philosophy and out of the crisis and death of philosophy), so now it is going to rise once again out of modern art and poetry, out of its supersession, out of what modern art has sought and *promised,* out of the clean sweep it has made of all the values and rules of everyday behavior.

Although the living values of intellectual and artistic creation are utterly contrary to the submissive intelligentsia's entire mode of existence, the latter wants to embellish its social position by claiming a sort of kinship with this creation of "values." Being more or less aware of this contradiction, this hired intelligentsia tries to redeem itself by an ambiguous glorification of artistic "bohemianism." The valets of reification acknowledge this bohemian experience as a moment of richness within extreme poverty, as a moment of the qualitative within everyday life, a qualitativeness which is excluded everywhere else. But the official version of this fairy tale must have an edifying ending: this moment of pure qualitativeness within poverty must finally arrive at ordinary "riches." Poor artists have produced masterpieces which in their time had no market value. But they are redeemed (their venture into the qualitative is excused, and even turned into an inspiring example) because their work, which at the time was only a by-product of their real activity, later turns out to be highly valued. Living people who struggled against reification have nevertheless ended up producing *their quota of commodities.* Invoking a sort of aesthetic Darwinism, the bourgeoisie applauds the bohemian values that have proved fit enough to survive and enter into its quantitative paradise. The fact that it is rarely the same people who possess the products at the stage of creation and at the stage of profitable commodities is discreetly downplayed as an unimportant and purely accidental detail.

The accelerated degradation of cultural ideology has given rise to a permanent crisis in this intellectual and artistic valorization, a crisis that dadaism brought out into the open. A dual movement has clearly characterized this cultural breakdown: on one hand, the dissemination of fake novelties automatically recycled with new packaging by autonomous spectacular mechanisms; and on the other hand, the public refusal to play along and the sabotage carried out by individuals who were clearly among those who would have been most capable of renewing "quality" cultural production (Arthur Cravan is a prototype of these people, glimpsed passing through the most radioactive zones of the cultural disaster without leaving behind them any commodities or memories).* The conjunction of these two demoralizing forces continues to aggravate the malaise of the intelligentsia.

After dadaism, and despite the fact that the dominant culture has succeeded in co-opting a sort of dadaist art, it is far from certain that artistic rebellion in the next generation will continue to be co-optable into consumable works. At the same time that the most elementary spectacular conmanship can exploit an imitation postdadaist style to produce all sorts of salable cultural objects, there exist in several modern capitalist countries centers of nonartistic bohemianism united around the notion of the end of art or the absence of art, a bohemianism that explicitly no longer envisages any artistic production whatsoever. Its dissatisfaction can only radicalize with the progress of the thesis according to which "the art of the future" (the phrase itself is misleading since it implies dealing with the future in terms of present specialized categories) will no longer be valued as a commodity, since we are discovering that it is only a subordinate aspect of the total transformation of our use of space, of feelings, and of time. All the real experiences of free thought and behavior that succeed in taking shape in these conditions are certainly moving in our direction, toward the theoretical organization of contestation.

We believe that the role of theorists—a role which is indispensable, but which must not be dominant—is to provide information and conceptual tools that can shed light on people's hidden desires and on the social crisis they are experiencing; to clarify things and show how they fit together; to make the new proletariat aware of the "new poverty" that must be named and described.

We are presently witnessing a *reshuffling of the cards of class struggle*—a struggle which has certainly not disappeared, but whose lines of battle have been somewhat altered from the old schema. The nation-state has not been transcended, but individual nationalisms have been incorporated into the framework of supernations, of two global blocs which are themselves composed of concentrated or dispersed multinational zones (e.g. Europe or the Chinese sphere of influence) within which there may be various modifications and regroupings of individual nations or ethnic regions (Korea, Wallonia, etc.).

In the context of the reality presently beginning to take shape, we may consider as proletarians all people who have no possibility of altering the social space-time that the society allots to them (regardless of variations in their degree of affluence or chances for promotion). The rulers are those who organize this space-time, or who at least have a significant margin of personal choice (even stemming, for example, from a significant survival of older forms of private property). A revolutionary movement is a movement that radically changes the organization of this space-time and the very manner of deciding on its ongoing reorganization (as opposed to merely changing the legal forms of property or the social origin of the rulers).

Already, all over the world, the vast majority now consumes the odious, soul-destroying space-time whose organization is "produced" by a tiny minority. (It should be noted that this minority produces literally nothing except this organization, whereas the "consumption" of space-time, in the sense we are using here, encompasses the whole of ordinary production, in which the alienation of consumption and of all life obviously has its roots.) The ruling classes of the past at least knew how to spend in a humanly enriching way the meager slice of surplus-value they managed to wrest from a static social production grounded on general scarcity; the members of today's ruling minority have lost even this "mastery." They are nothing but consumers of power—a power limited to organizing this miserable survival. And their sole purpose in so miserably organizing this survival is to consume that power. The lord of nature, the ruler, is degraded by the pettiness of his exercise of power (the scandal of the quantitative). Mastery without degradation would guarantee full employment—not of all the workers, but of all the forces of the society, of all the creative possibilities of everyone, for themselves individually and for dialogue with each other. Where then are the real masters? At the other pole of this absurd system. At the pole of refusal. The masters come from the negative, they are the bearers of the antihierarchical principle.

The distinction drawn here between those who organize space-time (together with their direct agents) and those who are subjected to that organization is intended to clearly reveal the polarization that is obscured by the intentionally woven complexity of the hierarchies of function and salary, which gives the impression that all the gradations are virtually imperceptible and that there are scarcely any more real proletarians or real capitalists at the two extremities of a social spectrum that has become highly flexible. Once this distinction is posed, other differences in status must be considered as secondary. It should not be forgotten, however, that an intellectual or a "professional revolutionary" worker is liable at any moment to tumble irretrievably into co-option—into one niche or another in one clan or another in the camp of the ruling zombies (which is far from being harmonious or monolithic). Until real life is present for everyone, the "salt of the earth" is always susceptible to going bad. The theorists of the new contestation can neither compromise with the ruling powers nor constitute themselves as a separate power without immediately ceasing to be such (their role as theorists will then be taken over by others). This amounts to saying that the revolutionary intelligentsia can realize its project only by suppressing itself—that the "intellectual party" can really exist only as a party that supersedes itself, a party whose victory is at the same time its own disappearance.

The Avant-Garde of Presence*
(excerpts)

[. . .] The dialectic of history is such that the Situationist International's theoretical victory is already forcing its adversaries to *disguise themselves* as situationists. Two main tendencies can now be distinguished in the impending struggle against us: those who proclaim themselves situationists without having any idea what they're talking about (the varieties of Nashism) and those who, conversely, decide to adopt a few situationist ideas minus the situationists and without mentioning the SI. The increasing likelihood of the confirmation of some of the simplest and least recent of our theses leads many people to appropriate aspects of one or another of them *without acknowledgment.* We are not, of course, concerned here with obtaining recognition and personal credit for priority. The only interest in pointing out this tendency is in order to denounce one crucial aspect of it: When these people draw on our theses in order to finally talk about some new problem (after having suppressed it as long as they could), they inevitably banalize it, eradicating its violence and its connection with the general subversion, defusing it and subjecting it to academic dissection or worse. This is the reason they have to suppress any mention of the SI. [. . .]

Free play confined within the terrain of artistic dissolution is only the co-option of free play. In spring 1962 the press began reporting on the "happenings" produced by the some of the avant-garde artists of New York. The happening is a sort of spectacle pushed to the extreme state of dissolution, a vaguely dadaist-style improvisation of gestures performed by a gathering of people within a confined space. Drugs, alcohol, and eroticism are often involved. The actions of the "actors" tend toward a mélange of poetry, painting, dance, and jazz. This form of social encounter can be considered as an instance of the old artistic spectacle pushed to the extreme, a hash produced by throwing together all the old artistic leftovers; or as a too aesthetically encumbered attempt to renovate the ordinary surprise party or the classic orgy. In its naïve striving to "make something happen," its absence of separate spectators, and its desire to liven up (however feebly) the impoverished range of present human relations, the happening can even be considered as an attempt to construct a situation in isolation, *on a foundation of poverty* (material poverty, the poverty of encounters, the poverty inherited from the artistic spectacle, and the poverty of the "philosophy" that has to considerably "ideologize" the reality of these events). In contrast, the situations defined by the SI can be constructed only on a foundation of material and spiritual richness. This amounts to saying that the first ventures in constructing situations must be the work/play of the revolutionary avant-garde; people who are resigned in one way or another to political passivity, to metaphysical despair, or even to being subjected to an art of total noncreativity, are incapable of participating in them. [. . .]

People urge us to present trivial projects that would be useful and convincing. But why should we be interested in convincing them? In any case, if we were to oblige them, they would immediately turn these projects against us, either by holding them up as proofs of our utopianism or by rushing to disseminate watered-down versions of them. In fact, those who are interested in and satisfied by such partial projects can solicit them from almost anyone else, but *not from us*. We contend that a fundamental cultural renewal will not be brought about by an accumulation of changes of details, but only *as a whole*. We are obviously in a good position to discover, a few years ahead of other people, all the potential gimmicks of the present extreme cultural decomposition. Since they are useful only in our enemies' spectacle, we merely make a few notes on them and file them away. Many of them are eventually discovered independently by someone or other and ostentatiously launched on the market. History has not yet "caught up" with the majority of them, however. Perhaps it never will with some of them. This is not simply a game, it is one more experimental verification of our perspectives.

We believe that modern art, wherever it was truly critical and innovative in the very conditions of its appearance, has fulfilled its role, a role of great importance; and that, despite the speculation on its products, it is still detested by the enemies of freedom. It suffices to note the fear it inspires even now among the cautiously de-Stalinizing rulers, how they panic at the slightest sign of its reappearance in their dominion after years of total repression. They denounce it as a leak in their ideology, because their power depends on that ideology's monopoly of information at every level. But the people in the West who profit from respectful prolongations and artificial revivals of the cultural ventures that were blocked long ago are the real enemies of modern art. We are its sole heirs.

We are against the conventional forms of culture, even in its most modern state; but not, obviously, in preferring ignorance, neoprimitivism, or petty-bourgeois common sense. There is an anticultural attitude that favors an impossible return to the old myths. Against such a current we are of course for culture. We take our stand on the other side of culture. Not before it, but *after it*. We contend that it is necessary to *realize* culture by superseding it as a separate sphere; not only as a domain reserved for specialists, but above all as a domain of a specialized production that does not directly affect the construction of life—not even the life of its own specialists.

We are not completely lacking in humor; but our humor is of a rather new kind. If someone wants to know how to approach our theses, without going into the fine points and subtleties, the simplest and most appropriate attitude is to take us completely seriously and literally.

How are we going to bankrupt the dominant culture? Two ways. Gradually at first, and then suddenly.* [. . .]

The Counter-Situationist Campaign in Various Countries
(excerpts)

The declaration published 25 June 1962 by the Situationist International concerning the trial of Uwe Lausen in Munich enumerated three types of negation the situationist movement has met with so far: police, as in Germany*; silence, for which France easily holds the record; and widespread falsification, in which northern Europe has provided the most fertile field of study over the last year. [. . .]

In *Internationale Situationniste* #7 (pp. 53–54) we mentioned the sort of manifesto in which Jörgen Nash attacked the SI in the name of the Scandinavian section. Reckoning on the considerable geographical dispersion of the Scandinavian situationists, Nash had not even consulted with all of them before his putsch. Surprised at not being unanimously followed and at finding himself countered on the spot by the partisans of the SI majority—who immediately circulated a definitive repudiation of his imposture—Nash at first feigned astonishment that things had gone to the point of a complete break with the situationists; as if the fact of launching a public surprise attack *full of lies* was compatible with carrying on a dialogue, on the basis of some sort of Nashist Scandinavian autonomy. The subsequent development of the conspiracy scarcely leaves any doubt as to his real objectives, since his new Swedish "Bauhaus," consisting of two or three Scandinavian ex-situationists plus a mass of unknowns flocking to the feast, immediately plunged into the most shopworn forms of artistic production (one need search no further than the initial production of this neo-Bauhaus: the "poems" of a certain Fazarkely, the sort of thing that would have been considered embarrassingly passé in 1930). A vacuous little Nashist journal entitled *The Situationist Times* appeared around the same time in Holland—a journal which has the peculiarity that it is "situationist" only in the sense that it is directed against the SI, its flock of occasional collaborators never having been (nor even claiming to have been) situationists, with the sole exception of one of the two editors [Jacqueline de Jong], who passed eighteen months in the SI and talks about it incessantly. The other editor is none other than Noël Arnaud, resuscitated from his Stalino-Pataphysical tomb. This eclectic assemblage also includes an ex-Lettrist and, even more posthumously, Boris Vian. In the polemic between Nashists and situationists in Scandinavia, the Nashists resorted, in addition to all the threats and violence they thought feasible, to the systematic spreading of false information (with the active collusion of certain journalists). The most flagrant lie, circulated in June, claimed that the SI had agreed to resume dialogue with them regarding their possible reinstatement in the group. In support of this contention they cited a supposed letter from the SI's Central Council that was a pure fabrication. But in the end, despite the fact that the extensive discussion of this affair in the Scandinavian press had shifted the debate to a terrain more favorable to Nashist disinformation than to the objective presentation of the SI's theses, all their efforts to gain time and all their petty maneuvers to prolong the confusion could not save the Nashists from appearing for what they are: alien to the SI; much more sociable, certainly, but much less intelligent. [. . .]

We don't want to attribute some particular perversity to Nash and his associates. It seems to us that Nashism is an expression of an objective tendency resulting from the SI's ambiguous and risky policy of consenting to act *within* culture while being against the entire present organization of this culture and even against all culture as a separate sphere. (But even the most intransigent oppositional attitude cannot escape such ambiguity and risk, since it still necessarily has to coexist with the present order.) The German situationists who were excluded at the beginning of 1962 expressed an opposition comparable to that of the Nashists—though with more frankness and artistic capacity—to the extent that such opposition contains elements of a legitimately arguable position. Heimrad Prem's statement at the Göteborg Conference (see *Internationale Situationniste* #7) complained about the situationist majority's continued refusal of a large number of offers to sponsor "creations" on the conventional avant-garde artistic plane where many people wanted to involve the SI, so as to bring things back to order and the SI back into the old fold of artistic praxis. Prem expressed the desire of the situationist artists to find an adequate field of activity in the here and now. This attitude, which merely seeks a renewal of art, is in total contradiction with situationist theory, which postulates that traditional, separate art can no longer be fundamentally renewed without other necessary reconstructions, without the free reconstruction of the entire society (the hypothesis of a constructed situation being a preliminary example of a post-artistic explosion that will disintegrate all the "conventional weapons" of traditional art). The Nashists have simply gone much further in their bad faith and in their complete indifference to any theory and even to conventional artistic activity, preferring the grossest commercial publicity. But Prem and his friends, though comporting themselves more honorably, had themselves certainly not completely avoided concessions to the cultural market. The SI has thus for a time included a number of artists of repetition incapable of grasping the present mission of the artistic avant-garde; which is not too surprising if one takes into account both the scarcely delineated stage of our project and the notorious exhaustion of conventional art. The moment when the contradictions between them and us lead to these antagonisms marks an advance of the SI, the point where the ambiguities are forced into the open and clearly settled. The point of no return, in our relations with the partisans of a renewal of conventional art under the aegis of a situationist school, was perhaps reached with the decision adopted at Göteborg to refer to artistic productions of the movement as "antisituationist" art. The contradictions expressed in Nashism are quite crude, but the development of the SI may lead to others at a higher level. [. . .]

DEFINITION
adopted by the SI Conference at Anvers
on the motion of J.V. Martin

Nashism (French: **Nashisme;** German: **Nashismus;** Italian: **Nascismo**): Term derived from the name of Nash, an artist who seems to have lived in Denmark in the twentieth century. Primarily known for his attempt to betray the revolutionary movement and theory of that time, Nash's name was detourned by that movement as a generic term applicable to all traitors in struggles against the dominant cultural and social conditions. Example: "But like all things transient and vain, Nashism soon faded away." **Nashist:** A partisan of Nash or of his doctrine. By extension, any conduct or expression evincing the aims or methods of Nashism. **Nashistique:** Popular French doublet probably derived by analogy to the English adjective **Nashistic.** **Nashisterie:** The general social milieu of Nashism. The slang term **Nashistouse** is vulgar.*

The SI cannot be a massive organization, and it will not even accept disciples, as do the conventional avant-garde groups. At this point in history, when the task is posed, in the most unfavorable conditions, of reinventing culture and the revolutionary movement on an entirely new basis, the SI can only be a Conspiracy of Equals, a general staff that *does not want troops.* We need to discover and open up the "Northwest Passage" toward a new revolution that cannot tolerate masses of followers, a revolution that must surge over that central terrain which has until now been sheltered from revolutionary upheavals: the conquest of everyday life. *We will only organize the detonation:* the free explosion must escape us and any other control forever.

One of the classic weapons of the old world, perhaps the one most used against groups delving into the organization of life, is to single out and isolate a few of their participants as "stars." We have to defend ourselves against this process, which, like almost all the usual wretched choices of the present society, has an air of being "natural." Those among us who aspired to the role of stars or who depended on stars had to be rejected. [. . .]

The same movement that would have us accept situationist followers would commit us to erroneous positions. It is in the nature of a disciple to demand certainties, to transform real problems into stupid dogmas from which he derives his role and his intellectual security. And later, of course, to demonstrate his modernity by revolting, in the name of those simplified certainties, against the very people who transmitted them to him. In this way, over a period of time generations of submissive elites succeed one another. We intend to leave such people outside and to resist those who want to transform the SI's theoretical problematics into a mere ideology. Such people are extremely handicapped and uninteresting compared with those who may not be aware of the SI but who are at least confronting their own lives. Those who have really *grasped* the direction the SI is going in can join with it, because the supersession we are talking about is to be found in reality, and we have to find it together. The task of being *more extremist* than the SI falls to the SI itself; this is even the first law of its continuation.

There are already certain people who, through laziness, think they can rigidify our project into a perfect program, one already present, admirable, and uncriticizable, in the face of which they have nothing more to do—except perhaps to declare themselves still more radical at heart, while abstaining from any activity on the grounds that everything has already been definitively said by the SI. We say that, on the contrary, not only do the most important aspects of the questions we have posed remain to be discovered—by the SI and by others—but also that the greater portion of what we have already discovered is not yet published due to our lack of all sorts of means; to say nothing of the still more considerable lack of means for the experiments the SI has barely begun in other domains (particularly in matters of behavior). But to speak only of editorial problems, we now think that we ourselves should rewrite the most interesting parts of what we have published so far. It is not a matter of revising certain errors or of suppressing a few deviationist seeds that have since blossomed into gross results* (e.g. Constant's technocratic concept of a situationist profession—see *Internationale Situationniste* #4, pp. 24–25), but of correcting and improving the most important of our theses, precisely those whose development has brought us further, on the basis of the knowledge since gained thanks to them. This will require various republications, although the SI's current difficulties in publishing are far from being resolved.

Those who think that the early situationist thought is already fixed in past history, and that the time has come for violent falsification or rapt admiration of it, have not grasped the *movement* we are talking about. The SI has sown the wind. It will reap a tempest.

All the King's Men

The problem of language is at the heart of all the struggles between the forces striving to abolish the present alienation and those striving to maintain it. It is inseparable from the very terrain of those struggles. We live within language as within polluted air. Despite what humorists think, words do not play. Nor do they make love, as Breton thought, except in dreams. Words *work*—on behalf of the dominant organization of life. Yet they are not completely automated: unfortunately for the theoreticians of information, words are not in themselves "informationist"; they contain forces that can upset the most careful calculations. Words coexist with power in a relation analogous to that which proletarians (in the modern as well as the classic sense of the term) have with power. Employed by it *almost* full time, exploited for every sense and nonsense that can be squeezed out of them, they still remain in some sense fundamentally alien to it.

Power* presents only the falsified, official sense of words. In a manner of speaking it forces them to carry a pass, determines their place in the production process (where some of them conspicuously work overtime), and gives them their paycheck. Regarding the use of words, Lewis Carroll's Humpty Dumpty correctly observes: "The question is which is to be master—that's all."* He adds that he himself (a socially responsible employer in this respect) pays overtime to those he employs excessively. We should also understand the phenomenon of the *insubordination of words,* their desertion or open resistance (manifested in all modern writing from Baudelaire to the dadaists and Joyce), as a symptom of the general revolutionary crisis of this society.

Under the control of power, language always designates something other than authentic experience. It is precisely for this reason that a total contestation is possible. The organization of language has fallen into such confusion that the communication imposed by power is exposing itself as an imposture and a dupery. An embryonic cybernetic power is vainly trying to put language under the control of the machines it controls, in such a way that information would henceforth be the only possible communication. Even on this terrain resistances are being manifested; electronic music could be seen as an attempt (obviously limited and ambiguous) to reverse the domination by detourning machines to the benefit of language. But there is a much more general and radical opposition that is denouncing all unilateral "communication," in the old form of art as well as in the modern form of informationism. It calls for a communication that undermines all separate power. Real communication dissolves the state.

Power lives off stolen goods. It creates nothing; it co-opts. If it determined the meaning of words, there would be no poetry but only useful "information." Opposition would be unable to express itself in language; any refusal would be nonverbal, purely lettristic. What is poetry if not the revolutionary moment of language, inseparable as such from the revolutionary moments of history and from the history of personal life?

Power's stranglehold over language is connected to its stranglehold over the totality. Only a language that has been deprived of all immediate reference to the totality can serve as the basis for information. News* is the poetry of power, the counterpoetry of law and order, the mediated falsification of what exists. Conversely, poetry must be understood as direct communication within reality and as real alteration of this reality. It is liberated language, language recovering its richness, language breaking its rigid significations and simultaneously embracing words and music, cries and gestures, painting and mathematics, facts and acts. Poetry thus depends on the richest possibilities for living *and changing* life at a given stage of socioeconomic structure. Needless to say, this relationship of poetry to its material base is not a subordination of one to the other, but an interaction.

Rediscovering poetry may merge with reinventing revolution, as has been demonstrated by certain phases of the Mexican, Cuban, and Congolese revolutions. Outside the revolutionary periods when the masses become poets in action, small circles of poetic adventure could be considered the only places where the totality of revolution subsists, as an unrealized but close-at-hand potentiality, like the shadow of an absent personage. What we are calling poetic adventure is difficult, dangerous, and *never guaranteed* (it is, in fact, the aggregate of behaviors that are *almost impossible* in a given era). One thing we can be sure of is that fake, officially tolerated poetry is no longer the poetic adventure of its era. Thus, whereas surrealism in the heyday of its assault against the oppressive order of culture and daily life could appropriately define its arsenal as "poetry without poems if necessary," for the SI it is now a matter of a poetry *necessarily* without poems. What we say about poetry has nothing to do with the retarded reactionaries of some neoversification, even one based on the least antiquated modernistic forms. Realizing poetry means nothing less than simultaneously and inseparably creating events and their language.

In-group languages—those of informal groupings of young people; those that contemporary avant-garde currents develop for their internal use as they grope to define themselves; those that in previous eras were conveyed by way of objective poetic production, such as *trobar clus* and *dolce stil nuovo**—are more or less successful efforts to attain a direct, transparent communication, mutual recognition, mutual accord. But such efforts have been confined to small groups that were isolated in one way or another. The events and celebrations they created had to remain within the most narrow limits. One of the tasks of revolution is to federate such poetic "soviets" or *communication councils* in order to initiate a direct communication everywhere that will no longer need to resort to the enemy's communication network (that is, to the language of power) and will thus be able to transform the world according to its desire.

The point is not to put poetry at the service of revolution, but to put revolution at the service of poetry. It is only in this way that revolution does not betray its own project. We don't intend to repeat the mistake of the surrealists, who put themselves at the service of the revolution right when it had ceased to exist. Bound to the memory of a partial and rapidly crushed revolution, surrealism rapidly turned into a reformism of the spectacle, a critique of a certain form of the reigning spectacle that was carried out from within the dominant organization of that spectacle. The surrealists seem to have overlooked the fact that every internal improvement or modernization of the spectacle is translated by power into its own encoded language, to which it alone holds the key.

Every revolution has been born in poetry, has first of all been made with the force of poetry. This phenomenon continues to escape theorists of revolution—indeed, it cannot be understood if one still clings to the old conception of revolution or of poetry—but it has generally been sensed by counterrevolutionaries. Poetry terrifies them. Whenever it appears they do their best to get rid of it by every kind of exorcism, from auto-da-fé to pure stylistic research. Real poetry, which has "world enough and time," seeks to reorient the entire world and the entire future to its own ends. As long as it lasts, its demands admit of no compromise. It brings back into play all the unsettled debts of history. Fourier and Pancho Villa, Lautréamont and the *dinamiteros* of the Asturias (whose successors are now inventing new forms of strikes),* the sailors of Kronstadt and Kiel, and all those around the world who, with us or without us, are preparing to fight for the long revolution are equally the emissaries of the new poetry.

Poetry is becoming more and more clearly the empty space, the antimatter, of consumer society, since it is not consumable (in terms of the modern criteria for a consumable object: an object that is of equivalent value for each of a mass of isolated passive consumers). Poetry is nothing when it is quoted; it needs to be *detourned,* brought back into play. Otherwise the study of the poetry of the past is nothing but an academic exercise. The history of poetry is only a way of running away from the poetry of history, if we understand by that phrase not the spectacular history of the rulers but the history of everyday life and its possible liberation; the history of each individual life and its realization.

We must leave no question as to the role of the "conservers" of old poetry, who increase its dissemination while the state, for quite different reasons, is eliminating illiteracy. These people are only a particular type of museum curator. A mass of poetry is naturally preserved around the world, but nowhere are there the places, the moments, or the people to revive it, communicate it, use it. And there never can be except by way of détournement, because the understanding of past poetry has changed through losses as well as gains of knowledge; and because any time past poetry is actually rediscovered, its being placed in the context of particular events gives it a largely new meaning. In any case, a situation in which poetry is possible must not get sidetracked into trying to restore poetic failures of the past (such failures being the inverted remains of the history of poetry, transformed into successes and poetic monuments). Such a situation naturally seeks the communication and possible triumph of *its own poetry.*

At the same time that poetic archeology is restoring selections of past poetry, recited by specialists on LPs for the neoilliterate public created by the modern spectacle, the informationists are striving to do away with all the "redundancies" of freedom in order to *simply trans-*

mit orders. The theorists of automation are explicitly aiming at producing an automatic theoretical thought by clamping down on and
eliminating the variables in life as well as in language. But bones keep
turning up in their cheese! Translating machines, for example, which
are beginning to ensure the planetary standardization of information
along with the informationist revision of previous culture, are victims
of their own preestablished programming, which inevitably misses
any new meaning taken on by a word, as well as its past dialectical
ambivalences. Thus the life of language—which is bound up with every
advance of theoretical understanding ("Ideas improve; the meaning
of words plays a part in that improvement")—is expelled from the
mechanical field of official information. But this also means that free
thought can organize itself with a secrecy that is beyond the reach of
informationist police techniques. A similar point could be made about
the quest for unambiguous signals and instantaneous binary classifi-
cation, which is clearly linked with the existing power structure. Even
in their most delirious formulations, the informationist theorists are
no more than clumsy precursors of the future they have chosen, which
is the same brave new world that the dominant forces of the present
society are working toward—the reinforcement of the cybernetic state.
They are the vassals of the lords of the technocratic feudalism that is
now constituting itself. There is no innocence in their buffoonery; they
are the king's jesters.

The choice between informationism and poetry no longer has anything to do with the poetry of the past, just as no variant of what the
classical revolutionary movement has become can anymore, anywhere,
be considered as part of a real alternative to the prevailing organization of life. The same judgment leads us to announce the total disappearance of poetry in the old forms in which it was produced and consumed and to announce its return in effective and unexpected forms.
Our era no longer has to *write poetic directives;* it has to carry them out.

Basic Banalities
(Part 2)

Summary of Part 1

The vast majority of people have always had to devote all their energy to SURVIVAL, thereby denying themselves any chance to LIVE. They continue to do so today as the WELFARE STATE imposes the elements of this survival in the form of technological conveniences (appliances, preserved food, pre-fabricated cities, Mozart broadcast for the masses).

The organization controlling the material equipment of our everyday life is such that what could potentially enable us to construct it richly plunges us instead into a poverty of abundance. Alienation becomes all the more intolerable as each convenience promises freedom and turns out to be only one more burden. We are enslaved by the means of liberation.

To be understood, this problem must be seen in the clear light of hierarchical power. But perhaps it isn't enough to say that hierarchical power has preserved humanity for thousands of years like alcohol preserves a fetus—by arresting either growth or decay. It should also be specified that hierarchical power represents the highest stage of private appropriation, and historically is its alpha and omega. Private appropriation can be defined as appropriation of things by means of appropriation of people, the struggle against natural alienation engendering social alienation.

Private appropriation entails an ORGANIZATION OF APPEARANCES by which its radical contradictions can be dissimulated: the servants must see themselves as degraded reflections of the master, thus reinforcing, through the looking glass of an illusory freedom, everything that increases their submission and passivity; while the master must identify himself with the mythical and perfect servant of a god or of a transcendence which is nothing other than the sacred and abstract representation of the TOTALITY of people and things over which he wields power—a power all the more real and unquestioned as he is universally credited with the virtue of his renunciation. The mythical sacrifice of the boss corresponds to the real sacrifice of the underling; each negates himself in the other, the strange becomes familiar and the familiar strange, each fulfills himself by being the inversion of the other. From this common alienation a harmony is born, a negative harmony whose fundamental unity lies in the notion of sacrifice. This objective (and perverted) harmony is sustained by myth—this term being used to designate the organization of appearances in unitary societies, that is, in societies where slave, tribal, or feudal power is officially consecrated by a divine authority and where the sacred allows power to seize the totality.

The harmony originally based on "GIVING oneself" contains a form of relationship that was to develop, become autonomous, and destroy it. This relationship is based on partial EXCHANGE (commodity, money, product, labor power...), the exchange of a part of oneself, which underlies the bourgeois notion of freedom. It arises as commerce and technology become preponderant within agrarian-type economies.

When the bourgeoisie seized power the unity of power was destroyed. Sacred private appropriation became secularized in capitalist mechanisms. Freed from the grip of power, the totality once again became concrete and immediate. The era of fragmentation has been nothing but a succession of attempts to recapture an inaccessible unity, to reconstitute some ersatz sacred behind which to shelter power.

A revolutionary moment is when "everything that reality presents" finds its immediate REPRESENTATION. All the rest of the time hierarchical power, increasingly deprived of its magical and mystical regalia, strives to make everyone forget that the totality (which has never been anything other than reality!) is exposing its fraudulence.

14

By directly attacking the mythical organization of appearances, the bourgeois revolutions unintentionally attacked the weak point not only of unitary power but of any hierarchical power whatsoever. Does this unavoidable mistake explain the guilt complex that is one of the dominant traits of bourgeois mentality? In any case, the mistake was undoubtedly inevitable.

It was a mistake because once the cloud of lies covering private appropriation was pierced, myth was shattered, leaving a vacuum that could be filled only by a delirious freedom and a splendid poetry. Orgiastic poetry, to be sure, has not yet destroyed power. Its failure is easily explained and its ambiguous signs reveal the blows struck at the same time as they heal the wounds. And yet—let us leave the historians and aesthetes to their collections—one has only to pick at the scab of memory and the cries, words, and gestures of the past make the whole body of power bleed again. The whole organization of the survival of memories will not prevent them from dissolving into oblivion as they come to life; just as our survival will dissolve in the construction of our everyday life.

And it was an inevitable process: as Marx showed, the appearance of exchange-value and its symbolic representation by money opened a profound latent crisis in the heart of the unitary world. The commodity introduced into human relationships a universality (a 1000-franc bill represents anything I can obtain for that sum) and an egalitarianism (equal things are exchanged). This "egalitarian universality" partially escapes both the exploiter and the exploited, but they recognize each other through it. They find themselves face to face, confronting each other no longer within the mystery of divine birth and ancestry, as was the case with the nobility, but within an intelligible transcendence, the Logos, a body of laws that can be *understood by everyone,* even if such understanding remains cloaked in mystery. A mystery with its initiates: first of all priests struggling to maintain the Logos in the limbo of divine mysticism, but soon yielding to philosophers and then to technicians both their positions and the dignity of their sacred mission. From Plato's Republic to the Cybernetic State.

Thus, under the pressure of exchange-value and technology (what we might call "mediation at your fingertips"), myth was gradually secularized. Two facts should be noted, however:

(a) As the Logos frees itself from mystical unity, it affirms itself both within and against that unity. Rational and logical structures of behavior are superimposed on the old magical and analogical ones, simultaneously negating and preserving them (mathematics, poetics, economics, aesthetics, psychology, etc.).

(b) Each time the Logos, the "organization of intelligible appearances," becomes more autonomous, it tends to break away from the sacred and become fragmented. In this way it presents a double danger for unitary power. We have already seen that the sacred expresses power's seizure of the totality, and that anyone wanting to accede to the totality must do so through the mediation of power—the repression of mystics, alchemists, and gnostics is sufficient proof of this. This also explains why present-day power "protects" specialists (though without completely trusting them): it vaguely senses that they are the missionaries of a resacralized Logos. Various historical movements represent attempts within mystical unitary power to found a rival unitary power based on the Logos: Christian syncretism (which makes God psychologically explainable), the Renaissance, the Reformation, and the Enlightenment.

The masters who strove to maintain the unity of the Logos were well aware that only unity can stabilize power. Examined more closely, their efforts can be seen not to have been as vain as the fragmentation of the Logos in the nineteenth and twentieth centuries would seem to prove. In the general movement of atomization the Logos has been broken down into specialized techniques (physics, biology, sociology, papyrology, etc.), but at the same time the need to reestablish the totality has become more imperative. It should not be forgotten that all it would take would be an all-powerful technocratic power in order for there to be a totalitarian domination of the totality, for myth's domination of the totality to be succeeded by the Logos's unitary cybernetic power. In such an event the vision of the Encyclopédistes (strictly rationalized progress stretching indefinitely into the future) would have known only a two-century postponement before being realized. This is the direction in which the Stalino-cyberneticians are preparing the future. In this context, peaceful coexistence should be seen as a preliminary step toward a totalitarian unity. It is time everyone realized that they are already resisting it.

15

We know the battlefield. The problem now is to prepare for battle before the pataphysician,* armed with his totality without technique, and the cybernetician, armed with his technique without totality, consummate their political coitus.

From the standpoint of hierarchical power, myth could be desacralized only if the Logos, or at least its desacralizing elements, were resacralized. Attacking the sacred was at the same time supposed to liberate the totality and thus destroy power. (We've heard that one before!) But the power of the bourgeoisie—fragmented, impoverished, constantly contested—maintains a relative stability by relying on the following ambiguity: Technology, which objectively desacralizes, subjectively appears as an instrument of liberation. Not a real liberation, which could be attained only by desacralization—that is, by the end of the spectacle—but a caricature, an imitation, an induced hallucination. What the unitary worldview previously transferred into the beyond (above), fragmentary power pro-jects (literally, "throws forward") into a state of future well-being, of brighter tomorrows proclaimed from atop the dunghill of today—tomorrows that are nothing more than the present multiplied by the number of gadgets to be produced. From the slogan "Live in God" we have gone on to the humanistic motto "Survive until you are old," euphemistically expressed as: "Stay young at heart and you'll live a long time."

Once desacralized and fragmented, myth loses its grandeur and its spirituality. It becomes an impoverished form, retaining its former characteristics but revealing them in a concrete, harsh, tangible fashion. God doesn't run the show anymore, and until the day the Logos takes over with its arms of technology and science, the phantoms of alienation will continue to materialize and sow disorder everywhere. Watch for those phantoms: they are the first signs of a future order. We must start to *play* right now if we want to avoid a future condemned to mere survival, or even a future in which survival itself will become impossible (the hypothesis of humanity destroying itself—and with it obviously the whole experiment of constructing everyday life). The vital objectives of a struggle for the construction of everyday life are the key, sensitive points of all hierarchical power. To build one is to destroy the other. Caught in the vortex of desacralization and resacralization, we aim above all to abolish (1) the organization of appearances as a *spectacle* in which everyone denies himself; (2) the *separation* on which private life is based, since it is there that the objective separation between owners and dispossessed is lived and reflected on every level; and (3) *sacrifice*. These three elements are obviously interdependent, just as are their opposites: participation, communication, and realization.* The same applies to their respective contexts: nontotality (a bankrupt world, a controlled totality) and totality.

16

The human relationships that were formerly dissolved in divine transcendence (the totality crowned by the sacred) settled out and solidified as soon as the sacred stopped acting as a catalyst. Their materiality was revealed. As Providence was replaced by the capricious laws of the economy, the power of men began to appear behind the power of gods. Today a multitude of roles corresponds to the mythical role everyone once played under the divine spotlight. Though their masks are now human faces, these roles still require both actors and extras to deny their real lives in accordance with the dialectic of real and mythical sacrifice. The spectacle is nothing but secularized and fragmented myth. It forms the armor of a power (which could also be called essential mediation) that becomes vulnerable *to every blow* once it no longer succeeds in disguising (in the cacophonous harmony where all cries drown each other out) its nature as private appropriation, and the greater or lesser dose of misery it allots to everyone.

Roles have become impoverished within the context of a fragmentary power eaten away by desacralization, just as the spectacle represents an impoverishment in comparison with myth. They betray its mechanisms and artifices so clumsily that power, to defend itself against popular denunciation of the spectacle, has no other alternative than to initiate such denunciation itself by even more clumsily replacing actors or ministers, or by organizing pogroms of prefabricated scapegoats (agents of Moscow, Wall Street, the Judeocracy, or the Two Hundred Families). Which also means that the whole cast has been forced to become hams, that style has been replaced by mannerisms.

Myth, as a motionless totality, encompassed all movement (pilgrimage can be considered as an example of adventure and fulfillment within immobility). On the one hand, the spectacle can seize the totality only by reducing it to a fragment or a series of fragments (psychological, sociological, biological, philological, and mythological worldviews); on the other, it is situated at the point where the process of desacralization converges with the efforts at resacralization. Thus it can succeed in imposing immobility only within the real movement, the movement that changes it despite its resistance. In the era of fragmentation the organization of appearances makes movement a linear succession of motionless instants (this notch-to-notch progression is perfectly exemplified by Stalinist "Dialectical Materialism"). Under what we have called "the colonization of everyday life," the only possible changes are changes of fragmentary roles. In terms of more or less inflexible conventions, one is successively citizen, parent, sexual partner, politician, specialist, professional, producer, consumer. Yet what boss doesn't himself feel bossed? The proverb applies to everyone: You may sometimes get a fuck, but you always get fucked!

The era of fragmentation has at least eliminated all doubt on one point: everyday life is the battlefield where the war between power and the totality takes place, with power having to use all its strength to control the totality.

What do we demand in backing the power of everyday life against hierarchical power? We demand *everything*. We are taking our stand in a generalized conflict stretching from domestic squabbles to revolutionary war, and we have gambled on the will to live. This means that we must survive as antisurvivors. Fundamentally we are concerned only with the moments when life breaks through the glaciation of survival, whether those moments are unconscious or theorized, historical (e.g. revolution) or personal. But we must also recognize that we are prevented from freely following the course of such moments (except during the moment of revolution itself) not only by the general repression exerted by power, but also by the requirements of our own struggles and tactics. We have to find ways of compensating for this "margin of error" by broadening the scope of these moments and demonstrating their qualitative significance. What prevents what we say about the construction of everyday life from being co-opted by the cultural and subcultural establishment (*Arguments*, academic thinkers with paid vacations) is the fact that all situationist ideas are faithful extensions of acts attempted constantly by thousands of people to try and prevent a day from being nothing but twenty-four hours of wasted time. Are we an avant-garde? If so, to be avant-garde means to move in step with reality.

17

We don't claim to have a monopoly on intelligence, but only on its use. Our position is strategic, we are at the heart of every conflict. The qualitative is our striking force.* People who half understand this journal ask us for an explanatory monograph thanks to which they will be able to convince themselves that they are intelligent and cultured—that is to say, idiots. Someone who gets exasperated and tosses it in the dump is making a more meaningful gesture. Sooner or later it will have to be understood that the words and phrases we use are still lagging behind reality. The distortion and clumsiness in the way we express ourselves (which a man of taste called, not inaccurately, "a rather irritating kind of hermetic terrorism") comes from our central position, our position on the ill-defined and shifting frontier where language captured by power (conditioning) and free language (poetry) fight out their infinitely complex war. To those who follow behind us we prefer those who reject us impatiently because our language is not yet authentic poetry—not yet the free construction of everyday life.

Everything related to thought is related to the spectacle. Almost everyone lives in a state of terror at the possibility that they might awaken to themselves, and this fear is deliberately fostered by power. Conditioning, the special poetry of power, has extended its dominion so far (all material equipment belongs to it: press, television, stereotypes, magic, tradition, economy, technology—what we call captured language) that it has almost succeeded in dissolving what Marx called the undominated sector, replacing it with another, dominated one (see below the composite portrait of "the survivor"). But lived experience cannot so easily be reduced to a succession of empty roles. Resistance to the external organization of life, i.e. to the organization of life as survival, contains more poetry than any volume of verse or prose, and the poet (in the literary sense of the word) is one who has at least understood or sensed this fact. But such poetry is in a most dangerous situation. Certainly poetry in the situationist sense of the word is irreducible and cannot be co-opted by power (as soon as an act is co-opted it becomes a stereotype, something conditioned by the language of power). But it is encircled by power. Power contains the irreducible by isolating it. But such isolation cannot last; something has to give. The two pincers are, first, the threat of disintegration (insanity, illness, destitution, suicide), and second, remote-controlled therapeutics. The first grants death, the second grants a lifeless survival (empty communication, "togetherness" of family or friends, psychoanalysis in the service of alienation, medical care, ergotherapy). Sooner or later the SI must define itself as therapeutic: we are ready to defend the poetry made by all against the false poetry contrived by power (conditioning). Doctors and psychoanalysts better get it straight too, or they, along with architects and other apostles of survival, may one day have to take the consequences for what they have done.

18

All unresolved, unsuperseded antagonisms weaken. Such antagonisms can evolve only by remaining imprisoned in previous, unsuperseded forms (anticultural art within the cultural spectacle, for example). Any radical opposition that fails or that is partially successful (which amounts to the same thing) gradually degenerates into reformist opposition. Fragmentary oppositions are like the teeth on cogwheels, they mesh with each other and make the machine go round—the machine of the spectacle, the machine of power.

Myth maintained all antagonisms within the archetype of Manicheanism. But what can function as an archetype in a fragmented society? The memory of previous antagonisms, presented in obviously devalued and unaggressive forms, appears today as the latest attempt to bring some coherence into the organization of appearances, so great is the extent to which the spectacle has become a spectacle of confusion and equivalences. We are ready to wipe out all trace of those memories by harnessing all the energy contained in previous antagonisms for a radical struggle soon to come. All the springs blocked by power will one day burst through to form a torrent that will change the face of the world.

In a caricature of antagonisms, power urges everyone to be for or against Brigitte Bardot, the *nouveau roman*, the 4-horse Citroën, Italian cuisine, mescal, miniskirts, the UN, the classics, nationalization, thermonuclear war, and hitchhiking. Everyone is asked their opinion about every detail in order to prevent them from forming one about the totality. However clumsy this maneuver may be, it might have worked if the salesmen in charge of peddling it from door to door were not themselves waking up to their own alienation. To the passivity imposed on the dispossessed masses is added the growing passivity of the directors and actors subjected to the abstract laws of the market and the spectacle and exercising less and less real power over the world. Signs of revolt are already appearing among the actors—stars trying to escape publicity, rulers criticizing their own power (Brigitte Bardot, Fidel Castro). The tools of power are wearing out; their desire for their own freedom is a factor that should be taken into account.

19

At the moment when slave revolts threatened to overthrow the power structure and reveal the relationship between transcendence and the mechanism of private appropriation, Christianity appeared with its grandiose reformism, whose central democratic demand was for the slaves to accede not to the reality of a human life—which would have been impossible without denouncing the exclusionary aspect of private appropriation—but rather to the unreality of an existence whose source of happiness is mythical (imitation of Christ as the price of the hereafter). What has changed since then? Anticipation of the hereafter has become anticipation of a brighter tomorrow; the sacrifice of real, immediate life is the price paid for the illusory freedom of an apparent life. The spectacle is the sphere where forced labor is transformed into voluntary sacrifice. Nothing is more suspect than the formula "To each according to his work" in a world where work is the blackmail of survival; to say nothing of "To each according to his needs" in a world where needs are determined by power. Any constructive project that tries to define itself autonomously and thus partially, and does not take into account that it is in fact defined by the negativity in which everything is suspended, becomes reformist. It is trying to build on quicksand as though it were a cement foundation. Ignoring or misunderstanding the context set by hierarchical power can only end up reinforcing that context. The spontaneous acts we see everywhere forming against power and its spectacle must be warned of all the obstacles in their path and must find a tactic taking into account the strength of the enemy and its means of co-option. This tactic, which we are going to popularize, is *détournement*.

20

Sacrifice must be rewarded. In exchange for their real sacrifice the workers receive the instruments of their liberation (comforts, gadgets), but this liberation remains purely fictitious since power controls the ways in which the material equipment can be used. Power uses to its own ends both the instruments and those who use them. The Christian and bourgeois revolutions democratized mythical sacrifice, the "sacrifice of the master." Today there are countless initiates who receive crumbs of power for putting to public service the totality of their partial knowledge. They are no longer called "initiates" and not yet "priests of the Logos"; they are simply known as specialists.

On the level of the spectacle their power is undeniable: the contestant on "Double Your Money" and the postal clerk chattering all day about all the mechanical features of his car both identify with the specialist, and we know how production managers use such identification to bring unskilled workers to heel. The true mission of the technocrats would be to unify the Logos—if only (due to one of the contradictions of fragmentary power) they themselves weren't so absurdly compartmentalized and isolated. Each specialist is alienated by being out of phase with the others; each knows everything about one fragment and no one grasps the totality. What real control can the atomic technician, the strategist, or the political specialist exercise over a nuclear weapon? What ultimate control can power hope to impose on all the gestures developing against it? The stage is so crowded with actors that chaos is the only master of the show. "Order reigns and doesn't govern" (*Internationale Situationniste* #6).

To the extent that the specialist takes part in the development of the instruments that condition and transform the world, he is preparing the way for the *revolt of the privileged*. Until now such revolt has been called fascism. It is essentially an operatic revolt—didn't Nietzsche see Wagner as a precursor?—in which actors who have long been pushed aside and see themselves becoming less and less free suddenly insist on playing the leading roles. Clinically speaking, fascism is the hysteria of the spectacular world pushed to the point of climax. In this climax the spectacle momentarily ensures its unity while at the same time revealing its radical inhumanity. Through fascism and Stalinism, which constitute its romantic crises, the spectacle reveals its true nature: it is a disease.

We are poisoned by the spectacle. All the elements necessary for a detoxification (that is, for our own construction of our everyday lives) are in the hands of specialists. We are thus highly interested in all these specialists, but in different ways. Some are hopeless cases: we are not, for example, going to try and show the specialists of power, the rulers, the extent of their delirium. On the other hand, we are ready to take into account the bitterness of specialists imprisoned in roles that are constricted, absurd, or ignominious. We must confess, however, that our indulgence has its limits. If, in spite of all our efforts, they persist in putting their guilty conscience and their bitterness in the service of power by fabricating the conditioning that colonizes their own everyday lives; if they prefer an illusory representation in the hierarchy to true fulfillment; if they persist in ostentatiously brandishing their specializations (their painting, their novels, their equations, their sociometry, their psychoanalysis, their ballistics); finally, if, knowing perfectly well—and soon *ignorance of this fact will be no excuse*—that only power and the SI hold the key to using their specialization, they nevertheless still choose to serve power because power, battening on their inertia, has chosen them to serve it, then fuck them! There's a limit to our generosity. They should understand all this, and especially the fact that the revolt of nonruling actors is henceforth linked to the revolt against the spectacle (see below the thesis on the SI and power).

21

The general disparagement of the lumpenproletariat stemmed from the use to which it was put by the bourgeoisie, which it served both as a regulating mechanism for power and as a source of recruits for the more dubious forces of order (cops, informers, hired thugs, artists . . .). Nevertheless, the lumpenproletariat embodies a remarkably radical implicit critique of the *society of work*. Its open contempt for both lackeys and bosses contains a good critique of work as alienation, a critique that has not been taken into consideration until now, not only because the lumpenproletariat was an ambiguous sector, but also because during the nineteenth and early twentieth century the struggle against natural alienation and the production of well-being still appeared as valid justifications for work.

Once it became known that the abundance of consumer goods was nothing but the flip side of alienation in production, the lumpenproletariat took on a new dimension: it expressed a contempt for organized work which, in the age of the Welfare State, is gradually taking on the proportions of a demand that only the rulers still refuse to acknowledge. In spite of the constant attempts of power to co-opt it, every experiment carried out on everyday life, that is, every attempt to construct it (an activity that has been illegal since the destruction of feudal power, where it was limited and reserved for the ruling minority), is concretized today in the critique of alienating work and the refusal to submit to forced labor. So much so that the new proletariat can be negatively defined as a "Front Against Forced Labor" bringing together all those who resist co-option by power. This is our field of action, the arena where we are gambling on the ruse of history against the ruse of power, backing the worker (whether steelworker or artist) who—consciously or not—rejects organized work and life against the worker who—consciously or not—accepts working at the dictates of power. In this perspective, it is not unreasonable to foresee a transitional period during which automation and the will of the new proletariat leave work solely to specialists, reducing managers and bureaucrats to the rank of temporary slaves. With the extension of automation, the "workers," instead of supervising machines, could devote their attention to watching over the cybernetic specialists, whose sole task would be to increase a production that, through a reversal of perspective, will have ceased to be the priority sector, so as to serve the priority of life over survival.

22

Unitary power strove to dissolve individual existence in a collective consciousness in such a way that each social unit subjectively defined itself as a particle with a clearly determined weight suspended as though in oil. Everyone had to feel overwhelmed by the omnipresent evidence that everything was mere raw material in the hands of God, who used it for his own purposes, which were naturally beyond individual human comprehension. All phenomena were emanations of a supreme will; any seemingly unexplainable perturbation was presumed to be a means toward some larger, hidden harmony (the Four Kingdoms, the Wheel of Fortune, trials sent by the gods). One can speak of a collective consciousness in the sense that it was simultaneously for each individual and for everyone: consciousness of myth and consciousness of particular-existence-within-myth. The power of the illusion was such that authentically lived life drew its meaning from what was not authentically lived. This is the reason for the priestly condemnation of life, the reduction of life to pure contingency, to sordid materiality, to vain appearance and to the lowest state of a transcendence that became increasingly degraded as it escaped mythical organization.

God was the guarantor of space and time, whose coordinates defined unitary society. He was the common reference point for all mankind; space and time came together in him just as in him all beings became one with their destiny. In the era of fragmentation, man is torn between a time and a space that no transcendence can unify through the mediation of any centralized power. We are living in a space-time that is out of joint, deprived of any reference point or coordinate, as though we were never going to be able to come into contact with ourselves, although everything invites us to.

There is a place where you create yourself and a time in which you play yourself. The space of everyday life, of our true realization, is encircled by every form of conditioning. The narrow space of our true realization defines us, yet we define ourselves in the time of the spectacle. To put it another way: our consciousness is no longer consciousness of myth and of particular-*being*-within-myth, but rather consciousness of the spectacle and of particular-*role*-within-the-spectacle. (I pointed out above the relationship between all ontology and unitary power; it should be recalled here that the crisis of ontology appears with the movement toward fragmentation.) Or to put it yet another way: in the space-time relation in which everyone and everything is situated, time has become the imaginary (the field of identifications); space defines us, although we define ourselves in the imaginary and although the imaginary defines us *qua* subjectivities.

Our freedom is that of an abstract temporality in which we are *named* in the language of power (these names being the roles assigned to us), our only margin of choice being limited to finding officially accepted *synonyms* for ourselves. In contrast, the space of our authentic realization (the space of our everyday life) is under the dominion of silence. There is no name to name the space of lived experience except in poetry—in language liberating itself from the domination of power.

23

By desacralizing and fragmenting myth, the bourgeoisie was led to demand first of all independence of consciousness (demands for freedom of thought, freedom of the press, freedom of research, rejection of dogma). Consciousness thus ceased being more or less consciousness-reflecting-myth, and became consciousness of successive roles played within the spectacle. What the bourgeoisie demanded above all was the freedom of actors and extras in a spectacle no longer organized by God, his cops, and his priests, but by natural and economic laws, "capricious and inexorable laws" defended by a new team of cops and specialists.

God has been torn off like a useless bandage and the wound has stayed raw. The bandage may have prevented the wound from healing, but it justified suffering, it gave it a meaning well worth a few shots of morphine. Now suffering has no justification whatsoever and morphine is far from cheap. Separation has become concrete. Anyone at all can put their finger on it, and the only answer cybernetic society has to offer us is to become spectators of the gangrene and decay, spectators of survival.

The drama of consciousness to which Hegel referred is actually the consciousness of drama. Romanticism resounds like the cry of the soul torn from the body, a suffering all the more acute as each of us finds himself alone in facing the fall of the sacred totality and of all the Houses of Usher.

24

The totality is objective reality, in the movement of which subjectivity can participate only in the form of realization. Anything separate from the realization of everyday life rejoins the spectacle—a hibernation in which survival is frozen and served out in slices. There can be no authentic realization except in objective reality, in the totality. Anything else is a farce. The objective realization that functions within the mechanism of the spectacle is nothing but the success of power-manipulated objects (the "objective realization in subjectivity" of famous artists, stars, personalities of *Who's Who*). On the level of the organization of appearances, every success—and even every failure—is inflated until it becomes a stereotype, which is then broadcast as though it were the only possible success or failure. So far power has been the only judge, though its judgment has been subjected to various pressures. Its criteria are the only valid ones for those who accept the spectacle and are satisfied to play a role in it. But there are no more artists on that stage, there are only extras.

25

The space-time of private life was harmonized in the space-time of myth. Fourier's harmony responds to this perverted harmony. As soon as myth no longer encompasses the individual and the partial in a totality dominated by the sacred, each fragment sets itself up as a totality. The fragment set up as a totality is, in fact, the totalitarian. In the dissociated space-time that constitutes private life, time—made absolute in the form of abstract freedom, the freedom of the spectacle—consolidates by its very dissociation the spatial absolute of private life, its isolation, its constriction. The mechanism of the alienating spectacle wields such force that private life reaches the point of being defined as that which is deprived of spectacles: the fact that someone escapes roles and spectacular categories is felt as an additional deprivation, a distressful feeling which power uses as a pretext to reduce everyday life to insignificant gestures (sitting down, washing, opening a door).

26

The spectacle that imposes its norms on lived experience itself arises out of lived experience. Spectacular time, lived in the form of successive roles, makes the space of authentic experience the area of objective powerlessness, while at the same time the objective powerlessness that stems from the conditioning of private appropriation makes the spectacle the ultimate of potential freedom.

Elements born of lived experience are acknowledged only on the level of the spectacle, where they are expressed in the form of stereotypes, although such expression is constantly contested and refuted in and by lived experience. The composite portrait of the survivors—those whom Nietzsche referred to as the "small ones" or the "last men"—can be conceived only in terms of the following dialectic of possibility/impossibility:

(a) Possibility on the level of the spectacle (variety of abstract roles) reinforces impossibility on the level of authentic experience.

(b) Impossibility (that is, limits imposed on real experience by private appropriation) determines the field of abstract possibilities.

Survival is two-dimensional. Against such a reduction, what forces can bring out what constitutes the daily problem of all human beings: the dialectic of survival and life? Either the specific forces the SI has counted on will make possible the supersession of these contraries, reuniting space and time in the construction of everyday life; or life and survival will become locked in an antagonism growing weaker and weaker until the point of ultimate confusion and ultimate poverty is reached.

27

Lived reality is spectacularly fragmented and labeled in biological, sociological, or other categories which, while being related to the communicable, never communicate anything but facts emptied of their authentically lived content. It is in this sense that hierarchical power, imprisoning everyone in the objective mechanism of private appropriation (admission/exclusion, see section #3), is also a dictatorship over subjectivity. It is as a dictator over subjectivity that it strives, with limited success, to force each individual subjectivity to become objectified, that is, to become an object it can manipulate. This extremely interesting dialectic should be analyzed in greater detail (objective realization in subjectivity—the realization of power—and objective realization in objectivity—which enters into the praxis of constructing everyday life and destroying power).

Facts are deprived of content in the name of the communicable, in the name of an abstract universality, in the name of a perverted harmony in which everyone realizes himself in an inverted perspective. In this context the SI is in the line of contestation that runs through Sade, Fourier, Lewis Carroll, Lautréamont, Surrealism, and Lettrism— at least in its least-known currents, which were the most extreme.

Within a fragment set up as a totality, each further fragment is itself totalitarian. Individualism treated sensitivity, desire, will, intelligence, good taste, the subconscious, and all the categories of the ego as absolutes. Today sociology is enriching the categories of psychology, but the introduction of variety into the roles merely accentuates the monotony of the identification reflex. The freedom of the "survivor" will be to assume the abstract constituent to which he has "chosen" to reduce himself. Once any real fulfillment has been put out of the picture, all that remains is a psycho-sociological dramaturgy in which interiority functions as a safety valve to drain off the effects one has worn for the daily exhibition. Survival becomes the ultimate stage of life organized as the mechanical reproduction of memory.

28

Until now the approach to the totality has been falsified. Power has parasitically interposed itself as an indispensable mediation between man and nature. But the relation between man and nature is based only on praxis. It is praxis which constantly breaks through the coherent veneer of lies that myth and its replacements try to maintain. It is praxis, even alienated praxis, which maintains contact with the totality. By revealing its own fragmentary character, praxis at the same time reveals the real totality (reality): it is the totality being realized by way of its opposite, the fragment.

In the perspective of praxis, every fragment is totality. In the perspective of power, which alienates praxis, every fragment is totalitarian. This should be enough to wreck the attempts that cybernetic power will make to envelop praxis in a mystique, although the seriousness of these attempts should not be underestimated.

All forms of praxis enter our project. They enter with their share of alienation, with the impurities of power; but we are capable of filtering them. We will elucidate the force and purity of acts of refusal as well as the manipulative maneuvers of power, not in a Manichean perspective, but as a means of developing, through our own strategy, this combat in which everywhere, at every moment, the adversaries are seeking to come to grips with one another but only clashing accidentally, lost in irremediable darkness and uncertainty.

29

Everyday life has always been drained to the advantage of apparent life, but appearance, in its mythical cohesion, was powerful enough to repress any mention of everyday life. The poverty and emptiness of the spectacle, revealed by all the varieties of capitalism and all the varieties of bourgeoisie, has revealed both the existence of everyday life (a shelter life, but a shelter for what and from what?) and the poverty of everyday life. As reification and bureaucratization grow stronger, the debility of the spectacle and of everyday life is the only thing that remains clear. The conflict between the human and the inhuman has been transferred to the plane of appearances. As soon as Marxism became an ideology, Marx's struggle against ideology in the name of the richness of life was transformed into an ideological anti-ideology, an antispectacle spectacle. (Just as in avant-garde culture the antispectacular spectacle is restricted to actors alone, antiartistic art being created and understood only by artists, so the relationship between this ideological anti-ideology and the function of the professional revolutionary in Leninism should be examined.) Manicheanism has thus found itself momentarily revived. Why did St. Augustine attack the Manicheans so relentlessly? It was because he recognized the danger of a myth offering only one solution, the victory of good over evil; he saw that the impossibility of such a solution threatened to provoke the collapse of all mythical structures and bring into the open the contradiction between mythical and authentic life. Christianity offered a third way, the way of sacred confusion. What Christianity accomplished through the force of myth is accomplished today through the force of things. There can no longer be any antagonism between Soviet workers and capitalist workers or between the bomb of the Stalinist bureaucrats and the bomb of the non-Stalinist bureaucrats; there is no longer anything but unity in the chaos of reified beings.

Who is responsible? Who should be shot? We are dominated by a system, by an abstract form. Degrees of humanity and inhumanity are measured by purely quantitative variations of passivity. The quality is the same everywhere: we are all proletarianized or well on the way to becoming so. What are the traditional "revolutionaries" doing? They are struggling to eliminate certain distinctions, making sure that no proletarians are any more proletarian than all the others. But what party is calling for the end of the proletariat?

The perspective of survival has become intolerable. What is weighing us down is *the weight of things in a vacuum*. That's what reification is: everyone and everything falling at an equal speed, everyone and everything stigmatized with an equal value. The reign of equal values has realized the Christian project, but it has realized it outside Christianity (as Pascal surmised) and more importantly, it has realized it over God's dead body (contrary to Pascal's expectations).

The spectacle and everyday life coexist in the reign of equal values. People and things are interchangeable. The world of reification is a world without a center, like the new prefabricated cities that are its decor. The present fades away before the promise of an eternal future that is nothing but a mechanical extension of the past. Time itself is deprived of a center. In this concentration-camp world, victims and torturers wear the same mask and only the torture is real. No new ideology can soothe the pain, neither the ideology of the totality (Logos) nor that of nihilism—which will be the two crutches of the cybernetic society. The tortures condemn all hierarchical power, however organized or dissimulated it may be. The antagonism the SI is going to revive is the oldest of all, it is radical antagonism and that is why it is taking up again and assimilating all that has been left by the insurrectionary movements and great individuals in the course of history.

30

So many other banalities could be examined and reversed. The best things never come to an end. Before rereading this text (which even the most mediocre intelligence will be able to understand by the third attempt) the reader would be well advised to pay particular attention to the following points—points as fragmentary as the preceding ones, but which must be discussed in detail and implemented. They concern a central question: the SI and revolutionary power.

Being aware of the crises of both mass parties and "elites," the SI must embody the supersession of both the Bolshevik Central Committee (supersession of the mass party) and of the Nietzschean project (supersession of the intelligentsia).

> (a) Every time a power has presented itself as directing a revolutionary upsurge, it has automatically undermined the power of the revolution. The Bolshevik Central Committee defined itself simultaneously as concentration and as representation. Concentration of a power antagonistic to bourgeois power and representation of the will of the masses. This duality led it rapidly to become no more than an empty power, a power of empty representation, and consequently to merge into a common form (bureaucracy) with a bourgeois power that was being pressured (by the Bolshevik threat) into following a similar evolution. The conditions for a concentrated power and mass representation

exist potentially in the SI when it notes that it possesses the qualitative and that its ideas are in everyone's mind. Nevertheless we refuse both concentrated power and the right of representation, conscious that we are now taking the only *public attitude* (for we cannot avoid being known to some extent in a spectacular manner) enabling those who find that they share our theoretical and practical positions to accede to revolutionary power: power without mediation, power entailing the direct action of everyone. Our guiding image could be the Durruti Column, moving from town to village, liquidating the bourgeois elements and leaving the workers to see to their own self-organization.*

(b) The intelligentsia is power's hall of mirrors. Opposing power, it never offers anything but passive cathartic identification to those whose every gesture gropingly expresses real opposition. The radicalism—not of theory, obviously, but of gesture—that could be glimpsed in the "Declaration of the 121,"* however, suggests some different possibilities. We are capable of precipitating this crisis, but we can do so only by entering the intelligentsia as a power against the intelligentsia. This phase—which must precede and be contained within the phase described in paragraph (a)—will put us in the perspective of the Nietzschean project. We will form a small, almost alchemical, experimental group within which the realization of the total man can be started. Nietzsche could conceive of such an undertaking only within the framework of the hierarchical principle. It is, in fact, within such a framework that we find ourselves. It is therefore of the utmost importance that we present ourselves without the slightest ambiguity (at the group level, the purification of the nucleus and the elimination of residues now seems to be completed). We accept the hierarchical framework in which we are placed only while impatiently working to abolish our domination over those whom we cannot avoid dominating on the basis of our criteria for mutual recognition.

(c) Tactically our communication should be a diffusion emanating from a more or less hidden center. We will establish nonmaterialized networks (direct relationships, episodic ones, contacts without ties, development of embryonic relations based on affinity and understanding, in the manner of the red agitators before the arrival of revolutionary armies). We will claim radical gestures (actions, writings, political attitudes, works) as our own by analyzing them, and we will consider that our own acts and analyses are supported by the majority of people.

Just as God constituted the reference point of past unitary society, we are preparing to create the central reference point for a new unitary society now possible. But this point cannot be fixed. As opposed to the ever-renewed confusion that cybernetic power draws from the inhuman past, it stands for the game that everyone will play, "the moving order of the future."

RAOUL VANEIGEM

Situationist International
Anti–Public Relations Notice

So you agree with the SI!

You want to join the SI!

We only ask of you a little preliminary work, to verify objectively (in your own interest as well as ours) how close you are to our concerns and your ability to participate fully in our undertaking. (*The SI does not want mere disciples.*)

1. Choose for yourself a point in the theses published by the SI that you consider important and develop some arguments and possible expansions of it. (Minimum one page typescript; no maximum.)

2. Choose for yourself, out of the same texts published by the SI, a point that can be criticized and destroy that position. (Same conditions.)

NOTE: This is not a meaningless game. The SI often proceeds like this in order to reexamine its own bases and develop new ideas. Perhaps you will chance on a point already criticized. But you might also initiate an appropriate critique of a position insufficiently questioned by us until now. Thus your critique, if it is well done, will be valid in any case; and it may even be useful in bringing up something new!

Now, the SI

"Each era forges its own human material, and if our era really needed theoretical works it would itself create the forces necessary for its satisfaction."
                        —Rosa Luxemburg, in *Vorwärts* (14 March 1903)

Now that the situationists already have a history and their activity has
carved out a very particular but undeniably central role for itself in the
cultural debates of the last few years, some people reproach the SI for
having succeeded and others reproach it for having failed.

In order to understand the real significance of these terms, as well
as almost all the intellectual establishment's judgments concerning
the SI, it is first necessary to *reverse* them. The SI's element of failure is
what is commonly considered to be its success—the artistic value that
is beginning to be appreciated in us; the fact that certain of our theses
have come to be sociologically or urbanistically fashionable; or simply
the personal success that is virtually guaranteed to any situationist
the moment he is excluded from the SI. Our element of success, which
is more profound, is the fact that we have resisted the mass of compromises that we have been offered; the fact that we have not clung to
our original pilot program but have proved that its main avant-garde
feature, in spite of some other more apparent ones, lay in the fact that
it had to lead further; and the fact that we have thus far been refused any
recognition within the established framework of the present order.

We have undoubtedly made many mistakes. We have often corrected or abandoned these mistakes, although it was precisely among them
that were found the elements which were succeeding or for which the
greatest aid was offered to bring them to fruition. It is easy to note the
shortcomings in our earliest publications—the extravagant verbiage,
the fantasies left over from the old artistic milieu, the holdovers from
the old politics; it is, moreover, in the light of the SI's later conclusions
that these earlier shortcomings are most easily criticizable. An inverse
factor has naturally left less trace in our writings, but has weighed
heavily on us: a nihilist abstentionism, a serious inability among many
of us to think and act beyond the first stammerings of positive dialogue. This lack is almost always accompanied by the most abstract
and pretentious insistence on a disembodied radicalism.

There is, however, a deviation that has threatened us more gravely than all the others: it was the risk of not differentiating ourselves
clearly enough from the *modern* tendencies of explanations and pro-

posals regarding the new society to which capitalism has brought us—tendencies which, behind different masks, all lead to integration into this society. Since Constant's interpretation of unitary urbanism this tendency has been expressed within the SI, and it is vastly more dangerous than the old artistic conception we have fought so much. It is more modern and therefore less obvious, and it certainly has a more promising future. Our project has taken shape at the *same time* as the modern tendencies toward integration. There is thus not only a direct opposition between them but also an air of resemblance, since the two sides are really contemporaneous. We have not paid enough attention to this aspect, even recently. Thus, it is not impossible to interpret Alexander Trocchi's proposals* in issue #8 of this journal as having some affinity—despite their obviously completely contrary spirit—with those pitiful attempts at a "psychodramatic" salvaging of decomposed art expressed for example by the ridiculous "Workshop of Free Expression" in Paris last May. But the point we have arrived at clarifies both our project and, inversely, the project of integration. All really modern nonrevolutionary ventures must now be recognized and treated as our number-one enemy. They are going to reinforce all existing controls.

We must not for all that abandon the extreme point of the modern world merely so as to avoid resembling it in any way, or even in order not to teach it anything that could be used against us. It is quite natural that our enemies succeed in partially using us. We are neither going to leave the present field of culture to them nor mix with them. The armchair advisors who want to admire and understand us from a respectful distance readily recommend to us the purity of the first attitude while they themselves adopt the second one. We reject this suspect formalism: like the proletariat, we cannot claim to be unexploitable under the present conditions; the best we can do is to strive to make any such exploitation entail the greatest possible risk for the exploiters. The SI has taken a clear stand as an alternative to the dominant culture, and particularly to its so-called avant-garde forms. The situationists consider that they must inherit and supersede art (which is dead) and separate philosophical reflection (whose corpse no one, despite all the present efforts, will succeed in "reviving") because the *spectacle* that is replacing this art and this thought is itself the heir of *religion*. And like the "critique of religion" in Marx's day (a critique that the present Left abandoned at the same time it abandoned all thought and action), the critique of the spectacle is today the essential precondition for any critique.*

The path of total police-state control over all human activities and the path of unlimited free creation of all human activities are one: it is the same path of modern discoveries. We are necessarily on the same path as our enemies—most often preceding them—but we must be there, without any confusion, as enemies. The best player will win.

The present era can test innumerable innovations, but it is incapable of putting them to good use because it is chained to the fundamental conservation of an old order. Over and over, in all our innovating formulations, we must stress the need for a revolutionary transformation of society.

The revolutionary critique of all existing conditions does not, to be sure, have a monopoly on intelligence; it only has a monopoly on its use. In the present cultural and social crisis, those who do not know how to use their intelligence have in fact no discernable intelligence of any kind. Stop talking to us about unused intelligence and you'll make us happy. Poor Heidegger! Poor Lukács! Poor Sartre! Poor Barthes! Poor Lefebvre! Poor Cardan! Tics, tics, and tics.* Lacking the method for using their intelligence, they end up with nothing but caricatural fragments of the innovating ideas that can simultaneously comprehend and contest the totality of our era. They are not only incapable of developing ideas, they don't even know how to skillfully plagiarize ideas developed by others. Once the specialized thinkers step out of their own domain, they can only be the dumbfounded spectators of some neighboring and equally bankrupt specialization of which they were previously ignorant but which has become fashionable. The former specialist of ultraleftist politics [Cardan] is awestruck at discovering, along with structuralism and social psychology, an ethnological *ideology* completely new to him: the fact that the Zuni Indians did not have any history appears to him as a luminous explanation for his own inability to act in our history. (Go laugh at the first twenty-five pages of *Socialisme ou Barbarie* #36.) The specialists of thought can no longer be anything but thinkers of specialization. We don't claim to have a monopoly on the dialectics that everyone talks about; we only claim to have a temporary monopoly on its use.

Some people still venture to object to our theories by gravely insisting on the necessity of practice, although those who speak at this level of methodological delirium have abundantly revealed their own inability to carry out the slightest practice. When revolutionary theory reappears in our time and can count only on itself to propagate itself *through a new practice,* it seems to us that this is already an important beginning of practice. This theory is at the outset caught in the framework of the new educated ignorance propagated by the present society, and is much more radically cut off from the masses than it was in the nineteenth century. We naturally share its isolation, its risks, and its fate.

To approach us one should therefore not already be compromised, and should be aware that even if we may be momentarily mistaken on many minor points, we will never admit having been mistaken in our *negative* judgment of persons. Our qualitative criteria are much too certain for us to debate them. There is no point in approaching us if one is not theoretically and practically in agreement with our condemnations of contemporary persons or currents. Some of the thinkers who are now going to plan and justify modern society have already justified and *ultimately conserved* more archaic forms of it when they were, for example, Stalinists. Now, without batting an eye, they are going to reenlist, just as coolly and cheerily as before, for a second debacle. Others, who fought them during the preceding phase, are now joining them in a common celebration of innovation. All the specializations of illusion can be taught and discussed by the tenured thinkers. But the situationists take their stand in the knowledge that is outside this spectacle: we are not thinkers sponsored by the state.

We have to organize a coherent encounter between the elements of critique and negation (whether as acts or as ideas) that are now scattered around the world; and between these critical and negative elements that have become conscious and the entire life of the bearers of them; and finally, between the people or the first groups that are at this level of intellectual knowledge and practical contestation. The coordination of these researches and struggles on the most practical plane (a new international linkup) is now inseparable from a coordination on the most theoretical plane (which will be expressed by several works presently being prepared by some of the situationists). For example, the present issue of this journal, in order to better elucidate certain aspects of our theses that have sometimes been presented too abstractly, gives a large place to a coherent presentation of items drawn from the ordinary daily news. The continuation of our projects will have to be expressed in fuller forms. This continuation will considerably exceed what we would have been able to undertake by ourselves.

While contemporary impotence blathers on about the belated project of "getting into the twentieth century," we think it is high time to eliminate the *dead time* that has dominated this century and to put an end to the Christian Era with the same stroke. Here as elsewhere, the road of excess leads to the palace of wisdom. Ours is the best effort so far toward *getting out of the twentieth century.*

Questionnaire

1. What does the word "situationist" mean?

It denotes an activity aimed at *creating* situations, as opposed to passively *recognizing* them in academic or other separate terms. At all levels of social practice or individual history. We replace existential passivity with the construction of moments of life, and doubt with playful affirmation. Up till the present philosophers and artists have only interpreted situations; the point now is to transform them. Since human beings are molded by the situations they go through, it is essential to create human situations. Since individuals are defined by their situation, they need the power to create situations worthy of their desires. This is the perspective in which poetry (communication fulfilled in concrete situations), the appropriation of nature, and complete social liberation must all merge and be realized. Our era is going to replace the fixed frontier of the extreme situations that phenomenology has limited itself to describing with the practical creation of situations; it is going to continually shift this frontier with the development of our realization. We want a phenomeno-praxis. We have no doubt that this will be the first banality of the movement toward the liberation that is now possible. What situations are to be transformed? At different levels it could be the whole planet, or an era (a civilization in Burckhardt's sense, for example), or a moment of individual life. On with the show! It is only in this way that the values of past culture and the hopes of realizing reason in history can find their true fulfillment. Everything else is in decay. The term situationist in the SI's sense is the total opposite of the current usage in Portugal, where "situationists" means supporters of the existing situation (i.e. supporters of Salazar's dictatorship).

2. Is the Situationist International a political movement?

The words "political movement" today connote the specialized activity of group and party bosses who derive the oppressive force of their future power from the organized passivity of their militants. The SI wants nothing to do with any form of hierarchical power whatsoever. The SI is neither a political movement nor a sociology of political mystification. The SI aims to represent the highest degree of international revolutionary consciousness. This is why it strives to illuminate and coordinate the gestures of refusal and the signs of creativity that are defining the new contours of the proletariat, the irreducible desire for freedom. Centered on the spontaneity of the masses, such activity is undeniably "political" in the sense that those rebellious masses are themselves political. Whenever new radical currents appear—as recently in Japan (the extremist wing of the Zengakuren), in the Congo, and in the Spanish underground—the SI gives them *critical* support* and thereby aids them practically. But in contrast to all the "transitional programs" of specialized politics, the SI insists on a permanent revolution of everyday life.

3. Is the SI an artistic movement?

A large part of the situationist critique of consumer society consists of showing to what extent contemporary artists, by abandoning the richness of supersession implicitly present (though not fully realized) in the 1910–1925 period, have condemned themselves to doing art as one does business. Since that time artistic movements have only been imaginary repercussions from an explosion that never took place, an explosion that threatened and still threatens the structures of this society. The SI's awareness of this abandonment and of its contradictory implications (emptiness and a desire to return to the initial violence) makes the SI the only movement able, by incorporating the survival of art into the art of life, to speak to the project of the authentic artist. We are artists only insofar as we are no longer artists: we come to fulfill art.

4. Is the SI an expression of nihilism?

The SI refuses the role that would be readily granted it in the spectacle of decomposition. The supersession of nihilism is reached by way of the decomposition of the spectacle; which is precisely what the SI is working on. Whatever is elaborated and constructed outside such a perspective will collapse of its own dead weight without needing any help from the SI. But it is also true that everywhere in consumer society wastelands of spontaneous collapse are offering a terrain of experimentation for new values that the SI cannot do without. We can build only on the ruins of the spectacle. Moreover, the fully justified anticipation of a total destruction precludes any construction that is not carried out in the perspective of the totality.

5. Are the situationist positions utopian?

Reality is superseding utopia. There is no longer any point in projecting imaginary bridges between the wealth of present technological potentials and the poverty of their use by the rulers of every variety. We want to put the material equipment at the service of everyone's creativity, as the masses themselves always strive to do in revolutionary situations. It's simply a matter of coordination or tactics. Everything we deal with is realizable, either immediately or in the short term, once our methods of research and activity begin to be put in practice.

6. Do you consider it necessary to call yourselves "situationists"?

In the existing order, where things take the place of people, any label is compromising. The one we have chosen, however, embodies its own critique, in that it is automatically opposed to any "situationism," the label that others would like to saddle us with. Moreover, it will disappear when all of us have become fully situationist and are no longer proletarians struggling for the end of the proletariat. For the moment, however ridiculous a label may be, ours has the merit of drawing a sharp line between the previous incoherence and a new level of rigor. Such incisiveness is just what has been most lacking in the thought of the last few decades.

7. What is original about the situationists, considered as a distinct group?

It seems to us that three notable points justify the importance that we attribute to ourselves as an organized group of theorists and experimenters. First, we are developing for the first time, from a revolutionary perspective, a new, coherent critique of this society as it is developing *now*. This critique is deeply anchored in the culture and art of our time, which can in fact be truly grasped only by means of such a critique (this work is obviously a long way from completion). Second, we make a practice of breaking completely and definitively with all those who oblige us to do so, and with anyone else who remains in solidarity with them. Such polarization is vital in a time when the various forms of resignation are so subtly intertwined and interdependent. Third, we are initiating a new style of relation with our "partisans": we absolutely refuse disciples. We are interested only in participation at the highest level, and in setting autonomous people loose in the world.

8. Why don't people talk about the SI?

The SI is talked about often enough among the specialized owners of decomposing modern thought; but they write about it very little. In the broadest sense this is because we refuse the term "situationism," which would be the only pigeonhole enabling us to be introduced into the reigning spectacle, incorporated in the form of a doctrine petrified against us, in the form of an ideology in Marx's sense. It is natural that the spectacle we reject rejects us in turn. Situationists are more readily discussed as individuals in an effort to separate them from the collective contestation, although this collective contestation is in fact the only thing that makes them "interesting" individuals. Situationists are talked about *the moment they cease to be situationists* (as with the rival varieties of "Nashism" in several countries, whose only common claim to fame is that they lyingly pretend to have some sort of relationship with the SI). The spectacle's watchdogs appropriate fragments of situationist theory without acknowledgment in order to turn it against us. It is quite natural that they get ideas from us in their struggle for the survival of the spectacle. But they have to conceal their source, not merely to protect their reputation for originality from charges of plagiarism, but because this source implies the broader, coherent context of these "ideas." Moreover, many hesitant intellectuals do not dare to speak openly of the SI because to speak of it entails taking a minimum position—saying what one rejects of it and what one accepts of it. Many of them believe, quite mistakenly, that to feign ignorance of it in the meantime will suffice to clear them of responsibility later.

9. What support do you give to the revolutionary movement?

Unfortunately there isn't one. This society certainly contains contradictions and is undergoing changes; this is what, in continually new ways, is making revolutionary activity possible and necessary. But such activity no longer exists—or does not yet exist—in the form of an organized movement. It is therefore not a matter of "supporting" such a movement, but of creating it: of inseparably defining it and experimenting with it. Admitting that there is no revolutionary movement is the first precondition for developing such a movement. Anything else is a ridiculous patching up of the past.

10. Are you Marxists?

Just as much as Marx was when he said, "I am not a Marxist."

11. Is there a relation between your theories and your actual way of life?

Our theories are nothing other than the theory of our real life and of the possibilities experienced or perceived in it. As fragmented as the available terrains of activity may be for the moment, we make the most of them. We treat enemies as enemies, a first step we recommend to everyone as an accelerated apprenticeship in learning how to think. It also goes without saying that we unconditionally support all forms of liberated behavior, everything that the bourgeois and bureaucratic scum call debauchery. It is obviously out of the question that we should pave the way for the revolution of everyday life with asceticism.

12. Are the situationists in the vanguard of leisure society?

Leisure society is an appearance that veils a particular type of production/consumption of social space-time. If the time of productive work in the strict sense is reduced, the reserve army of industrial life works in consumption. Everyone is successively worker and raw material in the industry of vacations, of leisure, of spectacles. Present work is the alpha and omega of present life. The organization of consumption plus the organization of leisure must exactly counterbalance the organization of work. "Free time" is a most ironic quantity in the context of the flow of a prefabricated time. Alienated work can only produce alienated leisure, for the idle (increasingly, in fact, merely semi-idle) elite as well as for the masses who are obtaining access to brief periods of leisure. No lead shielding can insulate either a fragment of time or the entire time of a fragment of society from the radiation of alienated labor, because that labor shapes the totality of products and of social life in its own image.

13. Who finances you?

We have never been able to be financed except, in a very precarious manner, by working in the present cultural economy. This employment is subject to the following contradiction: we have such creative abilities that we can be virtually assured of "success" in any field; yet we have such a rigorous insistence on independence and complete consistency between our project and each of our present creations (see our definition of antisituationist artistic production)* that we are almost totally unacceptable to the dominant cultural organization, even in the most secondary activities. The state of our resources follows from these conditions. In this connection, see what we wrote in issue #8 of this journal (p. 26) about "the capital that is never lacking for Nashist enterprises" and, in contrast, *our conditions* (on the last page of this issue).*

14. How many of you are there?

A few more than the original guerrilla nucleus in the Sierra Madre, but with fewer weapons. A few less than the delegates in London in 1864 who founded the International Working Men's Association, but with a more coherent program. As unyielding as the Greeks at Thermopylae ("Passerby, go tell them at Lakedaimon . . ."), but with a brighter future.*

15. What value can you attribute to a questionnaire? To this one?

Questionnaires are an obvious form of the pseudodialogue that is becoming obsessively used in all the psychotechniques of integration into the spectacle so as to elicit people's gleeful acceptance of passivity under the crude guise of "participation" and pseudoactivity. Taking such an incoherent, reified form of questioning as a point of departure, however, enables us to express precise positions. These positions are not really "answers," because they don't stick to the questions; they reply by posing new questions that supersede the old ones. Thus, real dialogue could begin after these responses. In the present questionnaire all the questions are *false*; our responses, however, are true.

Response to a Questionnaire
from the
Center for Socio-Experimental Art

1. Why are the masses not concerned with art? Why does art remain the privilege of certain educated sectors of the bourgeois class?

The importance of the theme of the present questionnaire and the limited space allotted for answers oblige us to be somewhat schematic. The situationists' positions on these topics have been elaborated in more detail in the SI's journals (*Internationale Situationniste, Der Deutsche Gedanke,* and *Situationistisk Revolution*)* and in the catalog published on the occasion of the "Destruction of RSG 6" demonstration in Denmark last June ["The Situationists and the New Forms of Action in Politics and Art"].

The masses, i.e. the nonruling classes, have no reason to feel concerned with any aspects of a culture or an organization of social life that have not only been developed without their participation or their control, but that have in fact been deliberately designed to prevent such participation and control. They are concerned (illusorily) only with the by-products specifically produced for their consumption: the diverse forms of spectacular publicity and propaganda in favor of various products or role models.

This does not mean, however, that art subsists merely as a "privilege" of the bourgeois class. In the past every dominant class had its own art—for the same reasons that a classless society will have none, will be beyond artistic practice. But the historical conditions of our time, associated with a major breakthrough in humanity's appropriation of nature and thus bearing the concrete project of a classless society, are such that major art in this period has necessarily been revolutionary. What has been called modern art, from its origins in the nineteenth century to its full development in the first third of the twentieth, has been an *anti-bourgeois* art. The present crisis of art is linked to the crisis of the workers movement since the defeat of the Russian revolution and the modernization of capitalism.

Today a *fake* continuation of modern art (formal repetitions attractively packaged and publicized, completely divorced from the original combativeness of their models) along with a voracious consumption of bits and pieces of previous cultures completely divorced from their real meaning (Malraux,* previously their most ludicrous salesman in the realm of "theory," is now exhibiting them in his "Culture Centers") are what actually constitute the dubious "privilege" of the new stratum of intellectual workers that proliferates with the development of the "tertiary sector" of the economy. This sector is closely connected to that of the social *spectacle:* this intellectual stratum (the requirements of whose training and employment explain both the quantitative extension of education and its qualitative degradation) is both the most direct producer of the spectacle and the most direct consumer of its specifically cultural elements.

Two tendencies seem to us to typify the contemporary cultural consumption offered to this public of alienated intellectual workers:

On one hand, endeavors such as the "Visual Art Research Group" clearly tend toward the integration of the population into the dominant socioeconomic system, along the lines currently being worked out by repressive urbanism and the theorists of cybernetic control. Through a veritable parody of the revolutionary theses on putting an end to the passivity of separated spectators through the *construction of situations,* this "Visual Art" group strives to make the spectators participate in their own impoverishment—taking its lack of dialectics to the point of "liberating" the spectator by announcing that it is "forbidden not to participate" (tract at the Third Paris Biennial).

On the other hand, "New Realism," drawing heavily on the form of dadaism (but not its spirit), is an *apologetic* junk art. It fits quite well into the margin of pseudofreedom offered by a society of gadgets and waste.

But the importance of such artists remains very secondary, even in comparison with advertising. Thus, paradoxically, the "Socialist Realism" of the Eastern bloc, which is not art at all, nevertheless has a more decisive social function. This is because in the East power is maintained primarily by selling ideology (i.e. mystifying justifications), while in the West it is maintained by selling consumer goods. The fact that the Eastern bureaucracy has proved incapable of developing its own art, and has been forced to adapt the forms of the pseudoartistic vision of petty-bourgeois conformists of the last century (in spite of the inherent ineffectuality of those forms), confirms the present impossibility of any art as a ruling-class "privilege."

Nevertheless, all art is "social" in the sense that it has its roots in a given society and even despite itself must have some relation to the prevailing conditions, or to their negation. Former moments of opposition survive fragmentarily and lose their artistic (or postartistic) value to the precise extent they have lost their oppositional core. With their loss of this core they have also lost any reference to the mass of postartistic acts (of revolt and of free reconstruction of life) that already exist in the world and that are tending to replace art. This fragmentary opposition can then only withdraw to an aesthetic position and harden rapidly into a dated and ineffectual aesthetic *in a world where it is already too late for aesthetics*—as has happened with surrealism, for example. Other movements are typical of degraded bourgeois mysticism (art as substitute for religion). They reproduce—but only in the form of solitary fantasy or idealist pretension—the forces that dominate present social life both officially and in fact: noncommunication, bluff, frantic desire for novelty as such, for the rapid turnover of arbitrary and uninteresting gadgets—Lettrism, for example, on which subject we remarked that "Isou, product of an era of unconsumable art, has suppressed the very idea of its consumption" and that he has "proposed the first art of solipsism" (*Internationale Situationniste* #4).

Finally, the very proliferation of would-be artistic movements that are essentially indistinguishable from one another can be seen as an application of the modern sales technique of marketing the same product under rival trademarks.

2. How can art be really "social"?

The time for art is over. The point now is to realize art, to really create on every level of life everything that hitherto could only be an artistic memory or an illusion, dreamed and preserved unilaterally. Art can be realized *only by being suppressed*. However, in contrast to the present society, which suppresses art by replacing it with the automatic functioning of an even more passive and hierarchical spectacle, we maintain that art can really be suppressed *only by being realized*.

2. (cont.) Does the political society in which you live encourage or discourage your social function as an artist?

This society has suppressed what you call the social function of the artist.

If this question refers to the function of employees in the reigning *spectacle,* it is obvious that the number of jobs to be had there expands as the spectacle does. The situationists, however, do not find this employment opportunity the least bit attractive.

If, on the other hand, we take this question as referring to the *inheriting of previous art* through new types of activity, beginning with contestation of the whole society, the society in question naturally discourages such a practice.

3. Do you think your aesthetics would be different if you lived in a socially, politically, or economically different society?

Certainly. When our perspectives are realized, aesthetics (as well as its negation) will be superseded.

If we were presently living in an underdeveloped country or in a country subjected to archaic forms of domination (colonialism or a Franco-type dictatorship), we would agree that artists can to a certain extent participate as such in popular struggles. In a context of general social and cultural backwardness the social function of the artist still retains a certain significance, and a not entirely sham communication is still possible within the traditional forms.

If we were living in a country governed by a "socialist" bureaucracy, where information about cultural and other experimentation in the advanced industrialized countries over the last fifty years is systematically suppressed, we would certainly support the minimum demand for dissemination of truth, including the truth about contemporary Western art. We would do this despite the inevitable ambiguity of such a demand, since the history of modern art, though already accessible and even glorified in the West, is nonetheless still profoundly falsified; and its importation into the Eastern bloc would first of all be exploited by hacks like Yevtushenko in their modernization of official art.

4. Do you participate in politics or not? Why?

Yes, but in only one kind: together with various other forces in the world, we are working toward the linking up and the theoretical and practical organization of a new revolutionary movement.

All the considerations we are developing here simultaneously demonstrate the need to go beyond the failures of previous specialized politics.

5. Does an association of artists seem necessary to you? What would be its objectives?

There are already numerous associations of artists, either without principles or based on one or another extravagant absurdity—mutual aid unions, mutual congratulation societies, alliances for collective careerism. Works that on the slightest pretext are proclaimed "collective projects" are fashionable at the moment, and are even put in the limelight at the pitiful Paris biennials, thus diverting attention from the real problems of the supersession of art. We regard all these associations with equal contempt and accept no contact whatsoever with this milieu.

We do believe that a coherent and disciplined association for the realization of a common program is possible on the bases worked out by the Situationist International, provided that the participants are so rigorously selected that they all demonstrate a high degree of creative originality, and that in a sense they cease to be "artists" or to consider themselves as artists in the old sense of the word.

It could in fact be questioned whether the situationists are artists at all, even avant-garde ones. Not only because almost everyone in the cultural scene resists acknowledging them as such (at least once the whole of the situationist program is involved) or because their interests extend far beyond the former scope of art. Their nature as artists is even more problematic on the socioeconomic level. Many situationists support themselves by rather dubious methods, ranging from historical research to poker, from bartending to running puppet theaters. It is striking that of the 28 members of the Situationist International whom we have had to exclude so far, 23 personally had a socially recognized and increasingly profitable role as artists: they were known as artists despite their membership in the SI. But as such they were tending to reinforce the position of our enemies, who want to invent a "situationism" so as to finish with us by integrating us into the spectacle as just one more doomsday aesthetic. Yet while doing this, these artists wanted to remain in the SI. This was unacceptable for us. The figures speak for themselves.

It goes without saying that any other "objectives" of any association of artists are of no interest to us, since we regard them as no longer having any point whatsoever.

6. How is the work you are presenting here related to these statements?

The enclosed work obviously cannot represent a "situationist art." Under the present distinctly antisituationist cultural conditions we have to resort to "communication containing its own critique," which we have experimented with in every accessible medium, from film to writing, and which we have theorized under the name of *détournement.* Since the Center for Socio-Experimental Art has limited its survey to the plastic arts, we have selected, from among the numerous possibilities of détournement as a means of agitation, Michèle Bernstein's antipainting *Victory of the Bonnot Gang.** It forms part of a series including *Victory of the Paris Commune, Victory of the Great Jacquerie of 1358, Victory of the Spanish Republicans, Victory of the Workers' Councils of Budapest,* and several other victories. Such paintings attempt to negate "Pop Art" (which is materially and "ideologically" characterized by *indifference* and dull complacency) by incorporating only *toy* objects and by making them meaningful in as heavy-handed a way as possible. In a sense this series carries on the tradition of the painting of battles; and also rectifies the history of revolts (which is not over) in a way that pleases us. It seems that each new attempt to transform the world is forced to start out with the appearance of a *new unrealism.*

We hope that our remarks here, both humorous and serious, will help to clarify our position on the present relationship between art and society.

For the Situationist International:
J.V. MARTIN, JAN STRIJBOSCH,
RAOUL VANEIGEM, RENÉ VIÉNET
6 December 1963

Address to Revolutionaries of Algeria and of All Countries

"Proletarian revolutions . . . pitilessly scoff at the hesitations, weaknesses, and inadequacies of their first efforts, seem to throw down their adversary only to see him draw new strength from the earth and rise again formidably before them, recoil again and again before the immensity of their tasks, until a situation is finally created that goes beyond the point of no return."
—Marx, *The Eighteenth Brumaire of Louis Bonaparte*

Comrades,

The collapse of the revolutionary image presented by the international Communist movement is taking place forty years after the collapse of the revolutionary movement itself. This time gained for the bureaucratic lie—that supplement to the continuing bourgeois lie—has been time lost for the revolution. The history of the modern world pursues its revolutionary course, but unconsciously or with false consciousness. Everywhere there are social confrontations, but nowhere is the old order destroyed, not even within the very forces that contest it. Everywhere the ideologies of the old world are criticized and rejected, but nowhere is "the real movement that suppresses existing conditions" liberated from one or another "ideology" in Marx's sense of the word: ideas that serve masters. Revolutionaries are everywhere, but nowhere is there any real revolution.

The recent collapse of the Ben-Bellaist image of a quasi-revolution in Algeria is a striking example of this general failure. The superficial power of Ben Bella represented the moment of rigid balance between the movement of the Algerian workers toward the management of the entire society and the bourgeois bureaucracy in the process of formation within the framework of the state. But in this official balance the revolution had nothing with which to further its objectives—it had already become a museum piece—whereas those in possession of the state controlled all power, beginning with that fundamental repressive instrument, the army, to the point of finally being able to throw off their mask, i.e. Ben Bella. Two days before the putsch, at Sidi Bel Abbes, Ben Bella added the ridiculous to the odious by declaring that Algeria was "more united than ever." Now he has stopped lying to the people and the events speak for themselves. Ben Bella fell as he had reigned, in solitude and conspiracy, by a *palace revolution*. He was ushered out by the same forces that had ushered him in: Boumédienne's army, which had opened the road to Algiers for him in September 1962. Ben Bella's regime ratified the revolutionary conquests that the bureaucracy was not yet able to repress: the self-management movement. The forces so well hidden behind the "Muslim Brother" Boumédienne have this clear goal: to eliminate all self-management. The June 19th Declaration sums up the policy of the new regime with a mixture of Western technocratic jargon and bombast about enforcing Islamic moral values: "We must put a stop to the current stagnation, which is already manifesting itself in lowered productivity, decreasing profitability, and a disturbing withdrawal of investments," while "keeping in mind our faith, our convictions, and the age-old traditions and moral values of our people."

The astonishing acceleration of practical demystification must now serve to accelerate revolutionary theory. The same society of alienation, of totalitarian control (here the sociologist predominates, there the police), and of spectacular consumption (here the cars and gadgets, there the words of the venerated leader) reigns everywhere, despite the diversity of its ideological and juridical disguises. The coherence of this society cannot be understood without an all-encompassing critique, illuminated by the inverse project of a liberated creativity, the project of everyone's control of all levels of their own history. This is the demand in acts of all proletarian revolutions, a demand until now defeated by the specialists of power who take over revolutions and turn them into their own private property.

To revive and bring into the present this *inseparable,* mutually illuminating project and critique means appropriating all the radicalism borne by the workers' movement, by modern Western poetry and art (as preface to an experimental research toward a free construction of everyday life), by the thought of the period of the supersession and realization of philosophy (Hegel, Feuerbach, Marx), and by the liberation struggles from the Mexico of 1910 to the Congo of today. To do this, it is first of all necessary to recognize, without holding on to any consoling illusions, the full extent of the defeat of the entire revolutionary project *in the first third of this century* and its official replacement, in every region of the world and in every domain of life, by delusive shams and petty reforms that camouflage and preserve the old order. The domination of bureaucratic state-capitalism over the workers is the opposite of socialism—this is a fact that Trotskyism has refused to face. Socialism exists wherever the workers themselves directly manage the entire society. It therefore exists neither in Russia nor in China nor anywhere else. The Russian and Chinese revolutions were defeated from within. Today they provide the Western proletariat and the peoples of the Third World with a false model which actually serves as a mere counterbalance to the power of bourgeois capitalism and imperialism.

A resumption of radicality naturally requires a considerable deepening of all the old attempts at liberation. Seeing how those attempts failed due to isolation, or were converted into total frauds, enables us to get a better grasp of the coherence of the world that needs to be changed. In the light of this rediscovered coherence, many of the partial explorations of the recent past can be salvaged and brought to their true fulfillment (the liberating content of psychoanalysis, for example, can be neither understood nor realized apart from the struggle for the abolition of all repression).* Insight into this reversible coherence of the world—its present reality in contrast to its potential reality—enables us to see the fallaciousness of half-measures and to recognize the presence of such half-measures each time the operating pattern of the dominant society—with its categories of hierarchization and specialization and its corresponding habits and tastes—reconstitutes itself within the forces of negation.

Moreover, the material development of the world has accelerated. It constantly accumulates more potential powers; but the specialists of the management of society, because of their role as guardians of passivity, are forced to ignore the possible use of those powers. This same development produces widespread dissatisfaction and objective mortal dangers which these specialized rulers are incapable of permanently controlling. The fundamental problem of underdevelopment must be resolved on a worldwide scale, beginning with the revolutionary overcoming of the irrational *overdevelopment* of productive forces in the framework of the various forms of rationalized capitalism. The revolutionary movements of the Third World can succeed only on the basis of a lucid contribution to global revolution. Development must not be a race to catch up with capitalist reification, but a satisfaction of all real needs as the basis for a genuine development of human faculties.

New revolutionary theory must move in step with reality, it must keep abreast with the revolutionary praxis which is starting up here and there but which yet remains partial, mutilated, and without a coherent total project. Our language, which will perhaps seem fantastical, is the very language of real life. History continues to present ever more glaring confirmations of this. If in this history the familiar is not necessarily known, it is because real life itself only appears in a fantastical form, in the upside-down image imposed on it by the modern *spectacle* of the world. In the spectacle all social life, including even the representation of sham revolutions, is written in the lying language of power and filtered by its machines. The spectacle is the terrestrial heir of religion, the opium of a capitalism that has arrived at the stage of a "society of abundance" of *commodities*. It is the illusion actually consumed in "consumer society."

The sporadic explosions of revolutionary contestation are countered by an international organization of repression, operating with a global division of tasks. Each of the blocs, or of the spinoff splinters of blocs, ensures the lethargic sleep of everyone within its sphere of influence, contributing toward maintaining a global order that remains fundamentally the same. This permanent repression ranges from military interventions to the more or less complete falsification practiced today by every constituted power. "The truth is revolutionary" (Gramsci) and all existing governments, even those stemming from the most liberatory movements, are based on lies inside and out. It is precisely this repression that constitutes the most resounding verification of our hypotheses.

Revolutionary endeavors of today, because they have to break all the rules of false understanding imposed by the "peaceful coexistence" of reigning lies, begin in *isolation,* in one particular sector of the world or in one particular sector of contestation. Possessing only the most rudimentary conceptions of freedom, they attack only the most immediate aspects of oppression. As a result, they meet with the minimum degree of aid and the maximum of repression and slander (they are accused of rejecting one existing order while necessarily approving of an existing variant of it). The more difficult their victory, the more easily it is confiscated by new oppressors. The next revolutions *can find aid in the world only by attacking this world as a whole.* The freedom movement of the American blacks, if it can assert itself incisively, will call into question all the contradictions of modern capitalism; it must not be sidetracked by the "black nationalism" and "black capitalism" of the Black Muslims. The workers of the United States, like those in England, are engaging in "wildcat strikes" against the bureaucratized unions that aim first of all at integrating them into the concentrated, semiregulated capitalist system. It is with these workers and with the students who have just won their strike at the University of California in Berkeley that a North American revolution can be made; and not with the Chinese atom bomb.

The movement drawing the Arab peoples toward unification and socialism has achieved a number of victories over classical colonialism. But it is more and more evident that it must finish with Islam, an obviously counterrevolutionary force as are all religious ideologies; it must grant freedom to the Kurdish people; and it must stop swallowing the Palestinian pretext that justifies the dominant policy in the Arab states—a policy that insists on the destruction of Israel and thereby perpetuates itself since this destruction is impossible. The repressive forces of the state of Israel can be undermined only by a *model of a revolutionary society realized by the Arabs*. Just as the success of a model of a revolutionary society somewhere in the world would mark the end of the largely sham confrontation between the East and the West, it would also mean the end of the Arab–Israel confrontation which is a miniature reproduction of it.

The revolutionary endeavors of today are *abandoned* to repression because it is not in the interest of any existing power to support them. So far, no practical organization of revolutionary internationalism exists to support them. We *passively watch* their combat and only the delusory babble of the United Nations or of the specialists of "progressive" state powers accompanies their death throes. In Santo Domingo US troops dared to intervene in a foreign country in order to back up fascist army officers against the legal government of the Kennedyist Caamaño, simply for fear that he would be overwhelmed by the people he had had to arm. What forces in the world took retaliatory measures against the American intervention? In the Congo in 1960 Belgian paratroopers, UN expeditionary forces, and the Mining Association's tailor-made state [Katanga] broke the impetus of the people who thought they had won independence, and killed Lumumba and Mpolo. In 1964 Belgian paratroopers, American transport planes, and South African, European, and anti-Castroist Cuban mercenaries pushed back the second insurrectional wave of the Mulelists.* What practical aid was provided by "revolutionary Africa"? A thousand Algerian volunteers, victors of a much harder war, would have been enough to prevent the fall of Stanleyville. But the armed people of Algeria had long been replaced by a classical army on lease to Boumédienne, who had other plans.

The next revolutions are confronted with the task of *understanding themselves*. They must totally reinvent their own language and defend themselves against all the forms of co-option prepared for them. The Asturian miners' strike (virtually continuous since 1962) and all the other signs of opposition that herald the end of Francoism do not indicate an inevitable future for Spain, but a choice: either the holy alliance now being prepared by the Spanish Church, the monarchists, the "left Falangists," and the Stalinists to harmoniously adapt post-Franco Spain to modernized capitalism and to the Common Market; or the resumption and completion of the most radical aspects of the revolution that was defeated by Franco and his accomplices on all sides—the revolution that realized truly socialist human relationships for a few weeks in Barcelona in 1936.

The new revolutionary current, wherever it appears, must begin to link up the present oppositional experiences and the people who bear them. While unifying such groups, it must at the same time unify the *coherent basis of their project.* The first gestures of the coming revolutionary era embody a new content, both visible and hidden, of the critique of present societies, and new forms of struggle; and also the irreducible moments of all the old revolutionary history that has remained in abeyance, moments which reappear like *ghosts.* The dominant society, which prides itself so much on its constant modernization, is thus going to meet its match, for it is at last beginning to produce its own modernized negation.

Long live the comrades who in 1959 burned the Koran in the streets of Baghdad!

Long live the workers' councils of Hungary, defeated in 1956 by the so-called Red Army!

Long live the dockers of Aarhus who last year effectively boycotted racist South Africa, in spite of their union leadership and the judicial repression by the Danish social-democratic government!

Long live the "Zengakuren" student movement of Japan, which actively combats the capitalist powers of imperialism and of the so-called "Communist" bureaucracies!

Long live the workers' militia that defended the northeastern districts of Santo Domingo!

Long live the self-management of the Algerian peasants and workers! The option is now between the militarized bureaucratic dictatorship and the dictatorship of the "self-managed sector" *extended to all production and all aspects of social life.*

Algiers, July 1965*

The Decline and Fall of the Spectacle-Commodity Economy

August 13–16, 1965, the blacks of Los Angeles revolted. An incident between traffic police and pedestrians developed into two days of spontaneous riots. Despite increasing reinforcements, the forces of order were unable to regain control of the streets. By the third day the blacks had armed themselves by looting accessible gun stores, enabling them to fire even on police helicopters. It took thousands of police and soldiers, including an entire infantry division supported by tanks, to confine the riot to the Watts area, and several more days of street fighting to finally bring it under control. Stores were massively plundered and many were burned. Official sources listed 32 dead (including 27 blacks), more than 800 wounded, and 3000 arrests.

Reactions from all sides were most revealing: a revolutionary event, by bringing existing problems into the open, provokes its opponents into an inhabitual lucidity. Police Chief William Parker, for example, rejected all the major black organizations' offers of mediation, correctly asserting: "These rioters don't have any leaders." Since the blacks no longer had any leaders, it was the moment of truth for both sides. What did one of those unemployed leaders, NAACP general secretary Roy Wilkins, have to say? He declared that the riot "should be put down with all necessary force." And Los Angeles Cardinal McIntyre, who protested loudly, did not protest against the violence of the repression, which one might have supposed the most tactful policy at a time when the Roman Church is modernizing its image; he denounced "this premeditated revolt against the rights of one's neighbor and against respect for law and order," calling on Catholics to oppose the looting and "this violence without any apparent justification." And all those who went so far as to recognize the "apparent justifications" of the rage of the Los Angeles blacks (but never the real ones), all the ideologists and "spokesmen" of the vacuous international Left, deplored the irresponsibility, the disorder, the looting (especially the fact that *arms and alcohol* were the first targets), and the 2000 fires with which the blacks lit up their battle and their ball. But who has defended the Los Angeles rioters in the terms they deserve?

We will. Let the economists fret over the $27 million lost, and the city planners sigh over one of their most beautiful supermarkets gone up in smoke, and McIntyre blubber over his slain deputy sheriff. Let the sociologists bemoan the absurdity and intoxication of this rebellion. The role of a revolutionary publication is not only to justify the Los Angeles insurgents, but to help elucidate their perspectives, to explain theoretically the truth for which such practical actions express the search.

In Algiers in July 1965, following Boumédienne's coup d'état, the situationists issued an "Address" to the Algerians and to revolutionaries all over the world which interpreted conditions in Algeria and the rest of the world *as a whole*. Among other examples we mentioned the movement of the American blacks, stating that if it could "assert itself incisively" it would unmask the contradictions of the most advanced capitalist system. Five weeks later this incisiveness was in the streets. Modern theoretical criticism of modern society and criticism in acts of the same society already coexist; still separated but both advancing toward the same realities, both talking about the same thing. These two critiques are mutually explanatory, and neither can be understood without the other. Our theory of "survival" and of "the spectacle" is illuminated and verified by these actions which are so incomprehensible to American false consciousness. One day these actions will in turn be illuminated by this theory.

Until the Watts explosion, black civil rights demonstrations had been kept by their leaders within the limits of a legal system that tolerates the most appalling violence on the part of the police and the racists—as in last March's march on Montgomery, Alabama. Even after the latter scandal, a discreet agreement between the federal government, Governor Wallace, and Martin Luther King led the Selma marchers on March 10 to stand back at the first police warning, in dignity and prayer. The confrontation expected by the demonstrators was reduced to a mere spectacle of a potential confrontation. In that moment nonviolence reached the pitiful limit of its courage: first you expose yourself to the enemy's blows, then you push your moral nobility to the point of sparing him the trouble of using any more force. But the main point is that the civil rights movement only addressed legal problems by legal means. It is logical to make legal appeals regarding legal questions. What is irrational is to appeal legally against a blatant illegality as if it was a mere oversight that would be corrected if pointed out. It is obvious that the crude and glaring illegality from which blacks still suffer in many American states has its roots in a socioeconomic contradiction that is not within the scope of existing laws, and that no future *juridical* law will be able to get rid of this contradiction in the face of the more fundamental laws of this society. What American blacks are really daring to demand is the right to really live, and in the final analysis this requires nothing less than the total subversion of this society. This becomes increasingly evident as blacks in their everyday lives find themselves forced to use increasingly subversive methods. The issue is no longer the condition of American blacks, but the condition of America, which merely happens to find its first expression among the blacks. The Watts riot was not a *racial* conflict: the rioters left alone the whites who were in their path, attacking only the white policemen, while on the other hand black solidarity did not extend to black store-owners or even to black car-drivers. Martin Luther King himself had to admit that the revolt went beyond the limits of his specialty. Speaking in Paris last October, he said: "This was not a race riot. It was a class riot."

The Los Angeles rebellion was a rebellion against the commodity, against the world of the commodity in which worker-consumers are *hierarchically* subordinated to commodity standards. Like the young delinquents of all the advanced countries, but more radically because they are part of a class without a future, a sector of the proletariat unable to believe in any significant chance of integration or promotion, the Los Angeles blacks take modern capitalist propaganda, its publicity of abundance, *literally*. They want to possess *now* all the objects shown and abstractly accessible, because they want to *use* them. In this way they are challenging their exchange-value, the *commodity reality* which molds them and marshals them to its own ends, and which has *preselected everything*. Through theft and gift they rediscover a use that immediately refutes the oppressive rationality of the commodity, revealing its relations and even its production to be arbitrary and unnecessary. The looting of the Watts district was the most direct realization of the distorted principle: "To each according to their *false* needs"—needs determined and produced by the economic system which the very act of looting rejects. But once the vaunted abundance is taken at face value and directly *seized,* instead of being eternally pursued in the rat-race of alienated labor and increasing unmet social needs, real desires begin to be expressed in festive celebration, in playful self-assertion, in the *potlatch* of destruction. People who destroy commodities show their human superiority over commodities. They stop submitting to the arbitrary forms that distortedly reflect their real needs. The flames of Watts *consummated* the system of consumption. The theft of large refrigerators by people with no electricity, or with their electricity cut off, is the best image of the lie of affluence transformed into a truth *in play*. Once it is no longer bought, the commodity lies open to criticism and alteration, whatever particular form it may take. Only when it is paid for with money is it respected as an admirable fetish, as a symbol of status within the world of survival.

Looting is a *natural* response to the unnatural and inhuman society of commodity abundance. It instantly undermines the commodity as such, and it also exposes what the commodity ultimately implies: the army, the police, and the other specialized detachments of the state's monopoly of armed violence. What is a policeman? He is the active servant of the commodity, the man in complete submission to the commodity, whose job is to ensure that a given product of human labor remains a commodity, with the magical property of having to be paid for, instead of becoming a mere refrigerator or rifle—a passive, inanimate object subject to anyone who comes along to make use of it. In rejecting the humiliation of being subjected to police, the blacks are at the same time rejecting the humiliation of being subjected to commodities. The Watts youth, having no future in market terms, grasped another *quality* of the present, and that quality was so incontestable and irresistible that it drew in the whole population—women, children, and even sociologists who happened to be on the scene. Bobbi Hollon, a young black sociologist of the neighborhood, had this to say to the *Herald Tribune* in October: "Before, people were ashamed to say they came from Watts. They'd mumble it. Now they say it with pride. Boys who used to go around with their shirts open to the waist, and who'd have cut you to pieces in half a second, showed up here every morning at seven o'clock to organize the distribution of food. Of course, it's no use pretending that food wasn't looted. . . . All that Christian blah-blah has been used too long against blacks. These people could loot for ten years and they wouldn't get back half the money those stores have stolen from them over all these years. . . . Me, I'm only a little black girl." Bobbi Hollon, who has sworn never to wash off the blood that splashed on her sandals during the rioting, adds: "Now the whole world is watching Watts."

How do people make history under conditions designed to dissuade them from intervening in it? The Los Angeles blacks are better paid than any others in the United States, but they are also the most *separated* from the California superopulence that is flaunted all around them. Hollywood, the pole of the global spectacle, is right next door. They are promised that, with patience, they will join in America's prosperity, but they come to see that this prosperity is not a fixed state but an endless ladder. The higher they climb, the farther they get from the top, because they start off disadvantaged, because they are less qualified and thus more numerous among the unemployed, and finally because the hierarchy that crushes them is not based on economic buying power alone: they are also treated as *inherently* inferior in every area of daily life by the customs and prejudices of a society in which all human power is based on buying power. Just as the human riches of the American blacks are despised and treated as criminal, monetary riches will never make them completely acceptable in America's alienated society: individual wealth will only make a *rich nigger* because blacks as a whole must *represent poverty* in a society of hierarchized wealth. Every witness noted the cry proclaiming the global significance of the uprising: "This is a black revolution and we want the world to know it!" *Freedom Now* is the password of all the revolutions of history, but now for the first time the problem is not to overcome scarcity, but to master material abundance according to new principles. Mastering abundance is not just changing the way it is shared out, but *totally reorienting it*. This is the first step of a vast, all-embracing struggle.

The blacks are not alone in their struggle, because a *new proletarian consciousness* (the consciousness that they are not at all the masters of their own activities, of their own lives) is developing in America among strata which in their rejection of modern capitalism resemble the blacks. It was, in fact, the first phase of the black struggle which happened to be the signal for the more general movement of contestation that is now spreading. In December 1964 the students of Berkeley, harassed for their participation in the civil rights movement, initiated a strike* challenging the functioning of California's "multiversity" and ultimately calling into question the entire American social system in which they are being programmed to play such a passive role. The spectacle promptly responded with exposés of widespread student drinking, drug use, and sexual immorality—the same activities for which blacks have long been reproached. This generation of students has gone on to invent a new form of struggle against the dominant spectacle, the *teach-in*, a form taken up October 20 in Great Britain at the University of Edinburgh during the Rhodesian crisis. This obviously primitive and imperfect form represents the stage at which people *refuse to confine their discussion of problems* within academic limits or fixed time periods; the stage where they strive to pursue issues to their ultimate consequences and are thus led to practical activity. The same month tens of thousands of anti–Vietnam war demonstrators appeared in the streets of Berkeley and New York, their cries echoing those of the Watts rioters: "Get out of our district and out of Vietnam!" Becoming more radical, many of the whites are finally going outside the law: "courses" are given on how to hoodwink army recruiting boards (*Le Monde*, 19 October 1965) and draft cards are burned in front of television cameras. In the affluent society disgust is being expressed for this affluence and *for its price*. The spectacle is being spat on by an advanced sector whose autonomous activity denies its values. The classical proletariat, to the very extent to which it had been provisionally integrated into the capitalist system, had itself failed to integrate the blacks (several Los Angeles unions refused blacks until 1959); now the blacks are the rallying point for all those who refuse the logic of this integration into capitalism, which is all that the promise of racial integration amounts to. Comfort will never be comfortable enough for those who seek what is not on the market, what in fact the market specifically eliminates. The level attained by the technology of the most privileged becomes an insult, and one more easily grasped and resented than is that most fundamental insult: reification. The Los Angeles rebellion is the first in history to justify itself with the argument that there was no air conditioning during a heat wave.

The American blacks have their own particular spectacle, their own black newspapers, magazines, and stars, and if they are rejecting it in disgust as a fraud and as an expression of their humiliation, it is because they see it as a *minority* spectacle, a mere appendage of a general spectacle. Recognizing that their own spectacle of desirable consumption is a colony of the white one enables them to see more quickly through the falsehood of the whole economic-cultural spectacle. By wanting to participate really and immediately in the affluence that is the official value of every American, they are really demanding the egalitarian *actualization* of the American spectacle of everyday life—they are demanding that the half-heavenly, half-earthly values of the spectacle be put to the test. But it is in the nature of the spectacle that it cannot be actualized either immediately or equally, *not even for the whites*. (The blacks in fact function as a perfect spectacular object-lesson: the threat of falling into such wretchedness spurs others on in the rat-race.) In taking the capitalist spectacle at its face value, the blacks are already rejecting the spectacle itself. The spectacle is a drug for slaves. It is designed not to be taken literally, but to be followed from just out of reach; when this separation is eliminated, the hoax is revealed. In the United States today the whites are enslaved to the commodity while the blacks are negating it. The blacks are asking for *more than the whites*—this is the core of a problem that has no solution except the dissolution of the white social system. This is why those whites who want to escape their own slavery must first of all rally to the black revolt—not, obviously, in racial solidarity, but in a joint global rejection of the commodity and of the state. The economic and psychological distance between blacks and whites enables blacks to see white consumers for what they are, and their justified contempt for whites develops into a contempt for passive consumers in general. The whites who reject this role have no chance unless they link their struggle more and more to that of the blacks, uncovering its most fundamental implications and supporting them all the way. If, with the radicalization of the struggle, such a convergence is not achieved, black nationalist tendencies will be reinforced, leading to the futile interethnic antagonism so characteristic of the old society. Mutual slaughter is the other possible outcome of the present situation, once resignation is no longer an option.

The attempts to build a separatist or pro-African black nationalism are dreams giving no answer to the real oppression. The American blacks have no fatherland. They are *in their own country* and they are *alienated.* So are the rest of the population, but the blacks are aware of it. In this sense they are not the most backward sector of American society, but the most advanced. They are the negation at work, "the bad side that makes history by provoking struggles" (*The Poverty of Philosophy*). Africa has nothing to do with it.

The American blacks are a product of modern industry, just like electronics or advertising or the cyclotron. And they embody its contradictions. They are the people whom the spectacle paradise must simultaneously integrate and reject, with the result that the antagonism between the spectacle and human activity is totally revealed through them. The spectacle is *universal,* it pervades the globe just as the commodity does. But since the world of the commodity is based on class conflict, the commodity itself is hierarchical. The necessity for the commodity (and hence for the spectacle, whose role is to *inform* the commodity world) to be both universal and hierarchical leads to a universal hierarchization. But because this hierarchization must remain *unavowed,* it is expressed in the form of unavowable, because *irrational,* hierarchical value judgments in a world of *irrational rationalization.* It is this hierarchization that creates *racisms* everywhere. The British Labour government has come to the point of restricting nonwhite immigration, while the industrially advanced countries of Europe are once again becoming racist as they import their subproletariat from the Mediterranean area, developing a colonial exploitation within their own borders. And if Russia continues to be anti-Semitic it is because it continues to be a hierarchical society in which labor must be bought and sold as a commodity. The commodity is constantly extending its domain and engendering new forms of hierarchy, whether between labor union leader and worker or between car-owners with artificially distinguished models. This is the original flaw in commodity rationality, the sickness of bourgeois reason, a sickness that has been inherited by the bureaucratic class. But the repulsive absurdity of certain hierarchies, and the fact that the entire commodity world is directed blindly and automatically to their protection, leads people to see—the moment they engage in a negating practice—that every hierarchy is absurd.

The rational world produced by the Industrial Revolution has rationally liberated individuals from their local and national limitations and linked them on a global scale; but it irrationally separates them once again, in accordance with a hidden logic that finds its expression in insane ideas and grotesque values. Estranged from their own world, people are everywhere surrounded by strangers. The barbarians are no longer at the ends of the earth, they are among the general population, made into barbarians by their forced participation in the worldwide system of hierarchical consumption. The veneer of humanism that camouflages all this is inhuman, it is the negation of human activities and desires; it is the humanism of the commodity, the solicitous care of the parasitical commodity for its human host. For those who reduce people to objects, objects seem to acquire human qualities and truly human manifestations appear as unconscious "animal behavior." Thus the chief humanist of Los Angeles, William Parker, could say: "They started acting like a bunch of monkeys in a zoo."

When California authorities declared a "state of insurrection," the insurance companies recalled that they do not cover risks at that level—they guarantee nothing beyond survival. The American blacks can rest assured that as long as they keep quiet they will in most cases be allowed to *survive*. Capitalism has become sufficiently concentrated and interlinked with the state to distribute "welfare" to the poorest. But by the very fact that they lag behind in the advance of socially organized survival, the blacks pose the problems of *life*; what they are really demanding is not to survive but to *live*. The blacks have nothing of their own to insure; their mission is to destroy all previous forms of private insurance and security. They appear as what they really are: the irreconcilable enemies, not of the great majority of Americans, but of the alienated way of life of the entire modern society. The most industrially advanced country only shows us the road that will be followed everywhere unless the system is overthrown.

Certain black nationalist extremists, to show why they can accept nothing less than a separate nation, have argued that even if American society someday concedes total civil and economic equality, it will never, on a personal level, come around to accepting interracial marriage. That is why *this American society itself must disappear*—in America and everywhere else in the world. The end of all racial prejudice, like the end of so many other prejudices related to sexual inhibitions, can only lie beyond "marriage" itself, that is, beyond the *bourgeois family* (which has largely fallen apart among American blacks)—the bourgeois family which prevails as much in Russia as in the United States, both as a model of hierarchical relations and as a structure for a stable *inheritance of power* (whether in the form of money or of social-bureaucratic status). It is now often said that American youth, after thirty years of silence, are rising again as a force of contestation, and that the black revolt is their Spanish Civil War. This time their "Lincoln Brigades" must understand the full significance of the struggle in which they are engaging and totally support its universal aspects. The Watts "excesses" are no more a political error in the black revolt than the

POUM's May 1937 armed resistance in Barcelona was a betrayal of the anti-Franco war. A revolt against the spectacle—even if limited to a single district such as Watts—calls *everything* into question because it is a human protest against a dehumanized life, a protest of *real individuals* against their separation from a community that could fulfill their *true human and social nature* and transcend the spectacle.*

December 1965

The Class Struggles in Algeria

One might almost think that the new Algerian regime's sole aim has been to confirm the brief analysis the SI made of it in the "Address to Revolutionaries" that we issued in Algiers soon after its inaugural putsch. Liquidating self-management is the total content of Boumédienne's regime, its only real activity; and that project began the very moment the state, through the deployment of the military force that was the only crystallization it achieved under Ben Bella, its only solid structure, *declared its independence* vis-à-vis Algerian society. The state's other projects—the technocratic reorganization of the economy, the social and juridical extension of its power base—are beyond the capacities of the present ruling class in the real conditions of the country. The mass of undecided, who had not been enemies of Ben Bella but who were disappointed by him and who waited to judge the new regime by its actions, can now see that it is ultimately doing nothing but establishing an autonomous state dictatorship and thereby declaring war on self-management. Even to formulate specific accusations against Ben Bella or to destroy him *publicly* seems to be beyond its power for a long time to come. The only remnant of "socialism" professed in Algeria is precisely that core of *inverted socialism,* that product of the general reaction within the workers' movement itself which the defeat of the Russian revolution bequeathed as a positive model to the rest of the world, including Ben Bella's Algeria: *the big lie of the police state.* Under such a regime the political enemy is not condemned for his real positions, but for the opposite of what he was; or else he suddenly fades into an organized silence—he never existed, either for the tribunal or for the historian. And Boumédienne, from the beginning one of those most responsible for the fact that Algerian self-management is only a caricature of what it needs to be, officially calls it "a caricature" in order to reorganize it in an authoritarian manner. In the name of an essence of self-management ideologically backed by the state, Boumé-dienne rejects self-management's actual fledgling manifestations.

The same inversion of reality determines the Boumédiennist cri-tique of the past. What Ben Bella is reproached for having done, or for having gone too far in, is precisely what he did not do and what he scarcely *pretended* to even strive for—the liberation of women or real support for the liberation struggles in Africa, for example. The present regime lies about the past because of its own profound unity with that past. The Algerian ruling class has not changed, it is reinforcing itself. It reproaches Ben Bella for having done poorly what he had in fact only pretended to do; for a revolutionariness that it itself has now ceased even simulating. The Algerian ruling class, before June 19 as well as after, is a bureaucracy in formation. It is pursuing its consolidation by partially changing the way its political power is shared out. Certain strata of this bureaucracy (military and technocratic) are predomi-nating over others (political and trade-unionist). The basic conditions remain the weakness of the national bourgeoisie and the pressure from the poverty-stricken peasant and worker masses, some of whom took over the self-managed sector when the former (European) ruling class fled the country. The merging of the Algerian bourgeoisie with the state bureaucracy is easier with the new ruling strata that Boumé-dienne represents; moreover, this evolution harmonizes better with the region of the global capitalist market to which Algeria is linked. In addi-tion, the bureaucratic strata that ruled with Ben Bella were less capable of an open struggle against the demands of the masses. Ben Bella and the unstable social *balance of power,* which was the temporary result of the struggle against France and the colonists, were overthrown at the same time. When they saw themselves supplanted, the previously predominant bureaucratic strata (the leaders of the FLN Federation of Greater Algiers and the General Union of Algerian Workers) hesitated and then rallied to the new regime because their solidarity with the state bureaucracy as a whole was naturally stronger than their ties to the mass of workers. The agricultural workers' union, whose congress six months before had adopted the most radical positions on self-man-agement, was the first to capitulate.

Among the bureaucratic forces in the lobbies of power around Ben Bella, two mutually antagonistic but related groupings had a special status: the Algerian Communist Party and the foreign leftists—nick-named *"pieds-rouges"*—who had put themselves at the service of the Alge-rian state. They were not so much in power as pretenders to power. A poor cousin of power, waiting to inherit it, this extreme left wing of the bureaucracy acquired its credentials as representative of the masses *through its connection with Ben Bella:* it drew its mandate not from the masses but from him. It dreamed of one day getting a monopoly on this power over the masses, this power that Ben Bella still shared on all sides. Since Ben Bella was personally its only access to present power and its main promise for the future, its only guarantee of being tolerated (its Sukarno),* the bureaucratic left demonstrated in his defense, but in an uncertain manner. Just as it respectfully flocked around the state, it placed itself on the terrain of the state to oppose the unfavorable shift of the relation of forces within the state. Here again the Boumédiennist critique of these elements, lumped together as "foreigners," in the name of a specifically Algerian Socialism, is entirely false. Far from "making theory for theory's sake" (*El Moudjahid,* 22 September 1965), the *pieds-rouges* represented an exhausted mixture of complete theoretical nullity and of unconscious or consciously hidden counterrevolutionary tendencies. Far from wanting to make adventurous "utopian experiments" in Algeria, they possessed nothing but mistakes or lies that had been *revealed as such a thousand times.* The best revolutionary ideas of the *pieds-rouges* were unsuitable not because they came from *too far away,* but because they were repeated much too late. It was a matter of history, not geography.

More radical and more isolated, at the extreme left of the Ben Bella regime, Mohammed Harbi was the thinker of self-management, but only by grace of the prince, in the bureaus of power. Harbi rose to the highest point reached by Algerian revolutionary thought: up to the idea of self-management, but not at all up to its consistent, effective practice. He understood its notion, but not its being. He occupied the self-contradictory position of *governmental* theorist of self-management. More accurately, he might be considered its court poet: soaring above practice, he eulogized self-management more than he theorized it. The *self-management state,* that logical monstrosity, had in Harbi its celebrator and its guilty conscience. Boumédienne's tanks in the streets meant a rationalization of the state, a state that wanted henceforth to free itself from the ridiculous self-contradictions of the Ben-Bellaist balance of power and from any guilty conscience and to simply *be a state.* It then became clear that Harbi, the unarmed prophet of self-management, had not envisaged *self-management's self-defense,* its defense on its own terrain, but only its defense through the mediation of Ben Bella. But if Harbi counted on Ben Bella alone to defend self-management, who did he count on to defend Ben Bella? The thinker of self-management was protected by Ben Bella, but who was going to protect his protector? He believed that Ben Bella, the incarnation of the state, would remain universally accepted in Algeria, although

Harbi himself only accepted his "good side" (his token recognition of self-management). But the real process advanced by way of his bad side: the forces that followed the opposite line of argument on Ben Bella were more capable of intervention. Ben Bella was not the resolution of the Algerian contradictions, he was only their temporary cover. History has shown that Harbi and those who thought like him were mistaken. They will now have to radicalize their ideas if they want to effectively fight the Boumédiennist dictatorship and actually *realize* self-management.

The fall of Ben Bella is a landmark in the collapse of global illusions regarding the "underdeveloped" version of pseudosocialism. Castro remains its last star, but he, who could previously argue with some plausibility that elections were unnecessary because the people were armed, is now demanding that all arms be turned in, and his police are rounding them up (Reuters, 14 August 1965). His second in command, Guevara, has already disappeared without any explanation being given to the masses from whom these leaders had demanded a blind personal confidence. Meanwhile the Algerians who are experiencing the fragility of Ben-Bellaist socialism are also discovering the value of all the so-called socialist camp's concern for their cause: the Chinese, Russian, and Cuban *states,* along with Nasser, are naturally rushing to outdo each other in fraternal greetings to Boumédienne's regime. Revolutions in the underdeveloped countries will continue to fail miserably as long as they recognize and emulate any existing model of socialist power, since those models are *all* manifestly false. The disintegrated official Sino-Soviet version of this socialism and the "underdeveloped" version of it mutually admire and reinforce each other and both lead to the same outcome. The first underdevelopment we have to get beyond is the worldwide *underdevelopment of revolutionary theory*.

The internal struggles of the Algerian bureaucracy, both during the war of independence and in the postwar 1962–1965 period, took the form of clan struggles, personal rivalries, inexplicable disputes among the leaders, obscure shifts of alliances. This was a direct continuation of the conditions prevailing around Messali Hadj since before the Algerian revolt. Not only was there a complete absence of theory, even ideology was only crudely and confusedly improvised; everything remained centered around superficial, abstract political questions. Since June 19 another period has begun: that of the confrontation between the ruling class and the workers, and this is the real movement that creates the conditions and need for a theory. As early as July 9, at a meeting of delegates from 2500 self-managed enterprises held at Algiers and chaired by Minister of Industry Boumaza, the delegates expressed to

the latter their insistence on self-management as an inviolable principle and made a series of critiques concerning the state's role in limiting
this principle. The delegates "questioned the multiplicity of overseers
(prefectures, ministries, party) and denounced the heavy taxation and
the state's nonpayment of debts; some delegates also brought up the
problem of layoffs, the 'draconian' demands of the foreign suppliers,
and the paralyzing role of the customs department" (*Le Monde*, 10 July
1965).

Those delegates knew what they were talking about. Since the June
19th Declaration [accompanying Boumédienne's coup]—in which the
term "self-management" is not even mentioned once—the regime has
been preparing the "stabilization" of the economic situation through
the strengthening of state control and the accelerated training of
"managerial staffs." It aimed to start collecting installment payments
as soon as possible for the more than 100,000 squatted lodgings; to
recover money "stolen from the state" in the self-managed enterprises;
to reduce the wearing out of poorly maintained equipment; and to
regularize all the illegal seizures carried out by the masses upon the
departure of the French. Since then, despite the fact that self-management is the most effective form for overcoming the paralyzing respect
for property (private or state) that has always been such an obstacle in
the workers' movement, the workers in the self-managed sector, await-
ing their several-months-overdue wages, are continually reproached
for having stolen a large part of what they have produced. The most
urgent goal of the Algerian state, which already has enough soldiers
and police, is to train 20,000 accountants a year.

The central struggle, veiled and open, immediately broke out between
the ruling class representatives and the workers precisely over the issue
of self-management. Boumaza's and Boumédienne's "reassuring" declarations didn't fool anyone. The "labor unrest" alluded to by *Le Monde*
on October 3 is a euphemism for the resistance of the sole bastion
of socialist revolution in Algeria (the self-managed sector) against the
most recent maneuvers of the ruling bureaucratic-bourgeois coalition.
The union leaders themselves could not remain silent: their official
status as representatives of the workers vis-à-vis the state and their
social status as left wing of the ruling class were at stake. The September articles in *Révolution et Travail*—in which genuine workers' demands
("when workers are reduced to poverty, self-management is violated")
are mixed with expressions of the union leaders' increasing alarm
(they "agree with the June 19th Declaration's analyses" but denounce
the technocrats and economists)—exactly reflect this situation of overlapping vertical and horizontal struggles. The increasing reference to

"economic anarchy" (which always really means self-management), the judicial measures against the self-managed sector (e.g. forcing the self-managed enterprises to pay back-taxes), which the newspapers talk about less, and the restitution of the Norcolor factory to its former owner—all this shows these "labor" leaders that soon they will no longer have a place in the ruling apparatus. The new pretenders are already there: the "scramble for power of dubious elements" that outrages *Révolution et Travail* expresses the ruling class's swing to the right. The techno-bureaucrats and the military have no possible allies but the representatives of the traditional bourgeoisie. At the same time that the officers, in the style of South American armies, are attaining bourgeois status (everyone knows about their BMWs, duty-free and 30% discounted), a multitude of Algerian bourgeois, following in the footsteps of the Norcolor owner, are returning to the country in the expectation of recovering their property, seized "under completely illegal conditions by unscrupulous persons" (Boumaza). Added to these challenges is the rapid increase in food prices. The workers, thoroughly aware of this process, are resisting *on the spot*: the repeated strikes in the Renault factories, the strikes of the press and parcel distributors and of the telephone and insurance workers, the demonstrations of the unpaid workers of Mitidja—these are the first steps of a movement of rage which, if it asserts itself effectively, is capable of sweeping aside the whole present regime.

Incapable of mastering a single one of their problems, the rulers are reacting with constant delirious conferences, constant torture in their prisons, and denunciations of the "slackening of moral standards." *El Moudjahid* (7 December 1965) attacks "the erotic sentimentalism of a young generation without political commitment" and the (accurate) views of those who "are tempted to reject religion as being a restraint on their taste for pleasure and on their liberation, which they take simply to mean their possibilities for pleasure, and who consider the contributions of Arab civilization as a step backward." The tone is no different from that used by the rulers in Washington or Moscow when they regretfully announce their lack of confidence in the young generation. And after a few months the new regime is emulating Ben Bella in its most ludicrous Islamic manifestation: the prohibition of alcohol.

The present opposition to the Boumédiennist dictatorship is two-fold: On one side, the workers are defending themselves in the enterprises (self-managed or not); their actions represent the real opposition. On another side, the leftists of the FLN apparatus are trying to re-form a revolutionary apparatus. The first effort of the Organisation de la Résistance Populaire, led by Zahouane and supported by the French Stalinists, was a hollow declaration that only appeared six weeks after the coup, a declaration that analyzed neither the present regime nor the means of opposing it. Its second appeal was addressed to the Algerian police, from whom it anticipated revolutionary support. This strategy proved to be somewhat of a miscalculation since by the end of September those police had arrested Zahouane and broken up his first clandestine network (Harbi himself had already been arrested in August). The ORP is continuing its activity, beginning to collect contributions "for Ben Bella" from Algerian workers in France and winning over the majority of the student leaders. This apparatus (underground or in exile) is counting on an economic-political crisis in Algeria in the near future to reestablish its influence with the struggling Algerian workers. In this Leninist perspective it will present itself, with or without the banner of Ben Bella, as the solution for a replacement of the Boumédiennist regime.

What is nevertheless going to prevent the establishment of a Bolshevik-type apparatus, striven for by so many militants? The time passed since Lenin and his failure, and the continued and evident degradation of Leninism, which is directly expressed by these leftists' allying with and fighting each other in every sort of variant—Khrushchevo-Brezhnevists, Maoists, sub-Togliattists, pure and semi-Stalinists, all the shades of Trotskyism, etc. All of them refuse, and are forced to refuse, to clearly face the essential problem of the nature of the "socialism" (i.e. of the class power) in Russia and China, and consequently also in Algeria. Their main weakness during the struggle for power is also the main guarantee of their counterrevolutionary role if they were to accede to power. These leftists will present themselves as a natural continuation of the personalized political confusion of the preceding period; but the real class struggle in Algeria has now brought that period to a close. Their doubts about Ben Bella overlapped with their doubts on the world (and on socialism) and will continue after Ben Bella. They don't say all they know and they don't know all they say. Their social base *and their social perspective* is that bureaucratic sector which came out worst in the power reshuffle and which wants to regain its old position. Seeing that they can no longer hope to dominate the regime, they turn toward the people in order to dominate the opposition. Nostalgic bureaucrats or would-be bureaucrats, they want to counterpose "the people" to Boumédienne, whereas Boumédienne has already revealed to the masses the real focus of opposition: state bureaucrat versus worker. But the most despicable aspect of their bolshevism is this glaring difference: the Bolshevik Party did not know the sort of bureaucratic power it was going to end up establishing, whereas these leftists have already been able to see, in the world and among themselves, that bureaucratic power which they wish to *restore* in a more or less purified form. The masses, if they have the chance to choose, will not choose this corrected version of a bureaucracy whose essential elements they have already had the opportunity of experiencing. The Algerian intellectuals who don't rally to the regime still have the choice between participating in this apparatus or seeking a direct linkup with the autonomous movement of the masses. As for the Algerian petty bourgeoisie (storekeepers, lower functionaries, etc.), it will naturally tend to support the new technocratic-military bureaucracy rather than the bureaucratic leftists.

The only road to socialism, in Algeria as everywhere else, passes through "an offensive and defensive pact with the truth," as a Hungarian intellectual put it in 1956. People in Algeria who got the SI's "Address" understood it. Wherever practical revolutionary conditions exist, no theory is too difficult. Villiers de l'Isle-Adam, a witness to the Paris Commune, noted, "For the first time one can hear the workers exchanging their opinions about problems that until now have been considered only by philosophers." The realization of philosophy, the critique and reconstruction of all the values and behaviors imposed by alienated life—this is the maximum program of *generalized self-management.* The leftist militants of the bureaucratic groups tell us that these theses are correct but that the time has not yet come when one can tell the masses everything. Those who argue in such a perspective never see this time as having come, and in fact they contribute toward making sure that it never does come. It is necessary to talk to the masses about *what they are already doing.* The specialized thinkers of revolution are the specialists of its false consciousness, who afterwards come to realize that they have done something entirely different from what they thought they were doing. This problem is aggravated here by the particular difficulties of underdeveloped countries and by the persistent theoretical weakness in the Algerian movement. Although the strictly bureaucratic fringe within the present opposition is extremely small, its very existence as a "professional leadership" is a *form* that weighs on and determines the content of that opposition. Political alienation is always related to the state. Self-management can expect nothing from *revived Bolsheviks.*

Self-management must be both the means and the end of the present struggle. It is not only what is at stake in the struggle, but also its adequate form. It is its own tool. It is itself the material it works on, and its own presupposition. It must totally recognize its own truth. The state power proposes the contradictory and absurd project of "reorganizing self-management"; it is in fact self-management that must *organize itself as a power* or disappear.

Self-management is the most modern and most important tendency to appear in the struggle of the Algerian movement, and it is also the one that is the least narrowly Algerian. Its meaning is universal. In contrast to the *Yugoslavian caricature* that Boumédienne wants to emulate, which is only a semi-decentralized instrument of state control ("We have to decentralize in order to better control the self-managed enterprises," Boumédienne openly admits in *Le Monde,* 10 November 1965), a subordinate level of central administration; and in contrast to the Proudhonian mutualism of 1848, which aimed at organizing on the margins of private property, real self-management—revolutionary self-management—can be won only through the armed abolition of the titles of existing property. Its failure in Turin in 1920 was the prelude to the armed domination of Fascism. The bases for a self-managed production in Algeria were spontaneously formed—as in Spain in 1936, as in Paris in 1871 in the workshops abandoned by the Versaillese—wherever the owners had to flee following their political defeat: on *vacant property.* These takeovers are a vacation from property and oppression, a temporary break from alienated life.

Such self-management, by the simple fact that it exists, threatens the society's entire hierarchical organization. It must destroy all external control because all the external forces of control will never make peace with it as a living reality, but at most only with its label, with its embalmed corpse. Self-management cannot coexist with any army or police or state.

Generalized self-management, "extended to all production and all aspects of social life," would mean the end of the unemployment that affects two million Algerians, but it would also mean the end of all aspects of the old society, the abolition of all its spiritual and material enslavements and the abolition of its masters. The present fledgling effort toward self-management can be controlled from above only because it consents to exclude below it that majority of the workers who don't participate in it or who are unemployed; and because even within its own enterprises it tolerates the formation of dominating strata of "directors" or management professionals who have worked their way up from the base or been appointed by the state. These managers are the state virus within that which tends to negate the state; they are a compromise. But the time for compromise is past, both for the state power and for the real power of the Algerian workers.

Radical self-management, the only kind that can endure and conquer, refuses any hierarchy within or outside itself. It must also reject in practice *any hierarchical separation of women* (an oppressive separation openly accepted by Proudhon's theory as well as by the backward reality of Islamic Algeria). The self-management committees, as well as all the delegates in the federations of self-managed enterprises, should be revocable at any moment by their base, this base obviously including all the workers, without any distinction between permanent and seasonal ones.

The only program for the Algerian socialist elements consists of the defense of the self-managed sector, not only as it is but as it must become. This defense must therefore counteract the purge carried out by the state with another purge within self-management: a purge carried out by its rank and file against everything that negates it from within. A revolutionary assault against the existing regime is only possible with a continued and radicalized self-management as its point of departure. By putting forward the program of quantitatively and qualitatively increased workers' self-management, one is calling on all the workers to directly take on the cause of self-management as their own cause. By demanding not only the defense of self-management but its extension to the point of *dissolving all specialized activity not answerable to self-management,* Algerian revolutionaries can show that this defense is the concern not only of the workers of the *temporarily self-managed* sector, but of all the workers, as the only way toward a definitive liberation. In this way they will demonstrate that they are struggling for the liberation of everyone and not for their own future domination as specialists of revolution; that the victory of "their party" must at the same time be its end as a separate party.

As a first step, it is necessary to envisage linking up self-management delegates with each other and with the enterprise committees that are striving for self-management in the private and state sectors; to disseminate and publish all information on the workers' struggles and the autonomous forms of organization that emerge out of them, and to extend and generalize these forms as the sole path for a profound contestation. At the same time, through the same clandestine relations and publications, it is necessary to develop the theory of self-management and its requirements, within the self-managed sector itself and before the masses of Algeria and the world. Self-management must become the sole solution to the mysteries of power in Algeria, and it must *know that it is that solution.*

Algiers, December 1965*

Contribution to a Councilist Program in Spain

A new current of social critique is developing in Spain, with which we are in considerable agreement. This current is not only faced with the task of opposing that particular retrograde form of power, the Franco regime. It has to oppose all the forms of global power, because it is preparing to confront the *next Spanish form* of capitalist power. Its aim is to form an alternative at the moment (which will not be long in coming) when the Franco regime comes to an end—so that a choice is presented between modern capitalism, as it exists in the European Common Market, and genuine socialism, i.e. workers' power, which exists nowhere in the world. This current is opposed to all the old organizations of the Spanish left, which are hostile to a struggle for such objectives. But there is also a struggle *within* this current, between a lucid critique of existing conditions and tendencies that still confusedly cling to fragments of old revolutionary ideologies. The difficulties of underground activity and the numerous forms of censorship imposed by the Franco regime complicate the work of clarification and objective discussion that is needed. The collapse of old leftist politics outside Spain provides the Spanish comrades with negative object lessons about what they must avoid. But the positive experience that could be provided by a new radical critique has been limited by the extremely restricted base of such a critique at the present time.

The first attempt of this current to express itself in Spain was the formation of the FLP (*Frente de Liberación Popular*). The FLP experience proved disappointing because (like the Algerian FLN in 1954) it consisted of groups issuing from the various traditional parties which decided to put aside the question of a program in order to engage in joint action. This coexistence of antagonistic perspectives was soon recognized by the radical wing as the main cause for a stagnation in the FLP's initial activity (reflected in insufficient linkups with striking workers) and for its inability to clarify the forthcoming crisis of Spanish society. The most advanced tendency that has emerged during the ensuing public discussion over the last few years has published the journal *Acción Comunista*, of which four issues have appeared since January 1965. According to the opening declaration of this journal: "The editorial committee of *Acción Comunista*, composed of revolutionary Marxist members of diverse workers organizations, is *beginning* with these collective articles to elaborate the political platform of a socialist revolution in Spain." The editors go on to say that this platform will need to be deepened and concretized, "counting on the contributions and critiques of all those who are in agreement with us on the two fundamental points of our platform: the necessity and possibility of a socialist alternative to the current development of capitalism in Spain, and the need for the formation of a genuine revolutionary workers party." We have been encouraged to make the present contribution to this discussion by the radical and staunchly internationalist perspectives that have been expressed by the *Acción Comunista* comrades, particularly in Lorenzo Torres's article "From Workers' Commissions to Workers' Councils" (in issue #2).

As we see it, the theoretical discussion initiated by *Acción Comunista* has already addressed four main issues: (1) how to characterize the economy and society of present-day Spain; (2) the general goal of a radical current in Spain; (3) the evaluation of the present state of the global revolutionary movement; and (4) the question of revolutionary organization. On the first two issues we are in complete agreement with the positions they have adopted. The discussion of the last two has been less extensive, and the arguments and ideas that have emerged have been less clear. In this context we are going to offer some observations which we hope will prove useful.

Acción Comunista has shown that Spain can no longer be considered an economically backward country—a dogma which continues to be maintained by all the traditional workers parties. The development of capitalism under Franco during the last decade (part of a global process) has transformed all the conditions in Spain. The ruling class no longer has its main base in a *land-owning bourgeoisie,* as was the case in the 1930s, but in an industrial bourgeoisie closely interlinked with international capital. This transformation is reflected in the scale of current expansion, in the rapid decrease of the agricultural pro-letariat (which is being channeled into the new factories), and in the success of Spanish manufactured goods on the international market (in Cuba, for example). It is this development, which has also been provoking a resurgence of worker struggles since 1962, that is leading the ruling class to seek more modern "European forms of exploita-tion" to replace the old Francoist forms. The neo-capitalist solution to the Franco regime has organized its political force, with the sup-port of the Church, in a pseudo-underground Christian-Democratic party that seeks to unite the oppositional Catholics. This party, due to the influence of the professors who belong to it, has up till now largely controlled the student opposition, and has taken particular care to prevent any juncture between workers' and students' actions (the recent episode in which students were surrounded by the police in a Barcelona convent that had granted them asylum illustrates this point). Being aware, however, that the Catholic labor unions will not suffice to guarantee a painless birth of the new regime they envision, the Christian Democrats are seeking other "workers organizations" capable of lulling the workers to sleep during the transition. They will find such elements in the Spanish Socialist Party, particularly among those who are calling for a technocratic renewal of this reformism, such as T. Galvan. The "national reconciliation" advocated by the Stalinist party is completely in favor of such collaboration (though the Spanish bourgeoisie's mistaken but ingrained fear of "reds" may cause it to reject this sincere offer of collaboration and assistance). The recent negotiations between the CNT and the Falangist unions are yet another reflection of this same tendency toward submission to bourgeois evolution.

The *Acción Comunista* comrades accept the present struggle for democratization while simultaneously pointing out its inevitable limits and putting forward their own perspectives. Specifically, they advocate participating in the workers' commissions and factory committees that already exist illegally or semilegally, in order to work toward a local, regional, and national coordination of these commissions to the point of transforming them into workers' councils. This change of function and unification of sovereign workers' assemblies would constitute a classic dual-power situation, concretely revealing the alternative between capitalism and workers' power. *Acción Comunista* does not present this outcome as a probability, but as a possibility which will depend on the consciousness of the masses and on the programmatic formulations that revolutionary elements will have been able to develop among those masses. None of the organized political groups have any conception of this sort of activity—as was shown by the example of the Madrid steelworkers' struggle, which was organized by a workers' commission outside the influence of any of those groups. Supporting the power of workers' councils, *Acción Comunista* advocates a model of socialist society incompatible with any bureaucratic domination, whether economic or political: "When a class has gone through the practical apprenticeship of struggle against a union bureaucracy (in this case the Falangist bureaucracy), it becomes easy for it to understand the dangers of *any* bureaucracy and the need for a genuine workers' democracy, within its own organizations as well as outside them . . . and the need for direct election of all its delegates, at the shopfloor, enterprise, and national level" (*Acción Comunista* #2, p. 22). If there is a significant bureaucratic danger at the moment of victory, it is even more obvious that the mere reconstitution of a "Popular Front" safeguarding the capitalist order, as sought by so many of the oppositional forces, amounts to the defeat of any post-Franco socialist perspective.

Although they are preparing to support in their country a total struggle against modern capitalism, and against the bureaucratic organizations whose inevitably reactionary role they denounce, not all of the *Acción Comunista* comrades seem to completely recognize the implications of this capitalist modernism or the role of this bureaucratic power in the world, or the interaction between the two (their simultaneous rivalry and solidarity). The theory of revolutionary organization is clearly inseparable from such a consistent analysis. In issue #1 (pp. 26–27), *Acción Comunista* declares itself in favor of "a total freedom of criticism concerning the numerous and increasingly evident negative aspects" of the so-called socialist countries (whose global crises have had the salutary effect of undermining some of the illusions held by the bureaucratically influenced underground organizations in Spain) and calls for "a scientific analysis of the social system of those countries." But this analysis is not sufficiently developed. The lack of precision regarding the nature of the oppression in Russian or China is still greater in the case of Cuba, Castro's "antidogmatism" seeming to have at least temporarily impressed some of the *Acción Comunista* editors. Similarly, the Marxian critique of *ideology* has as yet been taken up only vaguely in *Acción Comunista;* and without the foundation of that critique it is not possible to understand and effectively combat the bureaucracy of professional leaders. And in fact the democratic workers' organization that *Acción Comunista* evokes seems to be insufficiently distinguished from Leninism: the proposal that "permanent" members be limited to a minority in its "Central Committee" is certainly an inadequate precaution against the bureaucratization of the party itself. In another place *Acción Comunista* seems to accept the project of one big nonbureaucratic labor union, only to admit a few lines later that the predictable union divisions and the examples of co-opted trade unionism in the modern capitalist countries render such a project very dubious (since the unitary enterprise committees must maintain their sovereignty, there will be an inevitable open struggle between those assemblies and *any union*).

Devoting itself to a concrete discussion under difficult conditions, and having to begin by creating some of the very bases of information that need to be discussed, *Acción Comunista* has presented to its readers a number of classic texts of the workers movement. This presentation suffers from a certain empiricism, because it is not criticized by the editors from any specific perspective. Documents that are well worth reading—on the program of the Spartakus League, Christian Rakovsky's *Letter to Valentinov*, some texts from the First International, a forthcoming text from Lukács's *History and Class Consciousness*—are presented alongside Trotsky's 1936 analyses of the bureaucracy. Marx's *Address of the Central Council to the Communist League* (March 1850), reproduced in issue #4, is appropriate in the part where it urges the workers not to give up their political autonomy and warns them of the consequences of tagging behind the petty bourgeoisie, but very dangerous in the final section which advocates the most Jacobin sort of statist centralism. The first part is precisely applicable to Spain and its coming crisis. The latter has been disproved by the experience of all the proletarian revolutions of our time; and was already inapplicable to the situation of Spain in 1936, where regional autonomy was the basis enabling the expression of the most radical tendencies. The present position of *Acción Comunista* calls rather for a study of a party such as the *Kommunistische Arbeiter Partei* in 1920 Germany. Moreover, the rich experience of the Spanish revolution has been strangely neglected by *Acción Comunista*. The problem of revolution can only be posed in a global and total form. Just as it must not forget the scope of its terrain of struggle, revolution must not forget *its own past*. *Acción Comunista* is aware of this when it states that its militants are "at the forefront of all the fronts of struggle." The fundamental theoretical critique of politico-economic power, the understanding of the profound tendencies of modern society in its production of culture and its regimentation of everyday life, the cohesion of all the positions taken at the international level—these are fronts of the same unitary struggle. In this context, it seems to us that Eduardo Mena's article "Political Regression in Algeria" (issue #3) somewhat underestimates the bureaucratic factor in its condemnation of Boumédienne's reactionary coup. More disappointing is the reprinting in issue #4 of a particularly lame and superficial article on the Los Angeles uprising by Bertrand Russell and of another article by the Trotskyist economist Mandel, whose book (currently fashionable among the Parisian intelligentsia) *Treatise on Marxist Economics* by its title alone contradicts the whole revolutionary method of Marx, who limited himself to *criticizing* political economy as a discipline reflecting a society dominated by the logic of the commodity.

The first role of revolutionary organization, the very price of its right to existence, is certainly its *coherence,* the ruthless critique which must smash the "force of habit," the most powerful force of the old world among the masses. And the most important habits to smash are the "habits of the left" during a revolutionary situation. At such a moment, if you don't disarm Noske he will kill you. For forty years this *red police* role has primarily been carried out under the "Communist" label, whether in Barcelona in 1937 or more recently in Athens or Budapest.

Revolutionary coherence must also be concretized. It is necessary to make the workers aware of what they are capable of doing, and of the consequences of following a revolutionary strategy, whether it ends in victory or in defeat. When workers' councils appear, there can be no moderation on either side. A councilist program has everything to gain and nothing to lose from recognizing and facing all its implications. The old principle of battle—"Don't put your fate at stake without engaging all your forces"—is its principle, and its forces are precisely the awareness of, and desire for, what is *possible*. The enemies of workers' councils are quite justified in fearing the worst from councilist power, just as the councilists must fear the worst from the inevitable retaliation their agitation will provoke, whatever they do or don't do. The bourgeoisie and the bureaucracy are forced by all their interests (whether as established ruling class or as ruling class in the process of formation) to totally combat the aims of the councils. So you might as well express those aims openly to those who can recognize them as their program and their life.

Councilist power is the total enemy of existing "survival." It therefore cannot itself *survive* for very long without staking and winning its bet on the total transformation of all existing conditions and the immediate liberation of life. From the very beginning it must bring about the fundamental transformation of what is produced and how it is produced, reorienting people's needs and abolishing the whole commodity production system. It must transform the organization of the environment, the methods and goals of education, the implementation of justice, and the very definition of crimes. It must eliminate all hierarchies and the morality and religion that go with them. The deepening, the defense, and the illustration of such a program are the first tasks of any organization that proposes to unleash such forces. But the same program can be expressed by its other side: concrete methods of popular agitation. *Acción Comunista* is well aware that what will unite the present "opposition" in the immediate aftermath of the Franco regime will be respect for the capitalist order, organized into some sort of democratic national front. The way to make a clear break with this pseudo-opposition is to expropriate the foreign and domestic capital that owns the means of production. This project may seem rather abstract, and many people will be unable to imagine any solution to such a complex problem except some form of statist nationalization. To cut through this apparent complexity, let us propose a concrete example.

Advanced European capitalism's present organization of consumption is leading its privileged strata to buy houses in Spain. An article in *France-Soir* (11 November 1965) notes that "there are now kilometers of villas, whole strings of vacation-villages which have sprung up in six months on previously vacant beaches. For Spain this is an economic godsend; for the middle classes of France, Germany, and England it's a discovery of paradise—at only one million (old) francs apiece." The article goes on to quote a representative of the "Constructores Ibericos" real estate company: "Our buildings have been approved by 'Securitas,' which verifies construction quality throughout the world, and are also guaranteed for ten years by a Swiss insurance company." But the insurance companies of Europe could be upset in Spain as they were in 1905 by the "economic declaration" of the St. Petersburg Soviet, which announced that loans contracted by the Czarist government to fight the Russian people would in no case be honored by that people once they had liberated themselves. Those who take advantage of the low price of local labor power by investing in construction in Spain are economically supporting the regime that is responsible for that condition, as well as littering the countryside with "second homes" that will remain empty nine-tenths of the year. To this new form of exploitation, reflecting a contemptuous indifference toward the Spanish proletariat, a councilist program could respond by declaring right now that *all foreign real estate investments will be seized without compensation the moment workers' councils come to power.* The Spanish workers would be able to recognize the highest moments of their past in this project of direct expropriation; while the forces that strive for the democratization of capitalism will see it as the most intolerable action imaginable. But the international impact of this measure would be just as considerable. Everyone knows that the feeble, years-long anarchist campaign urging tourists to boycott Spain has completely failed. This campaign was carried on in the name of political issues that the masses have clearly forgotten. It went against the whole general development of modern society—the same development that has caused the 1936 revolution to be largely forgotten. This development is resulting in *poor people* going on vacations (eight million French people visited Spain during the summer of 1965) and no political voluntarism evoking some seemingly incomprehensible detail is going to have any notable effect on this trend. In contrast, a threat against the property of people capable of investing in Spain, in apartments that cost them a million old francs apiece, has the interest of bringing glaringly into view a wealthy class whose existence has been completely hidden in Europe since modern sociology's discovery that classes no longer exist. The European ruling class has been just as forgotten as the Spanish revolution: television never talks about it, and the Left only talks about what is talked about on television. Thus, this scientific demonstration of the existence of a privileged class could have the greatest practical effect, and not only on sociologists. According to a report of the National Institute of Statistics published in June 1965, half the wage laborers in France still have a monthly paycheck of less than 750 francs (for 27% of them, less than 562 francs). It is quite obvious that these workers would not be harmed by the decision of their Spanish comrades. On the contrary, this example, by revealing both the disease and the appropriate remedy, could have the most salutary influence in their own country. A workers' power in Spain would need such support from the masses of Europe, because it would immediately face the active hostility of all the European rulers and "middle classes." That sector's investment in "durable goods" in Spain reflects their confidence in the capitalist future of Spain. Our business is to create, against all present appearances, a totally opposite confidence.

Some Theoretical Topics That Need to Be Dealt With Without Academic Debate or Idle Speculation

What can be dealt with by radical theory must be prevented from being dealt with by speculation. As the situationist analysis of reality prepares the way for the practical realization of our project, this demand tends to become more widely applicable.

Knowledge is inseparable from the use that is made of it. The agitation that our irrefutable theories are beginning to foment in varying degrees in all the sectors of the old world is going to see to the improvement and correction of our good use of ideas and things. This is why, in a society of guaranteed abundance, we are the only ones who are not frightened by that abundance.

How to use theory is never problematical. The specialists of idle speculation—from *Socialisme ou Barbarie* to *Planète*—are only concerned with concealing who profits from their ideology of confusion. The situationists work in the opposite perspective. We pose only the questions to which the will to subversion of the greatest number can respond. Our aim is to give this will its maximum effectiveness.

The topics to consider listed briefly below will have the interest of shedding light on the revolutionary worth of whoever deals with them, and on the importance that must be accorded to them in current struggles.

Critique of political economy — Critique of the social sciences — Critique of psychoanalysis (in particular: Freud, Reich, Marcuse) — Dialectics of decomposition and supersession in the realization of art and philosophy — Semiology: contribution to the study of an ideological system — Nature and the ideologies of nature — The role of playfulness in history — History of theories and theories of history — Nietzsche and the end of philosophy — Kierkegaard and the end of theology — Marx and Sade — The structuralists.

The romantic crisis — The Preciosity movement* — The baroque — Artistic languages — Art and everyday creativity — Critique of dadaism — Critique of surrealism — Society and pictorial perspective — Self-parodying art — Mallarmé, Joyce, and Malevich — Lautréamont — Primitive arts — On poetry.

The Mexican revolution (Villa and Zapata) — The Spanish revolution — Asturias 1934 — The Vienna insurrection — The Peasant War (1525) — The Spartakist revolution — The Congolese revolution — The Jacqueries — Unknown revolutions — The English revolution — The communalist movements — The Enragés — The Fronde* — Revolutionary songs (study and anthology) — Kronstadt — Bolshevism and Trotskyism — The Church and the heresies — The different currents of socialism — Socialism and underdevelopment — Cybernetics and power — The state — The origins of Islam — Theses on anarchy — Theses for a final solution of the Christian problem — The world of the specialists — On democracy — The Internationals — On insurrection — Problems and theory of self-management — Parties and labor unions — On the organization of revolutionary movements — Critique of civil and penal law — Nonindustrialized societies — Theses on utopianism — Homage to Charles Fourier — Workers' councils — Fascism and magical thought.

On the repetitive in everyday life — Dreams and dreamlike ambiences — Treatise on the passions — The moments and the construction of situations — Urbanism and popular construction — Manual of subversive détournement — Individual adventure and collective adventure — Intersubjectivity and coherence in revolutionary groups

— Play and everyday life — Personal fantasies — On the freedom to love — Preliminary studies toward the construction of a base — Madness and entranced states of mind.

RAOUL VANEIGEM

Captive Words
Preface to a Situationist Dictionary

Popular assumptions, due to what they conceal, work for the dominant organization of life. One such assumption is the notion that language is not dialectical, thereby implying that all use of dialectics should be rejected. But in fact nothing is more clearly subject to dialectics than language, since it is a living reality. Thus, every critique of the old world has been made in the language of that world, yet directed against it and therefore automatically in a *different* language. Every revolutionary theory has had to invent its own terms, to destroy the dominant sense of other terms and establish new meanings in the "world of meanings" corresponding to the new embryonic reality needing to be liberated from the dominant trash heap. The same reasons that prevent our adversaries (the masters of the Dictionary) from definitively fixing language enable us to assert alternative positions that negate existing meanings. But we already know that these same reasons also prevent us from proclaiming any definitive certitudes. A definition is always open, never definitive. Ours have a historical value, they are applicable during a specific period, linked to a specific historical practice.

It is impossible to get rid of a world without getting rid of the language that conceals and protects it, without laying bare its true nature. As the "social truth" of power is permanent falsification, language is its permanent guarantee and the Dictionary its universal reference. Every revolutionary praxis has felt the need for a new semantic field and for expressing a new truth; from the Encyclopédistes to the Polish intellectuals' critique of Stalinist "wooden language" in 1956, this demand has continually been asserted. Because *language is the house of power,* the refuge of its police violence. Any dialogue with power is violence, whether passively suffered or actively provoked. When power wants to avoid resorting to its material arms, it relies on language to guard the oppressive order. This collaboration is in fact the most natural expression of all power.

From words to ideas is only a step—a step always taken by power and its theorists. All theories of language, from the simple-minded mysticism of Being to the supreme (oppressive) rationality of the cybernetic machine, belong to the same world: the discourse of power considered as the sole possible frame of reference, as the universal mediation. Just as the Christian God is the necessary mediation between two souls and between the soul and the self, the discourse of power establishes itself at the heart of all communication, becoming the necessary mediation between self and self. This is how it is able to co-opt oppositional movements, diverting them onto its own terrain, infiltrating them and controlling them from within. The critique of the dominant language, the *détournement* of it, is going to become an ongoing practice of the new revolutionary theory.

Since any new interpretation is called a *misinterpretation* by the *authorities,* the situationists are going to establish the legitimacy of such misinterpretation and denounce the fraudulence of the interpretations given and authorized by power. Since the dictionary is the guardian of present meaning, we propose to destroy it systematically. The *replacement* of the dictionary, that master reference of all inherited and domesticated language, will find its adequate expression in the revolutionary infiltration of language, in the détournement extensively used by Marx, systematized by Lautréamont, and now being put within everyone's reach by the SI.

Détournement, which Lautréamont called plagiarism, confirms the thesis, long demonstrated by modern art, that words are insubordinate, that it is impossible for power to *totally co-opt* created meanings, to fix an existing meaning once and for all. Which means that it is objectively impossible to create a "Newspeak."* The new revolutionary theory cannot advance without redefining its fundamental concepts. "Ideas improve," says Lautréamont. "The meaning of words plays a role in that improvement. Plagiarism is necessary. Progress depends on it. It sticks close to an author's phrase, exploits his expressions, deletes a false idea, replaces it with the right one." To salvage Marx's thought it is necessary to continually make it more precise, to correct it and reformulate it in the light of a hundred years of reinforcement of alienation and of the possibilities of negating alienation. Marx needs to be detourned by those who are continuing on this historical path, not moronically quoted by the thousand varieties of co-opters. On the other hand, power's own thought is becoming in our hands a weapon against power. Ever since it came to power, the bourgeoisie has dreamed of a universal language, a language which the cyberneticians of today are trying to implement electronically. Descartes dreamed of a language (a forerunner of Newspeak) in which thought would follow thought with mathematical rigor: the *mathesis universalis* or perpetuity of bourgeois categories. The Encyclopédistes,* dreaming (under feudal power) of "definitions so rigorous that tyranny could not tolerate them," paved the way for an eternal future power that would be the ultimate goal of history.

The insubordination of words, during the experimental phase from Rimbaud to the surrealists, has shown that the theoretical critique of the world of power is inseparable from a practice that destroys it. Power's co-option of all modern art and its transformation of it into the oppressive categories of its reigning spectacle is a sad confirmation of this. "Whatever doesn't kill power is killed by it." The dadaists were the first to express their distrust in words, a distrust inseparable from the desire to "change life." Following Sade, they asserted the right to *say everything*, to liberate words and "replace the Alchemy of the Word with a real chemistry" (Breton). The *innocence* of words is henceforth consciously refuted and language is revealed as "the worst of conventions," something that should be destroyed, demystified, liberated. Dada's contemporaries did not fail to stress its will to destroy everything, the danger it represented to the dominant sense. (Gide uneasily referred to it as a "demolition job.") After Dada it has become impossible to believe that a word is forever bound to an idea. Dada realized all the possibilities of language and forever closed the door on art as a specialty; it posed once and for all the problem of the realization of art. Surrealism was of value only insofar as it continued and extended this project; in its literary productions it was *reactionary*. The realization of art—poetry in the situationist sense—means that one cannot realize oneself in a "work," but rather realizes oneself, period. Sade's inauguration of "saying everything" already implied the abolition of literature as a separate domain (where only what is literary may be said). But this abolition, consciously asserted by the dadaists after Rimbaud and Lautréamont, was not a *supersession*. There is no supersession without realization, one cannot supersede art without realizing it. In fact, there has not even been any actual abolition, since even after Joyce, Duchamp, and Dada a new spectacular literature continues to thrive. This is because there can be no "saying everything" without the freedom to *do everything*. Dada had a chance for realization with the Spartakists, with the revolutionary practice of the German proletariat. The latter's failure made the failure of Dada inevitable. With its co-option (including that of virtually all its original protagonists) into subsequent artistic movements, Dada has become the literary expression of the nothingness of poetic activity, the art of expressing the nothingness of everyday freedom. The ultimate expression of this art of "saying everything" deprived of any doing is the blank page. Modern poetry (experimental, permutational, spatialist, surrealist, or neodadaist) is the antithesis of poetry, it is the artistic project co-opted by power. It abolishes poetry without realizing it, living off its own continual self-destruction. "What's the point of saving language," Max Bense asks resignedly, "when there is no longer anything to say?" Confession of a specialist! Muteness or mindless chatter are the sole alternatives of the specialists of permutation. Modern thought and art, guaranteeing power and guaranteed by it, move in the realm of what Hegel called "the language of flattery." Both contribute to the eulogy of power and its products, perfecting reification while banalizing it. Asserting that "reality consists of language" or that "language can only be considered in and for itself," the specialists of language arrive at the concepts of "language-object" and "word-thing" and revel in the panegyrics of their own reification. The thing becomes the dominant model and once again the commodity finds its realization and its poets. The theory of the state, of the economy, of law, of philosophy, of art—everything now has this apologetic character.

Whenever separate power replaces the autonomous action of the masses, whenever bureaucracy seizes control of all aspects of social life, it attacks language and reduces its poetry to the vulgar prose of its information. Bureaucracy appropriates language for its own use, just as it does everything else, and imposes it on the masses. Language—the material support of its ideology—is then presumed to communicate its messages and reflect its thought. Bureaucracy represses the fact that language is first of all a means of communication between people. Since all communication is channeled through bureaucracies, people no longer even need to talk to each other: their first duty is to play their role as receivers in the network of informationist communication to which the whole society is reduced, receivers of orders they must carry out.

This language's mode of existence is bureaucracy, its becoming is bureaucratization. The Bolshevik order born out of the failure of the soviet revolution imposed a whole series of more or less magical and impersonal expressions in the image of the bureaucracy in power. "Politburo," "Comintern," "Cavarmy," "Agitprop"—mysterious names of specialized agencies that really are mysterious, operating in the nebulous sphere of the state (or of the Party leadership) without any relation to the masses except insofar as they reinforce their subjection. Language colonized by bureaucracy is reduced to a series of blunt, inflexible formulas in which the same nouns are always accompanied by the same adjectives and participles. The noun governs; each time it appears the other words automatically fall in around it in the correct order. This "regimentation" of words reflects a more profound militarization of the whole society, its division into two basic categories: the caste of rulers and the great mass of people who carry out their orders. But the same words are also called on to play other roles, invested with the magic power to reinforce the oppressive reality, to cloak it and present it as the only possible truth. Thus there are no more "Trotskyists" but only "Hitlero-Trotskyists"; one never hears of Marxism but only of "Marxism-Leninism," and the opposition is automatically "reactionary" in the "Soviet regime." The rigidity with which these ritualistic formulas are sanctified is aimed at preserving the purity of this "substance" in the face of obviously contradictory facts. In this way the language of the masters is everything, reality nothing, or at most the shell of this language. People are required in their acts, their thoughts, and their feelings to behave as if the state was that reason, justice, and freedom proclaimed by the ideology. The ritual (and the police) are there to ensure conformity to this behavior (see Marcuse's *Soviet Marxism*).

The decline of radical thought considerably increases the power of words, the words of power. "Power creates nothing; it co-opts" (*Internationale Situationniste* #8). Words forged by revolutionary criticism are like partisans' weapons: abandoned on the battlefield, they fall into the hands of the counterrevolution. And like prisoners of war, they are subjected to forced labor. Our most direct enemies are the proponents and established functionaries of false critique. The divorce between theory and practice provides the central basis for co-option, for the petrification of revolutionary theory into ideology, which transforms real practical demands (for whose realization the premonitory signs are already appearing in the present society) into systems of ideas, into demands of reason. The ideologues of every variety, the watchdogs of the reigning spectacle, carry out this task, emptying the content from most corrosive concepts and putting them back into circulation in the service of maintaining alienation: dadaism in reverse. They become advertising slogans (see the recent Club Med prospectus). Concepts of radical critique suffer the same fate as the proletariat: they are deprived of their history, cut off from their roots. They become grist for power's thinking machines.

Our project of liberating words is historically comparable to the Encyclopédiste enterprise. The Enlightenment's language of "tearing apart" (to continue the Hegelian image) lacked the conscious historical dimension; it was a real critique of the decrepit feudal world, but it had no idea of what would emerge from it (none of the Encyclopédistes were republicans). It was, rather, an expression of the bourgeois thinkers' own internal tearing apart. Our language aims first of all at a practice that tears the world apart, beginning with tearing apart the veils that cloak it. Whereas the Encyclopédistes sought a quantitative enumeration, the enthusiastic description of a world of objects in which the bourgeoisie and the commodity were already victorious, our dictionary will express the *qualitative,* the possible but still absent victory, the repressed of modern history (the proletariat) and *the return of the repressed.* We propose the real liberation of language because we propose to put it into a practice free of all constraints. We reject any authority, linguistic or otherwise: only real life *allows* a meaning and only praxis verifies it. Debates over the reality or unreality of the meaning of a word, isolated from practice, are purely academic. We place our dictionary in that libertarian region which is still beyond the reach of power, but which is its only possible global successor.

Language remains the necessary mediation for comprehending the world of alienation (Hegel would say: the necessary alienation), the instrument of the radical theory that will eventually seize the masses because it is theirs. Only then will it find its own truth. It is thus essential that we forge our own language, the language of real life, against the ideological language of power, the terrain of justification of all the categories of the old world. From now on we must prevent the falsification or co-option of our theories. We use specific concepts already used by the specialists, but we give them a new content, turning them against the specialists that they support and against future salaried thinkers who might be tempted to besmear situationist theory with their own shit (as Claudel did with Rimbaud, and Klossowski with Sade). Future revolutions must invent their own language. Concepts of radical critique will be reexamined one by one in order to rediscover their truth. The word *alienation,* for example, one of the key concepts for the comprehension of modern society, must be disinfected after having passed through the mouths of people like Axelos [editor of *Arguments*]. All words have the same relation with power as does the proletariat: they are both its present servants and the instruments and agents of future liberation from it. Poor Revel! There are no forbidden words; in language, as it will be in every other domain, *everything is permitted.* To deny ourselves the use of a word is to deny ourselves a weapon used by our adversaries.

Our dictionary will be a sort of code book enabling one to decipher the news and rend the ideological veils that cover reality. We will give possible translations that will enable people to grasp the different aspects of the society of the spectacle, and show how the slightest signs and indications contribute to maintaining it. In a sense it will be a bilingual dictionary, since each word has an "ideological" meaning for power and a real meaning that we think corresponds to real life in the present historical phase. Thus we will be able at each step to determine the various positions of words in the social war. If the problem of ideology is how to descend from the heaven of ideas to the real world, our dictionary will be a contribution to the elaboration of the new revolutionary theory where the problem is how to effect the transition from language to life. The real appropriation of the words that work cannot be realized outside the appropriation of work itself. The inauguration of free creative activity will at the same time be the inauguration of true communication, freed at last. The transparency of human relations will replace the poverty of words under the old regime of opacity. Words will not cease to *work* until people do.

MUSTAPHA KHAYATI

The Role of Godard

In cinema Godard currently represents formal pseudofreedom and the pseudocritique of manners and values—the two inseparable manifestations of all fake, co-opted modern art. Everyone does everything to present him as a misunderstood and unappreciated artist, shockingly audacious and unjustly despised; and everyone praises him, from *Elle* magazine to Aragon-the-Senile.* Despite the absence of any real critiques of Godard, we see developing a sort of analogy to the famous theory of the increase of resistances in socialist regimes: the more Godard is hailed as a brilliant leader of modern art, the more people rush to his defense against incredible plots. Repetitions of the same doltish stupidities in his films are automatically seen as breathtaking innovations. They are beyond any attempt at explanation; his admirers consume them as confusedly and arbitrarily as Godard produced them, because they recognize in them the consistent expression of a *subjectivity*. This is true, but it is a subjectivity on the level of a concierge educated by the mass media. Godard's "critiques" never go beyond the innocuous humor typical of nightclub comedians or *Mad* magazine. His flaunted culture is largely the same as that of his audience, which has read exactly the same pages in the same drugstore paperbacks. The two most famous lines from the most read poem of the most overrated Spanish poet ("Terrible five o'clock in the afternoon—the blood, I don't want to see it" in *Pierrot le Fou*)—this is the key to Godard's method. The most famous renegade of modern art, Aragon, in *Les Lettres Françaises* (9 September 1965), has rendered an homage to his younger colleague which, coming from such an expert, is perfectly fitting: "Art today is Jean-Luc Godard . . . of a superhuman beauty . . . of a constantly sublime beauty. . . . There is no precedent to Godard except Lautréamont. . . . This child of genius." Even the most naïve can scarcely be taken in after such a testimonial from such a source.

Godard is a Swiss from Lausanne who envied the chic of the Swiss of Geneva, and then the chic of the Champs-Elysées, and his successful ascent up from the provinces might be seen as inspirational at a time when the system is striving to usher so many "culturally deprived" people into a respectful consumption of culture—even "avant-garde" culture if nothing else will do. We are not referring here to the ultimately conformist exploitation of any art that professes to be innovative and critical. We are pointing out Godard's directly conformist use of film.

To be sure, films, like songs, have intrinsic powers of conditioning the spectator: beauties, if you will, that are at the disposition of those who presently have the possibility of expressing themselves in that medium. Up to a point such people may make a relatively clever use of those powers. But it is a sign of the general conditions of our time that their cleverness is so limited, and that the extent of their ties with the dominant ways of life quickly reveals the disappointing limits of their enterprises. Godard is to film what Lefebvre or Morin is to social critique: each possesses the *appearance* of a certain freedom in style or subject matter (in Godard's case, a slightly free manner in comparison with the stale formulas of cinematic narration). But they have *taken this very freedom from elsewhere:* from what they have been able to grasp of the advanced experiences of the era. They are the *Club Med* of modern thought (see in this issue "The Packaging of 'Free Time' "). They make use of a caricature of freedom, as marketable junk, *in place of* the authentic. This is done on all terrains, including that of formal artistic freedom of expression, which is merely one sector of the general problem of pseudocommunication. Godard's "critical" art and his admiring art critics all work to conceal the present problems of a *critique of art*—the real experience, in the SI's phrase, of a "communication containing its own critique." In the final analysis the present function of Godardism is to forestall a situationist use of the cinema.

Aragon has for some time been developing his theory of the *collage* in all modern art up to Godard. This is nothing other than an attempt to interpret *détournement* in such a way as to bring about its co-option by the dominant culture. Laying the foundations for a Togliattist variant of French Stalinism, Garaudy and Aragon are setting up a "completely open" artistic modernism, just as they are moving "from anathema to dialogue" with the priests. Godard could become their *artistic Teilhardism.** In fact the collage, made famous by Cubism during the dissolution of plastic art, is only a particular case (a destructive moment) of détournement: it is displacement, the *infidelity of the element*. Détournement, originally formulated by Lautréamont, is a return to a superior fidelity of the element. In all cases, détournement is dominated by the dialectical devaluing/revaluing of the element within the development of a unifying meaning. But the collage of the merely devalued element has been widely used, well before being constituted as a Pop Art doctrine, in the modernist snobbism of the displaced object (making a spice bottle out of a chemistry flask, etc.).

This acceptance of *devaluation* is now being extended to a method of *combining neutral* and indefinitely interchangeable elements. Godard is a particularly boring example of such a use without negation, without affirmation, and without quality.

The Ideology of Dialogue

The situationists' practice of concretely breaking with apologists for any aspect of the present social order (particularly visible with regard to the *leading representatives* of the culture and politics of submission, and including as its extreme case the exclusion of certain members of the SI) has been subject to the greatest misunderstanding, although it follows quite directly from our basic positions. Certain commentators have propagated the most hostile interpretations of this practice, thereby causing concern among semi-informed people. The reality in this particular case is quite simple. Those who accept one or more variants of the prevailing pseudodialogue become the advocates of a new type of *free exchange* in the name of an abstract right to dialogue at any price (payable in avowed concessions to falsehood), and they reproach us for interrupting this *fake dialogue*. It is, however, only in this way that we are able to be the bearers of the reality of dialogue. On the question of exclusion, we believe that through experimentation we have made an advance in determining the requirements for the nonhierarchical organization of joint projects, which projects can be sustained only by the self-discipline of individuals proving themselves in the coherence of the theories and acts through which each member strives to merit his joint responsibility with all the others.

The one-sidedness of Stirner's notions on the relations of the egoist with the organization that he enters or leaves at whim (though it does contain a kernel of truth regarding *that aspect* of freedom) does not allow any independent basis for his passive and defenseless ghost of an "organization." Such an incoherent and undisciplined organization is at the mercy of any individual "egoist," who can cynically exploit it for his own ends while disdaining any social aims it might have (and in fact the Stirnerian individual can just as well enter the most reactionary association for his own personal profit). But a free association—"a bond, not a power"*—in which several individuals meet on a common basis cannot be passively subject to someone's individual whim. Those who wish neither to judge nor to command must be able to reject any person whose conduct would implicate them. When the SI excludes someone, we are calling him to account not for *his* life but for *ours*, for the common project that he would falsify (whether out of hostile intentions or through mere lack of discernment). Each side remains individually free (the fact that this freedom is generally impoverished is another problem, without which there would be no need for undertakings like the SI), and by throwing back on his own an individual who has always remained autonomous we are only expressing the fact that this autonomy was not able to fulfill itself within our common project. In rejecting someone in accordance with the rules of the game that he thought he had accepted, or had pretended to accept, it is our *own* resignation that we are rejecting.

It may be helpful to elucidate these remarks with excerpts from two letters recently addressed to one of our correspondents in East Europe.*

(*First letter.*) Our theoretical positions (on play, language, etc.) would not only risk becoming mendacious and valueless, they would *already* be without value if we held them in coexistence with some doctrinal dogmatism, whatever it might be. All of us believe, as you do, that "the freedom to travel all the unaccustomed paths" must be absolute (and not only on the artistic or theoretical plane, but in all aspects of practical life). For a thousand reasons, of which the experience of the Eastern bloc is the most obvious, we know that an ideology in power turns any partial truth into an absolute lie. . . . We are not a *power* in society, and thus our "exclusions" only express our freedom to distinguish ourselves from the confusionism around us or even among us, which confusionism is much closer to the actual social power and partakes of all its benefits. We have never wished to prevent anyone from expressing their ideas or doing what they want (and we have never sought to be in a position to exert such pressure). We merely refuse *to be ourselves mixed up with* ideas and acts that run contrary to our convictions and tastes. Note that this is all the more vital in that we have hardly any freedom to express our own convictions and tastes, due to their going so sharply against the mainstream. Our "intolerance" is nothing but a very limited response to the very strict intolerance and exclusion that *we run into everywhere,* particularly among the "intellectual establishment" (considerably more intense than the hostility the surrealists had to endure), and which we scarcely find surprising. Just as we are in no degree a controlling power in society, *we refuse to become one* someday by means of some political reshuffling (we are in this regard partisans of *radical self-management,* of workers' councils abolishing all separate state power or even separate "theoretical" power); and we are refusing to transform ourselves into any power whatsoever, even on the small scale that we would be allowed, when we refuse to enlist *disciples,* who would give us, along with the right of control and direction *over themselves,* a greater recognized social standing as representatives of one more artistic or political ideology. . . . One should not confuse the practical conditions of free thought here and in the East—or in Spain, for example. In countries where nothing can be openly expressed, it is obviously necessary to support the right of everyone to express themselves. But in places where everyone can express themselves (though under conditions of enormous inequality) any radical thought—without of course wishing to suppress this practical freedom—must first of all clear the way for its own "unaccustomed path," must assert its own right to exist without being "co-opted" and distorted by the social order which manifestly reigns behind this visible confusion and complexity and which ultimately possesses the *monopoly of appearances* (see our critique of the "spectacle" in the consumer society of commodity abundance). Finally, the reigning "tolerance" is one-way, and this on a global scale in spite of the antagonisms and complexity of the different types of exploitive societies. What the tolerant people who are in a position to express themselves tolerate, fundamentally, is the *established power* everywhere. You tell us that you live in X... If you were in Paris you would see how many of these tolerant leftist intellectuals turn out to be undecided, understanding, and tolerant toward the established conditions in X... or in Beijing. What they call "the sense of history" is their Hegelian adherence to *what they read in the daily papers.*

(*Second letter.*) A radically different point of departure in fact first of all restores the *truth* of the liberatory endeavors of the past. It is necessary to break clearly with the old confusion, and therefore with its partisans, whether they be open, cunning, or simply unconscious. We obviously have to bear the negative consequences of the attitude we have chosen, and we have to acknowledge this negativity. . . . We are in complete agreement with you on the interrelation of all aspects of the problem of the present avant-garde. We are in fact trying to initiate dialogue everywhere that that state of mind manifests itself in a radical direction. For that *state of mind* is itself divided by a struggle between its truth and its organized *co-option* by the ruling powers.

Interview with an Imbecile

Even worse than the old *Observateur,* the *Nouvel Observateur* is a veritable Niagara of stupidity (6,810,000 liters per second). A considerable portion of this flow is produced by two of its editors, Katia Kaupp and Michel Cournot, whose writings could serve as excellent historical documents for the study of the supreme phase of spectacular decomposition. Their combination of stupidity and stylistic vulgarity makes them perfect *Jean Nochers* of the Left (a Left which adheres to the dominant society as fundamentally as does Jean Nocher, apart from a few details concerning the "modernization" of this domination). For its launching, however, this magazine called on some guest celebrities. Its opening issue (19 November 1964) presented a five-page interview with a star thinker. We reproduce here a few of his most extraordinary statements. The parenthetical remarks are of course ours and not those of the *Nouvel Observateur* flunky who pretends to dialogue with the oracle.

"The young people I meet," says the imbecile, "are perhaps less hotheaded than in the past, but what I find most striking is that politically they are often at the same point as I am. My point of arrival is their point of departure. . . . And they have a whole lifetime ahead of them to build on the base that is my point of culmination." *(The young people who are not at the same point of political degradation would obviously never have been interested in meeting this imbecile. As for those who have the misfortune to be at that point, a hundred successive lifetimes "ahead of them" would never suffice to build anything on the base of his culmination, which has been revealed from every angle as an intellectual dead end.)*

"In France the 'yé-yé' phenomenon was used in order to turn the youth into a class of consumers." *(A perfect inversion of reality: it is because the youth of the modern capitalist countries has become a very important category of consumers that phenomena of the "yé-yé" sort appear.)*

"You can only be alluding to Marxist ideology. Today I don't know of any other: current bourgeois ideology is more notable for its absence than for its strength." *(Those who have read Marx know that his method is a radical critique of ideologies; but he who has only read Stalin can praise "Marxism" for having become the best of ideologies, the ideology that has had the strongest police.)*

"Socialism can be pure only as an idea or, perhaps, much later, if it becomes the regime of all societies. In the meantime its incarnation in a particular country implies that it must develop and define itself through innumerable relations with the rest of the world. In the forging of reality, the purity of the idea becomes tainted." *(Here is a Marxist ideologue really ideologizing: ideas are pure in the heavens and become rotten when they are incarnated. Since this thinker is himself real and has affirmed the principle that any realization in the world must entail a fundamental corruption, he implicitly both admits his own degradation in his "relations with the rest of the world" and justifies it on the grounds of inevitability. From all this we can appreciate his "advanced" state of decomposition.)*

Right after this, the imbecile quotes a Malian's statement which he greatly admires: "Our socialism is conditioned by the fact that we are a country without any outlet to the sea." *(Is it not also somewhat conditioned by the absence of an industrial proletariat in Mali? But this is just a trifling detail in the geopolitics of such a profound thinker!)*

To the idea that all the industrial societies have many features in common, the imbecile retorts: "To say that, one would have to prove that there is a class struggle in the socialist countries, that is, that the privileges accorded certain people are becoming stratified. Now, this is not at all the case. There are admittedly some very real inequalities; but the money obtained by a factory manager in the USSR cannot be reinvested anywhere: it is spent and cannot be replenished or augmented in his hands to become the basis of a class power." *(A basis which lies elsewhere: in the possession of the state. The extra money received by the privileged in the USSR is not the basis of their power, but a clear reflection of their power.)*

"The Soviets are shocked when one seems to believe that among them money can confer power." *(Of course, since it's the other way around!)*

"To be sure, these 'high-ranking functionaries' have numerous privileges; but to the very extent that the regime is authoritarian, there is a social instability, intermixing among different strata, demotion of leaders, a constant influx of newcomers from the base to the summit. If any conflicts were to occur in the USSR they would have the aspect of a reformism and not of a revolution." *(Thus the very arbitrariness serves to prove that there is no ruling class in the USSR. At this level of insult to one's intelligence, one could just as well argue that the free-enterprise capitalism of Marx's day was also socialist, since its economic laws ruined many industrialists and it sometimes happened that a worker would become a boss; hence the social instability, class intermixing, etc.)*

But the idea of a pure imbecile of this dimension would only be a "pure idea." Since such an imbecile actually exists, he must also firmly identify with a repressive power. After the armed revolt of the Hungarian proletariat—in one of those "socialist countries" where "one would have to prove" that class struggles could now exist—this same imbecile was so set on defending the interests of the Russian bureaucracy that he took a position *to the right of Khrushchev:* "The most serious mistake was probably Khrushchev's Report on Stalin, for the solemn public denunciation, the detailed exposure of all the crimes of a sacred personage who has represented the regime for so long, is a folly when such frankness is not made possible by a previous substantial rise in the standard of living of the population. . . . The result was to reveal the truth to masses who were not ready to receive it."

The thinker we have been talking about is Sartre. Anyone who still wants to seriously discuss the value (whether philosophical or political or literary—one can't separate the aspects of this hodgepodge) of such a nullity, so puffed up by the various authorities that are so satisfied with him, thereby reveals himself as not worth being taken seriously by those who refuse to renounce the *potential consciousness* of our time.

The Algeria of Daniel Guérin, Libertarian

In December 1965 Daniel Guérin published a pamphlet entitled *L'Algérie caporalisée?* which contains a rather bizarre analysis of Boumédienne's regime. According to Guérin, nothing happened in June. Faithful to an old schema, he sees only a "Bonapartism" in power both before and after the coup d'état, struggling classically on two fronts: against the "counterrevolution of the indigenous propertied classes" and against the threatening enthusiasm of the workers striving for self-management. And in foreign affairs he finds "the same desire on the part of both regimes for an adroit balancing act between capitalist and socialist countries" (p. 6). "None of the declarations of the so-called 'Council of the Revolution' contains any innovations whatsoever or any hints of an original program" (p. 10). However, when he drafted his main text, dated November 5, Guérin thought he detected some *potential* new developments as the putchists were being pushed, as if despite themselves, to the "right"—developments that *"seem to foreshadow* an antisocialist policy" (p. 11, our emphasis). One might suppose that Guérin disregards the considerable differences between the two regimes because he is carried away by the equal contempt that Ben Bella and Boumédienne might well arouse in a revolutionary who is a declared partisan of "libertarian socialism" and self-management. Unfortunately, this is not at all the case! He has no other revolutionary solution to recommend than the restoration of Ben Bella: "To rally a popular opposition to the colonels' regime in Algeria today without reference to Ben Bella, or while making a total political critique of Ben-Bellaism, would be an undertaking doomed to failure" (p. 17). And before June 19 the Ben Bella regime's numerous attacks on the workers, the exploits of its police and army—the same police and army that are still in place today, in fact—were for Guérin only "mistakes, weaknesses, and omissions" of an acceptable orientation. The king was badly advised or misinformed; never responsible. Since Guérin cannot be unaware of the open struggles of Ben Bella's regime against the masses (he himself provides some excellent documentation of them, notably apropos of the Congress of Agricultural Workers), he has to reconstruct history by totally separating Ben Bella from his regime. Page 12: "The sabotage of self-management, organized, of course, without Ben Bella's knowledge." Page 2: "As we can see more clearly today, Ben Bella never had his hands free: for nearly three years he was the tool, the prisoner, the hostage of Boumédienne." In other words, people thought Ben Bella was in power, but his downfall has shown that he wasn't. Such an astonishing retroactive demonstration could just as well be applied to the Czar, who was believed to be an autocrat before 1917. But Guérin overlooks this question: Who besides Ben Bella *made* Boumédienne, by hoisting himself into power with the aid of Boumédienne's arms? That Ben Bella later made some half-hearted and very inept attempts to get rid of his tool is another matter. It is because he was above all a bureaucrat that he was at first essentially in solidarity with, and eventually the victim of, bureaucrats more rational than he.

What, then, is the secret of this aberration of one of our famous leftist intellectuals, and one of the most ostensibly "libertarian" among them at that? With him it is no different than with all the others: it is the decisive influence of their vainglorious participation in *high society;* their common tendency, even more servile than a lackey's, to be swept off their feet with joy because they have spoken with the greats of this world; and the imbecility that makes them attribute such greatness to those who have condescended to talk to them. Whether they are partisans of the self-managing masses or of police-state bureaucracies, the "leftist intellectuals" of the period from which we are just emerging always have the same awestruck admiration for power and government. The closer they are to a governmental position, the more the leaders of the "underdeveloped" countries fascinate these ridiculous professors of leftist museology. In Simone de Beauvoir's memoirs, so revealing of the fundamental degradation of a whole generation of intellectuals, her narration of a dinner at the Soviet Embassy exposes a pettiness so irremediable and so shameless that she isn't even aware of it.

So here is the secret: Guérin "knew" Ben Bella. He "listened" to him from time to time: "When I had the privilege, at the beginning of December 1963, of a brief audience at the Villa Joly in order to present to the President a report resulting from my month of traveling around the country observing the self-managed enterprises, I had the impression that he had been prejudiced against my conclusions by Ali Mahsas and the Minister of Industry and Commerce, Bachir Boumaza" (p. 7).

Guérin really is for self-management, but, like Mohammed Harbi, it is in the pure form of its spirit incarnated as a privileged hero that he prefers to meet it, recognize it, and aid it with his sage advice. Daniel Guérin met the World-Spirit of self-management over a cup of tea, and everything else follows.

Domenach versus Alienation
(excerpts)

"Alienation, that key word for a whole system of politics, sociology, and critical thought—what does it cover? J.M. Domenach traces the astonishing itinerary of this concept of such diverse meanings, from Hegel to Jacques Berque. Then he takes another look at its content. It seems to him that the moment has come to renounce this 'hospital concept' where all the maladies of the century are lumped together, and to call into question the philosophy that developed it."

This prefatory note from the journal *Esprit* (December 1965) is not betrayed by the extraordinary impudence of Domenach's article "Let's Get Rid of Alienation," which opens the same issue. Domenach, prince of that notable province of contemporary confusionism, Christian leftism, reproaches the concept of alienation for being confused, for being used improperly, for having considerably evolved historically, and for having given rise to too many "vague and outmoded" formulas. If everything that was vague was therefore outmoded, religious thought would not have survived the rationalist clarification brought into the world by bourgeois society. But in a materially divided society, vague ideas and the vague use of precise concepts serve definite forces. The history of the concept of alienation, as Domenach recounts it in a few pages, is itself a perfect example of vague thought serving a specific confusionism. [. . .]

Domenach does not even want to "get rid of" the concept of alienation like the philosopher depicted in *The German Ideology* who wanted to liberate humanity from the idea of gravity so that there would be no more drownings. Domenach wants people to stop talking about alienation so that they will become *resigned to it*. This Christian, who naturally relies on Stalinist orthodoxy or the cybernetized "Marxism" of a Châtelet (acknowledging them all the more readily as Marxist since his very existence as a "leftist thinker" depends on such Marxism), removes his mask after enumerating a few items found in Châtelet, carefully selected for their incoherence, when he insinuates: "All these 'alienations' appear to emerge from a general human condition." Then, at the end of his discourse, he invites everyone to admit their "original alienation" and thus their Creator. In exchange, he offers this concession to the economistic and mechanistic Marxism that *all the modern priests are in the process of accepting:* the alienation banished from consciousness is to be replaced by the more "precise" concept of exploitation. While it is true that the general alienation in the East and the West is effectively based on the exploitation of the workers, the evolution of modern capitalism—and still more, of bureaucratic ideology—have largely succeeded in masking the Marxist analyses of exploitation at the stage of free competition and in making the handling of them less precise. In contrast, these parallel evolutions have brought alienation—which was originally a philosophical concept—into the reality of every hour of daily life. That is why this Christian believes that "the moment has come" to resume his original role ("It must be done, such is the will of the Lord") within the *new decor* of the era.

To be sure, in a society that needs to spread a *mass* pseudoculture and to have its spectacular pseudointellectuals monopolize the stage, many terms are naturally rapidly vulgarized. But for the same reasons, perfectly simple and illuminating words tend to disappear: such as the word *priest;* so that Domenach and his friends come to think that no one will ever again remind them of this embarrassing vulgarity. They are mistaken. Just as the secular efforts of a Revel (*En France*) to compile a list of words to forbid, a list that mixes a few fashionable trivialities with important contested terms, are ridiculous because one cannot hope to *simultaneously* suppress the theoretical discoveries of our time and the interested confusion to which they give rise in order to "return" to some simplified rationalism which *never had* the efficacy the nostalgic liberals now attribute to it. What all these vocabulary challengers lack is dialectics. In a recent *Le Monde* column Robert Le Bidois, who is usually less puristic, denounces all uses of the phrase "at the level of." Despite the many examples he gives of inept uses of that phrase, it should be understood that a society that is characterized by economic gradations and administrative hierarchies in all sectors of life and that is also familiar with the psychoanalytical unconscious (even if it represses a coherent use of such information)—it must be understood that such a society's language will not restrict its use of the concept of "level" to the literal spatial sense or to the figurative phrase "to be at the level of his task."

People like Domenach, being themselves valets of the establishment's cultural spectacle, which wants to quickly co-opt for its own use the most crucial terms of modern critical thought, will never want to admit that the truest and most important concepts of the era—alienation, dialectics, communism—are precisely marked by the organization around them of the greatest confusions and the worst misinterpretations. Vital concepts are *simultaneously* subject to the truest and the most false uses, along with a multitude of intermediary confusions, because the struggle between critical reality and the apologetic spectacle leads to a struggle over words, a struggle that is more bitter the more those words are central. The *truth* of a concept is not revealed by an authoritarian purge, but by the coherence of its use in theory and in practical life. It is of no importance that a priest at the pulpit renounces the use of a concept that he would in any case *never* have known *how* to use. Let us speak vulgarly since we're dealing with priests: alienation is the point of departure for everything—providing that one departs from it.

The Explosion Point of Ideology in China

The international association of totalitarian bureaucracies has completely fallen apart. In the words of the "Address" published by the situationists in Algiers in July 1965, the irreversible "collapse of the revolutionary image" that the "bureaucratic lie" counterposed to the whole of capitalist society, as its pseudonegation and actual support, has become obvious, and first of all on the terrain where official capitalism had the greatest interest in upholding the pretense of its adversary: the global confrontation between the bourgeoisie and the so-called socialist camp. This camp had in any case *never been socialist;* now, in spite of all sorts of attempts to patch it up, *it has ceased even to be a camp.*

The disintegration of the Stalinist monolith is already manifested in the coexistence of some twenty independent "lines," from Romania to Cuba, from Italy to the Vietnamese-Korean-Japanese bloc of parties. Russia, having this year become incapable of holding a joint conference of merely all the *European* parties, prefers to forget the era when Moscow reigned over the Comintern. Thus the *Izvestia* of September 1966 blames the Chinese leaders for bringing "unprecedented" discredit to "Marxist-Leninist" ideas, and virtuously deplores the confrontational style "in which insults are substituted for an exchange of opinions and revolutionary experiences. Those who choose this method confer an absolute value on their own experience and reveal a dogmatic and sectarian mentality in their interpretation of Marxist-Leninist theory. Such an attitude is inevitably accompanied by interference in the internal affairs of fraternal parties." In the Sino-Soviet polemic, in which each power is led to impute to its opponent every conceivable antiproletarian crime, being only obliged not to mention the *real crime* (the class power of the bureaucracy), each side can only arrive at the sobering conclusion that the other's revolutionariness was only an inexplicable mirage, a mirage which, lacking any reality, has now reverted to its old point of departure. Thus in New Delhi last February the Chinese ambassador described Brezhnev and Kosygin as "new czars of the Kremlin," while the Indian government, an anti-Chinese ally of this Muscovy, discovered that "the present masters of China have donned the imperial mantle of the Manchus." This denunciation of the new Middle Kingdom dynasty was further refined the following month in Moscow by the modernist state poet Voznesensky, who, evoking the menace of a new invasion of "the hordes of Kuchum," counts on "eternal Russia" to build a rampart against the Mongols who threaten to bivouac among "the Egyptian treasures of the Louvre."

The accelerating decomposition of bureaucratic ideology, as evident in the countries where Stalinism has seized power as in the others where it has lost every chance of seizing it, naturally began around issues of internationalism; but this is only the *beginning* of a general and irreversible disintegration. For the bureaucracy, internationalism could be nothing but an illusive proclamation in the service of its real interests, one *ideological* justification among others, since bureaucratic society is the *total opposite* of proletarian community. Bureaucratic power is based on possession of a nation-state and it must ultimately obey the logic of this reality, in accordance with the particular interests imposed by the level of development of the country it possesses. Its heroic age passed away with the ideological golden age of "socialism in a single country" that Stalin was shrewd enough to maintain by destroying the revolutions in China in 1927 and Spain in 1937. The autonomous bureaucratic revolution in China—as already shortly before in Yugoslavia—introduced into the unity of the bureaucratic world a dissolutive germ that has broken it up in less than twenty years. The general process of decomposition of bureaucratic ideology is now attaining its supreme stage in the very country where that ideology was most necessary, the country where, because of its general economic backwardness, the remaining ideological pretensions of revolution had to be pushed to their extreme: China.

The crisis that has continually deepened in China since the spring of 1966 constitutes an unprecedented phenomenon in bureaucratic society. The bureaucratic state-capitalist ruling class of Russia and East Europe, continually and necessarily exerting terror over the exploited majority, has of course often been torn apart by rivalries and antagonisms stemming from the objective problems it runs into as well as from the subjectively delirious style that a totally mendacious power is led to assume. But up till now the bureaucracy—which must be centralized due to its mode of appropriation of the economy, since it must draw from itself the hierarchical guarantee to all participation in its collective appropriation of the social surplus production—has always made its purges *from the top down*. The summit of the bureaucracy has to remain fixed because the whole legitimacy of the system depends on a fixed summit. It must keep its dissensions to itself (as it always has from the time of Lenin and Trotsky). Those who hold office may be replaced or liquidated, but the office itself must always retain the same indisputable majesty. The unexplained and unanswerable repression can then normally descend to each level of the apparatus as a mere implementation of what has been *instantaneously* decided at the top. Beria* must first be killed; then judged; then his faction can be hunted down; or in fact anybody can be hunted down because the power that is doing the liquidating thereby defines who and what that faction consists of and at the same time redefines itself as the sole power. But this is not what is happening in China. The persistency of the declared adversaries, in spite of the fantastic raising of bids in the struggle for total power, clearly shows that *the ruling class has split in two*.

A social disaster of such magnitude obviously cannot be explained, in the anecdotal style of bourgeois observers, as being the result of dissensions over foreign policy (on the contrary, the Chinese bureaucracy is quite unified in the docility with which it tolerates the insult of the crushing of Vietnam on its own doorstep). Neither could personal quarrels over succession to power have caused so much to be put at stake. When certain leaders are accused of having "kept Mao Tse-tung from power" since the end of the 1950s, everything leads one to believe that this is one of those retrospective crimes frequently fabricated during bureaucratic purges—Trotsky conducting the civil war on orders from the Mikado, Zinoviev supporting Lenin in order to work for the British Empire, etc.* The man who could have taken power from someone as powerful as Mao would not have slept as long as Mao was still around to come back. Mao would have died that very day, and nothing would have prevented his faithful successors from attributing his death to, say, Khrushchev. If the rulers and polemicists of the bureaucratic states certainly have a much better understanding of the Chinese crisis, their statements cannot for all that be taken any more seriously, for in talking about China they have to guard against revealing too much about themselves. The most deluded are the leftist debris of the Western countries, who are always the willing dupes of moldy sub-Leninist propaganda. They solemnly evaluate the role in Chinese society of the continuation of allowances to the capitalists who rallied to the "Communist" regime, or scrutinize the fray trying to figure out which leader represents genuine radicalism or workers' autonomy. The most stupid among them thought there was something "cultural" about this affair, until January when the Maoist press pulled the dirty trick on them of admitting that it had been "a struggle for power from the very beginning." The only serious debate consists in examining why and how the ruling class could have split into two hostile camps; and any investigation of this question is naturally impossible for those who don't recognize that the bureaucracy is a ruling class, or who ignore the specificity of this class and reduce it to the classical conditions of bourgeois power.

On the *why* of the breach within the bureaucracy, it can be said with certainty only that it was a matter in which the ruling class's very domination was at stake *since in order to settle it each side remained unyielding and neither hesitated to immediately risk their joint class power* by jeopardizing all the existing conditions of their administration of the society. The ruling class must thus have known that it could no longer govern as before. There is no question that the conflict involved the management of the *economy,* and that the collapse of the bureaucracy's successive economic policies is the cause of that conflict's extreme acuteness. The failure of the "Great Leap Forward"—mainly because of the resistance of the peasantry—not only put an end to the prospect of an ultravoluntarist takeoff of industrial production, but led to a disastrous disorganization whose effects were felt for several years.* Even agricultural production has scarcely increased since 1958 (the increase of food supplies has not even matched the rate of population growth).

It is less easy to say over what specific economic options the ruling class split. Probably one side (consisting of the majority of the Party apparatus, the union leaders, and the economists) wanted to continue, or increase more or less considerably, the production of consumer goods and to stimulate the workers' efforts with economic incentives; this policy would imply making some concessions to the peasants and especially to the factory workers, as well as increasing a hierarchically differentiated consumption for a good part of the bureaucracy. The other side (including Mao and a large segment of the higher-ranking army officers) probably wanted to resume at any price the effort to industrialize the country through an even more extreme recourse to terror and *ideological energy,* an unlimited superexploitation of the workers, and perhaps an "egalitarian" sacrifice in consumption for a considerable segment of the lower bureaucracy. Both positions are equally oriented toward maintaining the absolute domination of the bureaucracy and are calculated in terms of the necessity of erecting barriers against any class struggles that threaten that domination. In any case, the urgency and vital character of this choice was so evident to everyone that both camps felt they had to run the risk of immediately aggravating the conditions in which they found themselves by the disorder of their very schism. It is quite possible that the obstinacy on both sides is justified by the fact that there is no satisfactory solution to the insurmountable problems of the Chinese bureaucracy; that the two options confronting each other were thus equally unfeasible; and that some choice nevertheless had to be made.

As for figuring out *how* a division at the summit of the bureaucracy was able to descend from level to level—recreating at every stage remote-controlled confrontations which in turn incited or exacerbated oppositions throughout the Party and the state, and finally among the masses—it is probably necessary to take into account the survival of aspects of the ancient manner of administering China by provinces tending toward semiautonomy. The Peking Maoists' denunciation in January of "independent fiefs" clearly suggests this reality, and the development of the disturbances over the last few months confirms it. It is quite possible that the phenomenon of regionally autonomous bureaucratic power, which during the Russian counterrevolution was manifested only weakly and sporadically by the Leningrad organization, found firm and multiple bases in bureaucratic China, resulting in the possibility of a coexistence within the central government of clans and constituents holding entire regions of bureaucratic power as their personal property and bargaining with each other on this basis. Bureaucratic power in China was not born out of a workers' movement, but out of the military regimentation of peasants during a 22-year war. The army has remained closely interlinked with the Party, all of whose leaders have also been military chiefs, and it remains the principal training school of the peasant masses from which the Party selects its future cadres. It seems, moreover, that the local administrations installed in 1949 were largely based on the regions traversed by the different army regiments moving from the north to the south, leaving in their wake at every stage men who were linked to those regions by geographical origin (or by family ties: the propaganda against Liu Shao-ch'i and others has fully exposed this nepotistic factor in the consolidation of bureaucratic cliques). Such local bases of semiautonomous power within the bureaucratic administration could thus have been formed by a combination of the organizational structures of the conquering army with the productive forces it found to control in the conquered regions.

When the Mao faction began its public offensive against the entrenched positions of its adversaries by dragooning and indoctrinating students and schoolchildren, it was in no way for the purpose of directly initiating a "cultural" or "civilizing" remolding of the mass of workers, who were already squeezed as tightly as possible into the ideological straitjacket of the regime. The silly diatribes against Beethoven or Ming art, like the invectives against a supposed occupation or reoccupation of positions of power by a Chinese bourgeoisie that has obviously been annihilated as such, were only presented for the bene-

fit of the spectators—though not without calculating that this crude
ultraleftism might strike a certain chord among the oppressed, who
have, after all, some reason to suspect that there are still several obstacles in their country to the emergence of a classless society. The main
purpose of this operation was to make the *regime's ideology,* which is by
definition Maoist, appear in the street in the service of this faction.
Since the adversaries could themselves be nothing other than officially
Maoist, imposing a struggle on this terrain immediately put them in
an awkward position. It forced them to make "self-critiques," the insufficiency of which, however, expressed their actual resolution to hold
on to the positions they controlled. The first phase of the struggle can
thus be characterized as a confrontation of the *official owners of the ideology* against the majority of the *owners of the economic and state apparatus.*
But the bureaucracy, in order to maintain its collective appropriation
of society, needs the ideology as much as it does the administrative
and repressive apparatus; the venture into such a separation was thus
extremely dangerous if it was not quickly resolved.

The majority of the apparatus, including Liu Shao-ch'i himself
despite his shaky position in Peking, resisted obstinately. After their
first attempt to block the Maoist agitation at the university level by
setting up effectively anti-Maoist "work groups" among the students,
that agitation spread into the streets of all the large cities and everywhere began to attack, by means of wall posters and direct action, the
officials who had been designated as "capitalist-roaders"—attacks that
were not without errors and excesses of zeal. These officials organized
resistance wherever they could. It is likely that the first clashes between
workers and "Red Guards"* were in fact initiated by Party activists
in the factories under orders from local officials. Soon, however, the
workers, exasperated by the excesses of the Red Guards, began to intervene on their own. When the Maoists spoke of "extending the Cultural Revolution" to the factories and then to the countryside, they
gave themselves the air of having *decided* on a movement which had in
fact come about in spite of their plans and which throughout autumn
1966 was *totally out of their control.* The decline of industrial production;
the disorganization of transportation, irrigation, and state administration (despite Chou En-lai's efforts); the threats to the autumn and
spring harvests; the halting of all education (particularly serious in an
underdeveloped country) for more than a year—all this was the inevitable result of a struggle whose extension was solely due to the resistance
of the sector of the bureaucracy in power that the Maoists were trying
to make back down.

The Maoists, who have virtually no experience with struggles in urban environments, will have had good occasion to verify Machiavelli's precept: "One should take care not to incite a rebellion in a city while imagining that one can stop it or direct it at will" (*History of Florence*). After a few months of pseudocultural pseudorevolution, real class struggle has appeared in China, with the workers and peasants beginning to act for themselves. The workers cannot be unaware of what the Maoist perspective means for them; the peasants, seeing their individual plots of land threatened, have in several provinces begun to divide among themselves the land and equipment of the "People's Communes" (these latter being merely the new ideological dressing of the preexisting administrative units, generally corresponding to the old cantons). The railroad strikes, the Shanghai general strike (denounced, as in 1956 Budapest, as a favored weapon of the capitalists), the strikes of the great Wuhan industrial complex, of Canton, of Hupeh, of the metal and textile workers in Chungking, the peasants' attacks in Szechwan and Fukien—these movements came to a culmination in January, bringing China to the brink of chaos. At the same time, following in the wake of the workers who in September 1966 in Kwangsi had organized themselves as "Purple Guards" in order to fight the Red Guards, and after the anti-Maoist riots in Nanking, "armies" began to form in various provinces, such as the "August 1st Army" in Kwangtung. The national army had to intervene everywhere in February and March in order to subdue the workers, to direct production through "military control" of the factories, and even (with the support of the militia) to control work in the countryside. The workers' struggles to maintain or increase their wages—that famous tendency toward "economism" denounced by the masters of Peking—was accepted or even encouraged by some local cadres of the apparatus in their resistance to rival Maoist bureaucrats. But the main impetus of the struggle was clearly an irresistible upsurge from the rank-and-file workers—the authoritarian dissolution in March of the "professional associations" that had formed after the first dissolution of the regime's labor unions, whose bureaucracy had been deviating from the Maoist line, is a good demonstration of this. In Shanghai that same month the *Jiefang Ribao* condemned "the feudal tendencies of these associations, which are formed not on a class basis (*i.e., not on the basis of a Maoist total monopoly of power*) but on the basis of trades and which struggle for the partial and immediate interests of the workers in those trades." This defense of the real owners of the general and permanent interests of the collectivity was also distinctly expressed on February 11 in a joint directive from the Council of State and the Military Commission of the Central Committee: "All elements who have seized or stolen arms must be arrested."

While the settlement of this conflict—which has certainly cost tens of thousands of lives and involved fully equipped regiments and even warships—is being entrusted to the Chinese army, that army is itself divided. It has to ensure the continuation and intensification of production at a time when it is no longer in a position to ensure the unity of power in China. Moreover, the army's direct intervention against the peasants would present the gravest risks because it has been recruited largely from the peasantry. The truce sought by the Maoists in March and April, when they declared that all Party personnel were redeemable with the exception of a "handful" of traitors, and that the principal menace was now "anarchism," expressed not merely the anxiety over the difficulty of reining in the liberatory desires that the Red Guard experiences had awakened among the youth; it expressed *the ruling class's anxiety at having arrived at the brink of its own dissolution.* The Party and the central and provincial administration were falling apart. "Labor discipline must be reestablished." "The idea of excluding and overthrowing all cadres must be unconditionally condemned" (*Red Flag,* March 1967). A month earlier *New China* declared: "You smash all the officials . . . but when you have taken over some administrative body what do you have besides an empty room and some rubber stamps?" Rehabilitations and new compromises are following one another erratically. The very survival of the bureaucracy has ultimate priority, pushing its diverse political options into the background as mere means.

By spring 1967 it was evident that the "Cultural Revolution" was a disastrous failure and that this failure was certainly the most colossal of the long line of failures of the bureaucratic regime in China. In spite of the extraordinary cost of the operation none of its goals has been attained. The bureaucracy is more divided than ever. Every new power installed in the regions held by the Maoists is dividing in its turn: the "Revolutionary Triple Alliance" (Army-Party-Red Guard) has not ceased falling apart, both because of the antagonisms between these three forces (the Party, in particular, tending to remain aloof, getting involved only to sabotage the other two) and because of the continually aggravated antagonisms within each one. It seems as difficult to patch up the old apparatus as it would be to build a new one. Most importantly, *at least two-thirds of China is in no way controlled by the regime in Peking.*

Besides the governmental committees of partisans of Liu Shao-ch'i and the movements of workers' struggles that continue to assert themselves, the *warlords* are already reappearing in the uniforms of independent "Communist" generals, negotiating directly with the central power and following their own policies, particularly in the peripheral regions. General Chang Kuo-hua, master of Tibet in February, after street fighting in Lhasa used armored cars against the Maoists. Three Maoist divisions were sent to "crush the revisionists." They seem to have met with limited success since Chang Kuo-hua still controlled the region in April. On May 1 he was received in Peking, with negotiations ending in a compromise: he was entrusted to form a Revolutionary Committee to govern Szechwan, where in April a "Revolutionary Alliance" influenced by a certain General Hung had seized power and imprisoned the Maoists; since then, in June, members of a People's Commune seized arms and attacked the army. In Inner Mongolia the army, under the direction of Deputy Political Commissar Liu Chiang, declared itself against Mao in February. The same thing happened in Hopeh, Honan, and Manchuria. In May, General Chao Yungshih carried out an anti-Maoist putsch in Kansu. Sinkiang, where the atomic installations are located, was neutralized by mutual agreement in March, under the authority of General Wang En-mao; the latter, however, is reputed to have attacked "Maoist revolutionaries" in June. Hupeh was in July in the hands of General Chen Tsai-tao, commander of the Wuhan district, one of the oldest industrial centers in China. In the old style of the "Sian Incident,"* he arrested two of the main Peking leaders who had come to negotiate with him. The Prime Minister had to go there in person, and his obtaining the release of his emissaries was announced as a "victory." During the same period 2400 factories and mines were paralyzed in that province following an armed uprising of 50,000 workers and peasants. At the beginning of summer the conflict was in fact continuing everywhere: in June "conservative workers" of Honan attacked a textile mill with incendiary bombs; in July the coal miners of Fushun and the oil workers of Tahsing were on strike, the miners of Kiangsi were driving out the Maoists, there were calls for struggle against the "Chekiang Industrial Army" (described as an "anti-Marxist terrorist organization"), peasants threatened to march on Nanking and Shanghai, there was street fighting in Canton and Chungking, and the students of Kweiyang attacked the army and seized Maoist leaders. The government, having decided to prohibit violence "in the regions controlled by the central authorities," seems to be having a hard time of it even there. Unable to stop the disorders, it is stopping the *news* of them by expelling most of the rare foreigners in residence.

But at the beginning of August the fractures in the army have become so dangerous that the official Peking publications are themselves revealing that the partisans of Liu are "trying to set up an independent reactionary bourgeois kingdom within the army" and that "the attacks against the dictatorship of the proletariat in China have come not only from the higher echelons, but also from the lower ones" (*People's Daily*, August 5). Peking has gone so far as to openly admit that at least a third of the Army has declared itself against the central government and that even a large part of the old China of eighteen provinces is out of its control. The immediate consequences of the Wuhan incident seem to have been very serious: an intervention of paratroopers from Peking, supported by gunboats ascending the Yangtze from Shanghai, was repulsed after a pitched battle; arms from the Wuhan arsenal are also reported to have been sent to the anti-Maoists of Chungking. It should be noted, moreover, that the Wuhan troops belonged to the army group under the direct authority of Lin Piao, the only one considered completely loyal. Toward the middle of August the armed struggles have become so widespread that the Maoist government has come around to officially condemning this sort of continuation of politics by means that are turning against it, stating its firm conviction that it will win out by sticking to "struggle with the pen" instead of the sword.* Simultaneously it is announcing distribution of arms to the masses in the "loyal zones." But where are such zones? Fighting has broken out again in Shanghai, which had been presented for months as one of the rare strongholds of Maoism. In Shantung soldiers are inciting the peasants to revolt. The leaders of the Air Force are denounced as enemies of the regime. And as in the days of Sun Yat-sen,* Canton, toward which the 47th Army is moving in order to reestablish order, stands out as a beacon of revolt, with the railroad and transit workers in the forefront: political prisoners have been liberated, arms destined for Vietnam have been seized from freighters in the port, and an undetermined number of individuals have been hung in the streets. Thus China is slowly sinking into a confused civil war, which is both a confrontation between diverse regions of fragmented state-bureaucratic power and a clash of workers' and peasants' demands with the conditions of exploitation that the fragmented bureaucratic leaderships have to maintain everywhere.

Since the Maoists have presented themselves as the champions of absolute ideology (we have seen how successfully), they have so far naturally met with the most extravagant degree of respect and approbation among Western intellectuals, who never fail to salivate to such stimuli. K.S. Karol, in the *Nouvel Observateur* of February 15, learnedly reminds the Maoists not to forget that "the real Stalinists are not potential allies of China, but its most irreducible enemies: for them, the Cultural Revolution, with its antibureaucratic tendencies, is suggestive of

Trotskyism." There were, in fact, many Trotskyists who identified with it—thereby doing themselves perfect justice! *Le Monde,* the most unreservedly Maoist paper outside China, day after day announced the imminent success of Monsieur Mao Tse-tung, finally taking the power that had been generally believed to have been his for the past eighteen years. The sinologists, virtually all Stalino-Christians—this combination can be found everywhere, but particularly among them—have resurrected the "Chinese spirit" to demonstrate the legitimacy of the new Confucius. The element of silliness that has always been present in the attitude of moderately Stalinophile leftist bourgeois intellectuals could hardly fail to blossom when presented with such Chinese record achievements as: This "Cultural Revolution" may well last 1000 or even 10,000 years. . . . *The Little Red Book* has finally succeeded in "making Marxism Chinese." . . . "The sound of men reciting the *Quotations of Chairman Mao* with strong, clear voices can be heard in every Army unit." . . . "Drought has nothing frightening, Mao Tse-tung Thought is our fertilizing rain." . . . "The Chief of State was judged responsible . . . for not having foreseen the about-face of General Chiang Kai-shek when the latter turned his army against the Communist troops" (*Le Monde,* 4 April 1967; this refers to the 1927 coup, which was foreseen by everyone in China but which had to be awaited passively in order to obey Stalin's orders).* . . . A chorale sings the hymn entitled *One Hundred Million People Take Up Arms to Criticize the Sinister Book "How to Be a Good Communist"* (a formerly official manual by Liu Shao-ch'i). . . . The list could go on and on; we can conclude with this gem from the *People's Daily* of July 31: "The situation of the Proletarian Cultural Revolution in China is excellent, but the class struggle is becoming more difficult."

After so much ado the historical conclusions to be drawn from this period are simple. No matter where China may go from here, the image of the last revolutionary-bureaucratic power has shattered. Its internal collapse is added to the continuing disasters of its foreign policy: the annihilation of Indonesian Stalinism;* the break with Japanese Stalinism; the destruction of Vietnam by the United States; and finally Peking's proclamation in July that the Naxalbari "insurrection" was the beginning of a Maoist-peasant revolution throughout India (this a few days before it was dispersed by the first police intervention). By adopting such a delirious position Peking broke with the majority of its own Indian partisans—the last large bureaucratic party that remained loyal to it. At the same time, China's internal crisis reflects its failure to industrialize the country and make itself a credible model for the underdeveloped countries.

Ideology, pushed to its extreme, *shatters*. Its absolute use is also its absolute zero: the night in which all ideological cows are black. When, amidst the most total confusion, bureaucrats fight each other in the name of the same dogma and everywhere denounce "the bourgeois hiding behind the red flag," *doublethink* has itself split in two. This is the joyous end of ideological lies, dying in ridicule. It is not just China, it is our whole world that has produced this delirium. In the August 1961 issue of *Internationale Situationniste* we said that this world would become "at all levels more and more painfully ridiculous until the moment of its complete revolutionary reconstruction." This process now seems to be well on its way. The new period of proletarian critique will learn that it must no longer shelter from criticism anything that pertains to it, and that every existing ideological comfort represents a shameful defeat. In discovering that it is dispossessed of the false goods of its world of falsehood, it must understand that it is the specific negation of the totality of the global society. And it will discover this also in China. The global breakup of the *Bureaucratic International* is now being reproduced at the Chinese level in the fragmentation of the regime into independent provinces. Thus China is rediscovering its past, which is once again posing to it the real revolutionary tasks of the previously vanquished movement. The moment when Mao is supposedly "recommencing in 1967 what he was doing in 1927" (*Le Monde*, 17 February 1967) is also the moment when, for the first time since 1927, the intervention of the worker and peasant masses has surged over the entire country. As difficult as it may be for them to become conscious of their autonomous objectives and put them into practice, something has died in the total domination to which the Chinese workers were subjected. The *proletarian "Mandate of Heaven"* has expired.*

16 August 1967*

Two Local Wars

The Arab–Israel war was a dirty trick played by modern history on the good conscience of the Left, which was communing in the great spectacle of its protest against the Vietnam war. The false consciousness that saw in the National Liberation Front the champion of "socialist revolution" against American imperialism could only get entangled and collapse amidst its insurmountable contradictions when it had to decide between Israel and Nasser. Yet throughout all its ludicrous polemics it never stopped proclaiming that one side or the other was completely in the right, or even that one or another of their perspectives was revolutionary.

In immigrating into underdeveloped regions, the revolutionary struggle was subjected to a double alienation: that of an impotent Left facing an overdeveloped capitalism it was in no way capable of combatting, and that of the working masses in the colonized countries who inherited the remains of a mutilated revolution and have had to suffer its defects. The absence of a revolutionary movement in Europe has reduced the Left to its simplest expression: a mass of spectators who swoon with rapture each time the exploited in the colonies take up arms against their masters, and who cannot help seeing these uprisings as the epitome of Revolution. At the same time, the absence from political life of the proletariat as a class-for-itself (and for us the proletariat is revolutionary or it is nothing) has allowed this Left to become the "Knight of Virtue" in a world without virtue. But when it bewails its situation and complains about the "world order" being at odds with its good intentions, and when it maintains its poor yearnings in the face of this order, it is in fact attached to this order as to its own essence. If this order was taken away from it, it would lose *everything*. The European Left is so pitiful that, like a traveler in the desert longing for a single drop of water, it seems to aspire for nothing more than the meager feeling of an abstract objection. From the little with which it is satisfied one can measure the extent of its poverty. It is as alien to history as the proletariat is alien to this world. False consciousness is its natural condition, the spectacle is its element, and the apparent opposition of systems is its universal frame of reference: wherever there is a conflict it always sees Good fighting Evil, "total revolution" versus "total reaction."

The attachment of this spectator consciousness to alien causes remains irrational, and its virtuous protests flounder in the tortuous paths of its guilt. Most of the "Vietnam Committees" in France split up during the "Six-Day War" and some of the war resistance groups in the United States also revealed *their reality*. "One cannot be at the same time for the Vietnamese and against the Jews menaced with extermination," is the cry of some. "Can you fight against the Americans in Vietnam while supporting their allies, the Zionist aggressors?" is the reply of others. And then they plunge into byzantine discussions. Sartre hasn't recovered from it yet. In fact this whole fine lot does not actually fight what it condemns, nor does it really know much about the forces it supports. Its opposition to the American war is almost always combined with unconditional support of the Vietcong; but in any case this opposition remains spectacular for everyone. Those who were really opposed to Spanish fascism went to fight it. No one has yet gone off to fight "Yankee imperialism." The consumers of illusory participation are offered a whole range of spectacular choices: pacifist demonstrations; Stalino-Gaullist nationalism against the Americans (Humphrey's visit was the sole occasion the French Communist Party has demonstrated with its remaining faithful); the sale of the *Vietnam Newsletter* or of publicity handouts from Ho Chi Minh's state. Neither the Provos (before their dissolution) nor the Berlin students have been able to go beyond the narrow framework of anti-imperialist "action."

The antiwar movement in America has naturally been more serious since it finds itself face to face with the real enemy. Some of these young rebels, however, end up by simplistically identifying with the apparent enemies of their real enemies; which reinforces the confusion of a working class already subjected to the worst brutalization and mystification, and contributes to maintaining it in that "reactionary" state of mind from which one draws arguments against it.

Guevara's critique seems to us more important since it has its roots in real struggles, but it falls short by default. Che is certainly one of the last consistent Leninists of our time. But like Epimenides, he seems to have slept for the last fifty years to be able to believe that there is still a "progressive bloc," which for some strange reason is "lapsing." This bureaucratic and romantic revolutionary only sees in imperialism the ultimate stage of capitalism, struggling against a society that is socialist in spite of its imperfections.

The USSR's embarrassingly evident defects are coming to seem more and more "natural." As for China, according to an official declaration it remains "ready to accept all national sacrifices to support North Vietnam against the USA" (in lieu of supporting the workers of Hong Kong) "and constitutes the most solid and secure *rear guard* for the Vietnamese people in their struggle against imperialism." In fact, no one doubts that if the last Vietnamese were killed, Mao's bureaucratic China would still be intact. (According to *Izvestia,* China and the United States have already concluded a mutual nonintervention pact.)

Neither the Manichean consciousness of the virtuous Left nor the bureaucracy are capable of seeing the profound unity of today's world. Dialectics is their common enemy. Revolutionary criticism begins beyond good and evil; it is rooted in history and operates on the totality of the existing world. In no case can it applaud a belligerent *state* or support the bureaucracy of an exploitive state in the process of formation. It must first of all lay bare the *truth* of present struggles by putting them back into their historical context, and unmask the hidden aims of the forces officially in conflict. The arm of critique is the prelude to the critique by arms.

The peaceful coexistence of bourgeois and bureaucratic lies ended up prevailing over the lie of their confrontation. The balance of terror was broken in Cuba in 1962 with the rout of the Russians.* Since that time American imperialism has been the unchallenged master of the world. And it can remain so only by aggression since it has no chance of seducing the disinherited, who are more easily attracted to the Sino-Soviet model. State capitalism is the natural tendency of colonized societies, where the state is generally formed before the historical classes. The total elimination of its capital and its commodities from the world market is the deadly threat that haunts the American propertied class and its free-enterprise economy—this is the key to its aggressive rage.

Since the great crisis of 1929, state intervention has been more and more conspicuous in market mechanisms; the economy can no longer function steadily without massive expenditures by the state, the main "consumer" of all noncommercial production (especially that of the armament industries). This does not save it from remaining in a state of permanent crisis and in constant need of expanding its public sector at the expense of its private sector. A relentless logic pushes the system toward increasingly state-controlled capitalism, generating severe social conflicts.

The profound crisis of the American system lies in its inability to produce sufficient profits on the social scale. It must therefore achieve *abroad* what it cannot do at home, namely increase the amount of profit in proportion to the amount of existing capital. The propertied class, which also more or less possesses the state, relies on its imperialist enterprises to realize this insane dream. For this class, pseudocommunist state capitalism means death just as much as does *authentic* communism; that is why it is essentially incapable of seeing any difference between them.

The artificial functioning of the monopolistic economy as a "war economy" ensures, for the moment, that the ruling-class policy is willingly supported by the workers, who enjoy full employment and a spectacular abundance: "At the moment, the proportion of labor employed in jobs connected with national defense amounts to 5.2% of the total American labor force, compared with 3.9% two years ago. . . . The number of civil jobs in the national defense sector has increased from 3,000,000 to 4,100,000 over the last two years" (*Le Monde*, 17 September 1967). Meanwhile, market capitalism vaguely feels that by extending its territorial control it will achieve an accelerated expansion capable of balancing the ever-increasing demands of non-profit-making production. The ferocious defense of regions of the "free" world where its interests are often trifling (in 1959 American investments in South Vietnam were less than 50 million dollars) is part of a long-term strategy that hopes eventually to be able to write off military expenditures as mere business expenses in ensuring the United States not only a market but also the monopolistic control of the means of production of the greater part of the world. But everything works against this project. On one hand, the internal contradictions of private capitalism: particular interests conflict with the general interest of the propertied class as a whole, as with groups that make short-term profits from state contracts (notably arms manufacturers) or monopolistic enterprises that are reluctant to invest in underdeveloped countries, where productivity is very low in spite of cheap labor, preferring instead the "advanced" part of the world (especially Europe, which is still more profitable than saturated America). On the other hand, it clashes with the immediate interests of the disinherited masses, whose first move can only be to eliminate the indigenous strata that exploit them, which are the only strata able to ensure the United States any infiltration whatsoever.

According to Rostow, the "growth" specialist of the State Department, Vietnam is for the moment only the first testing ground for this vast strategy, which, to ensure its exploitive peace, must start with a war of destruction that can hardly succeed. The aggressiveness of American imperialism is thus in no way the aberration of a bad administration, but a necessity for the class relations of private capitalism, which, if not overthrown by a revolutionary movement, unrelentingly evolves toward a technocratic state capitalism. The history of the alienated struggles of our time can only be understood in this context of a still undominated global economy.

The destruction of the old "Asiatic" structures by colonial penetration gave rise to a new urban stratum while increasing the pauperization of a large portion of the superexploited peasantry. The conjuncture of these two forces constituted the driving force of the Vietnamese movement. Among the urban strata (petty bourgeois and even bourgeois) were formed the first nationalist nuclei and the skeleton of what was to be, from 1930 on, the Indochinese Communist Party. Its adherence to Bolshevik ideology (in its Stalinist version), which led it to graft an essentially agrarian program onto the purely nationalist one, enabled the ICP to become the leading force of the anticolonial struggle and to marshal the great mass of peasants who had spontaneously risen. The "peasant soviets" of 1931 were the first manifestation of this movement. But by linking its fate to that of the Third International, the ICP subjected itself to all the vicissitudes of Stalinist diplomacy and to the fluctuations of the national and state interests of the Russian bureaucracy. After the Seventh Comintern Congress (August 1935) "the struggle against French imperialism" vanished from the program and was soon replaced by a struggle against the powerful Trotskyist party. "As for the Trotskyists, no alliances, no concessions; they must be unmasked for what they are: the agents of fascism" (Report of Ho Chi Minh to the Comintern, July 1939). The Hitler–Stalin Pact and the banning of the Communist Party in France and its colonies allowed the ICP to change its line: "Our party finds it a matter of life or death . . . to struggle against the imperialist war and the French policy of piracy and massacre" (i.e. *against Nazi Germany*), "but we will at the same time combat the aggressive aims of Japanese fascism."

Toward the end of World War II, with the effective help of the Americans, the Vietminh was in control of the greater part of the country and was recognized by France as the sole representative of Indochina. It was at this point that Ho preferred "to sniff a little French shit rather than eat Chinese shit for a lifetime" and signed, to make the task of his colleague-masters easier, the monstrous compromise of 1946, which recognized Vietnam as both a "free state" and as "belonging to the Indochinese Federation of the French Union." This compromise enabled France to reconquer part of the country and, at the same time the Stalinists lost their share of bourgeois power in France, to wage a war that lasted eight years, at the end of which the Vietminh gave up the South to the most retrograde strata and their American protectors and definitively won the North for itself. After systematically eliminating the remaining revolutionary elements* (the last Trotskyist leader, Ta Thu Thau, was assassinated by 1946) the Vietminh bureaucracy imposed its totalitarian power on the peasantry and started the industrialization of the country within a state-capitalist framework. Improving the lot of the peasants, following their conquests during the long liberation struggle, was, in line with bureaucratic logic, subordinated to the interests of the rising state: the goal was to be greater productivity, with the state remaining the uncontested master of that production. The authoritarian implementation of agrarian reform gave rise in 1956 to violent insurrections and bloody repression (above all in Ho Chi Minh's own native province). The peasants who had carried the bureaucracy to power were to be its first victims. For several years afterwards the bureaucracy tried to smother the memory of this "serious mistake" in an "orgy of self-criticism."

But the same Geneva agreements enabled the Diem clique to set up, south of the 17th parallel, a bureaucratic, feudal, and theocratic state in the service of the landowners and comprador bourgeoisie. Within a few years this state was to nullify, by a few suitable "agrarian reforms," everything the peasantry had won. The peasants of the South, some of whom had never laid down their arms, were to fall back in the grip of oppression and superexploitation. This is the second Vietnam war. The mass of insurgent peasants, taking up arms once more against their old enemies, also followed once again their old leaders. The National Liberation Front succeeded the Vietminh, inheriting both its qualities and its grave defects. By making itself the champion of national struggle and peasant war, the NLF immediately won over the countryside and made it the main base of armed resistance. Its successive victories over the official army provoked the increasingly massive intervention of the Americans, to the point of reducing the conflict to an open colonial war, with the Vietnamese pitted against an invading army. Its determination in the struggle, its clearly antifeudal program, and its unitary perspectives remain the principal qualities of the movement. But in no way does the NLF's struggle go beyond the classical framework of national liberation struggles. Its program remains based on a compromise among a vast coalition of classes, dominated by the overriding goal of wiping out the American aggression. It is no accident that it rejects the title "Vietcong" (i.e. Vietnamese communists) and insists on its national character. Its structures are those of a state-in-formation: in the zones under its control it already levies taxes and institutes compulsory military service.

These minimal qualities in the struggle and the social objectives that they express remain totally absent in the confrontation between Israel and the Arabs. The specific contradictions of Zionism and of splintered Arab society add to the general confusion.

Since its origins the Zionist movement has been the contrary of the revolutionary solution to what used to be called the "Jewish question." A direct product of European capitalism, it did not aim at the overthrow of a society that needed to persecute Jews, but at the creation of a Jewish national entity that would be protected from the anti-Semitic aberrations of decadent capitalism. It did not strive to abolish injustice, but to transfer it. The original sin of Zionism is that it has always acted as if Palestine were a desert island. The revolutionary workers' movement saw the answer to the Jewish question in proletarian community, that is, in the destruction of capitalism and "its religion, Judaism"; the emancipation of the Jews could not take place apart from the emancipation of humanity. Zionism started from the opposite hypothesis. As a matter of fact, the counterrevolutionary development of the last half century proved it right, but in the same way as the development of European capitalism proved right the reformist theses of Bernstein. The success of Zionism and its corollary, the creation of the state of Israel, is merely a miserable by-product of the triumph of world counterrevolution. To "socialism in a single country" came the echo "justice for a single people" and "equality in a single kibbutz." The colonization of Palestine was organized with Rothschild capital, and the first kibbutzim were set up with European surplus-value. The Jews recreated *for themselves* all the fanaticism and segregation they had been victims of. Those who had suffered mere toleration in their society were to struggle to become in another country owners disposing of the right to tolerate others. The kibbutz was not a revolutionary supersession of Palestinian "feudalism," but a mutualist formula for the self-defense of Jewish worker-settlers *against the capitalist exploitive tendencies of the Jewish Agency.* Because it was the main Jewish owner of Palestine, the Zionist Organization defined itself as the sole representative of the superior interests of the "Jewish Nation." If it eventually allowed a certain degree of self-management, it was because it was sure that this would be based on the systematic rejection of the Arab peasant.

As for the Histadrut [the Israeli labor union], it was since its inception in 1920 subjected to the authority of world Zionism, that is, to the direct opposite of workers' emancipation. Arab workers were statutorily excluded from it and its activity often consisted of forbidding Jewish businesses to employ them.

The development of the three-way struggle between the Arabs, the Zionists, and the British was to be turned to the profit of the Zionists. Thanks to the active patronage of the Americans (since the end of World War II) and the blessing of Stalin (who saw Israel as the first "socialist" bastion in the Middle East, but also as a way to rid himself of some annoying Jews), it did not take long before Herzl's dream was realized and the Jewish state was arbitrarily proclaimed. The co-option of all the "progressive" forms of social organization and their integration within the Zionist ideal enabled even the most "revolutionary" individuals to work in good conscience for the building of the bourgeois, militaristic, rabbinical state that modern Israel has become. The prolonged sleep of proletarian internationalism once more brought forth a monster. The basic injustice against the Palestinian Arabs came back to roost with the Jews themselves: the State of the Chosen People was nothing but one more class society in which all the aberrations of the old societies were recreated (hierarchical divisions, tribal opposition between the Ashkenazi and the Sephardim, racist persecution of the Arab minority, etc.). The labor union assumed its normal function of integrating workers into a capitalist economy, an economy of which it itself has become the main owner. It employs more workers than the state itself, and presently constitutes the bridgehead of the imperialist expansion of the new Israeli capitalism. ("Solel Boneh," an important construction branch of the Histadrut, invested 180 million dollars in Africa and Asia from 1960 to 1966 and currently employs 12,000 African workers.)

And just as this state could never have seen the light of day without the direct intervention of Anglo-American imperialism and the massive aid of Jewish finance capital, it cannot balance its *artificial economy* today without the aid of the same forces that created it. (The annual balance of payments deficit is 600 million dollars, that is, more for each Israeli inhabitant than the average earnings of an Arab worker.) Since the settling of the first immigrant colonies, the Jews have formed a modern, European-style society alongside the economically and socially backward Arab society; the proclamation of the state of Israel only completed this process by the pure and simple expulsion of the backward elements. Israel forms by its very existence the bastion of Europe in the heart of an Afro-Asian world. Thus it has become doubly *alien:* to the Arab population, permanently reduced to the status of refugees or of colonized minority; and to the Jewish population, which had for a moment seen in it the earthly fulfillment of all egalitarian ideologies.

But this is due not only to the contradictions of Israeli society. From the outset this situation has been constantly maintained and aggravated by the surrounding Arab societies, which have so far proved incapable of any contribution toward an effective solution.

Throughout the British Mandate period the Arab resistance in Palestine was completely dominated by the propertied class: the Arab ruling classes and their British protectors. The Sykes-Picot Agreement put an end to the hopes of the Arab nationalism that was just beginning to develop, and subjected the skillfully carved up area to a foreign domination that is far from being over.* The same strata that ensured the Ottoman Empire's domination over the Arab masses turned to the service of the British occupation and became accomplices of Zionist colonization (by the sale, at very inflated prices, of their land). The backwardness of Arab society did not yet allow for the emergence of new and more advanced leaderships, and every spontaneous popular upheaval ran into the same co-opters: the "bourgeois-feudal" notables and their commodity: national unity.

The armed insurgence of 1936–1939 and the six-month general strike (the longest in history) were decided and carried out in spite of opposition from the leadership of all the "nationalist" parties. They were widespread and spontaneously organized; this forced the ruling class to join them so as to take over the leadership of the movement. But this was in order to put a check on it, to lead it to the conference table and to reactionary compromises. Only the victory of the fullest, most radical implications of that uprising could have destroyed both the British Mandate and the Zionist goal of setting up a Jewish state. Its failure heralded the disasters to come and ultimately the defeat of 1948.

That latter defeat signaled the end of the "bourgeois-feudality" as the leading class of the Arab movement. It provided the opportunity for the petty bourgeoisie to come to power and to constitute, with the officers of the defeated army, the driving force of the present movement. Its program was simple: Arab unity, a vaguely socialist ideology, and the liberation of Palestine (the Return). The Tripartite aggression of 1956* provided it with the best opportunity to consolidate itself as a ruling class and to find a leader-program in the person of Nasser, who was presented for the collective admiration of the completely dispossessed Arab masses. He was their religion and their opium. But the new exploiting class had its own interests and goals. The slogans used by the bureaucratic-military regime of Egypt to win popular support were already bad in themselves; in addition, the regime was incapable of carrying them out. Arab unity and the destruction of Israel (invoked successively as the liquidation of the usurper state or as the pure and simple driving of the Israeli population into the sea) were the core of this propaganda-ideology.

What ushered in the decline of the Arab petty bourgeoisie and its bureaucratic power was first of all its own internal contradictions and the superficiality of its options (Nasser, the Baath Party, Kassem, and the so-called Communist parties have never ceased fighting each other and compromising and allying with the most dubious forces).

Twenty years after the first Palestinian war, this new stratum has just demonstrated its total inability to resolve the Palestinian problem. It has lived by delirious bluff, for it was only able to survive by constantly raising the specter of Israel, being utterly incapable of effecting any radical solution whatsoever to the innumerable domestic problems. The Palestinian problem remains the key to the Arab power struggles. It is everyone's central reference point and all conflicts hinge on it. It is the basis of the objective solidarity of all the Arab regimes. It produces the "Holy Alliance" between Nasser and Hussein, Faisal and

Boumédienne, Aref and the Baath Party.*

The latest war has dissipated all these illusions. The total rigidity of "Arab ideology" was pulverized on contact with a reality that was just as hard but also permanent. Those who spoke of waging a war neither wanted it nor prepared for it, while those who spoke only of defending themselves actually prepared the offensive. Each of the two camps followed their respective propensities—the Arab bureaucracy that for lying and demagogy, the masters of Israel that for imperialist expansion. The most important lesson of the Six-Day War is a negative one: it has revealed all the secret weaknesses and defects of what was presented as the "Arab Revolution." The "powerful" military bureaucracy of Egypt crumbled to dust in two days, disclosing all at once the *secret reality* of its achievements: the fact that the axis around which all the socioeconomic transformations took place—the Army—has remained fundamentally the same. On one hand, it claimed to be changing everything in Egypt (and even in the Arab world as a whole); on the other, it did everything to avoid any transformation in itself, in either its values or its habits. Nasser's Egypt is still dominated by pre-Nasser forces; its bureaucracy is an agglomeration without coherence or class consciousness, united only by exploitation and the division of the social surplus-value.

As for the politico-military machine that governs Baathist Syria, it is entrenching itself more and more in the extremism of its ideology. But its rhetoric takes in no one anymore (except Pablo!).*Everyone knows that it did not fight and that it gave up the front without resistance because it preferred to keep its best troops in Damascus for its own defense. Those who have consumed 65% of the Syrian budget in the name of defending the country have definitively unmasked their own cynical lies.

Finally, the war has shown, to those who still needed showing, that a Holy Alliance with someone like Hussein can only lead to disaster. The Arab Legion [Jordanian Army] withdrew on the first day and the Palestinian population, which had suffered for twenty years under its police terror, found itself unarmed and unorganized in the face of the Israeli occupation forces. Since 1948 the Hashemite throne had shared the colonization of the Palestinians with the Zionist state. By deserting the West Bank it gave the Israelis the police files on all the Palestinian revolutionary elements. But the Palestinians have always known that there was no great difference between the two colonizations, and the blatancy of the new occupation at least makes the terrain of resistance clearer.

As for Israel, it has become everything that the Arabs had accused it of before the war: an imperialist state behaving like the most classic occupation forces (police terror, dynamiting of houses, permanent martial law, etc.). Internally a collective hysteria, led by the rabbis, is developing around "Israel's inalienable right to its Biblical borders." The war put a stop to the whole movement of internal struggles generated by the contradictions of this artificial society (in 1966 there were several dozen riots, and in 1965 alone there were no fewer than 277 strikes) and provoked unanimous support for the objectives of the ruling class and its most extremist ideology. It also served to shore up all the Arab regimes not involved in the armed struggle. Boumédienne could thus, from 3000 miles away, enter the chorus of political braggadocio and have his name applauded by the Algerian crowd before which he had not even dared to appear the day before, and finally obtain the support of a totally Stalinized ORP ("for his anti-imperialist policy"). Faisal, for a few million dollars, obtained Egypt's withdrawal from Yemen and the strengthening of his throne. Etc., etc.

As always, war, when not civil, only freezes the process of social revolution. In North Vietnam it has brought about the peasants' support, never before given, for the bureaucracy that exploits them. In Israel it has killed off for a long time any opposition to Zionism, and in the Arab countries it is reinforcing—temporarily—the most reactionary strata. In no way can revolutionary currents find anything there with which to identify. Their task is at the opposite pole of the present movement since it must be its absolute negation.

It is obviously impossible at present to seek a *revolutionary* solution to the Vietnam war. It is first of all necessary to put an end to the American aggression in order to allow the real social struggle in Vietnam to develop in a *natural way;* i.e. to allow the Vietnamese workers and peasants to rediscover their enemies at home: the bureaucracy of the North and the propertied and ruling strata of the South. Once the Americans withdraw, the Stalinist bureaucracy will seize control of the whole country—there's no getting around this. Because the invaders cannot indefinitely sustain their aggression; ever since Talleyrand it has been a commonplace that one can do anything with a bayonet except sit on it. The point is not to give unconditional (or even conditional) support to the Vietcong, but to struggle consistently and uncompromisingly against American imperialism. The most effective role is presently being played by those American revolutionaries who are advocating and practicing insubordination and draft resistance on a very large scale (compared to which the resistance to the Algerian war in France was child's play). The Vietnam war is rooted in America and it is from there that it must be rooted out.

Unlike the American war, the Palestinian question has no immediately evident solution. No short-term solution is feasible. The Arab regimes can only crumble under the weight of their contradictions, and Israel will be more and more the prisoner of its colonial logic. All the compromises that the great powers try to piece together are bound to be counterrevolutionary in one way or another. The hybrid status quo—neither peace nor war—will probably prevail for a long period, during which the Arab regimes will meet with the same fate as their predecessors of 1948 (probably at first to the profit of the openly reactionary forces). Arab society, which has produced all sorts of ruling classes caricaturing all the classes of history, must now produce the forces that will bring about its total subversion. The so-called national bourgeoisie and the Arab bureaucracy have inherited all the defects of those two classes without ever having known the historical accomplishments those classes achieved in other societies. The future Arab revolutionary forces that will arise from the ruins of the June 1967 defeat must know that they have nothing in common with any existing Arab regime and nothing to respect among the powers that dominate the present world. They will find their model in themselves and in the repressed experiences of revolutionary history. The Palestinian question is too serious to be left to the states, that is, to the colonels. It is too close to the two basic questions of modern revolution—*internationalism* and *the state*—for any existing force to be able to provide an adequate solution. Only an Arab revolutionary movement that is resolutely internationalist and antistate can dissolve the state of Israel while gaining the support of that state's exploited masses. And only through the same process will it be able to dissolve all the existing Arab states and create Arab unity through the power of the Councils.

Our Goals and Methods in the Strasbourg Scandal

The various expressions of shock and outrage in response to the situationist pamphlet *On the Poverty of Student Life,* which was published at the expense of the Strasbourg chapter of the National Student Union [UNEF], although having the salutary effect of causing the theses in the pamphlet itself to be rather widely read, have inevitably given rise to numerous misconceptions in the reportage and commentary on the SI's role in the affair. In response to all kinds of illusions fostered by the press, by university officials, and even by a certain number of unthinking students, we are now going to specify exactly what the conditions of our intervention were and explain the goals we were pursuing with methods we considered consistent with them.

Even more erroneous than the exaggerations of the press or of certain opposing lawyers concerning the amount of money the SI supposedly took the opportunity of pillaging from the treasury of the pitiful student union is the absurd notion, often expressed in the newspaper accounts, according to which the SI sunk so low as to campaign among the Strasbourg students in order to persuade them of the validity of our perspectives and to get a student government elected on such a program. We neither did this nor attempted the slightest infiltration of the UNEF by secretly slipping SI partisans into it. Anyone who has ever bothered to read us is aware that we have no interest in such goals and do not use such methods. What actually happened is that a few Strasbourg students came to us in the summer of 1966 and informed us that six of their friends—and not they themselves—had just been elected as officers of the Bureau of the local Student Association (AFGES), although they had no program whatsoever and were widely known in the UNEF as extremists who were in complete disagreement with all the factions of that decomposing body, and who were even determined to destroy it. The fact that they were elected (quite legally) was a glaring demonstration of the total apathy of the mass of students and of the total impotence of the Association's remaining bureaucrats. These latter no doubt figured that the "extremist" Bureau would be incapable of effectively implementing its negative intentions. Conversely, this was the fear of the students who had sought us out; and it was mainly for this reason that they themselves had declined to take part in this "Bureau": for only a coup of some scope, and not some merely humorous exploitation of their position, could save its members from the air of compromise that such a pitiful role immediately entails. To add to the complexity of the problem, while the students we were meeting with were familiar with the SI's positions and declared themselves in general agreement with them, those who were in the Bureau were for the most part ignorant of them, and counted mainly on those we were seeing to figure out what action would best correspond to their subversive intentions.

At this stage we limited ourselves to suggesting that all of them write and publish a general critique of the student movement and of the society as a whole, such a project having at least the advantage of forcing them to clarify in common what was still unclear to them. In addition, we stressed that their legal access to money and credit was the most useful aspect of the ridiculous authority that had so imprudently been allowed to them, and that a nonconformist use of these resources would have the advantage of shocking many people and thus drawing attention to the nonconformist aspects of the content of their text. These comrades agreed with our recommendations. In the development of this project they remained in contact with the SI, particularly through the SI's delegate, Mustapha Khayati.

The discussion and the first drafts undertaken collectively by those we had met with and the members of the AFGES Bureau—all of whom had resolved to see the matter through—brought about an important modification of the plan. Everyone was in agreement about the basic critique to be made and the main points that Khayati had suggested, but they found they were incapable of effecting a satisfactory formulation, especially in the short time remaining before the beginning of the school term. This inability should not be seen as the result of any serious lack of talent or experience, but was simply the consequence of the extreme *diversity* of the group, both within and outside the Bureau. Having originally come together on a very vague basis, they were poorly prepared to collectively articulate a theory they had not really appropriated together. In addition, personal antagonisms and mistrust arose among them as the project progressed. The only thing that still held them together was the shared desire that the coup have the most far-reaching and incisive effect. As a result, Khayati ended up drafting the greater part of the text, which was periodically discussed and approved among the group of students at Strasbourg and by the situationists in Paris—the only (relatively few) significant additions being made by the latter.

Various preliminary actions announced the appearance of the pamphlet. On October 26 the cybernetician Moles (see *Internationale Situationniste* #9, page 44), having finally attained a professorial chair in social psychology in order to devote himself to the programming of young functionaries, was driven from it during the opening minutes of his inaugural lecture by tomatoes hurled at him by a dozen students. (Moles was subsequently given the same treatment in March at the Musée des Arts Décoratifs in Paris, where this certified robot was to lecture on urbanistic methods for controlling the masses—this latter refutation being carried out by two or three dozen young anarchists belonging to groups that want to bring revolutionary criticism to bear on all modern issues.) Shortly after this inaugural class—which was at least as unprecedented in the annals of the university as Moles himself—the AFGES began publicizing the pamphlet by pasting up André Bertrand's comic strip *The Return of the Durruti Column,* a document that had the merit of stating in no uncertain terms what his comrades were planning on doing with their positions: "The general crisis of the old union and leftist bureaucracies was felt everywhere, especially among the students, where activism had for a long time had no other outlet than the most sordid devotion to the most stale ideologies and the most unrealistic ambitions. The last cohort of professionals who elected our heroes didn't even have the excuse that they had been misled. They placed their hope for a new lease on life in a group that didn't hide its intentions of sabotaging this decrepit militantism once and for all."

The pamphlet was distributed point-blank to the notables at the official opening ceremony of the university. Simultaneously, the AFGES Bureau announced that its only "student" program was the immediate dissolution of that Association, and convoked a special general assembly to vote on that question. This prospect immediately horrified many people. "This may be the first concrete manifestation of a revolt aiming quite openly at the destruction of society," wrote a local newspaper (*Dernières Nouvelles,* 4 December 1966). *L'Aurore* (November 26) referred to "the Situationist International, an organization with a handful of members in the chief capitals of Europe—anarchists playing at revolution, who talk of 'seizing power,' not in order to keep it, but in order to sow disorder and destroy even their own authority." And even in Turin the *Gazzetta del Popolo* of the same date expressed excessive concern: "It must be considered, however, whether repressive measures . . . may risk provoking disturbances. . . . In Paris and other university cities in France the Situationist International, galvanized by the triumph of its adherents in Strasbourg, is preparing a major offensive to take control of the student organizations." At this point we had to take into consideration a new decisive factor: the situationists had to defend themselves from being *co-opted* as a mere "news item" or intellectual fad. The pamphlet had ended up being transformed into an SI text: we had not felt that we could refuse to help these comrades in their desire to strike a blow against the system, and it was unfortunately *not possible for this help to have been less than it was.* This involvement of the SI gave us, for the duration of the project, a position as de facto leaders which we in no case wanted to prolong beyond this limited joint action: as anyone can well imagine, the pitiful *student milieu* is of no interest to us. Here as in other situations, we had simply tried to act in such a way as to make the new social critique that is presently taking shape reappear by means of the practice without concessions that is its exclusive basis. The unorganized character of the group of Strasbourg students had prevented the carrying out of an orderly dialogue, which alone could have ensured a minimal equality in decision-making, and had thus made necessary our direct inter-vention. The debate that normally characterizes a joint action under-taken by independent groups had scarcely any reality in this agglom-eration of individuals, who showed more and more that they were united in their approval of the SI and separated in every other regard.

It goes without saying that such a deficiency in no way constituted for us a recommendation for this group of students *as a whole,* who seemed more or less interested in joining the SI as a sort of easy way of avoiding having to express themselves autonomously. Their lack of homogeneity was also revealed, to a degree we had not been able to foresee, on an unexpected issue: at the last minute several of them got cold feet at the idea of aggressively distributing the pamphlet at the university's opening ceremony. Khayati had to explain to these people that one must not try to make scandals half way; that it is absurd to commit yourself to such a coup and then hope to reduce the risk by toning down its repercussions; that on the contrary, the success of a scandal is the only relative safeguard for those who have deliberately triggered it. Even more unacceptable than this last-minute hesitation on such an elementary tactical point was the possibility that some of these individuals, who had so little confidence even in each other, might at some point come to make statements in our name. Khayati was thus charged by the SI to have the AFGES Bureau declare that none of them was a situationist. This they did in their communiqué of November 29: "None of the members of our Bureau belongs to the Situationist Inter-national, a movement which for some time has published a journal of the same name, but we declare ourselves in complete solidarity with its analyses and perspectives." On the basis of this declared *autonomy,* the SI then addressed a letter to André Schneider, president of the AFGES, and Vayr-Piova, vice-president, to affirm its total solidarity with what they had done. The SI's solidarity with them has been maintained ever since, both by our refusal to dialogue with those who tried to approach us while manifesting a certain envious hostility toward the Bureau members (some even having the stupidity to denounce their action to the SI as being "spectacular"!) and by our financial assistance and public support during the subsequent repression (see the declaration signed by 79 Strasbourg students at the beginning of April in solidari-ty with Vayr-Piova, who had been expelled from the university; a penal-ty which was rescinded a few months later). Schneider and Vayr-Piova stood firm in the face of penalties and threats; this firmness, however, was not maintained to the same degree in their attitude toward the SI.

The judicial repression immediately initiated in Strasbourg (which has been followed by a series of proceedings in the same vein that are still going on) concentrated on the supposed illegality of the AFGES Bureau, which was, upon the publication of the situationist pamphlet, suddenly considered to be a mere "de facto Bureau" that was usurping the union representation of the students. This repression was all the more necessary since the holy alliance of bourgeois, Stalinists, and priests against the AFGES had even less support among the city's 18,000 students than did the Bureau. It began with the court order of December 13, which sequestered the Association's offices and administration and prohibited the general assembly that the Bureau had convoked for the 16th for the purpose of voting on the dissolution of the AFGES. This ruling (resulting from the mistaken belief that a majority of the students were likely to support the Bureau's position if they had the opportunity to vote on it), by freezing the development of events, meant that our comrades—whose only goal was to destroy their own position of leadership without delay—were obliged to continue their resistance until the end of January. The Bureau's best practice until then had been their treatment of the mob of reporters who were flocking to get interviews: they refused most of them and insultingly boycotted those who represented the worst institutions (French Television, *Planète*), thereby pressuring one segment of the press into giving a more accurate account of the scandal and into reproducing the AFGES communiqués less inaccurately. Since the battle was now taking place on the terrain of administrative measures and since the legal AFGES Bureau was still in control of the local section of the National Student Mutual, the Bureau struck back by deciding on January 11, and by implementing this decision the next day, to close the "University Psychological Aid Center" (BAPU), which depended financially on the Mutual, "considering that the BAPUs are the manifestation in the student milieu of repressive psychiatry's parapolice control, whose obvious function is to maintain . . . the passivity of all exploited sectors, . . . considering that the existence of a BAPU in Strasbourg is a disgrace and a threat to all the students of this university who are determined to think freely." At the national level, the UNEF was forced by the revolt of its Strasbourg chapter—which had previously been held up as a model—to recognize its own general bankruptcy. Although it obviously did not go so far as to defend the old illusions of unionist liberty that were so blatantly denied its opponents by the authorities, the UNEF nevertheless could not accept the judicial expulsion of the Strasbourg Bureau. A Strasbourg delegation was thus present at the general assembly of the UNEF held in Paris on January 14, and at the opening of the meeting demanded a preliminary vote on its motion to *dissolve the entire UNEF,* "considering that the UNEF declared itself a union uniting the vanguard of youth (Charter of Grenoble, 1946) at a time when labor unionism had long since been defeated and turned into a tool for the self-regulation of modern capitalism, working to integrate the working class into the commodity system; . . . considering that the vanguardist pretension of the UNEF is constantly belied by its subreformist slogans and practice; . . . considering that student unionism is a pure and simple farce and that it is urgent to put an end to it." The motion concluded by calling on "all revolutionary students of the world . . . to join all the exploited people of their countries in undertaking a relentless struggle against all aspects of the old world, with the aim of contributing toward the international power of workers' councils." Only two delegations, that of Nantes and that of the convalescent-home students, voted with Strasbourg to deal with this preliminary motion before hearing the report of the national leadership. (It should be noted, however, that in the preceding weeks the young UNEF bureaucrats had succeeded in deposing two other bureaus that had been spontaneously in favor of the AFGES position, those of Bordeaux and Clermont-Ferrand.) The Strasbourg delegation consequently walked out on a debate where it had nothing more to say.

The final exit of the AFGES Bureau was not to be so noble, however. Around this same time three situationists were excluded* from the SI for having jointly perpetrated—and been forced to admit before the SI—several slanderous lies directed against Khayati, whom they had hoped would himself be excluded as a result of this clever scheme (see the January 22 tract "Warning! Three Provocateurs"). Their exclusion had no connection with the Strasbourg scandal—in it, as in everything else, they had ostensibly agreed with the conclusions reached in SI discussions—but two of them happened to be from the Strasbourg region. In addition, as we mentioned above, some of the Strasbourg students had begun to be irritated by the fact that the SI had not rewarded them for their shortcomings by *recruiting* them. The excluded liars sought out an uncritical audience among them and counted on covering up their previous lies and their admission of them by piling new lies on top of them. Thus all those who had been *rejected* by the SI joined forces in the mystical pretension of "going beyond" the practice that had condemned them. They began to believe the newspapers, and even to expand on them. They saw themselves as masses who had actually "seized power" in a sort of Strasbourg Commune. They told themselves that they hadn't been treated the way a revolutionary proletariat deserves to be treated, and that their historic action had superseded all previous theories. Forgetting that their only discernable "action" in this affair was to have made a few meager contributions to *the drafting of a text,* they collectively compensated for this deficiency by inflating their illusions. This amounted to nothing more ambitious than collectively fantasizing for a few weeks while continually upping the dose of constantly reiterated falsifications.

The dozen Strasbourg students who had effectively supported the scandal split into two equal parts. This supplementary problem thus acted as a touchstone. We naturally made no *promises* to those who remained "partisans of the SI" and we clearly stated that we would not make any: it was simply up to them to be, unconditionally, partisans of the truth. Vayr-Piova and some of the others became partisans of falsehood with the excluded "Garnautins" (although certainly without knowledge of several excessive blunders in Frey's and Garnault's recent fabrications, but nevertheless being aware of quite a few of them). André Schneider, whose support the liars hoped to obtain since he held the title of AFGES president, was overwhelmed with false tales from all of them, and was weak enough to believe them without further investigation and to countersign one of their declarations. But after only a few days, independently becoming aware of a number of undeniable lies that these people thought it natural to tell their initiates in order to protect their miserable cause, Schneider immediately decided that he should publicly acknowledge his mistake: in his tract "Memories from the House of the Dead" he denounced those who had deceived him and led him to share the responsibility for a false accusation against the SI. The return of Schneider, whose character the liars had underestimated and who had thus been privileged to witness the full extent of their collective manipulation of embarrassing facts, struck a definitive blow in Strasbourg itself against the excluded and their accomplices, who had already been discredited everywhere else. In their spite these wretches, who the week before had gone to so much trouble to win over Schneider in order to add to the credibility of their venture, proclaimed him a notoriously feeble-minded person who had simply succumbed to "the prestige of the SI." (More and more often, recently, in the most diverse situations, liars end up in this way unwittingly identifying "the prestige of the SI" with the *simple fact of telling the truth*—a connection that certainly does us honor.)

Before three months had gone by, the association of Frey and consorts with Vayr-Piova and all those who were willing to maintain a keenly solicited adhesion (at one time there were as many as eight or nine of them) was to reveal its sad reality: based on infantile lies by individuals who considered each other to be clumsy liars, it was the very picture, involuntarily parodic, of a type of "collective action" that should never be engaged in; and with the type of people who should never be associated with! They went so far as to conduct a ludicrous *electoral campaign* before the students of Strasbourg. Dozens of pages of pedantic scraps of misremembered situationist ideas and phrases were, with a total unawareness of the absurdity, churned out with the sole aim of *holding on to the "power" of the Strasbourg chapter of the MNEF,* the minibureaucratic fiefdom of Vayr-Piova, who was eligible for reelection April 13. As successful in this venture as in their previous maneuvers, they were defeated by people as stupid as they were—the Stalinists and Christians, who were more naturally deft at electoral politics, and who also enjoyed the bonus of being able to denounce their deplorable rivals as "fake situationists." In the tract "The SI Told You So," put out the next day, André Schneider and his comrades were easily able to show how this unsuccessful attempt to exploit the leftovers of the scandal of five months before for promotional purposes revealed itself as the complete renunciation of the spirit and the declared perspectives of that scandal. Finally Vayr-Piova, in a communiqué distributed April 20, stated: "I find it amusing to be at last denounced as a 'nonsituationist'—something I have openly proclaimed ever since the SI set itself up as an official power." This is a representative sample of a vast and already forgotten literature. That the SI has become *an official power*—this is one of the typical theses of Vayr-Piova or Frey, which can be examined by those who are interested in the question; and after doing so they will know what to think of the intelligence of such theoreticians. But this aside, the fact that Vayr-Piova proclaims (whether "openly," or even "secretly," in a "proclamation" reserved for the most discreet accomplices in his lies) that he has not belonged to the SI since whenever was the date of our transformation into an "official power"—this is a *boldfaced lie.* Everyone who knows him knows that Vayr-Piova has never had the opportunity to claim to be anything but a "nonsituationist" (see what we wrote above concerning the AFGES communiqué of November 29).

The most favorable results of this whole affair naturally go beyond this new and opportunely much-publicized example of our refusal to enlist anything that a neomilitantism in search of glorious subordination might throw our way. No less negligible is the fact that the scandal forced the official recognition of the irreparable decomposition of the UNEF, a decomposition that was even more advanced than its pitiful appearance suggested: the *coup de grace* was still echoing in July at its 56th Congress in Lyon, in the course of which its sad president Vandenburie had to confess: "The unity of the UNEF has long since ended. Each association lives (*SI note: this term is pretentiously inaccurate*) autonomously, without paying any attention to the directives of the National Committee. The growing gap between the rank and file and the governing bodies has reached a state of serious degradation. The history of the proceedings of the UNEF has become nothing but a series of crises. . . . Reorganization and a revival of action have not proved possible." Equally comical were some side-effects stirred up among the academics, who felt that this was another current issue to petition about. As can be well imagined, we considered the position published by the forty professors and assistants of the Faculty of Arts at Strasbourg, which denounced the *fake students* behind this "tempest in a teacup" about false problems "without the shadow of a solution," to be more logical and socially rational (as was, for that matter, Judge Llabador's summing up) [see p. 503] than that wheedling attempt at approval circulated in February by a few decrepit modernist-in-stitutionalists gnawing their meager bones at the professorial chairs of "Social Sciences" at Nanterre (impudent Touraine, loyal Lefebvre, Maoist Baudrillard, cunning Lourau).

In fact, we want ideas to become *dangerous* again. We cannot be accepted with the spinelessness of a false eclectic interest, as if we were Sartres, Althussers, Aragons, or Godards. Let us note the wise words of a certain Professor Lhuillier, reported in the *Nouvel Observateur* (21 December 1966): "I am for freedom of thought. But if there are any Situationists in the room, I want them to get out right now." While not entirely denying the effect that the dissemination of a few basic truths may have had in slightly accelerating the movement that is impelling the lagging French youth toward an awareness of an impending more general crisis in the society, we think that the distribution of *On the Poverty of Student Life* has been a much more significant factor of clarification in some other countries where such a process is already much more clearly under way. In the afterword of their edition of Khayati's text, the English situationists wrote: "The most highly developed critique of modern life has been made in one of the least highly developed modern countries—in a country which has not yet reached the point where the complete disintegration of all values becomes patently obvious and engenders the corresponding forces of radical rejection. In the French context, situationist theory has anticipated the social forces by which it will be realized." The theses of *On the Poverty of Student Life* have been much more truly understood in the United States and in England (the strike at the London School of Economics in March caused a certain stir, the *Times* commentator unhappily seeing in it a return of the class struggle he had thought was over with). To a lesser degree this is also the case in the Netherlands—where the SI's critique, reinforcing a much harsher critique by events themselves, was not without effect on the recent dissolution of the "Provo" movement—and in the Scandinavian countries. The struggles of the West Berlin students this year have also picked up some aspects of the critique, though in a still very confused way.

But revolutionary youth have no alternative but to join with the mass of workers who, starting from their experience of the new conditions of exploitation, are going to take up once again the struggle to control their world and to do away with work. When young people begin to know the current theoretical form of this real movement that is everywhere spontaneously bursting forth from the soil of modern society, this is only a *moment* of the progression by which this unified theoretical critique (inseparable from an adequate *practical unification*) strives to break the silence and the general organization of separation. It is only in this sense that we find the result satisfactory. In speaking of revolutionary youth, we are obviously not referring to that alienated and semiprivileged fraction molded by the university—a sector that is the natural base for an admiring consumption of a fantasized situationist theory considered as the latest spectacular fashion. We will continue to disappoint and refute that kind of approbation. Sooner or later it will be understood that the SI must be judged not on the superficially scandalous aspects of certain manifestations through which it appears, but on its *essentially scandalous* central truth.

The Situationists and the New Forms of Action Against Politics and Art

Up till now our subversion has mainly drawn on the forms and genres inherited from past revolutionary struggles, primarily those of the last hundred years. I propose that we supplement our agitational expression with methods that dispense with any reference to the past. I don't mean that we should abandon the forms within which we have waged battle on the traditional terrain of the supersession of philosophy, the realization of art, and the abolition of politics; but that we should extend the work of the journal onto terrains it does not yet reach.

Many proletarians are aware that they have no power over their lives; they know it, but they don't express it in the language of socialism and of the previous revolutions.

Let us spit in passing on those students who have become militants in the tiny would-be mass parties, who sometimes have the nerve to claim that the workers are incapable of reading *Internationale Situationniste,* that its paper is too slick to be put in their lunch bags and that its price doesn't take into account their low standard of living. The most consistent of these students accordingly distribute the mimeographed image they have of the consciousness of a class in which they fervently seek stereotypical Joe Worker recruits. They forget, among other things, that when workers read revolutionary literature in the past they had to pay relatively more than for a theater ticket; and that when they once again develop an interest in it they won't hesitate to spend two or three times what it costs for an issue of *Planète.* But what these detractors of typography forget most of all is that the rare individuals who read their own bulletins are precisely those who already have the minimal background necessary to understand us right away; and that their writings are completely unreadable for anyone else. Some of them, ignoring the immense readership of bathroom graffiti (particularly in cafés), have thought that by using a parody of grade-school writing, printed on paper pasted on gutters like notices of apartments for rent, they could make the form correspond to the content of their slogans; and in this at least they have succeeded. All this serves to clarify what must not be done.

Our task is to link up the theoretical critique of modern society with the critique of it in acts. By detourning the very propositions of the spectacle, we can directly reveal the implications of present and future revolts.

I propose that we pursue:

1. *Experimentation in the détournement of photo-romances* and "pornographic" photos, and that we bluntly impose their real truth by restoring real dialogues (by adding or altering the speech bubbles). This operation will bring to the surface the subversive bubbles that are spontaneously but only fleetingly and half-consciously formed and then dissolved in the imaginations of those who look at these images. In the same spirit, it is also possible to detourn *any* advertising billboards—particularly those in subway corridors, which form remarkable sequences—by pasting pre-prepared placards onto them.

2. *The promotion of guerrilla tactics in the mass media*—an important form of contestation, not only at the urban guerrilla stage, but even before it. The trail was blazed by those Argentineans who took over the control station of an electronic bulletin board and used it to transmit their own directives and slogans. It is still possible to take advantage of the fact that radio and television stations are not yet guarded by

troops. On a more modest level, it is known that any amateur radio operator can at little expense broadcast, or at least jam, on a local level; and that the small size of the necessary equipment permits a great mobility, enabling one to slip away before one's position is trigonometrically located. A group of Communist Party dissidents in Denmark had their own pirate radio station a few years ago. Counterfeit issues of one or another periodical can add to the enemy's confusion. This list of examples is vague and limited for obvious reasons.

The illegality of such actions makes a sustained engagement on this terrain impossible for any organization that has not chosen to go underground, because it would require the formation within it of a *specialized subgroup*—a division of tasks which cannot be effectual without compartmentalization and thus hierarchy, etc. Without, in a word, finding oneself on the slippery slope toward terrorism. We can more appropriately recall the notion of propaganda by deed, which is a very different matter. Our ideas are in everybody's mind, as is well known, and any group without any relation to us, or even a few individuals coming together for a specific purpose, can improvise and improve on tactics experimented with elsewhere by others. This type of unconcerted action cannot be expected to bring about any decisive upheaval, but it can usefully serve to accentuate the coming awakening of consciousness. In any case, there's no need to get hung up on the idea of illegality. Most actions in this domain can be done without breaking any existing law. But the fear of such interventions will make newspaper editors paranoid about their typesetters, radio managers paranoid about their technicians, etc., at least until more specific repressive legislation has been worked out and enacted.

3. *The development of situationist comics.* Comic strips are the only truly popular literature of our century. Even cretins marked by years at school have not been able to resist writing dissertations on them; but they'll get little pleasure out of reading ours. No doubt they'll buy them just to burn them. In our task of "making shame more shameful still," it is easy to see how easy it would be, for example, to transform "*13 Rue de l'Espoir* [Hope Street]" into "*1 Blvd. du Désespoir* [Despair Boulevard]" merely by adding a few elements; or balloons can simply be changed. In contrast to Pop Art, which breaks comics up into fragments, this method aims at restoring to comics their content and importance.

4. The *production of situationist films.* The cinema, which is the newest and undoubtedly most utilizable means of expression of our time, has stagnated for nearly three quarters of a century. To sum it up, we can say that it indeed became the "seventh art" so dear to film buffs, film

clubs, and PTAs. For our purposes this age is over (Ince, Stroheim, the one and only *L'Âge d'or, Citizen Kane* and *Mr. Arkadin,* the lettrist films), even if a few traditional narrative masterpieces are yet to be unearthed in the film archives or on the shelves of foreign distributors. We should appropriate the first stammerings of this new language—in particular its most consummate and modern examples, those which have escaped artistic ideology even more than American "B" movies: newsreels, previews, and above all, filmed ads.

Although filmed advertising has obviously been in the service of the commodity and the spectacle, its extreme technical freedom has laid the foundations for what Eisenstein had an inkling of when he talked of filming *The Critique of Political Economy* or *The German Ideology.*

I am confident that I could film "The Decline and Fall of the Spectacle-Commodity Economy" in a way that would be immediately understandable to the proletarians of Watts who are unaware of the concepts implied in that title. Such adaptations to new forms will at the same time undoubtedly contribute to deepening and intensifying the "written" expression of the same problems; which we could verify, for example, by making a film called *Incitement to Murder and Debauchery* before drafting its equivalent in the journal, "Correctives to the Consciousness of a Class That Will Be the Last." Among other possibilities, the cinema lends itself particularly well to studying the present as a historical problem, to dismantling the processes of reification. To be sure, historical reality can be apprehended, known, and filmed only in the course of a complicated process of mediations enabling consciousness to recognize one moment in another, its goal and its action in destiny, its destiny in its goal and action, and its own essence in this necessity. This mediation would be difficult if the empirical existence of the facts themselves was not already a mediated existence, which only takes on an appearance of immediateness because and to the extent that consciousness of the mediation is lacking and that the facts have been uprooted from the network of their determining circumstances, placed in an artificial isolation, and poorly strung together again in the montage of classical cinema. It is precisely this mediation which has been lacking, and inevitably so, in presituationist cinema, which has limited itself to "objective" forms or re-presentation of politico-moral concepts, whenever it has not been merely academic-type narrative with all its hypocrisies. If what I have just written were filmed, it would become much less complicated—it's all really just banalities. But Godard, the most famous Swiss Maoist, will never be able to understand them. He might well, as is his usual practice, co-opt the above—lift a word from it or an idea like that concerning filmed advertisements—but he will never be capable of anything but brandishing little novelties picked up elsewhere: images or star words of the era, which definitely have a resonance, but one he can't grasp (Bonnot, worker, Marx, made in USA, Pierrot le Fou, Debord, poetry, etc.). He really is a child of Mao and Coca-Cola.

The cinema enables one to express anything, just like an article, a book, a leaflet, or a poster. This is why we should henceforth require that each situationist be as capable of making a film as of writing an article (see the "Anti–Public Relations Notice" in *Internationale Situationniste* #8). Nothing is too beautiful for the blacks of Watts.

RENÉ VIÉNET

Aiming for Practical Truth

Striving to present to the new revolutionary forces a model of theoretico-practical coherence, the SI must be ready at any moment to sanction, by exclusion or break, the failings, inadequacies, and compromises of those making of it—or recognizing in it—the most advanced experimental stage of their common project. If the insurgent generation that is determined to found a new society manifests an alertness, based on indisputable first principles, to smash every *attempt* at co-option, this is not because of a taste for purity, but out of a simple reflex of self-defense. In organizations prefiguring in their essential features the type of social organization to come, the least of requirements consists in not tolerating those people whom the established powers are able to tolerate quite well.

In its positive aspect, the practice of "exclusions" and "breaks" is linked to the question of membership in the SI and of alliance with autonomous groups and individuals. In its "Minimum Definition of Revolutionary Organizations," the 7th Conference stressed among other things the following point: "A revolutionary organization refuses to reproduce within itself any of the hierarchical conditions of the dominant world. The only limit to participating in its total democracy is that each member must have recognized and appropriated the coherence of its critique. This coherence must be both in the critical theory as such and in the relation between this theory and practical activity. The organization radically criticizes every ideology as separate power of ideas and as ideas of separate power."

The coherence of the critique and the critique of incoherence are one and the same movement, condemned to decay and to rigidify into ideology the moment separation is introduced between different groups of a federation, between different members of an organization, or between the theory and practice of an individual member. In the total struggle in which we are engaged, to yield an inch on the front of coherence is to allow separation to gain the upper hand all the way down the line. This is what spurs us to the greatest vigilance: to never take our coherence for granted, to remain alert to the dangers that threaten it in the fundamental unity of individual and collective behavior, and to anticipate and avoid these dangers.

The fact that a secret fraction* was able to form among us, but also that it was rapidly exposed, sufficiently indicates our rigor and our lack of rigor in transparency in intersubjective relations. Put another way, this means that the SI's influence stems essentially from this: it is capable of *setting an example*, both negatively, by showing its weaknesses and correcting them, and positively, by deriving new requirements from these corrections. We have often reiterated the importance of our not being mistaken in judging individuals; we have to prove this continually and thereby at the same time make it more impossible for people to be mistaken about us. And what goes for individuals goes for groups as well.

We recall the words of Socrates to one of the young men he was talking to: "Speak a little so I can see what sort of person you are." We are in a position to avoid this kind of Socrates and this kind of young man if the exemplary character of our activity ensures the radiating force of our presence in and against the reigning spectacle. To the mafiosi of co-option and to the losers who concoct rumors about our supposed "elitism" we should counterpose the antihierarchical example of continuous radicalization. We must not dissimulate any aspect of our experiences and we must establish, through the dissemination of our methods, critical theses, and agitational tactics, the greatest transparency concerning the collective project of liberating everyday life.

The SI should act like an axis which, receiving its movement from the revolutionary impulses of the entire world, precipitates in a unitary manner the radical turn of events. In contrast to the backward sectors that strive for tactical unity above all else (common, national, and popular fronts), the SI and allied autonomous organizations will meet each other only in the search for organic unity, considering that tactical unity is effective only where organic unity is possible. Group or individual, everyone must live in pace with the radicalization of events in order to radicalize them in turn. Revolutionary coherence is nothing else.

We are certainly still far from such a harmony of progression, but we are just as certainly working toward it. The movement from first principles to their realization involves groups and individuals, and thus their possible retardations. Only transparency in real participation cuts short the menace that weighs on coherence: the transformation of retardation into separation. The hostility of the old world we live in is at the root of everything that still separates us from the realization of the situationist project; but awareness of these separations already contains the means to resolve them.

It is precisely in the struggle against separations that retardation appears in various degrees; it is there that unconsciousness of retardation obscures consciousness of separations, thereby introducing incoherence. When consciousness rots, ideology oozes out. We have seen Kotányi keep the results of his analyses to himself, communicating them drop by drop with the tightfisted superiority of a water clock over time; and others (the most recently excluded) keeping to themselves their deficiencies in all respects, strutting like peacocks while lacking the tail. Mystical wait-and-see-ism and egalitarian ecumenicalism had the same odor. Vanish, grotesque charlatans of incurable infirmities!

The notion of retardation relates to the realm of play, it is connected with the notion of "game leader." Just as dissimulation of retardation or dissimulation of experiences recreates the notion of prestige, tends to transform the game leader into a boss, and engenders stereotyped behavior (roles, with all their neurotic outgrowths, their contorted attitudes, and their inhumanity), so transparency enables us to enter the collective project with the calculated innocence of Fourier's phalansterian players, rivaling each other ("composite" passion), varying their activities ("butterfly" passion), and striving for the most advanced radicality ("cabalist" passion).* But lightheartedness must be based on conscious, "heavy" relationships. It implies lucidity regarding everyone's abilities.

We have no interest in abilities apart from the revolutionary use that can be made of them, a use that acquires its sense in everyday life. The problem is not that some comrades live, think, fuck, shoot, or talk better than others, but that no comrade should live, think, fuck, shoot, or talk so poorly that he comes to dissimulate his retardations, to play the oppressed minority and demand, in the very name of the surplus-value he grants to the others because of his own inadequacies, a democracy of impotence in which he would flourish. In other words, every revolutionary must at the very least have the passion to defend his most precious attribute: his passion for individual realization, his desire to liberate his own everyday life.

If someone gives up engaging (and thus developing) all his abilities in the fight for his creativity, his dreams, his passions, he is in reality giving up on himself. In so doing, he has immediately debarred himself from speaking in his own name, much less from speaking in the name of a group embodying the chances for the realization of all individuals. An exclusion or break only concretizes publicly—with the logic of the transparency he lacked—his taste for sacrifice and his choice of the inauthentic.

On questions of membership or alliance, the *example* of real participation in the revolutionary project is the deciding factor. Consciousness of retardations, struggle against separations, passion to attain greater coherence—this is what must constitute the basis of an objective confidence among us, as well as between the SI and autonomous groups and federations. There is every reason to hope that our allies will rival us in radicalizing revolutionary conditions, just as we expect those who will join us to do so. Everything allows us to suppose that at a certain point in the extension of revolutionary consciousness each group will have attained such a coherence that the "game-leading" level of all the participants and the negligibility of retardations will enable individuals to vary their options and change organizations according to their passional affinities. But the momentary preeminence of the SI is a fact that must also be recognized and taken into account: a gratifying disgrace, like the ambiguous smile of the Cheshire Cat of invisible revolutions.

Because the International has today a theoretical and practical richness that only increases once it is shared, appropriated, and renewed by revolutionary elements (up to the point when the SI and the autonomous groups in turn disappear into the revolutionary richness), it must welcome only those wanting to take part in it who fully know what they are doing; that is, anyone who has demonstrated that in speaking and acting for himself, he speaks and acts in the name of many, whether by creating through the poetry of his praxis (leaflet, riot, film, agitation, book) a regroupment of subversive forces, or by his turning out to be the only one to maintain coherence in the process of the radicalization of a group. The advisability of his entry into the SI then becomes a tactical question to be debated: either the group is strong enough to cede one of its "game leaders"; or its failure is such that the game leaders are the only ones to have a say in the matter; or the game leader, due to unavoidable objective circumstances, has not succeeded in forming a group.

Wherever the new proletariat experiments with its liberation, autonomy in revolutionary coherence is the first step toward generalized self-management. The lucidity that we are striving to maintain concerning ourselves and the world teaches us that in organizational practice there's no such thing as too much precision or alertness. On the question of freedom, an error of detail is already a truth of state.

RAOUL VANEIGEM

Setting Straight Some Popular Misconceptions About Revolutions in the Underdeveloped Countries

1

The eminently revolutionary role of the bourgeoisie consists in having introduced the economy into history in a decisive and irreversible way. As the faithful master of this economy, the bourgeoisie has since its appearance been the real (though sometimes unconscious) master of "universal history." For the first time universal history ceased to be some metaphysical fantasy or some act of the World Spirit and became a material reality as concrete as the trivial existence of each individual. Since the emergence of commodity production, nothing in the world has escaped the implacable development of this neo-Fate, the invisible economic rationality: the *logic of the commodity*. Totalitarian and imperialist in essence, it demands the entire planet as its terrain and the whole of humanity as its servants. Wherever the *commodity* is present there are only slaves.

2

In response to the bourgeoisie's oppressive coherence in keeping humanity in *prehistory*, the revolutionary movement—a direct and unintended product of bourgeois capitalist domination—has for more than a century counterposed the project of a liberatory coherence that is the work of each and every one, the free, conscious intervention in the creation of *history*: the real abolition of all class divisions and the suppression of the economy.

3

Wherever it has penetrated—that is, almost everywhere in the world—the virus of the commodity never stops toppling the most ossified socioeconomic structures, enabling millions of human beings to discover through poverty and violence the historical time of the economy. Wherever it penetrates it spreads its destructive character, dissolving the vestiges of the past and pushing all antagonisms to their extreme. In a word, it hastens social revolution. All the walls of China crumble in its path, and scarcely has it established itself in India when everything around it disintegrates and agrarian revolutions explode in Bombay, in Bengal, and in Madras. The precapitalist zones of the world accede to bourgeois modernity, but without its material basis. There too, as in the case of the proletariat, the forces that the bourgeoisie has contributed toward liberating, or even creating, are now going to turn against the bourgeoisie and its native servants: the revolution of the underdeveloped is becoming one of the main chapters of modern history.

4

If the problem of revolution in the underdeveloped countries poses itself in a particular way, this is due to the very development of history: In these countries the general economic backwardness—fostered by colonial domination and the social strata that support it—and the underdevelopment of productive forces have impeded the development of socioeconomic structures that would have made immediately practicable the revolutionary theory elaborated in the advanced capitalist societies for more than a century. As they enter the struggle, none of these countries have any significant heavy industry and the proletariat is far from being the majority class. It is the poor peasantry that plays that role.

5

The various national liberation movements emerged well after the rout of the workers' movement resulting from the defeat of the Russian revolution, which right from its victory was turned into a counterrevolution in the service of a bureaucracy claiming to be communist. They have thus suffered—either consciously or with false consciousness—from all the defects and weaknesses of that generalized counterrevolution; and with the additional burden of their generally backward conditions, they have been unable to overcome any of the limits imposed on the defeated revolutionary movement. It is also precisely because of this defeat that the colonized and semicolonized countries have had to fight imperialism by themselves. But because they have fought only imperialism and on only a part of the total revolutionary terrain, they have only *partially* driven it out. The oppressive regimes that have installed themselves wherever national liberation revolutions believed themselves victorious are only one of the guises by which the *return of the repressed* takes place.

6

No matter what forces have participated in them, and regardless of the radicalism of their leaderships, the national liberation movements have always led the ex-colonial societies to *modern forms of the state* and to pretensions of modernity in the economy. In China, father-image of underdeveloped revolutionaries, the peasants' struggle against American, European, and Japanese imperialism ended up, because of the defeat of the Chinese workers' movement in 1925–1927, by bringing to power a bureaucracy on the Russian model. The Stalino-Leninist dogmatism with which this bureaucracy gilds its ideology—recently reduced to Mao's red catechism—is nothing but the lie, or at best the false consciousness, that accompanies its counterrevolutionary practice.

7

Fanonism* and Castro-Guevaraism are the false consciousness through which the peasantry carries out the immense task of ridding precapitalist society of its semifeudal and colonialist leftovers and acceding to a national dignity previously trampled on by reactionary colonists and ruling classes. Ben-Bellaism, Nasserism, Titoism, and Maoism are the ideologies that signal the end of these movements and their takeover by petty-bourgeois or military urban strata: the reconstitution of exploitive society with new masters and based on new socioeconomic structures. Wherever the peasantry has fought victoriously and brought to power the social strata that marshaled and directed its struggle, it has been the first to suffer their violence and to pay the enormous cost of their domination. Modern bureaucracy, like that of antiquity (in China, for example), builds its power and prosperity on the superexploitation of the peasants: ideology changes nothing in the matter. In China or Cuba, Egypt or Algeria, everywhere it plays the same role and assumes the same functions.

8

In the process of capital accumulation, *the bureaucracy fulfills what was only the unrealized ideal of the bourgeoisie.* What the bourgeoisie took centuries to accomplish "through blood and mud,"* the bureaucracy wants to achieve consciously and "rationally" within a few decades. But the bureaucracy cannot accumulate capital without accumulating lies: that which constituted the original sin of capitalist wealth is sinisterly referred to as "socialist primitive accumulation." Everything that the underdeveloped bureaucracies present as socialism, or imagine to be socialism, is nothing but a realized *neo-mercantilism.* "The bourgeois state minus the bourgeoisie" (Lenin) cannot go beyond the historical tasks of the bourgeoisie, and the most advanced industrial countries show to the less developed ones the image of their own development to come. Once in power, the Bolshevik bureaucracy could find nothing better to propose to the revolutionary Russian proletariat than to "follow the lessons of German state-capitalism." All the so-called socialist powers are nothing but underdeveloped imitations of the bureaucracy that dominated and defeated the revolutionary movement in Europe. Whatever the bureaucracy is able to do or is forced to do will neither emancipate the working masses nor even substantially improve their social condition, because those aims depend not only on the productive forces but also on *their appropriation by the producers.* However, what the bureaucracy will not fail to do is create the material conditions to realize both. Has the bourgeoisie ever done less?

9

In the peasant-bureaucratic revolutions only the bureaucracy aims consciously and lucidly at power. The seizure of power is the historical moment when the bureaucracy lays hold of the state and declares its independence vis-à-vis the revolutionary masses before even having eliminated the vestiges of colonialism and achieving effective independence from foreign powers. Upon entering the state, the new class suppresses all autonomy of the masses by pretending to suppress its own autonomy and to devote itself to the service of the masses. Exclusive owner of the entire society, it declares itself the exclusive representative of that society's superior interests. In so doing, the bureaucratic state is the fulfillment of the Hegelian State. Its separation from society sanctions at the same time the society's separation into antagonistic classes: the momentary union of the bureaucracy and the peasantry is only the fantastic illusion through which they jointly accomplish the immense historical tasks of the absent bourgeoisie. The bureaucratic power built on the ruins of precapitalist colonial society is not the abolition of class antagonisms; it merely substitutes new classes, new conditions of oppression, and new forms of struggle for the old ones.

10

The only people who are really underdeveloped are those who see a positive value in the power of their masters. The rush to catch up with capitalist reification remains the best road to reinforced underdevelopment. The question of economic development is inseparable from the question of who is the real owner of the economy, the real master of labor power. Everything else is nothing but the babble of specialists.

11

So far the revolutions in the underdeveloped countries have only tried to imitate Bolshevism in various ways. From now on the point is to go beyond it through the *power of soviets.* *

MUSTAPHA KHAYATI

Minimum Definition of Revolutionary Organizations

Since the only purpose of a revolutionary organization is the abolition of all existing classes in a way that does not bring about a new division of society, we consider an organization to be revolutionary if it *consistently and effectively* works toward the international realization of the absolute power of the workers' councils, as prefigured in the experience of the proletarian revolutions of this century.

Such an organization makes an integral critique of the world, or is nothing. By integral critique we mean a comprehensive critique of all geographical areas where various forms of separate socioeconomic powers exist, as well as a comprehensive critique of all aspects of life.

Such an organization sees the beginning and end of its program in the complete decolonization of everyday life. It thus aims not at the masses' self-management of the *existing world,* but at its uninterrupted transformation. It embodies the radical critique of *political economy,* the supersession of the commodity system and of wage labor.

Such an organization refuses to reproduce within itself any of the hierarchical conditions of the dominant world. The only limit to participating in its total democracy is that each member must have recognized and appropriated the *coherence of its critique.* This coherence must be both in the critical theory as such and in the relation between that theory and practical activity. The organization radically criticizes every *ideology* as *separate power* of ideas and as *ideas of separate power.* It is thus at the same time the negation of any remnants of religion and the negation of the prevailing social *spectacle* which, from news media to mass culture, monopolizes communication between people around their unilateral reception of images of their alienated activity. The organization dissolves any "revolutionary ideology," unmasking it as a sign of the failure of the revolutionary project, as the private property of new specialists of power, as one more fraudulent *representation* setting itself above real proletarianized life.

Since the *ultimate criterion* of the modern revolutionary organization is its comprehensiveness, such an organization is ultimately a critique of politics. It must explicitly aim to dissolve itself as a separate organization at its moment of victory.

Adopted by the 7th Conference of the SI (July 1966)

Three Postscripts to the Previous Issue

It seems to us that the insurrections of the blacks in Newark and Detroit have indisputably confirmed our 1965 analysis of the Watts riot ["The Decline and Fall of the Spectacle-Commodity Economy"]. In particular, the participation of numerous whites in the looting demonstrates that in its deepest sense Watts really was "a revolt against the commodity," an elemental reaction to the world of "commodity abundance." On the other hand, the danger represented by the *leadership* that is trying to constitute itself above the movement is now taking more definite shape: the Newark Conference has adopted the essential features of the Black Muslim program of black capitalism. Stokely Carmichael and the other "Black Power" stars are walking the tightrope between the *vague and undefined* extremism necessary to establish themselves at the head of the black masses (Mao, Castro, power to the blacks, and we don't even have to say what we're going to do about the 9/10 of the population who are white) and the *actual* unavowed paltry *reformism* of a black "third party," which would auction off its swing vote in the American political marketplace and which would eventually create, in the person of Carmichael and his colleagues, an "elite" like those that emerged out of the other American minorities (Poles, Italians, etc.), an elite that has so far never developed among the blacks.

* * *

In Algeria, too, Boumédienne has unfortunately proved the correctness of our analysis of his regime ["The Class Struggles in Algeria"]. Self-management there is now completely dead. We have no doubt we will eventually see it return under more favorable conditions. But for the moment no revolutionary network has succeeded in forming on the basis of the offensive resistance of the self-managed sector; and our own direct efforts toward this goal have been extremely inadequate.

* * *

Daniel Guérin wrote to us to say that our note about him ["The Algeria of Daniel Guérin, Libertarian"] was unfair and that he wanted to explain himself. We met him. He had to admit that we gave a correct account of his analysis of Algeria, which is at the opposite pole from ours. He complained only of having been presented as a sort of agent of Ben Bella. We stated that our note in no way suggests such an idea. Guérin explained his admiration for Ben Bella by psychological arguments whose sincerity we don't question: He had found Ben Bella very likable, particularly after thirty years of disappointments with his other militant anticolonialist North African friends, who have generally ended up becoming government officials. Ben Bella remained a man of the people, that was his good side. He became President of the Republic, that was his failing. Guérin already found Ben Bella's Algeria "miraculous" and reproached us for demanding a succession of additional miracles. We replied that such a succession was precisely our conception of revolution, and that any single "miracle" that remains miraculous (i.e. isolated and exceptional) will quickly disappear. We proposed to Guérin that he publish a text in response to our article; but he considered that his oral explanation was sufficient.

The Beginning of an Era

"Do you really believe that these Germans will make a political revolution in *our* lifetime? My friend, that is just wishful thinking," wrote Arnold Ruge to Marx in March 1843. Five years later that revolution had come. As an amusing example of a type of historical unconsciousness constantly produced by similar causes and always contradicted by similar results, Ruge's unfortunate statement was quoted as an epigraph in *The Society of the Spectacle,* which appeared December 1967. Six months later came the occupations movement, the greatest revolutionary moment in France since the Paris Commune.

The largest general strike that ever stopped the economy of an advanced industrial country, and the first *wildcat general strike* in history; revolutionary occupations and the beginnings of direct democracy; the increasingly complete collapse of state power for nearly two weeks; the resounding verification of the revolutionary theory of our time and even here and there the first steps toward putting it into practice; the most important experience of the modern proletarian movement that is in the process of constituting itself in its *fully developed* form in all countries, and the example it must now go beyond—this is what the French May 1968 movement was essentially, and this in itself *already* constitutes its essential victory.

Later on we will examine this movement's weaknesses and deficiencies, which were the natural consequences of the ignorance and improvisation and of the dead weight of the past that was still felt even where this movement best asserted itself; the consequences, above all, of the *separations* that all the joint forces for the preservation of the capitalist order narrowly succeeded in defending, with the bureaucratic political and labor-union machines exerting themselves to this end more intensely and effectively than the police at this life-or-death moment for the system. But let us first enumerate the evident characteristics at the *heart* of the occupations movement, where it was freest to translate its content into words and deeds. There it proclaimed its goals *much more explicitly* than any other spontaneous revolutionary movement in history; and those goals were much more radical and up-to-date than were ever expressed in the programs of the revolutionary organizations of the past, even at their best moments.

The occupations movement was the sudden return of the proletariat as a historical class, a proletariat now *enlarged* to include a majority of the salaried employees of modern society and still struggling for the real abolition of classes and of wage labor. The movement was a rediscovery of collective and individual history, an awakening to the possibility of intervening in history, an awareness of participating in an irreversible event where "nothing would ever be the same again." People looked back in amusement at the *strange* existence they had led a week before, at their outlived survival. It was a passion for bringing everything and everyone together, a holistic critique of all alienations, of all ideologies, and of the entire old organization of real life. In this process property was negated, everyone finding themselves at home everywhere. The *recognized desire* for genuine dialogue, completely free expression, and real community found their terrain in the buildings transformed into open meeting places and in the collective struggle. The telephones (which were among the few technical means still functioning) and the wandering of so many emissaries and travelers around Paris and throughout the entire country, between the occupied buildings, the factories, and the assemblies, manifested this real practice of communication. The occupations movement was obviously a rejection of alienated labor; it was a festival, a game, a real presence of people and of time. And it was a rejection of all authority, all specialization, all hierarchical dispossession; a rejection of the state and thus of the parties and unions; and of sociologists and professors, of the health-care system and repressive morality. Everyone awakened by the lightning chain reaction of the movement (one of the graffiti, perhaps the most beautiful, simply said: *"Quick"*) thoroughly despised their former conditions of existence and therefore those who had worked to keep them there, from the television stars to the city planners. Many people's Stalinist illusions, in various diluted forms from Castro to Sartre, were torn apart, as all the rival and interdependent lies of an era crumbled. International solidarity spontaneously reappeared: numerous foreign workers flung themselves into the struggle and many European revolutionaries rushed to France. The extensive participation of women in all aspects of struggle was an unmistakable sign of its revolutionary depth. There was a significant liberation from habits and customs. The movement was also a critique, still partially illusory, of the commodity system (in its lame sociological disguise as "consumer society"). And it already contained a *rejection* of art that did not yet recognize the historical *negation* of art (a rejection expressed in the poor abstract slogan, "Power to the imagination," which did not know how to put this power into practice, to reinvent everything; and which, lacking power, lacked imagination). Hatred of co-opters was expressed everywhere, though it did not yet reach the theoretico-practical knowledge of how to get rid of them (the neoartists, political neoleaders, and neospectators of the very movement that contradicted them). If the critique-in-acts of the spectacle of nonlife was not yet the revolutionary supersession of these co-opters, this was because the "spontaneously councilist" tendency of the May uprising was ahead of almost all the concrete means (including theoretical and organizational consciousness) that will one day enable it to transform itself into a power by being the only power.

Let us spit in passing on the banalizing commentaries and false testimonies by sociologists, retired Marxists, and all the doctrinaires of the old preserved ultraleftism or of the servile ultramodernism of spectacular society; no one who *experienced* this movement can deny that it contained everything we have said.

In *Internationale Situationniste* #10 (March 1966, p. 77), we wrote, "What might appear to be audacious speculation in several of our assertions, we put forward with the assurance that the future will bring their overwhelming and undeniable historical confirmation." And so it has happened.

Naturally we had prophesied nothing. We had simply pointed out what was *already present:* the material preconditions for a new society had long since been produced; the old class society had maintained itself *everywhere* by considerably modernizing its oppression, while developing an ever-increasing abundance of contradictions; the previously vanquished proletarian movement was returning for a second, more conscious and more total assault. Many people, of course, were already aware of these facts, so clearly demonstrated both by history and by present reality, and some people even stated them; but they did so abstractly and thus in a vacuum, without any echo, without any possibility of intervention. The merit of the situationists was simply to have recognized and pointed out the new focuses of revolt in modern society (focuses which do not at all exclude the old ones, but on the contrary bring them back to light): urbanism, the spectacle, ideology, etc. Because this task was carried out radically, it was able to stir up, or at least considerably reinforce, certain practical acts of revolt. If our enterprise struck a certain chord it was because *uncompromising* criticism was scarcely to be found among the leftisms of the preceding period. If many people *put our words into action* it was because we expressed the negative that had been lived by us and by so many others before us. What awakened in the spring of 1968 was nothing other than what had been sleeping in the night of "spectacular society," whose spectacles presented nothing but an eternal positive façade. But we had "cohabited with the negative" in accordance with the program we formulated in 1962 (see *Internationale Situationniste* #7, p. 10). We are not going into our "merits" in order to be applauded, but for the benefit of others who are going to act in similar ways.

Those who shut their eyes to this "critique within the mêlée" only saw an "immovable" force of modern domination which reflected their own renunciation. Their antiutopian "realism" was no more real than a police station or the Sorbonne were more real buildings before than after their transformation by arsonists or "Katangans."* When the subterranean phantoms of total revolution rose and extended their force over the entire country, it was all the forces of the old world that appeared as ghostly illusions dissipated in the daylight. After thirty miserable years that in the history of revolutions amounted to no more than a month, came this month of May that recapitulated thirty years.

To transform our desires into reality is a precise task, precisely the contrary of the intellectual prostitution that grafts its illusions of permanence onto any reality that happens to exist. Take Henri Lefebvre, for example, whom we already quoted in the preceding issue of this journal (October 1967) because in his book *Positions contre les technocrates* (Gonthier) he ventured a categorical conclusion whose scientific validity was revealed scarcely more than six months later: "The situationists . . . do not propose a concrete utopia, but an abstract one. Do they really imagine that one fine day or one decisive evening people will look at each other and say, 'Enough! We're fed up with work and boredom! Let's put an end to them!' and that they will then proceed into the eternal Festival and the creation of situations? Although this happened once, at the dawn of March 18, 1871 [the Paris Commune], that combination of circumstances will not occur again." A certain intellectual influence has been attributed to Lefebvre for certain of the SI's radical theses that he surreptitiously copied (see in this issue the reproduction of our 1963 tract *Into the Trashcan of History*),* but he reserved the truth of that critique for the past, even though it was born out of the *present* more than out of his academic reflections on the past, and he warned against the illusion that any present struggle could ever again achieve those results. Don't jump to the conclusion that Lefebvre is the only former thinker the event has made a complete fool of: those who avoided committing themselves to such ludicrous declarations nevertheless had the same convictions. Overcome by their shock in May, all the *researchers of historical nothingness* have admitted that no one had in any way foreseen what occurred. We must acknowledge a sort of exception to this in the case of all the sects of "resurrected Bolsheviks," of whom it is fair to say that for the last thirty years they have not for one instant ceased heralding the imminence of the revolution *of 1917*. But they too were badly mistaken: this was not at all 1917 and in any case they were hardly equal to Lenin. As for the remnants of the old non-Trotskyist ultraleft, they still needed at least a major economic crisis. They made any revolutionary moment contingent on its return, and saw nothing coming. Now that they have admitted that there was a revolutionary crisis in May they have to prove that some sort of *invisible* economic crisis was taking place in early 1968. As clueless and complacent as always, they are earnestly working on this problem, producing diagrams of increases in prices and unemployment. For them an economic crisis is no longer that terribly conspicuous objective reality that was so extensively experienced and described up through 1929, but rather a sort of eucharistic presence that is one of the foundations of their religion.

Just as it would be necessary to reissue the entire collection of *Internationale Situationniste* journals in order to show how greatly all these people were mistaken before May, so it would require a thick volume to go through all the stupidities and partial admissions they have produced since then. We will limit ourselves to citing the picturesque journalist Frédéric Gaussen, who felt that he could reassure the readers of *Le Monde* on 9 December 1966 that the few situationist maniacs who perpetrated the Strasbourg scandal had "a messianic confidence in the revolutionary capacity of the masses and in their aptitude for freedom." Since then Gaussen's aptitude for freedom has not progressed one millimeter, but we find him in the same paper, 29 January 1969, panic-stricken at finding everywhere "the feeling that revolutionary aspirations are universal." "Highschoolers in Rome, college students in Berlin, 'enragés' in Madrid, 'Lenin's orphans' in Prague, radical dissidents in Belgrade, all are attacking the same world, the Old World." And Gaussen, using almost the same words as before, now attributes to all those revolutionary masses the same "quasi-mystical belief in the creative spontaneity of the masses."

We don't want to dwell in triumph on the discomfiture of all our intellectual adversaries; not that this "triumph," which is in fact simply that of the modern revolutionary movement, is not quite significant, but because the subject is so monotonous and because the reappearance of history, the reappearance of direct class struggle recognizing *present-day* revolutionary goals, has pronounced such a clear verdict on the whole period that came to an end in May (previously it was the subversion of the existing society that seemed unlikely; now it is its preservation). Instead of going over what is already verified, it is henceforth more important to pose the new problems; to *criticize the May movement* and embark on the practice of the new era.

In all other countries the recent and generally confused quest for a radical critique of modern capitalism (private or bureaucratic) had not yet broken out of the narrow base it had in the student milieu. In complete contrast, whatever the government, the newspapers, and the ideologists of modernist sociology pretend to believe, *the May movement was not a student movement.* It was a revolutionary proletarian movement reemerging after half a century of suppression and generally deprived of everything. Its unfortunate paradox was that it was able to concretely express itself and take shape only on the very unfavorable *terrain* of a student revolt: the streets held by the rioters around the Latin Quarter and the mostly university buildings occupied in the same area. Instead of dwelling on the laughable historical parody of Leninist or Maoist-Stalinist students disguising themselves as proletarians or vanguard leaders of the proletariat, it must be realized that it was, on the contrary, the most advanced segment of the workers, unorganized and separated by all the forms of repression, that found themselves *disguised as students* in the reassuring imagery of the labor unions and the spectacular news. The May movement was not some political theory looking for workers to carry it out; it was the acting proletariat seeking its theoretical consciousness.

The *sabotage* of the university by a few groups of young and notoriously *antistudent* revolutionaries at Nantes and Nanterre (we are referring here to the "Enragés" and not, of course, to the majority of the "March 22nd Movement" who later imitated their actions) presented the *opportunity* to develop forms of direct struggle that dissatisfied workers, mainly young ones, had already initiated in the early months of 1968 (at Caen and Redon, for example). But this circumstance was in no way fundamental and could do the movement no harm. What was both significant and unfortunate was the fact that the unions were eventually able to control the *wildcat strike* that had been launched against their will and despite all their maneuvers. They accepted the strike they had been unable to prevent, which is the usual tactic of a union faced with a wildcat, although this time they had to accept one on a national scale. And by accepting this "unofficial" general strike they remained accepted by it. They kept control over the factory gates, simultaneously *isolating* the vast majority of the workers from the *real movement* and each plant from all the others. Thus the most unitary action and the most radical critique-in-action ever seen was at the same time a sum of isolations and a pageant of banal, officially approved demands. Just as the unions had to let the general strike spread *little by little,* winding up in virtual unanimity, so they strove to liquidate the strike little by little, using the terrorism of falsification and their monopoly of communication to coerce the workers in each separate enterprise to accept the crumbs they had *collectively rejected* on May 27. The revolutionary strike was thus reduced to a *cold war* between the union bureaucracies and the workers. The unions *acknowledged* the strike on the condition that the workers tacitly acknowledged, by their practical passivity, *that it would lead nowhere.* The unions did not "miss an opportunity" to act revolutionarily, because there is nothing revolutionary about any of them, from the Stalinists to the bourgeoisified reformists. They did not even act to bring about *substantial reforms,* because the situation was too dangerously revolutionary to play around with, even to try to exploit it to their own advantage. They very clearly wanted it to be brought to a halt immediately, at any cost. In this exceptional situation the Stalinists—admirably imitated in this hypocrisy by the semileftist sociologists (cf. Coudray in *La Brèche,* Éditions du Seuil, 1968)—though usually of such a contrary opinion, suddenly feigned an extraordinary respect for the competence of the workers, for their wise "decision," presented with the most fantastic cynicism as having been clearly debated, voted in full knowledge of the facts, and absolutely unequivocal: for once the workers supposedly knew what they wanted because "they did not want a revolution"! But all the obstacles and muzzles and lies that the panic-stricken bureaucrats resorted to in the face of this supposed *unwillingness* of the workers constitutes the best proof of their real will, unarmed but dangerous. It is only by forgetting the historical totality of the movement of modern society that one can blather on in this circular positivism, which thinks it sees a rationality everywhere in the existing order because it raises its "science" to the point of successively considering that order from the side of the demand and the side of the response. Thus the same Coudray [pseudonym of Cornelius Castoriadis] notes, "If you have these unions, a raise of 5% is the most you can get, and if 5% is what you want, these unions suffice." Leaving aside the question of their intentions in relation to their real life and their interests, what all these gentlemen lack at the very least is dialectics.

The workers, who as always and everywhere naturally had quite enough good reasons for being dissatisfied, started the wildcat strike because they sensed the *revolutionary situation* created by the new forms of sabotage in the universities and the government's successive mistakes in reacting to them. They were obviously as indifferent as we were to the forms and reforms of the university system; but certainly not to the critique of the culture, the environment, and everyday life produced by advanced capitalism, a critique that spread so quickly upon the first rip in that university veil.

By launching the wildcat strike, the workers *gave the lie to the liars* who spoke in their name. In most of the factories they proved incapable of really speaking on their own behalf and of *saying what they wanted*. But in order to say what they want it is first necessary for the workers to create, through their own autonomous action, the concrete conditions that enable them to speak and act, conditions that now exist *nowhere*. The absence, almost everywhere, of such dialogue and of such linking up, as well as the lack of theoretical knowledge of the autonomous goals of proletarian class struggle (these two factors being able to develop only together), prevented the workers from *expropriating the expropriators of their real life*. Thus the advanced nucleus of workers, around which the next revolutionary proletarian organization will take shape, came to the Latin Quarter as a *poor cousin* of a "student reformism" that was itself a largely artificial product of pseudoinformation or of the illusionism of the little leftist sects. This advanced nucleus included young blue-collar workers; white-collar workers from the occupied offices; delinquents and unemployed; rebellious highschoolers, who were often those working-class youth that modern capitalism recruits for the cut-rate education designed to prepare them for a role in developed industry ("Stalinists, your children are with us!" was one of the slogans); "lost intellectuals"; and "Katangans."

The fact that a significant fraction of French students took part in the movement, particularly in Paris, is obvious; but this cannot be considered as constituting the essence of the movement, or even as one of its main aspects. Out of 150,000 Parisian students at most 10–20 thousand were present during the least difficult times of the demonstrations, and only a few thousand during the violent street confrontations. The sole moment of the crisis involving students alone—admittedly one of the decisive moments for its extension—was the spontaneous uprising of the Latin Quarter on May 3 following the arrest of the leftist leaders in the Sorbonne. On the day after the occupation of the Sorbonne nearly half of the participants in its general assemblies, at a time when those assemblies had clearly taken on an insurrectional role, were still students worried about the conditions for their exams and hoping for some university reform in their favor. Probably a slight majority of the student participants recognized that the question of power was posed, but they generally did so as naïve constituents of the little leftist parties, as spectators of old Leninist schemas or even of the oriental exoticism of Maoist Stalinism. The base of these little leftist groups was indeed almost exclusively confined to the student milieu; and the *poverty* that was sustained there was clearly evident in virtually all the leaflets issuing from that milieu (vacuity of all the Kravetzes, stupidity of all the

Péninous). The best statements by the workers who came to the Sorbonne during the initial days were often received with a pedantic and condescending attitude by these students who fantasized themselves as experts in revolution, though they themselves were ready to salivate and applaud at the stimulus of the clumsiest manipulator proclaiming some stupidity while invoking "the working class." Nevertheless, the very fact that these groups manage to recruit a certain number of students is one more symptom of the discontent in present-day society: these little groups are the theatrical expression of a real yet vague revolt that is bargain-shopping for solutions. Finally, the fact that a small fraction of students really supported all the radical demands of May is another indication of the depth of the movement; and remains to their credit.

Although several thousand students, as individuals, were able through their experience of 1968 to break more or less completely with the position assigned to them in the society, the mass of students were not transformed by it. This was not in virtue of the pseudo-Marxist platitude that considers the student's social *background* (bourgeois or petty-bourgeois in the great majority of cases) as the determining factor, but rather because of his social destiny: the student's becoming is the truth of his being. He is mass-produced and conditioned for an upper, middle, or lower position in the organization of modern industrial production. Moreover, the student is being dishonest when he pretends to be scandalized at "discovering" this reason for his education, which has always been proclaimed openly. It is evident that the economic uncertainties of his optimum employment, and especially the dubious desirability of the "privileges" present society can offer him, have played a role in his bewilderment and revolt. But it is precisely because of this that the student is such a perfect customer, eagerly seeking his quality brand in the ideology of one or another of the little bureaucratic groups. The student who dreams of himself as a Bolshevik or a swaggering Stalinist (i.e. a Maoist) is playing both sides: Simply as a result of his studies he reckons on obtaining some modest position managing some small sector of the society as a cadre of capitalism, should a change in power never arrive to fulfill his wishes. And in case his dream of such a power change were to become a reality, he sees himself in an even more glorious managerial role and a higher rank as a "scientifically" warranted political cadre. These groups' dreams of domination are often clumsily revealed in the contempt their fanatics have the nerve to express toward certain aspects of workers' demands, which they often term "mere bread-and-butter issues." In this impotence that would be better advised to keep silent one can already glimpse the disdain with which these leftists would like to be able to respond to any future discontent among the same workers if these self-appointed specialists in the general interests of the proletariat ever managed to get their little hands on state power and police (as in Kronstadt, as in Beijing). But leaving aside the perspective of these germ-carriers of ruling bureaucracies, nothing serious can be recognized in the sociologico-journalistic contrasts between rebellious students, who are supposedly rejecting "consumer society," and the workers, who are supposedly still eager to participate in it. The consumption in question is only a consumption of commodities. It is a hierarchical consumption and it is increasing for everyone, but in a way that becomes increasingly hierarchical. The decline and falsification of the modern commodity's use-value is experienced by everyone, though to differing degrees. Everyone experiences this consumption of both spectacular *and* real commodities within a fundamental poverty, "because this poverty is not itself beyond privation, it is only an augmented privation" (*The Society of the Spectacle*). Like everyone else, the workers spend their lives passively consuming the spectacle and all the lies of ideologies and commodities. But they have fewer illusions than anyone about the concrete conditions imposed on them, about the price they have to pay, every moment of their lives, for the *production* of all that.

For all these reasons the students considered as a social stratum—a stratum itself also in crisis—were in May 1968 nothing but the *rear guard* of the whole movement.

The deficiency of almost all the students who expressed revolutionary intentions was, considering all their free time which they *could have* devoted to elucidating the problems of revolution, certainly deplorable, but quite secondary. The deficiency of the vast majority of workers, constantly leashed and gagged, was in contrast quite excusable, but decisive. The situationists' description and analysis of the *main stages* of the crisis have been set forth in René Viénet's book *Enragés and Situationists in the Occupations Movement* (Gallimard, 1968). We will merely summarize here the main points related in that book, which was written in Brussels during the last three weeks of July on the basis of then-existing documentation, but of which, it seems to us, no conclusion needs to be modified.

From January to March the Enragés group of Nanterre (whose tactics were later taken up in April by the March 22nd Movement) successfully carried out the sabotage of classes and university departments. The Paris University Council's bungling and too-belated repression, together with two successive shutdowns of the Nanterre

University, led to the spontaneous student riot in the Latin Quarter on May 3. The university was paralyzed by both the police and the strike. There was fighting in the streets throughout the following week. Young workers joined in, the Stalinists discredited themselves each day by incredible slanders, the leaders of SNESup [National Union of University Employees] and the little leftist groups revealed their lack of imagination and rigor, and the government responded successively and always at the wrong moment with force and inept concessions. On the night of May 10 the uprising that took over the neighborhood around Rue Gay-Lussac, set up sixty barricades, and held it for more than eight hours aroused the entire country and forced the government into a major capitulation: it withdrew the police forces from the Latin Quarter and reopened the Sorbonne that it could no longer keep running. From May 13 to May 17 the movement irresistibly advanced to the point of becoming a general revolutionary crisis, with the 16th probably being the crucial day, the day the factories began to declare themselves for a wildcat strike. The single-day general strike decreed for the 13th by the big bureaucratic organizations, with the aim of bringing the movement to a rapid end and if possible turning it to their own advantage, was in fact only a beginning: the workers and students of Nantes attacked the prefecture and those who occupied the Sorbonne opened it up to the workers. The Sorbonne immediately became a *"club populaire"* that made the language and demands of the clubs of 1848 seem timid by comparison. On the 14th the workers of Sud-Aviation at Nantes occupied their factory and locked up their managers. Their example was followed by two or three enterprises on the 15th and by several more after the 16th, the day the rank and file imposed the Renault strike at Billancourt. Virtually all the enterprises in the country were soon to follow;* and virtually all institutions, ideas, and habits were to be contested in the succeeding days. The government and the Stalinists made feverish efforts to bring the crisis to a halt by breaking up its main power: they came to an agreement on wage concessions that they hoped would be sufficient to lead to an immediate return to work. On the 27th the rank and file everywhere rejected those "Grenelle Accords." The regime, which a month of Stalinist devotion had not been able to save, saw itself on the brink of destruction. On the 29th the Stalinists themselves had to recognize the likelihood of the collapse of the de Gaulle regime and reluctantly prepared, along with the rest of the Left, to inherit its dangerous legacy: a social revolution that would have to be disarmed or crushed. If, in the face of the panic of the bourgeoisie and the wearing thin of the Stalinist braking force, de Gaulle had stepped down, the new regime would only have been a weakened but *officialized* version of the preceding de facto alliance: the Stalinists would have defended a Mendès-Waldeck [i.e. a Social-ist–Communist coalition] government, for example, with bourgeois militias, party activists, and fragments of the army. They would have tried to play the role not of Kerensky, but rather that of Noske.* De Gaulle, however, being more steadfast than the staff of his administra-tion, relieved the Stalinists by announcing on the 30th that he would strive to maintain himself in power by any means necessary; that is to say, by calling out the army and initiating a civil war in order to hold or reconquer Paris. "The Stalinists, delighted, were very careful not to call for a continuation of the strike until the fall of the regime. They imme-diately rallied around de Gaulle's proposal of new elections, regardless of what it might cost them. In such conditions, the immediate alter-native was either the autonomous self-affirmation of the proletariat or the complete defeat of the movement; councilist revolution or the Grenelle Accords. The revolutionary movement could not settle with the PCF [French Communist Party] without first having got rid of de Gaulle. The form of workers' power that could have developed in a post-Gaullist phase of the crisis, finding itself blocked both by the old reaffirmed state and by the PCF, no longer had any chance to hold back its onrushing defeat" (Viénet, *op. cit.*). The movement began to ebb, although the workers for one or more weeks stubbornly persisted in the strike that all their unions urged them to stop. Of course the bourgeoisie had not disappeared in France; it had merely been dumb-struck with terror. On May 30 it reemerged, along with the conformist petty bourgeoisie, to demonstrate its support for the state. But this state, already so well defended by the bureaucratic left, could not be brought down against its will as long as the workers had not elimi-nated the power base of those bureaucrats by imposing the form of their own autonomous power. The workers left the state this freedom and naturally had to suffer the consequences. The majority of them had not recognized the total significance of their own movement; and nobody else could do so in their place.

If, in a single large factory, between May 16 and May 30, a general assembly had constituted itself as a *council* holding all powers of deci-sion and execution, expelling the bureaucrats, organizing its self-de-fense, and calling on the strikers of all the enterprises to link up with it, this qualitative step could have immediately brought the movement to the *ultimate showdown,* to the final struggle whose general outlines have all been historically traced by this movement. A very large number of enterprises would have followed the course thus discovered. This factory could immediately have taken the place of the dubious and in every sense eccentric Sorbonne of the first days and have become the real center of the occupations movement: genuine *delegates* from the numerous councils that already virtually existed in some of the occupied buildings, and from all the councils that could have imposed themselves in all the branches of industry, would have rallied around this base. Such an assembly could then have proclaimed the expropriation of all capital, *including state capital*; announced that all the country's means of production were henceforth the collective property of the proletariat organized in direct democracy; and appealed directly (by finally seizing some of the telecommunications facilities, for example) to the workers of the entire world to support this revolution. Some people will say that such a hypothesis is utopian. We answer: It is precisely because the occupations movement was objectively at several moments *only an hour away* from such a result that it spread such terror, visible to everyone at the time in the impotence of the state and the panic of the so-called Communist Party, and since then in the conspiracy of silence concerning its gravity. This silence has been so total that millions of witnesses, taken in once again by the "social organization of appearances" which presents this period to them as a short-lived madness of youth (perhaps even merely of student youth), must ask themselves if a society is not itself mad if it could *allow* such a stupefying aberration to occur.

In such an eventuality, civil war would naturally have been inevitable. If armed confrontation had no longer hinged on what the government feared or pretended to fear concerning the supposed evil designs of the "Communist" Party, but had actually faced the consolidation of a direct, industrially based proletarian power (we are, of course, referring here to a total autonomous power, not to some "workers' power" limited to some sort of pseudocontrol of the production of their own alienation), then armed counterrevolution would certainly have been launched immediately. But it would not have been certain of winning. Some of the troops would obviously have mutinied; the workers would have figured out how to get weapons, and they certainly would not have built any more barricades—a good form of *political* expression at the beginning of the movement, but obviously ridiculous *strategically*. (And those like Malraux who claimed afterwards that tanks could have taken Rue Gay-Lussac much more quickly than the antiriot police did are certainly right on that point; but could they have afforded the political cost of such a victory? In any case, the state held its forces back and did not risk it; and it certainly didn't swallow this humiliation out of humanitarianism.) Foreign intervention would have inevitably followed, whatever some ideologues may think (it is possible to have read Hegel and Clausewitz and still be nothing more than a Glucksmann), probably beginning with NATO forces, but with the direct or indirect support of the Warsaw Pact. But then everything would once again have hinged on the European proletariat: double or nothing.

Since the defeat of the occupations movement, both those who participated in it and those who had to endure it have often asked the question: "Was it a revolution?" The general use in the press and in daily conversation of the cowardly neutral phrase, "the May events," is nothing but a way of evading answering or even posing this question. Such a question must be placed in its true historical light. In this context the journalists' and governments' superficial references to the "success" or "failure" of a revolution mean nothing for the simple reason that since the bourgeois revolutions *no revolution has yet succeeded:* not one has abolished classes. Proletarian revolution has so far not been victorious anywhere, but the practical process through which its project manifests itself has already created at least a dozen revolutionary moments of historic importance that can appropriately be termed revolutions. In none of these moments was the *total content* of proletarian revolution fully developed; but in each case there was a fundamental interruption of the ruling socioeconomic order and the appearance of new forms and conceptions of real life: variegated phenomena that can be understood and evaluated only in their overall significance, including their potential future significance.

Of all the partial criteria for judging whether a period of disruption of state power deserves the name of revolution or not, the worst is certainly that which considers whether the political regime in power fell or survived. This criterion, much invoked after May by the Gaullist thinkers, is the same one that enables the daily news to refer to the latest Third World military coups as revolutions. But the revolution of 1905 did not bring down the Czarist regime, it only obtained a few temporary concessions from it. The Spanish revolution of 1936 did not formally suppress the existing political power: it arose, in fact, out of a proletarian uprising initiated in order to defend that Republic against Franco. And the Hungarian revolution of 1956 did not abolish Nagy's liberal-bureaucratic government. Among other regrettable limitations, the Hungarian movement had many aspects of a national uprising against foreign domination; and this national-resistance aspect also played a certain, though less important, role in the origin of the Paris Commune. The Commune supplanted Thiers's power only within the limits of Paris. And the St. Petersburg Soviet of 1905 never even took control of the capital. All the crises cited here as examples, though deficient in their practical achievements and even in their perspectives, nevertheless produced enough radical innovations and put their societies severely enough in check to be legitimately termed revolutions.

As for judging revolutions by the amount of bloodshed they lead to, this romantic vision is not even worth discussing. Some incontestable revolutions have involved very little bloodshed—including even the Paris Commune, which was to end in a massacre—while on the other hand numerous civil confrontations have caused thousands of deaths without in any way being revolutions. It is generally not revolutions that are bloody, but the reaction's subsequent repression of them. The question of the number of deaths during the May movement has given rise to a polemic that the temporarily reassured defenders of order keep coming back to. The official version is that there were only five deaths, all of them instant, including one policeman. Those who claim this are the first to admit that this was an unexpectedly low number. Adding considerably to its improbability is the fact that it has never been admitted that any of the very numerous seriously wounded people could have died in the following days: this extraordinary good luck was certainly not due to rapid medical assistance, particularly on the night of the Gay-Lussac uprising. But if an easy coverup in underestimating the number of deaths was very useful *at the time* for a government up against the wall, it remained useful *afterwards* for different reasons.

But on the whole, the retrospective proofs of the revolutionariness of the occupations movement are as striking as those that its very *existence* threw in the face of the world at the time: The proof that it had established its own new legitimacy is that the regime reestablished in June never dared to prosecute those responsible for attacking the public order through overtly illegal actions, those who had partially divested it of its authority and even of its buildings. But the clearest proof, for those who know the history of our century, is still this: the Stalinists' relentless opposition to the movement at every stage confirms the presence of revolution.

While the Stalinists, as always, represented antiworker bureaucracy in its purest form, the little leftist bureaucratic embryos were straddling the fence. They all openly catered to the major bureaucratic organizations, as much out of calculation as out of ideology (except for the March 22nd Movement, which limited itself to catering to the manipulators who had infiltrated its own ranks: JCR [a Trotskyist group], Maoists, etc.). Locked in their delusory "left-versus-right" schemas, they could envisage nothing more than "pushing to the left" both a spontaneous movement that was much more extremist than they were and bureaucratic apparatuses that could not possibly make any concessions to left-ism in such an obviously revolutionary situation. Pseudostrategical illusions flourished: Some leftists believed that the occupation of one or another ministry on the night of May 24 would have ensured the victory of the movement (but other leftists maneuvered to prevent such an "excess," which did not enter into their own blueprint for victory). Others, prior to their later, more modest dream of maintain-ing a cleaned up and "responsible" administration of the university buildings in order to hold a "Summer University," believed that those buildings would become bases for urban guerrilla warfare. (All of them, however, were surrendered after the end of the workers' strike without being defended; and even the Sorbonne at the very time when it was the momentary center of an expanding movement could, on the crucial night of May 16 when all the doors were open and there were hardly any people there, have been retaken in less than an hour by a riot-police raid.) Not wanting to see that the movement had already gone beyond a mere political change in the state, or in what terms the real stakes were posed (a total, *coherent* awakening of conscious-ness in the enterprises), the little leftist groups worked against that perspective by disseminating moth-eaten illusions and by everywhere presenting bad examples of the bureaucratic conduct that the revolu-tionary workers were all rejecting in disgust; and finally, by the most pathetic parodying of all the forms of past revolutions, from parlia-mentarianism to Zapata-style guerrilla war, without their ludicrous dramatics having the slightest relation to reality. Fervent admirers of the errors of a vanished revolutionary past, the antiquated ideologists of the little leftist parties were naturally very ill-prepared to under-stand a *modern* movement. The March 22nd Movement, an eclectic aggregate of these old ideologies spiced up with a few fragments of modern incoherence, combined almost all the ideological defects of the past with the defects of a naïve confusionism. Co-opters were installed in the leadership of the very people who expressed their fear of "co-option," which was for them a vague and almost mystical peril since they lacked the slightest knowledge of elementary truths about either co-option or organization, or about the difference between a mandated delegate and an uncontrollable "spokesman"—a spokes-man [Daniel Cohn-Bendit] who was their de facto leader, since the main prestige and influence of the March 22nd Movement stemmed from its communication with reporters. Its laughable celebrities came before the spotlights to announce to the press that they were taking care not to become celebrities.*

The "Action Committees," which were spontaneously formed just about everywhere, were on the ambiguous borderline between direct democracy and infiltrated and co-opted confusionism. This contradiction created internal divisions in almost all of them. But there was an even clearer division between the two main types of organization that went by the same label. On one hand, there were committees formed on a *local* basis (neighborhood or enterprise ACs, occupation committees of certain buildings that had fallen into the hands of the revolutionary movement) or that were set up in order to carry out some specialized task whose practical necessity was obvious, notably the internationalist extension of the movement (Italian AC, North African AC, etc.). On the other hand, there was a proliferation of *professional* committees: attempts to revive the old trade-unionism, but usually for the benefit of semiprivileged sectors and thus with a clearly corporatist character; these committees served as tribunes for specialists who wanted to join the movement while maintaining their separate specialized positions, or even to derive some favorable publicity from it ("Congress of Cinema Workers," Writers Union, English Institute AC, etc.). The methods of these two types of AC were even more clearly opposed than their goals. In the former, decisions were executory and prefigured the revolutionary power of the councils; in the latter, they were abstract wishes and parodied the pressure groups of state power.

The occupied buildings, when they were not under the authority of "loyal labor-union managers" and insofar as they did not remain isolated as exclusive pseudofeudal possessions of their usual university users, constituted one of the strongest points of the movement (for example, the Sorbonne during the first few days; the buildings opened up to the workers and young slum-dwellers by the "students" of Nantes; the INSA taken over by the revolutionary workers of Lyon; and the Institut Pédagogique National). The very logic of these occupations could have led to the best developments. It should be noted, moreover, how a movement that remained paradoxically timid at the prospect of *requisitioning commodities* did not have the slightest misgivings about having already appropriated a part of the state's fixed capital.

If this example was ultimately prevented from spreading to the factories, it should also be said that the style created by many of these occupations left much to be desired. Almost everywhere the persistence of old routines hindered people from seeing the full scope of the situation and the means it offered for the action in progress. For example, *Informations, Correspondance Ouvrières* #77 (January 1969) objects to Viénet's book—which mentioned their presence at Censier—by declaring that the workers who had been with ICO for a long time "did not 'set up quarters' at the Sorbonne or at Censier or anywhere else; all were engaged in the strike at their own workplaces" and "in the assemblies and in the streets." "They never considered maintaining any sort of 'permanent center' in the university buildings, much less constituting themselves as a 'workers coordinating committee' or a 'council,' even if it were for 'maintaining the occupations' " (ICO considering this latter as tantamount to "participating in parallel organizations that would end up substituting themselves for the worker"). Further on, *ICO* adds that their group nevertheless held "two meetings a week" there because "rooms were freely available at the university departments, particularly at Censier, which was calmer." Thus the scruples of the ICO workers (whom we are willing to assume to be quite capable as long as they modestly limit themselves to striking at their own workplaces or in the nearby streets) led them to see in one of the most original aspects of the crisis nothing more than the possibility of switching from their usual café hangout by borrowing free rooms in a quiet university department. With the same complacency they also admit that a number of their comrades "soon stopped coming to ICO meetings because they did not find any response there to their desire to 'do something'." Thus, for these workers, "doing something" has automatically become a shameful inclination to substitute oneself for "the worker"—for a sort of pure, being-in-himself worker who, by definition, would exist only in his own factory, where for example the Stalinists would force him to keep silent, and where ICO would have to wait for all the workers to purely liberate themselves *on the spot* (otherwise wouldn't they risk substituting themselves for this still mute real worker?). Such an ideological acceptance of dispersion defies the essential need whose vital urgency was felt by so many workers in May: the need for coordination and communication of struggles and ideas, starting from bases of free encounter outside their union-policed factories. But the ICO participants have never, in fact, either before or since May, consistently followed out the implications of their metaphysical reasoning. Through their mimeographed publication a few dozen workers resign themselves to "substituting" their analyses for those that might spontaneously be made by the several hundred other workers who read it without having participated in writing it. Their issue #78 in February informs us that "in one year the circulation of *ICO* has risen from 600 to 1000 copies." But the Council for Maintaining the Occupations [CMDO], for example, which seems to shock the virtue of ICO by the mere fact that it occupied the Institut Pédagogique National, was able (to say nothing of its other activities or publications at the time) to get 100,000 copies of various of its texts printed for free, through an immediate agreement reached with the strikers of the IPN press at Montrouge. The vast majority of these texts were distributed to other striking workers; and so far no one has tried to show that the content of these texts could in the slightest way threaten to substitute itself for the decisions of any worker. And the strikers' participation in the linkups established by the CMDO in and outside Paris never contradicted their presence at their own workplaces (nor, to be sure, in the streets). Moreover, the striking typesetters who were members of the CMDO much preferred working elsewhere where there were machines available rather than remaining passive in "their" usual workplaces.

If the purists of worker inaction certainly missed opportunities to speak up and make up for all the times they have been forced into a silence which has become a sort of proud habit among them, the presence of a mass of neo-Bolshevik manipulators was much more harmful. But the biggest problem was still the extreme lack of *homogeneity* of the assembly, which in the first days of the Sorbonne occupation found itself, without having either wished it or understood it clearly, in the position of an exemplary center of a movement that was drawing in the factories. This lack of social homogeneity stemmed first of all from the overwhelming preponderance of students, in spite of the good intentions of many of them, a preponderance which was made even worse by the large number of visitors with merely touristic motivations. This was the objective base that made possible the most gross maneuvers on the part of bureaucrats like Péninou and Krivine. The ambiguity of the participants added to the essential ambiguity of the acts of an improvised assembly which by force of circumstances had come to represent (in all senses of the word, including the worst) the councilist perspective for the entire country. This assembly made decisions both for the Sorbonne (and even there in a poor and mystified manner: it never even succeeded in mastering its own functioning) and for the whole society in crisis: it wanted and proclaimed, in clumsy but sincere terms, unity with the workers and the negation of the old world. While pointing out its faults, let us not forget how much it was *listened to*. The same issue #77 of *ICO* reproaches the situationists for having sought in that assembly an exemplary act that would "enter into legend" and for having set up some heroes "on the podium of history." We don't believe we have ever built up anybody as a star on a historical tribune, but we also think that the superior irony affected by these lofty workerists falls flat: it *was* a historic tribune.

With the defeat of the revolution, the socio-technical mechanisms of false consciousness were naturally reestablished, virtually intact: when the spectacle clashes with its pure negation, no reformism can succeed in winning an increase, not even of 7%,* in the spectacle's concessions to reality. To demonstrate this to even the most casual observer it would suffice to examine the some *300 books* on May that have appeared in France alone in the year following the occupations movement. It is not the number of books in itself that merits being scoffed at or blamed, as certain people obsessed with the perils of co-option have felt obliged to declare (people who, moreover, have little to worry about on that score since they generally haven't come up with anything the co-opters would be interested in). This huge quantity reflects the fact that the historic importance of the movement has been deeply sensed, in spite of all the incomprehension and interested denials. What is deplorable is the fact that out of three hundred books there are scarcely a dozen that are worth reading: a few accounts or analyses that don't follow laughable ideologies, and a few collections of unfalsified documents. The misinformation and falsification prevalent everywhere are particularly evident in almost all the accounts of the situationists' activities. Leaving aside those books that limit themselves to remaining silent on this topic, or to a few absurd accusations, we can distinguish three main styles of falsification. The first pattern consists in limiting the SI's activity to Strasbourg, eighteen months before, as a remote initial triggering of a crisis from which it would later seem to have disappeared (this is also the position of the Cohn-Bendits' book [*Obsolete Communism: The Left-Wing Alternative*], which even manages not to say a word about the existence of the Nanterre "Enragés" group). The second pattern, presenting a positive lie and no longer merely a lie by omission, asserts, in spite of all indications to the contrary, that the situationists accepted some sort of contact with the March 22nd Movement; and many even go so far as to claim that we were an integral part of it. The third pattern presents us as an autonomous group of irresponsible maniacs springing up by surprise, perhaps even armed, at the Sorbonne and elsewhere in order to stir up disorder and shout extravagant demands.

It is difficult, however, to deny a certain continuity in the situationists' action from 1967–1968. This very continuity, in fact, seems to have been felt as an annoyance by those who through their quantity of ostentatious interviews or recruitments strove to be recognized as leaders of the movement, a role the SI has always rejected for itself: their stupid ambition leads some of these people to hide certain facts that they are a bit more aware of than are others. Situationist theory had a significant role in the origins of the generalized critique that gave rise to the first incidents of the May crisis and that developed along with that crisis. This was not only due to our intervention against the University of Strasbourg. Two or three thousand copies each of Vaneigem's and Debord's books [*The Revolution of Everyday Life* and *The Society of the Spectacle*], for example, had already been circulated in the months preceding May, particularly in Paris, and an unusually high proportion of them had been read by revolutionary workers (according to certain indications it also appears that these two books were *the most frequently stolen* from bookstores in 1968, at least relative to their circulation). By way of the Enragés group, the SI can flatter itself that it was not without importance in the very origin of the Nanterre agitation, which was to have such far-reaching effects. Finally, we don't think we remained too far behind the great spontaneous movement of the masses that dominated the country in May 1968, both in what we did at the Sorbonne and in the various subsequent forms of action carried out by the Council for Maintaining the Occupations. In addition to the SI itself and to a good number of individuals who acknowledged its theses and acted accordingly, many others defended situationist perspectives, whether unconsciously or as a result of direct influence, because those perspectives were to a large extent objectively implied by the present era of revolutionary crisis. Those who doubt this need only *read the walls* (those without this direct experience can refer to the collection of photographs published by Walter Lewino, *L'Imagination au pouvoir*, Losfeld, 1968).

It can thus be said that the systematic minimization of the SI is merely a detail corresponding to the current (and, from the dominant viewpoint, natural) minimization of the whole occupations movement. But the sort of jealousy felt by certain leftists, which strongly contributes to this minimization, is completely off base. Even the most "extreme-left" of the little groups have no grounds for setting themselves up as rivals to the SI, because the SI is not a group of their type, competing on their terrain of militantism or claiming like they do to be leading the revolutionary movement in the name of the "correct" interpretation of one or another petrified truth derived from Marxism or anarchism. To see the question in this way is to forget that, in contrast to these abstract repetitions in which old conclusions that happen still to be valid in class struggles are inextricably mixed in with a mass of conflicting errors and frauds, the SI had above all brought a *new spirit* into the theoretical debates about society, culture, and life. This spirit was assuredly revolutionary. It entered to a certain extent into a relation with the real revolutionary movement that was recommencing. And it was precisely to the extent that this movement also had a new character that it turned out to *resemble* the SI and partially appropriated its theses; and not at all by way of the traditional political process of recruiting members or followers. The largely new character of this practical movement is easily discernable in this very *influence* the SI exerted, an influence completely divorced from any directing role. All the leftist tendencies—including the March 22nd Movement, which included in its hodgepodge Leninism, Chinese Stalinism, anarchism, and even a dash of misunderstood "situationism"—relied very explicitly on a long history of past struggles, examples, and doctrines that had been published and discussed a hundred times. It is true that these struggles and publications had been smothered by Stalinist reaction and neglected by bourgeois intellectuals. But they were nevertheless incomparably more accessible than the SI's new positions, which had never had any means to make themselves known except our own recent publications and activities. If the SI's few known documents found such an audience it was obviously because a part of the advanced practical critique recognized itself in this language. We thus now find ourselves in a rather good position to say what May was essentially, even in its latent aspects; to make conscious the unconscious tendencies of the occupations movement. Others lyingly say that there was nothing to understand in this absurd outbreak; or describe, through the filter of their ideology, only a few older and less important aspects of the movement as if that was all there was to it; or simply draw from it new topics for their academic "studies" and consequenceless "conferences" and "debates." They have the support of major newspapers and influential connections, of sociology and mass-market circulation. We don't have any of that and we draw our right to speak only from ourselves. Yet what they say about May will inevitably fade in indifference and be forgotten; and what we say about it will remain, and will ultimately be believed and taken up again.

The influence of situationist theory can be read not only on the walls, but in the diversely exemplary actions of the revolutionaries of Nantes and the Enragés of Nanterre. In the press at the beginning of 1968 one can see the indignation that was aroused by the new forms of action initiated or systematized by the Enragés, those "campus hooligans" who one day decided that "everything disputable must be disputed" and ended up shaking up the whole university.

In fact, those who at that time met and formed the Enragés group had no preconceived idea of agitation. The only reason they had signed up as "students" was in order to get *grants*. It simply happened that broken-down streets and slums were less odious to them than concrete buildings, thickheaded self-satisfied students, and smooth-tongued modernist professors. In the former terrain they saw some vestiges of humanity, whereas they found only poverty, boredom, and lies in the cultural soup where Lefebvre and his honesty, Touraine and his end of class struggle, Bourricaud and his strongarms, and Lourau and his future were all splashing about in unison. Furthermore, they were familiar with the situationist theses and they knew that these thinkers of the university ghetto also were aware of them and used them to modernize their ideologies. They decided to let everyone know about this, and set about unmasking the lies, with the expectation of finding other playgrounds later on: they reckoned that once the liars and the students were routed and the university was destroyed, chance would weave them other encounters on another scale and that then "fortune and misfortune would take their shape."

Their avowed pasts (predominantly anarchist, but also surrealist and in one case Trotskyist) immediately worried those they first confronted: the old leftist sects, CLER Trotskyists, Daniel Cohn-Bendit and other anarchist students, all wrangling over the lack of future of the UNEF [National Student Union] and the function of psychologists. By making numerous exclusions without useless leniency they guarded against the success they rapidly encountered among a couple dozen *students*, as well as warding off various stupid would-be followers seeking a situationism without situationists in which they could give vent to all their obsessions and woes. As a result, the group which sometimes had as many as fifteen members more often consisted of a mere half-dozen agitators. Which turned out to be enough.

If the methods used by the Enragés—particularly the sabotage of lectures—are commonplace today in both universities and high schools, at the time they profoundly scandalized the leftists as well as the good students; the former sometimes even organized squads to protect the professors from the hails of insults and rotten oranges. The spread of the use of deserved insults and of graffiti, the call for a total boycott of exams, the distribution of leaflets on university premises, and finally the simple daily scandal of their existence drew upon the Enragés the first attempt at repression: Riesel and Bigorgne were summoned before the dean on January 25; Cheval was expelled from the campus at the beginning of February; Bigorgne was expelled from the university grounds later that same month and then banned from all French universities for five years at the beginning of April. Meanwhile the leftist groups began a more narrowly political agitation.

The old apes of the intellectual reservation, lost in the muddled presentation of their "thought," only belatedly started to get worried. But they were soon forced to drop their masks and make fools of themselves, as when Edgar Morin, green with spite amidst the hooting of students, screamed, "The other day you consigned me to the trashcan of history . . ." (Interruption: "How did you get back out?") "I prefer to be on the side of the trashcans rather than on the side of those who handle them, and in any case I prefer to be on the side of the trashcans rather than on the side of the crematories!" Or Alain Touraine, foaming at the mouth and howling: "I've had enough of these anarchists and more than enough of these situationists! Right now I am in command here, and if one day you are, I will go somewhere else where people know what it means to work!" A year later these profound perceptions were further developed in articles by Raymond Aron and René Étiemble protesting the impossibility of working under the rising tide of leftist totalitarianism and red fascism. From January 26 to March 22 violent class disruptions were almost constant. The Enragés participated in this continuous agitation while working on several projects that proved abortive, including the publication of a pamphlet projected for the beginning of May and the invasion and looting of the administration building with the aid of some revolutionaries from Nantes at the beginning of March. But even before having seen that much, Dean Grappin, speaking at a press conference on March 20, denounced "a group of irresponsible students who for several months have been disrupting classes and examinations and practicing guerrilla methods in the University. . . . These students are not connected with any known political organization. They constitute an explosive element in a very sensitive milieu." As for the pamphlet, the Enragés' printer did not progress as fast as the revolution. After the crisis they had to abandon the idea of publishing this text, which would have seemed intended to retrospectively demonstrate their prescience.

All this explains the interest the Enragés took in the evening of March 22, however dubious they already were about most of the other protesters. While Cohn-Bendit, already a star in the Nanterre skies, was debating with the less decided, ten Enragés took the initiative of occupying the Faculty Council room, where they were only joined 22 minutes later by the future "March 22nd Movement." Viénet's book describes how and why they withdrew from this farce.* In addition, they saw that the police were not coming and that with such people they could not carry out the only objective they had planned for the night: the complete destruction of the exam files. In the early hours of the 23rd they decided to exclude five of their number who had refused to leave the room out of fear that they would be "cutting themselves off from the masses" of students!

It is certainly piquant to find that the origin of the May movement involved a settling of accounts with the two-faced thinkers of the old *Arguments* gang. But in attacking this ugly cohort of state-appointed subversive thinkers, the Enragés were doing more than settling an old quarrel: they already spoke as an *occupations movement* struggling for everyone's real occupation of all the sectors of a social life governed by lies. And by writing "Take your desires for reality" on the concrete walls, they were already destroying the co-optive ideology of the "Power to the imagination" slogan that was pretentiously launched by the March 22nd Movement. Because they had desires, while the latter had no imagination.

The Enragés scarcely returned to Nanterre in April. The vague fancies of direct democracy ostentatiously proclaimed by the March 22nd Movement obviously could not be realized in such bad company, and they refused in advance the small place that would readily have been granted them as extremist entertainers to the left of the laughable "Culture and Creativity Commission." On the other hand, the taking up of some of their agitational techniques by the Nanterre students, even if within a confused "anti-imperialism" perspective, meant that the debate was beginning to be placed on the terrain the Enragés had wanted to establish. This was also demonstrated by the Parisian students' May 3 attack on the police in response to the university administration's latest blunder. The Enragés' violent warning leaflet, *Gut Rage*, distributed on May 6, chimed so perfectly with the real movement that the only people it outraged were the Leninists it denounced; in two days of street fighting the rioters had discovered its relevance. The Enragés' autonomous activity culminated as consistently as it had begun. They were treated as *situationists* even before entering the SI, in that the leftist co-opters picked up on some of their ideas while imagining that they could conceal the existence of their source through lavish performances in front of the reporters whom the Enragés had naturally rebuffed. The very term "Enragés," by which Riesel had given an unforgettable touch to the occupations movement, was later for a while given a spectacular "Cohn-Bendist" meaning.

The rapid succession of street struggles in the first ten days of May had immediately brought together the members of the SI, the Enragés, and a few other comrades. Their accord was formalized on May 14, the day after the occupation of the Sorbonne, when they federated as an "Enragés–SI Committee" which began that very day to publish texts thus signed. In the following days we carried out a more widespread autonomous expression of situationist theses within the movement. But this was not in order to lay down particular principles in accordance with which we would have claimed to shape or guide the real movement: in saying what we thought we also said *who* we were, while so many others were disguising themselves in order to explain that it was necessary to follow the correct line of their central committee. That evening the Sorbonne general assembly, which was effectively open to the workers, undertook to organize its own power, and René Riesel, who had expressed the most radical positions on the organization of the Sorbonne itself as well as on the total extension of the struggle that had begun, was elected to the first Occupation Committee. On the 15th the situationists in Paris addressed a circular to persons elsewhere in France and in other countries: *To the members of the SI and to the comrades who have declared themselves in agreement with our theses.* This text briefly analyzed the process that was going on and its possible developments, in order of decreasing probability: exhaustion of the movement if it remained limited "to the students before the antibureaucratic agitation has extended more deeply into the worker milieu"; repression; or finally, "social revolution?" It also contained an account of our activity up till then and called for immediate action to "publicize, support, and extend the agitation." We proposed as immediate themes in France: "the occupation of the factories" (we had just learned of the Sud-Aviation occupation that had taken place the night before); "the formation of workers' councils; the definitive shutdown of the universities; and the complete critique of all forms of alienation." It should be noted that this was the first time since the SI was formed that we ever asked anyone, however close they were to our positions, to do anything. All the more reason why our circular did not remain without response, particularly in the cities where the May movement was asserting itself most strongly. On the evening of the 16th the SI issued a second circular recounting the developments of the day and anticipating "a major confrontation." The general strike interrupted this series, which was taken up in another form after May 20 by the emissaries that the CMDO sent throughout France and to various other countries.

Viénet's book describes in detail how the majority of the members of the Sorbonne Occupation Committee, which was reelected *en bloc* by the general assembly on the evening of the 15th, soon after slunk away, yielding to the maneuvers and attempts at intimidation of an informal bureaucracy (UNEF, MAU, JCR, etc.) that was striving to surreptitiously recapture the Sorbonne. The Enragés and situationists thus found themselves with the responsibility for the Occupation Committee on May 16–17. When the general assembly of the 17th ended up neither approving the acts by which this Committee had carried out its mandate nor even disapproving them (the manipulators having prevented any vote in the assembly), we announced our departure from the played-out Sorbonne. Those who had grouped themselves around this Occupation Committee departed with us, and formed the core of the Council for Maintaining the Occupations. It is worth pointing out that the second Occupation Committee, elected after our departure, maintained its glorious bureaucratic existence without any further turnover until the return of the police in June. *Never again was there any question of the assembly daily electing revocable delegates.* This Committee of professionals soon even went so far as to suppress the general assemblies altogether, which from their point of view were only a cause of trouble and a waste of time. In contrast, the situationists can sum up their action in the Sorbonne with the single formula: "All power to the general assembly." It is thus amusing to hear people now talking about the situationists' having "taken power" in the Sorbonne, when the reality of this "power" was to constantly insist on direct democracy there and everywhere, to constantly denounce the co-opters and bureaucrats, and to demand that the general assembly fulfill its responsibilities by *making its own decisions and by seeing that they were carried out.*

By its consistent attitude our Occupation Committee had aroused the general indignation of the leftist manipulators and bureaucrats. If we had defended the principles and methods of direct democracy in the Sorbonne, we nevertheless had no illusions as to the social composition and general level of consciousness of that assembly. We were quite aware of the paradox of delegates being more resolute in their desire for direct democracy than were their mandators, and we saw that it couldn't last. But we were more than anything striving to put the not inconsiderable means with which the possession of the Sorbonne provided us at the service of the wildcat strike that had just started. Thus the Occupation Committee issued a brief communiqué at 3:00 p.m. on the 16th calling for "the immediate occupation of all the factories in France and the formation of workers' councils." All the other reproaches against us were almost nothing in comparison to the scandal provoked everywhere—except among the "rank-and-file" occupiers—by this "reckless" commitment of the Sorbonne. Yet at that very moment two or three factories were already occupied, some of the NMPP truckdrivers were trying to block the distribution of newspapers, and (as we were to learn two hours later) several Renault factories were successfully beginning to stop work. In the name of what, we wonder, could unauthorized individuals claim the right to manage the Sorbonne if they did not support the workers' right to seize all the property in the country? It seems to us that the Sorbonne, by declaring itself for such occupations, was making its last response that still remained at the level of the movement that the factories were fortunately to carry on, that is to say, at the level of the response the factories themselves had made to the first limited struggles in the Latin Quarter. This appeal certainly did not run counter to the intentions of the majority of people who were at the Sorbonne and who did so much to spread it. Moreover, as the factory occupations spread, even the leftist bureaucrats changed their minds and expressed their support of a *fait accompli* on which they had not dared to take a stand the day before, though they continued to vehemently oppose the idea of councils. The occupations movement did not really need the approval of the Sorbonne in order to spread to other factories. But beyond the fact that at that moment every hour counted in linking up all the factories with the action initiated by a few of them, while the unions were stalling everywhere in order to prevent a general work stoppage; and beyond the fact that we knew that such an appeal, coming from the Sorbonne Occupation Committee, would immediately be widely disseminated, even by radio—beyond all this, it seemed to us above all important to show the maximum toward which the struggle that was beginning should aim right away. But the factories did not go so far as to form councils, and the strikers who began to come to the Sorbonne certainly did not discover any exemplary model there.

It seems likely that this appeal contributed here and there to opening up perspectives of radical struggle. In any case, it certainly figured among the events of that day that awakened the greatest fears. At 7:00 in the evening the Prime Minister issued an official statement declaring that "in view of the various attempts announced or initiated by extremist groups to provoke a generalized agitation," the government would do everything possible to maintain "public peace" and republican order, "since university reform is turning into a mere pretext for plunging the country into disorder." At the same time, 10,000 state trooper reservists were called up. "University reform" was indeed merely a pretext, even for the government, which masked its retreat in the face of the Latin Quarter riot behind this suddenly discovered respectable necessity.

The Council for Maintaining the Occupations, which at first occupied the IPN on Rue d'Ulm, did its best during the remainder of the crisis, to which, from the moment the strike became general and came to a defensive standstill, none of the then-existing organized revolutionary groups any longer had the means to make a notable contribution. Bringing together the situationists, the Enragés, and some thirty to sixty other councilist revolutionaries (of whom less than a tenth could be considered students), the CMDO established a large number of linkups both within and outside France, making a special effort, toward the end of the movement, to communicate its significance to revolutionaries of other countries, who could not fail to be inspired by it. It published a number of posters and texts—around 200,000 copies of each in some cases—of which the most important were "Report on the Occupation of the Sorbonne" (May 19), "For the Power of the Workers' Councils" (May 22), and "Address to All Workers" (May 30). The CMDO, which had been neither directed nor organized by anyone for the future, "decided to dissolve itself on June 15. . . . The CMDO had not sought to obtain anything *for itself,* not even any sort of recruitment in view of a continued existence. Its participants did not separate their personal goals from the general goals of the movement. They were independent individuals who had grouped together for a struggle on determined bases at a specific moment; and who again became independent after its dissolution" (Viénet, *op. cit.*). The Council for Maintaining the Occupations had been "a bond, not a power."

Some people have reproached us, during May and since then, for having criticized everybody and for thus having presented the situationists' activity as the only acceptable one. This is not true. We approved the mass movement in all its depth and the remarkable initiatives of tens of thousands of individuals. We approved of the conduct of several revolutionary groups that we knew of in Nantes and Lyon, as well as the acts of all those who were in contact with the CMDO. The documents reproduced in Viénet's book clearly demonstrate that we also *partially* approved of a number of statements issued by some of the Action Committees.* It is certain that many groups or committees that were unknown to us during the crisis would have had our approval if we had been aware of them—and it is even more obvious that in being unaware of them we could in no way have criticized them. On the other hand, in regard to the little leftist parties or the March 22nd Movement, or people like Barjonet or Lapassade, it would indeed be surprising if anyone expected some polite approbation from us, considering our previous positions and the activity of these people during May.

Neither have we claimed that certain forms of action that characterized the occupations movement—with the possible exception of the use of critical comic strips—had a directly situationist origin. On the contrary, we see the origin of all these forms in "wildcat" *workers' struggles;* and for several years our journals have pointed them out as they developed and clearly specified where they came from.* Workers were the first to attack a newspaper building to protest against the falsification of news concerning them (Liège, 1961); to burn cars (Merlebach, 1962); to begin writing on the walls the formulas of the new revolution ("Here freedom ends," on a wall of the Rhodiaceta factory, 1967). On the other hand, we can point out, as a clear prelude to the Enragés' activity at Nanterre, the fact that on 26 October 1966 in Strasbourg a university professor was for the first time attacked and driven from his podium: that was the fate to which the situationists subjected the cybernetician Abraham Moles at his inaugural lecture.

All the texts issued by the situationists during the occupations movement show that we never spread any illusions as to the chances for a complete success of the movement. We knew that this objectively possible and necessary revolutionary movement had begun from a subjectively very low level: spontaneous and fragmented, unaware of its own past and of its overall goals, it was reemerging after a half century of repression and in the face of its still firmly entrenched bureaucratic and bourgeois vanquishers. A lasting revolutionary victory was in our eyes only a very slim possibility between May 17 and May 30. But the moment this chance existed, we showed it to be the *maximum* that had come to be at stake as soon as the crisis reached a certain point, and as something certainly worth risking. From our point of view the movement was already a historic victory, regardless of where it might go from there, and we thought that *even half* of what had already happened would already have been a very significant result.

Nobody can deny that the SI, in contrast in this regard, too, to all the leftist groups, refused to make any propaganda for itself. The CMDO did not raise any "situationist banner" and none of our texts of the period mentioned the SI except in the one instance when we responded to the impudent invitation for a common front issued by Barjonet the day after the Charléty meeting. Amid all the brand-name initials of groups pretending to a leadership role, not a single inscription mentioning the SI was to be found on the walls of Paris, even though our partisans were undoubtedly the best and most prolific writers of graffiti.

It seems to us—and we present this conclusion first of all for the comrades of other countries that will experience crises of this nature —that these examples show what can be done in the first stage of reappearance of the revolutionary proletarian movement by a few basically coherent individuals. In May there were only ten or twelve situationists and Enragés in Paris and none in the rest of France. But the fortunate conjunction of spontaneous revolutionary improvisation with a sort of aura of sympathy that existed around the SI made possible the coordination of a rather widespread action, not only in Paris but in several other large cities, as if there had been a preexisting nationwide organization. Even more far-reaching than this spontaneous organization, a sort of vague, mysterious situationist menace was felt and denounced in many places; those who embodied this menace were some hundreds or even thousands of individuals whom the bureaucrats and moderates called situationists or, more often, referred to by the popular abbreviation that appeared during this period, *situs*. We consider it an honor that this term, which seems to have originated as a pejorative term among certain student milieus in the provinces, served not only to designate the most extremist participants in the occupations movement, but also tended to evoke an image of vandals, thieves, or hoodlums.

We do not think we avoided making mistakes. It is again for the benefit of comrades who may later find themselves in similar situations that we will enumerate them here.

On Rue Gay-Lussac, where we came together in small spontaneously assembled groups, each of these groups met several dozen acquaintances or people who merely knew us by sight and came to talk with us. Then everyone, in the wonderful disorder found in that "liberated neighborhood," split up toward one or another "front line" or battle preparation long before the inevitable police attack. As a result, not only did all those people remain more or less isolated, but even our own groups were unable to keep in contact with each other most of the time. It was a serious mistake on our part not to have immediately asked everyone to remain grouped together. In less than an hour a group acting in this way would have inevitably snowballed and gathered together everyone we knew among the barricade fighters—among whom each of us ran into more friends than one chances to meet in Paris in a whole year. In this way we could have formed a band of two or three hundred people who knew each other and acted together, which was precisely what was most lacking in that dispersed fight. Of course, the vastly unequal forces (there were more than three times as many police surrounding the area as rioters, to say nothing of their superior arms) would have doomed this struggle to defeat in any case. But such a group would have made possible a certain freedom of maneuver, either by counterattacking at some spot or by extending the barricades to the east of Rue Mouffetard (an area rather poorly controlled by the police until very late) in order to open a path of retreat for all those who were caught in the dragnet (several hundred escaped only by chance, thanks to the precarious refuge of the École Normale Supérieure).

In and with the Sorbonne Occupation Committee we did virtually everything we could have done, considering the conditions and hurriedness of the moment. We cannot be reproached for not having done more to alter the architecture of that dismal edifice, which we didn't even have the time to scout out. It is true that a chapel remained there (closed), but our posters—and also Riesel in his statement in the general assembly on May 14—had appealed to the occupiers to destroy it as soon as possible. As for "Radio Sorbonne," it had no transmitter so we cannot be blamed for not having used it. It goes without saying that we neither considered nor prepared for setting the building on fire on May 17, as was rumored at that time following some obscure slanders on the part of certain leftist groups: the date alone suffices to show how ill-advised such a project would have been. Nor did we spread ourselves thin in routine details, however useful we may recognize them to have been. It is thus a pure fantasy when Jean Maitron states, "The Sorbonne restaurant and cooking . . . remained under the control of the 'situationists' until June. There were very few students among them, but many unemployed youth" (*La Sorbonne par elle-même*, Éditions Ouvrières, 1968, p. 114).* We must, however, reproach ourselves for this error: from May 16, 5:00 p.m. on, the comrades in charge of sending the leaflets and declarations of the Occupation Committee to be printed replaced the signature "Sorbonne Occupation Committee" with "Occupation Committee of the People's Free Sorbonne University" and no one thought anything about it. This was certainly a lapse of some importance because in our eyes the Sorbonne was of interest only as *a building seized by the revolutionary movement,* and this signature gave the impression that we acknowledged it as still having some legitimacy as a *university* (albeit a "people's free" one)—something we despise in any case and which was all the more unfortunate to seem to accept at such a time. A less important slip was made on May 17 when a leaflet composed by rank-and-file workers who had come from the Renault factory was circulated with the "Occupation Committee" signature. The Occupation Committee was quite right to provide these workers with means of expression without any censorship, but it should have been specified that this text was written by them and merely *printed* by the Occupation Committee; all the more so as these workers, while calling for a continuation of the "marches on Renault," still accepted the unions' phony argument according to which the factory gates should be kept closed so that the police could not derive from their being open a pretext or advantage for an attack.

The CMDO forgot to add to each of its publications the note "Printed by striking workers," which certainly would have been exemplary and in perfect accord with the theories those publications expressed, and which would have been an excellent reply to the usual union printshop label. A more serious error: while an excellent use was made of telephones, we completely overlooked the possibility of using the *teletype machines,* which would have enabled us to get in touch with a number of occupied buildings and factories in France and to transmit information throughout Europe. In particular, we neglected the network of astronomical observatories, which was accessible to us at least by way of the occupied Meudon Observatory.

But everything considered, we do not see how the SI's activities during the May movement merit any significant blame.

Let us now list the main *results* of the occupations movement so far. In France this movement was defeated, but in no way *crushed.* This is probably its most notable point and the one that presents the greatest practical interest. Probably never before has such a severe social crisis ended without a repression crippling the revolutionary current for a substantial period—a seemingly inevitable price that previously had to be paid for each moment of radical historical experience. Although of course numerous foreigners were administratively expelled from the country and several hundred rioters were convicted in the following months for various "common law" misdemeanors, there was no political repression properly speaking. (Although more than a third of the members of the CMDO had been arrested during the various confrontations, none of them were caught in this later roundup, their retreat at the end of June having been very successfully carried out.)* All the political leaders who did not manage to escape arrest at the end of the crisis were set free after a few weeks and not one of them was ever brought to trial. The government was forced to accept this new retreat merely to obtain a semblance of a calm reopening of the universities and a *semblance* of exams in fall 1968; this important concession was obtained as early as August by the mere pressure of the Medical Students Action Committee.

The depth of the revolutionary crisis has seriously thrown off balance "what was frontally attacked . . . the *well-functioning* capitalist economy" (Viénet), not so much, of course, because of the wage increases, which the economy can easily bear, nor even because of the total paralysis of production for several weeks, but primarily because the French bourgeoisie has *lost confidence in the stability of the country.* This—in conjunction with other aspects of the present international monetary crisis—led to the massive exodus of capital and the crisis of the franc as early as November 1968 (the French reserves of foreign currency dropped from 30 billion francs in May 1968 to 18 billion one year later). After the *delayed* devaluation of 8 August 1969, *Le Monde* began to notice that "May 1968 'killed' the franc as well as the

General."

The "Gaullist" regime was nothing but a trivial detail in this general calling into question of modern capitalism. Nevertheless, de Gaulle's power also received a mortal blow in May. We have previously shown how it was objectively easy for de Gaulle to reestablish himself in June, since the real struggle had already been lost elsewhere. But in spite of his reinstatement, de Gaulle, as the leader of the state that had survived the occupations movement, was unable to wipe out the blemish of having been the leader of the state that had been *subjected* to the scandal of such a movement's existence. De Gaulle, who in his personal style only served as a cover for anything that might occur—specifically, for the normal modernization of capitalist society—had claimed to reign by prestige. In May his prestige was subjected to a definitive humiliation that was subjectively felt by him as well as objectively expressed by the ruling class and the voters who always support that class. The French bourgeoisie is now searching for a more rational form of political power, one that is less capricious and dreamy and that will be more intelligent in defending it from the new threats whose emergence so dumbfounded it. De Gaulle wanted to wipe out the persistent nightmare, "the last phantoms of May," by winning on 27 April 1969 the referendum announced on 24 May 1968 but canceled that very night by a riot. He sensed that his tottering "stable power" had not recovered its equilibrium and he imprudently insisted on being quickly reassured by a factitious rite of reaffirmation of his cause. The demonstrators' slogans on 13 May 1968 [e.g. "Ten years is enough"] turned out to be right: de Gaulle's reign did not endure to its eleventh anniversary;* not, of course, due to the bureaucratic or pseudoreformist opposition, but because after the Gay-Lussac uprising everyone realized that Rue Gay-Lussac opened on to all the factories of France.

A generalized disorder, calling in question the very foundations of all institutions, has taken hold of most of the university departments and especially the high schools. If the state, limiting itself to the most vital sectors, succeeded in largely reestablishing the functioning of the scientific disciplines and the elite professional schools, elsewhere the 1968–1969 academic year has been a complete loss and diplomas have been devalued, though they are still far from being despised by the mass of students. Such a situation is in the long run incompatible with the normal functioning of an advanced industrial country, triggering a fall into underdevelopment by creating a qualitative bottleneck in secondary education. Even if the extremist current has in reality only retained a narrow base in the student milieu, this seems to be enough to maintain a process of continual deterioration: the occupation and sacking of the rectorate of the Sorbonne at the end of January, and a number of serious incidents since then, have shown that merely maintaining some sort of pseudoeducation constitutes a subject of considerable concern for the forces of order.

In the factories, where the workers have learned how to carry out wildcat strikes and where there is an implantation of radical groups more or less consciously opposed to the unions, the sporadic agitation has, despite the efforts of the bureaucrats, led to numerous partial strikes that easily paralyze the increasingly concentrated enterprises in which the different operations become increasingly interdependent. These tremors do not allow anyone to forget that the ground under the enterprises is still shaky, and that in May the *modern* forms of exploitation revealed both their interrelatedness and their new fragility.

With the deterioration of the old orthodox Stalinism (discernable even in the losses of the CGT in recent union elections), it is now the turn of the little leftist parties to lose their credibility through bungling maneuvers: almost all of them would have liked to *mechanically* recommence the May process in order to repeat their errors there. They easily infiltrated what remained of the Action Committees, which soon faded away. The little leftist parties are themselves splitting into numerous hostile tendencies, each one holding firm to some stupidity that prides itself on excluding all the stupidities of its rivals. The radical elements have become more numerous since May, but are still scattered—particularly in the factories. Because they have not yet proved capable of organizing a genuinely autonomous practice, the coherence they have to acquire is still distorted and obscured by old illusions, or verbosity, or sometimes even by an unhealthy unilateral "pro-situationist" admiration. Their only path, which is obviously going to be long and difficult, has nevertheless been mapped out: the formation of councilist organizations of revolutionary workers, federating with each other on the sole basis of total democracy and total critique. Their first theoretical task will be to combat and refute in practice the last form of ideology the old world will set against them: *councilist* ideology. At the end of the crisis the Toulouse-based *Révolution Internationale* group expressed a preliminary crude form of this ideology, quite simply proposing (we don't know, moreover, to whom) that workers' councils should be *elected* above the general assemblies, whose only task would thus be to ratify the acts of this wise revolutionary neoleadership. This Lenino-Yugoslavian monstrosity, since adopted by Lambert's "Trotskyist Organization," is almost as bizarre nowadays as the Gaullists' use of the phrase "direct democracy" when they were infatuated with referendary "dialogue." The next revolution will recognize as councils only sovereign rank-and-file general assemblies, in the enterprises and in the neighborhoods, whose delegates are answerable to those assemblies alone and always subject to recall by them. A councilist organization will never defend any other goal: it must translate into acts a dialectic that supersedes the rigid, one-sided extremes of spontaneism, on one hand, and of openly or covertly bureaucratized organization on the other. It must be an organization advancing *revolutionarily* toward the revolution of the councils; an organization that neither disperses at the first moment of declared struggle nor institutionalizes itself.

This perspective is not limited to France, it is international. The total significance of the occupations movement must be understood everywhere. Already in 1968 its example touched off, or pushed to higher levels, severe disorders throughout Europe and in America and Japan. The most remarkable immediate consequences of May were the bloody revolt of the Mexican students, which was able to be crushed due to its relative isolation, and the Yugoslavian students' movement against the bureaucracy and for proletarian self-management, which partially drew in the workers and put Tito's regime in great danger. What finally came to the rescue of the latter, more than the concessions proclaimed by the ruling class, was the Russian intervention in Czechoslovakia, which allowed the Yugoslavian regime to rally the country around itself by brandishing the menace of an invasion by a foreign bureaucracy. The hand of the new International is beginning to be denounced by the police of several countries, who believe they have discovered the directives of French revolutionaries in Mexico during summer 1968 and in the anti-Russian demonstration in Prague on 28 March 1969. The Franco government explicitly justified its recourse to martial law at the beginning of this year by stating that the university agitation in Spain risked developing into a general crisis of the French type.

England has been experiencing wildcat strikes for a long time, and one of the main goals of the Labour government is obviously to succeed in prohibiting them; but it was unquestionably this first experience of a general wildcat strike that led Wilson to strive with such urgency and determination to obtain repressive legislation against this type of strike this year. This careerist didn't hesitate to risk his career, and even the very unity of the Labour party-union bureaucracy, on the proposed "Barbara Castle Act,"* for if the unions are the direct enemies of wildcat strikes, they are nevertheless afraid of losing all importance by losing all control over the workers once the right to intervene against the real forms of class struggle is left solely to the state, without having to pass through their own mediation. On May 1 the antiunion strike of 100,000 dockers, printers, and metal workers against the threat of this law was the first political strike in England since 1926: it is most fitting that this form of struggle has reappeared against a Labour government. Wilson had to lose face by giving up his dearest project and handing back to the union police the task of repressing the 95% of work stoppages in England now caused by wildcat strikes. According to *Le Monde* (30 August 1969), however, the recent victory of the eight-week wildcat strike of the Port Talbot blast-furnace workers "has proved that the TUC leadership is incapable of fulfilling this role."

It is easy to recognize throughout the world the new tone with which a radical critique is pronouncing its declaration of war on the old society—from the graffiti on the walls of England and Italy to the extremist Mexican group *Caos,* which during the summer of 1968 called for the sabotage of the Olympics and of "the society of spectacular consumption"; from the acts and publications of the *Acratas* in Madrid to the shout of a Wall Street demonstration (AFP, April 12), "Stop the Show," in that American society whose "decline and fall" we already pointed out in 1965 and whose very officials now admit that it is "a sick society."

In Italy the SI was able to make a certain contribution to the revolutionary current as early as the end of 1967, when the occupation of the University of Turin served as the starting point for a vast movement; both by way of the publication of some basic texts (badly translated by publishers Feltrinelli and De Donato, but nevertheless rapidly sold out) and by way of the radical action of a few individuals (although the present Italian section of the SI was formally constituted only in January 1969). The slow evolution of the Italian crisis over the last twenty-two months—which has thus become known as "the creeping May"—first got bogged down in 1968 in the forming of a "Student Movement" that was much more backward even than in France, as well as being isolated—virtually the sole exemplary exception being the joint occupation of the city hall of Orgosolo, Sardinia, by students, shepherds, and workers. The workers' struggles also began slowly, but grew more serious in 1969 in spite of the efforts of the Stalinist party and the unions, who worked to fragment the threat by allowing one-day national strikes by category or one-day general strikes by province. At the beginning of April the Battipaglia insurrection, followed by the prison revolts in Turin, Milan, and Genoa, pushed the crisis to a higher level and reduced even more the bureaucrats' margin of maneuver. In Battipaglia the workers kept control of the town for twenty-four hours after the police opened fire, seizing arms, laying siege to the police holed up in their barracks and demanding their surrender, and blocking roads and trains. Even after the massive reinforcements of state troopers had regained control of the town and communications routes, an embryo of a council still existed in Battipaglia, claiming to replace the town government and expressing the inhabitants' direct power over their own affairs. If the demonstrations in support of Battipaglia throughout Italy were regimented by the bureaucrats and remained platonic, the revolutionary elements of Milan at least succeeded in violently attacking the bureaucrats and the police and ravaging the downtown area of the city. On this occasion the Italian situationists took up the French methods in the most appropriate manner.

In the following months the "wildcat" movements at Fiat and among the workers of the North have demonstrated, more clearly than has the complete collapse of the government, how close Italy is to a *modern* revolutionary crisis. The turn taken in August by the wildcat strikes at Pirelli in Milan and Fiat in Turin point to the imminence of a total confrontation.

The reader will easily understand the main reason we have dealt here both with the general significance of the new revolutionary movements and with their relation with the theses of the SI. Until recently, even those who readily recognized an interest in some points of our theory regretted that we ourselves made the whole truth of that theory contingent upon the return of social revolution, which they considered an incredible "hypothesis." Conversely, various activists with no real contact with reality, but taking pride in their eternal allergy to any relevant theory, posed the stupid question: "What is the SI's practical activity?" Lacking the slightest comprehension of the dialectical process through which the real movement "meets its own unknown theory," they all wanted to disregard what they believed to be an *unarmed critique*. Now this critique is arming itself. The "sunburst that in a flash reveals the features of the new world"* was seen in France in that month of May, with the intermingled red and black flags of workers' democracy. The followup will appear everywhere. If we have to a certain extent marked the return of this movement with our name, it is not in order to hold on to any of it or to derive any authority from it. From now on we are sure of a satisfactory consummation of our activities: the SI will be superseded.

Reform and Counterreform
in the Bureaucratic Bloc

It could almost be said that the history of the last twenty years has set itself the sole task of refuting Trotsky's analyses concerning the bureaucracy. Victim of a sort of "class subjectivism," Trotsky refused throughout his life to recognize in Stalinist practice anything but a temporary deviation of a usurping *stratum*, a "Thermidorian reaction." As an ideologue of the Bolshevik revolution, he was unable to become a theorist of proletarian revolution at the time of the Stalinist restoration. By refusing to recognize the bureaucracy in power for what it is, namely a *new exploiting class*, this Hegel of the revolution betrayed rendered himself incapable of making a genuine critique of it. The theoretical and practical impotence of Trotskyism (in all its variants) is largely attributable to this original sin of the master.*

In *Enragés and Situationists in the Occupations Movement* (chapter 1) we said, a month before the Russian invasion: "The bureaucratic appropriation of society is inseparable from a totalitarian possession of the state and from the exclusive reign of its ideology. The present rights of free expression and association and the absence of censorship in Czechoslovakia will in the very near future lead to one of these two alternatives: either a repression, which will reveal the sham character of these concessions; or a proletarian assault against the bureaucratic ownership of the state and the economy, which ownership will be unmasked as soon as the dominant ideology is deprived for any length of time of its omnipresent police. The outcome of such a conflict is of the greatest concern for the Russian bureaucracy, whose very survival would be threatened by a victory of the Czech workers." The first alternative was imposed by the intervention of "Soviet" tanks.

The basis of Moscow's total domination of the "socialist" countries was this golden rule proclaimed and practiced by the Russian bureaucracy: "Socialism must not go further than our army." Wherever that army has been the main force installing "Communist" parties in power, it has the last word each time its former protégés manifest any leanings toward independence that might endanger the totalitarian bureaucratic domination. The Russian socioeconomic system has been from the beginning the *ideal type* for the new bureaucratic regimes. But fidelity to this archetype has often conflicted with the specific requirements of the particular dominated societies; since the ruling-class interests of each satellite bureaucracy do not necessarily coincide with those of the Russian bureaucracy, interbureaucratic relations have always contained underlying conflicts. Caught between the hammer and the anvil, the satellite bureaucracies always end up clinging to the hammer as soon as proletarian forces demonstrate their desire for autonomy. In Poland or Hungary, as recently in Czechoslovakia, the national bureaucratic "revolt" never goes beyond replacing one bureaucrat with another.

As the first industrialized state conquered by Stalinism, Czechoslovakia has over the last twenty years occupied a "privileged" position in the international system of exploitation set up by the Russians after 1949, within the framework of the "socialist division of labor" directed by the Comecon. The naked totalitarianism of the Stalin era meant that upon their coming to power the Czech Stalinists could do nothing but servilely imitate the "universal socialist system." But in contrast to the other bureaucratic countries, where there was a real need for economic development and industrialization, the level of productive forces in Czechoslovakia was in complete contradiction with the objectives of the economic program of the new regime. After fifteen years of irrational bureaucratic management the Czech economy was on the brink of catastrophe, and its reform became a matter of life and death for the ruling class. This was the root of the "Prague Spring" and the adventurous liberalization attempted by the bureaucracy. But before going into the analysis of this "bureaucratic reform," let us orient ourselves by examining its origins in the purely Stalinist (or Novotnyist) period.

After the [1948] Prague coup, the integration of Czechoslovakia into the Eastern bloc's almost totally self-contained economic system made it the main victim of Russian domination. Since it was the most developed country it had to bear the costs of industrializing its neighbors, themselves yoked under a policy of superexploitation. After 1950 the totalitarian planning, with its emphasis on metallurgical and engineering industries, introduced a serious imbalance into the functioning of the economy which steadily grew worse. In 1966 investment in Czech heavy industry reached 47%, the highest rate in the world. This was because Czechoslovakia had to provide—at ridiculously low prices that did not even cover the costs of production and the wear and tear of the machinery—raw materials (in five years the USSR used up fifty years' worth of reserves from the Jachymov uranium deposits in Bohemia) and manufactured goods (machines, armaments, etc.) to the USSR and the other "socialist" countries, and later to the "Third World" countries coveted by the Russians. "Production for production's sake" was the ideology that accompanied this enterprise, the costs of which the workers were the first to bear. As early as 1953, in the wake of a monetary reform, the workers of Pilsen, seeing their wages decreasing and prices rising, revolted and were immediately violently repressed. The consequences of this economic policy were essentially: the Czech economy's increasing dependence on Soviet supplies of raw materials and fuel; an orientation toward foreign interests; a sharp decline in the standard of living following a decline in real wages; and finally a decline in the national income after 1960 (its growth rate fell from an average of 8.5% in 1950–1960 to 0.7% in 1962). In 1963, for the first time in the history of a "socialist" country, the national income fell rather than rose. This was the alarm signal for the new reform. Professor Ota Šik estimated that investment would have to be quadrupled in order to attain in 1968 the same national income growth as in 1958. From 1963 on it began to be officially admitted that "the national economy of Czechoslovakia is going through a period of serious structural imbalance, with limited inflationary tendencies appearing in all sectors of life and society, notably in foreign trade, the home market, and investments" (*Czechoslovakian Foreign Trade*, October 1968).

Voices began to be heard insisting on the urgency of transforming the economy. Ota Šik and his team began preparing their reform plan, which was to be more or less adopted after 1965 by the upper echelons of the state. The new Ota Šik plan made a rather daring critique of the functioning of the economy over the preceding years. It questioned the Russian tutelage and proposed that the economy be freed from rigid central planning and opened to the global market. To do this it was necessary to go beyond simple reproduction of capital, to put an end to the system of "production for production's sake" (denounced as an antisocialist crime after having been glorified as a fundamental principle of socialism), and to reduce the cost of production and raise the productivity index, which had gone from 7.7% in 1960 to 3.1% in 1962 and had fallen even further during the following years.

This plan, a model of technocratic reform, began to be implemented in 1965 and took full effect from 1967 on. It required a clean break with the administrative methods that had crushed all initiative: giving the producers an "interest" in the results of their work, granting autonomy to the different enterprises, rewarding successes, penalizing failures, encouraging through appropriate technical measures the development of profitable industries and enterprises, and putting the market back on its feet by bringing prices in line with the world market. Resisted by the hidebound administrative cadres, this program was applied only in small doses. The Novotnyist bureaucracy began to see the dangerous implications of such a venture. A temporary rise in prices that was not matched by a corresponding rise in wages enabled this conservative stratum to denounce the project in the eyes of the workers. Novotny himself presented himself as the defender of working-class interests and openly criticized the new measures at a workers' meeting in 1967. But the "liberal" wing, aware of the real interests of the bureaucratic regime in Czechoslovakia and sure of the support of the population, joined battle. As a journalist of *Kulturní Tvorba* (5 January 1967) put it, "For the people, the new economic system has become synonymous with the need for change"—*total change*. This was the first link in a chain of developments that would inevitably lead to far-reaching social and political changes. The conservative bureaucracy, having no real support to rely on, could only admit its failings and gradually bow out of the political scene: any resistance on its part would have rapidly led to an explosion analogous to that of Budapest in 1956. The June 1967 Fourth Congress of Writers (though writers and filmmakers had already been allowed a certain margin of artistic freedom) turned into a veritable public indictment of the regime. With their last strength the "conservatives" reacted by excluding a certain number of radical intellectuals from the Party and by putting their journal under direct ministerial control.

But the winds of revolt were blowing harder and harder, and nothing could any longer stem the popular enthusiasm for transforming the prevailing conditions of Czech life. A student demonstration protesting against an electricity shutdown, after being strongly repressed, turned into a meeting leveling accusations against the regime. One of the first discoveries of this meeting, a discovery which was to become the watchword of the whole subsequent oppositional movement, was the absolute insistence on *telling the truth*, in contrast to "the incredible contradictions between what is said and what is actually done." In a system based on the constant lies of ideology, such a demand becomes quite simply revolutionary; and the intellectuals did not fail to develop its implications to the limit. In the bureaucratic systems, where nothing must escape the Party–state totalitarianism, a protest against the slightest detail of life inevitably leads to calling in question the *totality* of existing conditions, to a human protest against the whole inhuman life that people are forced to lead. Even if it was limited to the Prague University campus, the student demonstration concerned all the alienated aspects of Czech life, which was denounced as unacceptable in the course of the meeting.

The neobureaucracy then took over the leadership of the movement and tried to contain it within the narrow framework of its reforms.

In January 1968 an "Action Program" was adopted, marking the rise of the Dubček team and the removal of Novotny. In addition to Ota Šik's economic plan, now definitively adopted and integrated into this new program, a certain number of political measures were proudly proclaimed by the new leadership. Almost all the formal "freedoms" of bourgeois regimes were guaranteed. This policy, totally unprecedented for a bureaucratic regime, shows how much was at stake and how serious the situation was. The radical elements, taking advantage of these bureaucratic concessions, were to reveal their real purpose as "objectively necessary" measures for safeguarding bureaucratic domination. Smrkovsky, the most liberal of the newly promoted members, naïvely expressed the truth of the bureaucratic liberalism: "Recognizing that even in a socialist society evolution takes place through constant conflicts of interest in the economic, social, and political domains, we should seek a system of *political guidance* that permits the settling of all social conflicts and avoids the necessity for extraordinary administrative interventions." But the new bureaucracy did not realize that by renouncing those "extraordinary interventions," which in reality constitute its only *normal* manner of governing, it would be leaving its regime open to a merciless radical critique. The freedom of association and of cultural and political expression produced a veritable orgy of critical truth. The notion that the Party's "leading role" should be "naturally and spontaneously recognized, even at the rank-and-file level, based on the ability of its Communist functionaries to work and command" (Action Program) was demolished everywhere, and new demands for autonomous workers' organizations began to be raised. At the end of spring 1968 the Dubček bureaucracy was giving the ridiculous impression of wanting to have its cake and eat it too. It reaffirmed its intention of maintaining its political monopoly: "If anticommunist elements attempt to attack this historic reality (*i.e. the right of the Party to lead*), the Party will mobilize all the forces of the people and of the socialist state in order to drive back and extinguish this adventurist attempt" (Resolution of the Central Committee, June 1968). But once the bureaucratic reform had opened participation in decision-making to the majority of the Party, how could the great majority outside the Party not also want to decide things for themselves? When those at the top of the state play the fiddle, how can they expect those at the bottom not to start dancing?

From this point on the revolutionary tendencies began to turn their critique toward denunciation of the liberal formalism and its ideology. Until then democracy had been, so to speak, "imposed on the masses" in the same way the dictatorship had been imposed on them, that is, by barring them from any real participation. Everyone knew that Novotny had come to power as a partisan of liberalization; and that a "Gomulka-type regression"* constantly threatened the Dubček movement. A society is not transformed by changing its political apparatus, but by overthrowing it from top to bottom. People thus came to the point of criticizing the Bolshevik conception of the Party as leader of the working class, and to demanding an autonomous organization of the proletariat; which would spell a rapid death for the bureaucracy. This is because for the bureaucracy the proletariat must exist only as an *imaginary* force; the bureaucracy reduces it—or tries to reduce it—to the point of being nothing but an appearance, but it wants this appearance to exist and to believe in its own existence. The bureaucracy bases its power on its formal ideology, but its *formal* goals become its actual content and it thus everywhere enters into conflict with *real* goals. Wherever it has seized the state and the economy, wherever the general interest of the state becomes an interest apart and consequently a real interest, the bureaucracy enters into conflict with the proletariat just as every consequence conflicts with the bureaucracy's own presuppositions.

But the oppositional movement following upon the bureaucratic reform only went half way. It did not have time to follow out all its practical implications. The relentless theoretical critique of "bureaucratic dictatorship" and Stalinist totalitarianism had scarcely begun to be taken up autonomously by the great majority of the population when the neobureaucracy reacted by brandishing the specter of the Russian threat, which had already been present from May on. It can be said that the great weakness of the Czechoslovakian movement was that the working class scarcely intervened as an autonomous and decisive force. The themes of "self-management" and "workers' councils" included in Ota Šik's technocratic reform did not go beyond the bureaucratic perspective of a Yugoslavian-style "democratic management." This was also true even of the alternative project, obviously drafted by labor-unionists, presented on 29 June 1968 by the Wilhelm Pieck factory. The critique of Leninism, presented by "certain philosophers" as being "already a deformation of Marxism since it inherently contains the logic of Stalinism," was not, as the asinine editors of *Rouge* would have it, "an absurd notion because it ultimately amounts to denying the leading role of the proletariat" (!), but the highest point of theoretical critique attained in a bureaucratic country. Dutschke himself was ridiculed by the revolutionary Czech students, his "anarcho-Maoism" being scornfully rejected as "absurd, laughable, and not even deserving the attention of a fifteen-year-old."*

All this criticism, which obviously could only lead to the *practical calling into question of the class power of the bureaucracy*, was tolerated and even sometimes encouraged by the Dubček regime as long as the latter could *co-opt* it as a legitimate denunciation of "Stalino-Novotnyist errors." The bureaucracy does indeed denounce its own crimes, but always as having been committed by *others:* it detaches a part of itself and elevates it into an autonomous entity that can be blamed for all the antiproletarian crimes (since the most ancient times, sacrifice has been bureaucracy's favored method for perpetuating its power). In Czechoslovakia, as in Poland and Hungary, nationalism has been the best argument for winning the population's support of the ruling class. The clearer the Russian threat became, the more Dubček's bureaucratic power was reinforced; his fondest desire would have been for the Warsaw Pact forces to remain indefinitely at the borders. But sooner or later the Czech proletariat would have discovered through struggle that the point is not to know what any given bureaucrat, or even the bureaucracy as a whole, momentarily represents as its goal, but to know what the bureaucracy really is, what it, *in conformity with its own nature*, will be historically forced to do. And the proletariat would then have taken appropriate action.

It was the fear of such a discovery that haunted the Russian bureaucracy and its satellites. Picture a Russian (or East German) bureaucrat in the midst of this "ideological" panic, how his brain—as sick as his power—is tortured, confused, stunned by these cries of independence, workers' councils, "bureaucratic dictatorship," and by the conspiracy of workers and intellectuals and their threat to defend their conquests arms in hand, and you will understand how in this clamorous confusion of truth and freedom, of plots and revolution, the Russian bureaucracy could cry out to its Czech counterpart: "Better a fearful end than a fear without end!"

If ever an event had cast its shadow ahead of itself long before it happened, it was, for those who know how to read modern history, the Russian intervention in Czechoslovakia. It was long contemplated and, despite all its international repercussions, virtually inevitable. By bringing into question the omnipotence of bureaucratic power, Dubček's adventurous—though necessary—effort began to imperil this same power wherever it was to be found, and thus became intolerable. Six hundred thousand soldiers (almost as many as the Americans in Vietnam) were sent to put a brutal stop to it. Thus when the "antisocialist" and "counterrevolutionary" forces, continually conjured up and exorcised by all the bureaucrats, finally appeared, they appeared not under the portrait of Benes* or armed by "revanchist Germans," but in the uniform of the "Red" Army.

A remarkable popular resistance was carried on for seven days—"the magnificent seven"—mobilizing virtually the entire population against the invaders. Paradoxically, distinctly revolutionary methods of struggle were taken up for the defense of a reformist bureaucracy. But what had not been carried out in the course of the movement could certainly not he carried out under the occupation: the Russian troops, having enabled the Dubčekists to brake the revolutionary process as much as possible while they were at the borders, also enabled them to control the whole resistance movement after August 21. They played exactly the same role the American troops do in North Vietnam: the role of ensuring the masses' unanimous support for the bureaucracy that exploits them.

The first reflex of the people of Prague, however, was to defend not the Palace of the Republic, but the radio station, which was considered the symbol of their main conquest: truth of information against organized falsehood. And what had been the nightmare of all the Warsaw Pact bureaucracies—the press and the radio—was to continue to haunt them for another entire week. The Czechoslovakian experience has shown the extraordinary possibilities of struggle that a consistent and organized revolutionary movement will one day have at its disposal. Equipment provided by the Warsaw Pact (in anticipation of a possible imperialist invasion of Czechoslovakia!) was used by the Czech journalists to set up 35 clandestine broadcasting stations linked with 80 emergency backup stations. The Soviet propaganda—so essential for an occupation army—was thus totally undermined, and the population was able to keep abreast of just about everything that was happening in the country and to follow the directives of the liberal bureaucrats or of the radical elements that controlled certain stations. For example, in response to a radio appeal aimed at sabotaging the operations of the Russian police, Prague was transformed into a veritable "urban labyrinth" in which all street signs and house numbers were removed and the walls were covered with May 1968–style graffiti. Defying all the police, Prague became a home of freedom and an example of the revolutionary détournement of repressive urbanism. Due to exceptional proletarian organization, *all* the newspapers were able to be freely printed and distributed under the nose of the Russians who asininely guarded the newspaper offices. Several factories were transformed into printing works turning out thousands of papers and leaflets—including a counterfeit issue of *Pravda* in Russian. The 14th Party Congress was able to meet secretly for three days under the protection of the workers of "Auto-Praha." It was this conference that sabotaged "Operation Kadar"* and forced the Russians to negotiate with Dubček. Nevertheless, by using both their troops and the internal contradictions of the Czechoslovakian bureaucracy, the Russians were eventually able to transform the liberal team into a sort of disguised Vichy-type government. Husák, who was thinking of his own future, was the principal agent responsible for canceling the 14th Congress (on the pretext of the absence of the Slovak delegates, who had in fact apparently stayed away on his recommendation). The day after the "Moscow Accords" he declared, "We can accept this accord, which will enable *sensible* men (*our emphasis*) to lead the people out of the present impasse in such a way that they will have no call to feel ashamed in the future."

The Czech proletariat, as it becomes more revolutionary, will have nothing to be ashamed of except its mistake in having trusted Husák, Dubček, or Smrkovsky. It already knows that it can count only on its own forces; and that one after the other Dubček and Smrkovsky will betray it just as the neobureaucracy collectively betrayed it by yielding to Moscow and falling in line with its totalitarian policy. Emotional attachment to one or another celebrity is a vestige of the miserable era of the proletariat, a vestige of the old world. The November strikes and the suicides somewhat slowed down the process of "normalization," which was not brought to completion until April 1969. By reestablishing itself in its true form, the bureaucratic power became more effectively opposed. The illusions all melted away one after the other and the Czechoslovakian masses' attachment to the reformist bureaucracy disappeared. By rehabilitating the "collaborators," the reformists lost their last chance for any future popular support. The workers' and students' revolutionary consciousness deepened as the repression became more severe. The return to the methods and "the narrow, stupid mentality of the fifties" is already provoking violent reactions on the part of the workers and students, whose diverse forms of linking up constitute the main anxiety common to Dubček, his successor, and their joint masters. The workers are proclaiming their "inalienable right to respond to any extreme measures" with their "own extreme countermeasures" (motion by the workers of the CKD to the Minister of Defense, 22 April 1969). The restoration of Stalinism has shown once and for all the illusory character of any bureaucratic reformism and the bureaucracy's congenital inability to "liberalize" its management of society. Its pretense of a "socialism with a human face" is nothing but the introduction of a few "bourgeois" concessions into its totalitarian world; and even these concessions immediately threaten its existence. The only possible *humanization* of "bureaucratic socialism" is its suppression by the revolutionary proletariat, not by a mere "political revolution," but by the total subversion of existing conditions and the practical dissolution of the Bureaucratic International.

The riots of 21 August 1969 have revealed to what extent *ordinary Stalinism* has been reestablished in Czechoslovakia, and also to what extent it is threatened by the proletarian critique: ten deaths, 2000 arrests, and the threats of expelling or prosecuting the puppet Dubček have not stopped the *national slowdown strike* through which the Czech workers are threatening the survival of the economic system of their indigenous and Russian exploiters.

The Russian intervention succeeded in slowing down the objective process of change in Czechoslovakia, but only at a tremendous cost for international Stalinism. The bureaucratic regimes of Cuba and Hanoi, being directly dependent on the "Soviet" state, could only applaud their masters' intervention—to the great embarrassment of their Trotskyist and surrealist admirers and the high-minded souls of the left. Castro, with a singular cynicism, justified the military intervention at great length as being necessitated by threats of a restoration of capitalism—thereby unmasking the nature of his own "socialism." Hanoi and the bureaucratic Arab powers, themselves the victims of foreign occupation, push their absurd logic to the point of supporting an analogous aggression because in this case it is carried out by their self-styled protectors.

As for those members of the Bureaucratic International that shed tears over Czechoslovakia, they all did so for their own national reasons. The "Czechoslovakian affair," coming right after the seismic shock suffered by the French Communist Party in the revolutionary crisis of May 1968, dealt the latter another serious blow. Now divided into old-fashioned-Stalinist, neo-Stalinist, and orthodox-Stalinist fractions, it is torn between loyalty to Moscow and its own interest on the bourgeois political chessboard. If the Italian CP was bolder in its denunciation, the reason lay in the rising crisis in Italy, particularly the direct blow struck against its "Togliattism." The nationalist bureaucracies of Yugoslavia and Romania found in the intervention an opportunity to consolidate their class domination, regaining the support of populations rendered fearful of a Russian threat—a threat that in their cases is more imaginary than real. Stalinism, which has already tolerated Titoism and Maoism as alternative images of itself, will always tolerate one or another sort of "Romanian independence" as long as it does not directly threaten its "socialist model" faithfully reproduced everywhere. There is no point in going into the Sino–Albanian critique of "Russian imperialism." In the logic of their "anti-imperialist" delirium, the Chinese in turn reproach the Russians for not intervening in Czechoslovakia like they did in Hungary (see *Peking News,* 13 August 1968) and then denounce the "odious aggression" perpetrated by "the Brezhnev-Kosygin fascist clique."

"The international association of totalitarian bureaucracies has completely fallen apart," we wrote in *Internationale Situationniste #11.* The Czechoslovakian crisis has only confirmed the advanced decay of Stalinism. Stalinism would never have been able to play such a great role in the crushing of the workers' movement *everywhere* if the Russian totalitarian bureaucratic model had not been closely related both to the bureaucratization of the old *reformist* movement (German Social Democracy and the Second International)* and to the increasingly bureaucratic organization of modern capitalist production. But now, after more than forty years of counterrevolutionary history, the revolution is being reborn everywhere, striking terror into the hearts of the masters of the East as well as those of the West, attacking them both in their differences and in their deep affinity. The courageous isolated protests expressed in Moscow after August 21 herald the revolution that will not fail to break out soon *in Russia itself.* The revolutionary movement now knows its real enemies, and none of the alienations produced by the two forms of capitalism—private-bourgeois or state-bureaucratic—can any longer escape its critique. Facing the immense tasks that lie before it, the movement will no longer waste its time fighting phantoms or supporting illusions.

How Not to Understand Situationist Books

If the SI's activity had not recently led to some publicly scandalous and threatening consequences, it is certain that no French publication would have reviewed our recent books. François Châtelet naïvely admitted as much in the *Nouvel Observateur* (3 January 1968): "One's first impulse when confronted with such works is purely and simply to exclude them, to leave this absolutist point of view of theirs in the realm of the absolute, the realm of the nonrelative and unmentioned." But having left us in the realm of the unmentioned, the organizers of this conspiracy of silence have within a few years seen this strange "absolute" fall back on their heads and turn out to be not very distinct from *present history,* from which they themselves were absolutely separated, all their efforts proving insufficient to prevent this "old mole" from making its way toward daylight. Châtelet's article is full of unwitting confessions of the state of mind of all the shysters of his ilk. Recalling the incidents at Strasbourg, this splendid prophet, just five months before May 1968, took comfort in reassuring himself while as usual misleading his imbecilic readers: "For a brief moment there was panic; there was fear that the contagion would spread (. . .) but everything returned (. . .) to order." He states that Debord and Vanei-gem, presenting "a denunciation that can be accepted or rejected only as a whole," have thereby disqualified themselves, and that they "dis-courage any criticism in advance" because "they consider it self-evi-dent that any objection to their positions can only come from foolish thinkers who are lackeys of 'power' and of the 'spectacle'." *Discouraging* the criticisms made by the miserable generation of intellectuals who have prostituted themselves in Stalinism and Argumentism and in philosophizing for *L'Express* and *Le Nouvel Observateur* is indeed one of our goals. The act of *criticizing us* does not make someone a stupidly spectacular and craven toady for the powers that be; on the contrary, it is because Châtelet briefly rallied to Stalinism in 1956, and has since transformed himself into a valet of the spectacle in a few somewhat more profitable trades, that he criticizes us so stupidly. Châtelet finds that, because we limit ourselves to a radical but "abstract" negation, we remain "in the empirical" and even "without concepts." Harsh words. But consider where they're coming from. We know that when the wine of critique is sufficiently diluted with dirty water, a hundred mediocre books are quickly saluted as highly conceptual by Châtelet and all the other castratos of the concept, who would like the unfortunate readers of *Le Nouvel Observateur* to believe that they have plenty of "concep-tual" knowledge. Moreover, this ex-Stalinist who would obviously have opposed the communism of 1848, gives a perfect expression of himself in what is perhaps the lamest remark that any cretin has ever applied to us. With the aim of disparaging us, but at the same time also, like the other Argumentists cuckolded by Stalinism, wishing to belittle the old demand for a proletarian revolution—which he believed had been exor-cised forever, buried by Stalinism and by his *Express*—Châtelet states that, although one might consider these books and the existence of the SI as "symptoms," as a "little glimmer flitting vaguely from Copen-hagen to New York," "situationism is *no more* the specter that haunts industrial society *than was communism* the specter that haunted Europe in 1848." It is we who emphasize this completely unintentional praise. Everyone will easily understand that we find it *already a gratifying accom-plishment* to be "mistaken" like Marx, rather than like Châtelet.

If the anger of these pretentious experts was already pretty strong, it became really extreme after the occupations movement arrived to contradict all their predictions. Pierre Viansson-Ponté (*Le Monde*, 25 January 1969) furiously dismisses Viénet's book with a dishonesty remarkable even for the editors of that paper. He sees nothing in it but "a virtually unreadable prose, a boundless pretension, and an unquenchable craving for publicity. (. . .) They conclude quite simply that the May revolt (. . .) heralds nothing less than a global revolution." Viansson-Ponté is nothing more than a moron. He begins his article with this pompous dictum: "Formerly, revolutionaries fell on the barricades or took power. They had no time to write their history, and they generally had no interest in doing so." He could hardly be more mistaken. Revolutionaries, among the best tendencies as among the worst, have *always written* a lot, for reasons that have been obvious to everyone except Viansson-Ponté, who is apparently not even aware that they have done so. To give just one example, in the single year 1871 a dozen important books written by survivors of the Paris Commune were published in Geneva and Brussels (Gustave Lefrançais's *Étude sur le mouvement communaliste à Paris*, Benoît Malon's *La troisième défaite du prolétariat français*, Lissagaray's *Les huit journées de mai derrière les barricades*, Georges Jeanneret's *Paris pendant la commune révolutionnaire*, etc., to say nothing of Marx's *La guerre civile en France*). But Viansson-Ponté wants blood. Unquestioningly accepting the official police line that there were very few deaths in May, he reproaches us for this paltry result: "The revolutionaries of May 1968, thank God, are still alive. (. . .) Now they write. A lot. The hands that only yesterday were throwing paving stones have now taken up the pen." We take pride in this passage from pen to paving stone and vice versa, considering it a preliminary step in the abolition of the division between manual and intellectual work. But doesn't this thoughtless necrophage realize that his ill-advised irony could be interpreted as an appeal for a bloodier police and military repression next time? And if such a repression happens, isn't it obvious that some of those who tried to deny the seriousness of the 1968 movement on the grounds that it didn't cause enough deaths run the risk of themselves being among the first victims of the inevitable spontaneous reprisals? In 1962 we wrote: "What is astonishing is rather that all the specialists of public-opinion polls remain so unaware of how close this public anger is to bursting forth, this anger that is arising for so many good reasons. One of these days they will be really astonished—at seeing the architects rounded up and hung in the streets of Sarcelles" (*Internationale Situationniste #7*, p. 19). Precisely because of its strength, which was due to the partial but nevertheless overwhelming participation of the proletarian masses, the May movement was *lenient*. But if, one of these days, we come to bloodier confrontations, the urbanists and the journalists (who are already denouncing the few blows recently given to the Stalinist Badia at Vincennes as "red fascism") will indeed be in great peril.

So it is that publications in France have felt obliged to devote several dozen articles to discussing our books. Nearly as many have appeared in the foreign press, the latter being somewhat more honest and informed. Some have even contained praises, which there is no point going into here. A general contradiction hangs over them all. Some of these authors, though believing they have discovered some striking insights in our writings, lack the most elementary political and theoretical knowledge that would enable them to really understand what our books are about, which requires considering each of them as a whole, within its entire context. A good example is the critic Henri-Charles Tauxe, in the Swiss newspaper *La Gazette Littéraire* (13 January 1968), who concludes his analysis (which at least has the merit of honestly trying to set out the content of the book he is reviewing) with this rumination: "One could certainly ask oneself a number of questions about the perspectives opened up by Debord, and in particular whether the very concept of revolution still has any meaning today." On the other hand, those of our critics who are well aware of the problems addressed in these books are led to falsify them, with a bad faith that is closely related to their particular positions and even to the particular platforms from which they speak. In order to avoid tedious repetition, we will limit ourselves to examining three typical attitudes, each manifesting itself in reaction to one of our books, attitudes represented respectively by an academic Marxist, a psychoanalyst, and an ultraleftist militant. In the process, we will note their primary motivations.

* * *

During the early 1950s Claude Lefort was a revolutionary and one of the main theorists of the journal *Socialisme ou Barbarie*—regarding which we stated in *Internationale Situationniste* #10 that it had sunk to run-of-the-mill academic speculation on the level of *Arguments* and that it was bound to disappear (which it confirmed by folding a month or two later).* By that time Lefort had already been separated from it for years, having been in the forefront of the opposition to any form of revolutionary organization, which he denounced as inevitably doomed to bureaucratization. Since this distressing discovery he has consoled himself by taking up an ordinary academic career and writing in *La*

Quinzaine Littéraire. In the 1 February 1968 issue of that periodical this very knowledgeable but domesticated man makes a critique of *The Society of the Spectacle.* He begins by acknowledging that the book has some merits. Its use of Marxian methodology, and even of détournement, has not escaped him, though he fails to notice its debt to Hegel. But the book nevertheless seems academically unacceptable to him for the following reason: "Debord adds thesis upon thesis, but he does not advance; he endlessly repeats the same idea: that the real is inverted in ideology, that ideology, changed in its essence in the spectacle, passes itself off for the real, and that it is necessary to overthrow ideology in order to bring the real back into its own. It makes little difference what particular topic he treats, this idea is reflected in all the others. It is only due to his exhaustion that he has stopped at the 221st thesis." Debord readily admits that he found, at the 221st thesis, that he had said quite enough, and had accomplished exactly what he had set out to do: make an "endless" description of what the *spectacle* is and how it can be overthrown. The fact that "this idea is reflected in all the others" is precisely what we consider the characteristic of a *dialectical book.* Such a book does not have to "advance," like some doctoral dissertation on Machiavelli, toward the approval of a board of examiners and the attainment of a diploma. (And as Marx put it in the Afterword to the second German edition of *Capital,* regarding the way the dialectical "method of presentation" may he viewed, "This reflecting may make it seem as if we had before us a mere *a priori* construction.") *The Society of the Spectacle* does not hide its *a priori* engagement, nor does it attempt to derive its conclusions from academic argumentation. It is written only to show the *concrete* coherent field of application of a thesis that already exists at the outset, a thesis deriving from the investigations that revolutionary criticism has made of modern capitalism. In our opinion, it is basically *a book that lacked nothing but one or more revolutions.* Which were not long in coming. But Lefort, having lost all interest in this kind of theory and practice, finds that the book is an ivory-tower world closed in on itself: "One would have expected this book to be a violent attack against its adversaries, but in fact this ostentatious discourse has no other aim than showing off. Admittedly it has a certain beauty. The style is flawless. Since any question that does not have an automatic response has been banished from the very first lines, one would search in vain for any fault." The misinterpretation is total: Lefort sees a sort of Mallarméan purity in a book which, as a *negative* of spectacular society (in which also, but in an inverse manner, any question that does not have an automatic response is banished at every moment), ultimately seeks nothing other than to *overthrow* the existing *relation of forces* in the factories and the streets.

After this general rejection of the book, Lefort still wants to play the Marxist regarding a few details in order to remind us that this is his specialty, the reason he gets assignments from intellectual periodicals. Here he begins to falsify in order to give himself the opportunity of introducing pedantic reminders of things that are obvious. He solemnly announces that Debord has changed "the commodity into the spectacle," a transformation that is "full of consequences." He ponderously summarizes what Marx says on the commodity, then falsely charges Debord with having said that "the production of the phantasmagoria governs that of commodities," whereas in fact the *exact opposite* is clearly stated in *The Society of the Spectacle,* notably in the second chapter, where the spectacle is defined as simply a *moment* of the development of commodity production. Lefort can thus arrive at the absurd conclusion that "according to Debord, all history is futile"! He also refers to Debord as "a strange offspring of Marx, intoxicated by the famous analysis of the fetishism of the commodity." We won't go into a debate about the best ways to become intoxicated—a matter that academics know little about—but we will note that Lefort was more surprised than we were when history suddenly returned in May 1968, that "bacchanalia of truth where no one remains sober" (Hegel)* in which one could already see *crowds* of people intoxicated by the discovery of the possibility of *destroying* the commodity and the spectacle at the heart of pseudolife. And Lefort, in *Le Monde* of 5 April 1969—still behind the times regarding what is happening, and even regarding what he knows, but less so than he was in February 1968—goes so far as to write that it isn't necessary to obsess, like "the bourgeois observers," about the reappearance of Trotskyist relics at the left of the Stalinist machine, because "the conditions are now present to permit a critique of the whole bureaucratic world and to base an analysis in new terms of the modern mechanisms of exploitation and oppression. (...) With the May movement, and with the initiatives that it has inspired among the young workers, something new is taking shape that owes nothing to the intervention of heroes: an opposition that does not yet know what to name itself, but that defies all the established authorities in such a way that it cannot be confused with the movements of the past." Better late than never! Only, as we have seen, in February 1968 the "conditions" were *already present,* although Lefort wanted to ignore them, and *he himself,* today, does "not yet" know what this opposition *names itself.*

* * *

We sink lower still with André Stéphane's *L'Univers contestationnaire* (Payot, 1969), the thirteenth chapter of which is a critique of Raoul Vaneigem's book [*The Revolution of Everyday Life*]. The publisher announces that "Stéphane" is the pseudonym of "two psychoanalysts." Judging from their stratospheric level of ineptitude and their ponderous parody of "orthodox Freudianism," there could just as well have been twenty-two of them, or the work could have been churned out by a computer programmed for psychoanalysis. Since the authors are psychoanalysts, Vaneigem is naturally insane. He is paranoid, which is why he has so perfectly expressed in advance the May movement and other distressing tendencies of modern society, all of which are nothing but fantasies, deliriums, a rejection of the object world and of the Oedipal problem, fusional narcissism, exhibitionism, sadistic impulses, etc. They crown their monument of hogwash by professing to "admire the book as a work of art." But unfortunately this book has fallen into bad hands: the May movement horrified our psychiatrists by its blind violence, its inhuman terrorism, its nihilistic cruelty, and its explicit goal of destroying civilization and perhaps even the planet. When they hear the word "festival" they reach for their electrodes; they insist that we get back to the serious, never doubting for a moment that they themselves are excellent representatives of the seriousness of psychoanalysis and of social life and that they can write about all that without provoking laughter. Even the people who were foolish enough to be the *customers* of this Laurel and Hardy of mental medicine told them that after May they felt less depressed and less dissociated. Fearing that this might result in a reduction of their income (after having been terrified at the thought of losing everything in May, when our ethereal absolutism threatened the very existence of money and the commodity system), our *socially integrated lunatics* write: "This was very clear in the case of certain patients, who seemed to consider that if Revolution (an infantile desire that they had abandoned) was possible, then *everything* would become possible; that it would no longer be necessary to abstain from anything . . ." These people would be an embarrassment to psychoanalysis if any dignity remained in that lamentable profession, that is, if the work of Freud had not already been torn to shreds by its co-option into bourgeois society over thirty years ago. But when these mental retards, driven by hate, fear, and the desire to maintain their profitable little prestige, venture to deal with an issue whose basis is obviously *political,* how do they manage? Here our mature and sensible defenders of "real" society, and of the principle that all is for the best in this best of all possible societies, reveal the full extent of their stupidity. For these psychoanalysts there is no question that this May movement, which they analyze with such brilliant penetration, consisted *exclusively of students* (these police dogs of the detection of the irrational have not for one moment found it *abnormal* and unexplainable that a mere outburst of student vandalism was able to paralyze the economy and the state of a large industrial country). Moreover, according to them all students are rich, living in comfort and abundance, without any discernable rational reason for discontent: they enjoy all the benefits and virtually none of the drawbacks of a happy society that has never been less repressive. Our psychoanalysts thus conclude that this socioeconomic happiness, evidently experienced in its purest state by *all* the May rebels, has revealed the inner, existential misery of people whose "infantile desire" has led them to a craving for the absolute, people whose immaturity makes them incapable of taking advantage of the "benefits" of modern society, thus demonstrating "an incapacity for libidinal expression in the external world due to internal conflicts. The most marvelous festivals cannot entertain someone who bears within himself boredom, that deficiency in the libidinal economy."

Reading these Stéphanes, one has to bear in mind that when they refer to "the most marvelous festivals," they are thinking of things like the "Sound and Light Show" at the Giza Pyramid. Their judgment of the automobile suffices to reveal the properly sublimated infantilism of these monogamous and responsibly voting "real adults": this splendid toy has provided a suitable replacement for the little electric train of their earlier years when they were resolving their Oedipus complexes, to the general satisfaction of their respectable families. Quoting (p. 215) a few ironic passages from Vaneigem on the current pseudo-satisfaction of social needs ("The Communards fought to the death so that you, too, could buy a Philips hi-fi stereo system"), they reject his paranoiac point of view with indignation and frankly declare that the Communards would have been thrilled to know that their sacrifice would assure for their descendants the right to live at Sarcelles and watch the television shows of Guy Lux. They conclude that Vaneigem "must truly have counterinvested materiality not to understand that buying a car may, at least provisionally, constitute a valid goal in itself, and that this acquisition may produce a great joy." They themselves must truly have counterinvested the slightest trace of rational thought to have made themselves the unconditional eulogists of this "great joy" at a time when the specialists of scientific examination, fragmented and socially disarmed though they be, are denouncing the dangers in all domains posed by the proliferation of this star-commodity (destruction of the urban environment, etc.); and when even those who are most alienated by the "possession" of a car never cease complaining about the specific conditions that are continually spoiling the "great joy" that this purchase supposedly guarantees them, according to the ads (to be sure, this discontent does not yet go so far as to grasp the fact that this spoiling is not caused by the inadequacies of this or that governmental administration, but simply by the obligatory multiplication of this pseudogood to the point of total congestion). Finally, our two psychiatrists are precise, sincere, and realistic only on a single point. In a note on page 99 they denounce certain persons "claiming to be psychoanalysts and Freudians" who, after a debate at the College of Medicine on the question of payment of psychoanalysts, wished to call in question the very necessity for such payment. "Now to anyone who is familiar with the effects of transference, it is clear that the money paid by the analysand guarantees him what we can schematically term 'autonomy' (once he pays the psychoanalyst, 'he no longer owes him anything')." Psychoanalysis has obviously never had any trouble articulating splendid psychoanalytic justifications of the necessity of paying. But if those who profit from it so as to consume more and live less are so comfortable psychoanalyzing Marxists, they don't make us forget that the most elementary Marxist critique reveals, with greater precision, their own *depth psychology* (to adopt their verbal style of analysis, it is no accident if the people say "he slipped the dough into his deep"),* their *economy*, and their *investments*. Here, then, is the origin of the book by these Stéphanes: their money was threatened. What worse delirium have they ever had to deal with? The psychiatrists have never seen a mode of production die! They are nevertheless beginning to feel some uneasiness.

At the end of 1966 Rector Bayen of Strasbourg declared to the press that *we should be dealt with by psychiatrists.* In the following year he saw the abolition of the "University Psychological Aid Centers" at Strasbourg and Nantes, and eighteen months later the collapse of his whole fine university world along with a great number of his hierarchical superiors. Finally, though a bit belatedly, the psychiatrists with which we were threatened have arrived, and have made this critique of Vaneigem. They have probably disappointed those who were hoping for a final solution of the situationist problem.

* * *

René Viénet's book [*Enragés and Situationists in the Occupations Movement*] has not had the honors of psychiatry, but has been criticized in an article in issue #2 of *Révolution Internationale*, the journal of an ultraleftist group that is anti-Trotskyist and non-Bordigist, but scarcely disengaged from Leninism: it is still striving to reconstitute the wise leadership of a true "party of the proletariat" which this time, however, promises to remain democratic once it manages to come into existence. This group's ideas are a bit too musty to be worth discussing here. Since we are dealing with people who have revolutionary intentions, we will merely point out a few of their specific *falsifications*. Such falsifications are in our opinion *much more inconsistent* with the activity of a revolutionary organization than the mere assertion of erroneous theories, which can always be discussed and corrected. Moreover, those who think they have to falsify texts in order to defend their theses thereby implicitly admit that their theses are otherwise indefensible.

Our critic says he is disappointed with the book, "especially since the several months' period of writing time should have made possible something better." In fact, although the book only appeared at the end of October 1968, it is clearly indicated in the introduction (p. 8) that it was completed July 26. It was then immediately sent to the publisher, after which no alterations were made apart from the addition of two short footnotes (pp. 20 and 209) explicitly dated October, concerning post-July developments in Czechoslovakia and Mexico.

Our critic then reproaches the book for "yielding to current fashion"—that is, in fact, to our own style, since it adopts the same sort of presentation as the previous issues of *Internationale Situationniste*—because it includes photos and comics; and he reproaches the situationists for being contemptuous of "the great infantile mass of workers" by aiming to *divert* them as do the capitalist press and cinema. He sternly notes that "it is above all the action of the Enragés and situationists that is described," only to add immediately: "which, moreover, is stated in the title." Viénet proposed to draw up an immediate report on our activities in the May period, accompanied with our analyses and some documents, considering that this would constitute a valuable documentation for understanding May, particularly for those who will have to act in future crises of the same type (it is with the same purpose that we have further taken up these questions in this issue). This experience may seem useful to some and negligible to others, depending on how they think and *what they really are*. But what is certain is that without Viénet's book this precise documentation would have been unknown (or known only fragmentarily and falsely) by many people. The title says clearly enough what it's about.

Without going so far as to insinuate that there is the slightest false detail in this report, our critic contends that Viénet has given too large a place to our action, that we have imagined it to have been "preponderant." "Reduced to its correct proportions, the place occupied by the situationists was certainly inferior to that of numerous other groups, or in any case not superior." We don't really know where the "certainty" of his comparison comes from, as if it were a matter of weighing the total amount of paving stones that each group threw in the same direction at the same building. The CRS and even the Maoists certainly had a "greater place" in the crisis than we had, a greater weight. The question is *in what direction* the force of one or another grouping was exerted. If we restrict ourselves to the *revolutionary* current, a great number of unorganized workers obviously had a weight so determinative that no group can even be compared with them; but this tendency did not become the conscious master of its own action. If—since our critic seems more interested in a sort of race among the "groups" (and perhaps he is thinking of *his?*)—we restrict ourselves to groups holding clearly revolutionary positions, we know very well that they were not so "numerous"! And in this case one would have to specify *which groups* one is referring to and *what they did*, instead of leaving everything in a mysterious vagueness, merely deciding that the specific action of the SI, in relation to these unknown groups, was "certainly inferior," and then—what is a bit different—"not superior."

In reality, *Révolution Internationale* reproaches the situationists for having said, for years, that a *new* setting out of the revolutionary proletarian movement was to be expected from a modern critique of the new conditions of oppression and the new contradictions those conditions were bringing to light. For *RI* fundamentally there is nothing new in capitalism, nor therefore in the critique of it; the occupations movement presented nothing new; the concepts of "spectacle" or of "survival," the critique of the commodity attaining a stage of abundant production, etc., are only empty words. It can be seen that these three series of postulates are all interlinked.

If the situationists were merely fanatics of intellectual innovation, *Révolution Internationale,* which knows everything about proletarian revolution since 1920 or 1930, would attach no importance to them. What our critic objects to is that we showed at the same time that these *new developments* in capitalism, and consequently the new developments in its negation, are *also rediscovering their connections* with the old truth of the previously vanquished proletarian revolution. This is very annoying to RI because it wants to possess this old truth *without any newness mixed in,* whether such newness arises within reality or in the theories of the SI or others. Here begins the falsification. *RI* excerpts a few sentences from pages 13 and 14 of Viénet's book, where he recapitulates these basic banalities of the unaccomplished revolution, and adds a bunch of marginal notes like a professor's red ink corrections:

"It's really wonderful that the SI 'readily' affirms what all workers and revolutionaries already knew"; "what a marvelous discovery!"; "obviously"; etc. But the excerpts from these two pages are, if we may say so, rather artfully selected. One of them, for example, is quoted exactly as follows: "The SI knew well (. . .) that the emancipation of the workers still clashed everywhere with bureaucratic organizations." What are the words deleted by this opportune ellipsis? Here is the exact sentence: "The SI knew well, *as did so many workers with no means of expressing it,* that the emancipation of the workers still clashed everywhere with bureaucratic organizations." *RI's* method is as obvious as the existence of class struggle, which this group seems to imagine itself the exclusive owner of—the class struggle to which Viénet was explicitly referring in response to "so many commentators" having the means of expressing themselves in books and newspapers who "agreed that the movement was unforeseeable."

And, always so as to deny that the SI has said in advance any truth on the nearness of a new period of the revolutionary movement, *RI,* which does not at all want this period to be new, asks ironically how the SI can claim to have foreseen this crisis; and why it didn't appear until exactly fifty years after the defeat of the Russian revolution—"why not thirty or seventy?" The answer is very simple. Even leaving aside the fact that the SI followed rather closely the rise of certain elements of the crisis (in Strasbourg, Turin, and Nanterre, for example), *we predicted the content, not the date.*

The *Révolution Internationale* group may very well be in total disagreement with us when it comes to judging the content of the occupations movement, as it is more generally at variance with the comprehension of its era and therefore with the forms of practical action that other revolutionaries have already begun to take up. But if we scorn the *Révolution Internationale* group and want no contact with it, it is not because of the content of its somewhat musty theoretical science, but because of the petty-bureaucratic *style* it is naturally led to adopt in order to defend that content. The form and content of its perspectives are thus in accord with each other, both dating from the same dismal years.

But modern history has also created the eyes that know how to read us.

Preliminaries on Councils and Councilist Organization

"The Workers' and Peasants' Government has decreed that Kronstadt and the rebelling ships must immediately submit to the authority of the Soviet Republic. I therefore order all who have revolted against the socialist fatherland to lay down their arms at once. Recalcitrants should be disarmed and turned over to the Soviet authorities. The commissars and other members of the government who have been arrested must be liberated at once. Only those who surrender unconditionally can expect mercy from the Soviet Republic. I am simultaneously giving orders to prepare for the suppression of the rebellion and the subjugation of the sailors by armed force. All responsibility for the harm that may be suffered by the peaceful population will rest entirely on the heads of the White Guard mutineers. This warning is final."

— Trotsky and Kamenev, *Ultimatum to Kronstadt*

"We have only one answer to all that: All power to the soviets! Take your hands off them—your hands that are red with the blood of the martyrs of freedom who fought the White Guards, the landowners, and the bourgeoisie!"

— *Kronstadt Izvestia #6**

During the fifty years since the Leninists reduced communism to electrification, since the Bolshevik counterrevolution erected the *Soviet State* over the dead body of the power of the soviets, and since "soviet" ceased to mean *council*, revolutions have continued to fling the Kronstadt demand in the face of the rulers of the Kremlin: *"All power to the soviets and not to the parties."* The remarkable persistence of the *real tendency* toward *workers' councils* throughout this half-century of efforts and repeated suppressions of the modern proletarian movement now imposes the councils on the new revolutionary current as the sole form of antistate dictatorship of the proletariat, as the sole tribunal that will be able to pass judgment on the old world and carry out the sentence itself.

The essence of the councils must be more precisely delineated, not only by refuting the gross falsifications propagated by social democracy, the Russian bureaucracy, Titoism, and even Ben-Bellaism, but above all by recognizing the insufficiencies in the fledgling practical experiences of the power of the councils that have briefly appeared so far; as well, of course, as the insufficiencies in councilist revolutionaries' very conceptions. The council's *ultimate tendency* appears negatively in the limits and illusions which have marked its first manifestations, and which have caused its defeat quite as much as has the immediate and uncompromising struggle that is naturally waged against it by the ruling class. The purpose of the council form is the *practical unification* of proletarians in the process of appropriating the material and intellectual means of changing all existing conditions and making themselves the masters of their own history. It can and must be the organization in acts of historical consciousness. But in fact it has nowhere yet succeeded in overcoming the separation embodied in *specialized* political organizations and in the forms of ideological false consciousness that they produce and defend. Moreover, although it is quite natural that the councils that have been major agents of revolutionary situations have generally been *councils of delegates*, since it is such councils which coordinate and federate the decisions of local councils, it nevertheless appears that the general assemblies of the rank and file have almost always been considered as mere assemblies of electors, so that the first level of the "council" is situated above them. Here already lies an element of separation, which can only be surmounted by treating local general assemblies of all the proletarians in revolution as the *ultimate, fundamental councils*, from which any delegation must derive its power.

Leaving aside the precouncilist features of the Paris Commune which so enthused Marx ("the finally discovered political form through which the economic emancipation of labor can be realized")—features which, moreover, can be seen more in the organization of the Central Committee of the National Guard, which was composed of delegates of the Parisian proletariat in arms, than in the elected Commune— the famous St. Petersburg "Council of Workers' Deputies" was the first fledgling manifestation of an organization of the proletariat in a revolutionary situation. According to the figures given by Trotsky in his book *1905*, 200,000 workers sent their delegates to the St. Petersburg Soviet; but its influence extended far beyond its immediate area, with many other councils in Russia drawing inspiration from its deliberations and decisions. It directly grouped the workers from more than 150 enterprises, besides welcoming representatives from 16 unions that had rallied to it. Its first nucleus was formed on October 13; by the 17th the soviet had established an Executive Committee over itself which Trotsky says "served it as a ministry." Out of a total of 562 delegates, the Executive Committee comprised only 31 members, of which 22 were actually workers delegated by the entirety of the workers in their enterprises and 9 represented three revolutionary parties (Mensheviks, Bolsheviks, and Social Revolutionaries); however, "the representatives of the parties had only consultative status and were not entitled to vote." Although the rank-and-file assemblies were presumably faithfully represented by their revocable delegates, it is clear that those delegates had abdicated a large part of their power, in a very *parliamentary* way, into the hands of an Executive Committee in which the "technical advisors" from the political parties had an enormous influence.

How did this soviet originate? It seems that this form of organization was discovered by certain politically aware elements among the ordinary workers, who for the most part themselves belonged to one or another socialist fraction. Trotsky seems to be quite unjustified in writing that "one of the two social-democratic organizations in St. Petersburg took the initiative of creating an autonomous revolutionary workers' administration" (moreover, the "one of the two" organizations that did at least immediately recognize the significance of this workers' initiative was the Mensheviks, not the Bolsheviks). But the general strike of October 1905 in fact originated first of all in Moscow on September 19, when the typographers of the Sytine printing works went on strike, notably because they wanted punctuation marks to be counted among the 1000 characters that constituted their unit of payment. Fifty printing works followed them out, and on September 25 the Moscow printers formed a council. On *October 3* "the assembly of workers' deputies from the printers, mechanics, carpenters, tobacco workers, and other guilds adopted the resolution to set up a general council (soviet) of Moscow workers" (Trotsky, *op. cit.*). It can thus be seen that this form appeared spontaneously at the beginning of the strike movement. And this movement, which began to fall back in the next few days, was to surge forward again up to the great historic crisis when on October 7 the railroad workers, beginning in Moscow, spontaneously began to stop the railway traffic.

The council movement in Turin of March–April 1920 originated among the highly concentrated proletariat of the Fiat factories. During August and September 1919 new elections for an "internal commission" (a sort of collaborationist factory committee set up by a collective convention in 1906 for the purpose of better integrating the workers) suddenly provided the opportunity, amid the social crisis that was then sweeping Italy, for a complete transformation of the role of these "commissioners." They began to federate among themselves as direct representatives of the workers. By October 30,000 workers were represented at an assembly of "executive committees of factory councils," which resembled more an assembly of shop stewards (with one commissioner elected by each workshop) than an organization of councils in the strict sense. But the example nevertheless acted as a catalyst and the movement radicalized, supported by a fraction of the

Socialist Party (including Gramsci) that was in the majority in Turin and by the Piedmont anarchists (see Pier Carlo Masini's pamphlet, *Anarchici e comunisti nel movimento dei Consigli a Torino*). The movement was resisted by the majority of the Socialist Party and by the unions. On 15 March 1920 the councils began a strike *combined with occupation of the factories* and *resumed production* under their own control. By April 14 the strike was general in Piedmont; in the following days it spread through much of northern Italy, particularly among the dockers and railroad workers. The government had to use warships to land troops at Genoa to march on Turin. While the councilist program was later to be approved by the Congress of the Italian Anarchist Union when it met at Bologna on July 1, the Socialist Party and the unions succeeded in sabotaging the strike by keeping it isolated: when Turin was besieged by 20,000 soldiers and police, the party newspaper *Avanti* refused to print the appeal of the Turin socialist section (see Masini, *op. cit.*). The strike, which would clearly have made possible a victorious insurrection in the whole country, was vanquished on April 24. What happened next is well known.*

In spite of certain remarkably advanced features of this rarely mentioned experience (numerous leftists are under the mistaken impression that factory occupations took place for the first time in France in 1936), it should be noted that it contained serious ambiguities, even among its partisans and theorists. Gramsci wrote in *Ordine Nuovo* (second year, #4): "We see the factory council as the historic beginning of a process that must ultimately lead to the foundation of the workers' state." For their part, the councilist anarchists were sparing in their criticism of labor unionism and claimed that the councils would give it a renewed impetus.

However, the manifesto circulated by the Turin councilists on 27 March 1920, "To the Workers and Peasants of All Italy," calling for a general congress of the councils (which never took place), formulates some essential points of the council program: "The struggle for conquest must be fought with arms of conquest, and no longer only with those of defense (*SI note: this is aimed at the unions, which the manifesto describes elsewhere as "organisms of resistance . . . crystallized into a bureaucratic form"*). A new organization must be developed as a direct antagonist of the organs of the bosses' government; for that task it must spring up spontaneously in the workplace and unite all the workers, because all of them, as producers, are subjected to an authority that is alien (*estranea*) to them, and must liberate themselves from it. . . . This is the beginning of freedom for you: the beginning of a social formation that by rapidly and universally extending itself will put you in a position to eliminate the exploiter and the middleman from the economic field and to become yourselves the masters—the masters of your machines, of your work, and of your life . . .”

The majority of the Workers' and Soldiers' Councils in the Germany of 1918–1919 were more crudely dominated by the Social-Democratic bureaucracy or were victims of its maneuvers. They tolerated Ebert's "socialist" government, whose main support came from the General Staff and the Freikorps. The "Hamburg seven points" (calling for the immediate dissolution of the old Army), presented by Dorrenbach and passed with a large majority by the Congress of Soldiers' Councils that opened December 16 in Berlin, were not implemented by the "People's Commissars." The councils tolerated this defiance, and the legislative elections that had been quickly set for January 19; then they tolerated the attack launched against Dorrenbach's sailors; finally, they tolerated the crushing of the Spartakist insurrection on the very eve of those elections.*

In 1956 the Central Workers' Council of Greater Budapest, constituted on November 14 and declaring itself determined to defend socialism, demanded "the withdrawal of all political parties from the factories" while at the same time pronouncing itself in favor of Nagy's return to power and free elections within a short time. It is true that this was during the time it was continuing the general strike despite the Russian troops' having already crushed the armed resistance. But even before the second Russian intervention the Hungarian councils had called for parliamentary elections: that is to say, they themselves were seeking to return to a dual-power situation at a time when they were in fact, in the face of the Russians, the only actual power in Hungary.*

Consciousness of what the power of the councils is and *must be* arises from the very practice of that power. But at an *impeded* stage of that power it may be very different from what one or another isolated member of a council, or even an entire council, thinks. *Ideology* opposes the truth in acts whose field is the system of the councils; and such ideology manifests itself not only in the form of hostile ideologies, or in the form of ideologies *about the councils* devised by political forces that want to subjugate them, but also in the form of an ideology *in favor of* the power of the councils that restrains and reifies their total theory and practice. A pure councilism will inevitably prove to be an enemy of the reality of the councils. There is a risk that such an ideology, more or less consistently formulated, will be borne by revolutionary organizations that are in principle in favor of the power of the councils. This power, which is itself *the organization of revolutionary society* and whose coherence is objectively determined by the practical necessities of this historical task grasped as a whole, can in no case escape the practical problem posed by *specialist organizations* which, whether enemies of the councils or more or less genuinely in favor of them, will inevitably interfere in their functioning. The masses organized in councils must be aware of this problem and overcome it. This is where councilist theory and the existence of authentically councilist organizations have a great importance. In them already appear certain essential points that will be at stake in the councils and in their own interaction with the councils.

All revolutionary history shows the part played in the failure of the councils by the emergence of a councilist ideology. The ease with which the spontaneous organization of the proletariat in struggle wins its first victories is often the prelude to a second phase in which counter-revolution works from the inside, in which the movement lets go of its reality in order to pursue the illusion that amounts to its defeat. Councilism is the artificial respiration that revives the old world.

Social democrats and Bolsheviks are in agreement in wishing to see in the councils only an auxiliary body of the party and the state. In 1902 Kautsky, worried because the unions were becoming discredited in the eyes of the workers, wanted workers in certain branches of industry to elect "delegates who would form a sort of parliament designed to regulate their work and keep watch over the bureaucratic administration" (*The Social Revolution*). The idea of a hierarchized system of workers' representation culminating in a parliament was to be implemented most convincingly by Ebert, Noske, and Scheidemann.* The way this type of councilism treats the councils was definitively demonstrated—for anyone who doesn't have shit for brains—as long ago as 9 November 1918, when the Social Democrats combatted the spontaneous organization of the councils on its own ground by founding in the *Vorwärts* offices a "Council of the Workers and Soldiers of Berlin" consisting of 12 loyal factory workers along with a few Social-Democratic leaders and functionaries.

Bolshevik councilism has neither Kautsky's naïveté nor Ebert's crudeness. It springs from the most radical base—"All power to the soviets"—and lands on the other side of Kronstadt. In *The Immediate Tasks of the Soviet Government* (April 1918) Lenin adds enzymes to Kautsky's detergent: "Even in the most democratic capitalist republics in the world, the poor never regard the bourgeois parliament as 'their' institution. . . . It is the closeness of the Soviets to the 'people,' to the working people, that creates the special forms of recall and other means of control from below which must now be most zealously developed. For example, the Councils of Public Education—periodic conferences of Soviet electors and their delegates convoked to discuss and control the activities of the Soviet authorities in this field—deserve our full sympathy and support. Nothing could be sillier than to transform the Soviets into something congealed and self-contained. The more resolutely we have to stand for a ruthlessly firm government, for the dictatorship of individuals *in certain processes of work* and in certain aspects of *purely executive* functions, the more varied must be the forms and methods of control from below in order to counteract the slightest hint of any potential distortion of the principles of Soviet government, in order tirelessly and repeatedly to weed out bureaucracy." For Lenin, then, the councils, like charitable institutions, should become pressure groups correcting the inevitable bureaucratization of the state's political and economic functions, respectively handled by the Party and the unions. The councils are a social component that, like Descartes's soul, has to be hooked on somewhere.

Gramsci himself merely cleanses Lenin in a bath of democratic niceties: "The factory commissioners are the only true social (economic and political) representatives of the working class because they are elected under universal suffrage by all the workers in the workplace itself. At the different levels of their hierarchy, the commissioners represent the union of all the workers in various levels of production units (work gang, factory department, union of factories in an industry, union of enterprises in a city, union of production units of mechanical and agricultural industries in a district, a province, a region, the nation, the world), whose councils and system of councils represent the government and the management of society" (article in *Ordine Nuovo*). Since the councils have been reduced to economico-social fragments preparing the way for a "future Soviet republic," it goes without saying that the Party, that "Modern Prince," appears as the indispensable political mediation, as the preexisting *deus ex machina* taking care to ensure its future existence: "The Communist Party is the instrument and historical form of the process of internal liberation thanks to which the workers, from being executants become initiators, from being masses become *leaders and guides,* from being muscles are transformed into minds and wills" (*Ordine Nuovo,* 1919). The tune may change, but the song of councilism remains the same: Councils, Party, State. To treat the councils fragmentarily (economic power, social power, political power), as does the councilist cretinism of the *Révolution Internationale* group of Toulouse, is like thinking that by clenching your ass you'll only be buggered half way.

After 1918 Austro-Marxism also constructed a councilist ideology of its own, in accordance with the slow reformist evolution that it advocated. Max Adler, for example, in his book *Democracy and Workers' Councils,* recognizes councils as instruments of workers' self-education which could end the separation between order-givers and order-takers and serve to form a *homogeneous people* capable of implementing socialist democracy. But he also realizes that the fact that councils of workers hold some power in no way guarantees that they have a coherent revolutionary aim: for that, the worker members of the councils must explicitly want to transform the society and bring about socialism. Since Adler is a theorist of *legalized dual power,* that is, of an absurdity that will never be capable of lasting as it gradually approaches revolutionary consciousness and prudently prepares a revolution for later on, he inevitably overlooks the single really fundamental element of the proletariat's self-education: revolution itself. To replace this irreplaceable terrain of proletarian homogenization and this sole mode of selection *for the very formation of the councils* as well as for the formation of ideas and coherent modes of activity within the councils, Adler comes to the point of imagining that there is no other remedy than this incredibly moronic rule: "The right to vote in workers' council elections must depend on membership in a socialist organization."

Leaving aside the social-democratic or Bolshevik ideologies *about* the councils, which from Berlin to Kronstadt always had a Noske or a Trotsky too many, councilist ideology itself, as manifested in past *councilist organizations* and in some present ones, has always had several general assemblies and imperative mandates too few. All the councils that have existed until now, with the exception of the *agrarian* collectives of Aragon, *saw themselves* as simply "democratically elected councils," even when the highest moments of their practice, when all decisions were made by sovereign general assemblies mandating revocable delegates, contradicted this limitation.

Only historical practice, through which the working class must discover and realize all its possibilities, will indicate the precise organizational forms of council power. On the other hand, it is the immediate task of revolutionaries to determine the fundamental principles of the *councilist organizations* that are going to arise in every country. By formulating some hypotheses and recalling the fundamental requirements of the revolutionary movement, this article—which should be followed by others—is intended to initiate a *genuine and egalitarian* debate. The only people who will be excluded from this debate are those who refuse to pose the problem in these terms, those who in the name of some sub-anarchist spontaneism proclaim their opposition to any form of organization, and who only reproduce the defects and confusion of the old movement—mystics of nonorganization, workers discouraged by having been mixed up with Trotskyist sects too long, students imprisoned in their impoverishment who are incapable of escaping from Bolshevik-type organizational schemas. The situationists are obviously partisans of organization—the existence of the *situationist organization* testifies to that. Those who announce their agreement with our theses while crediting the SI with a vague spontaneism simply don't know how to read.

Organization is indispensable precisely because it isn't everything and doesn't enable everything to be saved or won. Contrary to what butcher Noske said (in *Von Kiel bis Kapp*) about the events of 6 January 1919, the masses did not fail to become "masters of Berlin on noon that day" because they had "fine talkers" instead of "determined leaders," but because the factory councils' form of autonomous organization had not yet attained a sufficient level of autonomy for them to be able to do without "determined leaders" and separate organizations to handle their linkups. The shameful example of Barcelona in May 1937 is another proof of this: the fact that arms were brought out so quickly in response to the Stalinist provocation says a lot for the Catalonian masses' immense capacities for autonomy; but the fact that the order to *surrender* issued by the anarchist ministers was so quickly obeyed demonstrates how much autonomy for victory they *still lacked.* Tomorrow again it will be the workers' degree of autonomy that will decide our fate.

The councilist organizations that will be formed will therefore not fail to recognize and appropriate, as indeed a minimum, the "Minimum Definition of Revolutionary Organizations" adopted by the 7th Conference of the SI (see *Internationale Situationniste* #11). Since their task will be to work toward the power of the councils, which is incompatible with any other form of power, they will be aware that a merely *abstract* agreement with this definition condemns them to nonexistence; this is why their real agreement will be practically demonstrated in the nonhierarchical relations within their groups or sections; in the relations between these groups and with other autonomous groups or organizations; in the development of revolutionary theory and an integral critique of the ruling society; and in the ongoing critique of their own practice. Maintaining a unitary program and practice, they will refuse the old partitioning of the workers' movement into separate organizations (i.e. parties and unions). Despite the beautiful history of the councils, all the councilist organizations of the past that have played a significant role in class struggles have accepted separation into political, economic, and social sectors. One of the few old parties worth analysis, the *Kommunistische Arbeiter Partei Deutschlands* (KAPD, German Communist Workers' Party), adopted a councilist program, but by assigning to itself as its only essential tasks propaganda and theoretical discussion—"the political education of the masses"—it left the role of federating the revolutionary factory organizations to the *Allgemeine Arbeiter Union Deutschlands* (AAUD, General Workers' Union of Germany), a schema not far from traditional syndicalism. Even though the KAPD rejected the Leninist idea of the mass party, along with the parliamentarianism and syndicalism of the KPD (*Kommunistische Partei Deutschlands*—German Communist Party), and preferred to group together politically conscious workers, it nevertheless remained tied to the old hierarchical model of the vanguard party: professionals of Revolution and salaried propagandists. A rejection of this model (in particular, a rejection of the practice of separating the political organization from the revolutionary factory organizations) led in 1920 to the secession of some of the AAUD members, who then formed the AAUD-E (the 'E' for *Einheitsorganisation*—Unified Organization). By the very working of its internal democracy this new unitary organization aimed to accomplish the educative work that had until then devolved on the KAPD, and it simultaneously assigned itself the task of co-ordinating struggles: the factory organizations that it federated were supposed to transform themselves into councils at the revolutionary moment and take over the management of the society. Here again the modern watchword of workers' councils was still mixed with messianic memories of the old revolutionary syndicalism: the factory organizations would magically become councils when all the workers took part in them.

All that led where it would. After the crushing of the 1921 insurrection and the repression of the movement, large numbers of workers, discouraged by the waning prospect of revolution, abandoned factory struggle. The AAUD was only another name for the KAPD, and the AAUD-E saw revolution recede as fast as its membership declined. They were no longer anything but bearers of a *councilist ideology* more and more cut off from reality.

The KAPD's evolution into terrorism and the AAUD's increasing involvement in "bread and butter" issues led to the split between the factory organization and its party in 1929. In 1931 the corpses of the AAUD and the AAUD-E pathetically and without any sound or explicit bases merged in the face of the rise of Nazism. The revolutionary elements of the two organizations regrouped to form the KAUD (*Kommunistische Arbeiter Union Deutschlands*—German Communist Workers' Union). A consciously minority organization, the KAUD was also the only one in the whole movement for councils in Germany that did not claim to take upon itself the future economic (or economico-political as in the case of the AAUD-E) organization of society. It called on the workers to form autonomous groups and to themselves handle the linkups between those groups. But in Germany the KAUD came much too late; by 1931 the revolutionary movement had been dead for nearly ten years.

If only to make them cry, let us remind the retarded devotees of the anarchist–Marxist feud* that the CNT-FAI—with its dead weight of anarchist ideology, but also with its greater practice of liberatory imagination—was akin to the Marxist KAPD-AAUD in its organizational arrangements. In the same way as the German Communist Workers' Party, the Iberian Anarchist Federation saw itself as the *political* organization of the conscious Spanish workers, while its AAUD, the CNT, was supposed to take charge of the management of the future society. The FAI militants, the elite of the proletariat, propagated the anarchist idea among the masses; the CNT did the practical work of organizing the workers in its unions. There were two essential differences, however, the ideological one of which was to bear the fruit one could have expected of it. The first was that the FAI did not strive to take power, but contented itself with influencing the overall policies of the CNT. The second was that the CNT *really* represented the Spanish working class. Adopted on 1 May 1936 at the CNT congress at Saragossa, two months before the revolutionary explosion, one of the most beautiful programs ever proclaimed by a revolutionary organization was partially put into practice by the anarcho-syndicalist masses, while their leaders foundered in ministerialism and class-collaboration. With the pimps of the masses, García Oliver, Secundo Blanco, etc., and the brothel-madam Montseny, the antistate libertarian movement, which had already tolerated the anarcho-trenchist Prince Kropotkin, finally attained the historical consummation of its ideological absolutism: government anarchists.* In the *last* historical battle it was to wage, anarchism was to see all the ideological sauce that comprised its being fall back in its face: State, Freedom, Individual, and other musty ingredients with capital letters; while the libertarian militias, workers, and peasants were saving its honor, making *the greatest practical contribution ever* to the international proletarian movement, burning churches, fighting on all fronts against the bourgeoisie, fascism, and Stalinism, and beginning to *create a truly communist society.*

Some present-day organizations cunningly pretend not to exist. This enables them to avoid bothering with the slightest clarification of the bases on which they assemble any assortment of people (while magically labeling them all "workers"); to avoid giving their semi-members any account of the *informal leadership* that holds the controls; and to thoughtlessly denounce any theoretical expression and any other form of organization as automatically evil and harmful. Thus the *Informations, Correspondance Ouvrières* group writes in a recent bulletin (*ICO #84*, August 1969): "Councils are the transformation of strike committees under the influence of the situation itself and in response to the very necessities of the struggle, within the very dialectic of that struggle. Any other attempt, at any moment in a struggle, to declare the necessity of creating workers' councils reveals a councilist ideology, such as can be seen in diverse forms in certain unions, in the PSU, or among the situationists. The very concept of council excludes any ideology." These individuals clearly know nothing about ideology—their own ideology is distinguished from more fully developed ones only by its spineless eclecticism. But they have heard (perhaps from Marx, perhaps only from the SI) that ideology has become a bad thing. They take advantage of this to try to have it believed that any theoretical work — which they avoid as if it were a sin—is an ideology, among the situationists exactly as in the PSU. But their gallant recourse to the "dialectic" and the "concept" which they have now added to their vocabulary in no way saves them from an imbecilic ideology of which the above quotation alone is evidence enough. If one idealistically relies on the council "concept" or, what is even more euphoric, on the practical inactivity of ICO, to "exclude all ideology" in the real councils, one must expect the worst—we have seen that historical experience justifies no such optimism in this regard. The supersession of the primitive council form can only come from struggles becoming more conscious, and from struggles for *more consciousness*. ICO's mechanistic image of the strike committee's perfect automatic response to "necessities," which presents the council as automatically coming into existence at the appropriate time *provided that one makes sure not to talk about it,* completely ignores the experience of the revolutions of our century, which shows that "the situation itself" is just as ready to crush the councils, or to enable them to be manipulated and co-opted, as it is to give rise to them.

Let us leave this contemplative ideology, this pathetic caricature of the natural sciences which would have us observe the emergence of a proletarian revolution almost as if it were a solar eruption. Councilist organizations will be formed, though they must be quite the contrary of general staffs that would cause the councils to rise up on order. In spite of the new period of open social crisis we have entered since the occupations movement, and the proliferation of encouraging situations here and there, from Italy to the USSR, it is quite likely that genuine councilist organizations will still take a long time to form and that other important revolutionary situations will occur before such organizations are in a position to intervene in them at a significant level. One must not play with councilist organization by setting up or supporting premature parodies of it. But the councils will certainly have greater chances of maintaining themselves as sole power if they contain conscious councilists and if there is a real appropriation of councilist theory.

In contrast to the council as permanent *basic unit* (ceaselessly setting up and modifying councils of delegates emanating from itself), as the assembly in which all the workers of an enterprise (workshop and factory councils) and all the inhabitants of an urban district who have rallied to the revolution (street councils, neighborhood councils) must participate, a councilist organization, in order to guarantee its coherence and the authentic working of its internal democracy, must *choose its members* in accordance with what they explicitly want and what they actually can do. As for the councils, their coherence is guaranteed by the single fact that they are *the sole power;* that they eliminate all other power and decide everything. This practical experience is the terrain where people learn how to become conscious of their own action, where they "realize philosophy." It goes without saying that their majorities also run the risk of making lots of momentary mistakes and not having the time or the means to rectify them. But they know that their fate is the product of their own decisions, and that they will be destroyed by the repercussions of any mistakes they don't correct.

Within councilist organizations real equality of everyone in making decisions and carrying them out will not be an empty slogan or an abstract demand. Of course, not all the members of an organization will have the same talents (it is obvious, for example, that a worker will invariably write better than a student). But because in its aggregate the organization will have all the talents it needs, no hierarchy of individual talents will come to undermine its democracy. It is neither membership in a councilist organization nor the proclamation of an ideal equality that will enable all its members to be beautiful and intelligent and to live well; but only their real aptitudes for becoming more beautiful and more intelligent and for living better, freely developing in the only game that's worth the pleasure: the destruction of the old world.

In the social movements that are going to spread, the councilists will refuse to let themselves be elected to strike committees. On the contrary, their task will be to act in such a way as to encourage the rank-and-file self-organization of the workers into general assemblies that decide how the struggle is carried out. It will be necessary to begin to understand that the absurd call for a "central strike committee" proposed by some naïve individuals during the May 1968 occupations movement would, had it succeeded, have sabotaged the movement toward the autonomy of the masses even more quickly than actually happened, since almost all the strike committees were controlled by the Stalinists.

Given that it is not for us to forge a plan for all time, and that one step forward by the real movement of the councils will be worth more than a dozen councilist programs, it is difficult to state precise hypotheses regarding the relation of councilist organizations with councils during a revolutionary situation. A councilist organization—which knows itself to be *separated* from the proletariat—must cease to exist as a separate organization in the moment that abolishes separations; and it will have to do this even if the complete freedom of association guaranteed by the power of the councils allows various parties and organizations that are enemies of this power to survive. It may be doubted, however, that it is feasible to immediately dissolve all councilist organizations the very instant the councils first appear, as Pannekoek* wished. The councilists should speak as councilists within the council, rather than staging an exemplary dissolution of their organizations only to regroup them on the side and play pressure-group politics in the general assembly. In this way it will be easier and more legitimate for them to combat and denounce the inevitable presence of bureaucrats, spies, and ex-scabs who will infiltrate here and there. They will also have to struggle against fake councils or fundamentally reactionary ones (e.g. police councils) which will not fail to appear. They will act in such a way that the unified power of the councils does not recognize such bodies or their delegates. Because the infiltration of other organizations is exactly the contrary of the ends they are pursuing, and because they refuse any incoherence within themselves, councilist organizations will prohibit any dual membership. As we have said, all the workers of a factory must take part in the council, or at least all those who accept the rules of its game. The solution to the problem of whether to accept participation in the council by "those who yesterday had to be thrown out of the factory at gunpoint" (Barth)* will be found only in practice.

Ultimately, a councilist organization will stand or fall solely by the coherence of its theory and action and by its struggle for the complete elimination of all power remaining external to the councils or trying to make itself independent of them. But in order to simplify the discussion right off by refusing even to take into consideration a mass of councilist pseudo-organizations that may be simulated by students or obsessive professional militants, let us say that it does not seem to us that an organization can be recognized as councilist if it is not comprised of at least 2/3 workers. As this proportion might pass for a concession, let us add that it seems to us indispensable to correct it with this rider: in all delegations to central conferences at which decisions may be taken that have not previously been provided for by imperative mandates, workers must make up 3/4 of the participants. In sum, the inverse proportion of the first congresses of the "Russian Social-Democratic Workers' Party."

It is known that we have no inclination toward workerism of any form whatsoever. The above considerations refer to workers who have "become dialecticians," as they will have to become *en masse* in the exercise of the power of the councils. But on the one hand, the workers continue to be the *central* force capable of bringing the existing functioning of society to a halt and the *indispensable* force for reinventing all its bases. On the other hand, although a councilist organization obviously must not separate other categories of wage-earners, notably intellectuals, from itself, it is in any case important that the dubious importance the latter may assume should be severely restricted: not only by verifying, by considering all aspects of their lives, that such intellectuals are really councilist revolutionaries, but also by seeing to it that there are as few of them in the organization as possible.

A councilist organization will not consent to speak on equal terms with other organizations unless they are consistent partisans of proletarian autonomy; just as the councils will not only have to free themselves from the grip of parties and unions, but must also reject any tendency aiming to pigeonhole them in some limited position and to negotiate with them as one power to another. The councils are the only power or they are nothing. The means of their victory are already their victory. With the lever of the councils *plus* the fulcrum of the total negation of the spectacle-commodity society, the Earth can be raised.

The victory of the councils is not the end of the revolution, but the beginning of it.

RENÉ RIESEL

Notice to the Civilized Concerning Generalized Self-Management

"Never sacrifice present good for the good to come. Enjoy the moment. Avoid any matrimonial or other association that does not satisfy your passions from the very beginning. Why should you work for the good to come when it will exceed your desires anyway and you will have in the Combined Order only one displeasure, that of not being able to double the length of days in order to accommodate the immense range of enjoyments available to you?"

—Charles Fourier, *Notice to the Civilized Concerning the Next Social Metamorphosis*

1

Though it failed to go all the way, the May 1968 occupations movement has given rise to a confused popular awareness of the necessity of a supersession. The imminence of a total upheaval, felt by everyone, must now discover its practice: the passage to generalized self-management* through the establishment of workers' councils. The point to which the revolutionary upsurge has brought people's consciousness is now going to become a point of departure.

2

History is answering the question Lloyd George posed to the workers, a question which has since been taken up in chorus by all the servants of the old world: "You want to destroy our social organization, but what will you put in its place?" We know the answer thanks to the profusion of little Lloyd Georges who advocate the state dictatorship of a proletariat of their choice, counting on the working class to organize itself in councils in order to dissolve the existing dictatorship and elect another.

3

Each time the proletariat takes the risk of changing the world it rediscovers its historical memory. The project of establishing a society of councils—a project until now intermingled with the history of its crushing in different periods—reveals the reality of its past possibilities through the possibility of its immediate realization. This has been made evident to all the workers since May, when Stalinism and its Trotskyist residues showed by their aggressive weakness their inability to crush a council movement if one had appeared, and by their force of inertia their ability still to impede the emergence of one. Without really manifesting itself, a movement toward councils was implicitly present in the clash of two contradictory forces: the internal logic of the occupations and the repressive logic of the parties and labor unions. Those who still open their Lenin to find out what is to be done are only rummaging in the trashcan of history.

4

Many people intuitively rejected any organization not directly emanating from the proletariat negating itself as proletariat, and this feeling was inseparable from the feeling that an everyday life without dead time was finally possible. In this sense the notion of workers' councils is the first principle of generalized self-management.

5

May 1968 marked an essential phase in the long revolution: the individual history of millions of people, each day seeking an authentic life, linking up with the historical movement of the proletariat in struggle against the whole *system* of alienations. This spontaneous unity of action, which was the passional motive power of the occupations movement, can only develop its theory and practice unitarily. What was in everyone's heart is going to be in everyone's head. Having felt that they "could no longer live like before, nor even a little better than before," many people are inclined to prolong the memory of this exemplary moment of life and the briefly experienced hope of a great possibility —to prolong them in a line of force which, to become revolutionary, lacks only a greater lucidity on generalized self-management, i.e. on the *historical construction of free individual relations.*

6

Only the proletariat, by negating itself, gives clear shape to the project of generalized self-management, because it bears that project within itself objectively and subjectively. This is why the first specifics will come from the unity of its combat in everyday life and on the front of history; and from the consciousness that all demands are realizable right away, but only by the proletariat itself. In this sense the importance of a revolutionary organization will henceforth be measured by its ability to hasten its own disappearance in the reality of the society of the councils.

7

Workers' councils constitute a new type of social organization through which the proletariat puts an end to the proletarianization of everyone. Generalized self-management is simply the general framework in accordance with which the councils unitarily inaugurate a style of life based on ongoing individual and collective liberation.

8

It is clear from all these theses that the project of generalized self-management requires as many specifics as there are desires in each revolutionary, and as many revolutionaries as there are people dissatisfied with their everyday life. Spectacle-commodity society produces both the conditions that repress subjectivity and—contradictorily, through the refusal it provokes—the positivity of subjectivity; just as the formation of the councils, similarly arising out of the struggle against overall oppression, produces the conditions for a permanent realization of subjectivity without any limits but its own impatience to make history. Thus generalized self-management is linked to the capacity of the councils to realize the imagination historically.

9

Outside generalized self-management, workers' councils lose their sense. Anyone who speaks of the councils as separate economic or social organisms, anyone who does not place them at the center of the revolution of everyday life with the practice this entails, must be treated as a future bureaucrat and thus as a present enemy.

10

One of Fourier's great merits is to have shown the necessity of creating immediately—and for us this means from the inception of generalized insurrection—the objective conditions for individual liberation. For everyone the beginning of the revolutionary moment must mark an *immediate rise in the pleasure of living*—a consciously experienced entry into the totality.

11

The accelerating rate at which reformism, with its tricontinental bellyache, is leaving behind ridiculous leftist droppings—all those little Maoist, Trotskyist, and Guevaraist dungpiles—proves by its smell what the Right, and especially the socialists and Stalinists, have long sensed: partial demands are fundamentally contrary to a total change.

But trying to cut off the hydra heads of reformism one by one is futile. Better to overthrow the old ruse of history once and for all: this would seem to be the final solution to the problem of co-opters. This implies a strategy that sparks the general conflagration by means of increasingly frequent insurrectional moments; and a tactic of qualitative progression in which inevitably partial actions each entail, as their necessary and sufficient condition, the liquidation of the world of the commodity. It's time to begin the *positive sabotage* of spectacle-commodity society. As long as our mass tactics stick to the law of immediate pleasure there will be no need to worry about the outcome.

12

It is easy to mention here, merely as suggestive examples, a few possibilities which will quickly be surpassed by the practice of liberated workers: On every occasion—openly during strikes, more or less secretly during work—*initiate the reign of freeness* by giving away factory and warehouse goods to friends and revolutionaries, by making gift objects (radio transmitters, toys, weapons, clothes, ornaments, machines for various purposes), and by organizing "giveaway" strikes in department stores; *break the laws of exchange and begin the end of wage labor* by collectively appropriating products of work and collectively using machines for personal and revolutionary purposes; *depreciate the function of money* by spreading payment strikes (rent, taxes, installment payments, transportation fares, etc.); *encourage everyone's creativity* by starting up provisioning and production sectors exclusively under workers' control, even if this can only be done intermittently, while regarding this experimentation as necessarily groping and subject to improvement; *wipe out hierarchies and the spirit of sacrifice* by treating bosses and union bureaucrats as they deserve and by rejecting militantism; *act unitarily everywhere against all separations; draw theory from every type of practice and vice versa* by composing leaflets, posters, songs, etc.

13

The proletariat has already shown that it knows how to respond to the oppressive complexity of capitalist and "socialist" states by the simplicity of organization carried out *directly* by and for everyone. In our time questions of survival are posed only on the condition that they never be solved; in contrast, the problems of the history to be lived are clearly posed through the project of workers' councils—positively in that the councils are the basis of a unitary passional and industrial society, negatively in that they imply total opposition to the state.

14

Because they exercise no power separate from the decisions of their members, the councils tolerate no power other than their own. Encouraging antistate actions everywhere should thus not be understood to imply a premature creation of councils which would lack absolute power over their own areas, would be separated from generalized self-management, and would be inevitably emptied of content and susceptible to every kind of ideology. The only lucid forces that can presently respond to the history that *has* been made with the history *to be made* will be the revolutionary organizations that are developing, in the project of the councils, an equal awareness of the adversary to be combatted and the allies to be supported. An important aspect of such a struggle is manifesting itself before our eyes with the appearance of a *dual power.* In factories, offices, streets, houses, barracks, and schools a new reality is taking shape: contempt for bosses, regardless of their labels or their rhetoric. From now on this contempt must be pushed to its logical conclusion by demonstrating, through the concerted action of workers, that the bosses are not only contemptible but also useless, and that even from their own utilitarian point of view they can be eliminated with impunity.

15

Recent history will soon come to be seen, by rulers as well as revolutionaries, in terms of an alternative that concerns them both: generalized self-management or insurrectional chaos; new society of abundance or social disintegration, pillage, terrorism, and repression. The struggle within dual power is already inseparable from such a choice. Our coherence requires that the paralysis and destruction of all forms of government not be distinct from the construction of councils. If our adversary has even the slightest prudence it should realize that only an organization of new everyday relationships can prevent the spread of what an American police specialist has already called "our nightmare": small insurgent commandos bursting out of subway entrances, shooting from rooftops, taking advantage of the mobility and limitless resources of urban guerrilla warfare to fell the police, liquidate the servants of authority, stir up riots, and destroy the economy. But we don't have to save the rulers in spite of themselves. It will be enough to prepare the councils and ensure their self-defense by every means. In one of Lope de Vega's plays some villagers, driven beyond endurance by the exactions of a royal functionary, put him to death. When they are brought before the magistrate and charged to name the guilty party, all respond with the name of their village, "Fuenteovejuna." This tactic, used by many Asturian miners against pro-company engineers, has the drawback of smacking too much of terrorism and the *watrinage* tradition.* Generalized self-management will be our "Fuenteovejuna." It is no longer enough for collective action to discourage repression (imagine the powerlessness of the forces of order if during an occupations movement bank employees seized the funds); it must at the same time encourage progression toward a greater revolutionary coherence. The councils represent order in the face of the decomposition of the state, whose form is being contested by the rise of regional nationalisms and whose basic principle is being contested by social demands. To the pseudoproblems they see posed by this decomposition, the police can respond only by estimating the number of deaths. Only the councils offer a definitive solution. What prevents looting? The organization of distribution and the end of the commodity system. What prevents sabotage of production? The appropriation of the machines by collective creativity. What prevents explosions of anger and violence? The end of the proletariat through the collective construction of everyday life. There is no other justification for our struggle than the immediate satisfaction of this project —than what satisfies us immediately.

16

Generalized self-management has only one basis, one motive force: the exhilaration of universal freedom. This is quite enough to enable us right now to infer the rigor that will be necessary for its elaboration. Such rigor must henceforth characterize revolutionary councilist organizations; conversely, their practice will already contain the experience of direct democracy. This will enable us to concretize certain formulas more rigorously. A principle like "All power to the general assembly," for example, also implies that whatever escapes the direct control of the autonomous assembly will recreate, in mediated forms, all the autonomous varieties of oppression. Through its representatives, the whole assembly with all its tendencies must be present at the moment of decision. Even though the destruction of the state rules out a repetition of the "Supreme Soviet" farce, it is still necessary to take care that organization is simple enough to preclude the possibility of any neobureaucracy arising. But the abundance of telecommunications technologies—which might at first sight appear as a pretext for the continuation or return of specialists—is precisely what makes possible the constant control of delegates by the base, the immediate confirmation, correction, or repudiation of their decisions at all levels. Telex, computers, television, etc., are thus the inalienable possession of the primary assemblies, making it possible for those assemblies to be aware of and affect events everywhere. In the composition of a council (there will no doubt be neighborhood, city, regional, and international councils) it will be a good idea for the assembly to elect and control: an *equipping section* for the purpose of collecting requests for supplies, determining the possibilities of production, and coordinating these two sectors; an *information section* charged with keeping in constant touch with the experiences of other councils; a coordination section whose task it will be (to the extent permitted by the necessities of the struggle) to enrichen personal relationships, to radicalize the Fourierist project, to take care of requirements of passional satisfaction, to equip individual desires, to furnish whatever is necessary for experiments and adventures, to harmonize playful possibilities of organizing necessary tasks (cleaning, babysitting, education, cooking contests, etc.); and a *self-defense section*. Each section is responsible to the full assembly; delegates regularly meet and report on their activities and are revocable and subject to vertical and horizontal rotation.*

17

The logic of the commodity system, sustained by alienated practice, must be answered with the practice immediately implied by the social logic of desires. The first revolutionary measures will necessarily relate to reducing labor time and to the greatest possible reduction of forced labor. The councils will naturally distinguish between *priority sectors* (food, transportation, telecommunications, metallurgy, construction, clothing, electronics, printing, armament, health care, comfort, and in general whatever material equipment is necessary for the permanent transformation of historical conditions); *reconversion sectors,* whose workers consider that they can detourn them to revolutionary uses; and *parasitical sectors,* whose assemblies decide purely and simply to suppress them. The workers of the eliminated sectors (administration, bureaucratic agencies, spectacle production, purely commercial industries) will obviously prefer to put in three or four hours a week at some work they have freely chosen from among the priority sectors rather than eight hours a day at their old workplace. The councils will experiment with attractive forms of carrying out necessary tasks, not in order to hide their unpleasant aspects, but in order to compensate for such unpleasantness with a playful organization of it, and as far as possible to eliminate such tasks in favor of creativity (in accordance with the principle: "Work no, pleasure yes"). As the transformation of the world comes to be identical with the construction of life, necessary labor will disappear in the pleasure of history for itself.

18

To state that the councilist organization of distribution and production prevents looting and the destruction of machinery and goods is still to remain within a purely negative, antistate perspective. The councils, as organization of the new society, will eliminate the element of separation still present in this negativity by means of a *collective politics of desires*. Wage labor can be ended the moment the councils are set up, the moment the "equipment and provisions" section of each council organizes production and distribution in accordance with the desires of the plenary assembly. At that point, in tribute to the best Bolshevik prediction, urinals can be made out of gold and sterling silver, and dubbed "lenins."*

19

Generalized self-management implies the extension of the councils. At first, work areas will be taken over by the workers concerned, grouped in councils. In order to rid these first councils of their corporative, guildlike aspect, the workers will as soon as possible open them to their friends, to people living in the same neighborhood, and to volunteers coming in from the parasitical sectors, so that they rapidly take the form of local councils—which might themselves be grouped together in "Communes" of more or less equal size (perhaps 8000 to 10,000 people?).

20

The internal extension of the councils must be matched by their geographical extension. It will be necessary to vigilantly maintain the most complete radicality of the liberated zones, without Fourier's illusion as to the contagiousness of the first communes, but also without underestimating the seductiveness of any authentic experience of liberation once the intervening veils of falsification have been swept aside. The councils' self-defense thus illustrates the formula: "Armed truth is revolutionary."

21

Generalized self-management will soon have its own *code of possibilities*, designed to liquidate repressive legislation and its millennial domination. Perhaps it will appear during a period of dual power, before the judicial machinery and the penal system scum have been annihilated. The new rights of man humanity—everyone's right to live as they please, to build their own house, to participate in all assemblies, to arm themselves, to live as nomads, to publish what they think (to each his or her own wall-newspaper), to love without restraints; the right to meet, the right to the material equipment necessary for the realization of desires, the right to creativity, the right to the conquest of nature, the end of commodity time, the end of history in itself, the realization of art and the imagination, etc.—await their antilegislators.

RAOUL VANEIGEM

The Conquest of Space in the Time of Power

1

Science in the service of capital, the commodity, and the spectacle is nothing other than capitalized knowledge, fetishism of idea and method, alienated image of human thought. Pseudogreatness of man, its passive knowledge of a mediocre reality is the magical justification of a race of slaves.

2

It has been a long time since the power of knowledge has been transformed into power's knowledge. Contemporary science, experimental heir of the religion of the Middle Ages, fulfills the same functions in relation to the present class society: it compensates for people's everyday stupidity with its eternal specialist intelligence. Science sings in numerals of the grandeur of the human race, but it is in fact nothing other than the organized sum of man's limitations and alienations.

3

Just as industry, which was intended to free people from work through machinery, has so far done nothing but alienate them in the work of the machines, so science, which was intended to free people historically and rationally from nature, has done nothing but alienate them in an irrational and antihistorical society. Mercenary of separate thought, science works for survival and therefore cannot conceive of life except as a mechanical or moral formula. It does not conceive of man as subject, nor of human thought as action, and it is for this reason that it does not comprehend history as deliberate activity and makes people "patient(s)" in its hospitals.

4

Founded on the essential deceptiveness of its function, science can only lie to itself. Its pretentious mercenaries have preserved from their ancestor priests the taste and need for mystery. A dynamic element in the justification of states, the scientific profession jealously guards the laws of its guild and the "Machina ex Deo" secrets that make it a despicable sect. It is hardly surprising, for example, that doctors— those repairmen of labor-power—have illegible handwriting: it is part of the police code of monopolized survival.

5

But if the *historical* and *ideological* identification of science with temporal powers clearly reveals that it is a servant of states, and therefore fools no one, it was not until our own time that the last separations disappeared between class society and a science that had professed to be neutral and "at the service of humanity." The present impossibility of scientific research and application without enormous means has effectively placed spectacularly concentrated knowledge in the hands of the ruling powers and has steered it toward statist objectives. There is no longer any science that is not in the service of the economy, the military, and ideology. And the science of ideology reveals its other side, the ideology of science.

6

Power, which cannot tolerate a vacuum, has never forgiven the celestial regions for being terrains left open to the imagination. Since the origin of class society the unreal source of separate power has always been placed in the skies. When the state justified itself religiously, heaven was included in the *time* of religion; now that the state wishes to justify itself scientifically, the sky is in the *space* of science. From Galileo to Werner von Braun, it is nothing but a question of state ideology: religion wished to preserve its time, therefore no one was allowed to tamper with its space. Faced with the impossibility of prolonging its time, power must make its space boundless.

7

If the heart transplant is still a crude artisan technique that does not make people forget science's chemical and nuclear massacres, the "Conquest of the Cosmos" is the greatest spectacular expression of scientific oppression. The space scientist is to the smalltime doctor what Interpol is to the policeman on the beat.

8

The heaven formerly promised by priests in black cassocks is now really being seized by white-uniformed astronauts. Sexless and super-bureaucratized neuters, the first men to go beyond the atmosphere are the stars of a spectacle that hangs over our heads day and night, that can conquer temperature and distance, and that oppresses us from above like the cosmic dust of God. As an example of survival in its highest manifestation, the astronauts make an unintentional critique of the Earth: condemned to an orbital trajectory—in order to avoid dying from cold and hunger—they submissively ("for technical reasons") accept the boredom and poverty of being satellites. Inhabitants of an urbanism of necessity in their cabins, prisoners of scientific gadgetry, they exemplify *in vitro* the plight of their contemporaries: in spite of their distance they do not escape the designs of power. Flying billboards, the astronauts float in space or leap about on the moon in order to make people march to the time of work.

9

And if the Christian astronauts of the West and the bureaucratic cosmonauts of the East amuse themselves with metaphysics and secular morals (Gagarin "did not see God"; Borman prayed for the little Earth), it is in obedience to their spatial "assignment," which must be the essence of their religion; as with Saint-Exupéry, who spoke the lowest imbecilities from high altitudes, but whose essence lay in his threefold role of militarist, patriot, and idiot.

10

The conquest of space is part of the planetary hope of an economic system which, saturated with commodities, spectacles, and power, ejaculates into space when it arrives at the end of the noose of its terrestrial contradictions. Functioning as a new "America," space must serve the states as a new territory for wars and colonies—a new territory to which to send producer-consumers and thus enable the system to break out of the planet's limitations. Province of accumulation, space is destined to become an accumulation of provinces—for which laws, treaties, and international tribunals already exist. A new Yalta, the dividing up of space shows the inability of the capitalists and bureaucrats to resolve their antagonisms and struggles here on Earth.

11

But the revolutionary old mole, which is now gnawing at the foundations of the system, will destroy the barriers that separate science from the general knowledge that will be accessible to everyone when people finally begin making their own history. No more ideas of separate power, no more power of separate ideas. Generalized self-management of the never-ending transformation of the world by the masses will make science a basic banality, and no longer a truth of state.

12

Humanity will enter into space to make the universe the playground of the last revolt: the revolt that will go against the limitations imposed by nature. Once the walls have been smashed that now separate people from science, the conquest of space will no longer be an economic or military "promotional" gimmick, but the blossoming of human freedoms and fulfillments, attained by a race of gods. We will not enter into space as employees of an astronautic administration or as "volunteers" of a state project, but as masters without slaves reviewing their domains: the entire universe pillaged for the workers' councils.

EDUARDO ROTHE

The Latest Exclusions

On 21 December 1967 Timothy Clark, Christopher Gray, and Donald Nicholson-Smith were excluded from the SI, just as they were getting ready to publish a journal in England and begin a group activity there. (Charles Radcliffe had resigned a few weeks earlier for personal reasons.)

The divergences, which had been nonexistent or at least unnoticed in all other respects, suddenly appeared not in regard to their activity in England but on the issue of the SI's relations and possible action in the United States. Vaneigem had gone to New York in November as the delegate of all the situationists and carried out his mandate precisely, notably in discussions with the comrades with whom in everyone's opinion—including that of the British—we had the most developed contacts, and who have since formed our American section.* Vaneigem refused to meet a certain Ben Morea, publisher of the bulletin *Black Mask*, with whom our American comrades were in conflict on virtually every issue concerning revolutionary action and whose intellectual honesty they even questioned. Vaneigem had, moreover, already been obliged to break off a conversation with a certain Hoffman, who was admiringly expounding to him a *mystical* interpretation of his text "Basic Banalities," and who was currently the main collaborator in Morea's publications: the enormity of this fact naturally led Vaneigem no longer even to want to discuss our other, more general divergences with Morea.*

Everything seemed quite clear upon Vaneigem's return to Europe. But Morea wrote to the London situationists to complain of having been misrepresented to Vaneigem. Upon the insistence of the English comrades, who were concerned about fully clarifying the matter in the unlikely case that Morea himself was under some misapprehension, we wrote a collective letter detailing all the facts of the situation. The English agreed, however, that this would be the last response we would send him. Morea wrote once again to all of us saying that the reasons we had given were false pretexts and that the real dispute lay elsewhere; he insulted our New York friends and this time questioned Vaneigem's testimony. *Despite their express commitment*, the English responded again to Morea, saying that they no longer understood what was going on and that "someone" must be lying. They showed more and more indulgence toward Morea and more and more mistrust of our American friends; and even of Vaneigem, though refusing to openly admit it. We called on the three English to rectify this outrageous, publicly aired vacillation by immediately breaking with the falsifier and his mystical acolyte. They accepted this demand in principle, but equivocated and finally refused to implement it. We then had to break with them. In three weeks this discussion had given rise to two meetings in Paris and London and to the exchange of a dozen long letters. Our patience had been rather excessive, but what had at first seemed to be merely a surprising slowness in reasoning increasingly began to appear as an intentional (though still inexplicable) obstruction. Up to the moment of their exclusion, however, the discussion had never concerned anything but the details described here and the questions of method it so strangely raised regarding the SI's solidarity and general criteria for breaking (for the English never denied that Morea was teamed up with a mystical idiot).

Gray later passed through New York and sadly related, to whoever would listen, that his stillborn group had concerned itself directly with America in order to save the revolutionary project there from a detrimental incomprehension on the part of the continental European situationists (and of the Americans themselves). The English comrades themselves had not felt sufficiently appreciated. They hadn't dared to say so, but they were pained by the Continentals' lack of interest in *what they were going to do*. They were left isolated in their country—all surrounded by water. A more "theoretical" reason emerged *after* the discussion: England being (according to them) much closer to a revolutionary crisis than continental Europe, we "Continental" theorists were supposedly moved by spite at seeing that "our" theories would be realized somewhere else. The dubiousness of this historical law of Anglo-American revolutionism was demonstrated only five months later. But leaving aside the comical aspect of their belated self-justification, it has a rather ignoble side: The spite which they attributed to us over the supposedly impending foreign fulfillment of "our" theory would seem to imply that we are seeking revolutions in "our own" countries in order to have the chance to take up governmental positions. Their imputation of sordid motives to us seems rather to be a *projection* of the English ex-situationists' own hearkening back to the era before America's War of Independence, since they seem to want to direct the American revolutionary movement from London. This whole ridiculous geopolitical perspective naturally collapsed the moment they were excluded.

We should mention that during the two years we had known him, Donald Nicholson-Smith was well liked and in every way highly regarded by all of us. Unfortunately, once he returned to London he became less rigorous and less lucid, passing under the influence of two *poorly chosen* fellow situationists and of various persons outside the SI. When, six months later, he wrote us two letters asking to see us again in order to clear up the "misunderstanding," we regretfully felt obliged to refuse even a personal meeting. The whole affair had been too dubious, and the followup of Gray's activity has continued to be so.

Gray now publishes a rag called *King Mob* which passes, quite wrongly, for being slightly pro-situationist, and in which one can read eulogies to the eternal Morea. Since Morea is all that Gray has left, Gray and his acolytes have gone so far as to *conceal* certain of Morea's current writings that would be too embarrassing to reveal to the people in their entourage who they want to continue to respect their idol; and they make the ludicrous contention that Morea had the merit of transferring certain radical positions "from the situationist salon" to street fighting—they say this a year after the occupations movement!

Gray, too, tried to reestablish contact with us, but surreptitiously, through the intermediary of a certain Allan Green, who pretended not to know him but was unmasked at the second meeting. Fine work, and as cleverly conducted as might have been expected! The "unique" Garnautins must be turning over in their university graves in envy of such a worthy successor.

It will be noted that for nearly two years there have been no other exclusions. We must admit that this notable success is not entirely due to the real elevation of consciousness and coherent radicality of individuals in the present revolutionary period. It is also due to the fact that the SI, applying with increasing rigor its previous decisions on the preliminary examination of those wanting to join it, has during the same period refused some fifty or sixty requests for admission—which has spared us an equal number of exclusions.

The Elite and the Backward
(excerpt)

The situationists are undoubtedly very criticizable. So far, unfortunately, almost no one has made any of these critiques—that is, the intelligent and precise critiques, made without bad faith, that revolutionaries could make and will one day easily be capable of making regarding many of our theses and many aspects of our activity. But the manner in which many present-day revolutionaries spread inept objections or accusations, as if to repress the problem with the lamentable reflexes acquired during their previous period of defeats and nonexistence, only reveals a persistent leftist sectarian poverty, or even miserable *ulterior motives*.

Let us say first of all that, just as we find it quite natural that bourgeois, bureaucrats, and intellectual co-opters hate us, we recognize that would-be revolutionaries who claim to be opposed on principle to any form of organization based on a precise platform, entailing the practical co-responsibility of its participants, will naturally condemn us completely since we manifestly have a contrary opinion and practice. But all the others? It is a clear demonstration of dishonesty and an *implicit avowal of aims of domination* to accuse the SI of constituting a dominating organization when we have gone to great lengths to make it almost impossible to become a member of the SI* (which seems to us to destroy at the roots any concrete risk of our becoming a "leadership" vis-à-vis even the slightest fraction of the masses); and considering, in addition, that it is quite clear that we have never *exploited* our "intellectual prestige," either by frequenting any bourgeois or intellectual circles (much less by accepting any of their "honors" or remunerations), or by competing with the multitude of little leftist sects for the control or admiration of the miserable student public, or by trying to exert the slightest secret influence, *or even the slightest direct or indirect presence,* in the autonomous revolutionary organizations whose existence we and a few others have predicted, and which are now beginning to take shape.

Those who have never accomplished anything apparently feel that they have to attribute the scandalous fact that we *have* been able to accomplish something to imaginary goals *and means.* In reality, it is because we shock certain people by refusing contact with them, or even their requests for admission to the SI, that we are accused of being an "elite" and of aspiring to dominate those whom we don't even want to know! But what "elitist" role are we supposed to have reserved for ourselves? A theoretical one? We have said that the workers *must become dialecticians* and themselves take care of all their theoretical and practical problems.* Those who are concerned with running their own affairs need only appropriate our *methods,* instead of lapping up the latest rumors about us, and they will become that much more independent from us. [. . .]

Cinema and Revolution

Berlin Film Festival correspondent J.P. Picaper is awestruck by the fact that "in *The Gay Science* (an ORTF–Radio Stuttgart production, banned in France) Godard has pushed his admirable self-critique to the point of projecting sequences shot in the dark or even of leaving the spectator for an almost unbearable length of time facing a blank screen" (*Le Monde,* 8 July 1969). Without seeking more precisely what constitutes "an almost unbearable length of time" for this critic, we can see that Godard, following the latest fashions as always, is adopting a destructive style just as belatedly plagiarized and pointless as all the rest of his work, this negation having been expressed in the cinema* before he had ever begun the long series of pretentious pseudoinnovations that aroused such enthusiasm among student audiences during the previous period. The same journalist reports that Godard, through one of the characters in his short film *L'Amour,* confesses that "revolution cannot be put into images" because "the cinema is the art of lying." The cinema has no more been an "art of lying" than has any of the rest of art, which was dead in its totality long before Godard, who has not *even* been a modern artist, that is, who has not even been capable of the slightest personal originality. This Maoist liar is thus winding up his bluff by trying to arouse admiration for his brilliant discovery of a noncinema cinema, while denouncing a sort of inevitable falsehood in which he has participated, but no more so than have many others. Godard was in fact immediately *outmoded* by the May 1968 revolt, which caused him to be recognized as a spectacular manufacturer of a superficial, pseudocritical, *co-optive* art rummaged out of the trash-cans of the past (see "The Role of Godard" in *Internationale Situationniste* #10). At that point Godard's career as a filmmaker was essentially over, and he was personally insulted and ridiculed on several occasions by revolutionaries who happened to cross his path.

The cinema as a means of revolutionary communication is not inherently mendacious just because Godard or Jacopetti* has touched it, any more than all political analysis is doomed to duplicity just because Stalinists have written. Several new filmmakers in various countries are currently attempting to utilize films as means of revolutionary critique, and some of them will partially succeed in this. However, the limitations both in their aesthetic conceptions and even in their grasp of the nature of the present revolution will in our opinion prevent them for some time still from going as far as is necessary. We believe that at the moment only the situationists' positions and methods, as formulated by René Viénet in our previous issue ["The Situationists and the New Forms of Action Against Art and Politics"], are adequate for a directly revolutionary use of cinema—though political and economic conditions still present obvious obstacles to the creation of such films.

It is known that Eisenstein wanted to make a film of *Capital*. Considering his formal conceptions and political submissiveness, it can be doubted if his film would have been faithful to Marx's text. But for our part, we are confident that we can do better. For example, as soon as it becomes possible Guy Debord will himself make a cinematic adaptation of *The Society of the Spectacle* that will certainly not fall short of his book.

The Organization Question for the SI

1. Everything the SI has been known for up till now belongs to a period that is fortunately over. (More precisely, it can be said that that was our "second period," if the 1957–1962 activity that centered around the supersession of art is counted as the first.)

2. The new revolutionary tendencies of present-day society, however weak and confused they may still be, are no longer confined to a marginal underground: this year they are appearing in the streets.

3. At the same time, the SI has emerged from the silence that previously concealed it. It must now strategically exploit this breakthrough. We cannot prevent the term "situationist" from becoming fashionable here and there. We must simply act in such a way that this (natural) phenomenon works more for us than against us. To me, "what works for us" is not distinct from what serves to unify and radicalize scattered struggles. This is the SI's task as an organization. Apart from this, the term "situationist" could be used vaguely to designate a certain period of critical thought (which it is already no mean feat to have initiated), but one in which everyone is responsible only for what he does personally, without any reference to an organizational community. But as long as this community exists, it will have to distinguish itself from whoever talks about it without being part of it.

4. Regarding the necessary tasks we have previously set for ourselves, we should now concentrate less on theoretical elaboration (which should nonetheless be continued) and more on the communication of theory—which basically means practical linkups with whatever new gestures of contestation appear (by quickly increasing our possibilities for intervention, criticism, and exemplary support).

5. The movement that is hesitantly beginning is the beginning of our victory (that is, the victory of what we have been supporting and pointing out for many years). But we must not try to "capitalize" on this victory. (With each new affirmation of a moment of revolutionary critique, at whatever level, any advanced coherent organization must know how to lose itself in revolutionary society.) In present and forthcoming subversive currents there is much to criticize. It would be very poor taste for us to make this necessary critique while leaving the SI above it all.

6. The SI must now prove its effectiveness in a new stage of revolutionary activity—or else disappear.

7. In order to have any chance of attaining such effectiveness, we must recognize and state several truths about the SI. These were obviously already true before; but now that we have arrived at a point where this "truth is verifying itself," it has become urgent to make it more precise.

8. We have never considered the SI as an end in itself, but as a moment of a historical activity; the force of circumstances is now leading us to prove it. The SI's "coherence" is the relationship, striving toward coherence, between all our formulated theses and between these theses and our action; as well as our solidarity in those cases where the group is responsible for the action of one of its members (a collective responsibility that holds good regarding many issues, but not all). It cannot be some sort of mastery guaranteed to someone who would be reputed to have so thoroughly appropriated our theoretical bases that he would automatically derive from them a perfectly exemplary line of conduct. It cannot be a demand for (much less a pretension of) an equal excellence of everyone in all issues or activities.

9. Coherence is acquired and verified by egalitarian participation in the entirety of a collective practice, which simultaneously reveals shortcomings and provides remedies. This practice requires formal meetings to arrive at decisions, transmission of all information, and examination of all observed lapses.

10. This practice presently requires more participants in the SI, drawn from among those who declare their accord and demonstrate their abilities. The small number of members, rather unjustly selected until now, has been the cause and consequence of a ridiculous overvaluation "officially" accorded to each of them merely by virtue of the fact that they were SI members, even though many of them never demonstrated the slightest real capabilities (consider the exclusions that have occurred over the past year, whether of the Garnautins or the English). Such a pseudoqualitative numerical limitation both encourages stupidities and exaggeratedly magnifies the importance of each particular stupidity.

11. Externally, a direct product of this selective illusion has been the mythological recognition of autonomous pseudogroups, seen as gloriously situated at the level of the SI when in fact they were only feeble admirers of it (and thus inevitably soon to become dishonest vilifiers of it). It seems to me that we cannot recognize any group as autonomous unless it is engaged in autonomous practical work; nor can we recognize such a group as durably successful unless it is engaged in united action with workers (without, of course, falling short of our

"Minimum Definition of Revolutionary Organizations"). All kinds of recent experiences have shown the co-opted confusionism of the term "anarchist," and it seems to me that we must oppose it everywhere.

12. I think that we should allow SI members to constitute distinct tendencies oriented around differing preoccupations or tactical options, as long as our general bases are not put in question. Similarly, we must move toward a complete practical autonomy of national groups as soon as they are able to really constitute themselves.

13. In contrast to the habits of the excluded members who in 1966 pretended to attain—inactively—a total realization of transparency and friendship in the SI (to the point that one almost felt guilty for pointing out how boring their company was), and who as a corollary secretly developed the most idiotic jealousies, lies unworthy of a grade-school kid, and conspiracies as ignominious as they were irrational, we must accept only historical relationships among us (critical confidence, knowledge of each member's potentials and limits), but on the basis of the fundamental loyalty and integrity required by the revolutionary project that has been defining itself for over a century.

14. We have no right to be mistaken in breaking with people. We will have to continue to be more or less frequently mistaken in admitting people. The exclusions have almost never marked any theoretical progress in the SI: we have not derived from these occasions any more precise determination of what is unacceptable (the surprising thing about the Garnautin affair was that it was an exception to this rule). The exclusions have almost always been responses to objective threats that existing conditions hold in store for our action. There is a danger of this recurring at higher levels. All sorts of "Nashisms" could reconstitute themselves: we must simply be in a position to demolish them.

15. In order to make the form of this debate consistent with what I see as its content, I propose that this text be communicated to certain comrades close to the SI or capable of taking part in it, and that we solicit their opinion on this question.

GUY DEBORD
April 1968

Note added August 1969:

These notes of April 1968 were a contribution to a debate on organization that we were about to engage in. Two or three weeks later the occupations movement, which was obviously more pleasant and instructive than this debate, forced us to postpone it.

The last point alone had been immediately approved by the SI comrades. Thus this text, which certainly had nothing secret about it, was not even a strictly internal document. Toward the end of 1968, however, we discovered that truncated and undated versions of it had been circulated by some leftist groups, with what purpose I don't know. The SI consequently decided that the authentic version should be published in this journal.

When the SI was able to resume the discussion on organization in fall 1968, the situationists adopted these theses, which had been confirmed by the rapid march of events in the intervening months. The SI had meanwhile proved capable of acting in May in a manner that responded rather well to the requirements that these theses had formulated for the immediate future.

Since this text is now receiving a wider circulation, I think I should clarify one point, in order to avoid any misunderstanding regarding the relative openness proposed for the SI. I was not advocating any concession to "united action" with the semiradical currents that are already beginning to take shape; and certainly not any abandonment of our rigor in choosing members of the SI and in limiting their number. I criticized a bad, abstract use of this rigor, which could lead to the contrary of what we want. The admiring or subsequently hostile excesses of all those who speak of us from the viewpoint of excessively impassioned spectators should not be able to find a justification in a corresponding "situ-boasting" on our part that would promote the belief that the situationists are wondrous beings who have all actually appropriated in their lives everything they have articulated—or even merely agreed with—in the matter of revolutionary theory and program. Since May we have seen the magnitude and urgency this problem has assumed.

The situationists do not have any monopoly to defend, nor any reward to expect. A task that suited us was undertaken and carried out through good and bad, and on the whole it was carried out correctly, with the means available to us. The present development of the subjective conditions of revolution should lead toward formulating a strategy that, starting from different conditions, will be as good as that followed by the SI in more difficult times.

—G.D.

Miscellaneous
Publications

(1960–1969)

Preliminaries Toward Defining a Unitary Revolutionary Program

I. Capitalism: A Society Without Culture

1

Culture can be defined as the ensemble of means through which a society thinks of itself and shows itself to itself, and thus decides on all aspects of the use of its available surplus-value. That is to say, it is the organization of everything over and beyond the immediate necessities of the society's reproduction.

All forms of capitalist society today are in the final analysis based on the generalized and (at the mass level) stable division between directors and executants: those who give orders and those who carry them out. Transposed onto the plane of culture, this means the separation between "understanding" and "doing," the inability to organize (on the basis of continuous exploitation) the continually accelerating domination of nature toward any goal whatsoever.

For the capitalist class, dominating production requires monopolizing the understanding of productive activity, of work. To achieve this, work is on one hand increasingly parcelized, i.e. rendered incomprehensible to those who do it; and on the other hand, it is reconstituted as a unity by specialized agencies. These agencies, however, are themselves subordinated to the real directorate, which alone possesses the theoretical comprehension of the whole since it dictates the direction of production in accordance with its general directives. But this comprehension and these objectives are themselves subjected to a certain arbitrariness since they are cut off from practice and even from all realistic knowledge, which it is in no one's interest to transmit.

The total social activity is thus split into three levels: the workshop, the office, and the directorate. Culture, in the sense of active and practical comprehension of society, is likewise cut apart into these three aspects. These aspects are reunited (partially and secretly) only by people's constant transgression of the separate sectors in which they are regimented by the system.

2

The formative mechanism of culture thus amounts to a reification of human activities, a reification which fixates the living; which models the transmission of experience from one generation to another on the transmission of commodities; and which strives to ensure the past's domination over the future.

This cultural functioning enters into contradiction with capitalism's constant need to obtain people's adherence and to enlist their creative activity (within the narrow limits within which it imprisons them). In short, the capitalist order can survive only by ceaselessly fabricating a new past for itself. This can be seen particularly clearly in the cultural sector proper, whose publicity is based on the periodic launching of pseudoinnovations.

3

Work thus tends to be reduced to pure execution and thereby made absurd. As technology evolves, its application is trivialized; as work is simplified, it becomes more and more absurd.

But this absurdity also extends to the offices and laboratories: the ultimate determinations of their activity come from outside them, from the political sphere that runs the whole society.

On the other hand, as the activity of the offices and laboratories is integrated into the overall functioning of capitalism, the necessity to fully exploit this activity requires the introduction into it of the capitalist division of labor, that is, of parcelization and hierarchization. The logical problem of scientific synthesis then intersects with the social problem of centralization. The result of these changes is, contrary to appearances, a general lack of culture at all levels of knowledge: scientific synthesis is no longer carried out, science no longer comprehends itself. Science is no longer a real and practical clarification of people's relation with the world; it has destroyed the old representations without being able to provide new ones. The world as unified totality becomes indecipherable; certain specialists are the only people who possess a few fragments of rationality—fragments which they themselves are incapable of communicating, even to each other.

4

This state of things gives rise to a certain number of conflicts. The technical advances that are a natural tendency of the development of material processes (and largely even a natural tendency of the development of the sciences) often conflict with the technologies that selectively apply those advances in strict accordance with the requirements of exploiting the workers and thwarting their resistance. There is also a conflict between capitalist imperatives and people's elementary needs. Thus the contradiction between present nuclear practices and a still generally prevalent taste for living is echoed even in the moralizing protests of certain physicists. The alterations that man can now bring about in his own nature (ranging from plastic surgery to controlled genetic mutations) also demand an alteration of the society: its self-managed transformation through the abolition of all specialized directors.

Everywhere the vastness of the new possibilities poses the urgent alternative: revolutionary solution or science-fiction barbarism. The compromise represented by the present society is contingent on the preservation of a status quo which is in fact everywhere constantly out of its control.

5

Present culture as a whole can be characterized as alienated in the sense that every activity, every moment of life, every idea, every type of behavior, has a meaning only outside itself, in an "elsewhere" which, being no longer in heaven, is only the more maddening to try and locate: a utopia, in the literal sense of the word,* dominates the life of the modern world.

6

Having from the workshop to the laboratory emptied productive activity of all meaning for itself, capitalism strives to place the meaning of life in leisure activities and to reorient productive activity on that basis. Since production is hell in the prevailing moral schema, real life must be found in consumption, in the use of goods.

But for the most part these goods have no use except to satisfy a few private needs that have been pumped up to meet the requirements of the market. Capitalist consumption imposes a general reduction of desires by its regular satisfaction of artificial needs, which remain needs without ever having been desires—authentic desires being constrained to remain unfulfilled (or compensated in the form of spectacles). The consumer is in reality morally and psychologically consumed by the market. But above all, these goods have no social use because the social horizon does not extend beyond the factory; outside the factory everything is organized as a desert (dormitory towns, freeways, parking lots, etc.)—the terrain of consumption.

However, the society constituted in the factory has the exclusive domination over this desert. The real use of the goods is simply as status symbols which, in accordance with the inevitable tendency of industrial commodities, have at the same time become obligatory for everyone. The factory is symbolically reflected in leisure activities, though with enough room for individual variation to allow for the compensation of a few frustrations. The world of consumption is in reality the world of the mutual spectacularization of everyone, the world of everyone's separation, estrangement, and nonparticipation. The directorial sphere also strictly directs this spectacle, which is composed automatically and miserably in accordance with imperatives external to the society, imperatives to which absurd values are attributed. (The directors themselves, as living persons, can also be considered as victims of this automated directorial machine.)

7

Outside of work, the spectacle is the dominant mode through which people relate to each other. It is only through the spectacle that people acquire a (falsified) knowledge of certain general aspects of social life, from scientific or technological achievements to prevailing types of conduct and orchestrated meetings of international political celebrities. The relation between authors and spectators is only a transposition of the fundamental relation between directors and executants. It answers perfectly to the needs of a reified and alienated culture: the spectacle–spectator relation is in itself a staunch bearer of the capitalist order. The ambiguity of all "revolutionary art" lies in the fact that the revolutionary aspect of any particular spectacle is always contradicted and offset by the reactionary element present in all spectacles.

This is why capitalist society, in order to streamline its own functioning, must above all continually refine its mechanism of spectacularization. This is obviously a complex mechanism, for if its main role is to propagate the capitalist order, it nevertheless must not appear to the public as a mere capitalistic delirium; it must involve the public by incorporating elements of representation that correspond—in fragments—to social rationality. It must sidetrack the desires whose satisfaction is forbidden by the ruling order. For example, modern mass tourism presents cities and landscapes not in order to satisfy authentic desires to live in such human or geographical milieus; it presents them as pure, rapid, superficial spectacles (spectacles from which one can gain prestige by reminiscing about them). Similarly, striptease is the most obvious form of the degradation of eroticism into a mere spectacle.

8

The evolution and the conservation of art have been governed by these lines of force. At one pole, art is purely and simply co-opted by capitalism as a means of conditioning the population. At the other pole, capitalism grants art a perpetual privileged concession: that of pure creative activity—an isolated creativity which serves as an alibi for the alienation of all other activities (and which thus also makes it the most expensive and prestigious status symbol). But at the same time, this sphere reserved for "free creative activity" is the only one in which the question of what we do with life and the question of communication are posed fully and practically. In this sense art can reflect the basic antagonisms between partisans and adversaries of the officially dictated reasons for living. The established meaninglessness and separation give rise to the general crisis of traditional artistic means—a crisis linked to the experience of alternative ways of living or to the demand for such experience. Revolutionary artists are those who call for intervention, and who have themselves intervened in the spectacle in order to disrupt and destroy it.

II. Culture and Revolutionary Politics

1

The revolutionary movement can be nothing less than the struggle of the proletariat for the actual domination and deliberate transformation of all aspects of social life—beginning with the management of production and work by the workers themselves, directly deciding everything. Such a change would immediately imply a radical transformation of the nature of work and the development of new technologies designed to ensure the workers' domination over the machines.

This radical transformation of the meaning of work will lead to a number of consequences, the main one of which is undoubtedly the shifting of the center of interest of life from passive leisure to the new type of productive activity. This does not mean that overnight all productive activities will become in themselves passionately interesting. But to work toward making them so, by a general and ongoing reconversion of the ends as well as the means of industrial work, will in any case be the minimum passion of a free society.

In such a society, all activities will tend to blend the life previously separated between leisure and work into a single but infinitely diversified flow. Production and consumption will merge and be superseded in the creative use of the goods of the society.

2

Such a program proposes to people no reason to live other than their own construction of their own lives. This presupposes not only that people be objectively freed from real needs (hunger, etc.), but above all that they begin to develop real desires in place of the present compensations; that they refuse all forms of behavior dictated by others and continually reinvent their own unique fulfillments; and that they no longer consider life to be the mere maintaining of a certain stability, but that they aspire to the unlimited enrichment of their acts.

3

Such demands today are not based on some sort of utopianism. They are based first of all on the struggle of the proletariat at all levels, and on all the forms of explicit refusal or profound indifference that the unstable ruling society constantly has to combat with every means. They are also based on the lesson of the fundamental defeat of all attempts at less radical changes. Finally, they are based on the extremist strivings and actions appearing today among certain sectors of youth (despite all the efforts at disciplining and repressing them) and in a few artistic milieus.

But this basis is indeed utopian in another sense of the word, in that it involves inventing and experimenting with solutions to current problems without being preoccupied with whether or not the conditions for their realization are immediately present. (It should be noted that this utopian type of experimentation now also plays a key role in modern science.) This temporary, historical utopianism is legitimate; and it is necessary because it serves to incubate the projection of desires without which free life would be empty of content. It is inseparable from the necessity to dissolve the present ideology of everyday life, and therefore the bonds of everyday oppression, so that the revolutionary class can disabusedly discover present and future possibilities of freedom.

Utopian practice makes sense, however, only if it is closely linked to the practice of revolutionary struggle. The latter, in its turn, cannot do without such utopianism without being condemned to sterility. Those seeking an experimental culture cannot hope to realize it without the triumph of the revolutionary movement, while the latter cannot itself establish authentic revolutionary conditions without resuming the efforts of the cultural avant-garde toward the critique of everyday life and its free reconstruction.

4

Revolutionary politics thus has as its content the totality of the problems of the society. It has as its form the experimental practice of a free life through organized struggle against the capitalist order. The revolutionary movement must thus itself become an experimental movement. Henceforth, wherever it exists, it must develop and resolve as profoundly as possible the problems of a revolutionary microsociety. This comprehensive politics culminates in the moment of revolutionary action, when the masses abruptly intervene to make history and discover their action as direct experience and as festival. At such moments they undertake a conscious and collective construction of everyday life which, one day, will no longer be stopped by anything.

PIERRE CANJUERS* AND GUY DEBORD
20 July 1960

For a Revolutionary Judgment of Art

1

Chatel's article on Godard's film [*Breathless*] in *Socialisme ou Barbarie* #31 can be characterized as film criticism dominated by revolutionary concerns. The analysis of the film assumes a revolutionary perspective on society, confirms that perspective, and concludes that certain tendencies of cinematic expression should be considered preferable to others in relation to the revolutionary project. It is obviously because Chatel's critique thus sets out the question in all its fullness, instead of merely debating various questions of taste, that it is interesting and calls for discussion. Specifically, Chatel finds *Breathless* a "valuable example" supporting his thesis that an alteration of "the present forms of culture" depends on the production of works that offer people "a representation of their own existence."

2

A revolutionary alteration of the present forms of culture can be nothing less than the supersession of all aspects of the aesthetic and technological apparatus that constitutes an aggregation of spectacles separated from life. It is not in its surface meanings that we should look for a spectacle's relation to the problems of the society, but at the deepest level, at the level of *its function as a spectacle.* "The relation between authors and spectators is only a transposition of the fundamental relation between directors and executants. . . . The spectacle-spectator relation is in itself a staunch bearer of the capitalist order" ("Preliminaries Toward Defining a Unitary Revolutionary Program").

One must not introduce reformist illusions about the spectacle, as if it could be eventually improved from within, ameliorated by its own specialists under the supposed control of a better-informed public opinion. To do so would be tantamount to giving revolutionaries' approval to a tendency, or an appearance of a tendency, in a game that we absolutely must not play; a game that we must reject in its entirety in the name of the fundamental requirements of the revolutionary project, which can in no case produce an aesthetics because it is already entirely beyond the domain of aesthetics. The point is not to engage in some sort of revolutionary art-criticism, but to make a revolutionary critique of all art.

3

The connection between the predominance of the spectacle in social life and the predominance of a class of rulers (both being based on the contradictory need for passive adherence) is not a mere clever stylistic paradox. It is a factual correlation that objectively characterizes the modern world. It is here that the cultural critique issuing from the experience of the self-destruction of modern art meets up with the political critique issuing from the experience of the destruction of the workers' movement by its own alienated organizations. If one really insists on finding something positive in modern culture, it must be said that its only positive aspect lies in its self-liquidation, its withering away, its witness against itself.

From a practical standpoint, what is at issue here is a revolutionary organization's relation to artists. The deficiencies of bureaucratic organizations and their fellow travelers in the formulation and use of such a relationship are well known. But it seems that a completely conscious and coherent revolutionary politics must effectively unify these activities.

4

The greatest weakness of Chatel's critique is precisely that he assumes from the start, without even alluding to the possibility of any debate on the subject, that there is the most extreme separation between the creator of any work of art and the political analysis that might be made of it. His analysis of Godard is a particularly striking example of this separation. Having taken for granted that Godard himself remains beyond any political judgment, Chatel never bothers to mention that Godard did not *explicitly* criticize "the cultural delirium in which we live" and did not *deliberately intend* to "confront people with their own lives." Godard is treated like a natural phenomenon, a cultural artifact. One thinks no more about the possibility of Godard having political, philosophical, or other positions than one does about investigating the ideology of a typhoon.

Such criticism fits right into the sphere of bourgeois culture—specifically within its "art criticism" sector—since it obviously participates in the "deluge of words that camouflages every single aspect of reality." This criticism is one interpretation among many others of a work on which we have no hold. The critic assumes from the beginning that he knows *better than the author himself* what the author means. This apparent presumptuousness is in fact an extreme humility: the critic so completely accepts his separation from the artistic specialist in question that he despairs of ever being able to act on or with him (which would obviously require that he take into consideration what the artist was explicitly seeking).

5

Art criticism is a second-degree spectacle. The critic is someone who makes a spectacle out of his very condition as a spectator—a specialized and therefore ideal spectator, expressing his ideas and feelings *about* a work in which he does not really participate. He re-presents, restages, his own nonintervention in the spectacle. The weakness of random and largely arbitrary fragmentary judgments concerning spectacles that do not really concern us is imposed on all of us in many banal discussions in private life. But the art critic makes a show of this kind of weakness, presenting it as *exemplary*.

6

Chatel thinks that if a portion of the population recognizes itself in a film, it will be able to "look at itself, admire itself, criticize itself, or reject itself—in any case, to use the images that pass on the screen for its own needs." Let us first of all note that there is a certain mystery in this notion of using such a flow of images to satisfy authentic needs. Just how they are to be used is not clear. It would first of all seem to be necessary to specify which needs are in question in order to determine whether those images can really serve as means to satisfy them.

Furthermore, everything we know about the mechanism of the spectacle, even at the simplest cinematic level, absolutely contradicts this
idyllic vision of people equally free to admire or criticize themselves by
recognizing themselves in the characters of a film. But most fundamentally, it is impossible to accept this division of labor between uncontrollable specialists presenting a vision of people's lives to them and
audiences having to recognize themselves more or less clearly in those
images. Attaining a certain accuracy in describing people's behavior is
not necessarily positive. Even if Godard presents people with an image
of themselves in which they can undeniably recognize themselves more
than in the films of Fernandel, he nevertheless presents them with a
false image in which they recognize themselves falsely.

7

Revolution is not "showing" life to people, but bringing them to life. A
revolutionary organization must always remember that its aim is not
getting its adherents to listen to convincing talks by expert leaders, but
getting them to speak for themselves, in order to achieve, or at least
strive toward, an equal degree of participation. The cinematic spectacle is one of the forms of pseudocommunication (developed, in lieu of
other possibilities, by the present *class* technology) in which this aim
is radically unfeasible. Much more so, for example, than in a cultural
form such as a university-style lecture with questions at the end, in
which dialogue and audience participation, though subjected to rather
unfavorable conditions, are not absolutely excluded.

Anyone who has ever seen a film-club debate has immediately
noticed the dividing lines between the leader of the discussion, the
aficionados who regularly speak up at every meeting, and the people
who only occasionally express their viewpoints. These three categories are clearly separated by the degree to which they have mastered a
specialized vocabulary that determines their place within this institutionalized discussion. Information and influence are transmitted
unilaterally, from the top to the bottom, never from the bottom to the
top. Nevertheless, these three categories are quite close to one another
in their common confused powerlessness, as spectators making a show
of themselves, in relation to the real dividing line between them and
the people who actually make the films. The unilaterality of influence
is still more strict in relation to this division. The considerable differences among the various spectators' mastery of the conceptual tools
of film-club debates are ultimately diminished by the fact that those
tools are all equally ineffectual. A film-club debate is a subspectacle
accompanying the projected film; it is more ephemeral than written

criticism, but neither more nor less separated. In appearance a film-club discussion is an attempt at dialogue, at social encounter, at a time when individuals are increasingly isolated by the urban environment. But it is in fact the negation of such dialogue since these people have not come together to *decide* on anything, but in order to hold a discussion on a false pretext and with false means.

8

Leaving aside its external effects, the practice of this type of cinematic criticism immediately presents two risks to a revolutionary organization.

The first danger is that certain comrades might be led to formulate other criticisms expressing their different judgments of other films, or even of this one. Beginning from the same positions concerning the society as a whole, the number of different possible judgments of *Breathless,* though obviously not unlimited, is nevertheless fairly large. To give just one example, one could make a critique just as talented as Chatel's, expressing exactly the same revolutionary politics, but which would attempt to expose Godard's own participation in an entire sector of the dominant cultural mythology: that of the cinema itself (shots of the tête-à-tête with the photo of Humphrey Bogart, cut to the Café Napoléon). Belmondo—on the Champs-Élysées, at the Café Pergola, at the Rue Vavin intersection—could be considered as the image (largely unreal, of course, "ideologized") that the microsociety of *Cahiers du Cinéma* editors (and not even the whole generation of French filmmakers who emerged in the fifties) projects of its own existence; with its paltry dreams of flaunted subspontaneity; with its tastes, its real ignorances, but also its cultural enthusiasms.

The other danger would be that the impression of arbitrariness given by Chatel's exaltation of Godard's revolutionary value might lead other comrades to oppose any discussion of cultural issues simply in order to avoid the risk of lacking in seriousness. On the contrary, the revolutionary movement must accord a central place to criticism of culture and everyday life. But any examination of these phenomena must first of all be disabused, not respectful toward the given modes of communication. The very foundations of existing cultural relations must be contested by the critique that the revolutionary movement needs to really bring to bear on all aspects of life and human relationships.

GUY DEBORD
February 1961*

Theses on the Paris Commune

1

"The classical workers' movement must be reexamined without any illusions, particularly without any illusions regarding its various political and pseudotheoretical heirs, because all they have inherited is its failure. The apparent successes of this movement are actually its fundamental failures (reformism or the establishment of a state bureaucracy), while its failures (the Paris Commune or the 1934 Asturian revolt) are its most promising successes so far, for us and for the future" (*Internationale Situationniste #7*).

2

The Commune was the biggest festival of the nineteenth century. Underlying the events of that spring of 1871 one can see the insurgents' feeling that they had become the masters of their own history, not so much on the level of "governmental" politics as on the level of their everyday life. (Consider, for example, the *games* everyone played with their weapons: they were in fact playing with power.) It is *also* in this sense that Marx should be understood when he says that "the most important social measure of the Commune was its own existence in acts."*

3

Engels's remark, "Look at the Paris Commune—*that* was the dictatorship of the proletariat," should be taken seriously in order to reveal what the dictatorship of the proletariat is not (the various forms of state dictatorship over the proletariat in the name of the proletariat).

4

It has been easy to make justified criticisms of the Commune's obvious lack of a coherent organizational structure. But as the problem of political structures seems far more complex to us today than the would-be heirs of the Bolshevik-type structure claim it to be, it is time that we examine the Commune not just as an outmoded example of revolutionary primitivism, all of whose mistakes can easily be overcome, but as a positive experiment whose whole truth has yet to be rediscovered and fulfilled.

5

The Commune had no leaders. And this at a time when the idea of the necessity of leaders was universally accepted in the workers' movement. This is the first reason for its paradoxical successes and failures. The official organizers of the Commune were incompetent (compared with Marx or Lenin, or even Blanqui). But on the other hand, the various "irresponsible" acts of that moment are precisely what is needed for the continuation of the revolutionary movement of our own time (even if the circumstances restricted almost all those acts to the purely destructive level—the most famous example being the rebel who, when a suspect bourgeois insisted that he had never had anything to do with politics, replied, "That's precisely why I'm going to kill you").

6

The vital importance of the general arming of the people was manifested practically and symbolically from the beginning to the end of the movement. By and large the right to impose popular will by force was not surrendered and left to any specialized detachments. This exemplary autonomy of the armed groups had its unfortunate flip side in their lack of coordination: at no point in the offensive or defensive struggle against Versailles did the people's forces attain military effectiveness. It should be borne in mind, however, that the Spanish revolution was lost—as, in the final analysis, was the civil war itself—in the name of such a transformation into a "republican army." The contradiction between autonomy and coordination would seem to have been largely related to the technological level of the period.

7

The Commune represents *the only implementation of a revolutionary urbanism* to date—attacking on the spot the petrified signs of the dominant organization of life, understanding social space in political terms, refusing to accept the innocence of any monument. Anyone who disparages this attack as some "lumpenproletarian nihilism," some "irresponsibility of the *pétroleuses*,"* should specify what he believes to be of positive value in the present society and worth preserving (it will turn out to be almost everything). "All space is already occupied by the enemy. . . . Authentic urbanism will appear when the absence of this occupation is created in certain zones. What we call construction starts there. It can be clarified by the *positive void* concept developed by modern physics" ("Basic Program of Unitary Urbanism," *Internationale Situationniste* #6).

8

The Paris Commune succumbed less to the force of arms than to the force of habit. The most scandalous practical example was the refusal to use the cannons to seize the French National Bank when money was so desperately needed. During the entire existence of the Commune the bank remained a Versaillese enclave in Paris, defended by nothing more than a few rifles and the mystique of property and theft. The other ideological habits proved in every respect equally disastrous (the resurrection of Jacobinism, the defeatist strategy of barricades in memory of 1848, etc.).

9

The Commune shows how those who defend the old world always benefit in one way or another from the complicity of revolutionaries— particularly of those revolutionaries who merely *think about* revolution, and who turn out to still *think like* the defenders. In this way the old world retains bases (ideology, language, customs, tastes) among its enemies, and uses them to reconquer the terrain it has lost. (Only the thought-in-acts natural to the revolutionary proletariat escapes it irrevocably: the Tax Bureau went up in flames.) The real "fifth column" is in the very minds of revolutionaries.

10

The story of the arsonists who during the final days of the Commune went to destroy Notre-Dame, only to find it defended by an armed battalion of Commune artists, is a richly provocative example of direct democracy. It gives an idea of the kind of problems that will need to be resolved in the perspective of the power of the councils. Were those artists right to defend a cathedral in the name of eternal aesthetic values— and in the final analysis, in the name of museum culture— while other people wanted to express themselves then and there by making this destruction symbolize their absolute defiance of a society that, in its moment of triumph, was about to consign their entire lives to silence and oblivion? The artist partisans of the Commune, acting as specialists, already found themselves in conflict with an extremist form of struggle against alienation. The Communards must be criticized for not having dared to answer the totalitarian terror of power with the use of the totality of their weapons. Everything indicates that the poets who at that moment actually expressed the Commune's inherent poetry were simply *wiped out*. The Commune's mass of unaccomplished acts enabled its tentative actions to be turned into "atrocities" and their memory to be censored. Saint-Just's remark, "Those who make revolution half way only dig their own graves," also explains his *own* silence.*

11

Theoreticians who examine the history of this movement from a divinely omniscient viewpoint (like that found in classical novels) can easily demonstrate that the Commune was objectively doomed to failure and could not have been fulfilled. They forget that for those who really lived it, the fulfillment was *already there*.

12

The audacity and inventiveness of the Commune must obviously be measured not in relation to our time, but in terms of the political, intellectual, and moral attitudes of its own time, in terms of the *solidarity* of all the common assumptions that it blasted to pieces. The profound solidarity of presently prevailing assumptions (right and left) gives us an idea of the inventiveness we can expect of a comparable explosion today.

13

The social war of which the Commune was one episode is still being fought today (though its superficial conditions have changed considerably). In the task of "making conscious the unconscious tendencies of the Commune" (Engels), the last word has yet to be said.

14

For almost twenty years in France the Stalinists and the leftist Christians have agreed, in memory of their anti-German national front, to stress the element of national disarray and offended patriotism in the Commune. (According to the current Stalinist line, "the French people petitioned to be better governed" and were finally driven to desperate measures by the treachery of the unpatriotic right wing of the bourgeoisie.) In order to refute this pious nonsense it would suffice to consider the role played by all the foreigners who came to fight for the Commune. As Marx said, the Commune was the inevitable battle, the climax of 23 years of struggle in Europe by "our party."

GUY DEBORD, ATTILA KOTÁNYI, RAOUL VANEIGEM
18 March 1962*

The Situationists and the New Forms of Action in Politics and Art

The situationist movement can be seen as an artistic avant-garde, as an experimental investigation of possible ways for freely constructing everyday life, and as a contribution to the theoretical and practical development of a new revolutionary contestation. From now on, any fundamental cultural creation, as well as any qualitative transformation of society, is contingent on the continued development of this sort of interrelated approach.

The same society of alienation, totalitarian control, and passive spectacular consumption reigns everywhere, despite the diversity of its ideological and juridical disguises. The coherence of this society cannot be understood without an all-encompassing critique, illuminated by the inverse project of a liberated creativity, the project of everyone's control of all levels of their own history.

To revive and bring into the present this *inseparable,* mutually illuminating project and critique entails appropriating all the radicalism borne by the workers' movement, by modern poetry and art, and by the thought of the period of the supersession of philosophy, from Hegel to Nietzsche. To do this, it is first of all necessary to recognize, without holding on to any consoling illusions, the full extent of the defeat of the entire revolutionary project in the first third of this century and its official replacement, in every region of the world and in every domain of life, by delusive shams and petty reforms that camouflage and preserve the old order.

Such a resumption of radicality naturally also requires a considerable deepening of all the old attempts at liberation. Seeing how those attempts failed due to isolation, or were converted into total frauds, enables us to get a better grasp of the coherence of the world that needs to be changed. In the light of this rediscovered coherence, many of the partial explorations of the recent past can be salvaged and brought to their true fulfillment. Insight into this reversible coherence of the world—its present reality in relation to its potential reality—enables us to see the fallaciousness of half-measures, and to recognize the presence of such half-measures each time the operating pattern of the dominant society—with its categories of hierarchization and specialization and its corresponding habits and tastes—reconstitutes itself within the forces of negation.

Moreover, the material development of the world has accelerated. It constantly accumulates more potential powers; but the specialists of the management of society, because of their role as guardians of passivity, are forced to ignore the potential use of those powers. This same development produces widespread dissatisfaction and objective mortal dangers which these specialized rulers are incapable of permanently controlling.

Once it is understood that this is the perspective within which the situationists call for the supersession of art, it should be clear that when we speak of a unified vision of art and politics, this absolutely does not mean that we are recommending any sort of subordination of art to politics. For us, and for anyone who has begun to see this era in a disabused manner, there is no longer any modern art, just as there has been no constituted revolutionary politics anywhere in the world since the end of the 1930s. They can now be revived only by being *superseded,* that is to say, through the fulfillment of their most profound objectives.

The new contestation the situationists have been talking about is already emerging everywhere. Across the vast spaces of isolation and noncommunication organized by the present social order new types of scandals are spreading from one country to another, from one continent to another; and they are already beginning to communicate with each other.

The role of avant-garde currents, wherever they may appear, is to link these people and these experiences together; to help unify such groups and the coherent basis of their project. We need to publicize, elucidate, and develop these initial gestures of the forthcoming revolutionary era. They can be recognized by the fact that they concentrate in themselves new forms of struggle and a new content (whether latent or explicit): the critique of the existing world. Thus the dominant society, which prides itself so much on its constant modernization, is now going to meet its match, for it has finally produced a modernized negation.

Just as, on the one hand, we have been severe in preventing ambitious intellectuals or artists incapable of really understanding us from associating with the situationist movement, and in rejecting and denouncing various falsifications (of which Nashist "situationism" is the most recent example), so, on the other hand, we acknowledge the perpetrators of these new radical gestures as being situationist, and are determined to support them and never disavow them, even if many among them are not yet fully aware of the coherence of today's revolutionary program, but are only moving in that general direction.

We will limit ourselves to mentioning a few examples of acts that have our total approval. On January 16 of this year some revolutionary students in Caracas made an armed attack on an exhibition of French art and carried off five paintings, which they then offered to return in exchange for the release of political prisoners. The forces of order recaptured the paintings after a gun battle with Winston Bermudes, Luis Monselve, and Gladys Troconis. A few days later some other comrades threw two bombs at the police van that was transporting the recovered paintings, which unfortunately did not succeed in destroying it. This is clearly an exemplary way to treat the art of the past, to bring it back into play in life and to reestablish priorities. Since the death of Gauguin ("I have tried to establish the right to dare everything") and of Van Gogh, their work, co-opted by their enemies, has probably never received from the cultural world an homage so true to their spirit as the act of these Venezuelans. During the Dresden insurrection of 1849 Bakunin unsuccessfully proposed that the insurgents take the paintings out of the museums and put them on a barricade at the entrance to the city, to see if this might inhibit the attacking troops from continuing their fire. We can thus see how this skirmish in Caracas links up with one of the highest moments of the revolutionary upsurge of the last century, and even goes further.

No less justified, in our opinion, are the actions of those Danish comrades who over the last few weeks have resorted to incendiary bombs against the travel agencies that organize tours to Spain, or who have carried out pirate radio broadcasts warning of the dangers of nuclear arms. In the context of the comfortable and boring "socialized" capitalism of the Scandinavian countries, it is most encouraging to see the emergence of people whose violence exposes some aspects of the other violence that lies at the foundation of this "humanized" social order—its monopoly of information, for example, or the organized alienation of its tourism and other leisure activities—along with the horrible flip side that is implicitly accepted whenever one accepts this comfortable boredom. Not only is this peace not life, it is a peace built on the threat of atomic death; not only is organized tourism a miserable spectacle that conceals the real countries through which one travels, but the reality of the country thus transformed into a neutral spectacle is Franco's police.

Finally, the action of the English comrades [the "Spies for Peace"] who last April divulged the location and plans of the "Regional Seat of Government #6" bomb shelter has the immense merit of revealing the degree already attained by state power in its organization of the terrain and establishment of a totalitarian functioning of authority.

This totalitarian organization is not designed simply to prepare for a possible war. It is, rather, the universally maintained *threat* of a nuclear war which now, in both the East and the West, serves to keep the masses submissive, to organize *shelters* for *state power,* and to reinforce the psychological and material defenses of the ruling class's power. The modern urbanism on the surface serves the same function. In April 1962, in issue #7 of our French-language journal *Internationale Situationniste,* we made the following comments regarding the massive construction of individual shelters in the United States during the previous year:

> Here, as in every racket, "protection" is only a pretext. The real purpose of the shelters is to test—and thereby reinforce—people's submissiveness, and to manipulate this submissiveness to the advantage of the ruling society. The shelters, as a creation of a new consumable commodity in the society of abundance, prove more than any previous commodity that people can be made to work to satisfy highly artificial needs, needs that most certainly remain needs without ever having been desires. The new habitat that is now taking shape with the large housing developments is not really distinct from the architecture of the shelters; it merely represents a less advanced level of that architecture. The concentration-camp organization of the surface of the earth is the normal state of the present society in formation; its condensed subterranean version merely represents that society's pathological excess. This subterranean sickness reveals the real nature of the "health" at the surface.*

The English comrades have just made a decisive contribution to the study of this sickness, and thus also to the study of "normal" society. This study is itself inseparable from a struggle that has not been afraid to defy the old national taboos of "treason" by breaking the *secrecy* that is vital in so many regards for the smooth functioning of power in modern society, behind the thick screen of its glut of "information." The sabotage in England was later extended, despite the efforts of the police and numerous arrests: secret military headquarters in the country were invaded by surprise (some officials present being photographed against their will) and forty telephone lines of British security centers were systematically blocked by the continuous dialing of ultrasecret numbers that had been publicized.*

In order to salute and extend this first attack against the ruling organization of social space, we have organized this "Destruction of RSG-6" demonstration in Denmark.* In so doing, we are striving not only for an internationalist extension of this struggle, but also for its extension on the "artistic" front of this same general struggle.

The cultural creation that could be referred to as situationist begins with the projects of unitary urbanism or of the construction of situations in life, and the fulfillment of those projects is inseparable from the history of the movement striving to fulfill all the revolutionary possibilities contained in the present society. In the short term, however, a critical art can be carried out within the existing means of cultural expression, from cinema to painting—even though we ultimately wish to destroy this entire artistic framework. This critical art is what the situationists have summed up in their theory of *détournement*. Such an art must not only be critical in its content, it must also be self-critical in its form. It is a communication which, recognizing the limitations of the specialized sphere of established communication, "is now going to contain *its own critique*."

For this "RSG-6" event we have recreated the atmosphere of an atomic fallout shelter. After passing through this thought-provoking ambience, the visitor enters a zone evoking the direct negation of this type of necessity. The medium here used in a critical fashion is painting.

The revolutionary role of modern art, which culminated with dadaism, has been to destroy all the conventions of art, language, and behavior. Since what is destroyed in art and philosophy is nevertheless obviously not yet concretely eliminated from the newspapers and the churches, and since the advances in the arm of critique have not yet been followed by an armed critique, dadaism itself has become a recognized school of art and its forms have recently been turned into a reactionary diversion by neodadaists who make careers out of repeating the style invented before 1920, exploiting each pumped-up detail and using it to develop an acceptable "style" for decorating the present world.

However, the negative truth that modern art has contained has always been a *justified* negation of the society in which it found itself. In Paris in 1937 the Nazi ambassador Otto Abetz pointed to the painting *Guernica* and asked Picasso, "Did you do that?" Picasso very appropriately responded: "No. You did."

The negation and the black humor that were so prevalent in modern art and poetry in the aftermath of World War I surely merit being revived in the context of the *spectacle of World War III* within which we are now living. Whereas the neodadaists speak of charging with (aesthetic) positivity the plastic refusal previously expressed by Marcel Duchamp, we are sure that everything the world now offers us as positive can only serve to endlessly recharge the negativity of the currently permitted forms of expression, and in this roundabout way produce *the sole representative art of these times.* The situationists know that real positivity will come from elsewhere, and that from now on this negativity will collaborate with it.

Without having any pictorial preoccupations, and even, we hope, without giving the impression of any respect toward a now long outmoded form of plastic beauty, we have presented here a few perfectly clear signs.

The "Directives" exhibited on empty canvases or on detourned abstract paintings should be considered as slogans that one might see written on walls. The political proclamations that form the titles of some of the paintings are intended, of course, as a simultaneous ridicule and reversal of that pompous academicism currently in fashion which is trying to base itself on the painting of incommunicable "pure signs."

The "Thermonuclear Maps" immediately go beyond all the laborious strivings for a "new representationalism" in painting, because they unite the most freeform procedures of action-painting with representations *that can claim to be totally realistic* images of various regions of the world in the first hours of the next world war.

The series of "Victories"—similarly combining the most extreme ultramodern offhandedness with a minute realism à la Horace Vernet —revives the tradition of battle paintings. But in contradistinction to the reactionary ideological regression on which Georges Mathieu has based his paltry publicity scandals, the reversal here rectifies past history, changes it for the better, makes it more revolutionary and more successful than it actually was. These "Victories" carry on the totally optimistic détournement through which Lautréamont, quite audaciously, already disputed the validity of all the manifestations of misfortune and its logic: "I do not accept evil. Man is perfect. The soul does not fall. Progress exists. . . . Up till now, misfortune has been described in order to inspire terror and pity. I will describe happiness in order to inspire their contraries. . . . As long as my friends do not die, I will not speak of death."

GUY DEBORD
1963

On the Poverty of Student Life

Considered in Its Economic, Political, Psychological, Sexual, and Especially Intellectual Aspects, With a Modest Proposal for Doing Away With It

by
members of the Situationist International and students of Strasbourg University

To make shame more shameful still by making it public

It is pretty safe to say that the student is the most universally despised creature in France, apart from the policeman and the priest. But the reasons for which he* is despised are often false reasons reflecting the dominant ideology, whereas the reasons for which he is justifiably despised from a revolutionary standpoint remain repressed and unavowed. The partisans of false opposition are aware of these faults —faults which they themselves share—but they invert their actual contempt into a patronizing admiration. The impotent leftist intellectuals (from *Les Temps Modernes* to *L'Express*) go into raptures over the supposed "rise of the students," and the declining bureaucratic organizations (from the "Communist" Party to the UNEF [National Student Union]) jealously contend for his "moral and material support." We will show the reasons for this concern with the student and how they are rooted in the dominant reality of overdeveloped capitalism. We are going to use this pamphlet to denounce them one by one: the suppression of alienation necessarily follows the same path as alienation.

Up till now all the analyses and studies of student life have ignored the essential. None of them go beyond the viewpoint of academic specializations (psychology, sociology, economics) and thus they remain fundamentally erroneous. Fourier long ago exposed this "methodical myopia" of treating fundamental questions without relating them to modern society as a whole. The fetishism of facts masks the essential category, and the mass of details obscures the *totality*. Everything is said about this society except what it really is: a society dominated by *commodities and spectacles*. The sociologists Bourderon and Passedieu,* in their study *Les Héritiers: les étudiants et la culture*, remain impotent in face of the few partial truths they have succeeded in demonstrating. Despite their good intentions they fall back into professorial morality, the inevitable Kantian ethic of a *real democratization through a real rationalization of the teaching system* (i.e. of the system of teaching the system). Meanwhile their disciples, such as Kravetz,[1] compensate for their petty-bureaucratic resentment with a hodgepodge of outdated revolutionary phraseology.

Modern capitalism's spectacularization[2] of reification allots everyone a specific role within a general passivity. The student is no exception to this rule. His is a provisional role, a rehearsal for his ultimate role as a conservative element in the functioning of the commodity system. Being a student is a form of initiation.

This initiation magically recapitulates all the characteristics of mythical initiation. It remains totally cut off from historical, individual, and social reality. The student leads a double life, poised between his present status and the utterly separate future status into which he will one day be abruptly thrust. Meanwhile his schizophrenic consciousness enables him to withdraw into his "initiation group," forget about his future, and bask in the mystical trance of a present sheltered from history. It is not surprising that he avoids facing his situation, particularly its economic aspects: in our "affluent society" he is still a pauper. More than 80% of students come from income groups above the working class, yet 90% of them have less money than the lowest worker. Student poverty is an anachronism in the society of the spectacle: it has yet to attain the new poverty of the new proletariat. In a period when more and more young people are breaking free from moral prejudices and family authority as they are subjected to blunt, undisguised exploitation at the earliest age, the student clings to his tame and irresponsible "protracted infancy." Belated adolescent crises may provoke occasional arguments with his family, but he uncomplainingly accepts being treated as a baby by the various institutions that govern his daily life. (If they ever stop shitting in his face, it's only to come around and bugger him.)

---

1. Marc Kravetz, a slick orator well known among the UNEF politicos, made the mistake of venturing into "theoretical research": in 1964 he published a defense of student unionism in *Les Temps Modernes*, which he then denounced in the same periodical a year later.

2. It goes without saying that we use the concepts of *spectacle*, *role*, etc., in the situationist sense.

Student poverty is merely the most gross expression of the colonization of all domains of social practice. The projection of social guilty conscience onto the students masks the poverty and servitude of everyone.

But our contempt for the student is based on quite different reasons. He is contemptible not only for his actual poverty, but also for his complacency regarding every kind of poverty, his unhealthy propensity to wallow in his own alienation in the hope, amid the general lack of interest, of arousing interest in his particular lacks. The requirements of modern capitalism determine that most students will become mere *low-level functionaries*, serving functions comparable to those of skilled workers in the nineteenth century.[3] Faced with the prospect of such a dismal and mediocre "reward" for his shameful current poverty, the student prefers to take refuge in an unreally lived present, which he decorates with an illusory glamor.

The student is a stoical slave: the more chains authority binds him with, the freer he thinks he is. Like his new family, the university, he sees himself as the most "independent" social being, whereas he is in fact *directly subjected* to the two most powerful systems of social authority: the family and the state. As their well-behaved, grateful, and *submissive child*, he shares and embodies all the values and mystifications of the system. The illusions that formerly had to be imposed on white-collar workers are now willingly internalized and transmitted by the mass of future petty functionaries.

If ancient social poverty produced the most grandiose systems of compensation in history (religions), the student, in his marginal poverty, can find no other consolation than the most shopworn images of the ruling society, the farcical repetition of all its alienated products.

As an ideological being, the French student is always *behind the times*. The values and enthusiasms that are the pride of his closed little world have all long ago been condemned by history as laughable and untenable illusions.

Once upon a time the universities had a certain prestige; the student persists in the belief that he is lucky to be there. But he came too late. His mechanical, specialized education is as profoundly degraded (in comparison to the former level of general bourgeois culture)[4] as his own intellectual level, because the modern economic system requires a mass production of uneducated students who have been rendered

---

3. But without the revolutionary consciousness: the skilled worker did not have the illusion of promotion.
4. We are referring to the culture of Hegel or the Encyclopédistes, not to that of the Sorbonne or the École Normale Supérieure.

incapable of thinking. The university has become an institutional organization of ignorance. "High culture" is being degraded in the assembly-line production of professors, *all* of whom are cretins and most of whom would be jeered by any audience of highschoolers. But the student, in his mental menopause, is unaware of all this; he continues to listen respectfully to his masters, conscientiously suppressing all critical spirit so as to immerse himself in the mystical illusion of being a "student"—someone seriously devoted to learning *serious things*—in the hope that his professors will ultimately impart to him the ultimate truths of the world. The future revolutionary society will condemn all the noise of the lecture halls and classrooms as nothing but *verbal pollution*. The student is already a very bad joke.

The student is unaware that history is altering even his little "ivory tower" world. The famous "crisis of the university," that detail of a more general crisis of modern capitalism, remains the object of a deaf-mute dialogue among various specialists. It simply expresses the difficulties of this particular sector of production in its belated adjustment to the general transformation of the productive apparatus. The remnants of the old liberal bourgeois university ideology are becoming banalized as its social basis is disappearing. During the era of free-trade capitalism, when the liberal state left the university a certain marginal freedom, the latter could imagine itself as an independent power. But even then it was intimately bound to the needs of that type of society, providing the privileged minority with an adequate general education before they took up their positions within the ruling class. The pathetic bitterness of so many nostalgic professors[5] stems from the fact that they have lost their former role as guard-dogs serving the future masters and have been reassigned to the considerably less noble function of sheep-dogs in charge of herding white-collar flocks to their respective factories and offices in accordance with the needs of the planned economy. These professors hold up their archaisms as an alternative to the technocratization of the university and imperturbably continue to purvey scraps of "general" culture to audiences of future specialists who will not know how to make any use of them.

More serious, and thus more dangerous, are the modernists of the Left and those of the UNEF led by the FGEL "extremists," who demand a "reform of the university structure" so as to "reintegrate the university into social and economic life," i.e. so as to adapt it to the needs of

---

5. No longer daring to speak in the name of philistine liberalism, they invoke fantasized freedoms of the universities of the Middle Ages, that epoch of "the democracy of nonfreedom."

modern capitalism. The colleges that once supplied "general culture" to the ruling class, though still retaining some of their anachronistic prestige, are being transformed into force-feeding factories for rearing lower and middle functionaries. Far from contesting this historical process, which is subordinating one of the last relatively autonomous sectors of social life to the demands of the commodity system, the above-mentioned progressives protest against delays and inefficiencies in its implementation. They are the partisans of the future cybernetized university, which is already showing its ugly head here and there.[6] The commodity system and its modern servants—these are the enemy.

But all these struggles take place over the head of the student, somewhere in the heavenly realm of his masters. His own life is totally out of his control—*life itself* is totally beyond him.

Because of his acute economic poverty the student is condemned to a paltry form of *survival*. But, always self-satisfied, he parades his very ordinary indigence as if it were an original "lifestyle," making a virtue of his shabbiness and pretending to be a bohemian. "Bohemianism" is far from an original solution in any case, but the notion that one could live a really bohemian life without a complete and definitive break with the university milieu is ludicrous. But the student bohemian (and every student likes to pretend that he is a bohemian at heart) clings to his imitative and degraded version of what is, in the best of cases, only a mediocre individual solution. Even elderly provincial ladies know more about life than he does. Thirty years after Wilhelm Reich (that excellent educator of youth),[7] our would-be "nonconformist" continues to follow the most traditional forms of amorous-erotic behavior, reproducing the general relations of class society in his intersexual relations. His susceptibility to recruitment as a militant for any cause is an ample demonstration of his real impotence.

In spite of his more or less loose use of time within the margin of individual liberty allowed by the totalitarian spectacle, the student avoids adventure and experiment, preferring the security of the strait-jacketed daily space-time organized for his benefit by the guardians of the system. Though not constrained to separate his work and leisure, he does so of his own accord, all the while hypocritically proclaiming his contempt for "good students" and "study fiends." He accepts every type of separation and then bemoans the "lack of communication" in his religious, sports, political, or union "circles." He is so stupid and

---

6. See "Correspondence with a Cybernetician" in *Internationale Situationniste* #9 and the situationist tract "La tortue dans la vitrine" directed against the neoprofessor A. Moles.
7. See *The Sexual Struggle of Youth* and *The Function of the Orgasm*.

so miserable that he voluntarily submits himself to the University Psychological Aid Centers, those agencies of psycho-police control established by the vanguard of modern oppression and naturally hailed as a great victory for student unionism.[8]

But the real poverty of the student's everyday life finds its immediate fantasy-compensation in the opium of cultural commodities. In the cultural spectacle the student finds his natural place as a respectful disciple. Although he is close to the production point, access to the real Sanctuary of Culture is denied him; so he discovers "modern culture" as an *admiring spectator.* In an era when *art is dead* he remains the most loyal patron of the theaters and film clubs and the most avid consumer of the packaged fragments of its preserved corpse displayed in the cultural supermarkets. Consuming unreservedly and uncritically, he is in his element. If the "Culture Centers" didn't exist, the student would have invented them. He is a perfect example of all the platitudes of American market research: a conspicuous consumer, conditioned by advertising into fervently divergent attitudes toward products that are identical in their nullity, with an irrational preference for Brand X (Perec or Godard, for example) and an irrational prejudice against Brand Y (Robbe-Grillet or Lelouch, perhaps).

And when the "gods" who produce and organize his cultural spectacle take human form on the stage, he is their main audience, their perfect spectator. Students turn out *en masse* to their most obscene exhibitions. When the priests of different churches present their lame, consequenceless dialogues (seminars of "Marxist" thought, conferences of Catholic intellectuals) or when the literary debris come together to bear witness to their impotence (five thousand students attending a forum on "What are the possibilities of literature?"), who but students fill the halls?

Incapable of real passions, the student seeks titillation in the passionless polemics between the celebrities of Unintelligence: Althusser – Garaudy – Sartre – Barthes – Picard – Lefebvre – Lévi-Strauss – Hallyday* – Châtelet – Antoine, and between their rival ideologies, whose function is to mask real problems by debating false ones: Humanism – Existentialism – Structuralism – Scientism – New Criticism – Dialectico-naturalism – Cyberneticism – *Planète*-ism – Metaphilosophism.

---

8. With the rest of the population, a straitjacket is necessary to force them to appear before the psychiatrist in his fortress asylum. But with students it suffices to let them know that advanced outposts of control have been set up in their ghetto: they rush there in such numbers that they have to wait in line to get in.

He thinks he is avant-garde if he has seen the latest Godard, or bought the latest Argumentist book,[9] or participated in the latest happening organized by that asshole Lapassade. He discovers the latest trips as fast as the market can produce its ersatz version of long outmoded (though once important) ventures; in his ignorance he takes every rehash for a cultural revolution. His overriding concern is always to maintain his cultural status. Like everyone else, he takes pride in buying the paperback reprints of important and difficult texts that "mass culture" is disseminating at an accelerating pace.[10] Since he doesn't know how to read, he contents himself with fondly gazing at them.

His favorite reading matter is the press that specializes in promoting the frenzied consumption of cultural novelties; he unquestioningly accepts its pronouncements as guidelines for his tastes. He revels in *L'Express* or *Le Nouvel Observateur,* or perhaps he prefers *Le Monde,* which he feels is an accurate and truly "objective" newspaper, though he finds its style somewhat too difficult. To deepen his general knowledge he dips into *Planète,* the slick magical magazine that removes the wrinkles and blackheads from old ideas. With such guides he hopes to gain an understanding of the modern world and become politically conscious!

For in France, more than anywhere else, the student is content to be *politicized.* But his political participation is mediated by the same *spectacle.* Thus he seizes upon all the pitiful tattered remnants of a Left that was annihilated *more than forty years ago* by "socialist" reformism and Stalinist counterrevolution. The rulers are well aware of this defeat of the workers' movement, and so are the workers themselves, though more confusedly. But the student remains oblivious of it, and continues to blithely participate in the most laughable demonstrations that never draw anybody but students. This utter political ignorance makes the universities a happy hunting ground for the manipulators of the dying bureaucratic organizations (from the "Communist" Party to the UNEF), which totalitarianly program the student's political options. Occasionally there are deviationary tendencies and slight impulses toward "independence," but after a period of token resistance the dissidents are invariably reincorporated into an order they have never

---

9. On the *Arguments* gang and the disappearance of its journal, see the tract *Into the Trashcan of History* issued by the Situationist International in 1963.

10. In this regard one cannot too highly recommend the solution already practiced by the most intelligent, which consists of stealing them.

11. The latest adventures of the "Union of Communist Students" and its Christian counterparts demonstrate that all these students are united on one fundamental principle: unconditional submission to hierarchical superiors.

fundamentally questioned.[11] The "Revolutionary Communist Youth," whose title is a case of ideological falsification gone mad (they are neither revolutionary nor communist nor young), pride themselves on having rebelled against the Communist Party, then join the Pope in appealing for "Peace in Vietnam."

The student takes pride in his opposition to the "outdated" aspects of the de Gaulle regime, but in so doing he unwittingly implies his approval of *older crimes* (such as those of Stalinism in the era of Togliatti, Garaudy, Khrushchev, and Mao). His "youthful" attitudes are thus actually even more *old-fashioned* than the regime's—the Gaullists at least understand modern society well enough to administer it.

But this is not the student's only archaism. He feels obliged to have general ideas on everything, to form a coherent worldview capable of giving meaning to his need for nervous activity and asexual promiscuity. As a result he falls prey to the last doddering missionary efforts of the churches. With atavistic ardor he rushes to adore the putrescent carcass of God and to cherish the decomposing remains of prehistoric religions in the belief that they enrich him and his time. Along with elderly provincial ladies, students form the social category with the highest percentage of admitted religious adherents. Everywhere else priests have been insulted and driven off, but university clerics openly continue to bugger thousands of students in their spiritual shithouses.

In all fairness, we should mention that there are *some* tolerably intelligent students. These latter easily get around the miserable regulations designed to control the more mediocre students. They are able to do so precisely because they have *understood the system;* and they understand it because they despise it and know themselves to be its enemies. They are in the educational system in order to get the best it has to offer: namely, grants. Taking advantage of the contradiction that, for the moment at least, obliges the system to maintain a small, relatively independent sector of academic "research," they are going to calmly carry the germs of sedition to the highest level. Their open contempt for the system goes hand in hand with the lucidity that enables them to outdo the system's own lackeys, especially intellectually. They are already among the theorists of the coming revolutionary movement, and take pride in beginning to be feared as such. They make no secret of the fact that what they extract so easily from the "academic system" is used for its destruction. For the student cannot revolt against anything without revolting against his *studies,* though the necessity of this revolt is felt less naturally by him than by the worker, who spontaneously revolts against his condition as worker. But the student is a product of modern society just like Godard and Coca-Cola. His extreme alienation can be contested only through a contestation of the entire society. This critique can in no way be carried out on the student terrain: the student who defines himself as such identifies himself with a pseudovalue that prevents him from becoming aware of his real dispossession, and he thus remains at the height of false consciousness. But everywhere where modern society is beginning to be contested, young people are taking part in that contestation; and that revolt represents the most direct and thorough critique of student behavior.

It is not enough for theory to seek its realization in practice; practice must seek its theory

After a long period of slumber and permanent counterrevolution, the last few years have seen the first gestures of a new period of contestation, most visibly among young people. But the society of the spectacle, in its representation of itself and its enemies, imposes its own ideological categories on the world and its history. It reassuringly presents everything that happens as if it were part of the natural order of things, and reduces truly new developments that herald its *supersession* to the level of superficial consumer novelties. In reality the revolt of young people against the way of life imposed on them is simply a harbinger, a preliminary expression of a far more widespread subversion that will embrace all those who are feeling the increasing impossibility of *living* in this society, a prelude to the next revolutionary era. With their usual methods of inverting reality, the dominant ideology and its daily mouthpieces reduce this real historical movement to a socionatural category: the Idea of Youth. Any new youth revolt is presented as merely the eternal revolt of youth that recurs with each generation, only to fade away "when young people become engaged in the serious business of production and are given real, concrete aims." The "youth revolt" has been subjected to a veritable journalistic inflation (people are presented with the spectacle of a revolt to distract them from the possibility of participating in one). It is presented as an aberrant but necessary social safety valve that has its part to play in the smooth functioning of the system. This revolt against the society reassures the society because it supposedly remains partial, pigeonholed in the *apartheid* of "adolescent problems" (analogous to "racial issues" or "women's concerns"), and is soon outgrown. In reality, if there is a "youth problem" in modern society, it simply consists in the fact that young people feel the profound crisis of this society most acutely— and try to express it. The young generation is a product par excellence of modern society, whether it chooses integration into it or the most radical rejection of it. What is surprising is not that youth is in revolt, but that "adults" are so resigned. But the reason for this is historical, not biological: the previous generation lived through all the defeats and swallowed all the lies of the long, shameful disintegration of the revolutionary movement.

In itself, "Youth" is a publicity myth linked to the capitalist mode of production, as an expression of its dynamism. This illusory preeminence of youth became possible with the economic recovery after World War II, following the mass entry into the market of a whole new category of more pliable consumers whose consumer *role* enabled them to identify with the society of the spectacle. But the official ideology is once again finding itself in contradiction with socioeconomic reality (lagging behind it), and it is precisely the youth who have first asserted an irresistible rage to live and who are spontaneously revolting against the daily boredom and dead time that the old world continues to produce in spite of all its modernizations. The most rebellious among them are expressing a pure, nihilistic rejection of this society without any awareness of a perspective for superseding it. But such a perspective is being sought and developed everywhere in the world. It must attain the coherence of theoretical critique and the practical organization of this coherence.

At the most rudimentary level, the "delinquents" all over the world express with the most obvious violence their refusal to be integrated into the society. But the abstractness of their refusal gives them no chance to escape the contradictions of a system of which they are a spontaneous negative product. The delinquents are produced by every aspect of the present social order: the urbanism of the housing projects, the breakdown of values, the extension of an increasingly boring consumer leisure, the growing police-humanist control over every aspect of daily life, and the economic survival of a family unit that has lost all significance. They despise work, but they accept commodities. They want everything the spectacle offers them and they want it now, but they can't afford to pay for it. This fundamental contradiction dominates their entire existence, constricting their efforts to make a truly free use of their time, to express themselves, or to form any sort of community. (Their microcommunities recreate a primitivism on the margin of developed society, and the poverty of this primitivism inevitably recreates a hierarchy within the gang. This hierarchy, which can fulfill itself only in wars with other gangs, *isolates* each gang and each individual within the gang.) In order to escape this contradiction the delinquent must either resign himself to going to work in order to buy the commodities—to this end a whole sector of production is specifically devoted to seducing him into consumerhood (motorcycles, electric guitars, clothes, records, etc.)—or else he is forced to attack the laws of the commodity, either in a rudimentary manner, by stealing, or in a conscious manner by advancing toward a revolutionary critique of the world of the commodity. Consumption "mellows out" the behavior of these young rebels and their revolt subsides into the worst conformism. For the delinquents only two futures are possible: the awakening of revolutionary consciousness or blind obedience in the factories.

The *Provos* are the first supersession of the experience of the delinquents, the organization of its first political expression. They arose out of an encounter between a few dregs from the world of decomposed art in search of a career and a mass of young rebels in search of self-expression. Their organization enabled both sides to advance toward and achieve a new type of contestation. The "artists" contributed a few ideas about play, though still quite mystified and decked out in a patchwork of ideological garments; the young rebels had nothing to offer but the violence of their revolt. From the beginning the two tendencies have remained distinct; the theoryless masses have found themselves under the tutelage of a small clique of dubious leaders who have tried to maintain their "power" by concocting a "provotarian" ideology. Their neoartistic reformism has prevailed over the possibility that the delinquents' violence might extend itself to the plane of ideas in an attempt to supersede art. The Provos are an expression of the latest reformism produced by modern capitalism: the reform of everyday life. Although nothing short of an uninterrupted revolution will be able to change life, the Provo hierarchy—like Bernstein with his vision of gradually transforming capitalism into socialism by means of reforms —believes that a few improvements can transform everyday life. By opting for the fragmentary, the Provos end up accepting the totality. To give themselves a base, their leaders have concocted the ridiculous ideology of the "provotariat" (an artistico-political salad composed of mildewed leftovers of a feast they have never known). This new provotariat is contrasted with the supposedly passive and "bourgeoisified" proletariat (eternal refrain of all the cretins of the century). Because they despair of a total change, the Provos despair of the only force capable of bringing about that change. The proletariat is the motor of capitalist society, and thus its mortal threat: everything is designed to repress it—parties, bureaucratic unions, police (who attack it more often than they do the Provos), and the colonization of its entire life —because it is the only really menacing force. The Provos have understood none of this; they remain incapable of criticizing the production system and thus remain prisoners of the system as a whole. When an antiunion workers' riot inspired the Provo base to join in with the direct violence, their bewildered leaders were left completely behind and could find nothing better to do than denounce "excesses" and appeal for nonviolence. These leaders, whose program had advocated provoking the authorities so as to reveal their repressiveness, ended up by complaining that they had been provoked by the police. And they appealed over the radio to the young rioters to let themselves be guided by the "Provos," i.e. by the leaders, who have amply demonstrated that their vague "anarchism" is nothing but one more lie. To arrive at a revolutionary critique, the rebellious Provo base has to begin by revolting against its own leaders, which means linking up with the objectively revolutionary forces of the proletariat and dumping people like Constant and De Vries (the one the official artist of the Kingdom of the Netherlands, the other a failed parliamentary candidate who admires the English police). Only in this way can the Provos link up with the authentic modern contestation of which they are already one of the fledgling expressions. If they really want to change the world, they have no use for those who are content to paint it white.*

By revolting against their studies, the American students have directly called in question a society that needs such studies. And their revolt (in Berkeley and elsewhere) against the university hierarchy has from the start asserted itself *as a revolt against the whole social system based on hierarchy and on the dictatorship of the economy and the state.* By refusing to accept the business and institutional roles for which their specialized studies have been designed to prepare them, they are profoundly calling in question a system of production that alienates all activity and its products from their producers. For all their groping and confusion, the rebelling American youth are already seeking a coherent revolutionary alternative from within the "affluent society." Unfortunately, they remain largely fixated on two relatively incidental aspects of the American crisis—the blacks and Vietnam—and the small "New Left" organizations suffer from this fact. Their forms reflect a striving for genuine democracy, but the weakness of their subversive content causes them to fall into dangerous contradictions. Due to their extreme political ignorance and naïve illusions about what is really going on in the world, their hostility to the traditional politics of the old left organizations is easily rechanneled into unwitting acceptance of them. *Abstract* opposition to their society leads them to admire or support its most conspicuous enemies: the "socialist" bureaucracies of China or Cuba. A group like the "Resurgence Youth Movement" can in the same breath condemn the state and praise the "Cultural Revolution," that pseudorevolt staged by the most gargantuan bureaucracy of modern times: Mao's China. At the same time, these semilibertarian and nondirective organizations, due to their glaring lack of content, are constantly in danger of slipping into the ideology of "group dynamics" or into the closed world of the sect. The widespread consumption of drugs is an expression of real poverty and a protest against this real poverty: it is a fallacious search for freedom in a world without freedom, a religious critique of a world that has already superseded religion. It is no accident that it is so prevalent in the Beat milieu (that right wing of the youth revolt), where ideological refusal coexists with acceptance of the most ridiculous superstitions (Zen, spiritualism, "New Church" mysticism, and other rotten carcasses such as Gandhiism and Humanism). In their search for a revolutionary program the American students make the same mistake as the Provos and proclaim themselves "the most exploited class in society." They must henceforth understand that they have no interests distinct from all those who are subject to commodity slavery and generalized oppression.

In the Eastern bloc, bureaucratic totalitarianism is also beginning to produce its own forces of negation. The youth revolt there is particularly intense, but the only information on it must be derived from the denunciations of it in official publications and from the police measures undertaken to contain it. From these sources we learn that a segment of the youth no longer "respects" moral and family order (which still exists there in its most detestable bourgeois form), devotes itself to "debauchery," despises work, and no longer obeys the Party police. The USSR has set up a special ministry for the express purpose of combatting this new delinquency. Alongside this diffuse revolt, a more coherently formulated contestation is striving to express itself; groups and clandestine journals emerge and disappear depending on the fluctuations of police repression. So far the most important act has been the publication of the *Open Letter to the Polish Communist Party* by the young Poles *Kuron* and *Modzelewski,** which explicitly affirms the necessity of "abolishing the present production relations and social relations" and recognizes that in order to accomplish this, "revolution is inevitable." The Eastern intelligentsia is seeking to elucidate and make conscious the critique that the workers have already concretized in East Berlin, Warsaw, and Budapest*: the proletarian critique of bureaucratic class power. This revolt is in the difficult situation of having to pose and solve real problems at one fell swoop. In other countries struggle is possible but the goal remains mystified. In the Eastern bureaucracies the struggle is without illusions and the goals are known; the problem is to devise the forms that can open the way to their realization.

In England the youth revolt found its first organized expression in the antibomb movement. This partial struggle, rallied around the vague program of the *Committee of 100*—which was capable of bringing 300,000 demonstrators into the streets—accomplished its most beautiful action in spring 1963 with the "Spies for Peace" scandal.[12] For lack of radical perspectives, it inevitably fell back, co-opted by traditional political manipulators and noble-minded pacifists. But the characteristically English archaisms in the control of everyday life have not been able to hold out against the assault of the modern world; the accelerating decomposition of secular values is engendering profoundly revolutionary tendencies in the critique of all aspects of the prevailing way of life.[13] The struggles of the British youth must link up with those of the British working class, which with its shop steward movement and wildcat strikes is one of the most combative in the world. The victory of these two struggles is only possible if they work out common perspectives. The collapse of the Labour government is an additional factor that could be conducive to such an alliance. Their encounter will touch off explosions compared to which the Amsterdam Provo riot will be seen as child's play. Only in this way can a real revolutionary movement arise that will answer practical needs.

Japan is the only advanced industrialized country where this fusion of student youth and radical workers has already taken place.

The *Zengakuren*, the well-known organization of revolutionary students, and the *League of Young Marxist Workers* are the two major organizations formed on the common orientation of the *Revolutionary Communist League*. This formation is already tackling the problems of revolutionary organization. Simultaneously and without illusions it combats both Western capitalism and the bureaucracy of the so-called socialist countries. It already groups together several thousand students and workers organized on a democratic and antihierarchical basis, with all members participating in all the activities of the organization. These Japanese revolutionaries are the first in the world to carry on large organized struggles in the name of an advanced revolutionary program and with a substantial mass participation. In demonstration

---

12. In which the partisans of the antibomb movement discovered, made public, and then invaded several ultrasecret fallout shelters reserved for members of the government.

13. One thinks here of the excellent journal *Heatwave*, which seems to be evolving toward an increasingly rigorous radicality.*

after demonstration thousands of workers and students have poured into the streets to wage violent struggle with the Japanese police. However, the RCL lacks a complete and concrete analysis of the two systems it fights with such ferocity. It has yet to define the precise nature of bureaucratic exploitation, just as it has yet to explicitly formulate the characteristics of modern capitalism, the critique of everyday life, and the critique of the spectacle. The Revolutionary Communist League is still fundamentally a vanguard political organization, an heir of the best features of the classical proletarian organizations. It is presently the most important revolutionary grouping in the world, and should henceforth be a pole of discussion and a rallying point for the new global revolutionary proletarian critique.*

To create at last a situation that goes beyond the point of no return

"To be avant-garde means to move in step with reality" (*Internationale Situationniste* #8). The radical critique of the modern world must now have the *totality* as its object and as its objective. This critique must be brought to bear on the world's actual past, on its present reality, and on the prospects for transforming it. We cannot grasp the whole truth of the present world, much less formulate the project of its total subversion, unless we are capable of *revealing its hidden history*, unless we subject the entire history of the international revolutionary movement, initiated over a century ago by the Western proletariat, to a demystified critical scrutiny. "This movement against the whole organization of the old world came to an end long ago" (*Internationale Situationniste* #7). *It failed.* Its last historical manifestation was the Spanish proletarian revolution, defeated in Barcelona in May 1937. But its official "failures" and "victories" must be judged in the light of their eventual consequences, and their essential truths must be brought back to light. In this regard we can agree with Karl Liebknecht's remark, on the eve of his assassination,* that "some defeats are really victories, while some victories are more shameful than any defeat." Thus the first great "defeat" of proletarian power, the Paris Commune, was in reality its first great *victory*, in that for the first time the early proletariat demonstrated its historical capacity to organize all aspects of social life *freely*. Whereas its first great "victory," the Bolshevik revolution, ultimately turned out to be its most disastrous defeat.

The triumph of the Bolshevik order coincided with the international counterrevolutionary movement that began with the crushing of the Spartakists by German "Social Democracy." The commonality of the jointly victorious Bolshevism and reformism went deeper than their apparent antagonism, for the Bolshevik order also turned out to be merely a new variation on the old theme, a new guise of the old order. The results of the Russian counterrevolution were, internally, the establishment and development of a new mode of exploitation, *bureaucratic state capitalism,* and externally, the spread of a "Communist" International whose branches served the sole purpose of defending and reproducing their Russian model. Capitalism, in its bureaucratic and bourgeois variants, won a new lease on life, over the dead bodies of the sailors of Kronstadt, the peasants of the Ukraine, and the workers of Berlin, Kiel, Turin, Shanghai, and finally Barcelona.

The Third International, ostensibly created by the Bolsheviks to counteract the degenerate social-democratic reformism of the Second International and to unite the vanguard of the proletariat in "revolutionary communist parties," was too closely linked to the interests of its founders to ever bring about a *genuine socialist revolution* anywhere. In reality the Third International was essentially a continuation of the Second. The Russian model was rapidly imposed on the Western workers' organizations and their evolutions were thenceforth one and the same. The totalitarian dictatorship of the bureaucracy, the new ruling class, over the Russian proletariat found its echo in the subjection of the great mass of workers in other countries to a stratum of political and labor-union bureaucrats whose interests had become clearly contradictory to those of their rank-and-file constituents. While the Stalinist monster haunted working-class consciousness, capitalism was becoming bureaucratized and overdeveloped, resolving its internal crises and proudly proclaiming this new victory to be permanent. In spite of apparent variations and oppositions, a single social form dominates the world. The principles of the *old world* continue to govern our *modern world;* the traditions of dead generations still weigh on the minds of the living.

Opposition to this world offered from within it, on its own terrain, by supposedly revolutionary organizations is only an apparent opposition. Such pseudo-opposition, propagating the worst mystifications and invoking more or less rigid *ideologies,* ultimately helps consolidate the dominant order. The labor unions and political parties forged by the working class as tools for its own emancipation have become mere safety valves, regulating mechanisms of the system, the private property of leaders seeking their own particular emancipation by using them as stepping stones to roles within the ruling class of a society they never dream of calling into question. The party program or union statute may contain vestiges of "revolutionary" phraseology, but their practice is everywhere *reformist.* (Their reformism, moreover, has become virtually meaningless since capitalism itself has become officially reformist.) Wherever the parties have been able to seize power—in countries more backward than 1917 Russia—they have only reproduced the Stalinist model of totalitarian counterrevolution.[14] Elsewhere, they have become the static and necessary complement[15] to the self-regulation of bureaucratized capitalism, the token opposition indispensable for maintaining its police-humanism. Vis-à-vis the worker masses, they remain the unfailing and unconditional defenders of the bureaucratic counterrevolution and the obedient agents of its foreign policy. Constantly working to perpetuate the universal dictatorship of the economy and the state, they are the bearers of the biggest lie in a world of lies. As the situationists put it, "A universally dominant social system, tending toward totalitarian self-regulation, is only apparently being combatted by false forms of opposition—illusory forms that remain trapped on the system's own terrain and thus only serve to reinforce it. Bureaucratic pseudosocialism is only the most grandiose of these disguises of the old world of hierarchy and alienated labor."

As for student unionism, it is nothing but a parody of a farce, a pointless and ridiculous imitation of a long degenerated labor unionism.

The theoretical and practical denunciation of Stalinism in all its forms must be the basic banality of all future revolutionary organizations. It is clear that in France, for example, where economic backwardness has delayed awareness of the crisis, the revolutionary movement can be reborn only over the dead body of Stalinism. *Stalinism must be destroyed.** That must be the constantly repeated watchword of the *last* revolution of prehistory.

This revolution must once and for all break with its own prehistory and derive all its poetry from the future. Little groups of "militants" claiming to represent the "authentic Bolshevik heritage" are voices from beyond the grave; in no way do they herald the future. These relics from the great shipwreck of the "revolution betrayed" invariably end up defending the USSR; this is their scandalous betrayal of revolution. They can scarcely maintain their illusions outside the famous under-

---

14. The parties have striven to industrialize these countries through classic primitive accumulation at the expense of the peasantry, accelerated by bureaucratic terror.

15. For 45 years the French "Communist" Party has not taken a single step toward seizing power. The same is true in all the advanced countries that have not fallen under the heel of the "Red" Army.

developed countries, where they serve to reinforce theoretical under-development.[16] From *Partisans* (organ of reconciled Stalino-Trotskyist currents) to all the tendencies and semitendencies squabbling over the dead body of Trotsky within and outside the Fourth International, the same revolutionary *ideology* reigns, with the same theoretical and practical inability to grasp the problems of the modern world. Forty years of counterrevolution separate them from the Revolution. Since this is not 1920, they can only be wrong (and they were already wrong in 1920).

The dissolution of the "ultraleftist" *Socialisme ou Barbarie* group after its division into two fractions—"Cardanist-modernist" and "tradition-al Marxist" (*Pouvoir Ouvrier*)—is proof, if any were needed, that there can be no revolution outside the modern, nor any modern thought outside the reinvention of the revolutionary critique (*Internationale Situationniste* #9). Any separation between these two aspects inevitably falls back either into the museum of revolutionary prehistory or into the modernism of the system, i.e. into the dominant counterrevolution: *Voix Ouvrière* or *Arguments*.

As for the various anarchist groups, they possess nothing beyond a pathetic faith in the ideological label "Anarchy" in which they have pigeonholed themselves. The pitiful *Le Monde Libertaire*, obviously edited by *students*, attains the most incredible degree of confusion and stupidity. Since they tolerate each other, they would *tolerate anything*.

The dominant social system, which flatters itself on its constant modernization, must now be confronted with a worthy opponent: the equally modernized negation that it is itself producing.[17] Let the dead bury the dead. The practical demystifications of the historical movement are exorcizing the phantoms that haunted revolutionary consciousness; the revolution of everyday life is being confronted with the immensity of its tasks. Revolution and the life it announces must both be reinvented. If the revolutionary project remains fundamen-tally the same—the abolition of class society—this is because the con-ditions giving rise to that project have nowhere been radically trans-formed. But this project must be taken up again with a new radicality and coherence, learning from the failure of previous revolutionaries, so that its partial realization will not merely bring about a new division of society.

---

16. On their role in Algeria, see "The Class Struggles in Algeria" (*Internationale Situationniste* #10).

17. "Address to Revolutionaries of Algeria" (*Internationale Situationniste* #10).

Since the struggle between the system and the new proletariat can only be in terms of the *totality*, the future revolutionary movement must abolish anything within itself that tends to reproduce the alienation produced by the *commodity system*—the system dominated by commodified labor. It must be a living critique of that system, a negation embodying all the elements necessary for its *supersession*. As Lukács correctly showed, revolutionary organization is this necessary mediation between theory and practice, between humanity and history, between the mass of workers and the proletariat *constituted as a class*. (Lukács's mistake was to believe that the Bolshevik Party fulfilled this role.)* If they are to be realized in practice, "theoretical" tendencies and differences must immediately be translated into organizational questions. Everything ultimately depends on how the new revolutionary movement resolves the organization question; on whether its organizational forms are consistent with its essential project: the *international realization of the absolute power of workers' councils* as prefigured in the proletarian revolutions of this century. Such an organization must make a radical critique of all the foundations of the society it combats: commodity production; *ideology* in all its guises; the state; and the separations imposed by the state.

The rock on which the old revolutionary movement foundered was the separation of theory and practice. Only the supreme moments of proletarian struggles overcame this split and discovered their own *truth*. No organization has yet bridged this gap. *Ideology*, no matter how "revolutionary" it may be, always serves the rulers; it is the *alarm signal* revealing the presence of the enemy fifth column. This is why the critique of ideology must in the final analysis be the central problem of revolutionary organization. Lies are a product of the alienated world; they cannot appear within an organization claiming to bear the *social truth* without that organization thereby becoming one more lie in a world of lies.

All the positive aspects of the power of workers' councils must already be embryonically present in any revolutionary organization aiming at their realization. Such an organization must wage a mortal struggle against the Leninist theory of organization. The 1905 revolution and the Russian workers' spontaneous self-organization into soviets was already a critique in acts[18] of that baneful theory. But the Bolshevik movement persisted in believing that working-class spontaneity could not go beyond "trade-union consciousness" and was thus incapable of grasping "the totality." This amounted to decapitating

---

18. After the theoretical critique of it by Rosa Luxemburg.*

the proletariat so that the Party could put itself at the "head" of the revolution. Contesting the proletariat's historical capacity to liberate itself, as Lenin did so ruthlessly, means contesting its capacity to totally run the future society. In such a perspective, the slogan "All power to the soviets" meant nothing more than the conquest of the soviets by the Party and the installation of the party state in place of the withering-away "state" of the armed proletariat.

"All power to the soviets" must once again be our slogan, but literally this time, without the Bolshevik ulterior motives. The proletariat can play the *game* of revolution only if the stakes are the *whole world;* otherwise it is nothing. The sole form of its power, *generalized self-management,* cannot be shared with any other power. Because it represents the actual dissolution of all powers, it can tolerate no limitation (geographical or otherwise); any compromises it accepts are immediately transformed into concessions, into surrender. "Self-management must be both the means and the end of the present struggle. It is not only what is at stake in the struggle, but also its adequate form. It is itself the material it works on, and its own presupposition" ("The Class Struggles in Algeria").

A unitary critique of the world is the guarantee of the coherence and truth of a revolutionary organization. To tolerate the existence of an oppressive system in some particular region (because it presents itself as "revolutionary," for example) amounts to recognizing the legitimacy of oppression. To tolerate alienation in any one domain of social life amounts to admitting an inevitability of all forms of reification. It is not enough to be for the power of workers' councils in the abstract; it is necessary to demonstrate what it means concretely: the suppression of commodity production and therefore of the proletariat. Despite their superficial disparities, all existing societies are governed by the *logic of the commodity;* it is the basis of their totalitarian self-regulation. Commodity reification is the *essential* obstacle to total emancipation, to the free construction of life. In the world of commodity production, praxis is not pursued in accordance with autonomously determined aims, but in accordance with the directives of external forces. Economic laws take on the appearance of natural laws; but their power depends solely on the "unawareness of those who participate in them."

The essence of commodity production is the loss of self in the chaotic and unconscious creation of a world totally beyond the control of its creators. In contrast, the radically revolutionary core of generalized self-management is everyone's conscious control over the whole of life. The self-management of commodity alienation would only make everyone the programmers of their own survival—squaring the cap-italist circle. The task of the workers' councils will thus be not the self-management of the existing world, but its unceasing qualitative transformation: the concrete supersession of the commodity (that enormous detour in the history of human self-production).

This supersession naturally implies the abolition of work and its replacement by a new type of free activity, thereby eliminating one of the fundamental splits of modern society: that between an increas-ingly reified labor and a passively consumed leisure. Presently decom-posing groups like *Socialisme ou Barbarie* or *Pouvoir Ouvrier*,[19] although adhering to the modern watchword of Workers' Power, continue to follow the path of the old workers' movement in envisioning a reform-ism of labor through its "humanization." But work itself must now be attacked. Far from being "utopian," the abolition of work is the first condition for the effective supersession of commodity society, for the elimination within each person's life of the separation between "free time" and "work time"—those complementary sectors of alien-ated life—that is a continual expression of the commodity's internal contradiction between use-value and exchange-value. Only when this opposition is overcome will people be able to make their vital activity subject to their will and consciousness and see themselves in a world that they themselves have created. The democracy of workers' coun-cils is the solution to all the present separations. It makes impossible "everything that exists outside individuals."

The conscious domination of history by the people who make it —that is what the whole revolutionary project amounts to. Modern history, like all past history, is the product of social praxis, the (uncon-scious) result of human activities. In the era of totalitarian domina-tion, capitalism has produced its own new religion: the *spectacle*. The spectacle is the terrestrial realization of *ideology*. Never has the world been so inverted. "And like the 'critique of religion' in Marx's day, the critique of the spectacle is today the essential precondition of any cri-tique" (*Internationale Situationniste* #9).

Humanity is historically confronted with the problem of *revolu-tion*. The increasingly grandiose material and technological means are equaled only by the increasingly profound dissatisfaction of everyone. The bourgeoisie and its Eastern heir, the bureaucracy, are incapable of putting this overdevelopment (which will be the basis of the poetry of

---

19. In contrast, a group like ICO, by shunning any organization or coherent theory, condemns itself to nonexistence.

the future) to any good use precisely because they both must strive to *maintain an old order.* The most they can use it for is to reinforce their police control. They can do nothing but accumulate *capital,* and therefore *proletarians*—a proletarian being someone who has no power over his life and who knows it. It is the new proletariat's historical fortune to be the only consequent heir to the valueless riches of the *bourgeois world*—riches that it must transform and supersede in such a way as to foster the development of fully realized human beings pursuing the total appropriation of *nature* and of their own nature. This realization of human nature can only mean the unlimited multiplication and full satisfaction of the real *desires* which the spectacle represses into the darkest corners of the revolutionary unconscious, and which it can realize only fantastically in the dreamlike delirium of its advertising. The true fulfillment of genuine desires—which means the abolition of all the pseudoneeds and pseudodesires that the system manufactures daily in order to perpetuate its own power—cannot take place without the suppression and positive supersession of the commodity spectacle.

Modern history can be liberated, and its innumerable achievements can be freely put to use, only by the forces that it represses: the workers without power over the conditions, the meaning, and the products of their own activities. In the nineteenth century the proletariat was already the heir of philosophy;* now it has become the heir of modern art and of the first conscious critique of everyday life. It cannot suppress itself without at the same time realizing art and philosophy. To transform the world and to change life are one and the same thing for the proletariat,* the inseparable passwords to its suppression as a class, the dissolution of the present reign of necessity, and the finally possible accession to the reign of freedom. The radical critique and free reconstruction of all the values and patterns of behavior imposed by alienated reality are its maximum program. Free creativity in the construction of all the moments and events of life is the only poetry it can acknowledge, the poetry made by all, the beginning of the revolutionary festival. Proletarian revolutions will be *festivals* or nothing, for festivity is the very keynote of the life they announce. *Play* is the ultimate principle of this festival, and the only rules it can recognize are to live without dead time and to enjoy without restraints.*

November 1966*

In Short

(Two Summaries of Situationist Perspectives)

I

Internationale Situationniste is the journal of a group of theorists who over the last few years have undertaken a radical critique of modern society—a critique of what it really is and of all its aspects.

As the situationists see it, a universally dominant social system, tending toward totalitarian self-regulation, is only apparently being combatted by false forms of opposition—illusory forms that remain trapped on the system's own terrain and thus only serve to reinforce it. Bureaucratic pseudosocialism is only the most grandiose of these disguises of the old world of hierarchy and alienated labor. The developing concentration of capitalism and the diversification of its global operation have given rise, on one hand, to the forced consumption of commodities produced in abundance, and on the other, to the control of the economy (and all of life) by bureaucrats who own the state; as well as to direct and indirect colonialism. But this system is far from having found a permanent solution to the incessant revolutionary crises of the historical epoch that began two centuries ago, for a new critical phase has opened: from Berkeley to Warsaw, from the Asturias to the Kivu,* the system is being refuted and combatted.

The situationists consider that this opposition implicitly requires the real abolition of all class societies, of commodity production, and of wage labor; the supersession of art and all cultural accomplishments by their reentry into play through free creation in everyday life —and thus their true fulfillment; and the direct fusion of revolutionary theory and practice in an experimental activity that precludes any petrification into "ideologies," which reflect the authority of specialists and which always serve the specialization of authority.

The factors involved in this historical problem are the rapid extension and modernization of the fundamental contradictions within the present system, and between that system and human desires. The social force that has an interest in resolving these contradictions—and the only force that is capable of resolving them—is the mass of workers who are powerless over the use of their own lives, deprived of any control over the fantastic accumulation of material possibilities that they produce. Such a resolution has already been prefigured in the emergence of democratic workers' councils that make all decisions for themselves. The only intelligent venture within the present imbecilized world is for this new proletariat to carry out this project by forming itself into a class unmediated by any leadership.

The situationists declare that they have no interest outside the whole of this movement. They lay down no particular principles on which to base a movement which is real, a movement which is being born before our very eyes. Faced with the struggles that are beginning in various countries over various issues, the situationists see their task as putting forward the whole of the problem, elucidating its coherence, its theoretical and therefore practical unity. In short, within the various phases of the overall struggle they constantly represent the interest of the whole movement.

SITUATIONIST INTERNATIONAL
December 1965*

II

The only reason the situationists do not call themselves communists* is so as not to be confused with the cadres of pro-Soviet or pro-China antiworker bureaucracies, remnants of the great revolutionary failure that ultimately extended the universal dictatorship of the economy and the state.

The situationists do not constitute a particular party in competition with other self-styled "working-class" parties.

The situationists refuse to reproduce internally the hierarchical conditions of the dominant world. They denounce everywhere the specialized politics of the bosses of hierarchical groups and parties, who base the oppressive force of their delusory future class power on the organized passivity of their militants.

The situationists do not put forward any *ideological* principles on which to model and thus direct the movement of proletarians. They consider that up till now revolutionary ideology has only changed hands; the point is to dissolve it by opposing it with revolutionary *theory*.

The situationists are the most radical current of the proletarian movement in many countries, the current that constantly pushes forward. Seeking to clarify and coordinate the scattered struggles of revolutionary proletarians, they help to draw out the implications of their actions. Striving to maintain the highest degree of international revolutionary consciousness, with the new theoretical critique they have everywhere been able to predict the return of the modern revolution. They are feared not for the power they hold, but for the use they make of it.

The situationists have no interests separate from the interests of the proletariat as a whole. They expect everything and have nothing to fear from so-called excesses, which reflect the critical profundity of the new era and the positive richness of the liberated everyday life that is emerging.

In all the present struggles the situationists constantly bring to the forefront the project of abolishing "everything that exists separately from individuals" as the decisive issue for the movement working to negate the existing society.

The situationists disdain to conceal their views and aims. They openly declare that their only interest and only goal is a social revolution going to the point where all powers are concentrated in an international federation of workers' councils, the power of everyone over all aspects of everyday life—over all aspects of the economy, of the society, and of history. The point is therefore not to modify private or state property, but to abolish it; not to mitigate class differences, but to abolish classes; not to "improve" the present society, but to create a new society; not to achieve some partial success that would give rise to a new division, but to thoroughly reject every new disguise of the old world.

The situationists have no doubt that the only possible program of modern revolution necessarily entails the formation of councils of all the workers, who by developing a clear awareness of all their enemies will become the sole power.

Revolutionaries are now turning their attention especially to Italy, because Italy is on the eve of a general uprising toward social revolution.

ITALIAN SECTION OF THE SITUATIONIST INTERNATIONAL
November 1969*

May 1968
Documents

Communiqué

Comrades,

Considering that the Sud-Aviation factory at Nantes has been occupied for two days by the workers and students of that city,

and that today the movement is spreading to several factories (Nouvelles Messageries de la Presse Parisienne in Paris, Renault in Cléon, etc.),

THE SORBONNE OCCUPATION COMMITTEE calls for

the immediate occupation of all the factories in France and the formation of Workers' Councils.

Comrades, spread and reproduce this appeal as quickly as possible.

Sorbonne, 16 May 1968, 3:30 p.m.

Watch Out for Manipulators!
Watch Out for Bureaucrats!

Comrades,

No one should be unaware of the importance of the GA [general assembly] this evening (Thursday, May 16). Over the last two days several individuals, recognizable from having previously been seen peddling their various party lines, have succeeded in sowing confusion and in smothering the GAs under a barrage of bureaucratic manipulations whose crudeness clearly demonstrates the contempt they have for this assembly.

This assembly must learn how to make itself respected or disappear. Two points must be discussed above all:

WHO CONTROLS THE SECURITY MARSHALS? whose disgusting role is intolerable.

WHY IS THE PRESS COMMITTEE—which *dares to censor the communiqués* that it is charged to transmit to the news agencies—

composed of apprentice journalists who are careful not to disappoint the ORTF [National Radio–Television] bosses so as not
to jeopardize their future job possibilities?

Apart from that: Considering that the workers are beginning to occupy
several factories in France, FOLLOWING OUR EXAMPLE AND WITH
THE SAME RIGHT WE HAVE, the Sorbonne Occupation Committee
issued a statement approving of this movement at 3:00 this afternoon.
The central problem of this evening's GA is therefore to declare itself
by a clear vote supporting or disavowing this appeal of its Occupation
Committee. If it disavows the appeal it will have put itself on record as
reserving for students a right that it refuses to the working class; and
in that case it is clear that it will no longer want to concern itself with
anything but a Gaullist reform of the university.

OCCUPATION COMMITTEE OF THE
PEOPLE'S FREE SORBONNE UNIVERSITY
16 May 1968, 6:30 p.m.

Slogans to Be Spread Now by Every Means

(leaflets, announcements over microphones, comic strips, songs, graffiti, balloons on paintings in the Sorbonne, announcements in theaters
during films or while disrupting them, balloons on subway billboards,
before making love, after making love, in elevators, each time you raise
your glass in a bar):

OCCUPY THE FACTORIES

POWER TO THE WORKERS COUNCILS

ABOLISH CLASS SOCIETY

DOWN WITH SPECTACLE-COMMODITY SOCIETY

ABOLISH ALIENATION

TERMINATE THE UNIVERSITY

HUMANITY WON'T BE HAPPY TILL THE LAST BUREAUCRAT
    IS HUNG WITH THE GUTS OF THE LAST CAPITALIST*

DEATH TO THE COPS

FREE ALSO THE 4 GUYS CONVICTED FOR LOOTING
DURING THE MAY 6TH RIOT

OCCUPATION COMMITTEE OF THE
PEOPLE'S FREE SORBONNE UNIVERSITY
16 May 1968, 7:00 p.m.

Telegrams

PROFESSOR IVAN SVITAK PRAGUE CZECHOSLOVAKIA
THE OCCUPATION COMMITTEE OF THE PEOPLE'S FREE
SORBONNE SENDS FRATERNAL GREETINGS TO COM-
RADE SVITAK AND OTHER CZECHOSLOVAKIAN REVO-
LUTIONARIES STOP LONG LIVE THE INTERNATIONAL
POWER OF THE WORKERS COUNCILS STOP HUMANITY
WON'T BE HAPPY TILL THE LAST CAPITALIST IS HUNG
WITH THE GUTS OF THE LAST BUREAUCRAT STOP LONG
LIVE REVOLUTIONARY MARXISM

ZENGAKUREN TOKYO JAPAN
LONG LIVE THE STRUGGLE OF THE JAPANESE COMRADES
WHO HAVE OPENED COMBAT SIMULTANEOUSLY ON THE
FRONTS OF ANTI-STALINISM AND ANTI-IMPERIALISM STOP
LONG LIVE FACTORY OCCUPATIONS STOP LONG LIVE THE
GENERAL STRIKE STOP LONG LIVE THE INTERNATIONAL
POWER OF THE WORKERS COUNCILS STOP HUMANITY
WON'T BE HAPPY TILL THE LAST BUREAUCRAT IS HUNG
WITH THE GUTS OF THE LAST CAPITALIST STOP OCCUPA-
TION COMMITTEE OF THE PEOPLE'S FREE SORBONNE

POLITBURO OF THE COMMUNIST PARTY OF THE USSR THE
KREMLIN MOSCOW
SHAKE IN YOUR SHOES BUREAUCRATS STOP THE INTER-
NATIONAL POWER OF THE WORKERS COUNCILS WILL
SOON WIPE YOU OUT STOP HUMANITY WON'T BE HAPPY
TILL THE LAST BUREAUCRAT IS HUNG WITH THE GUTS OF
THE LAST CAPITALIST STOP LONG LIVE THE STRUGGLE OF
THE KRONSTADT SAILORS AND OF THE MAKHNOVSHCHI-
NA AGAINST TROTSKY AND LENIN STOP LONG LIVE THE
1956 COUNCILIST INSURRECTION OF BUDAPEST STOP

DOWN WITH THE STATE STOP LONG LIVE REVOLUTION-
ARY MARXISM STOP OCCUPATION COMMITTEE OF THE
PEOPLE'S FREE SORBONNE

POLITBURO OF THE CHINESE COMMUNIST PARTY GATE OF
CELESTIAL PEACE BEIJING
SHAKE IN YOUR SHOES BUREAUCRATS STOP THE INTER-
NATIONAL POWER OF THE WORKERS COUNCILS WILL
SOON WIPE YOU OUT STOP HUMANITY WON'T BE HAPPY
TILL THE LAST BUREAUCRAT IS HUNG WITH THE GUTS
OF THE LAST CAPITALIST STOP LONG LIVE FACTORY
OCCUPATIONS STOP LONG LIVE THE GREAT CHINESE
PROLETARIAN REVOLUTION OF 1927 BETRAYED BY THE
STALINIST BUREAUCRATS STOP LONG LIVE THE PRO-
LETARIANS OF CANTON AND ELSEWHERE WHO HAVE
TAKEN UP ARMS AGAINST THE SO-CALLED PEOPLE'S
ARMY STOP LONG LIVE THE CHINESE WORKERS AND
STUDENTS WHO HAVE ATTACKED THE SO-CALLED CUL-
TURAL REVOLUTION AND THE MAOIST BUREAUCRATIC
ORDER STOP LONG LIVE REVOLUTIONARY MARXISM
STOP DOWN WITH THE STATE STOP OCCUPATION COM-
MITTEE OF THE PEOPLE'S FREE SORBONNE

17 May 1968

Report on the
Occupation of the Sorbonne

The occupation of the Sorbonne that began Monday, May 13, has
opened a new period in the crisis of modern society. The events now
taking place in France foreshadow the return of the proletarian revolutionary movement in all countries. The movement that had already
advanced from theory to struggle in the streets has now advanced to
a struggle for control of the means of production. Modernized capitalism thought it had finished with class struggle—but it's started
up again! The proletariat supposedly no longer existed—but here it is
again.

By surrendering the Sorbonne, the government hoped to pacify
the student revolt, which had already succeeded in holding a section
of Paris behind its barricades an entire night before being recaptured

with great difficulty by the police. The Sorbonne was given over to the students in the hope that they would peacefully discuss their university problems. But the occupiers immediately decided to open it to the public to freely discuss the general problems of the society. This was thus a prefiguration of a council, a council in which even the students broke out of their miserable studenthood and ceased being students.

To be sure, the occupation was never complete: a chapel and a few remaining administrative offices were tolerated. The democracy was never total: future technocrats of the UNEF [National Student Union] claimed to be making themselves useful and other political bureaucrats also tried their manipulations. Workers' participation remained very limited and the presence of nonstudents soon began to be questioned. Many students, professors, journalists, and imbeciles of other professions came as spectators.

In spite of all these deficiencies, which are not surprising considering the disparity between the scope of the project and the narrowness of the student milieu, the exemplary nature of the best aspects of this situation immediately took on an explosive significance. Workers were inspired by the free discussion and the striving for a radical critique, by seeing direct democracy in action. Even limited to a Sorbonne liberated from the state, this was a revolutionary program developing its own forms. The day after the occupation of the Sorbonne the Sud-Aviation workers of Nantes occupied their factory. On the third day, Thursday the 16th, the Renault factories at Cléon and Flins were occupied and the movement began at the NMPP and at Boulogne-Billancourt, starting at Shop 70. Three days later 100 factories have been occupied and the wave of strikes, accepted but never initiated by the union bureaucracies, is paralyzing the railroads and developing into a general strike.

The only power in the Sorbonne was the general assembly of its occupiers. At its first session, on May 14, amidst a certain confusion, it had elected an Occupation Committee of 15 members revocable by it each day. Only one of the delegates, a member of the Nanterre–Paris Enragés group, had set forth a program: defense of direct democracy in the Sorbonne and absolute power of workers' councils as ultimate goal. The next day's general assembly reelected its entire Occupation Committee, which had as yet been unable to accomplish anything. In fact, the various specialized groupings that had set themselves up in the Sorbonne all followed the directives of a hidden "Coordination Committee" composed of self-appointed organizers, responsible to no one, doing everything in their power to prevent any "irresponsible" extremist actions. An hour after the reelection of the Occupation

Committee one of these "coordinators" privately tried to declare it dissolved. A direct appeal to the people in the courtyard of the Sorbonne aroused a movement of protests that forced the manipulator to retract himself. By the next day, Thursday the 16th, thirteen members of the Occupation Committee had disappeared, leaving two comrades, including the Enragés member, vested with the only delegation of power authorized by the general assembly—and this at a time when the urgency of the situation demanded immediate decisions: democracy was constantly being flouted in the Sorbonne while factory occupations were spreading all over the country. At 3:00 p.m. the Occupation Committee, rallying to itself as many Sorbonne occupiers as it could who were determined to maintain democracy there, launched an appeal for "the occupation of all the factories in France and the formation of workers' councils." To disseminate this appeal the Occupation Committee had at the same time to restore the democratic functioning of the Sorbonne. It had to take over or recreate from scratch all the services that were supposed to be under its authority: the loudspeaker system, printing facilities, interfaculty liaison, security. It ignored the squawking complaints of the spokesmen of various political groups (JCR [a Trotskyist group], Maoists, etc.), reminding them that it was responsible only to the general assembly. It intended to report to the assembly that very evening, but the Sorbonne occupiers' unanimous decision to march on Renault-Billancourt (whose occupation we had learned of in the meantime) postponed the meeting until 2:00 p.m. the next day.

During the night, while thousands of comrades were at Billancourt, some unidentified persons improvised a general assembly, which broke up when the Occupation Committee, having learned of its existence, sent back two delegates to call attention to its illegitimacy.

Friday the 17th at 2:00 p.m. the regular assembly saw its rostrum occupied for a long time by self-appointed marshals belonging to the FER [another Trotskyist group]; and then had to interrupt the session for the second march on Billancourt at 5:00.

That evening at 9:00 the Occupation Committee was finally able to present a report of its activities. It was, however, completely unable to get its actions discussed and voted on, in particular its appeal for the occupation of the factories, which the assembly did not take the responsibility of either disavowing or approving. Faced with such indifference, the Occupation Committee had no choice but to resign. The assembly proved equally incapable of protesting against a new invasion of the rostrum by the FER troops, whose putsch seemed to be aimed at countering the provisional alliance of JCR and UNEF bureaucrats.

The partisans of direct democracy realized, and immediately declared, that they had no further interest in the Sorbonne.

At the very moment that the example of the occupation is beginning to be taken up in the factories it is collapsing at the Sorbonne. This development is all the more serious since the workers have against them a bureaucracy infinitely more powerful and entrenched than that of the student or leftist amateurs. To add to the confusion, the leftist bureaucrats, echoing the CGT [the Communist Party-dominated labor union] in the hope of being accorded a little marginal role alongside it, abstractly separate the workers from the students. ("The workers don't need any lessons from the students.") But the students have in fact already given an excellent lesson to the workers precisely by occupying the Sorbonne and briefly initiating a really democratic debate. The bureaucrats all tell us demagogically that the working class is grown up, in order to hide the fact that it is enchained—first of all by them (now or in their future hopes, depending on which group they're in). They counterpose their lying seriousness to the "festivity" in the Sorbonne; but it was precisely that festiveness that bore within itself the only thing that is serious: the radical critique of prevailing conditions.

The student struggle has now been left behind. Even more left behind are all the second-string bureaucratic leaders who think it's a good idea to feign respect for the Stalinists at the very moment when the CGT and the so-called Communist Party are *terrified*. The outcome of the present crisis is in the hands of the workers themselves, if they succeed in accomplishing in their factory occupations the goals that the university occupation was only able to hint at.

The comrades who supported the first Sorbonne Occupation Committee—the Enragés–Situationist International Committee, a number of workers, and a few students—have formed a Council for Maintaining the Occupations. The occupations can obviously be maintained only by quantitatively and qualitatively extending them, without sparing any existing regime.

COUNCIL FOR MAINTAINING THE OCCUPATIONS
Paris, 19 May 1968

For the Power of the Workers' Councils

In the space of ten days workers have occupied hundreds of factories, a spontaneous general strike has brought the country to a standstill, and de facto committees have taken over many state-owned buildings. This situation—which cannot last, but must either extend itself or disappear (through repression or defeatist negotiations)—is sweeping aside all the old ideas and confirming all the radical hypotheses on the return of the revolutionary proletarian movement. The fact that the whole movement was *actually* triggered five months ago by a half-dozen revolutionaries of the "Enragés" group reveals even better how much the objective conditions were already present. The French example is already having repercussions in other countries, reviving the internationalism that is inseparable from the revolutions of our century.

The fundamental struggle is now between the mass of workers—who do not have direct means of expressing themselves—and the leftist political and labor-union bureaucracies which (even if merely on the basis of the 14% of the active population that is unionized) *control the factory gates* and the right to negotiate in the name of the occupiers. These bureaucracies are not workers' organizations that have degenerated and betrayed the workers; they are a mechanism for integrating the workers into capitalist society. In the present crisis they are the main protection of this shaken capitalism.

The de Gaulle regime may negotiate—essentially (even if only indirectly) with the PCF–CGT [French Communist Party and the labor union it dominates]—for the demobilization of the workers in exchange for some economic benefits; after which the radical currents would be repressed. Or the "Left" may come to power and pursue the same policies, though from a weaker position. Or an armed repression may be attempted. Or, finally, the workers may take the upper hand by speaking for themselves and becoming conscious of goals as radical as the forms of struggle they have already put into practice. Such a process would lead to the formation of workers' councils, making decisions democratically at the rank-and-file level, federating with each other by means of delegates revocable at any moment, and becoming the sole deliberative and executive power over the entire country.

How could the continuation of the present situation lead to such a prospect? Within a few days, perhaps, the necessity of starting certain sectors of the economy back up again *under workers' control* could lay the bases for this new power, a power which everything is already pushing to burst through the constraints of the unions and parties.

The railroads and printshops would have to be put back into operation for the needs of the workers' struggle. New de facto authorities would have to requisition and distribute food. If money became devalued or unavailable it might have to be replaced by vouchers backed by those new authorities. It is through such a *practical process* that the consciousness of the deepest aspirations of the proletariat can impose itself—the class consciousness that lays hold on history and brings about the workers' power over all aspects of their own lives.

COUNCIL FOR MAINTAINING THE OCCUPATIONS
Paris, 22 May 1968

Address to All Workers

Comrades,

What we have already done in France is haunting Europe and will soon threaten all the ruling classes of the world, from the bureaucrats of Moscow and Beijing to the millionaires of Washington and Tokyo. Just as we have *made Paris dance*, the international proletariat will once again take up its assault on the capitals of all the states and all the citadels of alienation. The occupation of factories and public buildings throughout the country has not only brought a halt to the functioning of the economy, it has brought about a general questioning of the society. A deep-seated movement is leading almost every sector of the population to seek a real transformation of life. This is the beginning of a revolutionary movement, a movement which lacks nothing but *the consciousness of what it has already done* in order to triumph.

What forces will try to save capitalism? The regime will fall unless it threatens to resort to arms (accompanied by the promise of new elections, which could only take place after the capitulation of the movement) or even resorts to immediate armed repression. If the Left comes to power, it too will try to defend the old world through concessions and through force. The best defender of such a "popular government" would be the so-called Communist Party, the party of Stalinist bureaucrats, which has fought the movement from the very beginning and which began to envisage the fall of the de Gaulle regime only when it realized it was no longer capable of being that regime's main guardian. Such a transitional government would really be "Kerenskyist" only if the Stalinists were beaten. All this will ultimately depend on the workers' consciousness and capacities for autonomous organization. The workers who have already rejected the ridiculous agreement that the union leaders were so pleased with need only discover that they cannot "win" much more within the framework of the existing economy, but that they can *take everything* by transforming all the bases of the economy on their own behalf. The bosses can hardly pay more; but they can disappear.

The present movement did not become "politicized" by going beyond the miserable union demands regarding wages and pensions, demands which were falsely presented as "social questions." It is *beyond politics:* it is posing *the social question* in its simple truth. The revolution that has been in the making for over a century is returning. It can express itself only in its own forms. It's too late for a bureaucratic-revolutionary patching up. When a recently de-Stalinized bureaucrat like André Barjonet calls for the formation of a common organization that would bring together "all the authentic forces of revolution . . . whether they march under the banner of Trotsky or Mao, of anarchy or situationism," we need only recall that those who today follow Trotsky or Mao, to say nothing of the pitiful "Anarchist Federation," have nothing to do with the present revolution. The bureaucrats may now change their minds about what they call "authentically revolutionary"; authentic revolution will not change its condemnation of bureaucracy.

At the present moment, with the power they hold and with the parties and unions being what they are, the workers have no other choice but to organize themselves in unitary rank-and-file committees directly taking over the economy and all aspects of the reconstruction of social life, asserting their autonomy vis-à-vis any sort of political or unionist leadership, ensuring their self-defense, and federating with each other regionally and nationally. In so doing they will become the sole real power in the country, the power of *workers' councils*. The only alternative is to return to their passivity and go back to watching television. The proletariat is "either revolutionary or nothing."

What are the essential features of council power?

- Dissolution of all external power.
- Direct and total democracy.
- Practical unification of decision and execution.
- Delegates who can be revoked at any moment by those who have mandated them.
- Abolition of hierarchy and independent specializations.
- Conscious management and transformation of all the conditions of liberated life.
- Permanent creative mass participation.
- Internationalist extension and coordination.

The present requirements are nothing less than this. Self-management is nothing less. *Beware of all the modernist co-opters*—including even priests—who are beginning to talk of self-management or even of workers' councils without acknowledging this *minimum,* because they want to save their bureaucratic functions, the privileges of their intellectual specializations, or their future careers as petty bosses!

In reality, what is necessary now has been necessary since the beginning of the proletarian revolutionary project. It's always been a question of working-class autonomy. The struggle has always been for the abolition of wage labor, of commodity production, and of the state. The goal has always been to accede to conscious history, to suppress all separations and "everything that exists independently of individuals." Proletarian revolution has spontaneously sketched out its appropriate forms in the councils—in St. Petersburg in 1905, in Turin in 1920, in Catalonia in 1936, in Budapest in 1956. The preservation of the old society, or the formation of new exploiting classes, has each time been over the dead body of the councils. The working class now knows its enemies and its own appropriate methods of action. "Revolutionary organization has had to learn that *it can no longer combat alienation by means of alienated forms of struggle*" (*The Society of the Spectacle*). Workers' councils are clearly the only solution, since all the other forms of revolutionary struggle have led to the opposite of what was aimed at.

ENRAGÉS–SITUATIONIST INTERNATIONAL COMMITTEE
COUNCIL FOR MAINTAINING THE OCCUPATIONS
30 May 1968

Graffiti*

In the decor of the spectacle,
the eye meets only things and their prices.

Commute, work, commute, sleep . . .

Meanwhile everyone wants to breathe and nobody can
and many say, "We will breathe later."
And most of them don't die because they are already dead.

Boredom is counterrevolutionary.

We don't want a world where the guarantee of not dying
of starvation brings the risk of dying of boredom.

We want to live.

Don't beg for the right to live—take it.

In a society that has abolished every kind of adventure
the only adventure that remains is to abolish the society.

The liberation of humanity is all or nothing.

Those who make revolutions half way only dig their own graves.

No replastering, the structure is rotten.

Masochism today takes the form of reformism.

Reform my ass.

The revolution is incredible because it's really happening.

I came, I saw, I was won over.

Run, comrade, the old world is behind you!

Quick!

If we only have enough time . . .

In any case, no regrets!

Already ten days of happiness.

At every moment something is happening.

Live in the moment.

Comrades, if everyone did like us . . .

We will ask nothing. We will demand nothing.
We will take, occupy.

Down with the state.

When the National Assembly becomes a bourgeois theater,
all the bourgeois theaters should be turned into national assemblies.
[*Written above the entrance of the occupied Odéon Theater*]

Referendum: whether we vote yes or no, it turns us into suckers.

It's painful to submit to our bosses;
it's even more stupid to choose them.

Let's not change bosses, let's change life.

Don't liberate me—I'll take care of that.

I'm not a servant of the people
(much less of their self-appointed leaders).
Let the people serve themselves.

Abolish class society.

Nature created neither servants nor masters.
I want neither to rule nor to be ruled.

We will have good masters as soon as everyone is their own.

"In revolution there are two types of people:
those who make it and those who profit from it."
(Napoleon)

Warning: ambitious careerists may now be
disguised as "progressives."

Don't be taken in by the politicos and their filthy demagogy.
We must rely on ourselves.
Socialism without freedom is a barracks.

All power corrupts. Absolute power corrupts absolutely.

We want structures that serve people,
not people serving structures.

The revolution doesn't belong to the committees, it's yours.
Politics is in the streets.

Barricades close the streets but open the way.

Our hope can come only from the hopeless.

A proletarian is someone who has no power over his life
and knows it.

Never work.

People who work get bored when they don't work.
People who don't work never get bored.

Workers of all countries, enjoy!

Since 1936 I have fought for wage increases.
My father before me fought for wage increases.
Now I have a TV, a fridge, a Volkswagen.
Yet my whole life has been a drag.
Don't negotiate with the bosses. Abolish them.

The boss needs you, you don't need the boss.

By stopping our machines together we will
demonstrate their weakness.

Occupy the factories.

Power to the workers' councils.
(an enragé)

Power to the enragés' councils.
(a worker)

Worker: You may be only 25 years old,
but your union dates from the last century.

Labor unions are whorehouses.

Comrades, let's lynch Séguy!*

Please leave the Communist Party as clean on leaving it
as you would like to find it on entering.

Stalinists, your children are with us!

Man is neither Rousseau's noble savage nor
the Church's or La Rochefoucauld's depraved sinner.
He is violent when oppressed, gentle when free.

Conflict is the origin of everything.
(Heraclitus)

If we have to resort to force, don't sit on the fence.

Be cruel.

Humanity won't be happy till the last capitalist is hung
with the guts of the last bureaucrat.*

When the last sociologist has been hung with the guts of
the last bureaucrat, will we still have "problems"?

The passion of destruction is a creative joy.
(Bakunin)

A single nonrevolutionary weekend is infinitely more bloody
than a month of total revolution.

The tears of philistines are the nectar of the gods.

This concerns everyone.

We are all German Jews.

We refuse to be highrised, diplomaed, licensed,
inventoried, registered, indoctrinated, suburbanized,
sermonized, beaten, telemanipulated, gassed, booked.

We are all "undesirables."

We must remain "unadapted."

The forest precedes man, the desert follows him.

Under the paving stones, the beach.

Concrete breeds apathy.

Coming soon to this location: charming ruins.

Beautiful, maybe not, but O how charming: life versus survival.

"My aim is to agitate and disturb people.
I'm not selling bread, I'm selling yeast."
(Unamuno)

Conservatism is a synonym for rottenness and ugliness.

You are hollow.

You will end up dying of comfort.

Hide yourself, object!

No to coat-and-tie revolution.

A revolution that requires us to sacrifice ourselves for it
is Papa's revolution.

Revolution ceases to be the moment it calls for self-sacrifice.

The prospect of finding pleasure tomorrow
will never compensate for today's boredom.

When people notice they are bored, they stop being bored.

Happiness is a new idea.

Live without dead time.

Those who talk about revolution and class struggle without
referring to everyday reality have a corpse in their mouth.

Culture is an inversion of life.

Poetry is in the streets.

The most beautiful sculpture is a
paving stone thrown at a cop's head.

Art is dead, don't consume its corpse.

Art is dead, let's liberate our everyday life.

Art is dead, Godard can't change that.

Godard: the supreme Swiss Maoist jerk.

Permanent cultural vibration.

We want a wild and ephemeral music.
We propose a fundamental regeneration:
concert strikes,
sound gatherings with collective investigation.
Abolish copyrights: sound structures belong to everyone.

Anarchy is me.

Revolution, I love you.

Down with the abstract, long live the ephemeral.
(Marxist-Pessimist Youth)

Don't consume Marx, live him.

I'm a Groucho Marxist.

I take my desires for reality
because I believe in the reality of my desires.

Desiring reality is great! Realizing your desires is even better!

Practice wishful thinking.

I declare a permanent state of happiness.

Be realistic, demand the impossible.

Power to the imagination.

Those who lack imagination cannot imagine what is lacking.

Imagination is not a gift, it must be conquered.
(Breton)

Action must not be a reaction, but a creation.

Action enables us to overcome divisions and find solutions.

Exaggeration is the beginning of invention.

The enemy of movement is skepticism.
Everything that has been realized comes from dynamism,
which comes from spontaneity.

Here, we spontane.

"You must bear a chaos inside you to give birth to a dancing star."
(Nietzsche)

Chance must be systematically explored.

Alcohol kills. Take LSD.

Unbutton your mind as often as your fly.

"Every view of things that is not strange is false."
(Valéry)

Life is elsewhere.

Forget everything you've been taught. Start by dreaming.

Form dream committees.

Revolution is the active passage from dream to reality.

Dare! This word contains all the politics of the present moment.
(Saint-Just)

Arise, ye wretched of the university.

Students are jerks.

The student's susceptibility to recruitment as a militant for
any cause is a sufficient demonstration of his real impotence.
(enragé women)

Professors, you make us grow old.

Terminate the university.

Rape your Alma Mater.

What if we burned the Sorbonne?

Professors, you are as senile as your culture,
your modernism is nothing but the modernization of the police.

We refuse the role assigned to us:
we will not be trained as police dogs.

We don't want to be the watchdogs or servants of capitalism.

Exams = servility, social promotion, hierarchical society.

When examined, answer with questions.

Insolence is the new revolutionary weapon.

Every teacher is taught, everyone taught teaches.

The Old Mole of history seems to be
splendidly undermining the Sorbonne.
(telegram from Marx, 13 May 1968)

Thought that stagnates rots.
To call in question the society you "live" in,
you must first be capable of calling yourself in question.

Take revolution seriously, but don't take yourself seriously.

The walls have ears. Your ears have walls.

Making revolution also means breaking our internal chains.

A cop sleeps inside each one of us. We must kill him.

Drive the cop out of your head.

Religion is the ultimate con.

Neither God nor master.

If God existed it would be necessary to abolish him.

Can you believe that some people are still Christians?

Down with the toad of Nazareth.

How can you think freely in the shadow of a chapel?

We want a place to piss, not a place to pray.

I suspect God of being a leftist intellectual.

The bourgeoisie has no other pleasure
than to degrade all pleasures.

Going through the motions kills the emotions.

Struggle against the emotional fixations that paralyze our potentials.
(Committee of Women on the Path of Liberation)

Constraints imposed on pleasure
incite the pleasure of living without constraints.

The more I make love, the more I want to make revolution.
The more I make revolution, the more I want to make love.

SEX: It's okay, says Mao, as long as you don't do it too often.

Comrades, 5 hours of sleep a day is indispensable:
we need you for the revolution.

Embrace your love without dropping your guard.

I love you!!! Oh, say it with paving stones!!!

I'm coming in the paving stones.

Total orgasm.

Comrades, people are making love in the Poli Sci classrooms,
not only in the fields.

Revolutionary women are more beautiful.

Zelda, I love you! Down with work!

The young make love, the old make obscene gestures.

Make love, not war.

Whoever speaks of love destroys love.

Down with consumer society.

The more you consume, the less you live.

Commodities are the opium of the people.

Burn commodities.

You can't buy happiness. Steal it.

See Nanterre and live. Die in Naples with Club Med.

Are you a consumer or a participant?

To be free in 1968 means to participate.

I participate.
You participate.
He participates.
We participate.
They profit.

The golden age was the age when gold didn't reign.

"The cause of all wars, riots, and injustices
is the existence of property."
(St. Augustine)

Happiness is hanging your landlord.

Millionaires of the world unite. The wind is turning.

The economy is wounded—I hope it dies!

How sad to love money.

You too can steal.

"Amnesty: An act in which the rulers
pardon the injustices they have committed."
(Ambrose Bierce)*

Abolish alienation.

Obedience begins with consciousness;
consciousness begins with disobedience.

First, disobey; then write on the walls.
(Law of 10 May 1968)

I don't like to write on walls.

Write everywhere.

Before writing, learn to think.

I don't know how to write but I would like to say beautiful things
and I don't know how.

I don't have time to write!!!

I have something to say but I don't know what.

Freedom is the right to silence.

Long live communication, down with telecommunication.

You, my comrade, you whom I was unaware of amid the tumult,
you who are throttled, afraid, suffocated—come, talk to us.

Talk to your neighbors.

Yell.

Create.

Look in front of you!!!

Help with cleanup, there are no maids here.

Revolution is an INITIATIVE.

Speechmaking is counterrevolutionary.

Comrades, stop applauding, the spectacle is everywhere.

Don't get caught up in the spectacle of opposition.
Oppose the spectacle.

Down with spectacle-commodity society.

Down with journalists and those who cater to them.

Only the truth is revolutionary.

No forbidding allowed.

Freedom is the crime that contains all crimes.
It is our ultimate weapon.

The freedom of others extends mine infinitely.

No freedom for the enemies of freedom.

Free our comrades.

Open the gates of the asylums, prisons, and other faculties.

Open the windows of your heart.

To hell with boundaries.

You can no longer sleep quietly once you've
suddenly opened your eyes.

The future will only contain what we put into it now.

Internal Texts

(1969–1971)

Provisional Statutes of the SI

Participation in the SI and National Sections

1. The SI is an international association of *individuals* who, having demonstrated an equality of capabilities—in general, not in every detail—for our common theoretical and practical activity, are equal in all aspects of its democratic management. Majority decision is executed by everyone; a minority has the *duty* to break if the issue in dispute seems to it to concern a fundamental matter among the previously recognized bases of agreement.

2. The SI organizes its activity on the basis of a division into national sections. This "national" criterion is understood in both geographical and cultural terms; it is possible, and in fact desirable, that each section be itself partially international in its composition. Each section is also "national" in the sense that it engages in a central advanced activity in a given country and does not seek to subdivide into regional subgroups in that country. A section might envisage such a subdivision within itself in certain exceptional geographical conditions, but the SI would continue to relate to the section only as a single unit.

3. A member of the SI is *ipso facto* a member of any national section where he expresses his decision to live and participate. Each member is responsible to the SI as a whole, and the SI is collectively responsible for the known behavior of each of its members.

4. The general assembly of all the members of the SI is the only decision-making power over all theoretical and practical choices. To the exact degree that there exist practical obstacles to the presence of everyone, the SI recognizes a system of delegates representing each of the members. These delegates may or may not bear specific, imperative mandates. Decisions made by delegates are revocable by those who have mandated them if the mandates have been left open; they are not revocable in cases in which a delegate has correctly executed a specific mandate.

Organization of National Sections

5. Each national section, on its own responsibility and within the general guidelines adopted by the entire SI, democratically decides on all its activities and tactics on its own terrain. It alone decides on all

aspects of the publications, contacts, and projects it sees fit to pursue. If possible it publishes a journal, the editorial management of which is entirely in its own hands. It goes without saying that personally undertaken projects or theoretical hypotheses cannot be limited by the section, nor by the SI as a whole—except in cases where they are manifestly hostile to the SI's very bases.

6. Each national section is the sole judge, in its region, of breaks with persons on the outside and of *admissions* to the section. It is responsible to the SI as a whole only for guarding against anything that might lower the general level of the SI (see Article #3) or introduce a notable inequality among participants. The entire SI automatically recognizes and upholds all these breaks and admissions as soon as it is informed of them.

7. Each section is master of its exclusions. It must immediately furnish the reasons and all pertinent documents to all the other sections. In cases where the *facts* are disputed by the excluded comrades, or in cases where another section requests a new discussion bearing on *the very basis* of the dispute, these exclusions are suspended until a general conference of the SI (or a meeting of delegates) makes the final decision. As a general rule, it is not admissible that theoretical or programmatic oppositions—even serious ones—be dealt with by exclusion before a general meeting of the SI can discuss the matter. But all practical failings must be dealt with on the spot. Any divergence or choice that does not require exclusion allows for resignation.

8. On any theoretical or tactical question that has not met with unanimity during a discussion, each member is free to maintain his own opinion (as long as he does not break practical solidarity). If the same problems and divergences are met with on several successive occasions, the members who are in agreement on one of the options have the right to openly constitute a *tendency,* and to draft texts to clarify and sustain their point of view, until there is some final resolution (by rediscovered unanimity, by a break, or by a practical supersession of the divergence). Such texts may be circulated throughout the SI and may also appear in the publications of one or more sections. A tendency bearing on a general tactical problem should normally itself be international (thereby tracing a division within several sections).

9. In exceptional cases in which a situationist finds himself isolated and yet active on a concrete terrain (a country where he alone acts in the name of the SI), he alone must determine his activity, while remaining answerable to the SI as a whole.

10. The present national sections can agree to temporarily share their contacts or activities in certain countries where no SI section exists, in accordance with considerations of common language or geographical proximity. Such apportionment must not be institutionalized nor must it notably increase the importance of one of the sections relative to the others.

11. Each national section will organize its own complete financial autonomy; but in this domain, too, it will, as its means permit, show solidarity with other sections that might be in need.

Coordination Between Sections

12. A general conference of the SI should meet as often as possible with all members, or at least the greatest possible number of them who can get there. In no case will it be held without the presence of at least one delegate from the section that would have the greatest difficulty in getting there.

13. To coordinate the SI's activity in the periods between conferences, meetings of *delegates* from the sections will be held as often as necessary. Each delegate disposes of the exact number of votes as the number of situationists from the section that has mandated him. In cases where two different positions exist within a section, such a section would have to have two delegates, each representing the number of votes supporting his position. Any member of the SI can participate and vote in these delegate meetings (in such a case, his vote obviously could not also be allotted to a delegate).

14. A section that cannot send a delegate to these meetings has the right to have itself represented by a situationist it chooses from another section, who will bear a specific mandate. The selected delegate should be informed far enough in advance to allow him to refuse to uphold a mandate if he disapproves of its content. The section that cannot attend would in that case have to ask another situationist to defend its point of view.

Adopted 30 September 1969 at the 8th SI Conference in Venice

Provisional Theses for the Discussion of New Theoretico-Practical Orientations in the SI

(excerpts)

[. . .] The "April Theses" [Debord's April 1968 "The Organization Question for the SI"] pointed out that the SI now needs to concentrate more on the dissemination of theory than on its elaboration (though the latter must also be continued). I want to call attention to the fact that in order to accomplish this, theory must *first of all be put in a condition in which it can be effectively disseminated.* The first step of theory's advance toward practice takes place within theory itself. The dissemination of theory is thus inseparable from its development. The task of giving all our formulated or implicit theses a systematic and completely dialectical development, one that will bring them not only to the point where no one can any longer be unaware of them, but also to the point where they circulate among the workers "like hotcakes" and finally spark a definitive awakening of consciousness (a scandal)—this is certainly a theoretical task. But it also has an immediately practical utility; more precisely, it is both necessary and banal at this time when the SI is more or less led to play double or nothing with history.

Let us consider, for example, the excellent project of a *Situationist Manifesto* ("situationist" in the sense that it is done by situationists). I think that some of the difficulty in conceiving or "imagining" it must be attributed to the fact that we have yet to attain a certain level of theoretical development. By this I mean: the SI's theory is solid and is already maturing without becoming old (it being the last theory, assuming that this era's decisive revolution is the last revolution). But beyond the fact that the SI's *Manifesto* must be translated into all the languages spoken by the modern proletariat and disseminated among the workers, it should be in a position to last at least as well as the *Communist Manifesto,* without having the latter's defects and inadequacies. It thus clearly cannot be a book, or an article (like the "Address to Revolutionaries of All Countries," for example) that would arbitrarily be called a "manifesto"; rather, it must be the geometric locus of the theory of modern society and the constant reference point of any future revolution. In this sense the project proposed by Guy* of settling our accounts with Marx, by precisely assessing the degree of accuracy of his analyses and predictions, is a preliminary project, though not a necessary one. More generally, our theory certainly runs through all the SI articles, from which it may easily be drawn; but in that form our theory has to be *reconstructed* by the reader. This theory must now be unified and synthesized, and for this end some additional analyses will be in order. In particular, the new simplicity of language we are seeking will certainly not be able to make our language *familiar* in the short run. Thus, before the *Manifesto* we might undertake the intermediate task of *scientifically* developing all our previously outlined themes (articles, pamphlets, books).

In contrast, it seems to me that René-Donatien's proposal of a *Wildcat Striker's Handbook* should be realized in the near future. To a brief history of the wildcat movement and a confirmation of its critique in acts of the unions, we could add a critique of the worker milieu and a brief final programmatic chapter (defeat of the revolutionary movement, bureaucracy, spectacle-commodity society, return of social revolution, workers' councils, classless society). This would be a premise for the *Manifesto* as well as a followup to *Student Poverty,* in that it might lead to a "Strasbourg of the factories."

Finally, it seems to me that the *Manifesto* project is the way in which we can consider the necessity of an overall advance in the relations among our theses as well as between them and the real movement, and that it thus presupposes the realization of virtually all the other projected theoretical works that have been formulated in the course of this debate. For example, René and Raoul's proposed pamphlet on workers' councils and the critique of Pannekoek; of the four major projects proposed by Guy, at least the analysis of the "two concomitant failures" (insofar as they concern the process of the formation of conscious revolutionary organizations and the critique of the present process of purely spontaneous struggle) and, linked to the critique of the councils of the past and of councilist ideology, the definition of the armed coherence (the outline of a program) of the new councils, which "will be situationist or nothing." Thus the "preface to the practical critique of the modernized old world" opens up the quest for a real antireformism and for new forms of mass or generalized action in the proletariat's development toward an autonomous movement, the first phase of which is manifested by sabotage, wildcat strikes, and above all by the new, *modern* demands. Besides this, it will still be necessary to come back to the question of historical class determination, notably that of the working class and its revolutionary *nature,* since it continues, because of its material position in society, to bear the consciousness of humanity as a whole. (Tony: "We must affirm that the workers

can become revolutionary, and that they are the only ones who will
be so *effectively*." Raoul: "The path of the worker is direct: because he
holds the fate of the commodity in his hands; all he has to do in order
to break free of his brutalization and stop being a worker is to become
conscious of his power. His positivity is immediate. The intellectual
is at best negative. . . . Our critique must now bear essentially on the
worker milieu, the motor of the proletariat.") Essential chapters are
thus: the analysis of American capitalism and American society with
its new déclassés; the critique of the most modern ideologies in relation to the *supersession* in acts of political economy and to the *delay* of
the revolution (urbanism as destruction of the city; automation seen
as automatically liberating; ecology as present-day society's moral
crisis, which compels it to envisage the necessity of *itself* transforming
production relations; and, linked to all the above, "situationism": the
critique of everyday life conducted by power itself); the analysis of the
material presence in work and in everyday life of all the fragmentary
elements of the totality, of the entire historical project, of that which
the disappearance of art, the withering away of philosophy, and the
bankruptcy of science were unable to abolish, but have on the contrary injected everywhere by making it a definitive acquisition of the
workers who are henceforth becoming their conscious inheritors. In
general, we need to pursue an international strategy of revolution by
way of politico-historical articles on different countries, that is to say,
to continue to translate *The Society of the Spectacle* into terms like those
of "The Decline and Fall of the Spectacle-Commodity Economy," and
even further in that direction. (A good translation of the former has
yet to appear in Italy.)

Another project I think it is useful to add is this: beginning with a
quick run-through of past revolutions (like Marx does in the *Manifesto*, Engels in the Introduction to *The Class Struggles in France*, Trotsky
in *1905*, Pannekoek in *Workers' Councils*), to develop an answer to the
question, "Why will the next revolution be the last one?" The history of
the workers' movement—aspects of which have been treated in numerous articles and whose line is most fully traced in "The Proletariat as
Subject and Representation" [Chapter 4 of *The Society of the Spectacle*],
along with Riesel's critique of its highest moments, the councils, in
Internationale Situationniste #12 ["Preliminaries on Councils and Councilist Organization"]—is still far from being an outworn topic on which
everything of consequence has already been said. But what seems to me
of even greater interest is to clarify why modern revolutions are henceforth, and for the first time, *exclusively proletarian,* and this at a time
that is witnessing a decisive transformation of the workers and of work

itself. Thus the revolutions of the past failed to attain, except margin-ally, that without which the modern revolution cannot even begin: the fact that victory can be achieved only by demanding the totality is now also expressed in the fact that there are no longer even any struggles except for the totality. One could start from a definitive critique and a *justification* of Russian Bolshevism (of Trotsky and Lenin) in relation to the real conditions of the Russian proletariat, those conditions being in their turn considered in relation to the conditions of the modern proletariat, which simultaneously make Bolshevism impossible and the councils necessary, "no longer at the periphery of a movement that is ebbing, but at the center of a movement that is rising." This would also be a verification of Marx's general thesis: As long as the existing production relations are not exhausted and have not entered into con-tradiction with the development of the productive forces (in the total historical sense that includes the development of the revolutionary class itself and of the consciousness that produces history), revolutions run the greatest risk, which so far has never been avoided, of being defeated and leading to a modernization of domination. Each revolu-tion sets loose all possibilities (in 1789 as in 1871 and 1917), but *in the final analysis* realizes only those that correspond to the level attained by the development of productive forces. Out of all the possibilities each revolution opens up for itself, it always seems to choose the nearest. All the possibilities are *there before it,* but some of them remain invisi-ble while others are in everybody's mind: it is obviously everyday life, the immediate relation with the existing world, that puts them there. This can just as well be expressed by saying that in all revolutions the negation is never absolute, that the *positive* plays a large part, whether as positive or inversely as *determining* the negation: if the condition of victory consists in reducing the former, it also always consists in rein-forcing the latter, in reducing the positive to its objective basis.

It also seems to me that we have arrived at a point where we must go over all of situationist theory from top to bottom and rewrite it, so as to deal with the mediations that were treated too rapidly and with the questions that were left open. The recognized value of writ-ing books, for example (books that in the present period the workers should begin to read), obviously stems from this necessity of super-seding the opening moment of hostilities on a new front of modern critique. [. . .]

In conclusion, we ourselves don't have a head start at this begin-ning of an era: it's the beginning of an era for us too. The SI was able to trace, condensed into a few phrases, a few of the fundamental alter-natives and perhaps all of the modern directions of development; but it is *precisely for this reason* that it is virtually a matter of beginning over again (except for the spectacle, the critique of everyday life, a few brief though excellent politico-historical texts on revolutions, and of course the analysis of May). Our most notable theoretical acquisition so far is our theoretical method, which must be verified in a number of concrete respects by deepening the theory itself in a decisive manner, precisely because "the force of spirit is only as great as its externalization." We have already written, in installments, our *German Ideology*, but our *1844 Manuscripts* will be the text Guy proposes for the historical détournement of Marx. We are beginning to consider our *Manifesto* at the same time as our *Critique of the Gotha Program*. Moreover, we don't come only from Hegel and Marx. *The Revolution of Everyday Life* has only opened the way; anti-utopia is an unexplored territory from which no one has returned so far. It is this anti-utopia, made possible on the bases of modern society, that must fill in the gaps left by Marx's "insufficiencies," just as it must itself be rendered dialectical and find a practical implementation. [. . .]

PAOLO SALVADORI
Milan, May 1970

Remarks on the SI Today

(excerpts)

1

I am in agreement with Paolo's text ("Provisional Theses," May 1970), apart from two slight differences. First, on page 5 of the French translation, I think it is necessary to dialectize somewhat more the question of the relation of Bolshevism to the backwardness of productive forces in Russia, by pointing out the very role of Lenin's Bolshevism as a factor of retardation and regression for that central part of the productive forces: the revolutionary class's *consciousness*. Elsewhere (page 7) Paolo characterizes this formulation regarding what the SI has so far been able to accomplish—"the element of *promise* still surpasses the element of accomplishment"—as a "slight exaggeration." On the contrary, I find this phrase to be completely true, without any exaggeration. With these theses of Paolo and a number of those expressed by various comrades, notably Raoul, René, and Tony (as well as Gianfranco's very correct insistence on our developing certain economic analyses more concretely), it seems to me that we have a substantial basis from which we can more and more concretely develop both our strategical analysis and our theoretico-practical activity.

2

However, a few points remain to be dealt with that are *preliminary* to this debate (though they have already been touched on in texts by René, René-Donatien, and myself). Paolo was right to parenthesize these preliminaries, for they have little direct relation with his programmatic outline; and he has taken care, in a final note, to make the very significance of his text *contingent* on their practical resolution. We must thus now make an effort to determine these difficulties more concretely—difficulties which are simultaneously *archaisms* in our own historical development and preconditions that we have to master before *really* undertaking the development of a more advanced perspective. [. . .]

4

After four months of this orientation debate we have not seen any theoretical divergences emerge; and this was fairly predictable. But one begins to wonder if these texts—which go in the same general direction and many of which contain excellent points—are not piling up like so many monologues *while scarcely being used*. To clarify what I mean regarding this underuse of theory: Just as Magritte could paint a pipe and then correctly write on the painting, "This is not a pipe," to declare that one does not separate theory and practice *is not yet to practice theory*. And putting revolutionary theory into practice is not at all messianically postponed until the victory of the revolution, it is required throughout the entire process of revolutionary activity. Similarly (and this too is only a theoretical observation, but a necessary one), we all naturally refuse to consider even the most fundamentally theoretical activity as separable from even the most distinctly practical activity. To formulate the most general revolutionary theory is inconceivable without a very precise practice, and vice versa. Even in a street fight you still have to think! But if we leave aside these dialectical truisms on extreme cases, we can consider the most common *concrete* situation in which dialecticians reveal themselves as such (even if many of them don't have the intellectual background enabling them to *talk* about dialectics or to *write* theory at the dialectical level). People meet each other. They talk about how they understand the world and what they think they can do in it. They judge each other while judging their world; and each judges the judgments of the others. They agree with or oppose each other's projects. If there is a common project, they have to know at different moments what this project has *become*. Their success or failure is measured by practice *and their consciousness of practice* (they may themselves, rightly or wrongly, characterize their failures and successes as secondary or decisive; the result may later be reversed and they may be aware of this or have forgotten it). Etc., etc. In a word, it is in this concerted and theorized action (which is also theory tested in action) that revolutionary dialecticians have to recognize as well as possible the *decisive elements* of a complex problem; the probable or modifiable (by them) *interaction* of these elements; the *essential character* of the moment as result, as well as the development of its negation. This is the *terrain of the qualitative* where individuals, their acts, meaning, and life know each other—and where it is necessary to *know how to know*. The presence of history in the everyday life of revolutionaries. You comrades will certainly say that the preceding lines are very banal; and this is quite true. [. . .]

6

Leaving aside the fact that all the issues of *Internationale Situationniste* have included a number of personal contributions (often notable and sometimes even discordant), it can be said that for the most part the anonymous portions of issues 1–5 were produced in a truly collective manner. Issues 6–9 were still done relatively collectively, mainly by Raoul, Attila, and me. But from number 10 on I have found myself left with *almost the entire responsibility* for preparing each publication. And what seems to me even more alarming and unhealthy is that I consider—unbiasedly, I hope—that these three issues are the best ones of the series! This situation was still somewhat obscured for me in numbers 10 and 11 by a small (but welcome) amount of collaboration from Mustapha (I'm still referring to the articles published without signature). We know that the departure of Mustapha right in the middle of the preparation of number 12 (though after he had turned in the article on Czechoslovakia) pushed things to a scandalous point, since at the same time the membership of the French section had doubled. I resigned soon thereafter from the position as "director" of the journal, mainly so as not to be an accomplice to a sort of spectacular lie, since we all had plenty of opportunity to be aware of our distance in this regard from our stated principles. A year has now gone by since this problem was posed, and the present editor-comrades are beginning to put themselves in a position to resolve it. If they succeed in this it will be by finally appropriating the methods that have "officially" been theirs for several years.

7

The deficiency of consciousness (on the asserted base of historical consciousness) regarding matters of *method* in carrying out various particular tasks obviously stems from a more general deficiency of consciousness. For two or three comrades, we can even note a deficiency of information, stemming from a lack of *reading* rather astonishing for theorists of the proletariat and realizers of philosophy and art. But this is only an epiphenomenon: it would be as vain to become indignant about it as it would be vulgar to joke about it. If some have not read what others quote and use, it is because they have had neither the *desire* nor the *need* to do so. I don't think this is because we have different *tastes*. It is simply that these comrades have discovered nothing to *do* that would have given them this desire and this need.

8

This deficiency of *collective* activity (I don't mean to say, of course, that we haven't collectively discussed, decided on, and carried out a certain number of actions or writings, even during the last two years) is mainly noticeable—in the French section—by a sort of general aversion to any critique aimed at a specific fact or at one of us. This was quite evident at the July 14 meeting. The slightest critique is felt as a total calling into question, an absolute distrust, a manifestation of hostility, etc. And this emotional reaction is not only expressed by the criticized comrade. The SI comrades are very quick and adept at judging the pro-situs* (the successive writings of the poor GRCA, for example), that is to say, something of very little importance. But almost everyone manifests a strange reluctance when it comes to judging anything about a member of the SI. They are visibly uneasy even when someone else of us does so. I cannot believe that some hollow politeness is at the origin of this. It must therefore be a certain fatigue that sets in the moment questions are broached that really concern our *movement:* things we *risk* succeeding or failing in. In any case a critique is never *carried further* by other comrades and no one (except occasionally the criticized comrade) strives to draw from it any conclusions that might be useful for our subsequent collective action. In this way the SI has a tendency to freeze into a sort of perpetual and admirable present (as if a more or less admirable past was continued in it). This not very historical or practical harmony is only broken in two situations, in one case really, in the other only apparently. When a critique is really taken seriously and given practical consequences (because the incident is so glaring that everyone demands this conclusion), an individual is excluded. He is cut off from the harmonious communion, perhaps even without ever having been criticized before, or only once briefly. The *apparent* break in our habitual comfort happens this way: A critique is made or a defect of our action is pointed out. Everyone goes along with this critique, often *without even bothering to express themselves* about it; the point seems clear and undeniable, but boring (and correspondingly little attention is given to really remedying it). But if someone has insisted on the point, everyone admits that the detail is indeed a bad thing. And everyone immediately decides that it must not continue, that things must change, etc. But since no one bothers with the practical ways and means, this decision remains a pious hope and the thing may well recur ten times; and by the tenth time everyone *has already forgotten the ninth.* The general feeling, expressed not so much in the responses as in the silences, is clearly: "Why make a drama out of it?" But this is a false idea because it's not a matter of a drama and the choice is not between drama and passivity. But in this way the problem, when it eventually is dealt with, is dealt with only dramatically, as many of our exclusions have shown. Between the extremes of breaking and complacency it thus seems that there is no place for real criticism. Such criticism is seen as pointless, as merely reflecting a bad mood (which is not to say that more genuine bad humor is not to be found among virtually all of us, in inverse proportion to our indulgence in overt criticism: in almost every personal encounter with a situationist one sees a sort of vague discontent that contrasts with the tranquility of most of our meetings).

9

It goes without saying that in speaking of "criticism" I am deploring not only the sleep of the "negative" aspect of criticism, but also of its "positive" side: usefully approving, developing, striving to reuse a theory or an act of one or another comrade. I mentioned our prompt critique of the errors of the pro-situs, not in order to say that it is not in itself justified, but in order to note that the pro-situs are not our principal reference point (any more than ICO or the leftist bureaucrats). Our principal reference point is ourselves, it is *our own operation.* The underdevelopment of internal criticism in the SI clearly reflects, at the same time that it contributes toward, the underdevelopment of our (theoretico-practical) action. [. . .]

11

I think that all this is only a symptom of a correctable deficiency: several situationists' *lack of cohabitation with their own practice.* I almost always remember the times I have been mistaken; and I acknowledge them rather often *even when no one reminds me of them.* I am led to think that this is because I am rarely mistaken, having never concealed the fact that I have nothing to say on the numerous subjects on which I am ignorant, and habitually keeping in mind several contradictory hypotheses regarding the possible development of events when I don't yet discern the qualitative leap. In speaking here for myself I would nevertheless like to believe that, as Raoul would put it, I am also speaking for some others. And, by anticipation, for all those comrades who will decide to consciously self-manage their own basic activity. [. . .]

15

The style of organization defined by the SI and that we have tried to implement is not that of the councils or even that which we have outlined for revolutionary organizations in general; it is *specific,* linked to our task as we have understood it so far. This style has had some obvious successes. Even now it is not a question of criticizing it for lacking effectiveness: if we successfully overcome the present problems of the phase of entering into a "new era," we will continue to be more "effective" than many others; and if we don't overcome them, it doesn't much matter if we have carried out a few publications and encounters a little slower or a little faster. I am thus not criticizing any ineffectiveness of this style of organization, but the essential fact that at the moment this style is not really being applied among us. If, in spite of all its advantages, our organizational formula has this sole fault of *not being real,* it is obvious that we must at all costs make it real or else renounce it and devise another style of organization, whether for a continuation of the SI or for a regroupment on other bases, for which the new era will sooner or later create the conditions. In any case, to take up Paolo's phrase, most of us "will not stop dancing." We must only stop pretending.

16

Since the present problem is not at the *simply theoretical* level (and since it is dissimulated when we carry on theoretical discussions, which are moreover virtually contentless since they immediately lead to a consequenceless unanimity), I don't think we can settle it by constituting formal tendencies (*much less by forgetting about it*). I think that each of us might first try to find with one other situationist, chosen by affinity and experience and after very *thorough* discussion, a theoretico-practical accord that takes account of all the elements we are already aware of (and of those that may appear in the process of continuing this discussion). This accord could then, with the same prudence, be extended to another, etc. We might in this way arrive at a few regroupments that would be capable of dialoguing with each other—whether to oppose each other or to come to an agreement. The process could be long (but not necessarily so) and it would probably be one way to put into practice the perspective evoked a few months ago but scarcely developed since of "rejoining the SI" (without formally suspending the present accord, but by here and now preparing *its future*). Suffice it to say that it is time to seek concrete individuals behind the now-evident *abstraction* of the "SI organization"; and to find out what they really want to do and can do. Without claiming that this will produce a stable assurance for the future, it would at least make it possible to bring into the open and deal with all the difficulties and discouraging impressions that have already been noted. We still have to talk about all this until acts permit us to shut up.

GUY DEBORD
27 July 1970

Declaration

The crisis that has continually deepened in the SI in the course of the last year, and whose roots go back much further, has ended up revealing all its aspects; and has led to a more and more glaring increase in theoretical and practical inactivity. But the most striking manifestation of this crisis (ultimately revealing what was precisely its original hidden center) has been several comrades' *indifference* in the face of its concrete development, month after month. We are quite aware that no one has in any way *expressed* this indifference. And that is precisely the heart of the problem, for what we have really been experiencing, behind abstract proclamations of the contrary, is this refusal to take any responsibility whatsoever in participating in either the decisions or the implementation of our *actual* activity, even at a time when it has been so indisputably threatened.

Considering that the SI has carried out an action that has been at least substantially correct and that has had a great importance for the revolutionary movement of the period ending in 1968 (though with an element of failure that we must account for); and that it has the *potential* to continue to make significant contributions by lucidly comprehending the conditions of the new period, including its own conditions of existence; and that the deplorable position in which the SI has found itself for so many months must not be allowed to continue—we have constituted a tendency.

Our tendency aims to break completely with the *ideology of the SI* and with its corollary: the miserable vainglory that conceals and maintains inactivity and inability. We want an exact definition of the SI organization's collective activity and of the democracy that is *actually possible* in it. And we want the *actual application* of this democracy.

After everything we have seen these last several months, we reject in advance *any abstract response*, any response that might still aim to simulate a comfortable euphoria by finding nothing specific to criticize or self-criticize in the functioning—or nonfunctioning—of a group in which so many people know so well what they have lacked. After what we have all seen for months regarding the question of our common activity, nothing can any longer be accepted as before: routine optimism becomes a lie, unusable abstract generalization becomes a dodge. Several of the best situationists have become *something else;* they don't talk about what they know and they talk about what they don't know. We want a radical critique—a critique *ad hominem.*

Without prejudging any later, more considered and serious responses they may make, we declare our disagreement with the American comrades, who have constituted a tendency on completely futile bases. At the present moment the infantile futility of pseudocritiques is a bluff as unacceptable as the noble generality of pseudocontentment; both are evasions of real criticism. Other comrades have for months never undertaken to respond in any manner whatsoever to the mass of clearly urgent questions pointed to *by facts themselves* and by the first, and *increasingly specific*, written critiques that we have been formulating for months. The very terrain of the scandal and of its denunciation have *expanded together* and any silence makes one directly complicitous in all the deficiencies. Let no one believe in our naïveté, as if we were putting forward here some new exhortation aimed at arousing the members against some incomprehensible and paralyzing inevitability —an exhortation that would meet with the same absence of response as all the preceding ones! We are quite aware that some of you have not wanted to respond.

This shameful silence is going to stop immediately because *we demand,* in the name of the rights and duties given us by the SI's past and present, that each member accept his responsibilities right now.

At this stage there is obviously no need to reiterate the central questions regarding which we await responses. Everyone is aware of them and they have already been put in writing. Let us simply say that we will naturally accept no response that is in contradiction with the actual practice of the person who formulates it.

If certain members have *hidden* goals different from ours, we want those goals to be brought out into the open and to be expressed, as they should be naturally, in distinct actions carried out under distinct responsibilities. And if anyone doesn't have any real goals, as strange as it seems to us that anyone would want to conserve the miserable *status quo ante*, let us only say that we will not contribute to covering for some glorified pseudocommunity of "retired thinkers" or unemployed revolutionaries.

Our tendency is addressing this declaration to all present members of the SI without distinction or exception. We want it to be clearly understood that we are not seeking the exclusion of anyone (and much less will we be satisfied with the exclusion of some scapegoat). But since we consider it very unlikely that a genuine accord can be arrived at *so belatedly* among everyone, we are prepared for any split, the dividing lines of which will be determined by the forthcoming discussion. In that eventuality, we will for our part do everything possible to make such a split take place under the most proper conditions, particularly by maintaining an absolute respect for truth in any future polemics, just as all of us have together maintained this truthfulness in all the circumstances in which the SI has acted until now.

Considering that the crisis has attained a level of extreme gravity, we henceforth reserve the right—in accordance with Article 8 of the statutes voted at Venice—to make our positions known outside the SI.

DEBORD, RIESEL, VIÉNET
Paris, 11 November 1970

Untitled Text

(excerpts)

Comrades,

In casting back into their nothingness the contemplatives and incompetents who counted on a perpetual membership in the SI, we have taken a great step forward. We must continue to advance; because now an era is over *for the SI too,* and is *better understood.* The undeniable success that we have registered in this case was so *easy*, and so *belated*, that certainly no one will think we have the right to settle back for a few weeks to gloat over it. Yet already over the last few weeks a certain lethargy has begun to manifest itself again (without, in my opinion, any longer having the previous excuses or semijustifications) when it comes to developing our present positions. [. . .]

(1) The SI recently was in danger of becoming not only inactive and ridiculous, but co-optive and counterrevolutionary. The lies multiplying within it were beginning to have a mystifying and disarming effect outside. The SI could, in the very name of its exemplary actions in the previous period, have become *the latest form of revolutionary spectacle*, and you know those who would have liked to maintain this role for another ten or twenty years.

(2) The process of alienation gone through by various past emancipatory endeavors (from the Communist League to the FAI,* or even, if this comparison should also be evoked in our case, surrealism) was followed by the SI in all its easily recognizable forms: theoretical paralysis; "party patriotism"; lying silence on increasingly evident faults; imperious dogmatism; wooden language addressed to the miners of Kiruna*—still rather far off, fortunately—and to Iberian exiles; invisible titles of ownership possessed by little cliques or individuals over one or another sector of our relations or activities, on the basis of their being "SI members" (like people used to invoke the privileges of being a "Roman citizen"); ideology and dishonesty. Naturally this process took place this time *in the present historical conditions*, that is to say, to a large extent in the very conditions created by the SI; so that many features of past alienations were precluded. This set of conditions could have made a counterrevolutionary subversion of the SI all the more dangerous if it had succeeded, but at the same time it made such a success difficult. I think that this danger virtually no longer exists: We have so thoroughly *smashed* the SI in the preceding months that there is scarcely any chance that that *title* and *image* could become harmful by falling into bad hands. The situationist movement—in the broad sense of the word—is now diffused more or less everywhere. And any of us, as well as some of the excluded members, could at any time, in the name of the SI's past and of the radical positions presently needing to be developed, speak *by himself* to the revolutionary current that listens to us; but that is precisely what Vaneigem will be unable to do.* On the other hand, if a neo-Nashist regrouping dared to form, a single pamphlet of twenty pages would suffice to demolish it. To smash the SI and reduce to nothing the dubious pretensions that would have been able to preserve it as an alienated and alienating model—this had become

at least our most urgent revolutionary duty. On the basis of these new measures of security we have fortunately implemented, we can now probably do better.

(3) The SI had (and still has, but fortunately with less of a monopoly on it) the most radical theory of its time. On the whole it knew how to formulate it, disseminate it, and defend it. It often was able to *struggle well* in practice; and some of us have often even been capable of conducting our personal lives in line with that theory (which was, moreover, a necessary condition to enable us to formulate its main points). But the SI has not applied its own theory *in the very activity of the formulation of that theory* or in the *general conditions of its struggle*. The partisans of the SI's positions have for the most part not been their creators or their real agents. They were only more official and more pretentious pro-situs. This has been the SI's main fault (avoidable or not?). To have gone so long without being aware of it has been its worst error (and to speak for myself, *my* worst error). If this attitude had prevailed, it would have been the SI's ultimate crime. As an organization, the SI has *partly* failed; and this has been the part in which it has failed. It was thus necessary to apply to the SI the critique it had applied, often so well, to the dominant modern society. (It could be said that we were rather well organized to propagate our program, but not our organizational program.)

(4) The numerous deficiencies that have marked the SI were *invariably* produced by individuals who *needed the SI* in order to personally be something; and that something was never the real, revolutionary activity of the SI, but its opposite. At the same time, they praised the SI to the extreme, both to make it seem that they subsisted in it like fish in water and to give the impression that their personal extremism was above any vulgar corroboration of facts and acts. And yet the alternative has always been quite simple: either we are fundamentally equal (and prove it) or we are *not even comparable*. As for us here, we can take part in the SI *only if we don't need it*. We must first of all be *self-sufficient*; then, secondarily, we may lucidly combine our *specific* (and specified) desires and possibilities for a collective action which, on that condition, *may* be the correct continuation of the SI. [. . .]*

GUY DEBORD
28 January 1971

Notes

Page 1. The humor or poetry of some of the signs in this list is obvious, but in other cases it will be obscure for the non-French reader. Quai des Orfèvres, for example, is the headquarters of the Paris Police Department and *placement* means not only job placement but also arrest. Saint-Anne's is a street name but also a well-known mental asylum. Some of the other oddities stem from the Parisian habit of naming stores after their street names, which are often rather picturesque, in some cases dating back to the Middle Ages. "Martyrs' Provisions," for example, was probably a grocery store located on Rue des Martyrs.

5. *The Court of Miracles* and *The Tower of Nesle:* allusions to two medieval tales (dramatized, respectively, by Victor Hugo and Alexandre Dumas).

6. *Ariadne:* woman in Greek mythology who gave Theseus the thread enabling him to find his way out of the Minotaur's labyrinth.

7. *DRIFTING:* Elsewhere in this book, the original French term *dérive* is used. See Debord's "Theory of the Dérive" (pp. 62–66).

7. *Saint-Germain-des-Prés:* Parisian neighborhood frequented by the Lettrists in the early 1950s. It was famous as the scene of postwar bohemianism and existentialism (Camus, Sartre, Simone de Beauvoir, etc.), but less visibly, in less trendy cafés and less reputable bars, Chtcheglov, Debord, and their friends pursued their own adventures, evoked in Debord's *Mémoires* and in two of his films (*On the Passage* and *In girum*), and recounted in detail in Jean-Michel Mension's *The Tribe.*

7. *Pigalle:* Parisian red light district. Chtcheglov's point is that the supposed presence of prostitution had nothing to do with Saint-Germain-des-Prés's cultural impact since Pigalle had far more prostitution yet exerted no particular influence.

7. Neither of these books was written.

8. "Ivan Chtcheglov participated in the ventures that were at the origin of the situationist movement, and his role in it has been irreplaceable, both in its theoretical endeavors and in its practical activity (the dérive experiments). In 1953, at the age of 19, he had already drafted—under the pseudonym Gilles Ivain—the text entitled "Formulary for a New Urbanism," which was later published in the first issue of *Internationale Situationniste.* Having

passed the last five years in a psychiatric clinic, where he still is, he reestablished contact with us only long after the formation of the SI. He is currently working on a revised edition of his 1953 text on architecture and urbanism. The letters from which the following lines have been excerpted were addressed to Michèle Bernstein and Guy Debord over the last year. The plight to which Ivan Chtcheglov is being subjected can be considered as one of modern society's increasingly sophisticated methods of control over people's lives, a control that in previous times was reflected in atheists being condemned to the Bastille, for example, or political opponents to exile." (Introductory note to Chtcheglov's "Letters from Afar," *Internationale Situationniste* #9 [1964], p. 38. For a passage from one of those letters, see Note 64.)

The version of Chtcheglov's "Formulary" reproduced in *Internationale Situationniste* #1 was abridged, as was the translation included in the first edition of the *SI Anthology.* The present text is a translation of the complete original version, which was published for the first time in 2006 in Chtcheglov's *Écrits retrouvés* (Éditions Allia). See also the biographical study by Jean-Marie Apostolidès and Boris Donné: *Ivan Chtcheglov, profil perdu* (Allia, 2006).

10. The quotation is from Marx's *The Poverty of Philosophy* (chap. 2).

11. *Claude Lorrain:* Two such paintings (Lorrain painted several of the same type) are included in Debord's film *The Society of the Spectacle.*

12. *author:* The quotation is from André Breton's *Le Revolver à cheveux blancs.*

12. This essay originally appeared in the Belgian surrealist journal *Les Lèvres Nues* #6 (September 1955).

14. Of the various persons disdainfully mentioned in this article, Clemenceau and Edgar Faure were politicians, Gide and Mauriac were writers, and Bugeaud and Gallifet were nineteenth-century generals (the first responsible for the conquest of Algeria, the second for the crushing of the Paris Commune).

14. This article appeared in *Potlatch* #23 (13 October 1955). The title echoes "Proposals for Irrationally Improving a City" (*Le Surréalisme au Service de la Révolution* #6, 1933).

14. The French word *détournement* means deflection, diversion, rerouting, misuse, misappropriation, hijacking, or otherwise turning something aside from its normal course or purpose. It has sometimes been translated as "diversion," but that word is confusing because of its more common meaning of idle entertainment. Like most other English-speaking people who have actually practiced détournement, I have chosen to retain the French spelling and pronunciation of the noun (*day-toór-nuh-maw*) and to anglicize the verb: to detourn (*dee-túrn*). For more on détournement (in addition to the passages in the present book listed in the Index), see *The Society of the Spectacle* ##204–209.

16. The two quoted phrases are from Isidore Ducasse's *Poésies*. Lautréamont was the pseudonym used by Ducasse for his other work, *Maldoror*. The "Plagiarism is necessary" passage was later plagiarized by Debord in *The Society of the Spectacle* #207.

17. The "metagraph," a genre developed by the Lettrists, is a sort of collage with largely textual elements. The two metagraphs mentioned here are both by Debord and can be found in his *Oeuvres* (p. 127).

18. The authors are detourning a sentence from the *Communist Manifesto:* "The cheapness of the bourgeoisie's commodities is the heavy artillery with which it batters down all Chinese walls, with which it forces the barbarians' intensely obstinate hatred of foreigners to capitulate."

19. In the first imagined scene a phrase from a Greek tragedy (Sophocles's *Oedipus at Colonus*) is put in the mouth of French Revolution leader Maximilien Robespierre. In the second, a phrase from Robespierre is put in the mouth of a truck driver.

20. *"Lenin Symphony":* Beethoven originally named his third symphony after Napoleon (seen as a defender and extender of the French Revolution), but when Napoleon crowned himself emperor he angrily tore up the dedication to him and renamed it "Eroica."

The implied respect in this passage for Lenin (like the passing references to "workers' states" in Debord's "Report on the Construction of Situations") is a vestige of the Lettrist International's early, less politically sophisticated period, when they seem to have been sort of anarcho-Trotskyist.

20. *Vendée:* a region in southwestern France, locale of a pro-monarchist revolt against the Revolutionary government (1793–1796).

21. This article was originally published in *Les Lèvres Nues* #8 (May 1956).

21. *Christian Dotremont:* Belgian poet who participated in the Revolutionary Surrealism movement of the 1940s and in Cobra (1948–

1951).

23. This article appeared in *Potlatch* #27 (2 November 1956).

31. *Andrei Zhdanov:* one of Stalin's most powerful officials, responsible for purging the arts and imposing the doctrine of "Socialist Realism."

32. *"Françoise Sagan phenomenon":* the way that this teenage writer became a supercelebrity, every detail of her life being considered newsworthy despite the relatively mediocre quality of her work. Spectacularization of vacuous and talentless personalities is of course commonplace nowadays, but in the 1950s it was seen as astonishing and the conventional culture critics were at a loss as to how to account for it.

34. Cobra participants included future SI members Constant and Asger Jorn.

35. The final break was provoked when the radical tendency (including Debord and Wolman) disrupted a Charlie Chaplin press conference in October 1952. The aesthete Lettrists, including the founder of Lettrism, Isidore Isou, disavowed this action. The disrupters responded with an open letter: "We believe that the most imperative expression of freedom is the destruction of idols, especially when those idols present themselves in the name of freedom. The provocative tone of our leaflet was an attack against a unanimous servile adoration. The disavowal by certain lettrists, including Isou himself, only reveals the constantly reengendered communication gap between extremists and ex-extremists."

Lettrist International participants included Henry de Béarn, Serge Berna, *Michèle Bernstein,* Jean-Louis Brau, Ivan Chtcheglov, *Mohamed Dahou, Guy Debord, Abdelhafid Khatib,* Jean-Michel Mension, Patrick Straram, *Alexander Trocchi,* and Gil J Wolman. Those italicized were later among the original members of the SI. (Chtcheglov was never an SI member, though he is listed in Raspaud and Voyer's book as a "membre de loin"—a fellow traveler—and was perhaps considered a sort of honorary member due to his important early contributions.)

37. The SI subsequently renounced any such "infiltration" of other groups, considering that simultaneous membership in two organizations tends to lead to manipulation.

43. This text was one of the preparatory documents for the July 1957 conference at Cosio d'Arroscia, Italy, at which the Situationist International was founded.

57. The original text says "updated in 1936," but that date has no particular significance in the history of surrealism. I suspect that it is a typo for 1956 (the year of the surrealist article that Jorn is criticizing).

59. *a few people:* Bernstein is probably referring to Ivan Chtcheglov and Patrick Straram, two LI members with whom she and Debord later resumed contact, though neither of them ended up joining the SI.

62. *dérive:* literally "drift" or "drifting." Like *détournement,* this term has usually been anglicized as both a noun and a verb.

A slightly different version of this text was first published in *Les Lèvres Nues* #9 (November 1956) along with accounts of two dérives.

64. "The *dérive* (with its flow of acts, its gestures, its strolls, its encounters) was *to the totality* exactly what psychoanalysis (in the best sense) is to language. Let yourself go with the flow of words, says the psychoanalyst. He listens, until the moment when he rejects or modifies (one could say *detourns*) a word, an expression, or a definition. The dérive is certainly a technique, almost a therapeutic one. But just as analysis unaccompanied with anything else is almost always *contraindicated,* so continual dériving is dangerous to the extent that the individual, having gone too far (not without bases, but . . .) without defenses, is threatened with explosion, dissolution, dissociation, disintegration. And thence the relapse into what is termed 'ordinary life,' that is to say, in reality, into 'petrified life.' In this regard I now repudiate my *Formulary*'s propaganda for a *continuous dérive.* It could be continuous like the poker game in Las Vegas, but only for a certain period, limited to a weekend for some people, to a week as a good average; a month is really pushing it. In 1953–1954 we dérived for three or four months straight. That's the extreme limit. It's a miracle it didn't kill us." (Ivan Chtcheglov, excerpt from a 1963 letter to Michèle Bernstein and Guy Debord, reprinted in *Internationale Situationniste* #9, p. 38.)

77. Reference to the famous "Parable of the Cave" in Book VII of Plato's *Republic,* in which people are chained in a cave facing a wall in such a way that they can see the real world only through shadows cast on the wall. They thus take those shadows for reality, and would be likely to resent and resist anyone who told them they were deluded and who tried to get them to turn around and look directly at the real world.

84. *Instructions pour une prise d'arme* is the title of a book by the nineteenth-century revolutionary Auguste Blanqui.

85. A later issue of *Internationale Situationniste* has the following note on Solidarity: "The majority of the British Solidarity group that is apparently demanding this boycott of the situationists are very combative revolutionary workers. We feel confident in stating that its shop-steward members have not yet read the SI, certainly not in French. But they have an ideological shield, their specialist of nonauthority, Dr. C. Pallis [Maurice Brinton], a well-educated man who has been aware of the SI for years and who has been in a position to assure them of its utter unimportance. His activity in England has instead been to translate and comment on the texts of Cardan [Cornelius Castoriadis], the thinker who presided over the collapse of *Socialisme ou Barbarie* in France. Pallis knows quite well that we have for a long time pointed out Cardan's undeniable regression toward revolutionary nothingness, his swallowing of every sort of academic fashion and his ending up becoming indistinguishable from an ordinary sociologist. But Pallis has brought Cardan's thought to England like the light that arrives on Earth from stars that have already long burned out—by presenting his least decomposed texts, written years before, and never mentioning the author's subsequent regression. It is thus easy to see why he would like to prevent this type of encounter." (*Internationale Situationniste* #11, p. 64).

86. The French word *urbanisme* usually means "city planning," but it also refers to the general policy and ideology of urban development. For more analysis of urban "territorial domination," see Chapter 7 of *The Society of the Spectacle.*

90. This text was originally presented by tape recording 17 May 1961 at a conference of the Group for Research on Everyday Life convened in Paris by Henri Lefebvre.

95. La Rochefoucauld, Maxim #195.

107. *The Bad Days Will End:* title of a nineteenth-century popular song.

107. *old mole:* "In the signs that bewilder the middle class, the aristocracy, and the poor prophets of regression, we do recognise our brave friend Robin Goodfellow, the old mole that can work in the earth so fast, that worthy pioneer—the Revolution" (Marx, speech at a dinner celebrating the founding of *The People's Paper,* London, 14 April 1856). Cf. "And when it [the revolution] has accomplished the second half of its preliminary work, Europe will leap up from its seat and exult: 'Well burrowed, old mole!' " (Marx, *The Eighteenth Brumaire of Louis Napoleon,* chap. 7). In both places Marx is alluding to Shakespeare's *Hamlet* (Act 1, Scene 5): "Well said, old mole! canst work i' the earth so fast?" Robin Goodfellow is a mischievous prankster in Shakespeare's *A Midsummer Night's Dream.* Elsinore Castle is the haunted locale where *Hamlet* takes place.

110. *The International:* The International Workingmen's Association, founded in 1864 and effectively dissolved following the 1872 split between the partisans of Marx and Bakunin. Usually referred to as the First International, as distinguished from the Second ("Socialist") and Third ("Communist").

110. *Makhnovists:* Ukrainian anarcho-communist peasant movement (1918-1921) led by Nestor Makhno. It allied with the Bolsheviks against the White Armies, then was betrayed and crushed by the Bolsheviks. See Peter Arshinov's *History of the Makhnovist Movement* and Voline's *The Unknown Revolution.* On the other revolutionary movements mentioned in this article, see Riesel's "Preliminaries on Councils and Councilist Organization" (pp. 348-362).

113. *sociologists:* For more detailed discussion of the limitations of these sociologists' insights, see *The Society of the Spectacle* ##196-200.

113. *G. Keller:* Asger Jorn resigned from the SI in April 1961, but for a year or two afterwards he maintained some collaboration with it under the pseudonym George Keller.

115. *in no position to judge:* Debord's modesty here is wickedly ironic, since he had by this time completed three films that were unquestionably of higher quality and more "situationist" than anything the Scandinavians may have produced.

115. *co-opted:* I previously translated the French term *récupération* as "recuperation," but that word normally has a different sense in English. Upon reconsideration I believe that the term is adequately, and more clearly, rendered by "co-option."

121. *Erostratus* burned down a famous Greek temple in 356 BC so that his name would be remembered for all time.

121. *Jacques:* French peasants who revolted in the Jacquerie of 1358; by extension, a jacquerie is any particularly violent peasant rebellion.

Enragés: extreme radical current during the French Revolution (1793-1794).

Fédérés: insurgents of the Paris Commune (1871), particularly those massacred during its last stand.

122. *"Crystal Night":* a Nazi-orchestrated "popular" reaction against Jews in Germany in 1938, so called because of the enormous number of store windows broken.

126. Reference to Mallarmé's poem *A Throw of the Dice Will Never Abolish Chance.* Vaneigem's meaning here is somewhat obscure (as is the poem), but he seems to be referring to the inadequacy of an indifferent alternation between arbitrary decisions and leaving things purely to chance. "Stéphane Mallarmé, in the great

poem that expresses and sums up the idea he pursued throughout his life, declares: *A Throw of the Dice Will Never Abolish Chance.* By the game of dice he symbolized pure thought, which is in essence Number. What he meant by chance is everything that escapes conscious thought and that arises out of its very lapses. He somberly proclaimed the failure of the human spirit, its inability to succeed in mastering itself" (André Rolland de Renéville, *Expérience Poétique*).

134. *Moïse Tshombe:* leader of Katangan secession movement. See Note 193.

136. A character in Dostoevsky's *The Brothers Karamazov* says, "But if God didn't exist then everything would be permitted."

137. *cuius regio eius religio:* "The ruler determines the religion of his subjects"—main provision of the Treaty of Augsburg (1555).

137. *Ubu cycle:* a series of grossly satirical plays by Alfred Jarry.

140. *Arthur Cravan:* poet, boxer, proto-dadaist perpetrator of scandals, and "deserter from 17 nations." He disappeared off the coast of Mexico in 1920.

142. *The Avant-Garde of Presence:* The article opens with a response to the critic Lucien Goldmann, who had referred to various more or less nihilistic artists (Beckett, Ionesco, etc.) as an "avant-garde of absence."

145. *"How are we going to bankrupt . . . suddenly"* is adapted from a passage in Hemingway's *The Sun Also Rises* (chap. 13).

145. *as in Germany:* In 1961-1962 the German situationists were subjected to a series of police harassments—searches, confiscation of SI publications, arrests for immorality, pornography, blasphemy, incitement to riot, etc. The SI conducted an international campaign on their behalf, even after the majority of them had been excluded from the SI for moderation and compromises in other regards. Uwe Lausen, who had not been excluded, was the only one to eventually be jailed (for three weeks); the others got fines and suspended sentences. See *Internationale Situationniste* #6, p. 6; #7, p. 51; #8, p. 64.

147. *Nashisterie, Nashistouse:* humorously vulgar French coinages. Rough English analogies might be "Nashistan" and "Nashtiness."

149. An example of the gross results: "The ex-situationist Constant, whose Dutch collaborators had already been excluded from the SI for having agreed to construct a church, now himself presents *models of factories* in his catalogue published in March by the Municipal Museum of Bochum. Apart from plagiarizing two or three poorly understood fragments of situationist ideas, this slippery character has nothing better to propose than to act as a public-relations man in integrating the masses into capitalist technological civilization; and he reproaches the SI for having abandoned his whole program of transforming the urban milieu, which he alone is carrying out. Under these conditions, yes!" (*Internationale Situationniste #6*, p. 6.)

Constant (Constant Nieuwenhuis) resigned from the SI in 1960. He is the same person later mentioned in *On the Poverty of Student Life* as one of the Provo hierarchy "leaders."

149. *Power:* The French word *pouvoir* can mean power in general, but it can also refer to the ruling powers, the ruling classes, the ruling system, or the particular regime in power.

149. The Humpty Dumpty quote is from Lewis Carroll's *Through the Looking Glass* (chap. 6).

150. The French word *information* also means "news."

151. *Trobar clus:* hermetic troubadour style. *Dolce stil nuovo:* 13th-century Italian poetic school culminating in Dante.

152. *Asturias:* mountainous region in northwest Spain where workers (primarily miners) carried out an extremely radical and violent insurrection in October 1934. They were referred to as *dinamiteros* because they often used sticks of dynamite for lack of other weapons.

In the early 1960s a later generation of Asturian workers carried out a daring series of wildcat strikes against the Franco regime. On the latter movement, see Guy Debord's unpublished article "La Grève asturienne" (*Oeuvres*, pp. 657–662).

157. *pataphysician:* reference to "pataphysics," the absurdist-nihilist philosophy of Alfred Jarry.

158. Many of the themes in "Basic Banalities" were later developed more clearly and fully in Vaneigem's *The Revolution of Everyday Life* (1967). Chapter 23 of that book deals with the "unitary triad": participation, communication, and realization, while Part I deals with their contraries: spectacle, separation, sacrifice, etc.

160. *striking force:* play on de Gaulle's contention that France needed to develop a strong military striking force.

172. *Durruti Column:* anarchist militia unit led by Buenaventura Durruti during the Spanish civil war.

172. *Declaration of the 121:* a "Declaration on the Right to Resist the Algerian War" signed by 121 French artists and intellectuals (September 1960). The French government responded with arrests and firings, and even prohibited news media from mentioning the name of any signer—which only resulted in more people signing. The "Declaration" polarized the intellectual community and contributed toward arousing French public opinion (the first demonstration against the war came a month later). Michèle Bernstein and Guy Debord were among the signers. See *Internationale Situationniste #5*, pp. 5–7, 12.

175. Trocchi's article, "Technique du coup du monde," stressed the cultural aspects of sub version and proposed establishing a sort of international network of alternative communities specializing in collective creation and experimentation. The English version, "Invisible Insurrection of a Million Minds," along with a follow-up piece, "Sigma: A Tactical Blueprint," appeared in *New Saltire #8* (London, 1963) and *City Lights Journal #2* (San Francisco, 1964). Both texts were reprinted in Andrew Murray Scott (ed.), *Invisible Insurrection of a Million Minds: A Trocchi Reader* (Polygon, 1991). *Internationale Situationniste #10* (p. 83) contains the following note: "Upon the appearance in London in fall 1964 of the first publications of the 'Project Sigma' initiated by Alexander Trocchi, it was mutually agreed that the SI could not involve itself in such a loose cultural venture, in spite of our interest in establishing contact with the more radical individuals who may be drawn to it, notably in the United States and England. It is therefore no longer as a member of the SI that our friend Alexander Trocchi has since developed an activity of which we fully approve of several aspects."

175. *critique of religion:* Allusion to Marx's *Introduction to a Critique of Hegel's Philosophy of Right* (1843): "the critique of religion is the essential precondition for any critique."

176. *Poor Heidegger! . . . Poor Cardan! Tics, tics, and tics:* echoes a passage in Isidore Ducasse's *Poésies* where he contemptuously dismisses various literary figures of his era. "Paul Cardin" was one of the pseudonyms of Cornelius Castoriadis. See Notes 85 and 191.

179. *critical support:* See, for example, the SI's "Contribution to a Councilist Program in Spain" (pp. 213–220); the comments on the Zengakuren in *On the Poverty of Student Life* (pp. 421–422); and the unpublished notes on the Congolese revolutionary movement reproduced in Debord's *Oeuvres* (pp. 692–698).

182. On "antisituationist art," see "The Fifth SI Conference in Göteborg" (pp. 114–117).

182. *Nashist enterprises:* The reference is to Jörgen Nash and others who had recently been excluded from the SI and who were trying to cash in on the situationists' notoriety by producing "situationist art" and founding a

"Second Situationist International" (see "The Counter-Situationist Campaign in Various Countries" (pp. 145-149).

As for the situationists' own conditions, they stated that they had no objection to publishers, film producers, patrons, etc., interested in financing situationist projects, whether disinterestedly or in the hope of making profits, as long as it was understood that the situationists would retain total control over the form and content of the projects.

Regarding the publication of radical texts, *Internationale Situationniste* #10 (p. 70) has the following note: "It is clear that there are presently only four possible types of publishing: state-bureaucratic; bourgeois semicompetitive (though subject to a tendency toward economic concentration); independent (wherever radical theory can be legally self-published); and clandestine. The SI—and any critical current anywhere—uses and will continue to use the latter two methods; it *may* in many cases use the second one (to obtain a qualitatively different level of distribution) because of the contradictions left open by anarchic competition and the lack of enforced ideological orthodoxy; and it is of course totally incompatible only with the first one. The reason is very simple: the competitive bourgeois type of publishing does not claim to guarantee any consistency between itself and its different authors; the authors are not responsible for a publishing firm's operation and, conversely, the publisher has no direct responsibility for their life or ideas. Only state-bureaucratic publishing (or that of parties representing such a bureaucracy in formation) is in complete solidarity with its authors: it has to endorse its authors in everything and its authors also have to endorse it. Thus it represents a *double impossibility* for any revolutionary expression."

183. *Sierra Madre:* mountain range in Cuba where Fidel Castro, Che Guevara, and a few companions began their guerrilla struggle against the Batista regime (1956). *The Greeks at Thermopylae:* a small band of Greek soldiers who fought to the death against the vastly superior forces of the Persian Empire (480 BC). See Herodotus's *History of the Persian Wars* (chap. 7). The quote is from the famous epigram of Simonides: "Stranger, when you come to Lakedaimon, tell them that we lie here, obedient to their will." (Translation by Kenneth Rexroth.)

183. *Der Deutsche Gedanke:* German-language journal: the only issue (1963) consisted mostly of translations of French SI articles. *Situationistisk Revolution:* Danish journal edited by J.V.

Martin.

184. *André Malraux:* French novelist and critic who became Minister of Culture under de Gaulle.

188. *Bonnot Gang:* French anarchist bandit gang (1911-1912).

191. "The discoveries of psychoanalysis have, as Freud suspected, turned out to be unacceptable for the ruling social order—or for any society based on repressive hierarchy. But Freud's 'centrist' position, stemming from his absolute, ahistorical identification of 'civilization' with repression by exploitation of labor, and thus his carrying out of a partially critical research within an uncriticized overall system, led psychoanalysis to become officially 'recognized' in all its degraded variants without being accepted in its central truth, namely its *potential* critical use. This failure is of course not exclusively attributable to Freud himself, but rather to the collapse in the 1920s of the revolutionary movement, the only force that could have brought the critical findings of psychoanalysis to some fulfillment. The subsequent period of extreme reaction in Europe drove out even the partisans of psychoanalytic 'centrism.' The psychoanalytic debris who are now in fashion (in the West, at least) have all developed out of this initial capitulation, in which an unacceptable critical truth was turned into acceptably innocuous verbiage. By surrendering its revolutionary cutting edge, psychoanalysis exposed itself *both* to being used by all the guardians of the present Sleep and to being disparaged for its insufficiencies by run-of-the-mill psychiatrists and moralists" (*Internationale Situationniste* #10, p. 63).

"Cardan [Cornelius Castoriadis], who here as elsewhere seems to think that it suffices to speak of something in order to have it, vaguely blathers on about 'imagination' in an attempt to justify the gelatinous flabbiness of his own thought. He latches onto psychoanalysis (just as does the official world nowadays) as a *justification* of irrationality and of the profound motivations of the unconscious, although the discoveries of psychoanalysis are in fact a weapon—as yet unused due to obvious sociopolitical reasons—for a *rational critique* of the world. Psychoanalysis profoundly ferrets out the unconscious, its poverty and its miserable repressive maneuvers, which only draw their force and their magical grandeur from a quite banal practical repression in daily life" (*Internationale Situationniste* #10, p. 79).

193. *Mining Association (Union Minière):* Belgian mining company with a concession for the mineral-rich Katanga region. In 1960 it supported the secession of Katanga from the newly independent Congo and was complicit in the murder of Patrice Lumumba, the first Congolese prime minister. *Mulelists:* insurgents led by Pierre Mulele.

194. This text was originally circulated clandestinely in Algeria (July 1965), then published as a five-language pamphlet (in Arabic, English, French, German, and Spanish) November 1965.

199. Berkeley student strike: i.e. the "Free Speech Movement." See David Lance Goines's *The Free Speech Movement.*

202. *Lincoln Brigades:* American volunteers who went to Spain to fight against Franco during the Spanish civil war (1936–1939).

203. *POUM (Partido Obrero de Unificación Marxista):* Spanish revolutionary Marxist organization, allied with the anarchists in opposing the machinations of the Stalinists within the anti-Franco camp. It was largely destroyed by the Stalinists in May 1937 through a series of repressions, arrests, and assassinations.

The concluding sentence ("A revolt against the spectacle . . .") is a détournement from Marx: "A social revolution involves the standpoint of the *whole*—even if it takes place in only one factory district—because it is a human protest against a dehumanized life, because it proceeds from the standpoint of the *single actual individual,* because the *community* against whose separation from himself the individual is reacting is the true community of man, true human nature" (*Critical Notes on "The King of Prussia and Social Reform,"* 1844).

205. *Sukarno* (president of Indonesia 1945–1967) "reigned à la Ben Bella, by basing his power on the obvious antagonism between the army and the most powerful Stalinist party of Asia" (*Internationale Situationniste* #10, p. 44)—until the army carried out a coup (1965) in which hundreds of thousands of Communists were massacred, and shortly afterwards removed Sukarno from power.

212. This text was originally published as a poster and circulated clandestinely in Algeria.

221. *Préciosité* (preciosity or preciousness) was a social style of extreme wit and refinement developed in certain French salons of the seventeenth century. Although from some angles it could be seen as silly and pretentious (Molière satirized the excesses of the movement in his play *Les Précieuses ridicules*), it also contained some suggestive innovations in the cultivation of aesthetic and amorous sensitivity. The *Carte de Tendre* (Map of Tenderness), an allegorical map purporting to show the way to a woman's affections which appeared in Madeleine de

Scudéry's novel *Clélie* (1656), was reproduced in *Internationale Situationniste* #3 (p. 14).

221. *The Fronde:* a complex series of revolts and social conflicts in seventeenth-century France (1648–1653).

223. *Newspeak:* the language imposed by the totalitarian regime in Orwell's *1984,* designed to make any alternative thinking ("thoughtcrime") or speech impossible by eliminating words and phrases conveying ideas of freedom, rebellion, etc.

224. *Encyclopédistes:* Diderot, d'Alembert, Montesquieu, Rousseau, Voltaire, and other eighteenth-century French thinkers who promoted the advancement of science and secular thought, encouraged reason, knowledge, education, and tolerance as a way of overcoming ignorance and superstition, and contributed to the *Encyclopédie* (1751–1780).

228. *Aragon-the-Senile:* popular designation for Louis Aragon after he became a Stalinist. During his earlier surrealist days he had once made a contemptuous reference to "Moscow-the-Senile."

230. *artistic Teilhardism:* i.e. a modernist artistic-Stalinist synthesis, by analogy to the modernist scientific-Catholic synthesis of Pierre Teilhard de Chardin.

231. *"a bond, not a power":* Marx's characterization of the First International.

231. The correspondent was Branko Vucicovic in Prague. The full text of the two letters can be found in Guy Debord's *Correspondance* (Volume 3, pp. 89–92 and 115–117).

242. *Lavrenti Beria,* head of Stalin's secret police, was arrested and executed immediately after Stalin's death in 1953.

242. *on orders from the Mikado, etc.:* Accusations fabricated during the Moscow Trials of 1936–1938 in which Stalin eliminated virtually all the former Bolshevik leaders except himself.

243. *Great Leap Forward (1958–1962):* Mao's pet scheme for ultrarapid industrialization, which resulted in economic chaos and famines killing tens of millions of people. Its failure caused Mao to be replaced as president of China by Liu Shao-chi (though he retained the powerful post of Chairman of the Communist Party).

245. *Red Guards:* youth enlisted by the Mao faction to attack the rival "revisionist" bureaucrats. Some groups of Red Guards, however, were actually set up and controlled by the anti-Mao faction. Others, though originally pro-Mao, ended up overflowing the control of the Maoist bureaucracy by taking the Maoist radical rhetoric seriously.

248. *Sian Incident:* In 1936 Kuomintang leader Chiang Kai-chek was imprisoned in Sian (Xi'an) by one of his own generals, who was in favor of an alliance with the Communist Party against the Japanese invaders. On Stalin's insistence Chiang was turned loose in exchange for his agreement to the united front between the CP and the Kuomintang that was effected a few months later.

249. *continuation of politics:* Reference to Clausewitz's maxim, "War is a continuation of politics by other means," with perhaps also an ironic allusion to Mao's saying, "Political power grows out of the barrel of a gun."

249. *Sun Yat-sen:* leader of the Chinese nationalist movement until his death in 1925.

250. *1927 coup:* On the advice of the Chinese Communist Party, the workers who had revolted and taken over Shanghai in 1927 welcomed Chiang Kai-chek's army into the city and allowed themselves to be disarmed; after which they were massacred. See Harold Isaacs's *The Tragedy of the Chinese Revolution.*

250. *annihilation of Indonesian Stalinism:* "None of these disasters, however, are so gross as the bloody downfall of Indonesian Stalinism, whose bureaucratic mania blinded it to the point of expecting to seize power only by way of plots and palace revolution, although it was in control of an immense movement—a movement it led to annihilation without ever having led it into battle (it is estimated that there have been over 300,000 executions)" (*Internationale Situationniste* #10, p. 65). See also Note 205.

251. The *"Mandate of Heaven"* is the traditional right of Chinese emperors to rule. When this mandate is lost—as revealed by inauspicious signs expressing the disfavor of Heaven—it is time for a revolution to establish a new dynasty.

251. This text was originally published as a pamphlet (August 1967). For simplicity's sake I have left all the Chinese proper names in the Wade-Giles system of romanization that was used in the original SI article, instead of the now-standard Pinyin system. (Peking is now Beijing, Mao Tse-tung is now Mao Zedong, etc.) A few of the alternative forms are indicated in the Index.

For an excellent and much more detailed account of the "Cultural Revolution," see Simon Leys's *The Chairman's New Clothes: Mao and the Cultural Revolution.* The book is long out of print, but a PDF can be viewed at www.bopsecrets.org/CF/leys.htm

254. *rout of the Russians:* Allusion to the "Cuban missile crisis," when Kennedy's threat of launching a nuclear war pressured Russia to remove the missiles it had installed in Cuba.

256. *eliminating the remaining revolutionary elements:* For a detailed account of the Vietnamese radical movements destroyed by the Stalinists, see Ngo Van's *In the Crossfire: Adventures of a Vietnamese Revolutionary* (translated by Ken Knabb et al., AK Press, 2010).

259. *British Mandate:* British protectorate over Palestine (1920–1948). *Sykes–Picot Agreement:* a secret agreement made between England, France, and Russia in 1916 to divide up the former Ottoman Empire possessions among themselves after the end of World War I. In 1917 the Bolsheviks discovered the document in the Russian state archives and publicly divulged and repudiated it, much to the embarrassment of the French and British governments.

260. *Tripartite aggression:* England, France, and Israel's joint attack on Egypt during the 1956 "Suez crisis."

261. *Baath Party:* Pan-Arab party, rival factions of which have ruled Syria and Iraq since the 1960s (until the 2003 US-led invasion overthrew the Iraqi branch). *Kassem:* Iraqi ruler, 1958–1963. *Aref:* Iraqi ruler, 1963–1966. *Hussein:* king of Jordan. *Faisal:* king of Saudi Arabia.

261. *Pablo:* pseudonym of Michalis N. Raptis, leader of a Trotskyist tendency.

269. *three situationists were excluded:* Théo Frey, Jean Garnault, and Herbert Holl, referred to as the "Garnautins."

278. *a secret fraction:* i.e. the "Garnautins." On the following page they are referred to as "the most recently excluded."

279. *composite, butterfly, cabalist:* Fourier's three "distributive passions." See *The Utopian Vision of Charles Fourier* (Beacon, 1971; ed. Beecher & Bienvenu), pp. 216–220.

283. See Frantz Fanon, *The Wretched of the Earth.*

284. *'through blood and mud':* See the chapters on "Primitive Accumulation" in Marx's *Capital.*

285. *the power of soviets:* i.e. the power of workers' councils. See Riesel's "Preliminaries on Councils and Councilist Organization" (pp. 348–362).

On Third World bureaucratic regimes, see *The Society of the Spectacle* #113.

291. *"Katangans":* nickname given to ex-mercenaries and other toughs who rallied to the May movement. Presumably some of them had fought in Katanga (see Note 193).

291. *Into the Trashcan of History:* In 1960 the SI initiated a boycott of anyone who collaborated with the journal *Arguments,* "in order to make an example of the most representative tendency of that conformist and pseudoleftist intelligentsia that has up till now laboriously organized a conspiracy of silence regarding us, and whose bankruptcy in all domains is beginning to be recognized by perceptive people" (*Internationale Situationniste* #5, p. 13). The SI noted various evidences of this bankruptcy and predicted the journal's imminent demise from sheer incoherence and lack of ideas; which was precisely what occurred in 1962.

As it happened, the last issue of *Arguments* contained an article by Henri Lefebvre on the Paris Commune that was largely plagiarized from the SI's "Theses on the Commune." The SI issued a tract, *Into the Trashcan of History*, calling attention to the contradiction that the lead article of a guest writer himself far above the general level of this journal—a journal pretending that the SI was of so little interest as to not be worth mentioning—was merely a watered-down version of a text that three situationists had written in a few hours. This tract was reprinted in *Internationale Situationniste* #12 in response to the numerous commentators who attributed to Lefebvre an important influence on the May 1968 movement due to "his" theses on the festive nature of the Commune.

For more on this topic, see "L'historien Lefebvre" (*Internationale Situationniste* #10, pp. 73–75).

298. By May 20 six million workers were on strike; within a few days the number had risen to eleven million.

Although many people continue to refer to May 1968 as a "student movement," these figures alone should suffice to refute that illusion, as they refuted many other then-current ideologies: "Those who spoke of Marcuse as the 'theorist' of the movement didn't know what they were talking about. They didn't even understand Marcuse, much less the movement itself. Marcusian *ideology*, already ridiculous, was pasted onto the movement in the same way that Geismar, Sauvageot, and Cohn-Bendit were 'designated' to represent it. But even these latter admitted that they knew nothing about Marcuse. If the May revolutionary crisis demonstrated anything, it was in fact precisely the opposite of Marcuse's theses: it showed that the proletariat has not been integrated and that it is the main revolutionary force in modern society. Pessimists and sociologists will have to redo their calculations, as will the spokespeople of underdevelopment, Black Power, and Dutschkeism" (René Viénet, *Enragés et situationnistes dans le mouvement des occupations*, pp. 153–154).

299. *Alexander Kerensky:* head of the Russian Provisional Government between the February 1917 revolution and the Bolsheviks' Octo-

ber 1917 coup. Evoked here as representative of devious counterrevolutionary maneuvering, as contrasted with the more overt action of Gustav Noske, the German socialist leader responsible for crushing the Spartakist insurrection in 1919.

303. "The March 22nd Movement was from the beginning an eclectic conglomeration of radicals who joined it as (supposedly) independent individuals. They all agreed on the fact that it was impossible for them to agree on any theoretical point, and counted on 'collective action' to overcome this deficiency. There was nevertheless a consensus on two subjects, one a ridiculous banality, the other a new standard. The banality was anti-imperialist 'struggle,' the heritage of the contemplative period of the little leftist groups that was about to end (Nanterre University, that suburban Vietnam, resolutely supporting the just struggle of insurgent Bolivia, etc.). The novelty was direct democracy within the organization. This was only very partially realized in the March 22nd Movement because of the participants' divided allegiances—the discreetly unmentioned or ignored fact that the majority of its members were simultaneously members of other groups.... The sociologists' and journalists' trumpeting of the 'originality' of the March 22nd Movement masked the fact that its leftist amalgam, while new in France, was a direct copy of the American SDS, itself equally eclectic and democratic and frequently infiltrated by various old leftist sects" (Viénet, *op. cit.,* pp. 37–39).

"Cohn-Bendit himself belonged to the independent semitheoretical anarchist group that publishes the journal *Noir et Rouge*. As much due to this fact as because of his personal qualities, he found himself in the most radical tendency of the March 22nd Movement, more truly revolutionary than the rest of the group whose spokesman he was to become and which he therefore had to tolerate. (In a number of interviews he has made increasing concessions to Maoism, as for example in the May 1968 issue of *Le Magazine Littéraire:* 'Maoism? I don't really know all that much about it! I've read some things in Mao that are very true. His thesis of relying on the peasantry has always been an anarchist thesis.') Insufficiently intelligent, informed confusedly and at second hand regarding present-day theoretical problems, skillful enough to entertain a student audience, frank enough to stand out from the arena of leftist political maneuvers yet flexible enough to come to terms with its leaders, Cohn-Bendit was an honest revolutionary, but no genius. He knew much less than he should have, and did not make the best use of what he did know. Moreover, because he uncritically accepted the role of a star, exhibiting himself for the mob of reporters from the spectacular media, his statements, which always combined a certain lucidity with a certain foolishness, were inevitably twisted in the latter direction by the deformation inherent in that kind of communication" (Viénet, *op. cit.,* pp. 38–39).

307. Allusion to the 7% wage increase offered in the Grenelle Accords.

311. "In the name of the Enragés, René Riesel immediately demanded the expulsion of two observers from the administration and of the several Stalinists who were present. An anarchist spokesman and regular collaborator of Cohn-Bendit asserted, 'The Stalinists who are here this evening are no longer Stalinists.' The Enragés immediately left the meeting in protest against this cowardly illusion" (Viénet, *op. cit.,* p. 34).

316. *Action Committees:* Besides numerous SI, Enragé, and CMDO texts, Viénet's book reproduces a critique of the health-care system by the National Center of Young Doctors, a critique of advertising by a group of ad designers, a manifesto against the commercial manipulation of soccer by the Soccer Players Action Committee, and leaflets by a Yugoslavian woman, by the North African Action Committee, by the strike committee of a large department store, by airline workers, by postal workers, and by several revolutionary groups.

Roger Grégoire and Fredy Perlman's booklet *Worker-Student Action Committees: France May '68* (Black and Red, 1969) gives a good first-hand account of some of other action committees that the SI was not aware of at the time.

316. *wildcat workers' struggles:* See, for example, the opening paragraphs of the 1962 article "The Bad Days Will End" (pp. 107–109).

319. *La Sorbonne par elle-même (Maitron et al.):* This book included some more serious misrepresentations regarding the situationists, including reproductions of CMDO texts that were knowingly falsified (critiques of the Stalinists deleted with no indication of the omissions, completely fabricated passages sympathetic to the CGT added, etc.). Following an account of their personal confrontation with Maitron upon his refusal to make a written apology for these misrepresentations, the situationists stated: "In our opinion, the number-one objective for the revolutionary movement that is presently taking shape—even more important and urgent than elaborating

a consistent theoretical critique or linking up with democratic rank-and-file committees in the factories or paralyzing the universities—is giving practical support for *an insistence on truth and nonfalsification.* This is the *precondition* and the *beginning* of all the rest. Whoever falsifies must be discredited, boycotted, spit on. When it is a matter of *systems of falsification* (as in the case of Stalinist bureaucrats or of bourgeois) it is obviously those systems that must be destroyed by a large-scale social and political struggle. But this very struggle must create its own conditions: when one is dealing with individuals or groups aiming to establish themselves anywhere in the revolutionary current, one must *not let them get away with anything.* By maintaining this insistence, the movement will fundamentally smash all the conditions of falsification that have accompanied and brought about its disappearance for the last half century. As we see it, all revolutionaries must now recognize it as their immediate task to denounce and *discourage,* by all means and whatever the price, those who continue to falsify." ("L'historien Maitron," *Internationale Situationniste* #12, pp. 89–90.)

320. Following the defeat of the movement in late June, the Enragés, situationists, and other CMDO members who were most directly implicated in the revolt escaped to Belgium for a few weeks until the momentary repression blew over.

321. Although he temporarily survived the May 1968 revolt, de Gaulle ended up resigning less than a year later after losing an April 1969 referendum.

323. An act proposed by Barbara Castle (UK Secretary of State for Employment and Productivity) that would have restricted strikes and curbed the power of the unions. Due to popular resistance it was not passed into law, but certain of its provisions were later enacted under Margaret Thatcher.

325. The quotation is from the Preface to Hegel's *The Phenomenology of Spirit.*

326. On Trotskyism, see *The Society of the Spectacle* ##112–113. On Leninism and Bolshevism, see ##98–106.

331. *"Gomulka-type regression":* Wladyslaw Gomulka had arrived in power in Poland in 1956 as a somewhat liberal bureaucrat, but had subsequently become more hardline.

331. *Rudi Dutschke:* leader of German SDS. *Rouge:* a French Trotskyist paper.

332. *Edvard Benes:* president of Czechoslovakia before the 1948 Stalinist takeover.

334. *"Operation Kadar":* i.e. an operation analogous to that carried out after the crushing of the 1956 Hungarian revolution, in which the Russians simply shot the Dubček-type liberal bureaucrats and installed their puppet János Kádár.

336. On Stalinism, see *The Society of the Spectacle* ##105–111. On German Social Democracy and the Second International, see ##95–97.

339. The article referred to is "Socialisme ou Planète" (*Internationale Situationniste* #10, pp. 77–79).

341. The quotation is from the Preface to Hegel's *The Phenomenology of Spirit.* The "famous analysis of the fetishism of the commodity" is in Marx's *Capital* (chap. 1, section 4).

344. *profonde* ("deep") is French slang for "pocket."

348. *Kronstadt:* In March 1921 the sailors of Kronstadt, who had been among the most ardent participants in the 1917 revolution, revolted against the Bolshevik government, calling for a genuine power of the soviets (democratic popular councils) as opposed to the rule of the "Soviet" state. Denounced as reactionaries, they were crushed by the Red Army under the leadership of Trotsky. See Ida Mett's *The Kronstadt Commune,* Paul Avrich's *Kronstadt, 1921,* or Israel Getzler's *Kronstadt 1917–1921: The Fate of a Soviet Democracy.*

On the 1917 Russian revolution in general, Trotsky's *The History of the Russian Revolution* is well worth reading, but it should be supplemented with Voline's *The Unknown Revolution* and Maurice Brinton's *The Bolsheviks and Workers' Control: 1917–1921* (included in the collection of Brinton's works, *For Workers' Power*). For a more personal first-hand account of the same period, see Emma Goldman's *My Disillusionment in Russia.*

351. *What happened next:* i.e. Mussolini's fascist coup (1922). On the Italian movement, see Paolo Spriano's *The Occupation of the Factories: Italy 1920.* For more detailed background, see Gwyn A. Williams's *Proletarian Order: Antonio Gramsci, Factory Councils and the Origins of Communism in Italy, 1911–1921.*

352. *Freikorps:* right-wing paramilitary units used to repress radical movements in the aftermath of World War I. On the German revolution, see Richard M. Watt's *The Kings Depart: Versailles and the German Revolution* or A.J. Ryder's *The German Revolution: 1918–1919.*

352. On the Hungarian revolution, see Andy Anderson's *Hungary '56.*

353. *Ebert, Noske, and Scheidemann:* "Socialist" leaders who crushed the German revolution.

358. *Anarcho-Marxist feud:* See *The Society of the Spectacle* #91. In the same book Debord examines the merits and defects of anarchism

(##92–94), of Marx's theories (##78–89), and of the various strands of "Marxism" (##95–113).

358. *Olivier, Blanco, Montseny:* anarchist leaders who became ministers in the Popular Front government during the Spanish civil war. *Anarcho-trenchists:* Kropotkin and other anarchists who supported World War I.

The best general histories of the Spanish revolution are Burnett Bolloten's *The Spanish Civil War* and Pierre Broué and Emile Témime's *Revolution and the War in Spain.* Some good first-hand accounts are George Orwell's *Homage to Catalonia,* Franz Borkenau's *The Spanish Cockpit,* and Mary Low and Juan Breá's *Red Spanish Notebook.* Other books worth reading include Vernon Richards's *Lessons of the Spanish Revolution,* Murray Bookchin's *To Remember Spain,* Noam Chomsky's *Objectivity and Liberal Scholarship,* Gerald Brenan's *The Spanish Labyrinth,* Sam Dolgoff's *The Anarchist Collectives,* Abel Paz's *Durruti: The People Armed,* and Victor Alba and Stephen Schwartz's *Spanish Marxism versus Soviet Communism: A History of the P.O.U.M.*

361. Anton Pannekoek, author of *Workers' Councils,* the classic work on this subject. See also *The Society of the Spectacle* ##116–119.

361. *Barth:* Probably Emil Barth, a German independent socialist who was briefly a member of the 1918 "Socialist" government before resigning in protest at its counterrevolutionary actions.

363. *generalized:* The sense is total, unlimited self-management: not the self-management of this or that sector of the existing system, but self-management extended to every region and every aspect of life.

368. *Watrinage:* the practice of assassinating an unpopular boss (from an engineer named Watrin, who was killed by striking French miners at the end of the nineteenth century).

On terrorism, see Debord's *Comments on the Society of the Spectacle;* the last half of Debord's *Preface to the Fourth Italian Edition of "The Society of the Spectacle";* and Gianfranco Sanguinetti's *On Terrorism and the State.*

369. For more detailed examination of these types of postrevolution issues, see Vaneigem's *Total Self-Management* (www.bopsecrets.org/CF/selfmanagement.htm) and Ken Knabb's *The Joy of Revolution* (www.bopsecrets.org/PS/joyrev4.htm).

370. *"lenins":* "When we are victorious on a global scale I think we will use gold for the purpose of building public lavatories in the streets of some of the largest cities. This would be the most 'just' and most educational way of utilizing gold" (Lenin, "The Importance of

Gold Now and After the Complete Victory of Socialism," on the occasion of Russia's return to the gold standard in 1921).

375. Members of the American SI section were Robert Chasse, Bruce Elwell, Jonathan Horelock, and Tony Verlaan.

375. Ben Morea and Allen Hoffman later formed the New York "Motherfuckers" group.

377. Although the situationists could easily have accumulated numerous members had they been so inclined, the SI's membership was rarely much more than a dozen.

In all, 63 men and 7 women from 16 different countries were members at one time or another. Most were from various west European countries; three were from the United States, two from Algeria, and one each from Congo, Hungary, Israel, Romania, Tunisia, and Venezuela.

378. *dialecticians:* "Proletarian revolution depends entirely on the condition that, for the first time, theory as understanding of human practice be recognized and lived by the masses. It requires that workers become dialecticians and put their thought into practice" (*The Society of the Spectacle* #123).

378. *expressed in the cinema:* Allusion to the Lettrist films of the early 1950s, which frequently contained such blank-screen passages, culminating in Debord's first film, *Howls for Sade* (1952), which contains no images whatsoever.

379. *Gualtiero Jacopetti:* director of *Mondo Cane* and other sensationalistic "shockumentaries."

389. "Utopia" literally means "nowhere."

393. Pierre Canjuers (pseudonym of Daniel Blanchard) was at this time a member of the *Socialisme ou Barbarie* group. This text, written when Debord was participating in that group's activities, is described in *Internationale Situationniste* #5 (p. 11) as "a platform for discussion within the SI, and for its linkup with revolutionary militants of the workers' movement."

For more on the interconnections between culture and society, see Chapter 8 of *The Society of the Spectacle.*

397. This text, written in February 1961, first appeared in *Notes Critiques: bulletin de recherche et d'orientation révolutionnaires* #3 (Bordeaux, 1962).

398. The Marx quotation and the following one by Engels are from *The Civil War in France.*

399. *pétroleuses:* Communard women who were rumored (probably falsely) to have burned down many Parisian buildings during the final days of the Commune by throwing bottles of petroleum.

401. *Louis-Antoine de Saint-Just,* one of the Jacobin leaders during the French Revolution, was

executed along with Robespierre in 1794.

401. This text, originally written in 1962 on the anniversary of the Commune (March 18), was reproduced in the tract *Into the Trashcan of History* (see Note 291).

405. The quotation combines three separate passages from "Geopolitics of Hibernation" (Debord does not indicate the ellipses).

405. The "Spies for Peace" scandal is recounted in detail in *Anarchy* #29 (London, July 1963).

405. *demonstration in Denmark:* "In June 1963 the SI organized a 'Destruction of RSG-6' demonstration in Denmark, under the direction of J.V. Martin. On this occasion the situationists distributed a clandestine reissue of the English tract *Danger: Official Secret—RSG 6,* signed 'Spies for Peace,' which revealed the plan and function of 'Regional Seat of Government #6.' A theoretical text, *The Situationists and the New Forms of Action in Politics and Art,* was also issued in Danish, English, and French. In one area an ugly reconstruction of a bomb shelter was set up; in another were exhibited Martin's 'Thermonuclear Maps' (détournements of Pop Art representing various regions of the globe during World War III)" (*Internationale Situationniste* #9, pp. 31–32).

As noted later in this article, the exhibition also included some painted "Directives" by Debord and some "Victories" by Michèle Bernstein. The "Victories" are also discussed at the end of "Response to a Questionnaire from the Center for Socio-Experimental Art" (p. 188) and a detail from one of them is reproduced in *Internationale Situationniste* #9, p. 43. One of the "Thermonuclear Maps" is reproduced in *Internationale Situationniste* #9, p. 32. Debord's "Directives" are reproduced in his *Oeuvres* (pp. 654–655).

408. *he:* In some passages of my translations from the SI I have followed the current practice of replacing formerly conventional masculine forms with gender-neutral ones (e.g. changing "man" to "humanity"). In other cases, however, I have retained the original terms in order to avoid a complicated recasting of what are already rather complex texts. In the present case, much of the incisiveness of the SI's critique of "the student" would be lost if the text was changed to plural or "his or her" forms.

Note also that "student" in this pamphlet always refers to college students. Grade school and high school students are referred to by different French terms.

409. *"Bourderon and Passedieu":* The actual names of these authors (transposed to make a sarcastic French play on words) are Pierre

Bourdieu and Jean-Claude Passeron.

413. *Hallyday:* rock star Johnny Hallyday, a sort of French Elvis, included in this list as an additional insult to the other "celebrities of Unintelligence" (all the rest of whom were prominent academic intellectuals).

419. For more on the Provos, see "Révolte et récupération en Hollande" (*Internationale Situationniste* #11, pp. 65–66) and Richard Kempton's *Provo: Amsterdam's Anarchist Revolt.*

420. Kuron and Modzelewski's *Open Letter* appeared in 1965. English translations appeared under several different titles: *An Open Letter to the Party; A Revolutionary Socialist Manifesto; Revolutionary Marxist Students in Poland Speak Out;* and *Solidarnosc, the Missing Link.*

420. *East Berlin, Warsaw, Budapest:* allusion to the East Berlin revolt of 1953 and the Polish and Hungarian revolts of 1956.

421. *Heatwave* editors Christopher Gray and Charles Radcliffe subsequently joined the SI.

Obsolete postal addresses of *Heatwave,* the Zengakuren, and the Japanese RCL (included in the original pamphlet) have been omitted.

422. The SI's judgment of the Revolutionary Communist League turned out to be mistaken in some respects. The RCL Zengakuren was not "the" Zengakuren, but only one of several rival ones (another was dominated by the Japanese Communist Party, others by various combinations of Trotskyists, Maoists, etc.). In the early sixties the Zengakuren faction that was to form the RCL did indeed have many of the positive features the SI attributed to it: it had a political platform distinctly to the left of Trotskyism, participated militantly in political struggles on many fronts, and seems to have had a fairly experimental approach to organizational and tactical questions. In 1963 it sent some delegates to Europe who met the situationists, and it later translated a few situationist texts into Japanese. At least by 1970, however, when an SI delegate (René Viénet) visited Japan, the RCL had devolved into a largely Leninist position and turned out to be not very different from leftist sects everywhere else.

422. *Karl Liebknecht:* one of the few German socialists to oppose World War I. He and Rosa Luxemburg founded the Spartakus League in 1916; they were both killed following the crushing of the Spartakist insurrection in January 1919.

424. The original text cites the Latin phrase *Carthago delenda est* ("Carthage must be destroyed") with which the ancient Roman senator Cato the Elder ended all his speeches. The sense is that the destruction of Stalinism must be constantly, and even obsessively, insisted

upon until it is carried out.

426. *Lukács:* See the last chapter of Lukács's *History and Class Consciousness.*

426. *Rosa Luxemburg:* See Luxemburg's article "Organizational Questions of Russian Social Democracy" (1904), in which she criticizes Lenin's *What Is To Be Done?* (1903).

429. *heir of philosophy:* "Just as philosophy finds its material weapons in the proletariat, so the proletariat finds its spiritual weapons in philosophy. . . . Philosophy cannot be realized without the supersession of the proletariat; the proletariat cannot be superseded without the realization of philosophy" (Marx, *Introduction to a Critique of Hegel's Philosophy of Right*).

429. " 'Transform the world,' said Marx. 'Change life,' said Rimbaud. For us these two commands are one and the same" (André Breton).

429. *enjoy without restraints:* The ending is stronger and more scandalous in the original: the French word *jouir* ("to enjoy") also means "to come" in the sexual sense.

429. *On the Poverty of Student Life* was originally published at the expense of the Strasbourg Student Union (see "Our Goals and Methods in the Strasbourg Scandal," pp. 263–272). With the possible exception of *The Society of the Spectacle,* it is the most widely reproduced situationist text. It has been translated into Chinese, Danish, Dutch, English, Farsi, Finnish, German, Greek, Indonesian, Italian, Japanese, Macedonian, Polish, Portuguese, Romanian, Russian, Spanish, Swedish, and probably several other languages, and its total printing is well over half a million.

430. *Berkeley:* reference to the 1964 Free Speech Movement. *Warsaw:* probably refers to the 1965 publication of Kuron and Modzelewski's *Open Letter to the Polish Communist Party* (see p. 420). *Asturias:* see Note 152. *Kivu:* region in eastern Congo.

431. This first text was appended to the original edition of "The Class Struggles in Algeria" (a poster distributed clandestinely in Algeria in December 1965). On a few later occasions it was separately reprinted by the SI, sometimes with minor variations (e.g. citing different examples of current struggles in subsequent years).

431. *"communists":* Many of the phrases in these two texts are in fact adopted or adapted from the *Communist Manifesto,* e.g. "The communists do not form a separate party opposed to other working-class parties. They have no interest separate and apart from those of the proletariat as a whole. They do not set up any sectarian principles of their own by which to shape and mold the proletarian movement." Numerous other situationist passages (for example, all three of the chapter titles in *On the Poverty of Student Life*) are also derived from Marx, particularly from his early writings of the 1840s.

432. This text appeared as an appendix in the pamphlet *Avviso al proletariato italiano sulle possibilità presenti della rivoluzione sociale* (1969). The present version incorporates a few sentences tadded in a reprinting the following year.

445. These graffiti are drawn primarily from Julien Besançon's *Les murs ont la parole* (Tchou, 1968), Walter Lewino's *L'Imagination au pouvoir* (Losfeld, 1968), Marc Rohan's *Paris '68* (Impact, 1968), René Viénet's *Enragés et situationnistes dans le mouvement des occupations* (Gallimard, 1968), Maurice Brinton's *Paris: May 1968* (Solidarity, 1968), and Gérard Lambert's *Mai 1968: brûlante nostalgie* (Pied de nez, 1988). Some were written by the situationists or the Enragés, or are quotes from SI writings, but many of the others clearly reflect a more or less situationist spirit, whether they were directly influenced by the SI, or because situationist ideas were in the air, or simply because the liberated reality was generating situationist-style feelings and insights. The other documents in this section are all drawn from Viénet's book.

448. *Georges Séguy:* head bureaucrat of the CGT, the largest French labor union, dominated by the Communist Party.

449. Détournement of the eighteenth-century slogan, "Humanity won't be happy till the last aristocrat is hung with the guts of the last priest."

456. The definition in Bierce's *The Devil's Dictionary* is actually: "Amnesty: The state's magnanimity to those offenders whom it would be too expensive to punish."

464. The SI members mentioned in these internal texts only by their first names are Attila Kotányi, Gianfranco Sanguinetti, Guy Debord, Mustapha Khayati, Paolo Salvadori, Raoul Vaneigem, René Riesel, René-Donatien Viénet, and Tony Verlaan.

471. *pro-situs:* pejorative term referring to fans, followers, and imitators of the SI. See "Theses on the SI and Its Time" ##25–38 in *The Real Split in the International*.

GRCA: Groupe Révolutionnaire Conseilliste d'Agitations (Revolutionary Councilist Agitational Group), one of the many situationist-influenced groups formed in the aftermath of May 1968.

477. *Communist League:* early international revolutionary organization (1847–1852). *FAI:* Iberian Anarchist Federation.

477. *Kiruna:* The SI had addressed a congratulatory telegram to wildcat strikers in Kiruna, Sweden (January 1970), and Vaneigem had later written an article about the strikes which appeared in the Danish SI journal.

477. *Vaneigem:* Raoul Vaneigem resigned from the SI on 14 November 1970 in response to the Debord–Riesel–Viénet "Declaration." His letter of resignation and the SI's "Communiqué Concerning Vaneigem" are reproduced in *The Real Split in the International*.

478. During the following year the remaining SI members decided to dissolve the organization. Its last publication, *The Real Split in the International* (April 1972; primarily written by Debord, though one of the texts was co-signed by Sanguinetti), examined the post-1968 SI crises in some detail, as well as new developments in the society as a whole. "Henceforth, situationists are everywhere and their task is everywhere."

Bibliography

For a continual update of this bibliography, see www.bopsecrets.org/SI/bibliog.htm.

Pre-SI and Early SI Texts

Gérard Berréby (ed.), *Documents relatifs à la fondation de l'Internationale Situationniste: 1948–1957* (Allia, 1985). This huge collection is now out of print, but Éditions Allia has published separate editions of most of the main texts from this period, as well as numerous other books by or about members of the SI or of pre-SI groups. Many are listed below; for others, see www.editions-allia.com.

Ruth Baumeister (ed.), *Fraternité Avant Tout: Asger Jorn's Writings on Art and Architecture* (nai010 Publishers, 2013) includes Danish and Swedish texts translated by Paul Larkin and French texts translated by Ken Knabb. The latter translations are also online at www.bopsecrets.org/SI/asger-jorn/index.htm. Baumeister has also written several books about Jorn.

Potlatch: 1954–1957 (Lebovici, 1985; Gallimard, 1996). The complete newsletters of the Lettrist International (LI), with a preface by Debord.

Jean-Louis Rançon (ed.), *Visages de l'avant-garde* (La Nerthe, 2020) presents and annotates some LI documents.

Serge Berna, *Écrits et documents* (Sandre, 2024; ed. Jean-Louis Rançon). Berna was the guy who masterminded the 1950 Notre-Dame scandal.

Gil J Wolman's *Défense de mourir* (Allia, 2001) includes all his LI texts and metagraphs plus numerous later works.

Guy Debord & Asger Jorn, *Fin de Copenhague* (1957; Allia, 2001). A collage collaboration.

Guy Debord & Asger Jorn, *Mémoires* (1958; Allia, 2004). See also Boris Donné's in-depth study of this book, *Pour Mémoires* (Allia, 2004).

Guy Debord's *Lettres à Marcel Mariën* (La Nerthe, 2015) were addressed to the editor of *Les Lèvres Nues,* the Belgian surrealist journal that included several texts by Debord and other LI members. The complete *Les Lèvres Nues* (1954–1958) were reissued by Allia in 1995.

Guy Debord, *Enregistrements magnétiques, 1952–1961* (Gallimard, 2010; ed. Jean-Louis Rançon) includes two CDs of Debord's recorded works.

Ivan Chtcheglov's *Écrits retrouvés* (Allia, 2006) includes recently discovered works. See also Jean-Marie Apostolidès & Boris Donné's *Ivan Chtcheglov, profil perdu* (Allia, 2006), a preliminary biographical study of this intriguing early figure whose psychogeographical explorations and visions inspired Debord.

Jean-Michel Mension's *La Tribu* (Allia, 1998), translated by Donald Nicholson-Smith as *The Tribe* (City Lights, 2001), is an illustrated series of reminiscences of the LI scene in Paris in the early 1950s with Debord, Wolman, Chtcheglov, Berna, Michèle Bernstein, Jean-Louis Brau, Éliane Brau, etc.

Ralph Rumney's *Le Consul* (Allia, 1999), translated by Malcolm Imrie as *The Consul* (City Lights, 2002), also includes some material on that scene, but it's mostly about Rumney's later life as artist and bohemian.

Michèle Bernstein's two quite interesting novels, *Tous les chevaux du roi* (1960; Allia 1998), translated by John Kelsey as *All the King's Horses* (Semiotext(e), 2008), and *La Nuit* (1961; Allia, 1999), translated by Clodagh Kinsella as *The Night* (Book Works, 2013), narrate the same story (loosely based on Bernstein and Debord's life in the late 1950s) in two different styles, the first parodying Françoise Sagan, the second parodying the *nouveau roman.*

Patrick Straram's *Les bouteilles se couchent* (Allia, 2006) is a fictional portrayal of the scene described in the Mension book, centering around the legendary Chez Moineau café.

Patrick Straram's *Lettre à Guy Debord* (Sens & Tonka, 2006) was written in 1960, after Straram had moved to Quebec.

Libero Andreotti & Xavier Costa (eds.), *Theory of the Dérive and Other Situationist Writings on the City* (Museu d'Art Contemporani de Barcelona, 1996) and Tom McDonough (ed.), *The Situationists and the City: A Reader* (Verso, 2010) are two anthologies of LI and early SI articles, the latter volume being the most comprehensive. See also Simon Sadler's study *The Situationist City* (MIT Press, 1998).

Gérard Berréby (ed.), *Textes et documents situationnistes, 1957–1960* (Allia, 2003) includes all the SI's publications from its first three years except the journals.

French SI Books

Internationale Situationniste: 1958–1969 (Van Gennep, 1970; Champ Libre, 1975; Fayard, 1997). 700-page facsimile reprint of all twelve issues of the French journal. Selections were translated by Christopher Gray in *Leaving the Twentieth Century: The Incomplete Work of the Situationist International* (Free Fall, 1974; Rebel, 1998). Ken Knabb's *Situationist International Anthology* (Bureau of Public Secrets, 1981; revised and expanded version, 2006; third edition: PM Press, 2024) is more accurate and much more comprehensive.

Raoul Vaneigem, *Traité de savoir-vivre à l'usage des jeunes générations* (Gallimard, 1967). Anonymous partial translation as *Treatise on Living for the Use of the Young Generations* (1970). Complete book translated as *The Revolution of Everyday Life* by John Fullerton & Paul Sieveking (Practical Paradise, 1972), and by Donald Nicholson-Smith (Rebel/Left Bank, 1983; revised 1994; Rebel, 2001; new translation: PM Press, 2012).

Guy Debord, *La Société du Spectacle* (Buchet-Chastel, 1967; Champ Libre, 1972; Gallimard, 1992). Translated as *Society of the Spectacle* by Fredy Perlman et al. (Black & Red, 1970; revised 1977; reprinted by AK Press, 2005); and as *The Society of the Spectacle* by Donald Nicholson-Smith (Zone, 1994), and by Ken Knabb (online, 2002; Rebel Press, 2004; revised and annotated edition, Bureau of Public Secrets, 2014; new edition: PM Press, 2024).

René Viénet, *Enragés et situationnistes dans le mouvement des occupations* (Gallimard, 1968). Includes numerous documents and illustrations. Translated as *Enragés and Situationists in the Occupation Movement, May '68* (Autonomedia/Rebel Press, 1992). Though published in Viénet's name, this book was actually collectively written by Debord, Khayati, Riesel, Vaneigem, and Viénet.

Guy Debord & Gianfranco Sanguinetti, *La véritable scission dans l'Internationale* (Champ Libre, 1972; Fayard, 1998). Translated by Michel Prigent & Lucy Forsyth as *The Veritable Split in the International* (Piranha, 1974; revised: Chronos, 1990); translated by John McHale as *The Real Split in the International* (Pluto, 2003).

Débat d'orientation de l'ex-Internationale Situationniste (Centre de Recherche sur la Question Sociale, 1974; Éditions du Cercle Carré, 2000). Internal SI documents, 1969–1971.

SI Texts in Other Languages

Most of the more original and important SI texts appeared in French. (The *SI Anthology* is drawn entirely from French texts except for the two Italian texts on pp. 431–432 and 464–468.) SI publications in other languages often represented the more eclectic, artistic, and opportunistic tendencies (notably in Italy, Germany, Scandinavia, and the Netherlands) that were repudiated early in the SI's history. In the later period, what would have become the British section never got off the ground, and the American and Italian sections scarcely lasted much longer, coming as they did in the middle of the post-1968 crises that were soon to lead to the SI's dissolution.

The American section's main publications were Robert Chasse's pamphlet *The Power of Negative Thinking* (New York, 1968) (a critique of the New Left, originally published shortly before Chasse joined the SI) and one issue of a journal, *Situationist International* #1 (New York, 1969). After their December 1969 resignation/exclusion, Chasse and Bruce Elwell produced a critical history of the American section, *A Field Study in the Dwindling Force of Cognition* (1970), which the SI never answered. The American journal was translated into French by Fabrice de San Mateo (Les Réveilleurs de la Nuit, 2012).

The Italian section published one issue of a journal, *Internazionale Situazionista* #1 (1969), and carried out a number of interventions in the crises and struggles in Italy. A complete French edition, *Écrits complets de la Section Italienne de l'Internationale Situationniste* (1969–1972), was translated by Joël Gayraud & Luc Mercier (Contre-Moule, 1988). Contre-Moule also published *Archives Situationnistes, volume 1* (1997), consisting of French translations of all the German and British SI texts.

The Scandinavian section published three issues of the Danish-language journal *Situationistisk Revolution* (1962, 1968, 1970). Some of its other activities were described in *Internationale Situationniste* #10, pp. 22–26.

Most of the major SI writings have been translated into English, German, Greek, Italian, and Spanish. Some have also been translated into Arabic, Chinese, Czech, Danish, Dutch, Farsi, Finnish, Hebrew, Hungarian, Indonesian, Japanese, Korean, Lithuanian, Macedonian, Norwegian, Polish, Portuguese, Romanian, Russian, Serbo-Croatian, Slovenian, Swedish, and Turkish.

Guy Debord's Films

Hurlements en faveur de Sade (Films Lettristes, 1952). 75 minutes.

Sur le passage de quelques personnes à travers une assez courte unité de temps (Dansk–Fransk Experimentalfilmskompagni, 1959). 20 minutes.

Critique de la séparation (Dansk–Fransk Experimentalfilmskompagni, 1961). 20 minutes.

La Société du Spectacle (Simar Films, 1973). 80 minutes.

Réfutation de tous les jugements, tant élogieux qu'hostiles, qui ont été jusqu'ici portés sur le film "La Société du Spectacle" (Simar Films, 1975). 25 minutes.

In girum imus nocte et consumimur igni (Simar Films, 1978). 100 minutes.

Shortly before his death, Debord also made a 60-minute video: *Guy Debord, son art et son temps,* in collaboration with Brigitte Cornand (Canal Plus, 1994).

Oeuvres cinématographiques complètes: 1952–1978 (Champ Libre, 1978; Gallimard, 1994) contains illustrated scripts of all six films. There is also a separate annotated edition of the voice-over text of *In girum* (Lebovici, 1990; Gallimard, 1999). The Gallimard annotated edition includes some additional documents as well as a number of reviews of *In girum* that were originally collected under the title *Ordures et décombres déballés à la sortie du film "In girum imus nocte et consumimur igni"* (Champ Libre, 1982). *Des contrats* (three of Debord's film contracts) was published by Le Temps Qu'il Fait (1995).

The *In girum* script was translated by Lucy Forsyth (Pelagian, 1991). Translations of the other five films by various translators were collected in Richard Parry (ed.), *Society of the Spectacle and Other Films* (Rebel Press, 1992). *Complete Cinematic Works* (AK Press, 2003; to be reprinted by PM Press in 2026) includes Ken Knabb's translations of all six scripts plus stills, documents, and extensive annotations.

All six of Debord's films plus the Cornand video were reissued in a three-DVD set (Gaumont Vidéo, 2005). This set is no longer available, but there are various versions of the individual films online. For links to them plus the latest news on Debord's films, see www.bopsecrets.org/SI/debord.films.

Thomas Y. Levin's informative early study *Dismantling the Spectacle: The Cinema of Guy Debord* (1989) is online at www.academia. edu/24931068/Dismantling_the_Spectacle_ The_Cinema_of_Guy_Debord. *Grey Room on Debord's Cinema* (MIT Press, 2013), a special issue including eight articles, is online at https://1000littlehammers.wordpress. com/2013/08/28/grey-room-on-debords/. There are also at least four books in French: Antoine Coppola's *Introduction au cinéma de Guy Debord et de l'avant-garde situationniste* (Sulliver, 2003); Guy-Claude Marie's *Guy Debord: de son cinéma en son art et en son temps* (Vrin, 2009); Fabien Danesi's *Le cinéma de Guy Debord* (Paris Expérimental, 2011); and Fabien Danesi, Emmanuel Guy & Fabrice Flahutez's *La Fabrique du cinéma de Guy Debord* (Actes Sud, 2013).

Post-SI Works

GUY DEBORD, *La Planète malade* (unpublished 1971 article; Gallimard, 2004), translated by Donald Nicholson-Smith as *A Sick Planet* (Seagull, 2008), online at https://www. e-flux.com/notes/506238/a-sick-planet.

—*Préface à la quatrième édition italienne de "La Société du Spectacle"* (Champ Libre, 1979; later included in the Gallimard edition of *Commentaires*). Translated by Lucy Forsyth & Michel Prigent as *Preface to the Fourth Italian Edition of "The Society of the Spectacle"* (Chronos, 1979).

—*A los libertarios/Aux libertaires* (1980). Anonymous declaration supporting imprisoned Spanish anarchists. Included in *Appels de la prison de Ségovie* (Champ Libre, 1980).

—*Considérations sur l'assassinat de Gérard Lebovici* (Lebovici, 1985; Gallimard, 1993). Translated by Robert Greene as *Considerations on the Assassination of Gérard Lebovici* (Tam Tam, 2001).

—(with Alice Becker-Ho), *Le "Jeu de la Guerre": Relevé des positions successives de toutes les forces au cours d'une partie* (Lebovici, 1987). Account of a board game (invented by Debord) with strategical commentaries. Translated by Donald Nicholson-Smith as *A Game of War* and published in a box with game board and cardboard pieces (Atlas Press, 2007).

—*Commentaires sur la société du spectacle* (Lebovici, 1988; Gallimard, 1992). Translated by Malcolm Imrie as *Comments on the Society of the Spectacle* (Verso, 1990).

—*Panégyrique, tome premier* (Lebovici, 1989; Gallimard, 1993). Autobiographical reflections. Translated by James Brook as *Panegyric, Volume I* (Verso, 1991). A revised edition of that translation was published along with Volume 2 (trans. John McHale) as *Panegyric, Volumes 1 & 2* (Verso, 2005).

—*"Cette mauvaise réputation . . ."* (Gallimard, 1993). Responses to various rumors and misconceptions about Debord. Translated by Bill Brown (2010) at www.notbored.org/this-bad-reputation.html

—*Oeuvres* (Gallimard, 2006; ed. by Jean-Louis Rançon in consultation with Alice Debord). This huge omnibus volume (1904 pages!) in the Gallimard "Quarto" series contains virtually everything Debord ever wrote—all of his books and all of his published articles, plus dozens of previously unpublished texts (from theses on the Congolese revolutionary movement to notes on poker strategy), plus selections from his correspondence.

—*Correspondance, volume 1: 1957–1960* (Fayard, 1999). Translated by Stuart Kendall & John McHale as *Correspondence: The Foundation of the Situationist International (June 1957–August 1960)* (Semiotext(e), 2009).

—*Correspondance, volume 2: 1960–1964* (Fayard, 2001).

—*Correspondance, volume 3: 1965–1968* (Fayard, 2003).

—*Correspondance, volume 4: 1969–1972* (Fayard, 2004).

—*Correspondance, volume 5: 1973–1978* (Fayard, 2005).

—*Correspondance, volume 6: 1979–1987* (Fayard, 2007).

—*Correspondance, volume 7: 1988–1994* (Fayard, 2008).

—*Correspondance, volume "0": 1951–1957* (Fayard, 2010). In addition to the earlier letters, this volume also includes various letters that were discovered too late to be included in the previous volumes. The whole series was edited by Patrick Mosconi with Alice Debord.

—*Le Marquis de Sade a des yeux de fille* (Fayard, 2004). Facsimile edition of certain early letters that were not included in the above-mentioned series.

Jean-François Martos's *Correspondance avec Guy Debord* (Le Fin Mot de l'Histoire, 1998) includes letters between Debord and Martos from 1981–1991. This book is no longer available, having been legally condemned for infringing on the copyright of Librairie Arthème Fayard, which had arranged with Debord's widow Alice (Becker-Ho) Debord to publish the multivolume edition cited above. See Martos's *Sur l'interdiction de ma "Correspondance avec Guy Debord"* (Le Fin Mot de l'Histoire, 1999).

—*La Librairie de Guy Debord* is a five-volume series (edited by Laurence Le Bras et al. and published by Éditions L'Échappé) reproducing all of Debord's personal notes on his readings, with detailed annotations:

—*La Librairie de Guy Debord: Stratégie* (L'Échappé, 2018). Debord's notes on Thucydides, Sun Tzu, Machiavelli, Napoleon, Clausewitz, etc.

—*La Librairie de Guy Debord: Poésie, etc.* (L'Échappé, 2019). Debord's notes on Homer, Li Po, Villon, Shakespeare, Swift, Baudelaire, Lautréamont, Apollinaire, Breton, Joyce, etc.

—*La Librairie de Guy Debord: Marx/Hegel* (L'Échappé, 2021). Debord's notes on Marx, Engels, Lukács, Korsch, Wittfogel, etc., and on Hegel and related works.

—*La Librairie de Guy Debord: Histoire* (L'Échappé, 2022). Debord's notes on various histories and historians.

—*La Librairie de Guy Debord: Philosophie* (L'Échappé, in preparation).

Debord also translated into French: *Protestation devant les libertaires du présent et du futur sur les capitulations de 1937* (text by the most radical anarchist current during the Spanish civil war: Champ Libre, 1979); *Stances sur la mort de son père* (classic Spanish poem by Jorge Manrique: Champ Libre, 1980; Le Temps Qu'il Fait, 1995); and Sanguinetti's *Véridique rapport* (see below).

GIANFRANCO SANGUINETTI (pseudonym Censor), *Rapporto veridico sulle ultime opportunità di salvare il capitalismo in Italia* (Milan, 1975). The anonymous first edition of this book, seemingly written by an enlightened conservative arguing that an alliance with the Communist Party was in the best interest of the Italian ruling class, was mailed to some 500 politicians and journalists and stirred up a lot of confused debate and speculation. A few months later Sanguinetti created a second scandal by revealing that he was the author. Translated into French by Guy Debord as *Véridique rapport sur les dernières chances de sauver le capitalisme en Italie* (Champ Libre, 1976). Translated into English by Len Bracken as *The Real Report on the Last Chance to Save Capitalism in Italy* (Flatland, 1997).

—*Del terrorismo e dello stato* (Milan, 1979). Translated into French by Jean-François Martos (1980) and by Jean-François Labrugère and Philippe Rouyau (1980), and thence into English by Lucy Forsyth and Michel Prigent as *On Terrorism and the State* (Chronos, 1982).

RAOUL VANEIGEM, *Terrorisme ou révolution* (introduction to Ernest Coeurduroy's *Pour la révolution,* Champ Libre, 1972). Translated as *Terrorism or Revolution* (Black Rose, 1975); reprinted in *Collection of Desires* (Paper Street, 2003).

—(pseudonym Ratgeb), *De la grève sauvage à l'autogestion généralisée* (Éditions 10/18, 1974). First two chapters translated by Paul Sharkey as *Contributions to the Revolutionary Struggle* (Bratach Dubh, 1981; Elephant, 1990). Third chapter translated by Ken Knabb as *Total Self-Management* (website, 2001). The whole book (combining those two translations) was reprinted in *Collection of Desires* (Paper Street, 2003) under the title *From Wildcat Strike to Total Self-Management*.

—(pseudonym J.F. Dupuis), *Histoire désinvolte du surréalisme* (Paul Vermont, 1977). Translated by Donald Nicholson-Smith as *A Cavalier History of Surrealism* (AK Press, 1999).

—*Le livre des plaisirs* (Encre, 1979). Translated by John Fullerton as *The Book of Pleasures* (Pending Press, 1983); reprinted in *Collection of Desires* (Paper Street, 2003).

—*Le mouvement du Libre-Esprit* (Ramsay, 1986; L'or des fous, 2005). Translated by Randall Cherry & Ian Patterson as *The Movement of the Free Spirit* (Zone, 1994).

—*Adresse aux vivants sur la mort qui les gouverne et l'opportunité de s'en défaire* (Seghers, 1990).

—*La résistance au christianisme: Les hérésies des origines au XVIIIe siècle* (Fayard, 1993). Translated by Bill Brown as *Resistance to Christianity: A Chronological Encyclopaedia of Heresy from the Beginning to the Eighteenth Century* (Eris, 2023).

—*Avertissement aux écoliers et lycéens* (Mille et Une Nuits, 1995). Translated by JML/Not Bored as *A Warning to Students of All Ages* (2000) and reprinted in *Collection of Desires* (Paper Street, 2003).

—*Nous qui désirons sans fin* (Le Cherche Midi, 1996).

—*Pour une Internationale du genre humain* (Le Cherche Midi, 1999).

—*Déclaration des droits de l'être humain* (Le Cherche Midi, 2001). Translated by Liz Heron as *A Declaration of the Rights of Human Beings: On the Sovereignty of Life as Surpassing the Rights of Man* (Pluto, 2003; translation revised by Donald Nicholson-Smith: PM Press, 2019).

—*Le Chevalier, la Dame, le Diable et la mort* (Le Cherche Midi, 2003).

—*Rien n'est sacré, tout peut se dire* (La Découverte, 2003).

—*Salut à Rabelais!* (Complexe, 2003).

—*Modestes propositions aux grévistes* (Verticales, 2004).

—*Voyage à Oarystis* (Estuaire, 2005).

—*Journal imaginaire* (Le Cherche Midi, 2006).

—*Entre le deuil du monde et la joie de vivre: Les situationnistes et les mutations des comportements* (Verticales–Gallimard, 2008).

—*Lettre à mes enfants et aux enfants du monde à venir* (Le Cherche Midi, 2012). Translated by Donald Nicholson-Smith as *A Letter to My Children and the Children of the World to Come* (PM Press, 2018).

—*Rien n'est fini, tout commence* (Allia, 2014). A lengthy series of conversations with Allia publisher Gérard Berréby in which Vaneigem looks back on his early life and his experiences as one of the key figures in the SI. Includes lots of anecdotes about Debord, Michèle Bernstein, Attila Kotányi, René Viénet, Mustapha Khayati, J.V. Martin, and other SI members. Illustrated with hundreds of photos. Extensive excerpts from the book were translated by Bill Brown as *Self-Portraits and Caricatures of the Situationist International* (Colossal Books, 2015).

(This is just a partial list of Vaneigem's post-SI works—he has been very prolific.)

RENÉ VIÉNET, *La dialectique peut-elle casser des briques?* (1973). 90-minute kung fu film with altered soundtrack. Keith Sanborn produced a videocopy with English subtitles entitled *Can Dialectics Break Bricks?* Another Viénet film, *Chinois, encore un effort pour être révolutionnaires* (1977), was translated by Donald Nicholson-Smith as *Peking Duck Soup.* Viénet also produced several other films, mostly about Mao's China.

Books About the Situationists

In French:

Jean-Louis Brau's *Cours camarade, le vieux monde est derrière toi!* (Albin Michel, 1968) and Éliane Brau's *Le Situationnisme ou la nouvelle Internationale* (Debresse, 1968) are confused and unreliable, but maybe of historical interest (the authors were in the 1950s LI scene).

Jean-Jacques Raspaud & Jean-Pierre Voyer's *L'Internationale Situationniste: protagonistes, chronologie, bibliographie (avec un index des noms insultés)* (Champ Libre, 1971) is a handy reference guide and index to the French journals.

Jean-François Martos's *Histoire de l'Internationale Situationniste* (Lebovici, 1989) is an "orthodox" view, recounting the SI's activities and perspectives largely by way of quotations from the SI's publications.

Pascal Dumontier's *Les situationnistes et Mai 68* (Lebovici, 1990) is an insightful and well-documented account of this period of the SI's practice.

Cécile Guilbert's *Pour Guy Debord* (Gallimard, 1996) is a lightweight aesthetic appreciation.

Gianfranco Marelli's *L'amère victoire du situationnisme* (French translation from the original Italian, Sulliver, 1998) examines the SI from an anarchist perspective, focusing on the co-option of certain aspects of the situationists in the aftermath of May 1968.

Frédéric Shiffter's *Guy Debord, l'atrabilaire* (Distance, 1999) is earnestly clueless.

Christophe Bourseiller's *Vie et mort de Guy Debord* (Plon, 1999) is a gossipy biography based in large part on interviews with people who knew Debord or who crossed his path at one point or another. The various anecdotes, rumors, and interpretations are often hostile and contradictory, and needless to say should be taken with a large grain of salt.

Laurent Chollet, *L'Insurrection situationniste* (Dagorno, 2000). I saw this volume in a Paris bookstore when it first came out, flipped to a section purporting to give detailed info on the American situ scene, found nine glaring errors of fact in a single paragraph, and did not bother to buy it.

Shigenobu Gonzalvez's *Guy Debord ou la beauté du négatif* (Mille et Une Nuits, 1998; expanded edition: Nautilus, 2002) includes the most extensive Debord bibliography up to that point.

Christophe Bourseiller (ed.), *Archives et documents situationnistes* (Denoël, 2001–2005) was a book-length journal of which five annual volumes appeared. The journals include useful bibliographical information along with other material of varying and often merely tangential interest or reliability (e.g. interviews with people who may or may not have had much to do with the SI or much understanding of what it was really about).

Sergio Ghirardi's *Nous n'avons pas peur des ruines: les situationnistes et notre temps* (Insomniaque, 2004) discusses the situationists from a more "Vaneigemist" perspective: the author focuses on Vaneigem's characteristic themes and often echoes Vaneigem's rhetorical style.

Stéphane Zagdanski's *Debord ou La diffraction du temps* (Gallimard, 2008) is erratically opinionated (among other things, the author is very pro-Heidegger and very anti-"sixties") but sometimes insightful.

Bessompierre's *L'amitié de Guy Debord* (Les Fondeurs du Brique, 2010) is a sympathetic personal account by a friend.

Jacob Rogozinski & Michel Vanni (eds.), *Dérives pour Guy Debord* (Van Dieren, 2011) is a collection of articles by diverse authors about various aspects of Debord.

Patrick Marcolini's *Le mouvement situationniste: une histoire intellectuelle* (L'Échappée, 2012) surveys the SI's influence on later currents and movements in Europe and America (political, academic, artistic, literary, architectural).

André Trillaud's *Debord, etc.* (Éditions 13 bis, 2013) is freewheeling and irreverent, sometimes pertinent, sometimes dubious.

Emmanuel Guy & Laurence Le Bras (eds.), *Guy Debord: un art de la guerre* (BNF/Gallimard, 2013) is a profusely illustrated collection of informative articles based on Debord's personal archives, which were acquired in 2012 by the Bibliothèque Nationale in Paris.

Éric Brun's *Les Situationnistes: Une avant-garde totale (1950–1972)* (CNRS, 2014) is a ponderous sociological study.

Anna Trespeuch-Berthelot's *L'Internationale Situationniste: de l'histoire au mythe (1948–2013)* (P.U.F., 2015) is an extensive examination of the "reception" and "mythification" of the SI in the decades following its dissolution.

Jean-Marie Apostolidès's *Debord le naufrageur* (Flammarion, 2015) is the most exhaustively researched Debord biography. Unfortunately, like his previous study, *Les Tombeaux de Guy Debord* (Flammarion, 2006), it is marred by the author's obsessive focus on psychoanalyzing Debord. Some of his speculative interpretations seem plausible, but others do not. Meanwhile, he has relatively little to say about Debord's subversive ventures beyond attributing them to his supposed character traits. In a volume of nearly 600 pages, there are only nine rather muddled pages on the May 1968 revolt and nothing whatsoever on the Strasbourg scandal.

Laurence Le Bras & Emmanuel Guy (eds.), *Lire Debord, avec des notes inédites de Guy Debord* (L'Échappé, 2016) includes 250 pages of Debord's notes in preparation for his films and for various unrealized projects, followed by numerous scholarly articles. Luc Mercier's *Présent fait aux lecteurs de "Lire Debord"* (Paris, 2023) is a recommended supplement. It corrects errors in the book, fills in references the editors were unaware of, and in the process elucidates numerous aspects of Debord and his projects. A PDF of it can be obtained from Luc at lmercier@mageos.com.

André Bertrand & André Schneider's *Le Scandale de Strasbourg* (Insomniaque, 2018) is an excellent, detailed, and abundantly illustrated account of the Strasbourg scandal by two of its main perpetrators.

Anselm Jappe, *Un complot permanent contre le monde entier: Essais sur Guy Debord* (L'Échappée, 2023) is by the author of the best book on Debord (see in the English section below).

Vanessa Theodoropoulou's *Le monde en situation: La révolte sensible de l'Internationale Situationniste* (Les Presses du Réel, 2024) is a comprehensive study of the constructive, imaginative, geographical, and behavioral "genres" invented by the early situationists.

Pol Charles, *Vaneigem l'insatiable* (L'Age d'homme, 2002).

Laurent Chollet, *Les situationnistes: L'utopie incarnée* (Gallimard, 2004).

Larent Six, *Raoul Vaneigem: L'éloge de la vie affinée* (Luce Wilquin, 2005).

Grégory Lambrette, *Raoul Vaneigem* (Libertaires, 2007).

Jean-Claude Bilheran, *Sous l'écorce de Guy Debord, le rudéral* (Sens & Tonka, 2007).

Toulouse-la-Rose, *Debord contre Debord* (Nautilus, 2010).

Fabien Danesi, *Le mythe brisé de l'Internationale Situationniste* (Les Presses du Réel, 2011).

Emmanuel Guy, *Le Jeu de la guerre de Guy Debord: L'émancipation comme projet* (Éditions B42, 2020).

Bertrand Cochard, *Guy Debord et la philosophie* (Hermann, 2021).

Emmanuel Roux, *Guy Debord: Abolir le spectacle* (Michalon, 2022).

In English:

Richard Gombin's *Les Origines du gauchisme* (Le Seuil, 1971), translated by Michael Perl as *The Origins of Modern Leftism* (Penguin, 1975), includes a relatively objective assessment of the SI's role leading up to May 1968.

David Jacobs & Chris Winks's *At Dusk: The Situationist Movement in Historical Perspective* (Perspectives, 1975; reissued 1999) is a Frankfurt School–influenced critique of the situationists by two ex-members of the situ group Point-Blank. I find it both turgid and unconvincing, but maybe I'm biased since it also includes some criticisms of "Knabbism."

Jean Barrot's *What Is Situationism: Critique of the Situationist International* (Unpopular Books, 1987) contends that Debord did not really understand capitalism. As Anselm Jappe put it: "The writer has clearly read neither Debord nor Marx."

Greil Marcus's *Lipstick Traces: A Secret History of the Twentieth Century* (Harvard, 1989) concentrates mostly on the presituationist ventures of the 1950s. The author relates those ventures enthusiastically, impressionistically, and ahistorically to other extremist cultural movements such as Dada and early punk, while showing little interest in or understanding of the SI's revolutionary aims and perspectives.

Elisabeth Sussman (ed.), *On the Passage of a Few People Through a Rather Brief Moment in Time: The Situationist International, 1957–1972* (MIT/Institute of Contemporary Art, 1989), an illustrated catalog of the 1989-1990 exhibition on the SI in Paris, London, and Boston, includes an assortment of academic articles devoted primarily to the early artistic and cultural aspects of the SI's venture.

Iwona Blazwick (ed.), *An Endless Adventure, an Endless Passion, an Endless Banquet: A Situationist Scrapbook* (Verso/ICA, 1989) includes an assortment of texts illustrating the (for the most part rather confused) influence of the SI in England from the 1960s through the 1980s.

Sadie Plant's *The Most Radical Gesture: The Situationist International in a Postmodern Age* (Routledge, 1992) effectively demonstrates that the situationists had virtually nothing in common with Baudrillard, Foucault, Lyotard, Deleuze, Guattari, and other "postmodernists" and "deconstructionists" with which they are so often ignorantly confused.

Anselm Jappe's *Guy Debord* (Via Valeriano, 1995), translated by Donald Nicholson-Smith (University of California Press, 1999; PM Press, 2018) is still the only book on Debord in either French or English that can be unreservedly recommended. Particularly useful for its extensive treatment of the Marxian connection usually ignored in culture-oriented accounts of the situationists. (The bibliography of the 2018 edition also includes more detailed comments on many of the books listed here.)

Simon Ford's *The Realization and Suppression of the Situationist International: An Annotated Bibliography 1972–1992* (AK Press, 1995) lists over 600 post-SI texts, mostly in English, about or influenced by the SI. Ford also authored *The Situationist International: A User's Guide* (Black Dog, 2005), which, like many of the other books listed here, does not live up to its extravagant title.

Stewart Home (ed.), *What Is Situationism? A Reader* (AK Press, 1996) presents an assortment of views, mostly hostile and uncomprehending, as is Home's own previous book, *The Assault on Culture* (Aporia/Unpopular Books, 1988; AK Press, 2002).

Len Bracken's *Guy Debord—Revolutionary* (Feral House, 1997) has the merit of focusing on the radical aspects of Debord's ventures. It has the fault of being rather sloppy: the translations are uneven, speculations are not always clearly distinguished from facts, and the numerous typos do not inspire confidence in the author's care for accuracy.

Ken Knabb's *Public Secrets* (Bureau of Public Secrets, 1997) includes considerable material about the SI and SI-influenced groups in the US and Europe.

Vincent Kaufmann's *Guy Debord: La révolution au service de la poésie* (Fayard, 2001), translated by Robert Bononno as *Guy Debord: Revolution in the Service of Poetry* (University of Minnesota Press, 2006), is a comprehensive and insightful examination of the cultural and "poetic" aspects of Debord's life and work. The political aspects are treated in a more perfunctory manner.

Andrew Hussey's *The Game of War: The Life and Death of Guy Debord* (Jonathan Cape, 2001) is riddled with factual errors. The author's crude interpretations of Debord's supposed personal motives are derived primarily from hostile sources and reflect a very superficial understanding of Debord's projects and perspectives.

Tom McDonough (ed.), *Guy Debord and the Situationist International* (MIT Press, 2002) presents a misleadingly one-sided selection of 150 pages of SI articles (mostly early ones on art and urbanism, with virtually nothing from the last two-thirds of the group's existence) insulated by a 300-page buffer zone of academic commentary. Were it not for the inclusion of a salutary polemic by T.J. Clark and

Donald Nicholson-Smith ("Why Art Can't Kill the Situationist International"), readers of the book would get the impression that the situationists were primarily important as avant-garde artists, and that their revolutionary ventures were merely incidental and outdated eccentricities.

Andy Merrifield's *Guy Debord* (Reaktion Books, 2005), though less obnoxiously glib than Hussey's book, contains little new information on Debord.

Stefan Zweifel et al. (eds.), *In girum imus nocte et consumimur igni—The Situationist International (1957–1972)* (JRP/Ringier/Museum Tinguely, 2006), a profusely illustrated catalog of a Switzerland/Netherlands exhibition, includes several articles in English, mostly hostile and unreliable, and there are numerous mistranslations and other errors.

Richard Gilman-Opalsky's *Spectacular Capitalism: Guy Debord and the Practice of Radical Philosophy* (Minor Compositions, 2011) rightly notes the continued political relevance of Debord (in contrast to Baudrillard, etc.), but in his concluding "Theses on Debord" the author presents ludicrously caricatural summaries of Debord's positions, with which he then pedantically explains his disagreements.

Mikkel Rasmussen & Jakob Jakobsen (eds.), *Expect Anything Fear Nothing: The Situationist Movement in Scandinavia and Elsewhere* (Nebula/Autonomedia, 2011) provides plentiful evidence of the cluelessness and silliness of the Nashists, the Spurists, *The Situationist Times,* the "Second Situationist International," etc., whose participants and sympathizers seem to have understood little or nothing of what Debord and the SI were actually about.

McKenzie Wark's *The Beach Beneath the Street: The Everyday Life and Glorious Times of the Situationist International* (Verso, 2011) is an assortment of glib articles focusing mostly on the less political participants in and around the early SI. The author's notion that the Nashists and their various cohorts can be regarded as significant rivals of Debord and the SI is laughable.

McKenzie Wark's *The Spectacle of Disintegration: Situationist Passages Out of the 20th Century* (Verso, 2013) is another glib hodgepodge, this time looking at a variety of post-SI ventures by T.J. Clark, Sanguinetti, Viénet, Debord, Alice Becker-Ho, etc.

Frances Stracey's *Constructed Situations: A New History of the Situationist International* (Pluto, 2014) is in no way a history of the SI, but simply another assortment of articles on a few aspects of the situationists' ventures, the most interesting of which is "The Situation of Women."

Olivier Assayas's *A Post-May Adolescence: Letter to Alice Debord and Two Essays on Guy Debord* (SYNEMA, 2012; translated by Rachel Zerner & Adrian Martin) is by the noted filmmaker who organized the reissuing of Debord's films in DVD format.

Jean-Pierre Voyer's *It's Crazy How Many Things Don't Exist: Selected Writings* (Cruel Hospice, 2015; translated by Isaac Cronin, Roger Grégoire & Linda Lanphear) includes some rabid attacks on Debord for not recognizing Voyer's amazing discovery that the economy and the spectacle "don't exist." Personally, I have found most of Voyer's writings (after the initial promise of his pamphlet *Reich: How to Use* and perhaps one or two of his earliest books) to be delirious, but a few people still swear by him.

Marco Briziarelli & Emiliano Armano (eds.), *The Spectacle 2.0: Reading Debord in the Context of Digital Capitalism* (University of Westminster Press, 2017) is a collection of academic articles.

Tom Bunyard's *Debord, Time and Spectacle: Hegelian Marxism and Situationist Theory* (Haymarket Books, 2018) is difficult in places, but the patience and clarity of the presentation make it more accessible and informative than the Russell book (see below).

James Trier's *Guy Debord, the Situationist International, and the Revolutionary Spirit* (Brill, 2019), yet another would-be history of the SI, prides itself on correcting the "Debordian slant" of the *SI Anthology* (regarding which, see www.bopsecrets.org/recent/responses.htm #Anthology).

Sam Cooper's *The Situationist International in Britain: Modernism, Surrealism, and the Avant-Garde* (Routledge, 2019) examines Alexander Trocchi, the English SI, King Mob, and later SI influences in the UK.

Tanya Loi's *We Make Revolution in Our Spare Time: The History and Legacy of the Situationist International* (Public Reading Rooms, 2019) discusses various archives and collections of SI-related material.

Alastair Hemmens & Gabriel Zacarias (eds.), *The Situationist International: A Critical Handbook* (Pluto Press, 2020) is a comprehensive collection of informative articles on a well-chosen range of topics.

Eric-John Russell's *Spectacular Logic in Hegel and Debord* (Bloomsbury Academic, 2021), an ambitious study relating *The Society of the Spectacle* to Hegel's *Science of Logic*, is often so dense that I doubt if many readers will get past the first few pages unless they are already very familiar with Hegel.

Edward John Matthews's two books, *Arts and Politics of the Situationist International* (Lexington Books, 2021) and *Guy Debord's Politics of Communication: Liberating Language from Power* (Lexington Books, 2024) are sympathetic and sometimes insightful, but more often simplistic and repetitive.

Mehdi El Hajoui & Anna O'Meara (eds.), *On the Poverty of Student Life* (Common Notions, 2022) presents several articles on the famous Strasbourg pamphlet followed by an illustrated bibliography of more than a hundred editions in twenty-one different languages.

Dominique Routhier's *With and Against: The Situationist International in the Age of Automation* (Verso, 2023) attempts to situate the SI in the context of the automation and cybernetics that were emerging in the 1950s and 1960s.

Online Archives

www.notbored.org/SI.html. The translations at this site are often awkward and the host's commentaries are sometimes questionable, but this is one of the most comprehensive and dedicatedly maintained archives of SI-related material in English.

https://libcom.org/tags/situationist-international. This large selection of texts is just one section of a huge site which includes collections of texts on numerous other radical topics and movements.

https://1000littlehammers.wordpress.com/situationist. This site includes PDFs of many of the books praised or criticized here.

The above three websites are among the most extensive and conveniently accessible on the Web. For others, present and to come, see the continually updated version of this bibliography at www.bopsecrets.org/SI/bibliog.htm.

The Blind Men and the Elephant
(Selected Opinions on the Situationists)

But even if this were not so, there would still be no reason to accept the tutelage of science, as is proposed, for example, by a self-styled "Situationist International," which imagines it is making a new contribution when in fact it is merely creating ambiguity and confusion. But is it not in such troubled waters that one fishes for a situation?

—Benjamin Péret in *Bief* #1 (1958)

This young group sees only one way out of this impasse: to renounce painting as an individual art in order to wield it within a new "situationist" framework. What a grotesque term! Such manifestos are interesting as symptoms of restlessness and discontent. This particular one contains a few trivial truths, but its authors cling too closely to phenomena and slogans, with the result that essential truth escapes them.

—*Die Kultur* (October 1960)

Their principal activity is an extreme mental derangement. . . . In the maximum number of languages the Situationist International sends letters from foreign countries filled with the most filthy expressions. In our opinion the Munich court gave them too much credit in condemning them to fines and imprisonment.

—*Vernissage* #9-10 (May–June 1962)

The situationist critics who hope to seize all the means of communication without having created any at any level, and to replace its diverse creations and trivialities with their own enormous triviality—these cretins are excretions of the Hitlerist or Stalinist type, one of the manifestations of its present extreme impotence, of which the most well known examples are the Nazi gangs of America and England.

—*Les Cahiers du Lettrisme* #1 (December 1962)

As previously happened with surrealism, the internal development of the Situationist International shows that when the crisis of language and poetry is pushed beyond certain limits it ends up putting in question the very structure of society.

—*La Tour de Feu* #82 (June 1964)

The concerns of this movement, supported by M. Bernstein and G. Debord among others, are in some sense comparable, a hundred years later, to those of the Young Hegelians and especially to the Marx of the *1844 Manuscripts*. . . . That is to say, they imagine that a revolution is possible and their program is aimed at making one.

—*Arts* (9 June 1965)

Behind the angry young men of Amsterdam we find a secret International. . . . The Provos provide the previously isolated theorists of the Situationist International with troops, "intelligent surrogates" capable of constituting the secular arm of an organization which itself prefers to remain more or less behind the scenes.

—*Figaro Littéraire* (4 August 1966)

These students have insulted their professors. They should be dealt with by psychiatrists. I don't want to take any legal measures against them—they should be in a lunatic asylum. . . . As for their incitement to illegal acts, the Minister of the Interior is looking into that.

—Rector Bayen, Strasbourg University (November 1966)

Their doctrine, if such a term can be used in describing their delirious ravings, . . . is a sort of radical revolutionism with an underpinning of nihilism. . . . A monument of imbecilic fanaticism, written in a pretentious jargon, spiced with a barrage of gratuitous insults of both their professors and their fellow students. It constantly refers to a mysterious "Situationist International."

—*Le Nouvel Alsacien* (25 November 1966)

This well-written text constitutes a systematic rejection of all forms of social and political organization in the West and the East, and of all the groups that are currently trying to change them.

—*Le Monde* (9 December 1966)

The accused have never denied the charge of misappropriating the funds of the Strasbourg Student Union. Indeed, they openly admit to having made the union pay some 5000 francs for the printing of 10,000 pamphlets, not to mention the cost of other literature inspired by the "Situationist International." These publications express aims and ideas which, to put it mildly, have nothing to do with the purposes of a student union. One need only read what the accused have written for it to be obvious that these five students, scarcely more than adolescents, lacking any experience of real life, their minds confused by ill-digested philosophical, social, political and economic theories and bored by the drab monotony of their everyday life, have the pathetic arrogance to make sweeping denunciations of their fellow students, their professors, God, religion, the clergy, and the governments and political and social systems of the entire world. Rejecting all morality and legal restraint, these cynics do not shrink from to advocating theft, the destruction of scholarship, the abolition of work, total subversion, and a permanent worldwide proletarian revolution with "unrestrained pleasure" as its only goal.

—Judge Llabador, Strasbourg District Court (13 December 1966)

The verbal gesticulations of the situationists do not hit home. . . . It is, moreover, curious to see the bourgeois press, which refuses to print information from the revolutionary workers movement, rushing to report and popularize the gesticulations of these buffoons.

—Le Monde Libertaire (January 1967)

A new student ideology is spreading around the world: a dehydrated version of the young Marx called "situationism."

—Daily Telegraph (22 April 1967)

Then appeared for the first time the disquieting figures of the "Situationist International." How many are there? Where do they come from? No one knows.

—Le Républicain Lorrain (28 June 1967)

Situationism is, of course, no more the specter that haunts industrial society than was communism the specter that haunted Europe in 1848.

—Le Nouvel Observateur (3 January 1968)

It's the tune that makes the song: more cynical in Vaneigem and more icy in Debord, the negative and provocative violence of their phraseology leaves nothing standing of what previous ages have produced except perhaps Sade, Lautréamont, and Dada. . . . A snarling, extravagant rhetoric that is always detached from the complexity of the facts upon which we reason not only makes the reading disagreeable but also staggers thought.

—Le Monde (14 February 1968)

M. Debord and M. Vaneigem have brought out their long-awaited major texts: the Capital and What Is To Be Done?, as it were, of the new movement. This comparison is not meant mockingly. . . . Under the dense Hegelian wrappings with which they muffle their pages several interesting ideas are lurking. M. Debord and M. Vaneigem are attempting, for the first time, a comprehensive critique of alienated society. . . . Their austere philosophy, now authoritatively set forth, may not be without influence on future Committees of 100, Declarations of the 121, and similar libertarian manifestations.

—Times Literary Supplement (21 March 1968)

These commando actions undertaken by a group of anarchists and "situationists," with their slogan: "Never work!" . . . How has a handful of irresponsible elements been able to provoke such serious decisions, affecting 12,000 students in Letters and 4000 in Law?

—L'Humanité (29 March 1968)

Those who want to understand the ideas lying behind the student revolts in the Old World ought to pay serious attention not only to the writings of Adorno and of the three M's—Marx, Mao, and Marcuse—but above all to the literature of the Situationists. . . . Debord's book . . . rejects the idea of proletarian revolution in the same way as it repudiates Socialist democracy, Russian or Chinese Communism, and traditional "incoherent anarchism." . . . One has to destroy all authority, especially that of the state, to negate all moral restrictions, to expose fossilized knowledge and all "establishments," to bring truth into the world of semblance, and to achieve what Debord calls "the fulfillment of democracy in self-control and action." He fails to say how to achieve this program.

—New York Times (21 April 1968)

The situationists . . . are more anarchist than the anarchists, whom they find too bureaucratic.

—Carrefour (8 May 1968)

WARNING: Leaflets have been distributed in the Paris area calling for an insurrectionary general strike. It goes without saying that such appeals have not been issued by our democratic trade-union organizations. They are the work of provocateurs seeking to provide the government with a pretext for intervention. . . . The workers must be vigilant to defeat all such maneuvers.

—*L'Humanité* (French Communist Party)
(20 May 1968)

. . . Daniel Cohn-Bendit, leader of the "enragés," whom the leftist intellectuals have presented as being disciples of the American Marcuse, although anyone who reads the French books of the "situationist" writers Vaneigem and Debord can see where Dany and his friends actually got their inspiration.

—*Le Canard Enchaîné* (22 May 1968)

Inside, in jampacked auditoriums, thousands applauded all-night debates that ranged over every conceivable topic, from the "anesthesia of affluence" to the elimination of "bourgeois spectacles" and how to share their "revolution" with the mass of French workers. . . . There were Maoists, Trotskyists, ordinary Communists, anarchists, and "situationists"—a tag for those without preconceived ideologies who judge each situation as it arises.

—*Time* (24 May 1968)

This explosion was provoked by a few groups in revolt against modern society, against consumer society, against technological society, whether communist in the East or capitalist in the West—groups, moreover, which do not know what they would put in its place, but which delight in negation, destruction, violence, anarchy, brandishing the black flag.

—Charles de Gaulle, speech to the nation
(7 June 1968)

The fact that the uprising took everyone by surprise, including the most sophisticated theoreticians in the Marxist, Situationist, and anarchist movements, underscores the importance of the May–June events and raises the need to re-examine the sources of revolutionary unrest in modern society.

—Murray Bookchin,
"The May-June Events in France" (July 1968)

Who is the authentic representative of the Left today: the Fourth International, the Situationist International, or the Anarchist Federation? Leftism is everything that is new in Revolutionary history, and is forever being challenged by the old. . . . The Strasbourg pamphlet . . . acted as a kind of detonator. And although we in Nanterre did not accept the Strasbourg interpretation of the role of minority groups, i.e. university students, in the social revolution, we did all we could in helping to distribute the pamphlet.

—Daniel & Gabriel Cohn-Bendit,
Obsolete Communism: The Left-Wing Alternative
(1968)

The notion of "spectacle" (drama, happening, mask) is crucial to the theories of what is probably the furthest out of the radical factions. . . . In our consumer-technologies, life is merely a bad play. Like Osborne's Entertainer, we strut about in a bankrupt sideshow playing parts we loathe to audiences whose values are meaningless or contemptible. Culture itself has become frippery and greasepaint. Our very revolutions are melodrama, performed under stale rules of make-believe; they alter nothing but the cast. . . . Compared to the Strasbourg absolutists, Monsieur Cohn-Bendit is a weather-beaten conservative.

—*Sunday Times* (21 July 1968)

. . . "situationists" (whose main contributions to the May Revolution were graffiti, joyful and nonsensical). . . . A group of "International Situationists"—a latterday incarnation of surrealism—seized the university loudspeaker system for a time and issued extravagant directives.

—Seale & McConville, *Red Flag, Black Flag:*
French Revolution 1968 (1968)

It would be wrong to underestimate certain antecedents, in particular the November 1966 takeover of the Strasbourg Student Union. . . . The observer cannot help being struck by the rapidity with which the contagion spread throughout the university and among the nonstudent youth. It seems that the slogans propagated by a small minority of authentic revolutionaries struck some sort of indefinable chord in the soul of the new generation. . . . This fact must be stressed: we are witnessing the reappearance, just like fifty years ago, of groups of young people totally devoting themselves to the revolutionary cause; revolutionaries who know from experience how to await the favorable moments to trigger or aggravate disturbances of which they remain the masters, then go back underground and continue the work of undermining and of preparing other sporadic or prolonged upheavals, so as to slowly destabilize the social edifice.

—*Guerres et Paix* #4 (1968)

. . . the Situationist International, which has its base in Copenhagen and which is controlled by the security and espionage police of East Germany.

—*Historama* #206 (December 1968)

The situationists . . . make use of street theater and spontaneous spectacles to criticize society and denounce new forms of alienation. . . . Even though the small situationist group concentrated principally on the student situation and the commercialization of mass culture, the spring revolt was less a questioning of culture than a political criticism of society.

—Alain Touraine,
The May Movement: Revolt and Reform (1968)

Their manifesto is the now famous book by Guy Debord, *The Society of the Spectacle*. In order to criticize the system radically, Debord, in an epigrammatic and Adorno-like style, constructs a concept of "spectacle" derived from Marx's, and especially Lukács's, conceptions of "commodity fetishism," alienation, and "reification."

—*L'Espresso* (15 December 1968)

Their general headquarters is secret but I think it is somewhere in London. They are not students, but are what are known as situationists; they travel everywhere and exploit the discontent of students.

—*News of the World* (16 February 1969)

You know, I more or less agree with the situationists; they say that it's all finally integrated; it gets integrated in spectacle, it's all spectacle.

—Jean-Luc Godard,
"Newsreel" interview (March 1969)

The occupation committee, which was re-elected every day, was not able to guarantee continuity, in addition to which situationist factions had gained a certain influence. On Thursday the 16th, the latter distributed a leaflet denouncing the "bureaucrats" who disagreed with their slogans and working methods. . . . The situationists set up a "council to maintain the occupations" which, in their inimitable Hegelianistic-Marxist terminology, expatiated on the same themes.

—Alain Schnapp & Pierre Vidal-Naquet,
The French Student Uprising (1969)

We should add that Vaneigem's very style is that of the slogans of May. He seems, moreover, to have been at the origin of many of the most successful and poetic phrases. . . . The author of *The Revolution of Everyday Life* gives us a key for understanding the role and place of the paranoiac mechanisms of our civilization.

—André Stéphane,
L'Univers contestationnaire (1969)

Historically, few doctrines have attempted to follow the thread we have been pursuing. I know of only two: personalism and, in the contemporary scene, situationism. . . . Built on ideological premises utterly opposed to those of personalism (the latter is strongly influenced by Christianity, which situationists reject), the movement actually advances (despite its criticism) the tenets of surrealism, which were genuinely revolutionary at the start and closely resembled those of situationism. . . . Situationism should be credited for advocating individual decision-making and the exercise of imagination free of the irrationality we have discussed. The individual is committed to scrutinize his daily existence and to create a potential new one.

—Jacques Ellul, *Autopsy of Revolution* (1969)

An advertising specialist summed up the action of the graffiti writers with this formula: "They are fighting advertising on its own terrain with its own weapons." . . . Those responsible are a small group of revolutionary students, half lettrist, half situationist.

—*France-Soir* (6 August 1969)

Too extreme for those of the Old Left intelligent enough to understand it and too incomprehensible for those of the New Left extreme enough to live it.

—Grove Press rationale for declining to
publish Viénet's book on May 1968 (1969)

It seems to me that the Situationist International's influence has been considerably underestimated by commentators on the May events. (It should be said that, sparing nothing and nobody, the Situationists devote a good deal of their activity to virulent attacks on those who are closest to their own thinking, and have thus alienated a good many intellectuals who would otherwise be sympathetic to their views.) . . . Distortion, which was adopted and widely used first by the Situationists—especially, though not exclusively, in strip cartoons—consists in adding to a drawing, for example, certain words or phrases that distort the original meaning. . . . If the new meaning dominates or at least disturbs the meaning usually perceived by the reader of the original, the desired aim is achieved. It may involve a sudden awareness, an invitation to reflection, to doubt, or at least to participation in the game that will produce a certain detachment from the thing criticized. . . . This practicable and cheap technique of counter-manipulation is all the more effective in that it is placed in the context of an event, a production, etc., that already possess an audience.

—Alfred Willener,
The Image-Action of Society (1970)

The Situationist pamphlet "Theses on the Commune" refers to the Commune as the greatest carnival of the nineteenth century, but to try to burn down the Louvre is merely symbolic. Revolutionary activity has to move beyond the symbolic into the phase of literalization of the stasis of "working" institutions in bourgeois society.

—David Cooper, *The Death of the Family* (1970)

Diderot wrote the preface to a Revolution and so the surrealists and the situationists have written the preface to a new Revolution. . . . Claims grew into contestation; the games and the playful demonstrations of the anarchist-situationist mini-group gave way to more serious activity.

—Posner (ed.), *Reflections on the Revolution in France: 1968* (1970)

The way out is beginning to become clear: it's there in the works of Wilhelm Reich and R.D. Laing, in the ideas in all of our heads in our maddest moments when we say to ourselves, "I can't say that, they'll think I'm nuttier than a fruit cake," very clearly in the ideas of the Situationist International.

—*Fusion* (Spring 1970)

Although the language and tone of the essay are markedly similar to those of the Situationist manifesto, there are important differences between Bookchin and the Situationists. He explains these (in a personal letter to the editor) as follows: "The Situationists have retained very traditional notions about the workers' movement, Pannekoek's 'council communism,' almost Stalinist forms of internal organization (they are completely monolithic and authoritarian in their internal organization), and are surprisingly academic."

—Lothstein (ed.), *"All We Are Saying . . ."* (1970)

In those mystical days of May . . . the poets of Paris were the International Situationists, who have attained a similar state of frenzied anti-doctrinal comic anarchism to the yippies, though suckled on Dada, not L.S.D.

—Richard Neville, *Play Power* (1970)

In the extreme case, the anarcho-situationist groups all but deny the persistence of traditionally recognized forms of oppression, and put forward a model of contemporary capitalism as dependent solely on psychological oppression, a strategy that sees class society defeated by the "return of the repressed," and an organization and tactics confined to the symbolically terrorist actions of small groups.

—*New Left Review* #64 (November 1970)

We are here concerned with only two small groups who alone set the scene for the May events and provided the insurrection with a dialectical backbone. These few outlaws, the Enragés and the Situationists, universally despised by political organizations and student bodies, have their base on the surrealistic fringes of the Left Wing. From there they have nurtured one of the most advanced, coherent revolutionary theories (though often plagued by academic arrogance and "in" references), which provoked a near-liquidation of the State.

—Stansill & Mairowitz (ed.),
BAMN (By Any Means Necessary) (1971)

When one reads or rereads the *Internationale Situationniste* issues it is quite striking to what degree and how often these *fanatics* have made judgments or put forward viewpoints that were later concretely verified.

—*Le Nouvel Observateur* (8 February 1971)

Internationale Situationniste 1958–1969 . . . provides a fascinating record of this groupuscule which began in the French tradition of political-cultural sectarianism and ended by playing a prominent part in the disturbances at Strasbourg University in 1966 and then in the more dramatic "events" of May 1968. Many of the slogans which achieved fame on the walls of Paris may be found here in some form, and the ideas which influenced the rebels so much were being worked out in these pages during the previous ten years. There is a certain irony in such a publication . . . here they are neatly packaged as a highly marketable commodity in a clearly spectacular way.

—*Times Literary Supplement* (19 February 1971)

The concept of the spectacle, which derives from the French Situationists . . . is a useful analytic device: it simplifies a world of phenomena that seem otherwise disparate. Surely the spectacle is conspicuous, once one learns to see it in its many dimensions.

—Todd Gitlin in *Liberation* (May 1971)

This revolt must be attributed to an awakening of awareness about the real nature of "consumer society"—an awakening (and its articulation) that has its source in the intellectual (and practical) activities of a small group of insolent but lucid insurgents: the Situationist International. By a paradox to which history holds the secret, the SI remained practically unknown in this country for over ten years, a phenomenon that verifies Hegel's reflection: "Every important revolution that leaps into view must be preceded in the spirit of an era by a secret revolution that is not visible to everyone, least of all to contemporaries, a revolution that is as difficult to express in words as it is to comprehend."

—*Le Nouveau Planète* #22 (May 1971)

The resolution unanimously passed by the Anarchist Congress calls for some explanation. The influence of the Situationist International, particularly negative on numerous Scandinavian, North American, and Japanese extra-parliamentary groups, has been active in France and Italy since 1967-68 with the aim of destroying the federated anarchist movement of these two countries—in the name of a theoretical discourse that the situationists generally submerge in a barrage of insolences and vague and tortuous phraseology.

—Communiqué of the Italian Anarchist Federation, *Umanità Nuova* (15 May 1971)

At the beginning of 1968 a critic discussing situationist theory mockingly characterized it as a "glimmer flickering vaguely from Copenhagen to New York." Alas, that same year the glimmer became a conflagration that spread through all the citadels of the old world. . . . The situationists have uncovered the theory of the underground movement that torments the modern age. While the pseudoinheritors of Marxism forgot the role of the negative in a world swollen with positivity, and simultaneously relegated dialectics to the museum, the situationists announced the resurgence of that same negativity and discerned the reality of the

same dialectics, whose language, the "insurrectional style" (Debord), they rediscovered.

—*Les Temps Modernes* #299–300 (June 1971)

It was not in America but among the Western European student movements that the recent renaissance of interest in Reich first began. In France, where he was practically unknown, his theories were initially rediscovered by the Situationists.

—*Liberation* (October 1971)

The Society of the Spectacle . . . has led the discussion among the entire ultraleft since its publication in 1967. This work, which predicted May 1968, is considered by many to be the *Capital* of the new generation.

—*Le Nouvel Observateur* (8 November 1971)

The situationists, although in many ways they are the heirs of surrealism, dadaism, and some millenarian trends, rejoin the modern currents in post-Marxism and even go further in their quasi-Marcusian analyses of alienation in capitalist-bureaucratic society, which is the purely political aspect of their ideas. . . . The enragés and the situationists had the chance to put their ideas into practice in the first Committee of Occupation of the Sorbonne (14–17 May 1968) which, under their influence, set up total direct democracy in the Sorbonne. . . . The members of the Situationist International go so far as to deny that they have any ideology at all since any ideology is alienating.

—Richard Gombin in *Anarchism Today,* ed. Apter & Joll (1971)

But the situationists never arrived at an adequate practice. Afraid to get their hands dirty in the confusion of radical activity (which they scorned as "militantism") they confined their interventions to the theoretical level.

—*Anarchy* #7 (London, Winter 1972)

The Situationists . . . constantly talk of "workers" (sic) councils . . . while demanding the abolition of work! Unfortunately they seem to confuse attacks on the work ethic and on alienated labor, both of which are justified and necessary, with attacks on work itself.

—*Workers' Councils and the Economics of a Self-Managed Society,* Solidarity (London, 1972)

Miss Martin said the "situationists" were a political movement active in France in the 18th century, and that there had been "talk" on the campus of a revival under that name in Berkeley.

—*San Francisco Examiner* (18 May 1972)

Debord and Sanguinetti . . . quote extensively from the bourgeois press in order to demonstrate the "importance" of the S.I. . . . They impute a revolutionary consciousness to openly reformist movements; when they say that "youth, workers, homosexuals, women and children dare to want everything that had been *forbidden* them" (thesis No. 12) they fail to see how movements which only question isolated aspects of bourgeois society are easily recuperated. . . . A large part of "61 theses" is concerned with a critique of the pro-situs and there is little to dispute about it. . . . In going beyond the S.I. . . . we face the same difficulties it confronted. . . . We make no pretensions about ourselves.

—*Point-Blank!* #1 (October 1972)

The manifesto published by the Strasbourg students did little more than restate the troubling dilemmas already examined by the radical existentialists. Its content was not particularly original—except, perhaps, in its interpretation of the capitalist system as a vast, cretinizing spectacle. . . . When all was said and done, the "theory" of the situationists was rather uninspiring. . . . The situationists described their "situation" but presented no real, strategic perspective for its transformation. The task of forging concrete solutions was left to Daniel Cohn-Bendit, the principal ideologue of the May revolt.

—Richard Johnson, *The French Communist Party Versus the Students* (1972)

The S.I., although it presented the "most developed, most comprehensive, most modern" revolutionary theory yet to be found anywhere, is still not the end-all of revolutionary theory and practice. The sexual politics of the new women's movement, coupled with the communal lifestyles and counter-institutions which have emerged, are among the American contributions which can aid in the development of a coherent post-Situationist critique of our conditions.

—*New Morning* (February 1973)

I could understand it, but it would be over the heads of our readers. Besides, why would they be interested in something that happened in *France* in 1968?

—Editor at Straight Arrow Books (April 1973)

Without some attempt at a coherent analysis of the general situation, why not accept, for example, the Situationists' explanation of May 68: everyone was all of a sudden fed-up and discovered alienation and hit the streets?

—*Internationalism Bulletin* #1 (New York, Summer 1973)

The notion of recuperation, first introduced by the Situationists, refers to the manner in which the repressive system seeks to neutralize or contain the attacks launched against it by absorbing them into the "spectacle" or by projecting its own meanings and goals onto these oppositional activities.

—Bruce Brown, *Marx, Freud and the Critique of Everyday Life* (1973)

In the confusion and tumult of the May Revolt the slogans and shouts of the students were considered expressions of mass spontaneity and individual ingenuity. Only afterward was it evident that these slogans were fragments of a coherent and seductive ideology and had virtually all previously appeared in situationist tracts and publications. . . . Mainly through their agency there welled up in the May Revolt an immense force of protest against the modern world and all its works, blending passion, mystery, and the primeval.

—Bernard E. Brown, *Protest in Paris: Anatomy of a Revolt* (1974)

Bernard E. Brown . . . portrays (and unsympathetically so) the elements of the French intelligentsia who raised the banners of unreason, passion and primitivism. The anarchists and the "situationists" upon whom he concentrates most, represent in this interpretation a traditional force of romantic but destructive politics, determined to resist progress.

New Republic (16 March 1974)

Other groups, like the Situationist International, are also important, though they lack an understanding of capital. . . . The communist revolution implies an action from the enterprise, to destroy it as such. The rebellions in the U.S. remained on the level of consumption and distribution. (This point was not fully understood in an interesting text by the Situationist International: *The Rise and Fall of the Spectacular Commodity Economy.*)

—Jean Barrot & François Martin, *Eclipse and Re-Emergence of the Communist Movement* (1974)

Pillaging and detourning in a lively and un-constrained manner a wealth of news clips, sequences filmed in the streets, ads with naked women, press photos, scenes from American westerns, second-rate war films, Soviet and Pol-ish films, flashes from fashion ads, mixing in quotations from Clausewitz, Marx, Machiavel-li, etc., interrupting the narrative to wickedly announce to the spectators that if the rhythm he has given the images continued it would become seductive, "but it won't continue," Debord develops the argument of his book without limiting himself to "illustrating" it. . . . If war, according to Clausewitz, is a con-tinuation of politics by other means, the cin-ema, according to Debord, is a continuation of theory with other weapons. One must have seen the film two or three times to enumerate all the carefully calculated strokes of genius, the riches lavished with a subtle irony and the outbursts of a lyricism of rage that suddenly grips the heart. . . . Debord's indignation (the word is too feeble) splashes out in superb im-ages of contemporary subversion from the As-turias to Gdansk and Gdynia, from Poznan to Budapest, from police actions all over the world to May 68. It is no longer a matter of filming the world, the point is to change it. . . . Brecht dreamt all his life of adapting *Capital* to the stage. Guy Debord has found a produc-er crazy enough and wise enough to permit him to re-form his *Society of the Spectacle* on the screen. Don't miss it.

—*Le Nouvel Observateur* (29 April 1974)

In his film *The Society of the Spectacle,* situa-tionist Guy Debord has undertaken "a total critique of the existing world, that is, of all aspects of modern capitalism and its general system of illusions." In bringing his book to the screen, the author has fulfilled his aim of creating a theoretical film. . . . Imagine a work of the same sort as *Capital* presented in the form of a western and you will get some idea of what Guy Debord's film is like. The sequences of this theoretical western are accompanied by a narration read from the book. The film is a montage of fashion ads, news clips, quotations from Marx, Machia-velli, Tocqueville, Clausewitz, and fragments from diverse films that have marked the his-tory of the cinema: *Potemkin, Ten Days That Shook the World, New Babylon, We From Kronstadt, Shanghai Gesture, They Died With Their Boots On, For Whom the Bell Tolls, Rio Grande, Johnny Guitar,* and *Mr. Arkadin.*

—*Le Monde* (9 May 1974)

The Makhnist Situationist International pig countergang created by the CIA from scratch in 1957 in France under the slogans "Kill the Vanguards!," "Workers Councils Now!," and "Create Situations!," is the paradigm exam-ple of a CIA synthetic all-purpose formation. The loose and programless anarchist "left cover" countergang on the SI model is ideal for the CIA for the recruitment of new agents, the launching of psywar operations, the det-onation of riots, syndicalist workers' actions (e.g., LIP strike), student power revolts, etc., the continual generation of new countergang formations, and infiltration, penetration and dissolution of socialist and other workers' organizations. . . . During the 1968 French general strike the Situationists united with Daniel Cohn-Bendit and his anarchist thugs in preventing any potential vanguard from assuming leadership of the strike—thus guar-anteeing its defeat. In the U.S. Goldner and his Situationist International offshoot group Contradiction have been assigned to play the same kind of role: namely to stop the Labor Committees from developing into a mass-based working-class party.

—*New Solidarity*
(National Caucus of Labor Committees)
(28 August and 6 September 1974)

What was basically wrong with the S.I. was that it focused exclusively on an intellectu-al critique of society. There was no concern whatsoever with either the emotions or the body. . . . In the last analysis they made the same mistake as all left-wing intellectuals: *they thought that everyone was plain thick.* The poor workers don't know what's going on, they need someone to tell them. But people in the streets, in the offices and factories know damn well what's going on, even if they can't write essays about all its theoretical ramifi-cations. The point is that they can't do any-thing about it. . . . Ultimately the problem is an *emotional,* not an intellectual one.

—Christopher Gray,
Leaving the Twentieth Century (1974)

The revolutionary hopes of the 1960s, which culminated in 1968, are now blocked or aban-doned. One day they will break out again, transformed, and be lived again with a dif-ferent result. . . . When that happens, the Sit-uationist programme (or anti-programme) will probably be recognized as one of the most lucid and pure political formulations of that earlier, historic decade, reflecting, in an extreme way, its desperate force and its privileged weakness. What then was its privileged weakness? ... They ignored the everyday fact of tragedy, both on a world and personal scale. They refused to face the need to find meaning in tragedy.

—John Berger in *New Society* (6 March 1975)

Apart from a lot of the dialectical jargon, which is just rubbish, there is much that is a bad case of "excuse me but didn't Hegel say that?" The grandeur of the rhetoric shows up the bathos of the suggested "practice" (e.g. creating situations, whatever that may mean), while the "revolutionary project" itself seems to lack any clear goals.

—*Time Out* (4 April 1975)

Coming from the decomposition of "left" lettristes and cultural dilettantes of the 50s, the Situationists simply carried to their logical conclusions the bourgeois "critiques" of capitalism contained in Dadaism and Surrealism. Parrotting what *Socialisme ou Barbarie* had taught them about economics, about the "workers councils" and "generalized self-management," the Situationists became the most coherent expression of petty bourgeois radicalism in the whole modernist carnival which accompanied May '68. ... But the proletariat did not begin a communist revolution in Paris '68. The Situationists and other modernists did not fail to notice this omission and from then on the viciousness of their anti-working class outbursts knew no limits. ... In *The Decline and the Fall of the "Spectacular" Commodity-Economy* (1965) the Situationists had already begun to talk about "the integration of the classical proletariat" to the "society of the spectacle."

—*World Revolution* #3 (April 1975)

But of course, it should have been obvious from the start that the Situationists do not have the slightest genuine concern with freedom. Their mask is far too transparent to conceal that familiar, vicious and authoritarian face beneath, the same old desire to dominate, rule and coerce other people. ... It is indeed fortunate for the human race, however, that there now exist truly radical individualist and libertarian movements which are actually dedicated to leading it out of the Twentieth Century—into the Twenty First, into a new world of greater freedom and prosperity and not, as would the Situationists, back into the Dark Ages of slavery and poverty.

—Chris R. Tame, *The Politics of Whim* (Radical Libertarian Alliance, 1975)

Situationism seems to have "caught on" in the U.S.A., particularly in California, that playground of the ideologies. ... The American situationists seem to be repeating the pattern of mutual exclusion and criticism as occurred in Europe, and to be employing a fairly impenetrable Hegelian vocabulary. ... Debord and Vaneigem are worth reading for their critique of modern consumer-culture (if you can arrange a few weeks free of work and booze).

—*Freedom* (10 May 1975)

Their strategy of interrupting the routines of daily life with guerrilla theatre in order to "create situations" was traceable to Lefebvre, although they asserted that he also took much from them. ... The Situationists created a mini-May in 1966, disrupting the university and publishing a very popular pamphlet, *De La Misère en milieu étudiant*, which was an application of the theory of the *Arguments* group to student life.

—Mark Poster, *Existential Marxism in Postwar France* (1975)

What is hidden behind the Censor case, where will the Censor scandal lead? First let us explain: Censor is the author of a book entitled *True Report on the Last Chance To Save Capitalism in Italy*, circulated in a limited edition in August among the men of power, then in October among the literati. At the time, everyone wondered who Censor was. Everyone assumed he had to be himself a man of power: Merzagora, Carli, Mattioli. The things he knew were too important and too precise. He had to be one of those three men. Instead, here is the surprise: a few days ago the real author revealed himself. He is not a man of power, but a little-known young man in his twenties by the name of Gianfranco Sanguinetti. "The first duty of the press today is to undermine all the bases of the constituted political order," wrote Marx in 1849. Sanguinetti-Censor has set out to accomplish precisely this task with his book. He is not modest, but on the whole he has done so effectively. ... Anyone who is familiar with the situationists knows that the immediate objectives of their philosophy are provocations and scandals carried out with coolness and precision. With his Censor coup, Sanguinetti has simply given a crowning manifestation of the situationist technique of scandal.

—*L'Europeo* (6 February 1976)

Situationalism: Species of Marxist cultural and political criticism propounded by L'Internationale Situationaliste, a tiny group of intellectual terrorists formed from the fusion of the Romanian surrealist Isidore Isou's Mouvement Lettriste with other nihilist and anti-cultural avant-gardists in 1957. Influenced by the Trotskyist surrealists Breton and Péret, as well as Lefebvre, de Sade, Lautréamont and Lewis Carroll. Specialists in staccato, sarcastic and heavily Hegelian denunciations of the Spectacle, art, advertising and consumption. . . . In its simplified form became a rationale for "action" and the propaganda of the deed during the decline of the student Left. Its executive has had British members, including the Scots novelist and junkie Alex Trocchi, but they have usually been swiftly expelled.

—David Widgery,
The Left in Britain: 1956–68 (1976)

Jorn's role in the Situationist movement (as in COBRA) was that of a catalyst and team leader. Guy Debord on his own lacked the personal warmth and persuasiveness to draw people of different nationalities and talents into an active working partnership. As a prototype Marxist intellectual Debord needed an ally who could patch up the petty egoisms and squabbles of the members. Their quarrels came into the open the moment Jorn's leadership was withdrawn in 1961. . . . Finally, 1966–8 saw the vindication of Debord's policy, sustained against every kind of opposition, of adhering rigidly to the uncompromising pursuit of a singleminded plan. When the time came—in Strasbourg in November 1966 and in Paris in May 1968—Debord was ready, with his two or three remaining supporters, to take over the revolutionary role for which he had been preparing during the last ten years. Incredible as it may seem, the active ideologists ("enragés" and Situationists) behind the revolutionary events in Strasbourg, Nanterre and Paris, numbered only about ten persons.

—Guy Atkins, *Asger Jorn,
the Crucial Years: 1954–1964* (1977)

Paris 1968 was rich in nameless wildness. . . . It was marred by a small group of embittered scene-creamers, who called themselves the Situationists, and who tried in typically French fashion to intellectualize the whole mood out of existence, and with their very name tried to colonize it. Failed activists

and mini-Mansonettes who boasted that all their books and pamphlets (Leaving the 20th Century, The Veritable Split in the Fourth International, etc.) had been produced from the proceeds of a bank robbery when even the most lavish of them could have been produced for the price of a few tins of cat-food from Safeways (one tiny exception being "Ten Days that Shook the University" by Omar Khayati). . . . Their heroes are a legion of mad bombers: Ravachol, Valerie Solanas, Nechayev, the IRA, et al.

—Heathcote Williams in *International Times*
(Autumn 1977)

Ducasse in one sense leads to the Orwell of *Politics and the English Language* and beyond, to Vaneigem and the Situationists who by shrewd use of collage and juxtaposition exposed both the poverty and richness of slogans, and the thinly veiled hypocrisy of a society which by not respecting words abuses people, and by insulting the intelligence creates a state of political cretinisation in which the various forms of authoritarian control may dominate.

—Alexis Lykiard, Introduction to his
translation of Ducasse's *Poésies* (1978)

Guy Debord rejects praise as well as blame. . . . Far from currying favor with his contemporaries, Debord denounces their compromises and resignations with the ferocity of a grand inquisitor. . . . The seduction of this author stems precisely from the rigor of his critique and the mastery of the form he gives to it. The publication of his *Oeuvres cinématographiques complètes,* and particularly of the text of his latest film, *In girum imus nocte,* confirms his position in the line of French writers—Pascal, Bossuet, Chamfort—who combine elegance, passion, and firmness. . . . We are going to die one day, soon. Let us therefore not be unworthy of our pride and our ambitions. This, I believe, is Guy Debord's message.

—*Le Monde* (20 January 1979)

In exploiting the hysteria of the record companies and the public over the Pistols, McLaren was drawing upon an avant garde movement too playful and fluid to be doctrinal. This was the Situationist International, or Situationism. . . . So, although professing the obligatory sympathy with the proletariat, the Situationists rejoiced, like students at a rag day, in scandal and shock tactics. . . . In this evaluation one may see the models for the subsequent behavior of Malcolm McLaren and the Pistols. . . . McLaren and Jamie Reid took Situationism to Glitterbest with more success. "It's wonderful to use it in rock n' roll," McLaren said.

—*Melody Maker* (June 1979)

Meanwhile, the notion of the spectacle elaborated by the S.I. falls behind what Marx and Engels understood by the term "ideology." Debord's book *The Society of the Spectacle* presents itself as an attempt to explain capitalist society and revolution, when in fact it only considers their forms, important but not determinant phenomena. . . . Its contradiction, and, ultimately, its theoretical and practical dead-end, is to have made a study of the profound through and by means of the superficial appearance. The S.I. had no analysis of CAPITAL: it understood it, but through its effects. . . . The S.I. saw the revolution as a calling into question more of the relations of distribution (cf. the Watts riot) than of the relations of production. It was acquainted with the commodity but not with surplus value.

—Jean Barrot,
"Critique of the Situationist International"
in *Red-Eye* #1 (Fall 1979)

Situationism is a product of the student rebellion, a glorification of the spontaneous happenings which it is felt will spring out of the favoured role of the student within society. It picks up phrases, here from Marxism and there from anarchism. It has an affinity with Blanquism and, when it does, often parades as Maoism or a revised form of Marxism-Leninism—to the indignation of orthodox Maoists or other Marxist-Leninists. But the situationists were virtually non-existent between situations, and unlikely ever to get around to doing anything so positive as attacking a Cabinet Minister.

—Stuart Christie, *The Christie File* (1980)

Shot in March 1978, this situationist maceration [*In girum imus nocte*] is now finally presented to the vulgum pecus of the Latin Quarter, Montparnasse, and the Olympic. . . . In 1973 Guy Debord presented his first film, *The Society of the Spectacle,* adapted from his book of the same name. Its moral: smash everything, hock the cinema, we have to live today. A détournement of the spectacle and thus of the cinema, a return to the essential, to immediate life. *In girum:* . . . a pavane for a disappointed love of the cinema, often irritating because of his self-satisfied indulging of his dear little ego. Strictly for in-group devotees.

—*Le Monde* (11 May 1981)

In girum imus nocte was completed in March 1978. . . . It was subjected to a complete blackout for the next three years. . . . Debord begins by attacking the spectators, the audience. The first image of the film is a photo of a "present-day film audience staring fixedly ahead," so that "the spectators see nothing but a mirror image of themselves on the screen." . . . But in his film Debord does not talk only about the cinema public. He talks about himself. . . . The same people who go into ecstasies over the self-portraits of famous painters, the memoirs of someone or other, or even Bakunin's *Confession* are suddenly outraged at having Debord "inflict his ego" on them. . . . Yet Debord recounts his life and loves quite simply. . . . And who better than he can render homage to his friends of long ago such as Ivan Chtcheglov . . . or expose the devastation that has since hit Paris? . . . But enough of all these scattered quotations from the text of the film. If you can't catch the pirate showing of it tonight on Channel 68, go see it at the cinema.

—*Libération* (3 June 1981)

I originally issued "The Blind Men and the Elephant" as a huge poster in 1975 (www.bopsecrets.org/PS/blindmen75.htm) and I later included the above augmented selection as an appendix in the first edition of the *SI Anthology* (1981). I haven't bothered to update it since that time. Over the decades the quantity of reactions has continually increased, but the main types of misunderstandings and falsifications remain much the same. In addition to the nearly one hundred books about the SI or Debord and the thousands of printed articles and reviews, Google currently shows more than seven million online results for "situationist" and over five million for "Guy Debord." Most of the later reactions are as laughably clueless as the earlier ones. In certain regards, however, the general level of comprehension has improved (particularly among those engaged in radical practices) because the society's increasingly evident spectacularization has made some of the situationists' insights more clear and undeniable.

Index

ABOUT PM

PM Press is an independent, radical publisher of critically necessary books for our tumultuous times. Our aim is to deliver bold political ideas and vital stories to all walks of life and arm the dreamers to demand the impossible. Founded in 2007 by a small group of people with decades of publishing, media, and organizing experience, we have sold millions of copies of our books, most often one at a time, face to face. We're old enough to know what we're doing and young enough to know what's at stake. Join us to create a better world.

JOIN THE FRIENDS OF PM PRESS BOOK CLUB!

Help support radical, independent publishing and get PM Press titles shipped to you each month.

WHAT?
A subscription bargain! You will automatically receive every new title delivered to your door each month and a 50% discount on all webstore purchases. On average we publish around thirty titles a year!

HOW DOES IT WORK?
Your card is billed once a month and we ship you our new books, until you tell us to stop. Or until our efforts succeed in bringing the revolution around. Or the financial meltdown of Capital makes plastic redundant. Whichever comes first. There's no catch. No hidden fees. There is no minimum number of months required.

WHY?
We are frequently asked why we offer such a great deal and how does it benefit PM Press. Your subscription fees provide us with a stable monetary platform that we can count on each month. All subscription fees go toward paying for the staggering cost of production. This steady source of income helps us to remain a truly independent publisher, unafraid to work with authors, artists, and activists who have traditionally been marginalized by mainstream publishers.

OPTIONS (all receive a 50% discount on purchases from our website)

- **$15 A MONTH** Get three e-Books each month
- **$30 A MONTH** Get all of our new books and pamphlets each month
- **$40 A MONTH** Get all PM Press releases (including CDs and DVDs)
- **$100 A MONTH** Everything plus PM merchandise and free downloads

For those who can't afford $30 or more a month, we have Sustainer Rates at $15, $10, and $5. Sustainers get a 50% discount on all purchases from our website.

pmpress.org/fopm

The Society of the Spectacle
Guy Debord

Translated and annotated by
Ken Knabb

PM Press, 2024
ISBN 979-8-887440-56-9
150 pages. $19.95

Guy Debord was the most influential figure in the Situationist International, the subversive group that helped trigger the May 1968 revolt in France. His book *The Society of the Spectacle,* originally published in Paris in 1967, has been translated into more than twenty other languages and is arguably the most important radical book of the twentieth century.

Contrary to popular misconceptions, Debord's book is neither an ivory-tower "philosophical" discourse nor a mere expression of "protest." It is a clarification of the most fundamental tendencies and contradictions of the social system in which we find ourselves, designed to facilitate its overthrow. This makes the book more of a challenge, but it is also why it remains so pertinent more than half a century after its original publication, while countless other social theories and intellectual fads have come and gone.

This meticulous new translation by Ken Knabb is the first in any language to include extensive annotations, clarifying the historical allusions and revealing the sources of Debord's "détournements."

Public Secrets

Ken Knabb

ISBN 978-0-93968-203-4

408 pages. $15.00

Distributed by PM Press

Collected Skirmishes of Ken Knabb: 1970–1997

Ken Knabb is well known for his translations of numerous works by Guy Debord and the Situationist International. *Public Secrets* is a comprehensive collection of his own writings over a period of three decades.

The first half of the book consists of two major new texts. "The Joy of Revolution" is a series of observations on the problems and possibilities of a situationist-style antihierarchical revolution. Beginning with a brief overview of the failures of Bolshevism and the inadequacies of reformism, it examines the pros and cons of a wide range of radical tactics, then concludes with some provocative speculations on what a global liberated society might be like. "Confessions of a Mild-Mannered Enemy of the State" is largely concerned with Knabb's situationist activities, but it also includes reminiscences of the sixties counterculture and accounts of his Zen practice and other later ventures.

The second half of the book presents a variety of pamphlets, posters, comics, and articles on Wilhelm Reich, Kenneth Rexroth, Gary Snyder, radical Buddhists, Japanese anarchists, Chinese dissidents, the 1970 Polish revolt, the 1979 Iranian uprising, and the 1991 Gulf war.

The aim throughout is to bring the real choices into the open and to incite people to make their own radical experiments.

The Revolution of Everyday Life

Raoul Vaneigem

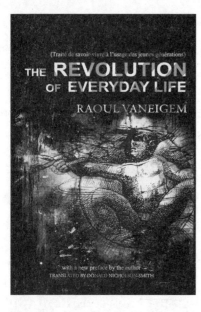

Translated by Donald Nicholson-Smith

ISBN: 978-1-60486-678-0

$20.00

6 x 9 • 288 pages

Originally published just months before the May 1968 upheavals in France, Raoul Vaneigem's *The Revolution of Everyday Life* offered a lyrical and aphoristic critique of the "society of the spectacle" from the point of view of individual experience. Whereas Debord's masterful analysis of the new historical conditions that triggered the uprisings of the 1960s armed the revolutionaries of the time with theory, Vaneigem's book described their feelings of desperation directly, and armed them with "formulations capable of firing point-blank on our enemies."

"I realise," writes Vaneigem in his introduction, "that I have given subjective will an easy time in this book, but let no one reproach me for this without first considering the extent to which the objective conditions of the contemporary world advance the cause of subjectivity day after day."

Vaneigem names and defines the alienating features of everyday life in consumer society: survival rather than life, the call to sacrifice, the cultivation of false needs, the dictatorship of the commodity, subjection to social roles, and above all the replacement of God by the Economy. And in the second part of his book, "Reversal of Perspective," he explores the countervailing impulses that, in true dialectical fashion, persist within the deepest alienation: creativity, spontaneity, poetry, and the path from isolation to communication and participation.

The present English translation was first published by Rebel Press of London in 1983. This new edition of *The Revolution of Everyday Life* has been reviewed and corrected by the translator and contains a new preface addressed to English-language readers by Raoul Vaneigem.